AFTER EVIL

Columbia Studies in Political Thought/Political History

Columbia Studies in Political Thought/Political History

||||||||||||||||||||||||||||||||||||||||||||||||||||||||||||||||||||||||||||||||||||

Dick Howard, General Editor

Columbia Studies in Political Thought/Political History is a series dedicated to exploring the possibilities for democratic initiative and the revitalization of politics in the wake of the exhaustion of twentieth-century ideological "isms." By taking a historical approach to the politics of ideas about power, governance, and the just society, this series seeks to foster and illuminate new political spaces for human action and choice.

Pierre Rosanvallon, *Democracy Past and Future*, edited by Samuel Moyn (2006)

Claude Lefort, *Complications: Communism and the Dilemmas of Democracy*, translated by Julian Bourg (2007)

Benjamin R. Barber, *The Truth of Power: Intellectual Affairs in the Clinton White House* (2008)

Andrew Arato, *Constitution Making Under Occupation: The Politics of Imposed Revolution in Iraq* (2009)

Dick Howard, *The Primacy of the Political: A History of Political Thought from the Greeks to the French and American Revolution* (2009)

ROBERT MEISTER

AFTER EVIL

A POLITICS OF HUMAN RIGHTS

Columbia

University

Press

New York

Columbia University Press

Publishers Since 1893

New York   Chichester, West Sussex

Copyright © 2011 Robert Meister

Paperback edition, 2012

Library of Congress Cataloging-in-Publication Data

Meister, Robert, 1947–

    After evil: a politics of human rights / Robert Meister.

      p. cm. — (Columbia studies in political thought/political history)

    Includes bibliographical references and index.

    ISBN 978-0-231-15036-1 (cloth : alk. paper)—ISBN 978-0-231-15037-8 (pbk. : alk. paper)—
ISBN 978-0-231-52095-9 (e-book)

  1. Human rights. I. Title. II. Series.

    JC571.M385   2010

    323.012—dc22

2010017186

Columbia University Press books are printed on permanent and durable acid-free paper.

This book is printed on paper with recycled content.

Printed in the United States of America

c 10 9 8 7 6 5 4

p 10 9 8 7 6 5 4

Cover image: "Untitled," Courtesy & © William Kentridge

CONTENTS

PREFACE | MY TASK

Most long books are revised to create the illusion that they could have been conceived all at once. I want you, my reader, to be under no such illusion. In a broad sense, this book is the reflection of an entire lifetime—what I now think about what I have thought since the mid-twentieth century. It reflects, more narrowly, a series of realizations I had between 1989 and 2009—the interval between the fall of communism and the collapse of global capitalism, when a discourse of sentimental humanitarianism promised to supplant that of hard-edged political struggle. For me, these were also the years following the completion of my book on Karl Marx, whose work originated in doubts about an earlier postrevolutionary appropriation of human rights by states claiming global hegemony. I had planned my next book on the relevance of U.S. constitutional thought, especially on questions of civil war and reconstruction, to political transformations then occurring throughout the world. This book, a critique of the dark side of the particular version of human rights that followed from U.S. global dominance, has overtaken the earlier project.

My successive realizations about what has been at stake in the changes of the past twenty years are a product of living and thinking through them. There is no way I could have come to these realizations all at once—and no way for me to give them a duly proportional emphasis as I revised every chapter. To help you follow what lies ahead I list here, at the outset, the realizations that I had so you can tie them together as you read.

- Political transitions are not just new beginnings; they are also what I call "survivor stories" that reflect a non-neutral judgment on the history that preceded them. In this respect, they are always about what the past will have been now that "we" have changed, and what it would have been had "we" changed sooner. Merely by occurring, political transitions thus instantiate a temporal reconstitution of the "we."

- A central problem in such transitions is how to view ongoing beneficiaries of an injustice now regarded as past. Once that injustice has been renounced, do their continuing advantages perpetuate it? Or are those who so claim rightly criticized for dredging up a past over which at least a moral victory has been achieved?

- A further problem is that it would be *good* to be a beneficiary of the past—whether it was just or not—provided that one arrives on the scene as a newcomer, rather than as an exploiter, oppressor, or successor-in-interest to those who were. *Birth* here is the prototype of morally innocent succession—that in virtue of which the sins of one's fathers should not be visited upon one. Correspondingly, *rebirth* is the paradigm of atonement—that in virtue of which an ongoing beneficiary should not be seen to perpetuate a past injustice he acknowledges and regrets.

- The modern theory of revolution (1789–1989) generally rejects the moral innocence of beneficiaries (and/or their potential for rebirth); it regards them as would-be perpetrators of social injustice unless they disgorge their unjust gains. Counterrevolutionaries react against this revolutionary identification of beneficiaries with perpetrators—they see the rise of revolutionary consciousness as itself morally damaging: insofar as it makes former victims capable of seizing power, it also makes them capable of inflicting even worse injustice than they suffered.

- Today's globally dominant view of human rights is no longer addressed to victims who would become revolutionaries but, rather, to beneficiaries who do not identify with perpetrators. It encourages them to acknowledge past evil as what they *would have* opposed so that future evil *will not have been* a repetition of it. The effect of such confession and conversion is to make the moment of its occurrence—which is always the present—*discontinuous* with the now repudiated past.

- A beneficiary who bears witness to the innocence of past victims can thus conceive of himself as a would-have-been rescuer rather than a would-be perpetrator. The question for the human rights convert is always whether it is already too late to rescue, or still too soon. By agonizing over the question of his own potential guilt as a bystander, the witness to human suffering tries to save his soul without necessarily relinquishing his position of advantage.

- Insofar as today's human rights consciousness is like a conversion experience, its moment of revealed truth is Auschwitz. Recognizing Auschwitz—

preventing *another* one—is now an article of faith for secular humanitarians in much the way that Pauline Christianity gave universal meaning to the experience of Jewish suffering without assuming responsibility for it. In post-Holocaust debates about human rights, the violence that Israel uses to defend itself has become a laboratory for the violence that the "world community" (and especially the U.S.) would be obliged to use in protecting *an* Israel that could not defend itself. The post-Holocaust security of Israel thus stands as the constitutive *exception* on which twenty-first-century humanitarianism is based.

- The way that "Israel's Holocaust" functions in how "the West" understands its humanitarian mission has changed during my lifetime. In the 1960s the question was whether one would have resisted Hitler *before* it was too late, and whether to resist one's own government before it commits similar crimes in Southeast Asia. As my generation came to power, however, its central question was whether nations with the power to do so should have intervened to stop Hitler.[1] Today the question is whether the "*world* community" has a responsibility to protect potential victims of another Holocaust by creating another Israel which the world community would then have a special duty to defend.

- The twenty-first-century doctrine of humanitarian intervention—the "Responsibility to Protect" (R2P)—is a culmination of my generation's globalized thinking. It proposes a new *nomos* of the Earth that would repudiate *past* violence (which always appears as something cyclical and uncontained) by endorsing exceptional violence—that of rescue and occupation.[2]

- Only when this book was nearly completed did I recognize that the "evil" in my title invokes the cyclical nature of violence (violence begetting violence) that humanitarian violence *puts* in its past. "After evil" thus corresponds to the Christian "revelation" described by René Girard that supersedes earlier religions based on human sacrifice by converting the surviving beneficiaries of such practices to belief in the universal innocence of past victims, as such.

- The revelation that we are already forgiven for the past evils we remember to confess is a consoling substitute for prophetic religions that do not let us off the hook in the present. This was the Qur'anic critique of the Judaeo-Christianity of Saint Paul; it is also a critique that strands of present-day Islamism make of today's imperialism of the human. When I finally reached this conclusion, I realized that it had been stated prophetically by my late friend Norman O. Brown in lectures on Islam, delivered in 1981, as a response to the Iranian revolution.

- This last realization brought me back to my original concern in 1989 that a new universalism of human rights was becoming the self-consciousness of U.S. capitalist hegemony following the cold war's end. If this is, as I argue, a successor to the counterrevolutionary project of the previous two centuries, we must ask whether it has also co-opted the revolutionary project. A prophetic answer could not be more urgent than it is now.

As the product of these realizations, *After Evil* is about the unexpected twenty-first century that is now under way. It thus concerns what the twentieth century was and what it would have been if its lessons were finally learned. The new century, as the projected future of that past, was to be one of both ethics and prosperity. Its core imperative was to *remember* as much evil as we can so as not to *repeat* it. The presence of memory was not, however, merely a means of nonrepetition—it had also become a *criterion*. By the turn of the new century humanitarians had thus come to see evil itself as a cyclicity of violence and counterviolence that can be *broken* by remembering what it *was*. From this perspective past evil cannot be repeated unless it is forgotten—and what happens next will *necessarily* be different if, but only if, it reminds us that we have turned away from the past. To *admit* as much past evil as possible is thus, implicitly, to set oneself *against* evil in the future.

This book shows the illusion of historical closure behind such a view—the idea that the opportunity for justice has been missed, and that compassion for past suffering is a moral state that justifies one's continuing to benefit from past conditions that one now would have opposed. In the chapters that follow I stress the intertemporal aspect of justice as a struggle against the *ongoing* effects of bad history. I no longer assume, as I did when I began, that the end of evil and the beginning of justice must coincide—but I still believe that the two must be linked. Today's version of humanitarian consciousness undermines this link to the extent that its prime directive (holding evil at bay) always justifies postponing justice—now is *never* the time. But if the past was evil, we would do better to conclude that justice must be something new. Such evil cannot be past until justice here and now becomes imperative.

AFTER EVIL

INTRODUCTION | DISAVOWING EVIL

A New Century of Human Rights?

This book questions a specific politics of human rights that represents itself as coming after evil, especially the evil of the twentieth century.[1] Unlike earlier versions of human rights that sought to hasten the advance of social equality,[2] today's commitment to human rights often seeks to postpone large-scale redistribution. It is generally more defensive than utopian, standing for the avoidance of evil rather than a vision of the good.[3] This is the version of human rights that entered the political mainstream as the twenty-first century began.

The mainstreaming of human rights was a long time coming. During most of the twentieth century, appeals to human rights were considered idealistic—perhaps a suitable program for the victors of world wars but not a practical alternative to *realpolitik*. By the time the cold war ended, however, references to the twentieth century as "a century of genocide" had become commonplace,[4] and its atrocities were condemned as uncontestable paradigms of evil that transcended cultural, religious, and ideological difference.[5] The denunciation of physical atrocity *as such* became an essential element in the fin de siècle conception of what it means to be human, and the foundational premise of human rights advocacy.

By the turn of the twenty-first century, lifelong advocates of human rights were celebrating the emergence of a world community that defined itself as being *against* such atrocity, always and everywhere. This new, no longer controversial, version of human rights gradually ceased to address the perpetrators of atrocity; they had already placed themselves in the category of the *in*human as now defined. It would be aimed primarily at third parties—potential rescuers, whether governments or NGOs, who had in the past done nothing (or too little) because of indifference, *realpolitik*, and ethical relativism, and could now regard their humanitarian intervention as legitimated by the physical suffering already occurring on the ground. Such a shift in ruling ideology had been advocated by supporters of human rights since the Holocaust. Following the cold war, however, the arguments previously addressed *to* great powers were appropriated *by* them to legitimate their vision of a new world order embracing both capitalism and humanitarianism in much the way that, after the defeat of Napoleon, the Rights of Man became the foundation of a global order built on both imperialism and nationalism.

The chapters that follow step outside the mainstream story of ascendant human rights, based on the universal meaning of Auschwitz, both to criticize it as a political ideology and to expound it (perhaps more fully than it has been) as a plausible ethical standpoint. These two projects go together. If large-scale physical cruelty is the ultimate evil, it would seem to follow that *rescue* provides sovereign power with a legitimation that comes ahead even of democracy. The priority of rescue over democracy explains the increasing receptivity of global superpowers to calls for humanitarian intervention: foreign military regimes seem ethically justified—something had to be done—regardless of the degree and character of their local political support. But the reality of rule by rescuers shows the darker, more Hobbesian side of human rights—the underlying politics of fear and insecurity on which global hegemony is now based. This book addresses the turn-of-the-century politics of human rights as both ideal and ideology by relating the wish for human rights to the fears and powers it invokes.

No one who has lived in the twentieth century could seriously argue (nor do I) that international condemnation of human rights violators is a bad thing, and no one could deny that the struggle for human rights against authoritarian regimes is often progressive. My critique is specific to a Human Rights Discourse that became globally predominant after the fall of Communism in 1989, a moment of apparent closure to the discourse of global revolution and counterrevolution that followed from the 1789 Declaration of the Rights of Man. The distinction I draw between these two discourses is historical—and not primarily conceptual. Conceptually, it might have seemed in 1948—the year of both the Genocide Convention and the Universal Declaration—that freedom from "crimes against humanity" was an obvious *extension* of the Rights of Man. And some progressive political thinkers of the cold war era could plausibly argue that Auschwitz and the French Revolution were alternative *foundations* for the *same* human rights. I do not here dispute such conceptual claims. In the chapters that follow, I, rather, use Human Rights Discourse, capitalized as a proper name, to designate the transformation of Auschwitz-based reasoning into a new discourse of global power that claims to supersede the cruelties perpetrated by both revolutionaries and counterrevolutionaries during the previous two centuries.

Before proceeding, however, I must acknowledge that the position of power from which human rights is now articulated is not merely that of a particular hegemonic enforcer, such as the U.S., but rather a "world community." This, too, reflects the changed global situation at the end of the twentieth century. During the cold war no "world community" existed, and the fifty-year nuclear stalemate made it unacceptably risky for either global superpower to intervene in cases of large-scale human rights abuse condoned or committed by the other. This constraint was still present after the 1975 Helsinki Accords led to the proliferation of Helsinki groups throughout Eastern Europe that were "watched" by Human Rights Watch NGOs in the West.[6] The fall of communism in 1989 eliminated the excuse that a humanitarian show of force could provoke nuclear countermeasures and also weakened the constraint on intervention. By the first Persian Gulf War in 1991, a self-described "world community" no longer doubted its power to prevail over evil. And after the 1994 Rwandan genocide, which outsiders could easily have interrupted,[7] the advocates of human rights intervention shifted from questioning whether "couldn't implies shouldn't" to arguing that "could implies should."

The mainstream version of Human Rights Discourse now assumes that the world community should intervene *when it can* to prevent the repetition in the twenty-first century of the undeniable evils that it had failed to prevent in the twentieth.[8] *Then* we needed to know more before trying to stop the genocides occurring before our eyes; we never knew enough until it was too late. But *now* visual evidence of genocide (bearing witness) is sufficient for human rights advocates to urge the world community to rescue first and investigate later. For an ethical intervener, such as the U.S., to be overly concerned today about its own potential role as an imperialist is, according to this view, at best an anachronism and at worst the same old craven excuse for doing nothing that allowed the horrors of the twentieth century to take place.[9] The fin de siècle unacceptability of this excuse cries out in David Rieff's 1995 call for U.S. intervention after the preventable genocide in Bosnia:

> To utter words like "Never again," as Clinton did at the opening of the Holocaust Museum, was to take vacuity over the border into obscenity as long as the genocide in Bosnia was going on and Clinton was doing nothing to stop

it. His words were literally meaningless. For if there was to be no intervention to stop a genocide that was taking place, then the phrase "Never again" meant nothing more than: Never again would Germans kill Jews in Europe in the 1940s. Clinton might as well have said, "Never again the potato famine," or "Never again the slaughter of the Albigensians."[10]

The ethical imperative of post–cold war Human Rights Discourse is to "get it right" this time—to rescue the victims of a likely massacre before it is too late. The journalist Paul Berman presents this conclusion as the terminus of a journey traveled by the generation of 1968, his and mine, which grew up in the aftermath of the Holocaust believing that "the way to judge anyone's moral character, including your own, was to pose a hypothetical question, . . . what would you have done . . . under the German occupation? . . . Would you have been a *résistant*? Or a *collabo*?"[11]

Our generation, according to Berman, made a mistake in applying its ethic of resistance to U.S. imperialism in Vietnam but got the ethic right in bringing about the downfall of Eastern European communism. The ultimate conclusion of the "68'ers" moral journey (reached, Berman thinks, only by the best of us) is that, if resisting Hitler was an ethical imperative for those subjected to him, it would have been even better for states with sufficient power to have intervened while his atrocities could have been stopped. Elsewhere Berman elaborates this lesson as creating "new possibility in the field of human rights and humanitarian action." He describes this view as follows:

> People with power . . . had a right to intervene in other societies . . . in spite of the sacred mandates of international law and the inviolability of borders. There was a right to intervene on humanitarian grounds, and to do so "without borders." More than a right—there was . . . a moral duty to use power to rescue the vulnerable. A duty to use this power wherever people were in desperate need. A duty for wealthy and powerful countries not to stand by, fat and happy, while the rest of the world went to hell. Or to put this entire argument the other way, the supremely oppressed had a right to be rescued.[12]

This doctrine, now widely known as the international community's "Responsibility to Protect"[13] likely victims of humanitarian disaster, frankly argues that the concept of a "crime against humanity" (first introduced at Nuremberg) supersedes the prior notion of a "war crime"—that unilaterally bombing the civilian population of another country, for example, is no longer a prima facie war crime when it is done to *stop* a crime against humanity occurring on the ground. "There are," according to Berman, "bombs that rescue."[14]

My question in this book is not whether the "international community" should have (at least) interrupted Auschwitz or the Rwandan genocide by relatively costless aerial bombing when these atrocities became known;[15] rather, I am concerned with the conception of ethics and politics that underlies Berman's broader conclusion. According to this conception, bombing, like foreign occupation, can be a justifiable form of political intervention by third parties if, and only if, it is a response to gross ethical barbarities occurring locally.[16] The ethical condemnation of atrocity, if not always the atrocity itself, must here precede intervention, which then becomes an act of rescue—ethical and *not* (at least initially) political.

This view can be stated as a post-idealistic (sadder-but-wiser) version of liberal political thought that places the undeniable evil of the Holocaust at its center:

- The evil of genocide, as a universal ethical truth, takes priority over the contestable, culturally relative notions of good on which politics might otherwise rest.
- Avoidance of that evil must now replace the pursuit of good (fact must replace illusion) as the ethical foundation of a universal politics-based *human* rights.
- If *committing* genocide is undeniably evil, *denying* genocide helps to make that evil possible.
- The denial of genocide by third parties thus contributed to the evils of the twentieth century.
- After those evils, third parties can no longer make the excuse that rescuing victims (when possible) would involve choosing sides in a political struggle.
- Those who deny genocide put politics (the pursuit of goods) ahead of ethics (the repudiation of evil).
- The ethics of non-evil must now come before a concern for whatever politics may follow from a bystander's act of rescue.

The ethically centered approach to human rights that triumphed after the fall of communism in 1989 implicitly superseded the politically centered version of the Rights of Man that had been the focus of struggles for equality and liberty since the French Revolution of 1789.[17] Third-party interveners in struggles inspired by the French Revolution tended to come in on the side of reaction, and thus against the Rights of Man. The new conception of human rights, however, sees the "world community" as the essential protector and foregrounds the position of the third-party intervener. The following presuppositions of the new discourse of human rights underscore its difference from the earlier view:

- Today's human rights *abuse* is essentially local—typified by the atrocities that neighbors inflict upon neighbor and not, for example, by the global maldistribution of wealth.
- Today's human rights *enforcement* is essentially global—a duty of third parties to intervene (across borders when necessary) to rescue neighbor from neighbor.
- Third-party *rescue* is fully justified by the human rights violations that neighboring combatants are inflicting, or have inflicted, on each other.
- The *means* used for human rights enforcement (which might include aerial bombardment, military invasion, or an embargo of essential goods and services) are exempt from being considered to be human rights violations in themselves.

The Evil That Is Past

My title, *After Evil*, refers not only to what follows the twentieth century but, more broadly, to the meaning of its pastness in the politics of the twenty-first—what the century of genocide *will have been* for those who live on. Those who participated in twentieth-century struggles imagined a future consensus on what evil *was*. This did not mean that all sides believed themselves to be on the side of good. It may be enough to believe that the *other* side thinks this and that its victory would leave one in a state of permanent disgrace. This is why revelations of atrocity may reinforce, rather than diminish, the intransigence of the side that commits them, and why ordinary individuals may fight desperately when they have some inkling of the brutalities that might eventually be disclosed. When one side envisions a future consensus on the meaning of evil, the other will often fight on to postpone that consensus.

Evil is, of course, generally a term of contestation rather than consensus. When Milton's Satan ("The Enemy") says "Evil, be thou my good," he inaugurates a war for the soul of mankind based on the meaning of the distinction between good and evil itself. If a struggle over the *meaning* of evil is the moral template for war, then consensus on the *fact* of evil is what it would mean for this war to end. The wars of the twentieth century ended with consensus on both the fact and evil of genocide.[18] Denying that genocide happened (for example, Holocaust denial) became not merely factual disagreement about the past but a way to challenge, as Satan did, the prevailing ethical consensus on the meaning of good and evil, and thus put reconciliation to an end.

As an effort to theorize the aftermath of the twentieth century, my project has turned out to be about the temporal dimension of human rights—the pasts they bring to closure, the futures they foreclose. Its argument is implicitly framed by other dates: the French Revolution of 1789 (with its Declaration of the Rights of Man and the Citizen)[19] and September 11, 2001—the equation of human rights with a war on terror. In the course of writing this book I have come to believe that the revolutionary conception of human rights that dominated the period between 1789 and 1989 has been supplanted by a counterrevolutionary conception of human rights that regards this two-hundred-year period as evil.

This book has become a critique of a historically specific politics of human rights that was formed by the moral repudiation of Nazism after 1945 and became the dominant ideology of capitalist democracy after the collapse of communism in 1989. My starting point is that the present political character of Human Rights Discourse is distinct from the broader concept of human rights associated with 1789, which was the topic of debate and struggle between the revolutionary and counterrevolutionary movements of the nineteenth and twentieth centuries.[20] That earlier conception, carried forward in the twentieth century welfare state and heavily represented in Eleanor Roosevelt's 1948 conception of a Universal Declaration of human rights, is now almost gone.[21] The post-1989 politics of human rights is not meant to be contested in the same *political* way as its predecessor—rather, it presents itself as an *ethical* transcendence of the politics of revolution and counterrevolution that together produced the horrors of the twentieth century—Nazism and communism. In the twenty-first century human rights is put forward as a cure for the mind-sets that made those now twinned evils intelligible to their proponents as moral goods. The new century was thus initially welcomed as coming *after* evil, a century in which the atrocities committed in the name of either revolution or counterrevolution are supposed to have become unthinkable and, if not, to justify the world community's humanitarian intervention to stop them. Today the invocation of human rights is often part of a political project fundamentally at odds with the revolutionary struggles based on human rights: it is the war cry of a self-described "international community" led by the victors in the cold war.[22]

The present discourse of human rights, unlike the Declaration of the Rights of Man that proclaimed a global revolutionary divide, attempts to move once divided societies from a moral psychology of struggle to one of reconciliation. Some scholars see overall progress in this development;[23] others take a contrary view.[24] In either case, a fundamental difference exists between human rights as a slogan of popular resistance and today's Human Rights movement, with its ostensibly less political focus on compassion for bodies in pain.

Human Rights Discourse is thus the name I give to the self-consciously *ethical* rejection of previous versions of the Rights of Man that were violently *against* the power of aristocracies, autocracies, and the like. Unlike previous conceptions of human rights that were a call to uprising and resistance, Human Rights Discourse operates today in the realm of intervention and rescue. It recasts the central dyads of revolutionary political thought— victim/perpetrator and victim/beneficiary—as nondivisive ethical relations among surviving witnesses to human cruelty. When it has its desired cultural effect, Human Rights Discourse is said to transform the attitudes that make it possible to engage in righteous struggle into those that make it possible to stop. The underlying hope of today's Human Rights Discourse is that victims of past evil will not struggle against its ongoing beneficiaries after the evildoers are gone.

Between Forgiveness and Vengeance?

To victims still suffering, forgiveness or vengeance often present themselves as two *competing* conceptions of the moral imperative that would remain after evil has ceased and before justice comes. There is thus an implicit assumption that surviving victims, or those who speak in their name, either have a duty to take vengeance (that they are obliged to do so) or that they really ought to forgive, and could be deservedly criticized if they are so damaged that they cannot do so.[25] There is, however, an obvious ethical problem with vengeance: it leads to a cycle of future vengeance that must be broken for justice to commence. The ethical problem with forgiveness is that forgivers can be deservedly criticized for failing to remember— and remembrance implies, if not vengeance, at least an unwillingness to let go of the desire for vengeance even after one decides that it is better not to act on it.[26] It is ironic, but nevertheless true, that we must *remember* that we wanted vengeance in order to know that we have truly forgiven.

This ethical tension between the imperatives to hold a grievance and to forgive is deeply evident in Hannah Arendt's account of forgiveness as a "new beginning"—a beginning aware of itself as beginning *again*:

> Forgiving attempts the seemingly impossible, to undo what has been done, and . . . [make] a new beginning when beginnings seemed to have become no longer possible. . . . Forgiving is the only strictly human action that releases us and others from the chain and pattern of consequences that all action engenders; as such forgiving is the capacity for action, for beginning anew.[27]

Here Arendt shows that forgiveness is paradoxical—indeed, strictly impossible—and that its importance is in the light it sheds on the simultaneously backward- and forward-looking aspects of political action in the present. The paradox is that a self-conscious politics of justice is always a matter of both doing and *un*doing. In looking forward there is an imperative to *do without* remembering; yet we must remember in order to *undo*.

Rather than work through Arendt's paradox, the mainstream literature on transitional justice tries to take a middle ground between forgiving and forgetting. It typically advises posttraumatic regimes in which it is wrong to indulge in vengeance but equally wrong to forget the past. Its goal is to avoid both pitfalls by remembering what happened in ways that fall far short of undoing it. This is often described as a stance somewhere "between vengeance and forgiveness."[28]

What does it mean to see forgiveness and vengeance as polar opposites *between* which one must *stand*? Forgiveness is a sovereign act—potentially an act of indifference, rather than compassion, that might be more humiliating than a punishment. From a sovereign standpoint, forgiveness is compatible with revenge—it might sometimes be the best revenge. The apparent need to choose between forgiveness and vengeance arises from the standpoint of former victims who are still unsure about whether they have won. For them successful vengeance could resolve this question by proving that victory was really theirs; but the thought that vengeance might fail, and perhaps even backfire, reinforces their anxiety that they may yet lose—not just politically but morally as well.

A rhetoric that locates itself between vengeance and forgiveness would be a weapon of the weak that provides at least an illusion of victory over those whose power they still have reason to fear. By taking this standpoint, the former victim tries not to think about who really won and eschews the temptation to engage in a political analysis that might open the question of whether that evil has finally been defeated.²⁹ Today's mainstream literature on transitional justice tends to assume that past victims never really win—their choice is whether to persist in struggle or to stop—and that stopping makes sense if they can declare a moral victory that seems to put oppression in the past.

Before Justice Comes

A recurring theme of this book is the inherently transitional character of Human Rights Discourse: it addresses a time between times, when evil has ended but before justice has begun.³⁰ There is, *ex hypothesi*, still time before a leap into justice and still a danger of relapse into the evil of the past. The question is whether it will always be *too soon* for justice until it is *too late*.

The *locus classicus* for thinking about a time between is Saint Paul's description of the Church in the time between the Resurrection and Christ's return in Judgment. Paul assured the members of his movement that everything necessary for messianic justice had already occurred, even though a time still remained in which the world would seem to go on as before. In addressing those who lived in this time between the forgiveness of sin and the coming of justice, Paul's task was to explain what it would mean to live as though everything had already changed because of Christ. Since the Crucifixion, Paul argued, everything necessary has already happened to bring about the forgiveness of past sin and reconcile mankind with God; since the Resurrection, nothing more will be necessary to establish God's promise to save mankind from death. Now is a time to wait in faith that the deferral of justice is necessary to allow *more* time for the world to acknowledge that everything has changed.

What kind of life is justified now? Paul's answer is not to live *as if* we were still in the pre-messianic past when sin was unforgiveable and hatred of the sinner was virtue; neither is it to live *as if* we were in the messianic future when God's justice has come and the sinner has already been punished. The former politicizes messianism; the latter aestheticizes it. Living in the now, for Paul, means living *as not*—not still in the past, not yet in the future—"but in the time it takes for time to come to an end."³¹ According to Paul, the sins that we commit *now*, after having forsaken sin, will be different from our earlier transgressions of law that have been pardoned, and will be judged by a different standard. Sin will henceforward take the form of behaving as we would if the past were not over; it must be judged as a failure of faith—the faith that we are already forgiven and are now free to forgive accordingly because the time itself has changed.

Echoing the rhetoric of Pauline Christianity, the fin de siècle discourse on human rights has instilled faith that times have changed in transitional societies such as South Africa, which have thus far been spared their Armageddons. In these societies, which seem in many ways *un*changed, the sins that come after sinning often take the form of returning to (dredging up) the past and violating the faith that things are already different—or *will* be once everyone accepts the change that has occurred. A further point is that societies entering a new era of human rights become convinced that they have been given *extra time* to change. The new question is whether this extra time must be prolonged because it is still too soon for justice, or whether it must be compressed so as to give justice greater exigency before it is too late. Meanwhile, to be saved (as in Augustine) or ethical (as in Kant) consists of living in a virtual reality in which one acts *as if* others had good-will even though they do not. What then is the difference between faith and fiction, between human rights as a second chance and as a missed opportunity in which the appearance of change substitutes for the reality? Agamben writes about the ethical distinction between living "as if" and living "as not":

> For Paul the redemption of what has been is the place of an exigency in the messianic. . . . The *as not* is by no means a fiction. . . . It has nothing to do with an ideal. . . . [T]hat which is not . . . is stronger than that which is. . . . [T]he messianic is the simultaneous abolition and realization of the *as if* . . . [T]he saved world coincides with the world that is irretrievably lost. . . . This means that he may not disguise the world's being-without-god in any way . . . and cannot pretend to save the appearance of salvation. The messianic subject does not contemplate the world as though it were saved.[32]

For Agamben, the heightened exigency of a salvation that has yet to occur is thus as much a part of Paul's messianism as putting evil in the past. Believing that there is *still* time, that it is not *too late*, has a different moral valence than believing that the moment for justice has been irretrievably missed, that it is postponed indefinitely, or that we have already been saved without deserving to be. For Paul, the time that remains is implicitly God-forsaken—God came and will return. This foreshortened time, a period of God's absence, has special meaning according to Paul because now is the time we have to change the world. Paul's messianism is not, primarily, the prophecy of an apocalypse but a way to live in the meantime. "The messianic is not the end of time, but the time of the end."[33]

Many of the most serious disagreements in politics concern the meaning of this transitional time: though some will argue that *the time has come* for change—"Never again"—others will argue that the next occurrence of evil will be the last—"the fire next time." Still others will say that what happened *last time* simply adds to what we already knew about past evil, which cannot be defended but which is so profound that redemption will require a miracle to change the human heart.

It is not necessary, however, to take a messianic view of the need for change in a time without God. To believe that we are living after evil and before justice is the essence of what it means to live in a secular age. Secularity is always a secondary concept, defined by whatever element of the sacred is absent from it, and by how that element of sacredness would be conceived.[34] In a post-Christian culture, secular history is still the time St. Paul carved out between two messianic moments. It is thus not merely transitional time (which could not go on forever) but also a gift of *more* time that would not have existed if the end of evil and the establishment of justice had occurred at once, as perhaps they should have. In my view, present-day Human Rights Discourse is an intermessianic (and implicitly antimessianic) secular theology in which former victims, and those who may have inflicted or benefited from their suffering, await a final judgment that some hope and others fear will never come. This conception of the secular age as a time between messianic moments implies that now is never the time for justice.[35]

To call Human Rights Discourse a secular theology is not necessarily a criticism; if it is, I don't know whether one would be criticizing that discourse for being secular (not theological *enough*) or for still being theological.[36] Secularization was, to begin with, a religious idea that originates *within* Judeo-Christian thought: it is what God does to himself when he creates the world and subsequently intervenes in its history. As a political idea, secularization arises out of the Roman separation of church and state. It occurs when the state usurps the legitimate spiritual function of the church, or when, perhaps surreptitiously, it relies on ideas that have already been delegitimated in their ecclesiastical form. Pauline Christianity gives believers extra time to confess and accept forgiveness for their sins before justice finally comes. Is Human Rights Discourse a secularization of this view?

Nothing in my view hinges on whether a fixed boundary between religion and politics has been breached. I am inclined to be suspicious of any ideology, religious or political, that makes people wait for justice, but I accept the legitimacy of asking in the aftermath of evil whether it is still too soon to demand justice. Neither of these views is more religious or political than its opposite. Those who insist that now *is* the time for justice thereby imply that it is *too late* for retrospection and forgiveness. This might seem to surrender some of the higher ground that Pauline Christians often claim. But Paul himself acknowledged that a moment for final justice must come, and he had to explain why his congregations should nevertheless view the delay in Christ's return as further evidence of God's grace rather than as a betrayal of God's promise. On the secular side, too, there are those who argue that it is *always* better to give people more time to change—a second chance—rather than risk their relapse into evil by demanding justice too urgently. There are also others who insist that we need to know what time it really is before saying that people should get a second chance.

The moral rhetoric of the second chance (and not the new beginning) is what distinguishes the fin de siècle discourse of human rights from earlier revolutionary versions. Rather than hastening the end, today's version of human rights buys more time for those who fear it may already be too late and provides hope that there is still an opportunity to avoid a final judgment on the past. This temporal logic is not unique to the field of human rights. Activists on global warming also argue that it is too late (the earth is past the tipping point) in order to persuade people to hope that it is not. We, the first-world beneficiaries of global warming, are promised in effect a second chance, not at ultimate success but at being judged differently for the policies we pursue from now on than we would be judged if global warming had happened before we understood the need for change.

Carving out a time in which our sins are no longer a continuation of the past is characteristic of periods of transitional justice. Such periods are typically marked by an unstable equipoise between Redemption and Reconstruction. Redeemers believe that the present actions must no longer be judged as a continuation of a past evil that has been confessed. Reconstructionists counter that the time for change has accelerated and is already running out. Both sides presuppose that their debate occurs in a special kind of time—accelerated time, abbreviated time, slow time, supplementary time—which comes before the onset of the future but after the end of the now discredited past.[37]

The main tropes of metahistory—including revolution, reaction, redemption, reconciliation, return, and rebirth (as well as catastrophe, upheaval, transition, and emancipation)—are all originally theological, but not in the sense of being spiritual rather than secular. They are, rather, about the *time* of change, the rate at which time *changes*, and the time it *takes* to change. The chapters that follow are always, more or less explicitly, about the changing temporalities in which claims to justice are made and contested. What does it mean for a great evil, such as Nazism, U.S. slavery, South African apartheid, or Stalinism to be over and done with?

Human Rights Discourse of the late twentieth century puts all such questions into a single metahistorical narrative that culminates in Human Rights Discourse itself. In this narrative, a moral consensus on evil is both necessary and sufficient to put it in the past; once this happens, resuming old political struggles can be repudiated as a potentially catastrophic effort to go *backward*. My initial response is that believing that the past was evil does not require one to believe that the evil is past. The problem, I argue, is when and whether a time for justice has come. But to make this argument I must take the reader on a considerable journey.

The Chapters Ahead

Our journey begins with the idea of launching a revolution against a form of social organization that fits to varying degrees the metaphor of a giant *labor* camp—such as a plantation, a mine, a factory, or even a prison. Variants of the labor camp may differ in their degree of centralization and homogeneity—and also in the type of mobility available to its subjects through, for example, escape, migration, and contractual consent. Using labor as a central metaphor—and not, for example, captivity, or poverty—focuses attention on the aspect of production and thereby opens the question of *who* benefits and *how* benefits accumulate. These questions about beneficiaries and their cumulative gains distinguish a revolution against a labor-camp system itself from mere overthrow of those who run it. To react against revolution—thus defined (to be "counterrevolutionary")—is to resist the moral equation of beneficiaries of injustice, with its direct perpetrators, and thus to preserve accumulated gains resulting from the system as a whole. Today's Human Rights Discourse contributes to the counterrevolutionary project of reassuring structural beneficiaries by focusing on violent crimes committed against the *bodies* of victims. Chapter 1 concludes that in Human Rights Discourse victims, thus defined, get to claim a moral victory when, and insofar as, the beneficiaries get to keep their gains.

Chapters 2 and 3 develop my argument in the context of two historical versions of the labor-camp model: South African apartheid and U.S. slavery. Both chapters focus on the conceptual process through which beneficiaries of both systems come to reidentify themselves as common *survivors* by bearing witness to the horrors of a *past* they now disavow. In the course of comparing South Africa and the United States (for example, on questions of "closure" versus "permanent recovery"), I consider what it means for an ongoing beneficiary to *put* injustice in the past by embracing the standpoint of a compassionate witness to it. If the beneficiary comes to see himself as, essentially, a "successor" to a now defunct regime, based on victimization, would it not be altogether *good* to be that beneficiary? Isn't this how European colonists, imbued by classical studies, viewed their unfortunate period of overlap with preexisting cultures, which could be honored and commemorated after they were gone?

Chapter 4 recommences my genealogy of Human Rights Discourse by adding questions arising from the critique of colonialism to those arising from the critique of capitalism. Just as capitalism raises questions of interpersonal justice between victim and beneficiary, colonialism raises questions of intertemporal justice about the relation of "settler" and "native": Who came first? Who will survive? And what is the relation of geographical space, cultural continuity, and biological extermination to the meaning of such survival? Colonies often functioned as labor camps within global capitalism, but colonialism itself had rationales that did not assume that the native and settler had a mutual need for the other's co-presence and ultimate survival. In addition to plantations, mines, and factories, it thus developed "reservations" (U.S.), "reserves" (British), and eventually "concentration camps," which appear first in colonized Africa and eventually in twentieth-century Europe. The main purpose of such *concentrations* was to reduce the space occupied by expendable populations: to *waste* them rather than use them—and eventually to eliminate them. Mid-twentieth century *death camps* used such violent methods of mass extermination that the whole idea of ethnic removal ("cleansing") is now associated with the threat of genocide.

Chapter 5 finds the core of Human Rights Discourse in the claim that death camps, exemplified by Auschwitz, are paradigmatically evil. One aspect of this paradigm is that the question of beneficiaries (nearly) drops out; a related aspect is that genocide, as such, becomes the ethical kernel of any critique of labor camps, reservations, and unjust regimes in general— what is ultimately wrong (once identified) is their noncommitment to the biological survival of subject populations. Human Rights Discourse adapts this argument ("no more death camps") after the cold war to allow the "international community" to intervene in former colonies for the purpose of rescuing human bodies without purporting to recolonize such "failed states."[38] The global "Responsibility to Protect" doctrine rests on a new paradigm, the *refugee* camp, which exists to save lives rather than to use or waste them and is therefore ethically distinguishable from both a labor camp and a colonial reservation. This ethical difference is large but not infinite. The inhabitants of refugee camps are rarely killed or exploited but are still disempowered, and they rarely benefit beyond having been saved. What matters in fin de siècle humanitarianism is simply to save them, and thus to be against their suffering and death. Here we reach the crux of the twenty-first-century conception of human rights, namely, that there is nothing worse than cruelty and that cruelty toward physical (animal) bodies is the worst of all. If the Holocaust now reveals genocide to be an absolute, and infinite, evil, then the only universal ethics after evil would be to put human rights, as a "Responsibility to *Protect*," ahead of *any* claim to justice (which will always be less absolute than the Holocaust). The chapter concludes by discussing the philosophical characteristics and limitations of this view, which authorizes third-party witnesses (and would-be rescuers) to claim ethical priority over militant believers in a new truth.

Chapter 6 explores the substantive centrality of the Holocaust to Human Rights Discourse as it emerged in the twentieth century. I treat this body of thought as a, perhaps, secular example of the "Jewish Question" originally asked and answered by St. Paul: Why are there *still* Jews now that Christ has given Jewish suffering a universal meaning? The first modern version of this question arose in the nineteenth century when the secular citizenship that Jews once sought in Christian states was extended to everyone and became the universal paradigm of citizenship as such. In similar fashion, the late-twentieth-century paradigm of universal *human* rights (such as the right of refugees to be saved) was self-consciously developed to prevent what happened to Jews in the Holocaust from happening again, to anyone. But now that Jewish history has once more been universalized, why do Jews still think that they are the *only* "Jews"? In confronting this question, I consider how the Holocaust has made the murdered Jew the paradigmatic human rights victim and modern Israel's survival the *constitutive exception* on which Human Rights Discourse is based. The parallel I draw between this discourse and Paul's Judeo-Christianity concludes with a discussion of militant Islamism as its political-theological "outside." Here I focus on the analogy between Crucifixion denial and Holocaust denial and whether giving universal value to past (Jewish) suffering brings the need for prophecy to an end.

Chapter 7 calls into question the fundamental mechanism of moral change on which a post-Auschwitz culture of human rights purports to rely—the conversion from "bystander" to "witness." Here the compassionate witness projects onto the actual victim feelings of *unfulfillment* that he already satisfies. How? Because the witness provides narrative fulfillment to the victim's story by putting it in his *own* remembered past. But the witness's real moral identification is not, I argue, with an actual victim but with a hypothetical *other* bystander who would have been an opponent by bearing witness in time. The chapter concludes with the question of whether beneficiaries ought to feel guilty about whether they would have been perpetrators rather than *just lucky* to be beneficiaries. The lucky are, by *definition*, those who benefit undeservedly but without doing anything wrong.

Chapter 8 returns to the position of beneficiaries and takes up a question previously set aside: Is it conceptually impossible (or just too hard) to account for the past history in structuring future benefit flows? Shifting to the register of law, I argue that we *already* use property rules to trace revenue flows retroactively and redirect them in the future and that, under the law of remedies, property can be created (or inferred) to account for past injustice. A "constructive trust," for example, is an equitable remedy for "unjust enrichment." This device treats unjustly acquired wealth as though it had been held in trust for victims, allowing them (and their successors in interest) access to revenue streams similar to those that would flow from ordinary (nonremedial) property rights. Once present beneficiaries of past injustice are regarded as constructive trustees, it does not matter whether they are personally guilty or not. A further point is that property rights (the effect of the past on the present) include embedded *options* (puts and calls) that could be separately priced and included in the corpus of such a constructive trust. This mode of valuation has recently been used to bring about a massive redistribution of global wealth based on property rights that have nothing to do with remedial justice. Although *any* use of such methods is, and should be, contestable, it is clear that barriers to using them for purposes of social reparation are not primarily conceptual. They are political and psychological barriers, reinforced by the comfort Human Rights Discourse gives to beneficiaries.

Chapter 9 considers the questions of why and whether perpetrators should be prosecuted. My focus here is Nuremberg, which stands as an exception to my general critique of recent "humanitarian" thought. I still disagree, however, with the now common interpretation of Nuremberg: that it advanced a transition from a "culture of impunity" to the "rule of law" by prosecuting only a few leading Nazis and (implicitly) giving amnesty to the rest. Today experts on transitional justice often favor declaring such amnesties explicitly, and in advance, so that there will not be a backlash if a few human rights trials need to be held. The real audience for such trials, they contend, is conformists in the old regime who now can think that they *would have been* opponents had they known what was really going on. What about the next "emergency"? As cultural conformists they can, henceforward, articulate the regret they *will feel* when "the full facts" are eventually known, while taking comfort from the fact that such knowledge will always come too late for them to be found blameworthy. I argue, against this view, that the central point of Nuremberg was to hold individuals responsible when it matters. The accused at Nuremberg were specifically not allowed the defense of a good faith belief that, following the Reichstag Fire, Jews and Communists really did pose a threat to the newly elected Nazi government. Contemporaneous statements alleging such a danger were, rather, part of the prosecution's case that defendants were collectively liable for conspiring to maximize Nazi power. When the Tribunal found sufficient evidence to hold defendants *individually* liable for their crimes, it did not go back and say that the constitutional "emergency" declared after the Reichstag was even partially exculpatory with respect to violating the international laws on which defendants were tried. The Bush administration understood and feared the possibility of Nuremberg-based prosecutions when it gave its officials what Nazi defendants lacked—legal opinion letters *stating* that the 9/11 emergency was a *full* defense. This way around Nuremberg has been rightly rejected by the Obama administration, which has reverted to the cultural argument that going forward with human rights trials would be unnecessary and divisive once "change has come." To the extent that this view prevails, a self-declared culture of human rights would become yet another "culture of impunity."

Chapter 10 considers the implications of this entire book for the work camp, death camp, and refugee camp as the basis of a late-twentieth-century dialectic of the "human." My underlying notion of humanitarianism as a counterreligion, rejecting the cruelty of whatever religion came before, here takes the foreground. I thus directly take up the moral psychology of conversion as both the expression and repression of the wish to kill a god who would demand human death. The underlying paradox, I argue, is that counterreligions treat the cruelty of human sacrifice as both a paradigm of injustice and as a reason to transcend justice itself with compassion (love) for the sacrificial victim. Claims of justice are thus neither originary nor self-sufficient—they always come after some form of human sacrifice (after evil). And they are often vague about what they reject in human sacrifice. Is it the *use* of human life that occurs in the work camp? Or the *useless expenditure* of human life that happens in the death camp? Or the *waiting* (to be saved/freed) that exists in the refugee camp? The question of whether *something* could redeem past human sacrifice, or justify collective self-sacrifice, pervades my concern throughout this book with issues such as revolution vs. compassion, exploitation vs. succession, St. Paul vs. Muhammad, messianism vs. the prophetic tradition—and the special roles projected onto "Jews" in each of these debates.

I conclude that such debates are still about justice, after all, but that justice itself is an intertemporal problem (the supersession of one time by another) and not simply an interpersonal problem. Both aspects of justice appear, I contend, in the recent clash between secular humanism (a variant of Judeo-Christian messianism) and resurgent forms of prophetic religion including, but not limited to, late-twentieth-century Islamism. The central issue (which has always arisen within, and not between, world "civilizations") is whether there is, finally, nothing worse than age-old human cruelty—returning to past evil—or whether something new has happened (or will have happened) that changes everything. My title, *After Evil*, evokes a time that comes *before justice* when justice may seem less urgent; this book is my attempt to keep its urgency alive.

1

THE IDEOLOGY AND ETHICS OF HUMAN RIGHTS

The *End* of Human Rights

What did it mean for the victors of the cold war to describe its end as a victory for human rights? In their institutional outcomes we can see obvious similarities between the "third-wave" *democratizations* of the late twentieth century and an earlier "age" of democratic *revolution*.[1] But there was also an obvious distinction: the third wave of democratizations had mostly occurred without revolutionary violence. Was it a final victory or a final defeat for human rights that they were now disentangled from the inevitable cruelties of revolutionary struggle?

Many historians of human rights regard it as a world-historical achievement to extract the humanitarian kernel or empathy for *all* who suffer from the political hell of revolutionary struggle in which *some* suffering is welcome as a means of change.[2] This view marks a rarely acknowledged shift in the meaning of human rights activism. Today the revolutionary is no longer the standard paradigm of a militant for human rights; his willingness to inflict suffering on enemies raises too many questions about politically motivated cruelty. Our new paradigm of human rights activism—the kind that seems unquestionably good—now consists of rescuing those who suffer, even if that suffering is inflicted in the name of revolution. If rescuing victims is what human rights activism does today, those on the ground who resist or attack the rescuers (perhaps for being *invaders* and *occupiers*) are no longer considered to be freedom fighters but rather are seen as enemies, and paradigmatic *violators*, of human rights as such.

By the twentieth century's end, the moral truth of human rights was often said to rest on a sympathetic identification with innocent victims on all sides that finally breaks the cycles of violence that revolutions too often produce.[3] In its new proximity to power, today's human rights establishment speaks with increasing hostility toward social movements that might once have been described as struggles for the Rights of Man and the Citizen. Such struggles are now described as enemies of the new Human Rights Discourse insofar as they engage in acts of "terror" or hesitate to condemn such acts elsewhere.

A few human rights scholars reject the mainstream view, arguing that a bland ideology of humanitarian*ism* had made it seem that the intervention by a "monolithic humanity" against local forms of resistance to authority could now be rationalized as largely benign. The legal theorist Costas Douzinas, for example, argues that revolutionary politics is at the core of human rights consciousness ("human rights are the necessary and impossible claim of law to justice") and that the myth of a pragmatic and compassionate humanitarianism brings this consciousness to an end. ("The end of human rights comes when they lose their utopian end.")[4]

There is truth in both positions. Demands for free elections and civil liberties that were revolutionary in 1789 and 1848 have become uncontroversial in the twenty-first century: it no longer *takes* a revolution to accomplish them, as it did in societies where feudal forms of power still prevailed. It is also true, however, that the ideology of postmodern humanitarianism understands itself as coming *after* a world politics based on revolution and counterrevolution. Post-1989 Human Rights Discourse must thus be understood as a critique and supersession of earlier ideas of revolutionary struggle in much the way that the post-1789 doctrine of the Rights of Man must be understood as a critique and supersession of the feudal ideas that it put in the past. In this respect it is *not* an unqualified triumph for those ideas.

Justice as Struggle

The main idea that post–cold war humanitarianism claims to supersede is the revolutionary concept of justice-as-struggle. Revolutionary ideologies (whether Marxist or not) typically had a social theory to show victims that their suffering has beneficiaries and a political practice aimed at provoking those beneficiaries into siding with the perpetrators when their benefits were threatened. By recognizing the beneficiaries of injustice as would-be perpetrators, victims would achieve the heightened "consciousness" necessary to liberate themselves through revolution.

The figure of the unreconciled victim dominated world political thought from the French Revolution of 1789 to the fall of communism in 1989. For unreconciled victims, justice itself would become a continuing struggle—not merely to defeat the evil regime but also to force remaining beneficiaries of past injustice to permanently relinquish their illegitimate gains. This was the final victory that the revolution aimed to achieve, the social question to be addressed when power had been won.

The revolutionary ideology of justice-as-struggle allowed former victims of the old regime to construct themselves as combatants, even after the fact, by regarding the initial victory over the perpetrators of oppression as merely the first stage in a longer struggle against the passive beneficiaries of the old regime.[5] Postrevolutionary justice thus became a form of militant struggle against the return of past evil. In practice this meant portraying the ongoing beneficiaries of past evil as a counterrevolutionary threat, thereby giving more of them reason to become the class-based enemies of revolution that they had always been according to unreconciled victims. In the grand narrative of revolution, the "foundational" violence necessary to seize power from the perpetrators of past injustice is followed by a potentially less limited violence against continuing beneficiaries (the Terror), which escalates when counterrevolutionary ideology is joined to popular insurgencies (the terror*ism* of *contras*) and supported from outside. This path is not inevitable; the victim-as-revolutionary can renounce it if he is willing to abandon his social program and/or accept defeat at the hands of the revolution's domestic and foreign enemies.[6] From this it follows, however, that revolutions do not succeed unless revolutionaries are willing to do whatever it takes to consolidate their gains.[7]

Because revolutionaries tend to repudiate the "merely moral" victory that could be claimed by abandoning their social program, the danger of moral defeat is always real; it will have already occurred if they give up the struggle for material justice; it may yet occur if they pursues that struggle until the revolution discredits itself through Terror. "While revolution," Koselleck notes, "was initially induced by its opponents as well as its proponents, once established in its legitimacy, it proceeded to continually reproduce its foe as a means through which it could remain permanent."[8]

Thus the political trajectory of revolutionary justice is to create enemies until it is eventually defeated by the enemies it creates—first morally and then politically.[9] In revolutionary justice the victim is to become victor; the problem with this concept is that nothing counts as winning except continuing the fight. But the problem with abandoning it is that nothing counts as justice if it is not worth the struggle.

On the counterrevolutionary side of the twentieth-century ideological divide, the defining fear was precisely that victorious victims would come to exercise a militant and punitive form of rule. Those who embraced a counterrevolutionary politics did not necessarily believe that their cause was just; some may even have accepted the revolutionary theory revealing them as beneficiaries of the suffering of others. This, however, only heightened their anxiety. For counterrevolutionaries it was often enough to believe that one's cause has made one hated by one's enemies (even justly hated) in order to conclude that rule by victorious victims would be worse than the status quo. To be a counterrevolutionary was to fear being ruled by those who regarded themselves as one's (former) victims—to fear them because the moral damage of victimhood itself, or of struggling against it, would make victims, if they were to achieve victory, capable of worse atrocities than those they suffered.

Disagreement over the moral damage suffered by victims has been at the heart of the political debates over revolution/counterrevolution: for revolutionaries, political militancy cleansed the victim of the moral damage that accompanies resentment. The counterrevolutionary saw the experience of victimhood as morally damaging in itself, and rejected the revolutionary faith that this damage would be overcome through the redemptive effects of struggle. From the counterrevolutionary perspective, the least just state would be that in which victors rule with the consciousness of victims. The fear that beneficiaries of injustice have of living under rulers who think they are still victims is the ethical basis for condoning regimes that they might otherwise concede are unjust.

Justice as Reconciliation

Following the cold war we are told that a culture of respect for human rights has narrowed or overcome the ideological divide between revolution and counterrevolution. This outcome appears as the desirable result of the techniques of transitional justice—including truth commissions and human rights trials[10]—that if practiced in just the right amount can bring about a cultural transformation that will leave liberal democracy secure.

I believe, however, that the real outcome must be described as a continuation of the counterrevolutionary project by other, less repressive means.[11] In transitional societies such as South Africa (the favored case for Human Rights Discourse), former victims establish that they were morally undamaged by allowing beneficiaries to keep most, if not all, of their gains from the discredited past without having to defend those gains as legitimate. Distributive justice is thus largely off the agenda of societies with new human rights cultures, except to the extent that redistribution can be divorced from retribution and recast as "reparation"—which in South Africa consisted of acknowledging past practices of repression that beneficiaries no longer have reason to deny or condone.[12] The result was to reinstate the distinction between perpetrators and beneficiaries that revolutionary politics denies, and thus to reassign political responsibility for past injustice from the class that benefited to the individuals who implemented the old regime's policies. By accepting the distinction between individual perpetrators and collective beneficiaries of injustice as essential to the "rule of law," the formerly revolutionary victim becomes "reconciled" to the continuing benefits of past injustice that fellow citizens still enjoy. He would thus appear "undamaged" in the sense that he now puts his victimhood firmly in the past.

In the moral narrative that culminates in today's Human Rights Discourse, the techniques of transitional justice save societies from the spiral of revolutionary violence by allowing beneficiaries of past injustice to see its victims as morally undamaged ("they didn't hate us after all"). Those who benefited passively from social injustice can now comfortably bear witness to the innocence of idealized victims whose ability to transcend their suffering reveals that they were never really a threat. The new social compact is an implicit agreement to treat unreconciled victims, who *still* equate the beneficiaries with perpetrators, as a true threat that may once have been legitimately feared but must now be repudiated. Those unreconciled victims who remain are compared to "extremists" on the other side whose reactionary embrace of violence plays on the fears of beneficiaries that they will be victimized in their turn. The political effect of recent Human Rights Discourse is thus to marginalize those on *both* sides who are still willing to fight on. In this social compact, victims get to claim a "moral victory" but only insofar as they are willing to regard it as victory enough. They show themselves *not* to have been morally damaged by reassuring continuing beneficiaries of evil that they will not now be treated as perpetrators. The "inhumanity" of twentieth-century violence—both revolutionary and counterrevolutionary—is the problem against which all civilized nations in the twenty-first century are now expected to make "war."[13]

In the twenty-first century the notion of human rights has devolved from an aspirational ideal to an implicit compromise that allows the ongoing beneficiaries of past injustice to keep their gains without fear of terrorism. The Human Rights movement also aims, of course, to persuade the passive supporters of the old order to abjure illegitimate *means* of counterrevolutionary politics—the repressive and fraudulent techniques of power that they once condoned or ignored. For the victim who was morally undamaged or subsequently "healed" or both, the past would be truly over once its horrors are acknowledged by national consensus. This consensus on the moral meaning of the past often comes at the expense of cutting off future claims that would normally seem to follow from it.

To put the point crudely, the cost of achieving a moral consensus that the past was evil is to reach a political consensus that the evil is past. The problem is obvious when we remind ourselves that the "victims" in the victim/beneficiary distinction are generally a larger and more lasting group than those who were victims of the physical cruelties inflicted by perpetrators. Why should the moral victory claimed by the smaller group of victims be considered sufficient for the larger group as well? The humanitarian answer is that acknowledgment and repair of moral damage merges both types of victimhood by reversing the logic of "consciousness-raising" through which unreconciled victims might have become revolutionaries. In practice, this reversal means that unreconciled victims who continue to demand redistribution at the expense of beneficiaries will be accused of undermining the consensus that the evil is past; it also means that continuing beneficiaries who act on their fears that victims are still unreconciled will be accused of undermining the consensus that the past was evil by "blaming the victim."

In the Human Rights Discourse that has become dominant since the cold war the meaning of "evil" itself has changed. It is no longer widely understood to be a system of social injustice that can have ongoing structural effects, even after the structure is dismantled. Rather, evil is described as a *time* of cyclical violence that is past—or can be *put* in the past by defining the present as *another time* in which the evil is remembered rather than repeated. The idea that we overcome evil through the way we speak in the present of a completed (or repeated) past owes as much to norms of grammar as to norms of ethics. In Human Rights Discourse a willingness to speak about what has been done *as* done is thought to be ethically (because grammatically?) inconsistent with repeating the past. Ongoing beneficiaries who deny that the past was evil are thus denounced for repeating it, but so, too, are victims who reject the new discursive norms for distinguishing the present from a now completed past.

The Question of Beneficiaries

The great bulk of recent literature on human rights focuses on the relations between former victims and perpetrators after an evil regime has been defeated. It thus addresses questions of impunity and disclosure—

trials as a means to truth and truth commissions as a way of achieving broader justice than limited trials could bring.

There is also in this literature some discussion of the justifiable anger former victims feel toward bystanders—those who knew (or should have known) and yet did nothing to resist or overthrow the oppressive regime, although they themselves had little to gain from it. An important strand of human rights scholarship blames systemic violations on the "passive injustice" (bad citizenship) of bystanders in the old regime.[14] From this perspective, a desired outcome of transitional justice is the creation of a vibrant civic culture of human rights activism—groups in civil society that will be vigilant in calling future abuses to the attention of the general public. Several recent writers on transitional justice identify the strengthening of such groups as a major goal of trials and truth commissions.[15] There is, however, very little discussion of the role of victims (seen more broadly) in relation to the structural beneficiaries, those who received material and social advantage from the old regime and whose continuing well-being in the new order could not have withstood the victory of unreconciled victims.

The apparent omission of the victim/beneficiary relation from Human Rights Discourse is not accidental. Its central aim is to exhort passive supporters of the old regime to become active opponents, a category into which some beneficiaries—for example, South African whites engaged in the anti-apartheid movement—may fall. By implying that beneficiaries may cleanse themselves in this way, Human Rights Discourse recognizes that those whose interests the perpetrators served were not necessarily their political constituents and that some eventual supporters might have become so only in response to terrorism.

But Human Rights Discourse does more than promote a more nuanced approach to beneficiaries: it also works to blur the moral distinction between beneficiary and bystander by suggesting that the general exoneration of *all* nonperpetrators would be more conducive to national "healing" than an inculpation of those whose interests were served. This means that those who must be won over to the new regime will inevitably include those who were conformists in the old regime—bystander and beneficiary alike. Because the recent literature on transitional justice focuses on overcoming the causes of past inaction that are common to beneficiary and bystander, it is much less concerned with tracing the persistent effects of unjust advantage from the past on social and economic relations under the successor regime. The implicit moral point is that opposing injustice is always costly and that *both* bystanders and beneficiaries are likely to be better off than they would have been had they actively resisted.[16] The most comprehensive and thoughtful writing on transitional justice thus considers the possibility of redistribution only as a series of "dilemmas" that place it at odds with the future establishment of a rule of law based on a consensus that "everyone" suffered in the past.[17]

The underlying reason why the literature on transitional justice does not focus on beneficiaries is that since "new democracies do not start with new citizens," they must offer "most of the compromised . . . a second chance."[18] They receive that second chance via the legal rituals through which the transitional regime assigns responsibility for the past to *others*—those who are now held individually answerable for acts they once performed with presumed official support.[19] Because this strategy is essential to the success of the specific forms of "democratization" supported by Human Rights Discourse, the outcome will inevitably disappoint those advocates of victims' rights who sought and expected broader cultural and economic transformations. The objective of Human Rights Discourse will thus have been achieved when those who happened to come out ahead in the old order acknowledge as evil the practices that produced their continuing advantage. This acknowledgment, however, leaves much of that advantage in place insofar as the accepted absence of a redistributive politics demonstrates, both morally and psychologically, the former victims' capacity to regard the evil as past and to get on with their lives.

What would it take to persuade those who merely benefited or stood by that, in victims' minds, the struggle against past evil has come to an end? This question underlies the plethora of recent books on creating a culture of human rights. The answer today almost always involves either trials or truth commissions. Significantly, the relative "success" of these alternatives is judged less by how effective they are in exposing and discrediting the most egregious perpetrators than by the procedural assurance the "rule of law" affords to those with more attenuated responsibility that they will not be subject to reprisal.[20] In this respect, the addressees of both truth commissions and trials are almost always the beneficiaries of the systemic injustices that were advanced in the context of "gross human rights violations" against individuals.[21]

We must note, however, that the survivor stories that appear in the great documents of transitional liberalism, such as the *Nunca Más* series[22] and the *Truth and Reconciliation Commission (TRC) Report*, are almost never *about* systemic injustice as such. Rather, they are about a narrow class of victims (those who suffered physical torment) and a narrow class of perpetrators (their active tormenters). Although one might argue that focusing on these particular atrocities puts a human face on structural injustice, much of the recent writing on human rights in political transitions explicitly rejects this interpretation as incompatible with reestablishing (or establishing) the "rule of law." The rule of law in the aftermath of evil is expressly meant to decollectivize both injury and responsibility and to redescribe systemic violence as a series of individual crimes.[23]

The central theme of this now familiar story of liberal transitions is to reduce the broad spectrum of collective injury to individual acts of cruelty and to suggest that the root of such cruelty may lie in the willingness to treat individuals as representatives of collective evil.[24] Beneficiaries of past injustice are expected (when the story works) to identify *with* individual victims (or at least with their pain) and also to see themselves as victims, now that they know the "truth" about the regime they once condoned.[25] (If they still identified with perpetrators, the story would not have worked.) Those who suffered from systemic oppression are expected, in turn, to identify with the innocence of passive beneficiaries who were *not* perpetrators and who would never again condone perpetrators' acts out of fear of what the victory of victims might mean. The primary problem addressed by Human Rights Discourse is not that the beneficiaries of past evil are inclined to deny that its victims were degraded in a material and physical sense but rather that they are inclined to believe that these victims must have been degraded morally as well. These beneficiaries may be willing to fight on (even to the death), not because they believe that their cause is just but instead because it has made them justly hated by an enemy whose triumph they would now have even greater reason to fear. The recent literature on political transitions presupposes and reifies the difference between winning and reconciling just discussed. A successful political transition, as the story goes, transforms a polarizing political culture in which choosing sides and winning are the paramount concerns into a pluralizing political culture in which winning is subordinated to the maintenance of institutional arrangements aimed at compromise and reconciliation.

Writers on transitional justice disagree about the compatibility of providing political reassurance to nonvictim groups and promoting critical self-reflection on their responsibility for the past.[26] From the standpoint of creating an *effective* transitional regime, bystanders are beneficiaries who are yet to be blamed and beneficiaries are bystanders who are yet to be absolved. But why should inaction be more blameworthy for citizens whose interests were served by the evil they condoned than for those who were relatively unaffected? Is it necessary to choose? Or should these categories remain fluid, perhaps over generations?[27] The success of transitional justice depends on keeping these questions alive: *measuring* the persistence of unjust advantage must thus continue so that the desirability of correcting it can be continually debated. This debate becomes the substance of *transitional* liberalism as a *sui generis* project that is distinct from liberalism itself.

In transitional justice, the revolutionary project of social reconstruction can neither be rejected in principle nor pursued in practice.[28] This is not the expected result of the Rawlsian theory of justice, with its "maximin" principle benefiting the worst off. In transitional justice, by contrast, the "worst off" are also, and more importantly, *victims*—and the most relevant issue is whether their demand for benefits will return society to the logic of revolution and civil war from which it has so recently escaped. The "worst off" citizens of states recovering from a traumatic past will thus be effectively barred from demanding redistribution if, in making such demands, they must first represent themselves as the unreconciled "victims" of past evil. For this reason, justice-as-reconciliation is, in important ways, reconciliation to *continuing inequality* as a morally acceptable aftermath of past evil.[29] Because distributive justice will inevitably have a retributive side in states recovering from traumatic histories, the project of "transition" presents itself as a period of grace in which redistributive claims in the name of victims are indefinitely deferred.

In a still *recovering* nation, former victims of the old regime cannot attempt to win without challenging the consensus that the historical evil is truly past: the passive beneficiaries of a defeated evil have a lighter burden; they have no need to defend a past that former victims still need to attack. Transitional justice (the liberalism of Human Rights Discourse) is not in this respect an exceptional *form* of liberalism. Rather, it expresses through a dislocation in *time* the fissure inherent in all liberalism as ambivalence about the moral significance of victimhood itself. The transitional version of liberalism authorizes and presupposes the very wish for revolutionary justice that it seeks to censor. It relies on fantasies of genocidal guilt and punishment that will remain potent enough to suggest that the project of recovery may never end. Instead of "burying the past" to avoid reliving it, transitional liberalism is haunted by a past that it fears will return. The result is a political discourse that enshrines the logic of historical transition in much the same way that the discourse of the personal "recovery movement" makes permanent the logic of incurable disease.[30]

My claim that actually existing liberalism substitutes a model of permanent transition for the urgent pursuit of justice is not original. For Karl Marx, liberal democracies based on the Rights of Man are always transitional in the sense that feudal oppressors have been morally defeated (or "put in the past"), even while the beneficiaries of that oppression continue to prosper. Liberal rationalizations of capitalism, he argued, treat capitalism as though it might have started yesterday and never acknowledge that capitalism perpetuates the unjust inequalities of the old regime—which comes to mean *whatever* injustice the free market system now regards as *past*. So capitalism, which always follows a presumptively unjust historical precursor, gets a free ride, because its beneficiaries no longer have to justify their unequal starting points: they keep and accumulate their gains while allowing ongoing losers the moral consolation of knowing that no one defends the predations of the past—whether feudal, absolutist, authoritarian, or (nowadays) even communist.[31] Marx used class analysis as a way to think about this problem, and I believe that something like it needs to be reinvented as a way to address the specific historical circumstances in which Human Rights Discourse has emerged as a global substitute for resistance to local authoritarianism.[32] A plausible class analysis of transitional justice would focus on the ways in which this form of government rules in the name of the victims of past injustice but in the interests of the beneficiaries. This would be objectionable on its face if we assume that no evil can be truly past as long as its beneficiaries continue to profit from it. By the end of the twentieth century, however, this apparently straightforward assumption had become problematic insofar as it seemed to authorize justice-as-struggle no matter what. "The decisive issue," as the sociologist John Torpey says, is now "the extent to which *economic disadvantage in the present* is relevant."[33]

To criticize transitional justice today, we must go beyond a class analysis showing that the "haves" came out ahead and take a new look at the moral psychology that underlies a liberalism that regards itself as inherently "transitional." Edmund S. Morgan, an eminent historian of race in America, identifies the ambivalent feelings of sympathy and fear that can result from the very process of *persuading* beneficiaries of injustice that the past was evil:

> What neither white nor black historians seem to understand . . . is the nature of the guilt feeling that supports white racism. . . . Guilt feelings are a continuation of that embarrassment, and racism is a way of exorcising it by blaming the victims and their descendants. . . . Blacks have been given equality under the law. But they have never been forgiven for the embarrassment of their ancestors' sufferings.[34]

Morgan's mode of analysis is rare in recent Human Rights Discourse, because that discourse stresses the need for the broadest possible consensus about the evils done by perpetrators without considering the psychological effect on beneficiaries. Mainstream human rights literature is, implicitly, an effort to ease the beneficiary's mind by troubling it just enough to acknowledge from a position of safety the undeserved nature of the advantages he still enjoys. The now established techniques of transitional justice (memorials, truth commissions, etc.) thus aim to convince beneficiaries that their ongoing advantages will not be denounced as continuations or revivals of past injustice. When such techniques succeed, passive beneficiaries of the old order will join with former victims in opposing a return to the politics of fear itself—their new common enemy.[35] In this respect, the human rights culture to be established in the twenty-first century is a continuation, by more benign means, of the counterrevolutionary project of the twentieth—to assure that beneficiaries of past oppression will largely be permitted to keep the unjustly produced enrichment they presently enjoy.

Emptying the Present

The mainstream literature on transitional justice has been characterized by the attempt to establish a decisive split between the past and the future so that the present is defined as a purely transitional moment, most narrowly seen as closure, more broadly as reconciliation.[36] This literature uses history to establish that the past is *over*—that its evils (such as slavery, apartheid, fascism, and communism) are not coming back. In laying the past to rest, the project of transitional justice blocks the "tiger's leap into the past" that characterizes what the philosopher Walter Benjamin called "redemptive" justice.[37] Now that cyclical violence is assumed to epitomize evil, Benjamin's description of revolutionary militancy—fighting on as though even the dead must be saved—is exactly the mind-set against which humanitarians unite.[38] Human rights are on the agenda today because the idea of urgent revolution (in Benjamin's sense) is not.

The beneficiaries of past injustice occupy a position in Human Rights Discourse that corresponds to those who are saved but not yet judged in Pauline Christianity in which all mankind is the passive beneficiary of the death by execution of God himself. Paul's letters are addressed to Christian converts—those who have renounced past sin and *then* live on in the hope (and fear) that they will be judged on the basis of that renunciation rather than the original sin for which they already have been promised eventual forgiveness. Because Christians who do not immediately die upon conversion can expect to sin again, they need something to *say* about the new sins committed in this transitional time that is consistent with their Pauline faith that their old sins have been forgiven. Justification by *faith* alone does not mean that they are sinless or that all new sins will also be forgiven in the end. (A sin against one's faith may be worse than a sin before conversion.) To be justified, rather, is "to be 'declared' just, to be 'counted as' just."[39] This means that any sins committed henceforward are no longer the *same* sins as before.[40] To be *justified* in Paul's sense, *one need not have been just*. Justification requires, instead, that something new has been revealed, something that those who would be saved did not always know. Now that we know the truth about the Holocaust or apartheid or that we were trapped in a cycle of violence begetting violence that we could not see, we can regard our new knowledge as changing everything that matters, at least morally. This is what it means, Paul argues, to be *converted* from sin in a world that otherwise seems unchanged.

Human Rights Discourse follows the Pauline script for confessed sinners who have escaped just punishment through a miracle of a new beginning. Even if they commit new sins, they accept, indefinitely, the status of "recovering" sinner and believe that they are never more in danger of relapse than when they think they have finally "recovered" from the sins that are already forgiven. From a Pauline perspective, living on after evil requires the faithful to reject any idolatry of the present that assumes the time for judgment is now. Human Rights Discourse, as a successor to this view, provides a way to say that any given moment is too soon or too late for historical justice; now is never the time.

Becoming the Victim

The message of Human Rights Discourse about the present is not entirely the program of peace and reconciliation that it might seem to be on the surface. It is also a declaration of war against a new enemy. Carl Schmitt made a similar point about human rights consensus expressed by the Treaty of Versailles in 1919, the subsequent establishment of the League of Nations in that same year, and the Kellogg-Briand Pact of 1928 outlawing aggressive war. "The solemn declaration of outlawing war," he said, "does not abolish the friend-enemy distinction, but, on the contrary, opens new possibilities by giving an international *hostis* declaration new content and new vigor."[41]

> When a state fights its political enemy in the name of humanity it . . . seeks to usurp a universal concept against its military opponent . . . in the same way that one can misuse peace, justice, progress, and civilization in order to claim these as one's own and to deny the same to the enemy. (p. 54)

Such a development is, he said, a way to create "a potential or actual alliance, i.e., a coalition" (p. 57).

> It is . . . erroneous to believe that a political position founded on economic superiority is "essentially unwarlike," . . . War is condemned but executions, sanctions, punitive expeditions, pacifications, protection of treaties, international police, and measures to assure peace remain. The adversary is thus no longer called an enemy but a disturber of peace and is thereby designated to be an outlaw of humanity. . . . But this allegedly non-political . . . system cannot escape the logic of the political. (pp. 78–79)

Schmitt here anticipated the rhetorical demands that Human Rights Discourse would place on liberal politicians still fighting, as Woodrow Wilson did, "to make the world safe for democracy." His words might be read today as forecasting a time in which Human Rights Discourse allows the U.S. to fight wars of aggression only on the condition that they are not described as such, and to threaten even the use of nuclear weapons if this is what it takes to rescue the victims of crimes against humanity. "Whoever invokes humanity wants to cheat," Schmitt says. "To . . . invoke and monopolize such a term probably has certain incalculable effects, such as denying the enemy the quality of being human and declaring him to be an outlaw of humanity; and a war can thereby be driven to the most extreme inhumanity" (p. 54).

In stressing the dehumanization of the enemy, Schmitt may not have fully understood a further implication of his argument: that adopting a Human Rights Discourse allows potential rescuers to identify with the presumed innocence of *victims*. It is *they*, the newly vulnerable, who must now be protected from being violated by the "inhuman." What does it now mean for us, as surviving beneficiaries of the barbaric twentieth century, to deal with the anxieties of success by identifying ourselves with its victims? The force of this question is, perhaps, clearest at a personal level. Individuals who suffer cannot understand themselves as "victims" without understanding what it would mean for there to be a perpetrator.[42] This is not to say that the language of victimhood is appropriate only if there *is* an identifiable perpetrator. The point, rather, is that to speak in the voice of the victim one must speak *as if* there were an agent responsible for one's loss. Thus one cannot conceive of oneself as the victim of atrocity or injustice without first being able to imagine, and then to project onto another, the intention of committing it. To be a victim is precisely to experience oneself as the object of hostile desires that one does not experience oneself as having. The subject of that desire (to torture, intimidate, humiliate, etc.) is always imagined as someone else who can then be properly blamed for acting on them. Thus blaming is a direct way of experiencing oneself as the *object* (victim) of desires on which it would be reprehensible to act. It is also and indirectly a way of innocently reexperiencing the desires that would make one capable of having victims in one's turn.

At the level of collective history, Human Rights Discourse functions in similar ways to construct the innocence of victims. That discourse begins with the commonsense premise that there is a significant difference between suffering an atrocity and committing it. It exhorts us, always, to identify with victims whose suffering it graphically depicts by inviting us to imagine ourselves as victims of desires that we no longer condone. But this humanitarian act of identification is also the ideological basis for using military force against those whom we believe have forfeited their claims to a common humanity by avowing and/or acting upon such now forbidden desires. The tragic irony is that our own atrocities become (indirectly) thinkable by projecting onto our enemy the desire to commit atrocity. This is a version of Schmitt's argument that is echoed in a different key by Walter Benjamin: "There is no document of civilization which is not at the same time a document of barbarism."[43]

Splitting of the Victim

Nothing that I have said so far is meant to deny the commonsense view that victims can suffer terror and loss without consciously fantasizing about doing likewise, and perpetrators may inflict suffering out of indifference without consciously thinking of themselves as past or potential victims. My point is, rather, about the mental drama that plays out when we identify with the victim in order to put victimhood in the past. The problem of internalizing social justice/injustice was well understood by both Socrates and Jesus, whose teachings stressed (in different ways) that identifying oneself as the victim of persecution corrupts the soul, even (or especially) if one *is* such a victim, and makes one capable of *having* victims in one's turn.[44] Although the psychoanalyst Melanie Klein does not profess to be concerned with the justice of our feelings of persecution, she helps us understand the structure of such feelings in ways that can illuminate their potential for moral damage.[45]

Klein described *individual* psychology as the dynamics of a *group* that is already in our heads. The mind, according to Klein, is populated by multiple subjectivities that have affective feelings toward each other: the internalized others that we experience as who we are; the externalized parts of the self that we experience as who we *are not*.[46] To have a mind is to be *mindful* of the difference between how it feels and how it looks to be ourselves. The *thought* of feelings that we do not *feel* as our own is thus a large part of the content of our interior life, as is the process of attributing our own feelings to others whose minds we experience but whose interiority we do not share. Klein's theory of the splitting-off of affect both sociologizes the individual and psychologizes the group.

Klein's central insight into the relation of group and individual is that our interpersonal conflicts also have an internal (intrapsychic) dimension: they involve relations between the version of the self with which we identify as "good" and a version of the self from which we (perhaps unsuccessfully) dissociate as bad (because it threatens the good self). We thus get rid of parts of the self by projecting them onto the others in our head, and perhaps also by actually transmitting those feelings to others who identify themselves through the feelings we shed. "A projection is what I disown in myself and see in you; a projective identification is what I succeed in having you experience in yourself, although it comes from me in the first place."[47] This interpersonal "transference" of affect in the clinical situation is a possible window into the unconscious projection of affect onto the *internalized* other. By recognizing and avowing the very feelings that the patient unconsciously disavows, the analyst feels them instead of the patient and on the patient's behalf.[48]

"Projective identification" is Klein's clinical term for the phenomenon of reexperiencing our own feelings as though we were their object and not the feeling subject. This, she argues, is the internal process through which we defend against our sense of loss, abandonment, or betrayal by identifying ourselves as *innocent* (undeserving) objects of persecution. In politics, projective identification can refer to either one's recognition in others of what one refuses to acknowledge in oneself or to one's rediscovery in outside reality of what one does not wish oneself to be.[49]

An essential part of projective identification is the "splitting" of the self into "good" and "bad." According to Klein, we "idealize" the good self (who becomes the innocent victim) and demonize the bad self, whose feelings of hostility would provoke the persecution that we fear. We do not, however, avow these "split-off" feelings of hostility as our own. Instead, we project them onto the internalized figure of our persecutor and experience the good (or innocent) self as their object. We thus reexperience our split-off feelings of aggression toward others as if it were aggression directed by others against us. Desire thus posits a version of the self as both its *subject* ("I") and its *object* ("me"). We desire to *be* what we would otherwise have and to *have* what we would otherwise be.[50] The liberal subject, for example, posits itself as "being" free and its totalitarian enemy as "lacking "(and therefore *wanting*) the freedom that the liberal subject "has." His very freedom thus becomes the unobtainable *thing* that the imagined terrorist would both desire and hate in him.[51]

Our liberalism rests more generally on a splitting victimhood in Klein's sense. On the one hand, it produces idealized victims—victims without enemies—who are candidates for the extensive redistribution that could be justified on Rawlsian principles. Such victims would not treat better-off individuals who bear the burden of distributive justice as would-be perpetrators of past injustice and would regard doing so as a form of demonization. On the other hand, liberalism produces victims who pose a credible threat to those who must pay. Their victimhood requires a judgment on the past: it demands to win in ways that the Rawlsian conception precludes.[52] These two conceptions of victimhood are fused in societies with histories of traumatic conflict—the very societies in which liberal principles are most appealing. Each authorizes a revolutionary (or transformative) wish that the other forecloses. In this respect, the liberal project (wish) is inherently defensive with respect to an anxiety it cannot state in liberal terms.

The moral psychology of "splitting" is central to my critique of fin de siècle Human Rights Discourse.[53] I argue that, through the work of human rights trials and truth commissions, beneficiaries can live out the fantasy of loving one split-off version of the victim and fearing the other, who can consequently be treated as a threat. Yet for all this, the whole victim never appears as an object of their affective thought. This point has been made by scholars of postwar Germany, who note the rapidity with which "philosemitism" (the identification of Germany with its missing Jews) replaced anti-Semitism as a cultural norm. A postwar German political leadership that demonized Hitler and idealized the Good German (who mourns the "vanished Jew") made it possible for all Germans to keep their "inner" Jew alive.[54]

We can thus see that the aspect of Human Rights Discourse that Schmitt called "warlike" is *at once* a basis for community and for hatred—community based on hatred of the purveyors of hate. As an emergent ideology of the "world community," Human Rights Discourse does not move beyond the paranoid stance of demonizing all demonizers to a state in which we realize that our aggression toward the split-off bad victim might destroy the good victim. Melanie Klein suggests that the way to move past both these positions begins with the recognition that the good and bad objects are one.[55] Here she develops Freud's insight that, at the level of the unconscious, wishes and deeds are the same, and that civilization requires us to punish ourselves unconsciously for wishes that we thereby repress.[56] For Klein, the clear implication is that self-accusatory depression is the inner cost of repressing our murderous wishes toward the dead, and others who betray our attachment and trust by leaving or injuring us.[57] Such depression can be individual, cultural, or both. The literary critic Jacqueline Rose develops the implications of the Kleinian view in an illuminating book, which claims that national identity is, at the level of affect, a product of the collective fantasies through which individuals learn to both avow guilt and avoid punishment for the crimes they did not commit.[58]

Repoliticizing Liberalism

The limitations of recent Human Rights Discourse are linked to those of liberalism itself, not necessarily the ideal versions where the "worst off" are favored but the real, historical versions where the worst-off have the moral psychology of victims. Real liberalism, the kind that people fight for, gains its moral purchase as a historically specific afterlife of a historically specific evil. It is not a theoretical exception to the paranoid politics of friend and foe but, rather, an ideology of constant vigilance that chooses its enemies carefully.[59] This Schmittian form of liberalism represents the political choice to demonize the demonizers—those unreconciled remnants of an illiberal past that haunt the continuing beneficiaries of the old order. The liberalism that keeps these demons at bay—a "liberalism of fear"—is the moral psychology that underlies the Human Rights Discourse.

"The liberalism of fear" was distinguished from other liberalisms by the political theorist Judith Shklar. A refugee from Nazism, she was educated by a generation of Harvard faculty, senior and junior, who sought to turn postwar liberalism into a fighting creed.[60] Their notion of "totalitarianism" carried forward the ideological mobilization of World War II into the cold war by refusing to distinguish between communism and fascism as mortal enemies of American liberalism.[61]

Shklar had read her Schmitt and understood (despite her deep suspicion of all cold war ideologies) that to have political purchase liberalism needed enemies. The question facing postwar liberals was how to find the *right* enemies, enemies that could be fought by an inclusive polity that did not demonize particular groups, internal or external.[62] Her eventual solution, echoing Franklin D. Roosevelt, was to define the true enemy of liberalism as "fear itself."

By making liberalism a fighting creed, Shklar implicitly conceded that it must become *political* in Schmitt's sense. In normal times, she argued, hate is what we hate; fear is what we fear. Hating and fearing are thus the exceptions on which liberal sovereignty rests—the feelings we have when that sovereignty itself is at risk. At these exceptional moments there is always something to hate more than hate itself and to fear more than fear itself—we hate and fear the enemy, whom we come to see as spreading hatred and fear. Shklar's embrace of non-neutral liberalism (a liberalism that is frankly *against* something) presupposes that cruelty, especially physical cruelty, is worse than all other forms of injustice because the fear that it produces in its victim makes him *capable* of cruelty. Shklar's double condemnation of political cruelty explicitly repudiates all utopian hopes, because their immediate political effect is to desensitize us to the cruelties that might be committed in their name. This is true, she argued, even of a "*liberalism* of hope" (such as that of her Harvard contemporary, John Rawls), which she expressly contrasted with her own "liberalism of fear."[63] For her, international humanitarian intervention would seem to be the only way that tyrannical and/or brutal regimes could be removed without intentional cruelty.[64]

Human rights interventionism—threatened in Schmitt's time by the newly established League of Nations and carried out in our time by the U.S.—would thus become the political cruelty that can be authorized as an exception to Shklar's normative politics of *anti*cruelty. This is the militant liberalism that comes after evil and that regards itself as a political alliance against evil's return. By making liberalism a political doctrine in precisely Schmitt's sense,[65] she self-consciously mobilizes its friends to fight for what Schmitt dismissed as "liberal pathos"—the hypocritical revulsion at human cruelty that gives liberal political ideas what he called "a double face."[66] Shklar believed that physical cruelty is even worse than hypocrisy and is the only thing worth fighting against.[67] She could easily have accepted Schmitt's response that the difference between them comes down to rationales for war—the choice of enemies that precedes our ability to feel compassion for our friends. Shklar's point, shared with many humanitarians, is that we should feel compassion for as many people as possible and *really hate* those who refuse to enter our *no-hate zone*.

Her contemporary, George Kateb, goes further, arguing that political evil *itself* is the result of the human temptation to struggle *against* evil in pursuit of some utopian goal, such as social justice:

> It may be that evils on the greatest scale come about when governments and political groups persuade people to believe that there is evil greater than moral evil, or good greater than moral goodness. . . . [W]hen morality is dislodged from its supremacy, terrible evils result. . . . On the other hand the production

of evil on behalf of fighting moral evil or trying to achieve a positive moral good has also been enormous. . . . Inflamed identity pursues its purposes without regard to moral limits: I mean respect for individual human beings, for what we now call human rights.[68]

To overcome evil, thus conceived, through human rights is to become more sensitive to the (primarily physical) pain of individuals. For Schmitt hypocrisy, rather than cruelty, was the worst thing. Kateb agrees with Shklar that this conception of politics itself had made mass cruelty, and ultimately genocide, conceivable in the twentieth century.[69]

Thinking the Unthinkable

Making future cruelty unthinkable was to be a foundational premise of the fin de siècle human rights culture. Why, then, do images of genocidal massacre during the twentieth century figure so prominently in the iconology of the twenty-first?[70] The superficial message is to warn us of the dangers of genocide so that we would fear and avoid them at all cost. What does it really mean to first imagine genocide and then avoid it *at all cost*?

As the world embarks on the twenty-first century, genocide has never been more thinkable—especially the genocide of which we may be victims. It is now conventional to argue that genocide has occurred, for example, in Darfur, by publishing photographs of dead bodies and daring the viewer to refuse empathy. Empathy here means connecting a new image to earlier, iconic images of genocide through which the viewers' own imagined victimhood becomes morally intelligible.[71] That very intelligibility is also, however, a form of distancing, and hence a psychological mechanism of defense.[72]

The imaginability of genocide as a defense against the fear of genocide is a disturbing point to acknowledge. To say that genocide is morally intelligible (that it *must* be for us to fear it) is not to say that it is now, or ever could have been, morally justified; instead, it is to note that most genocides are not mere acts of inadvertence or insensitivity but rather moments of intense moral concentration invoking high concepts—including those of human rights and democracy—that are also invoked to keep the fear of genocide at bay. If we cannot grasp the moral *logic* of genocide, we will never understand how Human Rights Discourse (which may, for a period of time, seem well established in places like Sarajevo) has dissolved into what commentators glibly describe as "primordial group hatreds" and how that same discourse can later reemerge as a self-conscious return to civilized values.[73] When countries have gone through such seemingly inexplicable changes, those who imagine themselves to "live on" tend to speak as though "that was another time" while also insisting that a return to that time is now unthinkable (even as they fear it). For them, evil as a political concept refers to a period of time—and its repudiation to a moment of political conversion puts that time affectively in the past. It is thus apparent that both the fact of genocide and the fear of it lie at the foundation of the particular form of Human Rights Discourse that has moved from the periphery to the center of ethical thought since 1945—and that the relation between the fact and the fear is less straightforward than Human Rights Discourse would lead us to believe.

As I have described, fin de siècle Human Rights Discourse represents a post-Holocaust standpoint toward the system of sovereign states created by the Peace of Westphalia. It assumes—often explicitly—that the continuing legitimacy of territorial rule by a national state rests on the simultaneous existence and repression of the genocidal thoughts, both active and passive, that founded the nation.[74] The ethical responsibility of sovereign states is thus to actively suppress these thoughts by *protecting* the internal populations potentially endangered by them. Since the Holocaust, and later atrocities seen to resemble and even repeat it, each state's overarching "Responsibility to Protect" is now widely thought to be underpinned by a *right* of the "world community" (or any state strong enough) to intervene for the specific purpose of *rescuing* inhabitants of another state that is unwilling or unable to protect them.[75]

Protecting and rescuing victims would thus become the common ethical basis for legitimating the nation-state, the world community, and the occasions on which one nation-state might intervene, both militarily and politically, in the governance of a state that had failed to meet this basic responsibility to some or all of its people. As the hallmark of early twenty-first-century political thought, the UN document proclaiming the "Responsibility to Protect"[76] crystallized the lessons of the twentieth century around the need for what one writer calls a "weak cosmopolitanism"[77] that would curb the inherent tendencies of nation-states to scapegoat, expel, and ultimately exterminate internal populations.

Behind this conclusion lies the view that stopping evil (rather than bringing justice) has become the ethical basis for all politics, and that justice-based politics discredits itself if it does not aim to stop evil *first*. This view would not have been as broadly embraced in 2001 if the twentieth-century struggles over capitalism and colonialism had been active. By then, however, evil was widely equated with the *cyclicity* of violence (mobilizing friends against the enemy) that was embraced in Schmitt's "concept of the political" and that other thinkers would trace back to age-old practices of human sacrifice (scapegoating) on which primitive religions were based.[78] Scapegoating internal victims and fighting a limited war against outsiders had always been the means by which communities renewed their internal taboos against murdering one another: by making the object of their violence (nearly) unanimous they foreclosed something even worse—an internal contagion of violence that would destroy them from within. The twin lessons of Auschwitz and Hiroshima, as the argument goes, is that there is *now* nothing worse, because the scapegoating mechanism that Schmitt thought necessary to contain internal violence had unleashed the uncontainable violence of genocide, and because the use of nuclear war to stop the next cycle of mass killings (Cambodia) could result in omnicide.[79] By the late twentieth century the persecutions and war that Schmitt considered to be the periodic *exceptions* to legality on which political legitimacy rests had been reconceived as the normal condition of large parts of humanity—what he goes so far as to consider the "nomos" of modern politics itself.[80] Today the asserted priority of ethics over politics is based on the sacredness of human life and is symptomatic of a political condition in which defenselessness is presupposed.[81] Human rights interventionism thus understands itself as a refusal to rationalize persecutory violence as one moment in a cycle in which states make war in order to make peace. Recent humanitarians regard the *cyclicity* of violence—violence that begets violence—as itself the paradigm of evil and views the rescue of innocent victims as a *break* in this cycle rather than a continuation of it.

Thus described, human rights have become a discourse of revelation-followed-by-conversion that is modeled on certain Christian accounts of the Cross. In these accounts, Christ's sacrifice is meant to reveal the cruelty of all sacrifice (because the victim is innocent) and thus to bring the cycle of sacrifice to an end through concern for the suffering of humans as such (love one another).[82] The wars fought by professedly Christian rules would thereby become wars of rescue—crusading wars of peace—aimed to ward of the return of the earlier, cyclical forms of violence.[83] (This notion that a *Christian* Emperor fights as a defender of humanity against the return of pagan sacrifice goes back to the distinction made by Eusebius between the imperial wars of Rome before and after its conversion.)[84] For those who claim to be *converted* by the events of Auschwitz or Hiroshima or both, new ways to save the innocent from a return to twentieth-century violence are not more of the same; instead, they are a way of bearing witness to the cyclicity of that violence so as to end it. Ethical wars are those fought by self-professed rescuers to oppose a cycle of violence and prevent those still engaged in it from obtaining the means of omnicide, now generically called "weapons of mass destruction." In the new discourse of human rights the ultimate evil is physical cruelty, the intentional infliction of bodily suffering; consequently, the response to bodily suffering is the ultimate test of affirmative moral responsibility.

The Ethics and Politics of Rescue

What has been new and ethically distinctive in fin de siècle human rights was strikingly formulated by the French philosopher Emmanuel Lévinas. "The supreme ordeal of the will," he said," is not death, but suffering,"[85] But "suffering," he also said, "remains ambiguous: it is already the present of the pain . . . but, as consciousness, the pain is always yet to come."[86] Lévinas concluded that the present and future suffering of another is always "useless" (*un*justified) and that attempting to rationalize it is the source of all immorality."[87] He is not here referring primarily to the growing medicalization of humanitarian invention,[88] although he does think analgesia is a paradigmatically ethical response to physical pain.[89] His main point is that ethics *resists* the tendency to see a situation in its ever more total historical context and concentrates instead on the questions presented by proximity to suffering.[90]

Ethical proximity is not, for Lévinas, merely a spatial concept—both space and time can be proximate or distant; rather, it calls into question our right to be *where, when* (and also *who*) we are when faced with another's anguish.[91] That question is whether we are to remain indifferent to the other's call. The ethical imperative that precedes all contextualization reminds me that "I might be the Messiah . . . I have come to save the world. And of course I forget that; we are all Messiahs who forget it. . . . [but] I am unique and . . . can do something no one else can do in my place, and that is *not foreseen by law or justice*" (emphasis added).[92]

For Lévinas, an ethics based on proximity is a *spatializing* discourse within time[93] that distinguishes itself from "temporalizing" rhetorics of memory and identity,[94] which he holds accountable for the atrocities of the twentieth century. Temporal narratives, he suggests, rationalize continuing indifference to suffering before our eyes as necessary to the redemption of an ancestor or comrade who may seem closer through kinship or ideology than one who could be rescued here and now. Ethical proximity is thus, according to Lévinas, a pure moment of approach—the moment we come to be answerable for the suffering before us.

Calls for humanitarian intervention in such situations thus claim to be ethical, rather than political, in exactly Lévinas's sense: they presuppose that a "responsibility for the other human being is . . . anterior to every question." A distinctively *humanitarian* response to killing in Bosnia, Rwanda, or Darfur does not ask who arrived first, what have they done to each other, or which of them is allergic and which is the allergen. The ethical point—for Lévinas, the whole point—is that those who approach must answer to the unavoidable presence of the others, even before deciding what to do.[95] Like today's humanitarian politics, the first imperative of Lévinasian ethics is to avoid historical contextualization. It does this by *assigning* to historical enemies a responsibility to coexist in the same place, regardless of the broader political context, and thus provides an implicit rationale for the politics-without-redistribution that today's purely ethical interventions presuppose.[96] Such a moment of ethical *approach* is illustrated by the journalist Philip Gourevitch's account of the return of "a certain Girumuhatse" to share a house with the surviving members of the family he butchered during the 1994 Rwanda genocide.[97]

Lévinas understood that a political question is implicit in his claim that *ethics* always puts peace ahead of justice. The political question arises, according to Lévinas, from the relationship between the Two and a Third[98]—a witness-rescuer-redeemer. When a Third arrives on the scene of the Two, his decision about *whom* to rescue gives the victim's suffering the ethical weight of genuine alterity—what Lévinas calls "infinite" weight—while reducing the otherness of the perpetrator to that of the enemy whose suffering does not count (Lévinas would call this "totalizing" him).[99] "If you're for the other," Lévinas says, "you're for the neighbor"—and not yet *against* anyone. "But," he continues, "if your neighbor attacks another neighbor or treats him unjustly . . . [t]hen alterity takes on another character, in alterity we can find an enemy. . . . There are people who are wrong."[100] Lévinas tacitly agrees with Schmitt that it is always a third party who defines the difference between two kinds of otherness—that of the friend for whose suffering he is ultimately responsible and that of the enemy whose suffering does not count.[101] In Lévinas, however, the role of the Third does not begin by defining whom to be against (by *making* enemies) but rather in carving out an exception to his antecedent responsibility for the suffering of enemy and nonenemy alike so that he can rescue one from the other.[102] His concept of the ethical, like Schmitt's concept of the political, is essentially triangular:[103] "The third party is other than the neighbor but also another neighbor, and also the neighbor of the other, and not simply their fellow. . . . What, then, are the other and the third party with respect to one another? Birth of the question."[104]

The Lévinasian Third, however, does not begin as a sovereign but rather as an ethical rescuer who comes to occupy the place of the Two[105]—he figuratively steps into the line of fire to stop them from killing each other and justifies his own use of force only when attacked for no other reason than being an occupier. In this respect, Lévinas anticipates the developments in Human Rights Discourse that grounds sovereignty itself in a domestic government's "Responsibility to Protect" the human inhabitants of its territory and international military as a distinctively ethical response to attacks on aid workers and peacekeepers.

Reading Lévinas with Schmitt suggests that an ethics of rescue is also a politics of global power in a post-Auschwitz world where the potential for human rights violations exists wherever rescuers do not rule. Does this mean that the matter of human rights is just another imperialism—a pretext for occupying territory that is no less political than the pretexts of earlier colonial occupiers who originally came to save the "natives" from killing one another, and then sent soldiers to rescue those earlier rescuers from natives who had shown their "inhumanity" by attacking innocent third parties who had come to help? That rescue is inherently non-neutral (there is always a victim and perpetrator) can put rescuers in need of permanent protection. Viewed historically (and now politically), we know that the rescue of "natives" from one another has been a pretext for colonial invasion, and that colonial administrations make former victims their agents in systems of divide-and-rule (thereby leaving them vulnerable when colonial rule ends).[106] Third-party interveners who lack a viable exit strategy are always open to attack as de facto occupiers. As a consequence, *reluctance* to occupy (or colonize) a violent society can be a pretext for a potential rescuer *not* to intervene, even while genocide is occurring on the ground. Human Rights Discourse defines itself today as a rejection of this pretext and distinguishes itself from earlier imperialisms based on the claim that, even when it invades and occupies, it does so for ethical, and *not* political, reasons. In doing this it relies on a weak version of Lévinas's concept of the ethical.

For Lévinas himself, rescue is the only ethical basis for being *anywhere*: those who are not there *for* the others should always question their right to occupy another's "place in the sun." This means that those who attack rescuers are always in the wrong: as enemies of all mankind, there is *nowhere* they deserve to be. It also makes it ethical for the rest of us to postpone political questions that might be asked in advance about the interveners who respond to the "cry" of human suffering, even though their motives will *always* be questioned if they stay. For the rescuers themselves, knowing what will happen (how their intervention will *look*) must always come *later*—the ethical imperative to rescue comes first. Unlike proponents of today's "Responsibility to Protect" doctrine, Lévinas does not simply argue that the risks of humanitarian intervention are a "lesser evil" than allowing atrocity to occur.[107]

The Lévinasian kernel of Human Rights Discourse is that suffering is meaningless when it is not *for* anyone, but that the self-imposed travails of those who rescue (at least to the extent of providing humanitarian aid) represents the "high-mindedness that is the honor of a still uncertain, still vacillating, modernity emerging at the end of a century of unutterable suffering."[108] This describes the interiority of a Lévinasian third party (the peacekeeper) who intervenes between the two in order to stop the repetition of bad history. For the intervener, the ethical question is always one of patience: how long?[109]

Lévinas calls "the time of patience itself . . . the dimension of the political" insofar as politics itself is ethically driven: "in patience . . . the will is transported to a life *against someone* and *for someone*."[110] The Third thus *makes* an enemy of anyone who attacks his rescue operation.[111] By infinitizing the suffering of those to be saved, he defines his own ethical responsibility through the difference between doing *to* (the perpetrator) and doing *for* (the victim). The difference between accusative and dative thus becomes the grammatical basis for Lévinas's claim that substituting the self *for* the other is a way to move beyond the damaging self-absorption of doing things *to* the other *for* the self. This grammatical point also suggests, however, that Lévinas's ethics, and humanitarianism in general, is less concerned with what one *does* than with the responsibility to choose between *two* others. That this generally unacknowledged choice presents itself as the imperative to *do* something before it is *too late* sheds light on Human Rights Discourse as an attitude toward itself. Here conduct is ethically justified by keeping faith with the situation as immediately presented, even if the result is merely to postpone the inevitable end.

Today it is the *patience* of the long-suffering rescuer that makes the use of force seem ethical, *not* political. This argument has been made in support of aerial bombardment to stop atrocities inflicted or condoned by local authorities and, more recently, to support the supply of food and medicine (perhaps by air-drop) to local populations whose government refuses aid from the "international community" following a natural disaster.[112] For Lévinas, the essence of such ethical responsibility is that its demands are always too much for third parties, who always arrive too late to meet them but must nevertheless respond.

The ultimate futility of humanitarian intervention does not, however, lead Lévinas to conclude that its main benefit is to make the rescuers feel morally better about themselves. Ethical *responsibility* has nothing to do with either virtue or justice as other philosophers commonly understand these terms. Its ultimate product, according to Lévinas, is simply the postponement of death and suffering in others. If nothing is *worse* than useless suffering—not even injustice—then a politics that puts the good (or justice) first would be inherently *un*ethical, according to Lévinas. Peace is thus the highest aim of ethics—and not justice in any sense that might require breaching peace: ethical responsibility, for Lévinas, is an adjournment of the politics of hastening the future and that of undoing the past. In the *presence* of the other, he argues, it inaugurates a different *kind* of time, a time of doing what one can.[113] The ethical point of intervention/rescue is never, according to Lévinas, to "settle accounts";[114] rather, it is to prolong the time we have in which to bear our responsibilities to those in need.[115]

Extra time, according to Lévinas, is always *created*. He thus sees the time of survivorship as a paradigm of temporality as such. "To be temporal," Lévinas says, "is both to be for death [in the Heideggerian sense] and to still have time, to be *against* death" (emphasis added).[116] If extra time is the most Lévinasian ethics can produce, there is nothing ethical that counts as final victory—a point agreeable to Lévinas, for whom the very idea of winning lies entirely within the struggle between Two. What he eventually calls "diachrony" identifies the radical noncoincidence between past and present as a correlative to the radical noncoincidence of self and others: it is thus both interpersonal and intertemporal.

Like Lévinasian ethics, today's discourse of human rights confronts the charge that its motives are political, not ethical. The point of this charge is that occupying violent places to provide security is always political—that, even in Hobbes, the intervention of a third-party sovereign is needed to end the "war of all against all." From that point on, security *means* support for the sovereign—his enemies become our enemies, both foreign and domestic. An ethics that makes *security* its prime directive is also a political justification for third parties to use exceptional violence to *stop* violence and, potentially, to invade, occupy, and rule an otherwise violent place.[117] Those who oppose such intervention as "imperialist" typically do so by stressing the continuing political role of the third-party intervener (such as the U.S.) in creating and perpetuating enmity between the original Two.

The ethical counterargument is that *politicizing* rescue in this way has always been an excuse for third parties to turn away from those who suffer. After Auschwitz, this argument concludes, we must never again let ethical indifference masquerade as *realpolitik*. Instead of reducing ethics to security, Human Rights Discourse (and Lévinas) regard themselves as elevating ethics to its highest imperative—the "Responsibility to Protect" human life.

Unthinking Auschwitz

To read Human Rights Discourse as implicitly (and unhappily) Lévinasian is to become more sensitive to the Schmittian underpinnings that we have already found in Shklar and Kateb. We can understand, for example, how proponents of universal human rights see global interventions in the local as central to their enterprise, while local interventions in the global are at best peripheral and no longer justifiable if any violence ensues. Thus the bombings of Belgrade or Baghdad have been justified as violence in the cause of human rights, whereas far less violent protests against global causes of suffering—for example, the Seattle riots against the World Trade Organization (WTO) and the Chiapas rebellion against North American Free Trade Agreement (NAFTA)—are no longer considered to fall within the category of human rights–based interventions.

A perverse effect of a globalized "ethic" of protecting local human rights is to take the global causes of human suffering off the political agenda. In the emergent global discourse on human rights, "nothing essential to a person's human essence is violated if he or she suffers as a consequence of military action or of market manipulation from beyond his own state when that is permitted by international law."[118] Any violent action taken against global injustice thus runs the risk of being considered a violation of universal human rights (perhaps even "terrorism") in the locality where it occurs. In this way, the global primacy of ethics crystallizes around our horror at the inhuman act (the "gross" violation of human rights) rather than, for example, the unjust international distribution of wealth or the harmful effects of global climate change.

The exceptionality and memory of genocide has become the morally incomparable act that called a humanitarian *world* community into being in much the way that regicide lies at the origin of modern nation-states.[119] Today the wish for genocide—to be *all* without the others—is what that world community now makes taboo. It is the *repression*, however, not the absence of such a wish that is the true goal of the fin de siècle project of human rights. This kind of argument is nothing new. Freud argued that mass (or group) psychology originates in both the wish to kill the father and repression of the anxiety that one has already acted on that wish, at least in one's mind.[120] Subsequent scholarship extended Freud's theory to portray the social contract and the modern state as a relation between the real and fantasmatic scenarios of regicide and fratricide that mark its revolutionary founding.[121] If these are the originary crimes that bound the nation-state, what binds the late twentieth century "world community" is belief in Auschwitz as the crime that had become unthinkable, not because it could not happen but because it had.

The ethical imperative "Never *again*" implies that naming "genocide" adds a distinctive element of horror to any atrocity so named—the revulsion appropriate to a taboo, repeatedly violated, that has been violated once again. *Naming* genocide thus became the first step in human rights intervention that is defined by the ultimate moral duty to put humanity ahead of all politics.[122] This form of argument presupposes a radical shift of moral orientation after 1945 in which "the Holocaust" rather than "the Revolution"—French, Russian, or arguably Haitian[123]—becomes the event that defines the relation between ethics and politics. Stated as an imperative, justice-as-reconciliation prescribes the ethical duty of neighbors always to assure each other that "now" is never the time for historical reckoning.

Although twenty-first-century Human Rights Discourse has never been formulated as a comprehensive political theory, it is clear that global politics (insofar as it successfully avoids issues of wealth and resource distribution) is now focused on humanitarian intervention to stop atrocities committed at the local level.[124] There is thus a widely professed ethical commitment to view local cruelties (especially the infliction of physical suffering) as an uncontestable evil, the amelioration of which would justify global intervention in ways that earlier forms of imperialism (in retrospect) did not. The primacy of the global over the local, which was once the basis of a directly political imperialism, is here ostensibly humanized and offset by the primacy of the ethical over the political.

Even after the U.S. debacle in Iraq undermined the generality of this argument, many human rights activists want the U.S. out of Iraq so that it can go into Darfur, where its role could be presumptively ethical once again.[125] Suppose we, as ethical Americans, do decide to rescue in Darfur before we have a plan for reconstruction or an exit strategy—isn't such indifference to the politics that comes later what it means, after Auschwitz, to refuse to look away when "it" happens again? The core proposition of Human Rights Discourse—"Responsibility to Protect"—is, at its best, and also at its worst, an ethical argument against political contextualization *while* people are killing each other. Even though states and multilateral bodies rarely intervene to stop the killing in time, the strong humanitarian argument is that they *should* do so when they *can*. It is better, the argument goes, to be criticized politically for having acted too soon than to be criticized ethically for having waited until it was too late. This argument has been qualified post-Iraq but has not been abandoned.[126]

The Human Rights Discourse described in this chapter fits the needs of a globalization that regards the struggles over capitalism and colonialism as finished. The *excesses* of proximity are what the world market cannot tolerate, and integration of the local economy into the global is the promised reward for violent societies that make the desired transition to a culture of human rights. Instead of demanding justice now, the subjects of transitional justice are expected to show patience and to understand that, from the perspective of a watching world, the real point of their transition is to bring closure to the past.

In justice-as-reconciliation, beneficiaries seek to rationalize their continuing advantage as an ethical repudiation of *both* the perpetrators of past evil and the morally damaged victims who emerged from it. This was true in South Africa, which was the *beau ideal* of turn-of-the-century transitions—the high point of an era on which we may look back with nostalgia as the horrors of our new century emerge. By waiting out the era of anticolonial revolutions allied with global communism, South Africa was largely spared the trauma of revolution, civil war, and genocidal violence: twentieth-century political history doesn't get much better. But the fact that South Africa did not become another Algeria or Mozambique is more than a matter of historical luck. The fin de siècle idea of justice-as-reconciliation was itself a supersession of the revolutionary model of justice as permanent struggle on behalf of unreconciled victims of past *in*justice.

For former victims who were unsure of their victory, the outcome was better than the revolution would have been—forgiveness as the capacity for vengeance that has been, voluntarily, forgone. In the following chapter we consider the South African process of Truth and Reconciliation as also, and more importantly, a way of winning—and go on to ask the question it suppressed, "Who won?" The answer, which is not obvious, depends on which war one thinks has ended—the war against colonialism, against capitalism, against minority rule—and on what counts as winning.

2

WAYS OF WINNING

The War Is Over

I visited South Africa in 1998 to learn more about the process of truth and reconciliation as an alternative to the model of revolutionary struggle described in chapter 1. Soon after my arrival, I found myself across the dinner table from an Afrikaner adviser to Thabo Mbeki and a member of parliament for the African National Congress (ANC) who had been imprisoned during the last years of apartheid. He was freed when the rapprochement talks began to negotiate the return of the ANC exiles, many of whom were under death sentence in absentia.

Over dinner, he told me that his counterpart in that negotiation happened to be the officer who tortured him in prison. There was a pause. He went on, "Not mentioning that fact was hard for me. It helped, of course, that we had won." Winning had made it psychologically possible for him to meet his former torturer daily without acknowledging their shared past.[1]

After a pause, I asked my interlocutor the question that I had come to South Africa to study. "You won," I said. "You have turned the tables on this man and on the regime he served. But what of those more passive victims of apartheid who have not yet 'won' in the obvious sense of assuming power from their former oppressors? Could a Truth and Reconciliation Commission (TRC) grant these noncombatants a moral victory without also granting them material justice?"

"That is the question," my interlocutor agreed.

From its inception, the TRC attempted to answer this question by articulating a coherent conception of what it would mean to have won a legitimate struggle against injustice. Its stated goal was to mark South Africa's transition from a period of struggle over apartheid to a "new future" based on the creation of a shared "human rights culture."[2] This goal embodied the growing belief of many who had advocated a South African revolution that what happened instead would be better, even morally, than what might have been achieved through successful armed struggle.[3]

What happened instead, however, was a negotiated compromise in which the ANC achieved majority rule without militarily defeating the white minority. The broadest terms of the compromise are well described by the historian George Fredrickson:

> The entrenchment of market capitalism and the recognition of most existing white property rights was the price that had to be paid to open up the political system to Africans by some means short of actually driving the whites from power after a prolonged and bloody revolutionary struggle. . . . Major reform, with revolutionary implications for the racial status order but not for the character of other social and economic relationships, is one way to describe what has taken place in South Africa.[4]

The legislation establishing the TRC effectively gave it two years to transform this political compromise into a moral victory over apartheid.[5] Its central assumption was that the struggle against apartheid had been won morally, if not militarily, and that the nation as a whole could *realize* that victory by achieving a consensus that apartheid was an evil that must never be repeated.[6] What could it mean to "live on" after this moral victory?[7] Was *having won* consistent with pursuing the rest of the agenda for which the liberation movement struggled? Or must the historic struggles against capitalist exploitation and settler colonialism be abandoned now that majority rule had been achieved? Was *having won* the democratic struggle for majority rule consistent with continuing the struggle against capitalist exploitation (and *for* workers' rule)? With having won the struggle against settler colonialism (and *for* native rule)? Who had won *those* struggles if they were now to be abandoned? The symbolic task of the TRC was to enact a backward-looking logic of *having won* that could supersede the forward-looking goal of *winning* all three struggles at once.

How successful was the TRC in representing its own process as a substitute for the logic of revolutionary struggle? It was so successful that in most narratives of the South African "miracle" it is longer appropriate to ask, "Who won?" They typically describe the "miracle" itself as a near-Gandhian conversion from the goal of winning to the project of fostering reconciliation. The remainder of this chapter challenges such narratives and also questions their underlying assumption that a struggle for justice is *ended* through reconciliation rather than, for example, by success.

Gandhi did not himself see reconciliation as a value independent of justice and incompatible with struggle. He believed in *struggling* for justice and developed ways to win that do so without violence. In a famous parable he asks his Indian reader, still living under British rule, to imagine that a thief has entered his bedroom, and that, upon turning on the light, he discovers that the thief is his own father. Would he not be embarrassed for his father's shame? Gandhi's parable is not about the importance of reconciliation as this term is conventionally understood. It shows, rather, that in certain situations reconciliation is a way of winning. In the scenario Gandhi describes, for example, the father's exposure as the thief transforms his own guilt into shame, and the thief's exposure as the father transforms the appropriate reaction of his victim/son from outrage into embarrassment.[8] This shows us (as victims/sons/successors) how to exercise our power by transcending the inappropriate impulse to struggle against those who are already disgraced and superseded. Being embarrassed for their shame, Gandhi suggests, is how a moral victory should *feel*. His lesson was that Indian independence should not be considered transitional; it was to be won before being granted.[9] A similar lesson could be drawn from the TRC. But the stress on stories of personal forgiveness in discussions of its work has diverted attention from the more complex political notion of *victory* as a moral relationship to an evil that does not end until justice has already been achieved.

Deconstructing Victimhood

How did the TRC attempt to reconcile the moral attitudes that made South Africans capable of engaging in righteous struggle with the moral attitudes that would make them capable of ending it? My answer to this question was adumbrated in chapter 1. If the category of unreconciled victimhood is constructed by the ultimate refusal to distinguish between the perpetrators and beneficiaries of evil, then it can be deconstructed in the aftermath of struggle through institutional practices that reinstate such a distinction. The success of the TRC's project of justice-as-reconciliation would effectively delegitimate and marginalize the "unreconciled victim" of revolutionary theory who sees the beneficiaries of oppression as would-be perpetrators, and who wages righteous struggle against perpetrator and beneficiary alike.

Justice-as-reconciliation replaces the unreconciled victim of revolutionary theory with the victim who was morally undamaged by past oppression. This lack of moral damage is demonstrated by the victim's retrospective willingness to distinguish, after all, between perpetrators and beneficiaries. The passive beneficiary of injustice can identify fully with the victim, much as the comfortable reader of a literary melodrama is expected to identify with the victim of the social injustices therein portrayed. The condition of this identification is to distinguish between all other grievous injuries done to victims and the distinctively moral kind of damage that would make victims capable of doing injustice in their turn and thus *in*capable of legitimate rule.[10]

According to this liberal script, passive beneficiaries of social injustice will not feel guilt but rather will identify with the innocence of idealized victims whose ability to transcend their suffering reveals that they were never really a threat. This new social compact between undamaged victims and passive beneficiaries presupposes that the unreconciled victim has been damaged by the past and that the beneficiaries of past evil would have been justified in hearing that victim's voice as a threat. Reconciled victims, however, get to "win" in this liberal scenario and to be relatively safe, but only on the condition that they demand little more than this from their putative victory. For them moral victory must be victory enough. As explained in chapter 1, the acknowledgment of moral damage on the part of victims reverses the logic of "consciousness-raising" through which unreconciled victims might have become revolutionaries in the period when evil still ruled. The TRC process thus treats reconciliation as a moral (and not merely political) imperative that is no less part of our conception of justice than the capacity for righteous struggle against injustice.

The idea of moral damage was centrally at stake in what may have been the defining moment of the TRC's public hearings: the appearance of Winnie Mandela. To many South Africans, black and white, she represented the unreconciled victim for whom the anti-apartheid struggle was not yet over. The agenda of her hearing was to demonstrate that she was also (therefore?) morally damaged—a genuine victim whose persecution had made her capable of criminal behavior in her turn. Time and again, Archbishop Tutu pleaded with her to admit her moral damage, and each time she responded with reserve.[11] The overall effect was to construct her as the very figure that the TRC meant to marginalize. She now implicitly represented the antitype of Nelson Mandela, the reconciled, and morally undamaged, victim who was fit to rule because his victory was also moral.[12] The greatest appeal of justice-as-reconciliation does not lie in its fuzzy notion of "forgiving" but rather in the fact that it provides a clear notion of "winning," something the revolutionary model of justice lacks.

Viewing the TRC process as a way of winning allows us to better understand its portrayal of reconciliation as a historically specific form of justice rather than a compromise with injustice. If the TRC's underlying project is to deconstruct revolutionary victimhood, then success depends upon the specific truth to be established when its official procedures are done. The truths that lead to reconciliation are those that enable victims to distinguish once again between the perpetrators and beneficiaries of past evil—and thus to allow reconciled beneficiaries to live *off* that evil without being deemed to have revived it.

The crucial, and controversial, assumption behind the TRC is that an evil *can* be truly dead even though its beneficiaries continue to prosper from it. Those of us who are troubled by this assumption will find it natural to respond by reverting to the revolutionary logic of justice-as-struggle, described earlier: "The evil still lives," we will say, "the struggle continues." This response may be appropriate in South Africa where, by some measures, the level of social inequality is greater now than it was under apartheid. If the vast majority of South Africans continue to suffer from the effects of racialized exploitation, then perhaps the project of justice-as-reconciliation is an ideological means of preserving those effects without resort to overt repression.[13] This is the critique that diehard revolutionaries would make of reconciliation, the chosen path of the ANC after the release of Nelson Mandela in 1990. It required a *political* response.

The *TRC Report*

Viewed politically, the TRC signifies the ANC's abandonment of its revolutionary goals as a way of winning the armed struggle that began after Sharpeville in March 1960. The TRC could not accomplish this, however, by simply portraying the ANC as the victor in a righteous struggle—there was too much compromise for that, and no decisive battle. Rather, its final *Report* found moral victory in the ANC's willingness to renounce the logic of righteous struggle in order to confront the moral damage inflicted on those who followed its strategy of making South Africa "ungovernable" in the mid-1980s.

The fundamental challenge of the *Report* was, thus, not merely to decide "who won" the struggle that was about to end but to end the struggle proactively by redefining what it would mean to have won. Through the TRC process, many victims of apartheid would be assured a moral victory, at least, with possible economic benefits to come. The *TRC Report* is fundamentally an effort to seize that moral victory, and to distinguish it from the political and economic compromises that also occurred.[14]

Archbishop Tutu makes this clear in the foreword to the *Report*:

> The bulk of victims have been black and I have been saddened by what has appeared to be a mean-spiritedness in some of the leadership in the white community. They should be saying: "How fortunate we are that these people do not want to treat us as we treated them. How fortunate that things have remained much the same for us except for the loss of some political power." . . . Can we imagine the anger that has been caused . . .? Should our land not be overwhelmed by black fury leading to orgies of revenge, turning us into a Bosnia, a Northern Ireland or a Sri Lanka?[15]

This comment illustrates the degree to which the moral logic of revolution and civil war still lies behind the rationale for reconciliation as the archbishop conceives it. He had famously said at Chris Hani's funeral in 1993, "We are marching toward victory." But the real victory was to be "a victory of peace and reconciliation over the violence and alienation of apartheid."[16] Now, in October 1998, Tutu declared that the victory had been won, and that the absence of reprisal was a sign of moral superiority on the part of those who struggled and suffered, a moral superiority that seals their right to rule.

Tutu's claim to moral victory was a form of Christian politics, but it should not be confused with the Christian self-abnegation that Nietzsche dismissed as "slave morality." The archbishop was, rather, proposing a peculiarly Nietzschean Christianity in which the goodness of those who suffered is and ought to be shaming to those who stood by.[17] He intended his *Report* to show that whites were saved without deserving it, and that nonwhites, particularly blacks, were their saviors. What is the appropriate moral attitude of the saved? The archbishop's answer was that a feeling of relief is not enough: humility and contrition were also necessary.[18] TRC Commissioner Wynand Malan, in stating his "Minority Position," objected to precisely this aspect of Tutu's view—effectively its core argument—as ultra vires because it is a religious and moral claim about political communities rather than a finding of fact about individuals. In this respect, he believed, the *Report* participated in the divisive logic of apartheid itself.[19]

Commissioner Malan's dissent came close to asking the central questions about the TRC's political success. Its *Report* implied that the moral superiority of the black community was to be established through self-restraint, a refusal to rule as it had been ruled. Did this mean that redistributive initiatives, if there are any, must come from *white* beneficiaries of apartheid, rather than being imposed by majority rule? Did it mean that redistribution by majority rule would only be legitimate when there are enough black beneficiaries of the new order to pay a significant share? Would the black majority sacrifice the moral superiority that the *Report* conferred upon them if they were to demand material redress at the expense of whites? These are not questions that the *Report* directly answers. Despite its multivocal tone, it carefully avoids the moral relativism that Malan believes to be the only way forward—the recognition that in a land of "multiple truths" bygones must finally be bygones. There is, however, a thread of argument in the *Report* that Malan seems to miss: the decision to include the ANC among the perpetrators of human rights violations, and the ANC's subsequent effort to suppress the *Report*.[20] The precise issue here was whether the *Report*'s moral endorsement of the ANC's militant struggle against apartheid should have put the violence of the liberation movement in a category different from the acts of violence committed in support of the regime.[21]

In a fundamental sense the *Report* is, as its critics charge, a legitimation of ANC rule, but the form of that legitimation is unusual. The TRC does not argue that ANC rule will be just because it was the victor in a righteous struggle. Instead, the TRC bases the legitimacy of ANC rule on its willingness to renounce the logic of struggle and to confront the moral damage inflicted by that logic on all those who followed its "ungovernability strategy." This was clearly not the legitimation that then Deputy President Mbeki wanted, but President Mandela, in accepting the TRC's *Report* "with all its imperfections," may have recognized that it gave the ANC both penance and absolution. The TRC had, in effect, made the crimes of the ANC and the apartheid government morally equivalent *after* the struggle without conceding that they *had been* morally equivalent while evil still reigned. As a consequence of the TRC itself, the ANC was *now* morally undamaged by its revolutionary struggle, and thus it was fit to rule.

In the large literature on "transitional justice," nothing like the 1998 *TRC Report* exists, both in its scope and critical self-awareness.[22] While decrying the unmet need for economic redistribution,[23] the *Report* argued that the "psychic and subjective" elements of social transformation must come, first, as a necessary precondition for any "material and redistributive" elements that might follow.[24] Its rejection of the revolutionary assumption that redistribution comes first presupposes a deep discontinuity between the moral impulses that demand the eradication of past injustice and those that allow us to create a consensus that the evil that produced such injustice is truly past.[25] The former follow the moral logic of just war; the latter, the logic of reconciliation and peacemaking.

From the TRC's perspective, the "human rights culture" that would follow apartheid was not merely a political compromise that ended revolutionary struggle. Instead, it reflects a postrevolutionary conception of justice as something other than a first step toward redistributing the illegitimate gains of past oppression.

The Transition to Liberalism

Chapter 1 considered the ever growing literature on the transition to liberal democracy after periods of state-sponsored oppression. There I argued that a common theme in this literature is that successful transitions depend upon constructed narratives that allow the victims and beneficiaries of past injustice to both share and suppress their fear of reenacting past struggle. The point of survivors' justice, thus conceived, is to go forward on a common moral footing—not because the past has been forgiven or forgotten but because continuing to struggle against an evil that is gone is no longer appropriate, and may be morally equivalent to reviving it.

South Africa's TRC was, by design, a culmination of this fin de siècle project.[26] It followed the example of previous truth commissions in reducing the politics of revolution and counterrevolution to the moral psychology of violence and the fear of violence. The TRC's critics correctly state that it was not required to embrace this limited conception of its role: its mandate explicitly permitted it to consider the cumulative social injustice produced by apartheid (which began in 1948) and by earlier forms of racialized exploitation as the *context* of the revolutionary and counterrevolutionary violence that occurred between 1960 and 1994, the period of the TRC's official mandate.[27] This period began with the Sharpeville massacres of 1960, the moment when the anti-apartheid movement embraced the strategy of revolutionary armed struggle. Within its mandated period, the TRC focused further on 1978–89,[28] the years immediately following successful communist revolutions in Mozambique and Angola (1974), Cambodia and Vietnam (1975), and massive unrest in Soweto (1976). These events had made it possible for the Botha government, which came to power in 1978, to recast the defense of apartheid in South Africa as a "total strategy" against the "total onslaught" of global communism.[29]

The TRC thus dealt, by choice, with precisely those aspects of apartheid that had most in common with other "securitocratic" responses to revolution (and, in the Eastern bloc, to counterrevolution) during the final years of the cold war. An implicit assumption of the *Report* is that whites had reason to fear the consequences of majority rule in 1976 when they believed South Africa was in danger of becoming another Mozambique or Angola.[30] Perhaps for this reason, the responsibility of the U.S. and British governments for supporting Botha's "total strategy" was never addressed by the TRC, which took this issue no further than did its predecessors, the Latin American truth commissions. By the 1990s the generally accepted precondition for creating a new "human rights culture" was the repudiation by the Left of whatever revolutionary aims might have excused extralegal repression by the state as the lesser of two evils.[31] Nonwhites in South Africa were thus allowed their moral victory over apartheid only after whites had "won" the cold war.[32] A major success of the TRC process was to make the white fear of black revolution politically inexpressible thereafter by substituting the figure of the undamaged victim for those who, once in power, would be capable of even worse misrule.

The Afrikaner journalist Rian Malan argues, however, that South African whites themselves were morally damaged by the belief that blacks could justly hate them. For some, this damage took the form of tolerating an otherwise abhorrent regime; for antiapartheid whites, like him, it was expressed in the delusion that they could cleanse themselves by opposing it.[33] His point, although he does not say so, is an extension of the Socratic argument that injustice truly harms those who become morally capable of inflicting it, the perpetrators. Here he ascribes a similar moral damage to beneficiaries who knew enough to become opponents, or who believe that they would have been opponents if they had known then what they know now.

When Malan turned against the apartheid regime, he did not regard himself as an early adopter of the feelings that most beneficiaries would later come to have that they could (and should) have safely opposed it. Instead, he took the revolutionary view of justice-as-struggle, described in chapter 1, in which beneficiaries are regarded as would-be perpetrators *unless* they become opponents *while there is still time*. His remarkable book, *My Traitor's Heart*, shows why this view was unsustainable. It recounts how he, as an anti-apartheid journalist, had often put himself in the position of being saved from "bad" Africans by "good" Africans, whom he had thereby endangered. But the blacks who would make him safe, Malan concludes, were no less the figments of his imagination than the blacks who would kill him merely for being white. Those whites who chose to cross the racial divide were implicitly daring blacks not to kill them because they were white, while also daring whites not to kill them as they would a black who posed a similar threat. They never ceased to make themselves the beneficiaries of apartheid.

Malan thus argues that his earlier effort to be a "Just White Man" was never a way of making race irrelevant; it was, rather, how his racism expressed itself before he could acknowledge it. His book reconnects the split-off sides of the psyche of the South African white who refused to be a bystander by challenging him to confront the figure of the black who was the object of his fears (pp. 124–92). The "bad" African is still the morally damaged victim (described in chapter 1) who seemed to legitimate whatever actions the apartheid regime took to ease the insecurities of the passive white beneficiary. The "good" African, however, would distinguish the beneficiary-as-opponent from beneficiaries as would-be perpetrators—he is, essentially, another split-off projection of Malan himself.[34] He concludes from this experience that apartheid was never based on an abstract belief in white superiority as such but, rather, on an idealization of the "good" African, with whom one can identity, and a fear of being slaughtered by the "bad" African, who must either be eliminated or controlled. "When the chips were down," he confesses, even his seemingly courageous opposition to the apartheid regime would be taken as a mode of camouflage, the affectation of albinism (I only look white) that would not save him.[35] He was thus a double traitor, betraying both his Afrikaner people and his professed antiapartheid cause.

> In the end there was no middle ground anywhere, no refuge from choice, not even in myself. I had always been two people, you see—a Just White Man appalled by the cruelties Afrikaners committed against Africans, and an Afrikaner appalled by the cruelties Africans inflicted on each other, and might one day inflict on us. There were always these two paths open before me, these two forces tugging at my traitor's heart.[36]

Malan's 1990 diagnosis of his own ambivalent attitudes toward apartheid, even when resisting it, applies equally to conclusions that many white beneficiaries would later draw from processes culminating in the TRC: that they had been saved by Nelson Mandela (the undamaged victim) from Winnie Mandela (the unreconciled victim), whom even *he* would now repudiate as a threat. This diagnosis resembles the account given by Melanie Klein and her followers of "mock reparation" as a defense against paranoid anxieties. Here one disavows one's hostile thoughts toward the bad other by identifying with an idealized version of the other who remains morally undamaged by those thoughts, and was hence never *really* a threat. Behind this defense are fantasies of omnipotence, the illusion that the external object of one's positive or negative feelings has become in reality what he is in one's own mind—and, thus, that one's internalized destroyer is now potentially (and fantasmatically) one's rescuer. Klein saw the elation that often accompanies "mock" reparation as "manic" because the external reality of those objects as still damaged is now wished away.[37]

What it meant for Malan to refuse to be a bystander bears an uncanny similarity to the hypothetical refusal of those continuing beneficiaries who profess to be convinced by the results of proceedings such as the TRC. These proceedings make it safe for continuing beneficiaries of past injustice to *imagine* themselves as opponents, and to blame their past passivity on ignorance and fear. When the mock reparation process worked, passive beneficiaries of apartheid were relieved of guilt for crimes that they did not personally commit and would not have condoned had they known then about the victims what they know now. They thus gained temporal distance by ceasing to think of the objects of their potential guilt as still being damaged, especially by themselves, in the specific sense that they stood to be accused as would-be perpetrators. Why? Because those victims who were now recognized as "innocent" were not morally damaged and had thus *never been* the kind of threat that had once led apartheid's beneficiaries to support (or condone) its perpetrators. The TRC process thus allowed white beneficiaries of apartheid to become its *would-have-been* opponents, in much the way that Rian Malan *had been* when it mattered: they were symbolically rescued by Nelson Mandela (the undamaged victim) from Winnie Mandela (the unreconciled victim), whom even *he* would now repudiate as a threat.

Is this how surviving beneficiaries *should* think about the feelings that they would have had while evil ruled, if only they had known its true character and extent? Not necessarily. As TRC chair, Archbishop Tutu clearly recognized the possibility that beneficiaries of past evil would see themselves as susceptible to future victimization when the full extent of past atrocity is known.[38] To avoid this scenario, the *TRC Report* allowed them to identify themselves as fellow survivors and hence transform their latent guilt into a sense of shame over their impotence in evil times.[39] Some previously unreconciled victims would in turn express embarrassment for their shame, implicitly abandoning the wish to carry on old struggles until material justice was achieved.[40] The TRC successfully marginalized those on *both* sides who were still willing to fight by establishing a *future* moral equivalence between them: henceforth unreconciled victims who might advocate continuing acts of terrorism could be condemned equally with vigilantes on the other side who prey upon the beneficiary's fear of such terrorists.[41] Following the *TRC Report*, only *extremists* would still believe that those who were lucky enough to benefit from apartheid still condoned what the perpetrators of that system did to its victims.

The essential claim of the TRC was not that postapartheid South Africa had become just but that a redistribution of affect must precede any lasting redistribution of wealth and social power.[42] The ongoing beneficiary position was to first achieve moral distance from the past by acknowledging forms of cultural and racial insensitivity that are *no longer* acceptable. This did not mean that actions based on inappropriate feelings were either forgivable or forgiven. It meant, rather, that there would be hardly anyone left who still needed to be forgiven for them.[43]

Justice as Closure?

What follows, then, from the struggle for the soul of the beneficiary in an emerging "human rights culture?" Is relieving him of guilt an alternative to structural reform or a precondition for it, as many of the TRC commissioners hoped? To what extent may structural reform collectively disadvantage the vicarious beneficiaries of a past evil (for example, through reverse discrimination), and in what situations would structural reform be experienced and symbolized as a collective (and perhaps vicarious) punishment that treats all nonvictims as perpetrators?

In the U.S., as in South Africa, the transitional devices for separating questions of historical truth from questions of distributive justice are precisely this kind of manic response—fantasies of forgiving our victims for the guilt that we would otherwise feel. This is one way to relieve our anxiety about the self-destructive aspects of continuing to hate, but it does not address the victim as anything more than an internalized accuser, a part of the self. In effect, we cope with our fantasies of eliminating or controlling the victim we fear by internalizing a "good" victim who has recognized and coped with his (justifiable) hatred of us. In this way we continue to deny that the good victim and the bad victim are one, and that reparative justice is necessary to reintegrate our experience of them.

Freud was the first to describe the roles that identification, ambivalence, and fantasy play in our emotional responses to traumatic loss, a process he called "the work of mourning." He understood that the immediate experience of survivorship is often accompanied by a sense of elation and triumph (which is what we do with our feeling of hatred and aggression toward the lost or injured object) and that these manic feelings are often followed by depressive bouts of intense self-criticism which are oddly unaccompanied by shame or remorse. What explains this pattern, he said, is that in our inner experience (fantasy) being a victim and having a victim are the same: that is, we understand what it means to be victimized by imagining ourselves to be the objects of our own aggressive fantasies about others. For this reason, victims of loss must always forgive themselves for the crimes that they did *not* commit as part of the work of mourning and recovery.[44] This is the kernel of moral truth on which justice-as-reconciliation rests—the pathological guilt of victimhood, which stands in the way of recovery.[45]

The moral error of justice-as-reconciliation, however, is to suggest that those who inflicted injury or benefited from it must focus on recovery and *self*-forgiveness. The problem here is not only to understand the respects in which they were *like* victims because they, too, were driven by fantasies of being punished and thus projected the inner sources of their anxiety onto those whom they consequently feared. If this were enough, beneficiaries and perpetrators would merely need to recover from their own inner fears to be reconciled with former enemies. This euphoric (manic) substitute for reparation occurs, for example, when German youth become the bearers of a missing *yiddishkeit* or American Boy Scouts act out the role of the "Vanished Indian." Consuming (incorporating) one's earlier victim implicitly preserves the beneficiary's triumph and is not a form of reparation.[46]

Based on Freud, we can question whether either the "undamaged" or the "unreconciled" victim really exists in present-day South Africa, except as a projection of the moral anxieties of the rescued beneficiaries. The rapid creation of a racially integrated South African ruling class[47] did not correspond to the picture of undamaged victims whose moral victory is to demand nothing more. In the new South Africa, there is now a widespread perception that some morally damaged victims have benefited the most from apartheid's demise,[48] while the degree of inequality between rich and poor may be even greater than it was when apartheid still seemed invulnerable.[49] We have seen that justice-as-reconciliation has a moral logic that makes sense as a critique of justice-as-struggle, but we must now consider the degree to which it blocks the possibility of large-scale societal change that would require genuine reparative sacrifice and that remains the kernel of truth in the revolutionary idea.

Melodrama, Pain, and Pastness

What is the notion of a moral victory over the past on which my account of the TRC rests?[50] Describing the TRC's moral view as a "way of winning" would be an oxymoron to liberal philosophers, for whom morality is not essentially connected to the concept of victory. A follower of John Rawls, for example, would make a sharp distinction between retributive justice, based on historically given identities, and distributive justice, which must abstract from those very identities so that no one can be said to have "won."

The liberalism of the TRC, however, reasons in a different moral register than that of either retributive or distributive justice. It reasons, rather, in the moral register of melodrama. "The connotations of the word [melodrama]," according to the literary scholar Peter Brooks, "include the indulgence of strong emotionalism; moral polarization and schematization; extreme states of being, situations, actions; overt villainy, persecution of the good, and final reward of virtue; inflated extravagant expression; dark plotting, suspense, breathtaking peripety."[51]

The written accounts of the ANC's work[52] are powerful examples of "the melodramatic imagination" described by Brooks. Their focus is overwhelmingly on intense confrontations, acts of torture, bodies in pain; their dramatic project is to equate the experience of pain with the achievement of truth and the infliction of cruelty with evil. In revealing the truth about pain, melodramatic performance thus enacts a partial victory over evil: suffering is redeemed, and the victim is vindicated in the end. To describe the work of a *truth* commission as falling under a genre of *fiction* (melodrama) seems insensitive to the real human pain that is reported. My point is not that the truth about what happened was (or might as well have been) a falsehood but, rather, that the narrative through which that truth is told assumes an audience that regards itself *as sensitive* to human suffering in just the way melodramatic fiction does.

Who reads social melodrama, and why? Social melodrama is not written in the voice of the victim crying out against the oppressor and is not generally addressed to victims of the suffering portrayed. Instead, it is meant to be read by people who may *want* to feel bad about the conditions described but who would be made highly uncomfortable if the victim were portrayed as blaming them. In social melodrama the victim is always constructed as innocent (morally undamaged by suffering) so that the melodrama's audience, which is likely to include beneficiaries of such suffering, can understand themselves as bystanders who are capable of feeling compassion without fear. The victim of unjust suffering becomes an object of melodramatic sympathy by being depicted as someone morally superior to the threat that he or she may have become in real life.

Viewed in this way, social melodrama is emphatically different from a literature of social reconstruction, which would exhort the bystander to confront his beneficiary position and ask why the victimary position should be allowed to exist. Such literatures present systemic victimization as a matter of social choice and ask, "Why wait?"[53] In deferring such utopian demands, the work of truth commissions (and the vast literature about them) constructs moral evil as insensitivity to the pain of others that results from feelings of political urgency, whether ethically motivated or not. The moral victory available to victims of torture and atrocity is produced by the telling of their story in a way that makes readable the body in pain. This way of winning, however, raises an obvious question about the melodramatic conventions of the truth commission itself: to what extent should intentionally inflicted pain, especially physical pain, be privileged over other forms of injury in political discourse?

Physical pain, even when its causes are social and historical, has a different temporality than other kinds of injury. "The most crucial fact about pain," Elaine Scarry remarks, "is its presentness." Pain, the intensely conscious physical pain on which Scarry dwells, reduces us to an inner world in which there is nothing but pain and the fear that what is happening now will never end.[54] For this very reason, however, physical pain is also a paradigm case of adversity that can be put in the past. To feel such pain is to desire its end; for pain to end means precisely that it is no longer felt.

Past physical pain and the pain of others can, of course, be imagined and remembered, but the pain of another time/person that becomes an object of memory and imagination is not the pain we experience, when he have it, as a world unto itself. Because imagination and memory are incompatible with *feeling* pain, they can sometimes be used to anaesthetize pain that is still happening. Unlike imagined or remembered pain, however, one's own present pain is "the only [perceptual state] that has no object. . . . [P]ain is like seeing or desiring but not like seeing x or desiring y."[55] Scarry's point is well expressed by the poet Emily Dickinson:

> Pain has an element of blank;
> It cannot recollect
> When it began, or if there were
> A day when it was not.[56]

This description of pain is atypical of the way we speak of the social, rather than physical, injuries that are the ordinary subject of demands for justice. Historical injustice is decidedly *not* "an element of blank." It often can "recollect when it began" and *typically* evokes "a day when it was not."

Although physical pain can be unjustly inflicted (like the acts of torture reported by the TRC), the experience of physical pain while it is undergone is atypical of the experience of injustice that is primarily social and historical. Physical pain is brought to an end by imagination and memory, but social injustice cannot be experienced as such without evoking imagination and memory—and it cannot be imagined or remembered without being simultaneously reexperienced through victimary identification. Political and social injury are in this respect unlike physical pain that is still happening, but have at least a metaphorical connection to physical pain that is *over*. A pain understood to be physical is no longer felt when it is over; but to understand an injury as historical or social is to experience one's present victimhood as *repetition* of the past.[57] The special connection between pain and presentness is so strong that philosophers can reasonably ask why we should have any "bias" between past and future pain: would we really prefer to remember a past pain than to know that we will experience a worse pain in the future followed by amnesia?[58] In melodramas of pain, such as the TRC, there is an exaggerated "time bias" regarding the pain of others: such exercises claim to enlarge, perhaps to maximize, the amount of past pain that is *remembered* in order to limit, perhaps minimize, the experience of its *repetition* in the future. Evoking physical pain as the clearest form of social injury thus becomes an ideological means to force closure on social grievance by allowing those whose pain has stopped to stand in for all who still suffer the consequences of an injustice that is past. We cannot, however, reach this conclusion without first considering how proponents of Human Rights Discourse attempt to avoid it.

Trauma, Narrativity, and Truth

Present-day melodramas of human rights typically rely on the concept of "trauma" to connect physical and social injury. "Trauma," which had previously referred to physical blows or wounds, took on a new meaning in nineteenth-century litigation over railroad accidents causing brain or spinal injury. These "traumatic" injuries, which may or may not have been experienced as especially painful when they occurred, resulted in recurring pain, which was describable for legal purposes as a repetition of the original trauma that had never really ended. From this medical concept, according to the philosopher Ian Hacking, the psychologization and moralization of trauma followed, and hence the analogy of social injustice to the kind of physical pain that cannot be put in the past when it stops.[59]

Unlike the felt pain of torture (the *kind* of pain that Scarry characterizes by its "presentness"), traumatic pain is not necessarily conscious. Trauma must, rather, be *made* conscious in order to be put in the past (remembered) rather than repeated. It is this broadening of physical pain to include traumas that are not fully conscious that becomes the prototype in Human Rights Discourse for social injuries that do not stop hurting the victim when the perpetrator stops. The pain of torture, for example, would persist in the form of trauma until it is *expressed* as a healing social narrative that I have described here as melodrama. Physical torture, thus conceived, appears to be the prototype of all injustice, not merely because the torture victim's pain is prototypically intense but because as *bodily* pain it can be described, independently of its historical and cultural context, as a violation of *human* rights.[60] Cultural historians have compared the inherent *latency* of physical trauma—the old wound that does not heal—to the effect on society of the written inscription of an archive that records past suffering.[61]

What, then, are we to make of the cultural inscription of an archival record of bodily pain? Behind the privileging of torture in today's Human Rights Discourse lies the foundational assumption, well described by the cultural critic Lauren Berlant, that "pain is the only sign readable across the hierarchies of social life."[62] The notion that the true self is the self in pain, she argues, promotes the illusion that a nation can be built (or repaired) through "channels of affective identification and empathy . . . when the pain of intimate others burns into the conscience of classically privileged national subjects" (p. 53). According to Berlant, "This tactical use of trauma to describe the effect of social inequality . . . overidentifies the eradication of pain with the achievement of social justice" (p. 54).[63] Berlant's striking argument can be read as a critique of the conception of moral victory reflected in the TRC. For her "pain is merely banal, a story always already told" (p. 77). Her point is not about expressions of bodily pain itself (such as a scream); instead it is that bodies in pain are "readable" only through narrative conventions that connect individual suffering to social justice. Among these conventions is the genre I have described here as humanitarian *melodrama*.

Berlant's criticism should thus lead us to ask about the specificity of melodrama as genre. Why, for example, is the temporal relation between (first) suffering torture and (then) describing it commonly narrated as a public step from humiliation to dignity—and hence a story of moral victory? We might with equal plausibility see the public *description* of one's own past torture as degrading and the continued ability to maintain silence as noble. If we took this view, we could easily read the victim's willingness to provide a "graphic" account of his own degradation as *pornographic*.[64]

Melodrama and pornography are not, however, the only narrative genres that make pain readable. Still other conventions apply to the visual and literary portrayal of bodily afflictions in Hell—the eschatological paintings of Hieronymous Bosch come to mind. Here the imagined audience is split between onlookers in heaven (already in the picture) who view with apparent satisfaction the well-deserved torments of Hell[65] and those of us (not yet in the picture) who have anxiety that we may yet deserve something similar. It is thus not bodily pain itself but the narrative genre used to depict it that creates moral feeling in the audience. If accounts of physical pain used the conventions of pornography or eschatology, they might evoke feelings in their audience of moral superiority or moral vulnerability or both.

In the stories told by, and about, the TRC we can see the conventions of melodrama at work to create admiration for the victim's virtues (whether those of innocence or heroism) without creating a fear of retribution for the victim's pain. Here the victim's original torture is narrated as a secret humiliation and defeat and its public exposure as a dramatic reversal of fortune that brings about eventual moral victory. Such narratives take place against a scene of private darkness followed by one of public light. (Past torture *had to be* done in secret—it could not have been broadcast; the description of that torture *has to be* public, it cannot be covered up if healing is to occur.) The melodrama populates this scenic background with characters who then *displace* their feelings of humiliation and triumph onto one another using mechanisms of projection and introjection discussed throughout this book.[66] We thus see in melodramas of human rights that *torture* itself would have been mere physical exercise were it not for the interrogator's projective identification with the inflicted pain as something that he completely understands but does not *feel*. The victim's subsequent *confession under torture*, as well as his resistance to it, would then become an introjection of the interrogator's presumed desire to hear certain things but not others. How, then, are we expected to read the interrogator's confession of torture to the TRC?[67] In the melodrama of the TRC titled *Perpetrators Hearing*, the torturers (such as De Kock and Benzien) confess to insensitivity—not having felt the pain they projected onto their victim. As a result of this confession they now profess to admire, rather than despise, the victims who underwent that pain.

Without questioning the possibility of such individual transformations, we must note that the confession *of* torture elicited by truth commissions is no *less* fictitious (and no more *true*) than confessions elicited *under* torture may have been. Peter Brooks's sequel to his study of melodrama, *Troubling Confessions*, argues that confessions of the pain one felt and the pain one caused are both equally fictitious. "Confessions," he says,

> no doubt speak *of* guilt, but don't necessarily speak *the* guilt. . . . There is probably something true in most confessions, but the kind and nature of that truth is not always evident—and not always evidence. At worst . . . the performance of confession . . . produce[s] the guilt needed in order to confess.[68]

The former torturer is not, however, the only one expected to produce the feelings needed by the melodramatic genre of the truth commission. A torture victim must himself project feelings of triumph, which may take the form of forgiveness (if he is capable of it) or, at the very least, of vindication. We who watch the melodrama are also under an imperative to have certain feelings and not others. For us *not* to show compassion for the torments of past victims would be reprehensible; for us *not* to profess admiration for the moral qualities of those who underwent such torments would also be blameworthy. Worst of all, however, would be for us, as onlookers, to take pornographic pleasure in depictions of their pain as the torments of a Hell that might have been enjoyable to souls safely ensconced in an authoritarian Heaven. (What conception of Heaven is *not* authoritarian?)

The TRC must be considered the high-water mark of fin de siècle Human Rights Discourse because it largely succeeded in getting participants and onlookers to profess the feelings it made imperative and to disavow the feelings it made criticizable. In its *Report* the TRC listed twenty thousand traumatized victims, mostly combatants in the revolutionary struggle to defeat apartheid, and mentioned in only a general way the millions more (presumably nonarchived) victims of apartheid and the systems of racialized exploitation that preceded it.[69] Although the commission's stated purpose was to make continuing beneficiaries of apartheid more sympathetic to the needs of the poor when future redistributive measures are considered,[70] its effect was to give these beneficiaries hope that large numbers of nontraumatized victims would be inspired and humbled by the public example of victims who suffered *real pain* and yet escaped *moral damage*.

In the TRC's melodramatic version of the truth, those victims who were named and later reconciled became the official heroes of past struggle, but all who suffered could vicariously share their triumph by considering it a moral victory for victims generally. Berlant criticizes this conception of moral victory as "a logic of fantasy reparation involved in the conversion of the scene of pain and its eradication to the scene of the political itself" (p. 57). The fantasy she describes is not necessarily that of the victim of injustice; it primarily exists in the mind of the anxious beneficiary, still haunted by the specter of revolutionary politics,[71] and is a public form of the "mock reparation" that has been discussed.

Nonrevolutionary Closure

Throughout this book I ask whether the cost of achieving a consensus that the past is evil is to agree, also, that the evil is past. The TRC clearly attempted to do both in its model of justice-as-reconciliation. But, by reducing the scope of social injustice to pain and the scope of political evil to cruelty, it largely failed to confront the forms of structural injustice produced by apartheid that continue after majority rule. Quite possibly the TRC succeeded in persuading the beneficiaries and perpetrators of apartheid that the past was evil. Banal stories of pain and acknowledgment will often serve this purpose for a time. But that consensus will not last unless the beneficiaries also come to believe that the time of evil is now past in the lives of those who suffered under apartheid. For many South Africans, however, the pastness of apartheid is not a fact but rather an ideological construction that rationalizes their continuing disadvantage.

My ideological critique of Human Rights Discourse is that it continues, rather than transcends, the counterrevolutionary project to the extent that victims of the old regime let its beneficiaries keep their gains in the new. This is, I believe, a moral advance over the uglier forms of counterrevolution—it allows reconciled victims a moral victory—but it remains a political compromise that gives beneficiaries more long-term security than they might have gotten through counterrevolutionary means.

Do my misgivings about justice-as-reconciliation make me nostalgic for the revolutionary project of the twentieth century? Yes, in the limited sense that we need to oppose, politically and ethically, the ways in which Human Rights Discourse protects the beneficiaries of past injustice. I believe, however, that an adequate successor to the revolutionary project must begin with the recognition that moral victory is a sine qua non for political victory—but without thereby dropping the demand for distributive justice.

For me, the salient question would be how to reconcile the moral attitudes that make it possible (and legitimate) to engage in revolutionary struggle with the moral attitudes that make it possible (and legitimate) to stop.

A loss of sympathy for justice-as-struggle was, I think, a moral blind spot in the sensibility that Shklar, Kateb, and many other advocates of victim-based approaches to human rights brought to the fin de siècle understanding of the twentieth century's cruelties.[72] Aristotle famously said that *tragic* catharsis evokes both fear and pity. My argument is that the social *melodramas* of reconciliation allow continuing beneficiaries of injustice to pity victims without fearing them, because the victims' grief is now disconnected from their sense of grievance. The flawed idea behind the TRC is that those who rule will do so in the name of victims who have ceased to struggle. In this respect, the *TRC Report* represents what happened to the beneficiaries of apartheid in South Africa as an opportunity for redemption instead of retribution. Was the TRC a failure because, over a decade later, the beneficiaries of apartheid have moved on with little redemptive sacrifice or penance for the past?

On balance, I believe, the TRC must *still* be considered a success to the extent that it allowed many black South Africans to claim a moral victory over apartheid. I do not refer here to the relatively small number of victims who personally found forgiveness during the hearings or to the larger number who may have done so while observing them. The collective moral victory over apartheid was, rather, achieved through national discussion of the miraculous nature of what was happening.[73] In this respect the TRC process transfigured a nation that had long lived in a state of disgrace. This is, perhaps, all that it could mean for an old score to be settled in the short run.

Long-term moral victory is impossible, however, if the claim to justice is fully and finally foreclosed. Archbishop Tutu has consistently recognized this. Although he opened the TRC by saying that its task was closure ("to lay [the] ghosts of the past so that they will not return to haunt us"),[74] he *closed* it by holding forth the possibility of future justice and warning darkly of the alternatives. The archbishop clearly meant this warning to be taken seriously. His introduction to the supplementary volumes of the *TRC Report* (2003) called the project of reconciliation a "sham."[75] On the matter of reparation, he elaborated in a press interview as follows:

> They (victims) have waited long, too long for their reparations. . . . They go to work in town, which is still largely white . . . they leave that to return to the squalor. I cannot explain why those people do not say to hell with Tutu and

the Truth Commission, the Mandelas and all these people. To hell with these people. We are going on a rampage. And my white compatriots still take that for granted.[76]

On the tenth anniversary of the TRC in 2006 the archbishop and Charles Villa-Vicencio (who as TRC research director was responsible for the *Report*) called redistribution and reparation the commission's "unfinished business."[77] They also endorsed the efforts of the TRC's chief prosecutor Dumisa Ntsebeza (who in the end had prosecuted no one) to bring suit in U.S. courts under the Alien Tort Claims Act against corporations profiting from apartheid.[78]

Such misgivings were not, however, widely noted outside South Africa. The dominant view was that of the TRC's deputy chair, Alex Boraine, who continues to present it as a model for bringing "closure" to historical injustice elsewhere.[79] What follows if, as Archbishop Tutu now believes, the TRC has not brought closure? Are the alternatives to closure what he called a "rampage" of vengeance? Another call for forgiveness? A wish to forget?

Tutu's political theology allowed most South Africans to believe that they had the gift of extra time—that the final reckoning with apartheid was deferred. Now that the ANC's moral victory is eroding (along with the multiracial consensus it produced), there is increasing reason to believe that time is running out. How, then, should we view his legacy for the politics of the twenty-first century?

To call his view a secularized theology is not itself a criticism. The philosopher Hans Blumenberg points out, as we have seen, that secularization is a "reoccupation" of the space left empty by Christian theology.[80] What we seek in such a space is not justice as such: there would be no further need for world-transformation if the decisive events in our history (the Holocaust, Hiroshima, apartheid, etc.) "have already occurred" (pp. 134–35). In confessing the present truth of these events, we seek the mysterious quality that St. Paul called "justification." The philosopher Paul Ricoeur explains that being justified is "something that comes to a man—from the future to the present." If declaring sinners justified was the religious message of Christ's death, then secularizing it means postponing justice long enough so that individual "justification" (getting one's own story straight) is still possible.[81]

The TRC superseded the conviction that it is already too late to be saved[82] by giving South Africans time to feel *justified*. During apartheid, as the Pauline logic goes, the beneficiaries of evil hid behind the letter rather than the spirit of the law and felt righteous because they had been law-

abiding. The religious message of the TRC is that South African beneficiaries must recognize that their everyday functioning under apartheid had
been invisible to them as sin. At the same time, however, victims must also
stop believing that legal recourse was appropriate for sins of the past. This
step beyond reliance on the law changed everything by requiring "an absolution that does not remove from the world the consequences of ... guilt."[83]
The TRC gave beneficiaries of apartheid an opportunity to feel at once
responsible and absolved (guilty and forgiven), which is a secular version of
feeling "justified" in Paul's sense.[84]

Sorrow and Disgrace

We have seen that the moral register of the TRC, and other stagings
of transitional justice, is not that of justice in its ordinary sense: it is not
retributive justice (the perpetrators should be punished); it is not reparative justice (the beneficiaries should pay). And, unlike theories of *basic* justice, such as that of John Rawls, theories of transitional justice do not ask
why there should *be* disadvantaged social positions. (Under what conditions could there be inequality *without* victimization?) The moral register
of transitional justice is social melodrama, perhaps a kind of poetic justice,
if it is justice at all.

In social melodrama the plight of undamaged victims is represented in
hyperrealistic and graphic detail as a struggle between good and evil. This
aims, as we have seen, to make us feel bad, but in a good way, as compassionate witnesses. Compassion is pathos without sorrow that creates a
broad potential audience for melodrama. As escapist entertainment, melodramas of social justice stir fantasies of rescue that reassure their audience
of its innermost virtues. Social melodrama is aimed at those who may want
to feel compassion for the conditions described, but haven't *yet*, because
recognizing those conditions also makes them feel afraid. Here the victim
is always good (morally undamaged by suffering) and thus poses no threat
to persons in the onlooker's social position who would believe themselves
capable of similar compassion once their fears are eased. Very frequently
the victims portrayed are helpless women and their children, and the clear
implication is that these children, unless rescued, may well grow up to
become unreconciled victims eventually capable of becoming perpetrators
themselves. In such a morally complicated situation there is *heightened*
pathos for the *loss* of innocence to come. John Coetzee's novel, *Disgrace*,
provides a view of South Africa's transition that is *anti*melodramatic.[85] For

his disgraced protagonist, David Lurie, the question is not whether we are sorry but "what are we going to do now that we are sorry?"[86]

In early Christian writings the moral valence of the sorrow that comes after renouncing sin can be either positive or negative.[87] Positive sorrow is said to come from God and to be a source of repentance and eventual blessedness. Those who feel it are therefore praised and comforted by early Christian writers.[88] But there is also in the monastic tradition a blameworthy sorrow—the way of feeling bad that Saint Gregory of Nyssa ascribes to Cain and Judas.[89] Saint John Cassian described this second kind of sorrow as "harsh, impatient, rough, full of rancor and barren grief and punishing despair, crushing the one whom it has embraced and drawing him away from any effort and salutary sorrow."[90] It is marked by a belief that the condition of the human sinner is never to be sorry enough. Bad sorrow always wants to be sorrier than it is; it always fears that it will deaden and decay because it comes from renouncing sin without believing in redemption. This describes the sorrow felt by ongoing beneficiaries of past injustice who ease their anxieties by expressing heightened compassion.

Walter Benjamin anticipated my criticism of compassion as a numbing form of sorrow by associating it with the monastic sin of *acedia*. *Acedia* was manifested in monks as a slowness to perform penitential tasks.[91] Here the ascetic monk comes to believe that he is shunning worldly goods as though they were evil to no end—that he is *not* redeeming himself and that all his abstinence and penitence will have had no meaning in the afterlife.[92] The Desert Fathers[93] moralized against *acedia* as the specific form of sin that a penitent commits if his sadness (*tristitia*) substitutes itself for work.[94] This fills him with shame, they said, which he allays by endlessly commiserating with the problems of his fellow penitents as a diversion from performing his own penance.[95] For this reason they considered *acedia* to be a sin in itself—the sin that comes after giving up sin without doing what comes next.[96] In *acedia*, however, the monk feels bad about feeling good—and the sin of moral torpor (crushing boredom) becomes in this way its own punishment.[97] My critique of humanitarian compassion is slightly different: I argue that it makes us feel good about feeling bad, creating the delusion that compassion is its own reward.[98]

Coetzee's *Disgrace* is not merely about disgrace but also about the now archaic concepts of *acedia* and *tristitia*. Although he does not use these words, his great theme is the gap in works that lies between becoming penitent and achieving redemption. The question raised throughout *Disgrace* is what it means to have more time after the sinning stops. What kind of state are we in, Coetzee asks, when the words of confession and apology do not reconcile, expiate, heal, or comfort?[99] If disgrace is what comes between acknowledging that the past was evil and putting evil in the past, then *acedia* is the sin of spiritual lethargy that comes from being bored with that acknowledgment. Coetzee's novel raises questions about whether, and in what ways, such boredom can be overcome. It suggests that whipping up retrospective feelings of compassion for victims merely makes one's disgrace seem all the more inevitable. If so, *acedia* might be overcome by penitential works that do not require self-conscious identification with past victims, such as Lurie's care for animals in the novel.[100]

The treatment of animals is, for Coetzee, the paradigm of a moral difference between penitence as an imperative to *undergo sorrow* and bearing compassionate witness as a way of *feeling sorry*.[101] His next novel, *Elizabeth Costello*, asks what it really means to use "the language of the stockyard and the slaughterhouse" to characterize the crime of Auschwitz as treating "people like animals." Does it mean that we must identify with (imagine ourselves in the place of) victims at Auschwitz? Or that we must refuse to be bystanders today when we are surrounded by stockyards and slaughterhouses about which the beneficiaries profess to not really know ("in that special sense")?[102]

The compassionate carnivore, who disregards the abbatoir while continuing to eat meat is, for Coetzee's protagonist, Elizabeth Costello, the figure of the passive beneficiary (the Good German) par excellence.[103] Where animal suffering is concerned, "pain is pain." This claim on behalf of animal rights is at the core of a conception of *human* rights, which seeks to make us better able to imagine bodily pain that is not our own.[104] Coetzee brings this point back to the sin of compassion-*fatigue* that could follow confessing the world's indifference to Auschwitz.[105] Compassion-fatigue clearly stands in relation to Auschwitz as *acedia* once stood in relation to sin. The figure of Elizabeth Costello illustrates what it might now mean to battle *acedia* through a militant refusal to acquiesce in the infliction on any sentient being of the treatment humans now accord to animals. This position (which Coetzee may well endorse) can also be read as a reductio ad absurdum of the view that the object of ethics is to produce compassion in the beneficiaries of suffering.[106]

Is compassion for suffering as such, whether human or animal, the form that penitence should take after Auschwitz? Is a life of heightened empathy the way to sustain a robust politics of sorrow? Such a view is persuasive only if we invest what the literary scholar Carolyn Dean calls "the fragility of empathy" with the full moral condemnation once directed at *acedia*. Curing such moral torpor would then require a tireless search for new sites of suffering that would revive our feeling for the past suffering about which we did nothing and thus hold off the return of indifference. Our priestly intercessors in the cultivation of the feelings that replace *acedia* would be those journalists and photographers who can help us imagine how victims *really feel* and model how it looks to feel for them.[107]

Feeling sorry *for others*, however, plays only a minor role in the core medieval texts on overcoming acedia. Cassian discusses "the shedding of tears,"[108] but these are tears of *compunction* for one's *own* bad feeling rather than compassion for the innocent suffering of others.[109] In these modern Benedictine texts, recuperating the thought of the Desert Fathers, tears are a "stage" in the mortification of the sinner, leading to a purification of feeling. But here the goal is not, as in compassion, to achieve intensified feeling but, rather, a form of *condescension* in the precise sense of imitating Christ's looking down from the cross.[110] As an imitation of Christ, the tears of the penitent are not for innocent victims but for guilty sinners who have been saved.

Outside monasticism, the medieval church prescribed a range of penitential rites far wider than the auricular confession and private absolution practiced today. Penances could be public as well as private, communal as well as individual, and could consist of pilgrimages and tariffs as well as prayer. The historian Mary C. Mansfield notes that medieval rites of penance played a central role of "communal peacemaking" and "diplomacy," where they where a "face-saving religious ritual" that fostered reconciliation within and between communities. An important purpose of these rites was not only the cancellation of guilt before God but also what Mansfield calls "the public humiliation of sinners."[111]

Mansfield points out that, "by 1200, there were three types of penance: private penance, nonsolemn public penance, and solemn public penance." In stressing its political function she notes that "confession of public sins obviously does not reveal anything that man or god does not know; instead it implies submission to the discipline of the church."[112] Nevertheless, the practice of public penitence in medieval cities raises the question of what could it mean to take seriously the idea of being sorry for the past. If this acknowledgment is genuine, what should we then *do*?

Sorry States

In European thought the concept of Purgatory is still the source of most of our ideas about what it means to stop sinning without achieving grace. Purgatory took hold in Catholic thought in the late twelfth century as an alternative to damnation for those, like the "beneficiaries" of evil, who repented their sins too late to be saved or whose postbaptismal vices (including the sin of *acedia*) were ultimately redeemable.[113]

According to the historian Jacques Le Goff, "Purgatory is a place, but it is also a time, since one definition of Purgatory is that it is a Hell of limited duration."[114] Purgatory is also, according to Le Goff, a "sphere of penance on the borderline between spiritual life and material and social life."[115] Spiritually the denizens of Purgatory are recipients of God's grace who have confessed and repented of sin. Their time in Purgatory, however, is marked by the material consequences of the evil for which they were responsible: it is taken up with prayer, corporeal suffering, and works of penitence.[116] Moreover, Purgatory is understood as both a place and time where the extent of the penitent's suffering and work can be mitigated by the prayers, sacrifices, and indulgences of those who survive.[117] In addition to making remembrance a spiritual contract between named individuals, living and dead, the concept of Purgatory gave "work" a new moral meaning.[118] The work of prayer, abstinence, and self-mortification became something the monastic orders were willing to sell for a fee—they claimed to act not merely on behalf of their own salvation but to redeem the named individuals in Purgatory with whose remembrance they were charged. In its medieval origin the moral significance of work was thus a two-way relationship between the living and the dead based on memory, penitence, and the redemptive value of pain.

Based on the foregoing account, the genealogy of several of the concepts at stake in my general argument about the afterlives of evil can be traced to the concept of Purgatory:

- *Suffrage.* In its medieval Christian origin, suffrage (the vote) is an intercessory prayer for the soul of a sinner. Souls in Purgatory sought the intercessions, or votes, of Saints (the already saved), who could speed the prayers of sinners to Heaven. No less important, however, were the suffrages of those whom one had loved and of those whom one had injured. From this idea we can derive the notion that the suffrage of victims matters, especially in a political order recovering from past evil, and that the idea of mass suffrage is rooted not only in Athenian democracy but also in a Christian political theology (such as that of Lincoln) in which all are, equally, sinned against and sinning.
- *Tolerance.* What is required to save a soul in Purgatory is the granting of an indulgence or dispensation for sin. Another word for this is "tolerance." Thus tolerance, in its medieval origin, is a response to penitence and makes forgiveness depend on one's willingness to pay, hence linking mercy to a type of justice.

- *Confession.* Both the auricular confession of sin and the public expression of sorrow are preconditions for entering the state of Purgatory. Without confession, and consequent sorrow, the sinner's prayers and works will not count toward salvation.[119]

- *Exomologesis.* The practice of exomologesis required the sinner to humble himself in sackcloth and ashes, abjure ordinary pleasures of food and drink, and (through constant prayer) abase himself by glorifying God.[120] As a ritual of public penance, medieval exomologesis also functioned as a trial run for Purgatory.

- *Sadness.* To be truly sorry is also to be sad. Sadness (*tristitia*) is itself a state of sin as well as the lethargic moral condition (*acedia*) of those who have withdrawn from sin.[121] It is thus the affective condition of souls entering Purgatory.

- *Work.* Penitence requires works (*satisfactio operis*) to overcome the lethargy typically associated with renouncing sin. As a theological concept, work was the invention of medieval monks (both anchorite and cenobite) to overcome the torpor that follows after sin and which is itself a sin. The intense moral value attached to willingly performed work (not the labors of slaves or serfs) rested on the premise that such self-inflicted suffering was necessary to the purgation of sin. Morally valuable work was thus performed in sadness but with the ultimate hope of redemption.[122]

Suffrage, tolerance, confession, exomologesis, sorrow, and work are spiritually intense disciplines, involving agony, ecstasy, and prayer, but only in rare exemplars (of which St. Francis was one) did they elicit the sinner's compassion for other sufferers. Compassion *itself* was not considered morally valuable—although it might be a sign of divine grace—because the capacity of a medieval sinner to accept and withstand pain was a necessary element in his redemption. The holy sufferer was thus an object of admiration, not of pity. Sorrow, both divine and human, was reserved for human sin itself and not the pain a merciful God required as expiation.[123] As a virtual participation in the suffering of his world, compassion drives out the bystander's indifference; in doing so, however, it also promises relief. Like medieval souls in Purgatory, the modern objects of media compassion now receive suffrages from all mankind in accordance with the salvific message of Human Rights Discourse.

But who is to be saved in our postreligious version of Purgatory *inter vivos*—the perpetrator, the victim, or the compassionate witness? Coetzee ends *Disgrace*, as we have seen, with a vision of his protagonist doing good works for dying animals without self-pity or complaint; these figures resonate with the depiction in Human Rights Discourse of the humanitarian aid worker who devotes his life (or precious youth) to solitary and necessary service in places like Darfur.[124] The exceptionality of their work is, I think, an essential part of the story—those of us who bear witness are not expected to see them as exemplary precursors on a path to redemption that we must all eventually follow; their examples of how a turn toward works would *look* tend, rather, to reinforce the sense of helplessness and futility that a compassionate witness is generally meant to feel. Despite (perhaps even because) such saintly figures exist in Human Rights Discourse, I would continue to argue that its real aim is to reassure the compassionate witness of his own redemption.

What would it mean to think of Purgatory as a state that is not merely moral and spiritual but also political? And what would it mean to think of political states as forms of Purgatory? Dante's *Purgatorio*, an account of how belated penitents can redeem themselves, provides a useful contrast to today's Human Rights Discourse. The inhabitants of Purgatory, as Dante describes them, suffer greatly, but they also see their suffering as a means of relief from the burdens of the past. Those who once sought sin, he says, must now seek suffering.[125] Such souls do not call forth Dante's compassion, and those he meets tend to moralize against anyone who would feel sorry for them. Purgatory, for them, is a workplace that allows hope that their penance may finally be accepted as sufficient, and Dante's up-to-the-minute report on their progress is that sorrow conjoined with hope requires work. The suffering they seek, moreover, is not everlasting: it is of limited duration and diminishes over time.[126] The difference between Hell and Purgatory, according to Dante, does not hinge on the sin itself but rather on the difference between *punishment* seen as deserved suffering without hope and *penance* seen as deserved suffering that leads to expiation.[127]

Is the state of Purgatory, as Dante describes it, also a description of the appropriate moral attitude for survivors of an evil time for whom repentance came too late? Our answer to these questions must be mixed. The too-lateness of repentance is a topic mostly avoided by the mainstream literature on transitional justice, which is addressed to former bystanders who now believe that they might have acted differently had they felt then the compassion for victims that they feel now. But compassion for past victims is itself an experience of *lag* between the end of evil and the time of justice, based on the assumption that patience is required of the *victims*. In Dante's *Purgatory*, by way of contrast, belated sorrow is one's ticket of admission. Thereafter one's own works, supported by the suffrages and tolerances of others, become the way out—the path to purgation. *Im*patience on the part of *sinners* is the dominant mood in Purgatory—a feeling that it is (almost) too late to make things right and that the time has come to hurry.

The need for a purgative element in political transitions (even those that make no claim to revolutionary significance) is why I focus throughout this book on the moral psychology of continuing beneficiaries of past evil who no longer condone it. For them, I have argued, believing that the past was evil is only the beginning, not the end, of the necessary transition. Here I disagree with liberal approaches to transitional justice, which rest heavily on the assumption that changed belief is a goal worth achieving for its own sake. These theories assume that it is *never* too late for repentance and *always* too soon for justice. I assume, along with Dante, that, even when repentance comes too late, justice can never come too soon.

My concern is not with the validity of transitional justice as an indefinite deferral of justice on the time line of eternity, but with how an apparently secular "reoccupation" of that theology makes the present seem more legitimate than the past, whether or not justice happens in the future. Here, I would suggest, many white South Africans who engaged with the TRC process as it actually occurred would equate salvation with having simply "gotten off," because they converted just in time—before a final reckoning.[128]

Dante's account of Purgatory is, however, equally limited as a path to social justice. It makes no assumption, for example, that an individual's purgation of sin of Purgatory must take a form that is beneficial to others whom he meets along the way.[129] Although Dante's conception of Purgatory tells us who should pay the price of penance (and how they should think of themselves while doing so), it tells us nothing about who (if anyone) should benefit from the heavy price that the penitent should be willing to pay to save his own soul. This is not to say that purgatorial practice altogether ignores interpersonal redistribution. There are traces of redistribution in the idea that living descendants must pay something to speed the expiation of past generations as well as in the complementary idea that dying sinners are obliged to bequeath alms to the living who will intercede for them. The moral argument for almsgiving, however, stresses that the purchase and performance of sacramental good works (such as masses said in remembrance of the dead) are more important than help for those who suffer in life. St. Thomas More, for example, opposed using church wealth for the poor by arguing (as paraphrased by Steven Greenblatt) that "the miseries of the poor are vastly exceeded by the unspeakable miseries of souls in Purgatory, and the good that alms can do for the living is vastly exceeded by what the same alms can do for the dead."[130]

More's notion of redistributing wealth to save the dead is a striking alternative to contemporary views of social reconstruction that encourage the living, as survivors of evil, to regard *themselves* as saved. The analogy between transitional justice and Purgatory thus raises questions that in a secular context are essentially redistributive: Who must gain from the sacrifices and works required to expiate the past? These questions are essentially ways to limit our concern with redeeming the dead to issues of political identity that can be set aside in the name of future interests.

Justice as Afterlife

A great achievement of Western modernity was to put relations among the living at the center of concerns about justice. The high-water mark in this development was the French Revolution's Declaration of the Rights of Man, which rejected in the name of *human* rights the customary rights that functioned as a dead hand of the past. Jeremy Bentham said that the Declaration had been mistaken to state a forward-looking politics of interest in the backward-looking language of rights. The future-oriented concept of utility would allow the living to produce the greatest possible good, or at least what is best for the greatest possible number of them; the backward-oriented concept of rights would cause permanent conflict between the distinct historical identities that define winners and losers in the present. The fundamental difference between identity and interest— history and happiness—could not, according to Bentham, be elided by such "nonsensical" concepts as the Rights of Man.[131]

Most present-day liberals would agree with Bentham that the *confusion* of interests and identities causes ongoing political disorder, but many believe that the concept of human (as distinct from historical) rights can facilitate the *transition* from identity to interest politics. Here the *need* to move from identity to interest politics becomes part of the rhetoric of postponement—liberals invoke it to perpetuate the effects of past injustice on the basis of society's need to move on while refusing to address the ways in which forward-looking interests are themselves the products of past historical identities from which illegitimate advantages were reaped. (Whatever Bentham's shortcomings, he did not believe in postponing justice.)

We can best address the complexities of transitional justice by speaking of them metaphorically as "afterlives of injustice." There would be no problem of postponement if we had only interests but no identities or only identities but no interests. This would occur if we were to imagine ourselves in a hypothetical "original position" in which everyone was not yet born[132] or a hypothetical "final position" in which everyone is already dead.[133] But politics as we know it arises because we are in neither the original nor the final position. We are, rather, *alive*—already born but not yet dead—and our lives are partial continuations of the identities of others who lived before.

The living approach one another with undeserved gains, unsatisfied grievances, and unmitigated disgrace that it is already too late to undo. They are, in this sense, the expected future of an unforgotten past. In another sense, however, the living have also come *too soon* for final justice.

The genius of the TRC was to reconceptualize what would otherwise have been a *mere* compromise as, rather, the redemption of a time. Before the compromise, it was said, each side believed it was *too late* for the apartheid regime to change: revolutionaries believed that revolution was long *overdue*; counterrevolutionaries believed that they had *already* been judged and condemned. The compromise, however, showed that there was *still time* for apartheid's beneficiaries to avoid final judgment and for its victims to escape moral damage. In South Africa the project of transitional justice was not necessarily a way to produce more justice, but it was certainly a way to produce *more time*.

But what does it mean to have more time, and how is this time different from the time that came before? It means, at the very least, that *the time is no longer right* for revolution, if it ever was. Beyond this, however, it is not clear whether that time is *past* or *still to come*. The TRC left open the question of what followed from the fact that the beneficiaries of apartheid *still had time* to change. Did it mean that it was *now too late* for revolution? Or did it mean that South Africans now had a *second chance*? The transition from Mbeki to Zuma suggests South Africa's partial return to the once normal political cleavages based on race and class and a new concern with whether the country is to be ruled by those who were morally damaged by a past that is not yet entirely past.[134]

The idea that transitional time can be indefinitely prolonged leads to the example of the postslavery U.S., which constitutionalized the idea of a permanent recovery. We must now consider what this meant as the U.S. stands at its own Mandela moment—the election of a president with overwhelming black support who did not, thereby, provoke overwhelming white opposition. Many whites—a near majority—voted for Obama, and many Republicans described his victory as a moment of national redemption rather than historical reproach. Did this mean that our 150-year period of recovery from slavery was finally over, that change had come? This claim hinges on the historically exceptional character of Mandela/Obama as undamaged victims and the unexpected capacity of beneficiaries to recognize them as such and set aside their fear of being treated as would-be perpetrators. At such apparently self-legitimating moments, the struggle over historical redress is arguably transcended by the hope for national regeneration.

Chapters 1 and 2 have explored the political logic of such miraculous moments as *exceptions* to the claim that real change must be revolutionary in the simple sense that beneficiaries of past injustice do not emerge as winners. Here the victims' triumph over moral damage leaves beneficiaries relatively secure in their material gains. I have suggested throughout that claims of legitimation-by-miracle must be understood alongside other types of temporal legitimation in which the present time appears as normal in contrast to some past (and/or future) time. Claims about a national "miracle" privilege the *now* as the time of exception—"we are the ones we have been waiting for"[135]—in much the way that belief in a national "emergency" does. The two can indeed converge to the extent that they depend on the exceptional character of a charismatic leader who brings moral regeneration at a time of peril. Carl Schmitt thus saw such moments of "self-empowering novelty" as filled with the "audacity and joy in the *danger* of having no need for justification" (my emphasis).[136] That danger, of course, can consist of infinitizing the moral virtue of the leader but also of hypervigilance for signs of moral damage, such as racism, corruption, or dictatorial tendencies. (Speaking of "a Hitler" conveys the dual sense that a self-legitimating leader *could* claim extraordinary powers, on the one hand, and for this very reason be exceptionally vulnerable to political assassination, on the other—*sic semper tyrannus.*) To the extent that a Mandela or Obama show themselves to be undamaged by *not* being antiwhite and pro-redistribution, they will give questions of race, class, and political corruption a heightened, *now*-based salience for successors' governments (such as those of Mbeki and Zuma), which must decide whether to take up or avoid the question of reconstruction.[137] Racism can here be renewed in the form of antiracism and class exploitation continued as an expansion of free markets. The basis of this argument is that the moral regeneration of beneficiaries has *already* occurred and that the present is not a continuation of the past.

The U.S. after Lincoln was the historical laboratory for such developments. Chapter 3 steps backward in time to explore the significance of Lincoln's legacy for the late-twentieth-century project of transitional justice.

3

LIVING ON

Permanent Recovery

South Africa's politics of "closure" is not the only form that transitional justice can take: it is also possible to defer closure in order to make permanent the project of national recovery. This was the path eventually taken by post–Civil War America, where the historical victims of slavery could never claim to be a national majority and now claim to have finally "overcome" only as a consequence of Barack Obama's election as president.

For most of its history, however, the United States has been an aspirationally liberal political order that made the transition from slavery a permanent part of its constitutional identity. When viewed from the perspective of South Africa's still unfinished transition, the checkered history of U.S. constitutional development sheds light on how the consequences of a morally unacceptable past can be simultaneously perpetuated and transcended. This chapter considers the U.S. experience of *prolonging* transition (perhaps indefinitely) as both a positive and negative prototype for recent attempts to end evil by postponing justice.

Viewed narrowly, the official period of Reconstruction in U.S. history is atypical of the recent democratic "transitions" discussed elsewhere in this book. There was no negotiated transfer of power and no prior agreement on alternative forms of justice (or alternatives to justice) that would allay the fears of former rulers and their beneficiaries who relinquished power to avoid the horrors of protracted civil war. We Americans actually fought our Civil War, and our period of postwar Reconstruction was a form of victor's justice that impeded reconciliation between North and South for as long as it lasted. When sectional reconciliation finally occurred, decades later, it came at the cost of abandoning the effort to achieve a semblance of justice for the victims of slavery and their descendants. That project was suspended for nearly a century and remains unfinished today.

Unlike more recent democratic transitions, the U.S. failed in the aftermath of the Civil War to produce an official moral narrative about its unforgotten past. There was, as we shall see, only one full prosecution of war crimes committed against combatants and little effort until recently to document the historical record of slavery and its effects.[1] The U.S. Civil War put to rest the question of slavery, but, as Kirk Savage says, "The question of what this nation had become without slavery remained, and still remains, unsettled." Our period of Reconstruction left war memorials of various kinds, including the Civil War amendments to our Constitution.[2] The Civil War amendments were, however, ambiguous in their historical meaning. They could be read at different periods and from different perspectives as both an amnesty for the past and an aspiration for the future, like the work of recent truth commissions that combine forgiveness with a pledge of "*nunca más.*"[3]

Temporalities of Transition

The preceding chapters have considered the special characteristics of transitional time: the time after evil has been brought to a close that is *still* a time before justice. I have argued that transitional justice is not another paradigm of justice—an answer to the question of who does what *to* whom *for* whom and at *whose expense*. The project of transitional justice is concerned instead with the temporality of justice—what *will have* happened if the past is properly understood; what *would have* happened had we known then what we now understand. If successful, this project of intertemporal reconciliation makes the continuing *absence* of justice today more acceptable than it would have been when evil prevailed.

I have thus contrasted transitional justice with revolution—which it defers. The occurrence of revolution—the belief that it *has* occurred—means that "more of the same" is no longer sufficient to legitimate the future. Between past time (T_1) and future time (T_2) there will now have been a revolutionary time (T_R) that is a special exception to normal time. (T_R) interrupts the past and refounds the future by bringing about an irreversible breach between "now" and "then."

The concept of revolution as a new beginning is thus, and always has been, the limit point to be excluded from the domain of transitional justice. In revolution, what Walter Benjamin calls a "summary" judgment is made on the past:[4] that judgment's *presumed* legitimacy sums up the moral meaning of the past and becomes the legal basis of a new political order that follows.[5] This concept of a revolutionary moment is not alien to the U.S.: we Americans grow up with it. In our refounding as an independent state there was not (at least in retrospect) a period of *transition* between the time when we were ruled by the bad old King of England, and the moment when We the People came to rule ourselves.[6]

A theory of transitional justice would cover the entire domain that excludes revolutionary justice as its constitutive exception. Such a theory assumes that there can be a kind of secular time that effectively keeps (T_1) from returning and (T_2) from arriving that is *not* (T_R). This transitional time (T_T) can be of indefinite length. It can be constitutionalized as a time of indefinite duration, potentially permanent, except for the fact that its end must always be conceivable as a time when *change has finally come.*

The U.S. Civil War and Reconstruction could have been a Second American Revolution.[7] Instead, they resulted in a state of permanent national recovery enshrined in the constitutional jurisprudence of the Civil War amendments. This jurisprudence gave the U.S. additional time to be *against* the evils that led to our Civil War and to avoid the outbreak of another one. As an alternative to revolution, transitional justice represents the elongation (perhaps even hypertrophy) of the time (T_T) between (T_1) and (T_2). Transitional justice thus deals with all cases in which $(T_R) \neq 0$.[8] In such cases preventing the *return* of civil war (or avoiding a future one) is a project that can seem no less morally desirable than bringing past evil to an end by hastening the moment of *change.*

In a state of indefinite, perhaps permanent, *transition*, former victims do not become the new beneficiaries. Such a transitional state may stop doing bad things *to* the former victims, but it still exists largely *for the sake of* ongoing beneficiaries of the old order: there is no paradigm shift in the way who/whom questions are stated. But *within* the grammar of transitional justice, revolutionary language can still affect the way now/then questions are to be addressed. In this interpretive debate, "revolution" represents the limit case in which there has been *sufficient* time to address past injustice. This rhetorical point, however, is now *off* the scale of other ways of characterizing the continuing and completed aspects of past evil and also the relationship of its degree of pastness to the conditionality of present actions (what they would have meant if the past were otherwise). In transitional regimes, such as the U.S., we thus develop a lexicon of "R" words that contrast with *Revolution.*

- *Recovery.* To be in recovery is to be engaged in restoring something lost in the past. As we shall see, Lincoln's Gettysburg Address set forth a post–

Civil War project of U.S. national recovery, which was about rehabilitating, and ultimately restoring, the Jeffersonian ideals of 1776. Recovery in Lincoln's sense would not have been merely atonement for the sin of slavery; it would, rather, have been an ongoing effort to save the national soul. Thus his stated war aim was for the U.S. to *survive* a period of moral danger without destroying *itself*. A state of permanent recovery, so conceived, would be a process of constant *self-examination* to allay anxiety that the patterns of the past will be repeated.

- *Reconstruction* is a strong, forward-looking version of national recovery that moves it toward the limit point of revolution. The Reconstruction-era South was divided between the friends and foes of the new social order—a clash between revolutionary and reactionary social forces in which federal intervention was usually on the side of the former.[9] By treating peace as a continuation of the Civil War through politics, the project of radical Reconstruction provided much less assurance to the defeated beneficiaries of past injustice than we see in most of today's models of transitional justice.[10]

- *Redemption* was the ideology of anti-Reconstruction resistance in the American South. Defeated Southern whites, while still underrepresented in Congress, saw Freedmen and Carpetbaggers as virtual terrorists operating with the tacit or explicit collusion of federal military officials. These feelings gave rise to semiclandestine resistance movements (*Contras*), such as the Ku Klux Klan, which purported to rescue defenseless women and children from atrocities condoned in the name of Reconstruction.[11] The self-identified "Redeemers" sought through both direct action and political influence to vindicate the honor and ideals of the Antebellum South and constructed a new social movement around the idea that "the South shall rise *again*."[12] Although the Redeemers are rarely studied as a social movement by historians of the U.S., their nineteenth-century success was the twentieth-century model for U.S.-sponsored "freedom fighters" against communist-inspired projects of social reconstruction elsewhere in the world.[13]

- *Rebirth*. Birth itself is, specifically, *not* a transition but rather a beginning; *re*birth is a second beginning—a moment of beginning *again*. Lincoln followed St. Paul, as we shall see, in viewing *recovery* as a form of *rebirth*. The association of birth with moral innocence, and rebirth with moral cleansing, is a consequence of the biblical rejection of intergenerational guilt in Ezekiel 18:20: "the son shall not suffer for the iniquity of the father."[14] The Christian idea of rebirth as moral renewal, however, is not the same as *going back* to one's beginning. Rather, the moral slate is wiped clean even though the sins committed in one's "former" life are still remembered as one's own. To restate this point contentiously, rebirth assumes that the amnesia of one's original birth was a nonpathological and morally desirable state and promises a return to that same desirable state but without the amnesia. The moral value of rebirth requires one to remember prior experiences while nevertheless regarding them as discontinuous with one's present state of mind. Rebirth is thus described as, ethically, even better than forgetting: the "born again" are often so persuaded of their newfound innocence that they can be reminded of their evil past without suffering embarrassment. If birth is the paradigm of moral innocence, rebirth is the ethical paradigm of successful atonement.[15]

The Lincolnian Legacy

Since Lincoln's Gettysburg Address, America has stood for the possibility that a living constitution can be persuasively reinterpreted, as a result of historical trauma, to make a new beginning. The forward-looking Lincoln (the Lincoln we commemorate) lifted Americans above the unendurable cycle of guilt and recrimination by moving the United States from a sense of being unwilling perpetrators of evil, first to the recognition that we are all "victims" and then to the acceptance of the common national identity as "survivors."

As a figure in this chapter, my Lincoln is a mixture of fact and myth. The real Lincoln was a complex figure whose prewar views were tempered by political expediency and whose postwar aspirations can only be inferred from his conduct during the last few weeks of his life.[16] There is, however, ample evidence that his war aims changed in the months before Gettysburg from the restoration of a "union" to the rebirth of a "nation."[17] The Lincoln of national memory now stands for a constitutional politics based on *reidentification* (with its implication of national rebirth and new identity) as opposed to a constitutional politics of *representation* with its implication that preexisting identities are fixed, or have become so, and require recognition. The latter is the view that I associate with the position of Woodrow Wilson in the American political tradition and, more generally, with those who believe that (aside from the immorality of slavery itself) Lincoln would have been wrong to suppress the desire of the Southern states for self-determination.

In recasting of the Jeffersonian legacy to oppose secession and free the slaves, Lincoln reversed the order of ideas in Jefferson's Declaration of

Independence. Liberty is no longer merely listed among inalienable rights but is stated as a preconception (we were "conceived in liberty"); just as important, Jefferson's notion that "all men are created equal" becomes for Lincoln a "proposition" to which "this nation" must "now" affirmatively rededicate itself.[18]

Why us? Why now? Lincoln's implicit answer to these questions evoked the perspective of "the world," an international context in which our Civil War was already a notable event. He had long believed that slavery "deprives our republican example of its just influence in the world," which would ultimately inspire "all lovers of liberty everywhere" to embrace the egalitarian principles of our Declaration of Independence.[19] At Gettysburg Lincoln implied that the commitment to human equality had survived the European defeats of 1848 to be reborn in the United States.[20] Our Civil War was a *test*, he said, of whether "any nation so conceived and so dedicated" can "long endure" in a counterrevolutionary world.[21] That test, however, was no longer merely a matter of perseverance in our original revolutionary beliefs. It was, rather, to transform the moral logic that had led the nation from Revolution to Civil War into one of common survivorship and collective rebirth. How did he propose to achieve this result?

The conception of national recovery and rebirth that I call "Lincolnian" denies that the constitutional problem of the Civil War is how to fit the Negro into the framework of competing sovereignties on which our federal system is based. That view—the basis of previous sectional compromises—would have conceded that partition could be a mutually agreeable alternative to federal union and that (on suitable terms) repatriation could be a plausible alternative to emancipation for the African American. Lincoln may have believed something like this for most of his life,[22] but the Lincoln we remember did not. From the received Lincolnian perspective on the U.S. Civil War, the problem is slavery, not sovereignty. Slavery is, moreover, a national problem—a problem for both North and South, for both black and white. The precise nature of that problem, however, is not necessarily to set things right for the individual victims of enslavement but rather to help the entire nation recover from what pop psychologists might call its "toxic guilt."

For Lincoln himself, the problem of redemption from national guilt was a secular version of the Pauline problem of enslavement to sin.[23] He said as much in his Second Inaugural, and in the Gettysburg Address he described the meaning of the Civil War—our "new birth of freedom"—as a rebirth from what St. Paul might have called our national slavery to slavery. Lincoln knew that abolitionists had also used this imagery—it had been the basis of the movement for *northern* secessionism after the *Dred Scott* deci-sion[24]—and he appropriated it to represent the Civil War as a struggle to free the Union from its own slavery, its own original sin. Lincoln's Gettys-burg Address became in effect our national "survivor story," and the Second Inaugural Address a national recovery program from the near-death expe-riences of slavery and civil war.

These redemptive metaphors were more than rhetorical gestures. Many of Lincoln's Old World contemporaries, such as Bismarck and Cavour, had linked national resurgence and victimary identity in order to justify the use of military force to "reunify" their nations.[25] Lincoln raised the Ameri-can Civil War to a higher moral plane than other wars of national reunifica-tion by portraying the Union itself as the victim of slavery and the war against secession as its struggle for redemption and rebirth.[26] In Lincoln's survivor story, the suffering of war substitutes and atones for the suffering of slavery: black and white, South and North, would cease to regard each other as victims and perpetrators—all would become *survivors* of the war to end slavery.

Here Lincoln assumes that the slaves identify with the victorious rescu-ers who suffered grievously to make them free. This nontriumphal identifi-cation with victory by the North does not, however, give redemptive meaning to their suffering as slaves. Their suffering is *wasted*, its moral sig-nificance obliterated, by the fact that the whole nation sacrificed for them and thus shared an experience of victimhood that before the war belonged only to the slave. For Lincoln, America's national recovery from its collec-tive trauma would now be based on a collective pledge to remember the past in order to avoid repeating it, a limbic state that honors reticence about the necessary stages of our moral development as a nation.[27]

There are at least two possible variants of Lincoln's American survivor story. The first allows former perpetrators to identify themselves as victims in order to become survivors. This is the variant that promises "to bind up the *nation's* wounds" (emphasis added) by placing the North and South on an equal moral footing as survivors of slavery and the war to end it. A sec-ond variant requires former perpetrators to both identify with their victims and see themselves from their victims' point of view. Here the war is itself a recompense for "every drop of blood drawn with the lash."[28] These two vari-ants introduce a profound ambiguity in their depiction of precisely who the historical victims are (slaves or Southerners?) and of what would trigger a traumatic memory of the past (racism or the accusation of racism?).

Although both variants depend upon a mutuality of identification, they differ significantly in how the new collective identity is defined. In the first variant the healing comes through a dedication (for Lincoln a *rededication*) to a set of higher principles of human equality originally embodied in the Declaration of Independence; in the second variant the "scourge of war" atones for the national sin of slavery. Superficially the latter claim resembles the abolitionist (and Radical Republican) idea that the victory of the Union Army represents an apocalyptic judgment on the sin of the morally guilty South.[29] In Lincoln's rendition, however, the suffering of the Union Army meant that the Southern sin of slavery had been assumed by the morally innocent North, implying that through this vicarious sacrifice the nation as a whole might be cleansed and reborn.[30]

Lincoln's Second Inaugural Address merged the biblical language of judgment and retribution with that of sacrifice, forgiveness, and renewal. After quoting the passage, "Woe unto the world because of offenses!" (Matt. 18:7), Lincoln insists that God "gives to *both* North and South this terrible war as the woe due to those by whom the offense came" (emphasis added). His well-known conclusion is not, however, that the postwar world will be a living hell—the final judgment of a righteous God on a sinful nation.[31] Lincoln suggests, rather, that the living are the undeserving beneficiaries of the sacrifice of those who (as he said at Gettysburg), "gave their lives that . . . [the] nation might live." A Lincolnian attitude of "malice toward none" and "charity for all" is appropriate to a once guilty people that has been forgiven through a redeeming act of grace.[32] Viewed as a peace strategy, Lincoln's national "survivor story" provided a moral framework under which many in the defeated South could accept a Northern victory as something other than a humiliating punishment for slavery and secession.[33]

The prospect of former enemies living in the same place under one government is a problem for peacemakers in any civil war. To the extent that this prospect is unthinkable, a final peace is also unthinkable.[34] The argument that surrender will lead to severe retaliation, or even genocide, has always been used by wartime leaders to make the losing side fight on, especially when it knows that its aims and conduct in the war are seen as morally reprehensible by its enemy.[35] This was certainly the view that many Southern leaders took of the consequences of defeat. Exhorting his troops in November 1863, Lee said, "A cruel enemy seeks to reduce our fathers and our mothers, our wives and our children, to abject *slavery*, to strip them from their homes. Upon you these helpless ones rely" (emphasis added).[36] His rhetoric suggests that, as the war drags on, the Confederate Army is also fighting against slavery—the enslavement of the South as the cruel punishment that a formerly slave-holding society might be thought by its enemies to deserve. From Lee's perspective, the only honorable peace was a negotiated settlement that would have preserved the capacity of both sides to make war and, thus ratified, at least implicitly, the existence of two nations.

Lincoln's story of national survival presents the alternative vision of how a civil war can end.[37] It demonstrates how the processes of aggression and identification (both conscious and unconscious) are no less part of the logic of victim and perpetrator than of the logic of forgiveness and reconciliation. But nations in recovery are often ambivalent in their choice of heroes. Lincoln is honored in American history because his war aim was to refound the Republic on unconditional surrender rather than on a moral compromise. Also honored is Lee, who rejected the North's belief that it was warring against evil as, *itself*, an evil to be resisted at all cost. By respecting Lee's war aim alongside Lincoln's, the post–Civil War U.S. was able to treat Lincoln's victory as total while treating Lee's surrender as strategic. But we have also seen that the North's willingness to be magnanimous in victory brought eventual reconciliation to the defeated South at the expense of justice for the victims of slavery.

Forgiving and Forgetting

The potential conflict between reconciliation and truth in the construction of a posttraumatic political identity is the source of a further ambiguity in Lincoln's national survivor story. His story is, at the very least, a form of amnesty[38]—an effort to take the nation past the divisive traumas of slavery and civil war. In the aftermath of civil war or revolution, amnesty is always an appealing alternative to purges, political prosecutions, and lustration laws.[39] Such postwar amnesties assume that there is both a desire to forget and a need to remember.

Although the Lincoln we remember is generally credited with the sort of moral vision we now ascribe to Mandela and Tutu, Lincoln the president faced a very different task in linking amnesty to a military and political strategy for winning an ongoing civil war. His wartime amnesty policy was partly based on the urgency of restoring loyalist governments in federally occupied Louisiana and Arkansas and of finding enough collaborators to avoid large-scale disorder in the rest of the occupied South.[40] There was, nevertheless, a principled basis for Lincoln's view of amnesty. Throughout the war he had disagreed with those in his own party who believed that at the moment of secession the Southern state governments ceased to exist (and that Congress could henceforth administer defeated Confederate states as federal territories). His position was, rather, that secession had been illegal because the union was "indestructible." It followed that the states in rebellion continued to be members of the Union but that individuals, especially political leaders, were engaged in illegal acts of rebellion.[41] The task of reconstruction therefore required granting a sufficient number of individual amnesties so that the states (which had always consisted of their loyal citizens) could resume self-government.[42]

Based on this constitutional theory, Lincoln issued his Proclamation of Amnesty and Reconstruction of December 1863. It granted a full pardon to ordinary citizens and soldiers participating in the rebellion on condition that they sign an oath of loyalty to the United States, and that they agree to abide by all wartime acts of Congress and presidential proclamations on the subject of slavery. Ineligible for this automatic pardon-by-oath were officials of the "so-called Confederate Government," high-ranking Confederate military and naval officers, persons who resigned their seats in Congress or their military and naval commissions to join the rebellion in violation of their oaths of office, and all persons who mistreated prisoners of war. These individuals could not have their rights restored without further action by the president or Congress.[43] Lincoln thus left open the possibility of either trials or amnesty for top Confederates and war criminals at all levels.

Trials were a serious possibility toward the end of the war. In the North stories had been widely circulated of atrocities in Southern prison camps, and leaders of the Confederacy, including Jefferson Davis, were alleged to be personally implicated.[44] Andersonville became the leading symbol of these atrocities. Its commanding officer died, however, in February 1865, and Captain Henry Wirz, the second in command, was the only person tried for war crimes in the aftermath of the Civil War.[45]

The question of what to do with Jefferson Davis raised other problems for Lincoln's theory of postwar responsibility. After Davis was captured in flight shortly after Lincoln's assassination, a serious effort was made to try the president of the defeated Confederacy for treason in the federal court in Virginia—which (not coincidentally) was presided over by the chief justice of the United States, Salmon P. Chase.[46] Before the trial took place, however, the Fourteenth Amendment was ratified, and Chase came to believe that Section Three (barring former federal officials who served the Confederacy from again holding federal office) constituted a legal punishment that precluded any further prosecution of those to whom it applied. The Supreme Court, in the end, never upheld Chase's view on this matter. His fellow judge on the circuit court disagreed. But, fortified by the chief justice's position, President Andrew Johnson effectively disposed of the treason charge against Davis by issuing a universal amnesty proclamation for all unpardoned Confederates on Christmas Day, 1868.[47]

In practical effect, if not intent, the Fourteenth Amendment had become a kind of amnesty that allowed those Confederate officials who had left U.S. government service to be punished for violating their oath of office but for nothing else.[48] But Chase's claim that Section Three of the Fourteenth Amendment is a self-executing punishment had only backward-looking implications for the nation as a whole; for this reason the record of prosecutions and amnesties from 1865 through 1868 conveys no clear moral message about the meaning of the Civil War,[49] as large elements of the Confederate power structure regained dominance in the defeated South.[50]

Given the limbo occupied by the Fourteenth Amendment between amnesty and Reconstruction, we must thus consider the role of Lincoln's notion of common survivorship as rebirth (what President Obama calls "One People") in linking the Thirteenth Amendment abolishing slavery (it is gone) to the Fourteenth (through which the U.S. addresses the continuing presence of its slaveholding past) and, finally, the Fifteenth (through which the descendants of slaves obtain voting rights, but without the constitutional protection of their own statehood).[51]

Reconstruction, Amnesty, or Both?

Our national debate over the value and limits of Lincolnian recovery largely takes the form of a struggle that still goes on today over the meaning of the Fourteenth Amendment. There are three broad approaches to interpreting the Fourteenth Amendment, each based on a different version of Lincoln's legacy.

The first view represents the Fourteenth Amendment as the victory of the North, and its values, over the South. This is the Radical Republican interpretation of Lincoln's legacy and is represented in the current literature by scholars such as Bruce Ackerman and Akhil Amar, who see the abolition of slavery by the Thirteenth Amendment as the unfinished business taken up by the Fourteenth.[52] In this approach the Fourteenth should be interpreted counterfactually—*as though* slavery had been defeated by the moral equivalent of a successful slave revolt that inserted the project of abolition into the Constitution itself.[53] Thus conceived, the revolutionary struggle against slavery will not be over as long as its aftereffects persist in institutions of both private and public power. Accordingly, the three Civil War amendments must be read together as a continuation by other means of the project of Reconstruction that was interrupted by the Compromise of 1876.

The second view is that Lincoln's legacy was to free the slaves without upsetting Chief Justice John Marshall's framework of national union based on divided sovereignty. This view of Lincoln appears in Woodrow Wilson's *History of the American People*[54] and is reflected in such mainstream interpretations of the Fourteenth Amendment as that of John Hart Ely, which stress the primacy of electoral democracy and the need to correct its distortions in areas where there is no floating majority, but rather a series of permanent minorities that the courts call "discrete and insular."[55] Here, what it means for the struggle against slavery to be over (because of the Thirteenth Amendment) is that "We the People" simply reinterpreted the Fourteenth as though slavery had never existed. According to this approach, constitutional justice proceeds as though the issues arising out of slavery are similar to those that affect other inside-outsiders in a federal system of sovereign states—a problem of popular majoritarianism as such that has nothing to do with our particular history of oppressing a particular group.

Finally, there is the view presented here of the Fourteenth Amendment as an instrument of national recovery from a traumatic history. National recovery as a redemptive project would, for Lincoln, transcend both victims' justice for former slaves and victors' justice against the perpetrators of slavery. The point of survivors' justice, as Lincoln conceived it, is to go forward now on a common moral footing—not because the past has been either forgiven or forgotten but because continuing to struggle against an evil that is gone is no longer appropriate. Inasmuch as my attribution of this idea to Lincoln may be novel (I have not directly encountered it in the literature), it is worth developing in contrast to the better-known Radical Republican view of constitutional rupture and the Marshall-Wilson claim of continuity.

The Struggle Continues

According to the Radical Republican interpretation of the Fourteenth Amendment, the surrender of the Confederate armies was only the beginning of the Northern conquest of the South. That conquest would be completed by a political, social, and economic transformation of slave society.[56] This argument implies that the U.S. is not an appropriate case study of the aftermath of evil because we freed the slaves without abolishing slavery. The basis of such a claim is that, although the preexisting legal slots of slave and slave owner were evacuated, they are still *conceptually* integral to our Constitution. Why? Because Lincoln, having conquered parts of the South, became (in his official capacity) the last slaveholder and could then become the Great Emancipator by exercising the preexisting power of a master to free his slaves. From this perspective the Emancipation Proclamation exercised a form of manumission that was only possible within the framework of slavery. What the conventional understanding of "abolition" *abolished* was entirely consistent with the distinction within the law of slavery itself between free Negroes and slave Negroes: it simply emptied the latter category, leaving Negroes, as such, without constitutional standing to claim rights deriving from the abolition of slavery.[57]

The question raised by the Radical view is how to interpret the Thirteenth Amendment. Was it simply a national version of the Emancipation Proclamation? Or should it have been read as a sweeping revision of our entire legal framework to eliminate all traces of legitimation for the slave idea? If slavery were merely, the radicals say, a lack of self-ownership in the narrow sense defined by the law of slavery itself, then the Thirteenth Amendment, in effect, nationalized this form of private property in order to reprivatize it as self-ownership. (For one brief moment the U.S. government must have owned slaves so that it could legitimately "free" them within the logic of slavery itself.) That slaves were finally *given* freedom meant that they no longer had to *buy* it as they might have done previously.[58]

But *manumission* did not complete the abolition of slavery by defining the propertyless wage worker as self-owned. It implied, rather, that slavery had always been based on contract because manumission was, even though the possibility of manumission was anomalous in a system of hereditary enslavement based on the law of chattel.[59] The contractual afterlife of slavery implied that those who suffered its indignities *might* have done so willingly and that the coercive aspects of it need only be eliminated to make clear that the inferior social status of former slaves would be ratified by freedom of choice and freedom of association. This happened in the U.S. following the end of Reconstruction in 1876.

Most radical scholars who argue today for a "Reconstruction-based" reading of the Fourteenth Amendment via the Thirteenth believe that this unfinished revolution should recommence. They view the imperative of continuing Reconstruction as a constitutional adoption of the "jeremiad" tradition of Yankee abolitionism—a prophetic spirit of reform based on the nation's own higher values.[60] For holders of this view there is no peace after a just war until its righteous aims have been fulfilled by eliminating the lingering aftereffects of slavery. Here the link between continuing *dis*advantage and past slavery qualifies a victimary group for remedial justice, but also *caps* the remedy to whatever it takes to remove that disadvantage. There is thus no room to argue that, but for their history of slavery, the racially identified victim group would have *naturally* come out ahead and that its hypothetical position of advantage should be actualized.[61]

Traces of Sovereignty

The anti-Reconstructionist interpretation of U.S. constitutional development, epitomized by Woodrow Wilson, allows slavery to be treated, for constitutional purposes, as though it never happened. In this approach the framework of victim-perpetrator-beneficiary (Slave–South–North) is superseded by a framework that stresses the rule of a "people" in a geographical territory through the displacement or subordination (or both) of prior inhabitants. At its core this framework takes the independent settler-colony as the paradigm of modern statehood, modifications of which then turn upon the *question* of settler sovereignty with respect to the native. The native/settler question, and its implications, is considered more globally in chapter 4. With respect to the U.S. (and the comparison with apartheid-era South Africa), we must focus narrowly here on how the postcolonial model foregrounds the relationship between citizenship and territorial rule.

The broad Wilsonian model I have in mind is based less on Jeffersonian democracy than Marshallian federalism. Marshall's question was no longer what rights (perhaps "natural") the settlers of a colony have to overthrow rule by the mother country but, rather, what rights the federally protected citizens of sovereign have when they move on to settle in other such states or in territory still inhabited by "natives." Here the only federally enforceable individual rights derive from the positive law of the several sovereign states and the need for federal protection of citizens of one state who were living elsewhere. "Protection against what?" one might ask. Against being victimized by the local inhabitants, whether through laws enacted by a majority of self-governing state citizens or through violence inflicted by the native denizens of a territory in which the U.S. claimed preemptive power to protect the citizens of its several states.

An individual's right to federal protection is not here conceived abstractly as a *human* right.[62] In the Marshall-Wilson model it is, rather, traceable to a *state's* equal claim to sovereignty in the interstate system coupled with the rights of its citizens to move about and do business in other states. Before the Civil War such federally protected constitutional rights were not applicable to the laws of one's own state, where an electoral minority was still subject to majority rule in the strong Madisonian sense. But elsewhere in the union *all* out-of-state citizens were a constitutionally protected minority in the sense that they must be given the same legal privileges and immunities that the local majority creates for itself. The paradigmatic holder of constitutional rights was thus a citizen of *one* state residing in *another*, and the paradigmatic constitutional right was an *exception* to the power of in-state majorities to discriminate against their own local minorities.[63] This idea was Chief Justice John Marshall's great contribution to world political thought.[64] It meant that individual rights were a consequence of actual (and, arguably, potential) statehood under the Constitution and that stateless individuals lacked rights to federal protection in every state or territory in which they traveled or resided and could thus be subject to mob rule.

Three groups fell into the category of stateless sojourner, each in different ways and to differing degrees. The first were legally resident aliens. They may have had limited rights as "persons" to live in the United States "under the protection" of its laws, but they were not entitled to nondiscrimination with respect to the privileges and immunities of state citizens. They could thus be forbidden to own property, denied licenses to practice their professions, and so forth.[65] Under the Marshallian scheme, aliens would become entitled to full federal protection only if they were first naturalized by a state.[66] Foreign nationals could still be protected, however, by private international law, which included principles of interjurisdictional comity as modified by treaties between the United States and other sovereign nations.[67]

A second category of stateless residents included the descendants of the indigenous population of every state at the time of its white settlement. The treatment of such persons as "dependent sovereign nations" was originally thought necessary to legitimate U.S. acquisition as federally administered "territories" of their former habitations and eventually became grounds for denying them birthright citizenship in the United States after the Civil War. Yet the theory of tribal sovereignty was never considered strong enough to support a claim to foreign citizenship, much less to separate statehood, within the federal framework.[68]

Finally, the category of statelessness briefly, but significantly, included the descendants of Africans who entered the country as slaves. The great antebellum legal scholar John Codman Hurd provided the most coherent (and hence most troubling) account of how hereditary slavery could continue to exist in places where there is no recognized legal power of one person, originally, to enslave another. His answer rested on the doctrine of comity as a core principle of transnational private law—and on his juris-prudential view that the principles of comity adopted in each forum are a matter of local positive law and thus can vary from state to state. In resting the presence of slaves *here* on the presumed legitimacy of the power to enslave *elsewhere*, Hurd sought to explain not merely how slavery could legally exist in places where it was regarded as a violation of natural law, but also how it could exist in *some* such places and not in others.[69]

The kernel of truth in the *Dred Scott* opinion, according to Hurd, was that Marshallian federalism could only recognize rights in the interstate diaspora that were traceable to the federally recognized sovereignty of a "people." In the fugitive slave cases the Court had already determined that slaveholders would be federally protected out of state in the exercise of their state-created rights. Chief Justice Taney's 1858 *Dred Scott* decision raised the question of whether parallel claims could be made on behalf of an interstate diaspora of Negroes who asserted their freedom through the effect of state liberty laws or equivalent federal legislation governing the territories. Because he could not argue that slave and free states were unequal in their power to confer individual rights, Taney was constrained to argue that blacks and whites were unequal in their standing to assert the sovereignty of a people for purposes of federal protection. His conceptual leap in *Dred Scott* was to assume that persons actually born in the United States without the protection of its laws must be constitutionally ineligible for naturalization. This reasoning was historically flawed and morally embarrassing, as Hurd well knew.[70] He nevertheless accepted Taney's inference from the logic of Marshallian federalism that, if freed slaves had federal protection in any state, the institution of slavery would be unsustainable. Why? Because any person of black African descent who was about to be recaptured would have a right to federal judicial review of the question of whether he had, in fact, gained freedom while traveling in another state. Inasmuch as the Fugitive Slave Clause of the Constitution (Art. IV, 3.2) denied such a right, neither Congress nor the states had power to confer citizenship on persons who might thereby claim federal protection from the summary process that the clause would otherwise require.

This genealogy of U.S. antidiscrimination law suggests that the Fourteenth Amendment is, in effect, a negative template of the jurisprudence of *Dred Scott* insofar as it "overturn[ed] the *Dred Scott* decision by making all persons born within the United States and subject to its jurisdiction citizens of the United States."[71] By placing the relation of federal and state citizenship squarely under the U.S. Constitution, it preserved the underlying premise of *Dred Scott* that the congressional power to confer U.S. citizenship was limited to foreign nationals and indigenous tribes.[72] Under the

Fourteenth Amendment, however, a *state* was required to extend citizenship on an equal basis to all persons born or naturalized in the United States who resided within its borders. Having established residency as the only constitutionally legitimate criterion of state citizenship, the Fourteenth Amendment went on to forbid the states from discriminating against their internal minorities based on criteria, largely unspecified, that were clearly no longer limited to citizenship in another state. Viewed as an extension of Taney's logic in *Dred Scott*, the Fourteenth Amendment allowed for the creation of virtualized statehood (admitting a *virtual Liberia* to the Union) so that African Americans, dispersed throughout the country, could have the same kind of right to nonvictimization throughout the U.S. that they could have gotten originally only by having their own state.

Although Americans can now claim similar rights to nonvictimization under the Fourteenth Amendment through identities based on race, religion, gender, age, and disability, these rights are all conceived by analogy with the right of out-of-state citizens under local majority rule. We thus begin by imagining ingathered "nations" of blacks, women, the elderly, the disabled, and so forth—able to make laws suitable to themselves and under which their present legally created disadvantages would be fully offset by legal advantages. This is the mythical moment of "separate but equal." Protection under the Fourteenth Amendment kicks in when federal courts recognize the diasporic nature of all such groups in order to enforce their rights not to be *disadvantaged* by laws as they are. Under this paradigm of nondiscrimination, individual rights appear as traces of the equality of sovereign and distinct peoples, some of whom, through brutality or historical accident, have imposed their concepts of normality on others.[73]

Once we go down the path of virtualized statehood there is no limit to the number of overlapping identities that can become eligible for a right to rescue. Viewed from a pre–Civil War perspective, the significance of the Fourteenth Amendment was that every native-born American was now in some respects to be treated as "out of state"—even while at home. Thus a right to nondiscrimination is no longer linked to a collective right to self-determination in another state but, rather, is based on U.S. citizenship as defined by the Fourteenth Amendment.[74]

A Nation in Recovery

I have thus far described two interpretations of the Fourteenth Amendment and Reconstruction, both of which I will distinguish from what I take to be the authentic Lincolnian approach. The first interpretation stresses the fact that slavery was a deeply embedded feature that was defeated only as a result of a struggle that included the efforts of the slaves themselves.[75] The second interpretation stresses the fact that slavery is dead and that the struggle against it is now over. Each of the approaches I have discussed takes account of only one of these two facts—and each is limited for that very reason.

The vision of Lincoln developed in this chapter stands apart from both views. His genius was to accommodate both the element of struggle and the element of the pastness of that struggle in his model of transitional liberalism as a national story of survival and rebirth. In taking this view, Lincoln imagined a future America as a morally appropriate afterlife to the kind of evil that slavery was. He understood that our history of slavery had made Americans different from what they might have been according to the social contract model embraced by our first founders. It had made us not a nation of free and equal people meeting up for the first time in a state of nature but, rather, a nation of the wounded, a nation in recovery.

My capsule summary of Fourteenth Amendment jurisprudence suggests, however, that the approach to national recovery that I have called Lincolnian was not fully articulated until 1954, when the great case of *Brown v. Board of Education*, outlawing segregation in the public schools, began America's "*Second* Reconstruction," which was considerably more Lincolnian than the first Reconstruction. Constitutional scholars were at first unable to see this. Herbert Wechsler, a civil rights liberal, famously criticized the Court's reasoning in *Brown* and called for a constitutional argument that was "neutral" between the desire of blacks to associate with whites and the desire of whites not to associate with blacks.[76] The *Plessy* Court had held that discrimination on the basis of race was not the same as discrimination against blacks—how could it be, if segregated railroad cars reached their destination at the same time? Thus Wechsler was troubled by the fact that, although segregation laws were, on their face, no more restrictive on blacks than on whites, the Court's ruling seemed to restrict the associative preferences of whites for the benefit of blacks and was therefore non-neutral.[77] But strict neutrality of the kind demanded by Wechsler would not be necessary if the Equal Protection Clause is interpreted as Lincolnian recovery from slavery. The primary purpose of the Fourteenth Amendment would, rather, be to memorialize and discharge the continuing burden that a history of slavery places on our public institutions. This is what the Warren Court said when it overruled *Plessy* on the grounds that, as a matter of law, racial segregation is inherently stigmatizing to blacks.

Because of *Brown*, we interpret the Equal Protection Clause to forbid discrimination *against blacks* even before it forbids discrimination *based on race*. This interpretation is, in essence, that the United States survived its legacy of slavery by making a constitutional commitment not to repeat the patterns and practices deriving from it—that we, as a nation, have broken free of our slavery to slavery itself. Once the Fourteenth Amendment is read—via the Gettysburg Address—as part of our national survival story, each new *repetition* of a pattern or practice of racism becomes legally actionable as a new *violation* of civil rights. Because it is *not* new, each violation justifies the imposition of remedies more drastic and far-reaching than would be necessary in a country that did not bear our particular historic burdens.

The paradigmatic constitutional argument of the Second Reconstruction, based on *Brown*, is that national recovery from a history of racial oppression requires both a continuing awareness of the dangers of relapse and a constant vigilance against the repetition of past patterns and practices. This argument implies that we can never recover from our past unless we believe ourselves to be in permanent recovery—that we are never in greater danger of reviving racism than when we believe ourselves to have overcome it. The debate over the continuing need for race-based policies to *avoid* discrimination is, in this sense, similar to arguments about whether a recovering alcoholic must always "beware the first drink." In the jurisprudence of the Warren era, the notion of a permanent recovery constrains and motivates the pursuit of racial justice under our Constitution in much the same way that the problem of incurable addiction constrains and motivates the alcoholic's pursuit of sobriety and that the problem of inexpiable sin constrains and motivates the Christian's pursuit of salvation.

In a society recovering from slavery, echoes of the past are not merely offensive; there may be a specifically cognizable *wrong* in the reenactment—however symbolic—of the role of a historic oppressor in a manner that forces the victim's role on persons with historical reasons to fear it. A history of slavery also augments the specific *harm* of racially discriminatory conduct—both because of the conscious fears it may evoke and because a replication of patterns and symbols of racial subordination (which are not the same as slavery itself) can induce a repetition of the internalized trauma of slavery in the unconscious—where remembering and reliving are indistinguishable. The foregoing arguments suggest that a heightened awareness of racial oppression—itself a product of liberation—can actually increase the harm of subsequent discrimination while also being a necessary stage in identifying the wrong.[78]

What are the advantages of entering a state of permanent transition, such as Lincoln sought for the U.S.? The usual claim for the Lincolnian model is that the alternative could have been worse: a return to civil war or the beginning of a race war (on the Haitian model) around the question of black Jacobinism, which freed slaves would certainly have lost.[79] If this may have happened, the argument goes, it is better to live in a time when everyone *believes* that things have changed radically—that they are not a continuation of past evil—even though everything *appears* to be nearly the same as it was when evil ruled. The techniques for producing and performing this belief draw heavily on St. Paul's account of messianic time in which everything seems the same but *is not*. The strongest case in favor of transitional justice must therefore rest on the moral quality of the time it creates.

In recent years the moral logic of this "Lincolnian" model of national recovery from slavery has been extended to support other claims to rights based on past stigmatization, exploitation, or abuse. The crucial step here is to reinterpret what might otherwise be deemed a mere injury (resulting perhaps from accidental exclusion) as, rather, a result of a repressed identi-fication between the victims and the rest of us—now seen as unwitting per-petrators of abuse against our "other" selves. Once victim and perpetrator learn to think of each other as common survivors of a traumatic history, this enlarged identity can be asserted to give even relatively minor injuries the added significance of a *return* to a historical pattern of abuse that the nation as a whole has committed itself to overcome.[80]

We should not, however, assume that a Lincolnian approach to justice as recovery from trauma is preferable to approaches that stress material resti-tution or distributive justice.[81] National recovery is, essentially, a survivor story, and in Lincoln's own story of America it was not essential for indige-nous peoples to survive. He assumed that we, as their successors, were to *survive them*. Since Lincoln, we have become a single nation based on the equality of newcomers and natives and *also* on the denial of the general proposition that indigeneity confers a special right to self-determination.[82] The aftermath of Confederate defeat was also an era of heightened extermi-nation of native "savages" as the railroads moved west and immigration from Europe increased.[83] Under the Fourteenth Amendment (ratified in 1868), citizenship would henceforth be based on naturalization and birth— all children of immigrants would thus be born "Americans." But settler citi-zenship based on natality was both an erasure of the rights of "natives," ratifying the ways in which the word "native" had already come to mean something different from "born here" in the sense we now use to distin-guish naturalized immigrants from citizens by birth. Notwithstanding the Fourteenth Amendment, however, natives were not considered American citizens by birth. Even today the rights of "dependent sovereign peoples"— as distinct from ordinary minority "groups"—remain an anomaly under the logic of the Fourteenth Amendment.[84] Thus there are troubling affinities between the Lincolnian vision of Reconstruction and the claims made by our national survivor story to a manifest destiny that may not have appeared inevitable to the absent victims of a settler colonial state after its frontier "closed."[85]

Remembering to Forget

The distinctively Lincolnian approach to Reconstruction that I have developed in this chapter now stands alongside the two previous approaches without fully superseding them. Although each of the three approaches to Fourteenth Amendment jurisprudence is distinct and identifiable, none is dominant, and each begets, in a dialectical fashion, the conditions that make the other two plausible. The contrast between the three is reflected in the ongoing U.S. debate about affirmative action.

Viewed as reparations, affirmative action programs almost always do too little too late. Reparations in their essence aim at closure; they can be discharged within a finite period of time, perhaps a generation or two beyond the lifetime of the original victims.[86] Affirmative action is potentially interminable precisely because it is *not* a form of reparation but, rather, a defense mechanism that guards against the return of racism.[87] Defense mechanisms typically reproduce the wishes that they disavow; affirmative action does this by constructing an antiracist self as always a potential victim of a racism that is unconsciously its own. Insofar as the practices of affirmative action that we use to disprove our racism are also repetitive defenses against it, they fall within a fundamentally different moral register than reparative obligations. As a form of cultural self-analysis their duration is indefinite.[88]

Nonfinality has become the essential characteristic of most affirmative action programs in the minds of defenders and critics alike. The standard criticism is not that they do too little but that there is no limit to how long they must go on—nothing seems to count as "enough." Defenders of these programs also essentialize their nonfinality, but view it as a positive feature because it grounds our future on the principle of "Never again." The debate over the continuing need for race-based policies to avoid discrimination is in this sense again similar to arguments about whether a recovering alcoholic must always suspect himself of being a latent drunk. Does "being in recovery" *mean* that nothing counts as having recovered?

Both sides of the affirmative action debate exemplify the Lincolnian project of "recovery"—both in its virtues and defects. The essence of that is to replace racism with a fear of racism, revolutionary politics with a fear of revolutionary politics, and so on. A deep ambivalence is thus built into it. On the one hand, we are committed to hypervigilance ("strict scrutiny") with respect to any pattern or practice that seems to reenact the past. (This is how we suppress the fantasy of eliminating objects of our guilt.) On the other hand, there is resistance to the notion that structural reform should come at the expense of only some segments of society, when all are equally guilty and hence equally absolved. (This is how we suppress the fantasy of being punished by the objects of our guilt.)

We can illustrate this psychology, on one side, by quoting Justice Scalia's concurring opinion in a case that limits affirmative action to remedies against perpetrators of racism—not mere beneficiaries.

> Under our Constitution there can be no such thing as either a creditor or a debtor race. . . . To pursue the concept of racial entitlement—even for the most admirable and benign of purposes—is to reinforce and preserve for future mischief the way of thinking that produced race slavery, race privilege, and race hatred. In the eyes of the government, we are just one race here. It is American.[89]

What unites Justice Scalia's "Americans" is a demonization of the racists of the past and a persecutory fear that those racists will return to haunt us. As idealized Americans we are committed to fight those racists in whatever guise they may present themselves. We are thus able to deny that we are them or that we may once again become them. Instead, our own racial aggressions are projected outward and reexperienced as threats.[90]

A similar moral psychology appears in Justice O'Connor's later opinion for the Court in *Grutter v. Bollinger* that cautiously upholds for the time being race-conscious admissions criteria that fall short of being racial *quotas*.[91] O'Connor shares with Scalia the wish to delegitimate any prima facie argument for redistribution based on race. "Narrow tailoring," she says, "requires that a race-conscious admissions program not unduly harm members of any racial group" (p. 341). This means that racial balance is not to be pursued for its own sake but rather with "reference to the educational benefits that diversity is designed to produce" (p. 330). O'Connor defines these benefits as essentially a matter of the ongoing legitimation of national elites:

> In order to cultivate a set of leaders with legitimacy in the eyes of the citizenry, it is necessary that the path to leadership be visibly open to talented

and qualified individuals of every race and ethnicity . . . so that all members of our heterogeneous society may participate in the educational institutions that provide the training and education necessary to succeed in America. (p. 332)

O'Connor notably refuses to embrace the idea that the legitimating function of race-conscious policies is, *in principle*, permanent. "Race conscious admissions policies," she says, "must be limited in time." In practice, however, this means that there must be "periodic reviews to determine whether racial preferences are still necessary to achieve student body diversity" (342). So, although racial preferences must, in principle, be subject to sunset provisions in order to avoid the taint of redistributive policy, the need for reviewing whether they are needed will remain a permanent feature of political legitimation in the U.S. O'Connor's view of affirmative action is thus similar to Freud's view of psychoanalysis: the therapy is, in principle, terminable (otherwise, why undertake it?), but in practice we must never act as though we are fully cured.[92]

In a Lincolnian world of heightened scrutiny about race, both the beneficiaries of the past evil and those with claims against them can now be seen as equally guilty of returning to the past and hence of discrimination. Here the politics of equality becomes to a significant extent a matter of *not forgetting to remember* and then *remembering to forget*. This has been evident in forms of race-conscious policy that the Court proposed in *Bakke* and upheld in *Grutter*: we cannot fail to remember race in testing the outcome of admissions decisions by the standard of diversity; but we must also remember to forget race in judging individual applicants.

Preserved in this way of thinking is Lincoln's own ambivalence about allowing the slaves to *have won* the Civil War. His strategy, as we have seen, was to represent the slaves as the beneficiaries of suffering and sacrifice by *both* the North and South, a penance that could already have been large enough to atone for the sins committed under slavery itself. Our jurisprudence of affirmative action preserves this ambivalence by viewing the descendants of slaves as the beneficiaries of white sacrifice, beginning with the Civil War, and as the victims of legalized discrimination (and also of constitutionally sanctioned slavery that preceded it). Like Lincoln's "Second Inaugural," mainstream affirmative action jurisprudence is poised between two white fantasies: the fantasy of black gratitude for having been rescued and of black hatred for having been persecuted. Both these fantasies are examples of projective identification; in neither are the interests of present-day blacks themselves politically negotiable.

The figure of Lincoln authorizes all Americans to entertain fantasies of guilt for the crimes of racism that they do not actually commit as well as fantasies of rage over the crimes of racism that were not actually committed against them. The Lincolnian model views justice, inevitably, as an afterlife of evil in which political relations will be based on a mutual recognition of the capacity for sin, which, as a matter of generational accident, may have been more fully realized on one side than on the other. The result is a political culture of national recovery based on hypervigilance against the surfacing of the guilty wish to sin and hypersensitivity about any claim for remedial justice that implies the appropriateness of selective punishment for the guilt we all share. The damage done to victims is honored, but only to the extent (and because) it is not an effective basis for political demands. After evil, a humbled nation in recovery must split the concept of social justice into a backward-looking therapy for the injustice of the past and a forward-looking approach to the distribution of the remainders of that injustice. This Janus-like face of political justice is more typical than exceptional in posttraumatic societies as we enter the twenty-first century.

Nondiscrimination and Redistribution

Posttraumatic constitutions do not merely enshrine abstract principles of justice; they also memorialize particular histories of injustice. We cannot interpret such constitutions without also reinterpreting these histories in a way that both preserves and transcends the antagonistic identities that made the nation. It was thus appropriate that the *Brown* Court, after renouncing racial segregation as a continuation of the sin of slavery, decreed that the remedy should come "with all deliberate speed."[93] This is not, of course, as simple as it might seem. The tools of statistics tell us to what extent the inequalities between groups explain the inequalities within them;[94] they do not tell us which inequalities to measure or how to group individuals for the purpose of meaningful comparison.[95] So, before applying these techniques of rectification, we would still have to decide what goods should be equally distributed over which groups.

In both non-Lincolnian views, equality functions as the baseline norm for social restitution. To the extent that inequalities in social outcome can be measured, they can also be offset and, in principle, eliminated. The extent to which their median benefit is still higher than that of the population as a whole (including both victim and nonvictim) is what makes them continuing beneficiaries of wrongs that they now disavow. It is this differential that must be purged before the evil can finally be past.

The choice of methodology here depends upon assumptions that are both historically and socially relative. It is worth listing the most important of these:

- The primary goods to be equalized are limited to those that the nonvictim group provides for itself. It is that group's greater access to these particular goods that makes them, still, beneficiaries of the evil to which they are now retrospectively opposed and which gives them something more to do before the past is laid to rest.
- What makes statistical measures relevant after evil is the ethical assumption that one kind of difference *should* make no difference in the distribution of another,[96] combined with the historical argument that it *has* made a difference. The idea that persons who are otherwise diverse should be treated *as* equals is a necessary part of the argument that past refusal to do so has produced a difference in advantage that *remains illegitimate.*[97]
- Statistical analyses are thus the abstract measure of the extent to which one set of group differences explains another, but the choice of groups to compare is based on a narrative of past evil overcome. The victimary identity against which inequalities are measured is *both* ethical and historical.
- In states of permanent transition, the crux of political debate concerns *when*, *why*, and *which* beneficiaries should pay. In this debate the antecedent desires of the historical victims themselves play only a minor role. That role is largely counterfactual—a reminder of the irretrievability of their loss. That said, the cumulative gains of beneficiaries can *always* be relinquished *later* (as long as there are still beneficiaries), which means that it is never necessary for beneficiaries to disgorge them *now*.
- Redistributing affect (feelings) within the minds of beneficiaries as a form of purgation can thus defer and provisionally substitute for a redistribution of wealth.

The foregoing assumptions are historically contingent, and all are open to question. Such questions, however, are precisely those on which we claim to reach consensus at moments in history when we decide to put evil in the past. Assuming that beneficiaries have, in fact, reached consensus, they can use the methods of statistical sociology to determine whether they have set things right.[98] Their cumulative differential gain (which is what makes them beneficiaries) would constitute the fund from which the costs of redistribution can legitimately be paid. Any remaining arguments would then be over patience versus urgency: Why hurry? Why wait? Leaving the present pattern of distribution in place is no less a deliberate policy choice than changing it would be. That beneficiaries perceive a further difficulty is an indication that a consensus has not been reached on the evils of the past and that many still accept a presumption of legitimacy for the status quo.[99] What, then, is the political form in which victimary identities can mobilize in order to confront beneficiaries who must then *react*?

Let My People Stay

Despite the *dis*analogy between the U.S. Civil Rights movement (which sought integration) and the Exodus (which implies separatism), most chroniclers of black liberation have invoked what the political theorist Michael Walzer calls "Exodus politics"[100] to describe the uneasy cohabitation of freed slaves with the ongoing beneficiaries of their former oppression. In Exodus politics, liberation consists of two elements: manumission ("Let my people go") and nation building.

In Western political culture, the Exodus story is the prototypical model for liberation movements of all kinds—a model on which most national independence movements, and many separatist movements, continue to rely, either explicitly or implicitly. The point of comparing liberation movements to the Exodus is to chart a conceptual path from victimhood to emancipation to nationhood and, finally, to sovereignty.[101] But what if the freedom that comes after slavery is not a claim to nationhood or to any kind of territorial home?

If the Exodus story is the *locus classicus* for the study of a victimhood that seeks nationhood (self-rule), then postslavery black liberation in the U.S. would seem to suggest an alternative path in which a different Moses might have tried to reintegrate freed slaves into the society of Pharaonic Egypt. The promised land of black liberation was also the land of black affliction: the post-slavery U.S.[102] The genius of Martin Luther King Jr., as the successor to what I call the Lincolnian model, was to fuse the liberation theology of the Exodus with a messianic theology (based on St. Paul) in which the final role of Israel (God's people) was to bring redemption to the oppressors (Egyptian, Romans, and white Americans). In the context of our broader study of transitional justice, Civil Rights–era America is a case where the demand for liberation is not "let my people go" but, rather, "let my people stay."

It is only by saving white America, King preached, that black Americans could free themselves. If King presented himself as a Moses to blacks, his message to whites was that of St. Paul—that they still have time to be saved.[103] By interpreting Moses *through* Paul, King tied the political mobilization implied by the Book of Exodus to the moral logic of passive resistance implied by Romans. This was not merely a moral repudiation of political violence; it was also an interpretation of liberation, not as a way of leaving Egypt but instead as a way of confronting Rome: "One day we shall win freedom, but not only for ourselves. We shall so appeal to your heart and conscience that we shall win *you* in the process, and our victory will be a double victory."[104]

Like St. Paul, who addressed the "Romans" *as* a Jew, King here addressed white Americans *as* a black with the message that both sin and salvation must be conceived in terms that transcended the black/white divide in U.S. history. His was a theology for the *meanwhile*, in which the messianic mission of American blacks was to save everyone. He thus constructed the message of the race within the Empire as something *more* universal than Empire itself—an alternative universalism of the kind that Paul attributed to the Jews.[105] Ahead of justice, King thus placed the duty to love one another in the present.[106] This was the link between King's Mosaic promise to liberate his people and his Pauline mission to save everyone. "In essence, King unknowingly made the subject of the Civil Rights movement the 'White beneficiary' [of racial discrimination], rather than the African American."[107]

That beneficiary was ultimately the northern white liberal who could still enjoy the advantages of racialized inequality while saving his own soul through conversion to King's cause of nonviolent change. By using nonviolence as a *tactic*, King shifted the moral burden of refighting the Civil War to those in the South who wished to preserve the status quo. Time and again his nonviolent demonstrations would *provoke* white Southerners to revert to the violent symbolism of slavery a full century after slavery had been abolished —calling out the dogs (Bull Connor), raising the Confederate Battle Flag (Lester Maddox), and brutally beating peaceful demonstrators. It would thus be the southern segregationists, and not the Civil Rights movement, who would be accused by a watching North of violating the Lincolnian peace at a time when nationwide media, both broadcast and print, were reaching maturity. Insofar as civil rights protesters anticipated (while not seeming to provoke) a violent *response*, they called forth a federal duty to rescue (what we now call a Responsibility to Protect) that would eventually extend the reach of the Equal Protection clause to authorize a reoccupation of southern political space by federal marshals and federal courts. Southern *contras* were here recast from their role as "Redeemers" of a way of life to quintessential perpetrators of human rights abuses.[108]

The moral effect of King's nonviolence depended on its implicit power to unleash violence. On his own side, this power was largely exercised through restraint—King's movement was all that stood between white liberals and a growing black nationalism, impatient with the pace of change. It was also true, however, that maintaining nonviolence *within* King's movement required an organizational discipline that was the very opposite of passivity. This internal discipline gave the Civil Rights movement the capacity to mobilize violence effectively, had its leadership so chosen. By 1968 it had become clear that King's movement was both the only alternative to black violence (his assassination "unleashed riots") and that it could not "go too far" without producing a violent white reaction.[109]

From the perspective developed in chapters 1 and 2, King's strategy contrasts with both justice-as-struggle, the view that treats beneficiaries as would-be perpetrators, and also with the Gandhian model of justice-as-reconciliation, in which everything necessary for self-rule (*swaraj*) is conceived to be already in place. If Lincolnianism was a harsh repudiation of anyone who returns to the violent ways of the past, then King's strategy of *non*violence showed how this legacy could be turned against whites who resort to racialized violence. It was, finally, King who gave Americans a coherent conception of what the Lincolnian legacy of permanent recovery might be in contrast to the search for "closure" that characterized aspects of South Africa's TRC process. The measure of King's success was the extent to which the federal use of force, when it finally came, was on the side of his movement.[110]

King's *divisive* political strategy was, perhaps, best understood by his contemporaneous adversary, George Wallace, the racist governor of Alabama, who played the anti-King on the national political stage. The Wallace phenomenon was not merely "white backlash," as northern media described it. Viewed from the outside (as Wallace viewed it), King's political strategy had been to show that blacks were morally undamaged by racism, and thus to separate the race issue, which northern liberals were willing to address in narrow terms, from the class issue, which raised the question of who was benefiting from racialized exploitation.[111] I thus interpret Wallace and King together as the dialectical adversaries produced by the Lincolnian model of Americanism.

Both their national strategies were compromises arising out of the need to address a regional conflict in national terms. Wallace did so in a way that attempted to mobilize the class forces that King was trying to demobilize until the end. King's movement was, however, something more than a neutralization of the white-worker alliance that had been the foundation of New Deal liberalism. It also gave clearer meaning to the Lincolnian approach by portraying himself as *both* the Moses who led his people to freedom and the Paul who taught them to see salvation in patience and a "hope that does not disappoint" (Rom. 5:5).

The Civil War Virus: Lincoln vs. Wilson

Lincoln's reinterpretation of Thomas Jefferson at Gettysburg is not the only version of U.S. politics that was exported to the world. In the aftermath of World War I, Woodrow Wilson revived the pre-Lincolnian interpretation of Jefferson as a proposed basis for world order. Unlike others who stress the relation between popular sovereignty and individual rights, Wilson focused on the Jeffersonian relation between the state and the nation.

States were created by sovereign "peoples," Wilson believed. Liberalism might later define the relation of ruler and ruled *within* a people, but nationalism—in this case ethno-nationalism—would create that people and define its boundaries.[112] If all nation-states functioned in world politics as the virtual representatives of their own "peoples" in diaspora, so his logic goes, then each national state would protect its permanent minorities out of fear that members of its own "people" might suffer retaliation while living as minorities elsewhere.[113] The postcolonial relation between national and international politics, as Wilson conceived it, is a kind of hostage arrangement based on the tacit acknowledgment that the "peoples" of the world are already dispersed and that their potential ingathering is a legal fiction needed to protect their rights wherever they might be.[114]

In Wilson's terms, groups asserting protected minority status anywhere *must* imagine themselves as both vulnerable to victimhood where they are and as hegemonic victimizers somewhere else.[115] The heightened imaginability of ethno-national violence is thus an unavoidable structural presupposition of the interstate system in which nation-states based on victimhood feel entitled to use their sovereign status in the international community to protect conationals who live as minorities elsewhere. If the point of demanding nationhood is to protect a diasporic people from further victimization, it follows that a state does not violate Wilsonian principles by resisting, at least up to a point, attempts at self-help by separatist minority groups that threaten to "strand" members of the present "majority" within a smaller state in which the present "minority" rules. The obvious problem is that a previously subjugated minority allowed to rule in the name of former victims will almost inevitably have permanent minorities of its own. In the words of one scholar, "the effort of the state to become a nation aroused the determination of the nation to become a state."[116] Those who assert protected minority status from a Wilsonian perspective thus become hypothetical threats to their current oppressors (people who could do the same to "us"), thereby allowing "us" to rationalize continuing oppression on the grounds of self-defense. Whenever "otherness" is asserted as a counterhegemonic claim, a long-term cycle of mutual threat and reprisal is always a danger.[117]

The troubling truth is that many civil wars throughout the world are based on such a cycle and many nations that see themselves as Lincolnian survivors are doomed to fight civil wars against secessionist claims grounded in a cultural, and often a political, version of Wilsonianism. Whenever past victims claim as much sovereignty as it takes to turn the tables, the regressive logic of atrocity and reprisal is set loose. No reader of Nietzsche can be sure that the perpetrators of past discrimination are wrong to hear "the voice of the victim" as a threat;[118] and no follower of Paul can ignore the appeal of conversion from evil, now seen as a cycle of violence, to make a new beginning. For Lincolnians, the appeal of using the violence of renewal to survive originary violence is reason enough to choose the politics of national unity and resist all separatist claims.

A dark implication, however, of our discussion of both Lincoln and Wilson has been that survivor stories often rationalize abuses that produce new demands for separation based on the sovereign coequality of peoples. Secessionist movements, in turn, produce victims who may become survivors with new stories of their own. This cycle is not universal, but it is observable, and it suggests that Lincolnian and Wilsonian perspectives may be both interdependent and mutually subversive at a deeper level. By this I mean that each story has a tendency to undermine its own premises and motivate acceptance of the other.[119] Today we might describe postmodern thinkers as "cultural Wilsonians" insofar as they believe that marginalized groups, especially minorities, should not be judged according to the norms imposed by those who represent the hegemonic culture. From this perspective, liberation in its most general form is based on the critique of cultural imperialism (including that of the Lincolnian "survivor story"), and colonial oppression becomes the paradigm of all injustice—which is initially the affront of not being heard and understood and ultimately the threat of genocide.

4

THE DIALECTIC OF RACE AND PLACE

Race, Ethnicity, and Territory

Large-scale murder, even the destruction of entire populations, is not a product of modernity. The sacking and pillaging of conquered cities, and the rape and massacre of their inhabitants, has occurred across religious traditions and cultures. The Greeks did it to Troy; the Romans did it to Carthage—and both Greeks and Romans built national legends around the significance of those deeds. To their enemies in the ancient world, the Persians, Akkadians, Assyrians (and so forth) were legendary for their willingness to destroy cities and kill or transport entire populations. The deliberate killing of entire populations was not, moreover, a policy avowed only by those classified as "barbarians" in the Greco-Roman imaginary. Thucydides describes a debate among Athenian democrats about whether the inhabitants of a defeated city should be put to death: they were. Massive as these killings sometimes were, their purpose was to terrify and/or eliminate the population of a specific place that had been conquered rather than to remove from the face of the earth a specific genealogy and thus to purify a "race."[1]

The conceptual apparatus of modern genocide—its specific link to racism—arises out of the political logic of colonialism and anticolonialism as distinctive constellations of state power.[2] Before considering the philosophical implications of the genocide taboo, we must recover the conceptual framework within which genocide became all too thinkable within the framework of modernity. This chapter is concerned with the phenomenon of genocide before the concept and its origins in late medieval and early modern conceptions of race, ethnicity, and territory.[3]

Modern colonialism originates in an act of violent usurpation/conquest or in an unopposed claim to possession of territory that is already inhabited.[4] It differs, however, from the military conquests of ancient kingdoms and empires, which sometimes involved the annihilation of the defeated, and also from the ancient migrations of groups that resulted in the rule of some over others. The distinctive feature of modern colonialism is the conception (after 1492) that the *entire earth* is subject to what Carl Schmitt calls a "nomos,"—a fundamental norm for apportioning terrestrial space. According to this norm, rulership over *land* was based on a preexisting freedom of the *sea*, and the appropriation of overseas colonies was thus conceived as an *exception* to the international law that disfavored the imperialism of invading neighboring states across borders.[5] Because the claimed (appropriated) colonial "possession" had been exempted from the international law that governs tyranny on the land and piracy on the sea and would eventually reconcile modern Europe's overseas empires with a denial that supposedly enlightened Europeans could reconcile their modern overseas empires with rejecting a "right of conquest" as a legitimate basis for empire within Europe itself. Instead, the sovereignty of modern European states would be grounded on *rebellions* against imperial control—the struggle of their inhabitants to purify themselves as "peoples"[6] from foreign contamination. But before this became the basis for popular self-rule in Europe, it was the basis for colonial powers to assert their *race* (broadly indistinguishable from nationhood) as a *nomos* for dividing and ruling an ethnically mapped earth.[7]

What distinguishes European colonies acquired after 1492 from the suzerainties of ancient empires and the wanderings of ancient tribes is an *imagined* relation, both spatial and temporal, between a territory's prior inhabitants, its colonial possessors, and its eventual citizens as an independent state.[8] Both the colonial and anticolonial mind can conceive of genocide because they both can (must?) imagine the same territory without its current inhabitants. Relations among current occupants appear within the framework of colonialism to be essentially matters of temporal succession. Thus, in the colonial dialectic, everything depends on who came first and who will remain. From the perspective of colonialism, any present time of simultaneous cohabitation of racialized ethnicities must be seen as historically abnormal and, perhaps, ephemeral.

Modern colonialism introduces into world political thought a fundamental distinction between "native" and "settler" and, eventually, the related distinction between ethnicity and race.[9] As developed in this chapter, the distinction between "native" and "settler" is essentially political—it is about the role of indigeneity in a territorial state. The native's identity is based on *priority* and *place* (they preceded the settlers as occupants of the territory to be settled), and the settler's identity, insofar as it is translocal, can be said to be based on a cluster of purportedly global theories of history and human development that converge around the concept of *race*. Long before race had biological explanations—before such explanations were thinkable—it had been a political and religious concept relating origins (both temporal and geographic) to destinations. Racialized thinking is essentially translocal and transtemporal: it foregrounds the *successive* occupation of presently inhabited space. By doing so, it also makes imaginable divine or human intervention in a race's historical trajectory across the earth. If a "race" can imagine its own spatial migration over time—race is what remains the same, regardless of location—it can also imagine itself as the object of extermination in any given place, as biblical Jews could easily do.[10] For them Israel was not a site of cartographic origin but a promised destiny (a destination) to which only a purified remnant would return—not merely to home but to a path.

To use the concepts of race and place in this way after 1492 is to take the perspective of the metropole toward the local. From the metropolitan perspective of a would-be settler, the concept of "place" plays a role that is, at least superficially, innocent in identifying the colonial territory with the cartographic space of a state, initially empty and to be filled (or "colored") in by a form of political rule that it otherwise lacks.[11] The presence of prior occupants, however, is not a mere accident or complication for colonizing peoples—even when they claim that their "discovery" of a place (its effective *placement* on their own world map) preceded their need to conquer its subsequently hostile inhabitants.[12] As expatriate colonizers, they are not rooted where they are and may thus entertain a cosmopolitan fantasy that they would be the "same" people anywhere. Contrary to the cosmopolitan ethic, however, metropolitan colonials never "forget where they come from."[13] Their ethical perspective is *not* cosmopolitan to the extent that the distinctiveness of indigenous populations poses a political and moral problem for them. The essence of that problem, from the settler's standpoint, is what it could mean to respect local *culture* and *ethnicity*, where these very concepts represent the political residue that is left of indigeneity in a cartographic space where the settler's eventual presence is presupposed. This presupposition lies at the core of colonial *thought*, even if an active policy of settlement is not pursued as a means of more fully possessing a particular colony.

Thus the metropolitan map of colonialism eventually becomes filled with the ethnic names of local places—a process that explicitly links ethnicity and territory while giving this linkage political significance in and for the outside world that imposed and recognized it. At the broadest level, that political significance is obvious—there would not be a global *map* filled with homelands if people were always "at home." Some people (the discoverer, the mapmaker, the conqueror, the settler) are necessarily *not* at home wherever in that world they happen to be. It is *they* who identify cartographic space (territory) with origin rather than location and thus create a map that presupposes the mobility rather than the stability of populations. To the extent that this map itself appears to be natural (the world), the political distinction between race and ethnicity remains dynamic rather than fixed in any given locale.[14]

We can thus say that when members of ethnic groups arrive at another place, their identity (whether as colonial settlers or as migrant workers) is racialized. Sometimes groups respond to such racialization by clinging or returning to the ethnicity associated with their cartographic origins. In these cases they are seeking to "re-ethnicize." The reidentification of U.S. Negroes as African Americans is an example of this phenomenon. Similarly, the Jewish idea of a "return" to Jerusalem has served for centuries as an ideology of voluntary re-ethnicization on the part of diasporic Jews suffering from racialized oppression. As Rebecca Solnit writes,

> Race itself, this identification with an ethnicity also imagined as an origin, has for the last century tended to generate a kind of ethnic nationalism whose insistency on the inseparability of race and place is itself mystical. . . . Israel itself was founded on the idea that the legacy of blood entitled the Jews to a legacy of land . . . I've always been as much appalled as awestruck that a people . . . could remain so attached to an absent place of origin that everyplace else could be framed as a temporary exile . . . no matter how long they stayed. Becoming native[15] is a process of forgetting and embracing where you are.[16]

In contrast with the fiction of ethnicity as something inherently local, the fiction of race is all about the fact and possibility of migration without assimilation. It is thus, on the one hand, an alternative to the ethnic rootedness of populations and, on the other, an exception to their free mobility.[17] Races are in this respect the collective subjects of actual and potential migration in a (consequently) ethnicized world. A "racial" identity bespeaks a place of origin from which one is absent, a place of occupation in the present, and perhaps also a historical destination that may be either a return to the first or a fuller inhabitation of the second.

Note, however, that the refiguring of racialized groups as "natives" is not necessarily liberatory. Involuntary re-ethnicization occurred under South African apartheid when the families of migrant workers were relocated to their tribal "homelands" in order to suppress political resistance by a hyperexploited racialized labor force on which the mines and factories relied.[18]

The nineteenth-century scheme for a voluntary colonization of Liberia by freed slaves also relied on the double meaning of "African" as both a racial and ethnic designator. Here Africans, conceived as a geographically mobile race, were to be re*settled* in a place inhabited by the natives of so-called Africa. The concept of a "liberia" (rule by the free/freed) illustrates the colonial concept that a race, defined by its origin and destination, should rule the indigenous occupants of a place.

Why, then, do most Americans use the term "ethnic" to refer to immigrants rather than "indigenous peoples"? One reason is that the "race question" has been more salient than the "native question" in U.S. politics, especially since the "closing of the frontier."[19] In the apparent absence of a native question, political differences among settler identities would be described as "ethnic"—especially as the term "race" came to be associated with biological racism. But the term "ethnicity" was not merely a substitution for earlier uses of "race" to designate settler groups in America.[20] By circumventing the native question, the American "invention of ethnicity" allowed descendants of all settlers to be members of a single race, American, into which even blacks might conceivably "integrate" by regarding *themselves* as "African Americans."[21] This use of the term "ethnicity"[22] became common just as colloquial uses of "race" (and ideologies of biological racism) were becoming disreputable.

The peculiarly American exclusion of the native from the race/ethnicity distinction reflects what some scholars call its "liberal tradition," which *dilutes* the importance of Old World origins and identities once people get to this New World.[23] In America, that backward-looking significance of diverse origins is the freedom and mobility that America itself made possible.[24] The common racial identity of ethnic Americans is thus *revealed* by their political assimilation—a relation between originary choice and final destination that distinguishes them from the descendants of both slaves and natives.[25] In this twentieth-century conception of Americanism, the European concept of race is not merely *purified* of the taint of biological determinism; it is also *intensified* in its moral force. Like a European's "race," an American's "freedom" is an inner differentiating quality (something we *have* before anything we *do*) that can be instantly recognized by those who share it, and either admired or resented by those who lack it.[26]

Racialized Thought

"Freedom" is the name Americans give to the hidden originary essence that allows us to consider immigrants as "ethnics" and thus to distance ourselves from the settler-native question. This ideology seems to remove the taint of biological *racism* from the "ethnic" settler's self-understanding and thus eliminate the most objectionable aspect of the colonial idea of race. The concept of race, when ostensibly purified of its biological racism, allows Americans of diverse national and religious origin to distinguish themselves from the descendants of slaves and indigenous peoples on the grounds of freedom alone. Behind this apparent purification, however, there is also an *intensification* of race as a political concept, which now suggests that some noninhabitants of the nationally claimed territory were spiritually destined to arrive and that some present inhabitants may be spiritually unsuited to remain.[27] Our American freedom has become the pure *thing* (like a European's race) that makes us experience hatred of our power in the world as a hatred of what we essentially *are*. Thus the ideology of "Americanism" both generalizes and preserves the European concept of "race" as the translocal exercise of power, while equating such power not with purity of biological descent but with the moral significance of freedom itself.

In the dialectic of race and place described in this chapter, "Americanism" can be best described as racialized antiracism that distills racialized thinking as a translocal standpoint toward "place" based on whatever shared inner quality—perhaps our own tolerance of diversity—that those who hate us ultimately lack. This antiracist racialism is, of course, the general form of racialized thought in the postcolonial world. The racialism that refuses to recognize itself as such has been well described by the French political theorist, Étienne Balibar, who stresses that

> nationalism cannot be defined as an ethnocentrism except precisely in the sense of the product of a *fictive* identity. To reason any other way would be to forget that "peoples" do not exist naturally any more than "races" do, either by virtue of their ancestry, a community of culture or pre-existing interests. But they do have to institute in real (and therefore in historical) time their imaginary unity *against* other possible entities.[28]

As Balibar reminds us, there is no natural ontology of races and ethnicities. The concepts of race and ethnicity are, rather, part of political theory, and it is as such that they must be understood and criticized. Balibar at one point insists that "there is in fact no racism without theory,"[29] Elsewhere he says:

> Theoretically, racism is a philosophy of history . . . which makes history the consequence of a hidden secret revealed to men about their own nature

and their own birth. It is a philosophy which makes visible the invisible cause of the fate of societies and peoples; not to know that cause is seen as evidence of degeneracy or the historical power of the evil. . . . The "secret," the discovery of which it endlessly rehearses, is that of a humanity eternally leaving animality behind and eternally threatened with falling into the grasp of animality.[30]

Racialized thinking (which Balibar simply calls "racism") is therefore always relatively universal with respect to nationality, because it is, logically, the form of political identification that transcends (or even undermines) mere ethnic occupancy of a cartographic space. As a theoretical construct, a race is something *within* a given nation—its hidden part that comes to be viewed as originary.[31] A discourse of "race" is thus the initial way in which the *human* is understood as something translocal—and therefore a category through which we can understand the *merely local* as something less than fully human.

Although Balibar does not forcefully say so, the idea of the "secular Jew" is the prototype for his account of the relation between racism and universalism. The claim that a secular (converted, assimilated, nonobservant) Jew is *still* nevertheless a Jew—that secularity is just *another way* of remaining Jewish—is precisely what he means by racialized thinking, and the anti-Semitic variant of this claim is what he means by racism. Such thinking is, perhaps originally, a precipitate of the way St. Paul constructs the Jewish-Christian difference in his *Epistle to the Romans*. Here Paul argues that Gentiles who become part of "Israel" through joining the brotherhood of Christ are different people (subject to different standards) than "the Jews" who always remain Jews, whether they accept Christ as their Messiah or not.[32] "The Jews" for Paul (and here he includes himself) have an originary relation to God that precedes Christ and a separate path to redemption. For them, accepting Christ is another way of being Jewish; for Gentiles (the Nations), it is the *only* way to join the people of Israel. As the self-declared Jewish emissary to the Nations, Paul proclaims that only *some* Jews will be saved but that the salvation originally promised to the Jews alone is now available to God's new people, a new Israel defined as the Church itself.[33] Thus is born the question of who the *real* Jew is: not all Jews are really Jews, and some non-Jews can claim to be the true Jews.[34] The Jewish notion of purity based on ritual is here replaced with a notion that Balibar would call "racial." Because those who *remain* Jews consider themselves to be the *only* Jews, they can be hated for their racism by those Gentiles who think that *they* are the *real* Jews. Here, as in subsequent history, antiracism appears as the originary form of racism itself: the racialized other is hated for *being* racist.[35]

If the racialized conception of the Jew created by Paul is no longer that of a nation, neither is it quite that of a religion in the new sense that he invents. True religion, according to Paul, is about the meaning of Jewish *history* for the world. What happened to the Jews now has universal religious significance, which is, according to Paul, different from the significance it will come to have henceforward for Jews themselves. The significance of Judaism as a separate religion is thus no longer exhaustive of the religious significance that Judaism has for the world. The identity of the "the Jew" rather appears as a counteruniversal, standing between the "nation" and the "human" in much the way that Balibar's idea of "race" does. Race is, for Balibar a concept that is ambiguously both biological and creedal, but it is always highly theorized in just the way that Paul's political theology theorizes the Jewish-Christian difference.

A race is, as we have seen, an identity not localized in space but rather defined in its relation to time. Instead of occupying a place, races have origins and possible destinations. The very idea of a "people" as the political subject that *constitutes* a state—what it both rules and represents—is carved out of the relatively more universal concept of a race that is only contingently related to the cartographic *place* the state occupies. Insofar as a "people" defines itself from *within* a prior conception of race, there will always be tension between seeing peoplehood as a dilution of race through the accident of territorial assimilation and seeing it as an intensification of race through the project of political purification. Michel Foucault took note of this project and provocatively described it as the "race war" underlying the modern discourse of political sovereignty over a place, but it is more accurately described as a struggle over the meaning and relevance of the concept of "race" itself.

Balibar's use of the pejorative term "racism" to designate racialized ways of thinking can distract us from his principal insight into the link between racial thinking and the humanitarian view that racists are inhuman.[36] Today "racism" is the name critics apply to the particular theories of colonial domination that are superseded by nationalism in much the same way that "feudalism" became the generic name that historians of the modern state gave to the particular rationalizations of aristocratic rule that it superseded. Foucault argues that the modern state created the constitutional prototypes of "race war" in the broad sense of constituting a people within the people (a race) that rules in order to purify itself and purifies itself in order to rule.

It is thus race in the sense of an originary difference (whether cultural or biological) that comes to explain why the nation needs to rule itself rather than be submerged into a larger entity or divided into smaller ones. Race in this sense is the "hidden" element in the nation that makes its people "equal" and enables nations to produce a "fictitious ethnicity," a "populism," that substitutes in a postfeudal world for the rule of family aristocracy.[37] "What theoretical racism calls 'race' or 'culture' (or both together)," says Balibar, "is therefore a continued origin of the nation, a concentration of the qualities which belong to the nationals 'as their own.'" But racial thinking, according, to Balibar, is not merely "supernational" in the sense of designating a "superrace" and a "subrace" within the nation itself; it is also what Balibar calls "supranationalist" in the sense of defining

> communities of language, descent and tradition which do not, as a general rule, coincide with historical states, even though they always obliquely refer to one or more of these. This means that the dimension of universality of theoretical racism . . . permits a "specific universalization" of nationalism. . . . . There actually is a racist "internationalism" or "supranationalism" which tends to idealize timeless transhistorical communities such as the "Indo-Europeans," "the West," "Judaeo-Christian civilization" and therefore communities which are at the same time both closed and open.[38]

The fact that the "race" is both within the nation and outside the nation, according to Balibar, makes "racism more nationalistic than nationalism itself . . . an *excess* of nationalism"[39] rather than an atavistic remnant of primitive culture.

From Balibar's insight into the relation between racism and nationalism it follows that ideological antiracism—the attribution of racist attitudes to ethnic immigrants—is the new form that racialized thinking takes today. In postcolonial globalized societies, the cultural unassimilability of certain immigrants is the essential (racial) marker distinguishing them from those who identify with a global culture that celebrates the "human race" as such and who practice a kind of "meta-racism" that aims to "*explain racism* and to ward it off."[40] In this respect, even the avowed antiracist—the democrat who replaces the study of "racial belonging" with the study of "racist conduct" (race relations)—participates in a form of metropolitan knowledge of hidden cultural differences that naturalizes a propensity to commit racist acts as a substitute for race itself.

Balibar thus describes such analyses of culturally induced racial bias as themselves a "differentialist racism" (pp. 22–23). As he points out:

> The idea of a "racism" without "race" is not as revolutionary as one might imagine. . . . A racism which does not have the pseudo-biological concept of race as its main driving force has always existed . . . Its prototype is

anti-Semitism. Modern anti-Semitism [as distinct from "theological anti-Judaism"] . . . is *already* a "culturalist" racism. Admittedly, bodily stigmata play a great role in its phantasmatics, but . . . the Jew is more truly a Jew the more indiscernible he is. His essence is that of a cultural tradition, a ferment of moral disintegration. . . . In many respects the whole of current differential-ist racism may be considered, from the formal point of view, *as a generalized anti-Semitism.* (pp. 23–24)

Balibar here refers to the ranking of "individuals or groups in terms of their greater aptitude for—or resistance to—assimilation" (p. 24) based on hidden (or inner) characteristics: the ineluctable "Islamism" of Arabs as much as the inner "Judaism" of Jews.[41] The techniques that Balibar describes as "differentialist racism" are nowhere more apparent than in the post-9/11 efforts to avoid "racial profiling" of Arabs by "discovering" an "inner" (cultural) difference within Islam that separates "good Muslims" (who love freedom and embody a kind of Protestant Ethic) from "bad Muslims" (religious fanatics who hate freedom and do not value human life, whether their own or others). Only the "bad Muslims" become suicide bombers, or so the argument goes, and it is they who must first be identified and then controlled to defend the global interests of humanity. This is the prototype of racism directed against European Muslims—Europe's new Jews—who are hated for expressing racial hatred (in this case) toward the Jews themselves. A Judeo-Christian world thus measures the acceptability of resident Muslims by their willingness to be assimilated as most Jews have been. Balibar's analysis implies that the Muslim-Jewish difference is still no less definitive of Western Christendom (now transformed into Judeo-Christendom) than it was during the First Crusades, when Muslims were conceived as armed Jews.[42]

Having elaborated the dynamic relations between ethnicity, race, and nation that underlie the ideologies of modern democratic states, we are once again confronted with anti-Semitism as the paradigm of modern racism. As Balibar suggests, the "inverted" racism of pre-Holocaust anti-Semitism—rooting out the "hidden" Jew (the really Jewish Jew) who only pretends to be assimilated—has become the template for present-day discrimination against Arabs in the West. That discrimination is, through the process of ideological inversion, based on *their* propensity to anti-Semitism—another "hidden" trait (presumptively based on cultural origin) that can be rooted out through special tests designed to look behind their merely superficial adherence to Western ideas of tolerance. The essential test (especially post-9/11) is refusal to denounce, as terrorism, any militant action directed against the premise that a Jewish state in Palestine is an exceptional responsibility of the (now Judeo-Christian) world community after the Holocaust. Those Muslims (the "real" or "bad" Muslims) who regard the military defeat of Israel as desirable, or even thinkable, are thus taken to reveal a hidden cultural propensity toward the kind of anti-Semitism that is supposed to make the Holocaust, and its potential repetition, thinkable as well.

We are thus confronted in greater specificity with the question posed at the beginning of this chapter about the unthinkability of genocide. If anti-Semitism is the prototype of modern racial thinking ("differentialist racism" in Balibar's sense), it is also the specific version of racism that first made genocide thinkable—not in the sense that the Nazi attempt to exterminate European Jewry is the first historical example of a genocide but in the sense that the name "genocide" itself was invented to capture the specificity of what the Nazis intended to accomplish and the magnitude of their eventual success. The 1948 Genocide Convention defines what they did as the paradigmatic crime against humanity, illegal and prosecutable everywhere, and a complete justification for any wars (up to and including world wars) that are necessary to prevent, stop, or punish states and nonstate actors that engage in genocide.

As the foregoing discussion suggests, the assumption that Nazi anti-Semitism made genocide conceivable is deeply embedded in the post-Holocaust reorientation of human rights thinking around the prohibition of genocide—a reorientation that, at the very least, made anti-Semitism unspeakable (if not unthinkable) in all societies in which human rights thinking has taken hold. In these societies (which believe themselves to constitute a world community of humanitarian values), denouncing Jews as such is not only unacceptable; anti-Semitism is also regarded as an external manifestation of an inner quality that is now considered paradigmatically inhuman—so much so that, as early as 1950, equating it with "Hitlerism" became a basis for Aimé Césaire to attack the racist inhumanity of colonialism itself:

> We must study how colonization works to *decivilize* the colonizer . . . to awaken him to buried instincts, to covetousness, violence, race hatred, and moral relativism . . . [until] the poison has been distilled into the veins of Europe . . .
>
> People are surprised . . . they hide the truth from themselves . . . that it is Nazism, yes, but that before they were its victims they were its accomplices; that they tolerated that Nazism before it was inflicted upon them . . . because until then it had been applied only to non-European peoples.

... Yes, it would be worthwhile ... to reveal to the very distinguished, very humanistic, very Christian bourgeois of the twentieth century that without his being aware of it he has a Hitler inside him, that Hitler *inhabits* him ... and that, at bottom, what he cannot forgive Hitler for is not ... *the humiliation of man as such*, it is ... the humiliation of the white man, and the fact that [Hitler] applied to Europe colonialist procedures.[43]

My purpose here is not to pursue Césaire's specific analogy between colonialism and the methods of the Holocaust but rather to explore the ways in which the logics of race, ethnicity, and nation implied the possibility of eliminating entire populates before the word "genocide" itself became associated with a taboo. Before treating Hitler's extermination of the Jews as the paradigm case it has now become, it is useful here to take up a less familiar, earlier case in which the logic of native/settler played out with genocidal consequences.

The Irish Example

At the beginning of this chapter I suggested that "race" and "ethnicity" are protean concepts within colonial discourse that can be filled in with whatever fears and fantasies the settlers wish to project onto their difference with the natives. In its late medieval origin the colonial idea of "race" had little if anything to do with physical characteristics or "mere appearances" like skin color. As early as twelfth-century Europe the concept of "race" was used to distinguish diasporic settler nations from indigenous "tribes"— primordially rooted in a specific place. The great "nations" of the Franks, Germans, Slavs, Normans, and so forth, were thus originally conceived as "races" that settled the land of indigenous "tribes" long before they came to regard themselves as "nations" that were entitled to become "states."[44]

The history of Ireland is a case in point. Anglo-Norman colonization of Ireland began in the 1150s by dispensation of the pope. The remnants of this Old English colonization of Ireland remained largely Catholic, distinguishing themselves from both the Gaelic Catholics and the Anglo-Irish and lowland Scots who would follow.[45] After Henry VIII's decision to break with the Catholic Church, "the English occupation of Ireland ... would take on the qualities of a true colonization, distinct from the invasive migrations culminating in near-assimilations that preceded it. . . . Campaigns of vast brutality were launched to subdue the population again and again."[46]

England thus developed a scheme to "plant" the "waste" land of Ireland, and, under Elizabeth and James, the establishment of the Irish Plantations, such as Londonderry and Munster, were "intertwined" with the Plantations of Virginia, using the same techniques of conquest, population removal, and deforestation to create new landed estates for the younger sons of British aristocrats and gentry, especially from Devon and Cornwall.[47] The subsequent Cromwellian "Settlement" of Scots-English in Ulster brutally suppressed an Irish rebellion.[48] It did not take long for the Anglo-Irish[49] to identify themselves as a settler race—no longer merely English and with their own claims to Ireland.[50]

The core conceptual apparatus of native/settler is already present in England's treatment of Ireland.[51] If, however, the Anglo-Irish settlers experienced their pastoral fantasies as memories of an English "home," it is clear that (what we would now call) their genocidal fantasies regarding actual pastoralists were entirely focused on Ireland.[52] After the seventeenth-century colonization of Ireland, the colonists continued to actively imagine themselves as the victims of savage massacres by Gaelic-speaking hordes; they consequently had little public compunction about imagining an Ireland in which the natives were gone and settlers had become the real "Irish" (a people capable of mounting, by the 1790s, an independence struggle of their own, modeled on the American Revolution).[53] This aspect of the Anglo-Irish imaginary is nowhere more clearly articulated than in the writings of the satirist Jonathan Swift, dean of St. Patrick's Cathedral in Dublin, whose view of the native question in Ireland is already informed by a substantial body of literature comparing native Irish practices to those of Amerindians and Hottentots.

As early as 1700, native Irish immigrants to England are described as "white negroes."[54] This took on a redoubled significance as British colonialism was extended to the Americas, India, and Africa in the eighteenth and nineteenth centuries: as Great Britain's expanded imperial reach gave Irish Protestants (the settler "race" of Ireland) a prominent role in colonial administration elsewhere, "native" Irish emigrants would be treated as "black" in the far colonies.[55] In the postcolonial U.S., the racialization of Irish immigrants took an even more bizarre turn. The early settlers from Ireland—mostly Protestant Ulstermen—began to call themselves "Scotch Irish," first to distinguish themselves from indigenous peoples (Gaels and Amerindians) and then to distinguish themselves from the "black Irish" who immigrated after the Potato Famine. Although "the label Scotch-Irish was unknown in Ireland,"[56] it is now used to designate the native ethnic stock of an increasingly diverse America.[57]

The general significance of the Irish example is that a distinction between the native and settler occupants of place underlies the emergence of both race and nation—so much so that it grounds the national consciousness of the settler races at home. Even English national identity can be used as an example, especially if we focus on its narrative reconstruction through nineteenth-century tales of the colonization of Saxons by Normans, such as Sir Walter Scott's *Ivanhoe*.[58] This and other Romantic fictions about the feudal origins of European nation-states are, essentially, stories of conflict between settler and native, retold as foundational struggles that would anticipate the singular national consciousness that was to come.[59]

Here we can already see the dialectic of settler and native—of race and place—that made conceivable the modern politics of collective extermination. As pure dialectic, it is inherently reversible: the settler can declare himself to be a native and declare the native to be a foreigner.[60] When, for example, the Dutch settler becomes an Afrikaner and the Puritan settler an American, the new story is that the indigenous peoples were just earlier settlers. They are, within the terminology used, a different *race*—invaders from a different time and therefore subject to displacement, absorption, extermination, or all three. Within the moral logic of colonialism, the aboriginal is a mere local placeholder who is replaceable in his tribal "homeland" by settler races.[61] When such substitution occurs, the removed "Bantu" in Africa or the removed "Indian" in North America becomes a domestic alien in the land of his birth. As a racialized denizen, he is protected by neither the laws of the state (as a citizen) nor the laws of his tribal homeland, and thus he becomes the quintessential victim of genocide and genocidal imagination.[62]

Colonialism and Revolution

The political theory of classical liberalism was ideally suited to the founding of "new" societies in colonial contexts precisely because it treated the specificity of the colonial distinction between race and place as theoretically peripheral. In Locke's account of the Social Contract, for example, the lingering presence of prior occupants is largely irrelevant to the legitimacy of the form of government created by individuals who might as well have come together in an empty space. The understanding that colonialism is *essentially* a form of state rule by settler over native is also largely absent from Thomas Jefferson's original enunciation of principles of self-determination.[63] Thus he frames the U.S. War of Independence as a struggle between settlers and the mother country over the issue of home rule—notwithstanding the question of settler rule over natives that remains in the background.

Jefferson himself, however, was fully aware that he had made this choice. As both a student of Native American cultures and a speculator in tribal lands, he understood that the claim of settlers to self-determination as a natural right was fundamentally at odds with a parallel claim that could be made on behalf of aboriginal peoples. Nevertheless, he knew that after the French and Indian Wars, the British could claim a permanent role in North America as mediator between settler and native, both of whom were, equally, subjects of the Crown. To counter this argument, Jefferson reluctantly concluded that establishing an independent settlers' republic required the involuntary cession of tribal lands and, tragically, the eventual reduction, removal, or elimination of their populations. Like the paradox of Jefferson's support for slavery, his complex attitude toward indigenous peoples is fundamental to a full understanding of the principles of 1776 as a foundational expression of *both* liberalism and settler colonialism.[64]

As the example of Jefferson suggests, the colonial dialectic of native and settler is no less a part of modern revolutionary thought than is the dialectic of victim/beneficiary discussed in earlier chapters. The U.S. Declaration of Independence is thus implicitly about proximity and distance. (We who have come together in this place have the right *not* to be ruled from afar so that we can exercise the right we *do* have to rule or displace those who were here before us.) The Declaration is also about wealth and power. (England is still exploited by its landed aristocracy; but because Americans *work* the land they own, they can reject all prior claims to the soil, whether feudal or indigenous.) In forging an ideology of the settler bourgeoisie, Jefferson brings the anticolonial and antifeudal forms of revolutionary thought into near harmony by sidestepping the topic of race and rhetorically locating the oppressor at a spatial distance.

In the two centuries that followed Jefferson, his two potentially distinct arguments for revolution have always been partially present in each other—and always somewhat at odds. In the U.S. Revolution, these contrapuntal claims produced a racialized split in the revolutionary subject, who sees himself as victim, rather than agent, of colonial oppression—while being both victim and agent simultaneously. In Fanon's enunciation of the Algerian revolutionary position, the racially split colonial subject becomes conscious of himself as an agent whose capacity for suicidal violence mirrors the genocidal violence of colonial rule. Both the French and the Russian revolutions were conducted through the clear, class-based discourse of victim/beneficiary described in earlier chapters, but both also produced new forms of imperialism and nationalism as responses to the political insecurities that these two revolutions created on all sides. In both cases, it appears that the two forms of revolutionary discourse that were in counterpoint for Jefferson are effectively unconscious with respect to each other—to enunciate one is to repress the other.

Our present discussion of native and settler puts us in a position to restate and amplify the schematic account in previous chapters of the revolutionary struggle between victim and beneficiary. In concrete circumstances, the specific revolutionary demands of victims and beneficiaries can be enunciated from the standpoint of either settler or native; and the demands of settlers and natives can be enunciated from the standpoint of either victim or beneficiary. The colonial and class paradigms of revolutionary thought might thus be seen as two dials on the same ideological clock, moving at different historical speeds, sometimes occluding each other, sometimes not. Precisely how they relate in a given ideology of conflict can vary. (Natives, for example, can be represented in revolutionary ideology as victims of parasitical settlers, as beneficiaries of immigrant labor, or as alter egos that cannot be simultaneously recognized alongside settlers as occupants of a common space.) Each dial, however, can be independently reset in relation to the other through an act of real or symbolic violence. When a violent event occurs to reset the historical clock—when someone assumes (or is assigned) the role of *perpetrator*—the axes of victim/beneficiary and native/settler become less orthogonal and are sometimes overlapping. To the extent that this occurs, the "truth" can then be told according to the temporality of either colonial or class struggle and sometimes as though these separate narratives were functionally one and the same.

The Roots of Genocide

The secular logic of genocide arises from the moral psychology of place and race within the colonial project. To understand this, we can rely, once again, on Melanie Klein's concept of projective identification, discussed in earlier chapters. The essential idea (restated in Klein's terminology) is that the settler reexperiences his own aggression toward the native in the form of fear of the native's hostility toward him. In fearing the native's "primitive" racism (which is already a response to colonization), the settler defends against guilt for displacing the native. By identifying himself as the *object* of his own feelings toward the native, the settler reexperiences them as feelings of racial antipathy on the part of the natives. In the dialectic of race and place, the role of the colonist is to think, "These people hate us because of our [. . .]." "Race" is the term of art that fills in the political blank: it acquires whatever biological, religious, linguistic, or cultural content is necessary to describe a difference between the settler and the native place-holder that precedes the settler's occupation of the native's place.[65] The settler perfectly understands the depth of these ascribed feelings of racialized hatred, for they are merely his own original feelings projected onto others.

It should be noted that two imaginaries of genocide are embedded in such an account of projective identification.[66] The first is the genocide of the native against the settler—the racially motivated "massacres" of innocents by savages that are the foundation of settler colonialist lore. The second is the massacre of natives by settlers. The unconscious moral logic of the colonial experience bases the settlers' genocide against the native on the settlers' repressed fear or fantasy of being subjected to genocidal actions by the native.

In his now classic *Wretched of the Earth*, Frantz Fanon theorized that in order to liberate himself from colonialism the (black) native must embrace this projected willingness to exterminate the (white) settler.[67] Fanon urges the "good native" to embrace the "bad" identity that embodies the settler's terror. Jean-Paul Sartre famously read this claim as the next stage in revolutionary consciousness and saw the native's will to fight the colonist to the death as a higher form of the totalizing dialectic of master and slave described by Hegel and Marx.[68] Read in a broader context, however, Fanon's argument is that the settler/native dialectic is distinct from, and even potentially broader than, that of master and slave. In *Black Faces, White Masks* he sets forth the paradigm of anticolonial struggle as lacking the mutuality of recognition present in the Hegelian-Marxist view of class struggle.

> Here the master laughs at the consciousness of the slave. What he wants from the slave is not recognition but work.
> In the same way, the slave here is in no way identifiable with the slave who loses himself in the object and finds in his work the source of his liberation.
> The Negro wants to be like the master.
> Therefore he is less independent than the Hegelian slave.
> In Hegel the slave turns away from the master and turns toward the object.
> Here the slave turns towards the master and abandons the object.[69]

In colonialism the relationship is not initially one of *subjugation* mediated by something they have in common, an object which is simultaneously the product of the slave's labor and the object of the master's need; rather, it is based on originary *displacement*—of one occupying the place of another, both physically and psychically. Fanon demonstrates that the conceptual root of genocide lies in the prior lack-of-relation between native and settler as mutually exterior occupants of the same ground.

Fanon's theory of colonialism is thus less an extrapolation of Sartre's (and Hegel's) account of the struggle for recognition from master/slave to white/black than an anticipation of Lévinas's ethical argument (discussed in chapter 5) against the politics of recognition and particularly against Hegel's view that inclusion based on mutual respect is the ethical goal of the struggle for recognition.[70] According to Lévinas, the philosophy that regards recognition as the *end* of struggle is itself a formula for murder because it does not ask about the struggle's *beginning*. It does not ask, in particular, whether one has already *taken the place* of the other whom one will eventually recognize as another self.[71] Fanon's argument anticipates the later position of Lévinas by taking the "totalizing discourse" of white/black and, most generally, self/other outside the special context of relations of production (master/slave, capitalist/worker) and placing them in the arguably more general context of occupying a space in which the other, as such, does not (or need not) exist at all except as a projection of the self, an alter ego. In this context, which is typical of the colony, the willingness of the native to exterminate or expel the settler is simply a return-to-sender of the genocidal message of colonialism itself.

The genocidal logic of colonialism is well illustrated by the concept of "the vanishing Indian" in U.S. history.[72] The availability of this concept to American culture is a direct result of the decision to define "American" as a racial identity (eventually a series of racial identities) possessed by settlers as distinct from aboriginals.[73] That definition came about a century before the U.S. Revolution, after a highly organized political alliance of Algonquins posed a serious threat to the settler population in Massachusetts during what became known as King Philip's War, named for the executed leader of an antisettler rebellion whose near success ended the settlers' willingness to cohabit with the ethnic placeholders who preceded them. Following King Philip's War, the aboriginal population of New England was no longer considered "American" but something else—denizens "skulking" within a racialized settler state.[74] To be "American" was no longer a matter of residency alone but also a matter of race in the sense that I have defined.

As a consequence of this ideological shift, the "true" Americans (the settlers) could represent themselves as the heirs of the "good Indians" who had somehow faded away. In claiming to be their heirs, later Americans (the new "natives") would dress up as Indians (as in the Boston Tea Party) and develop a wide range of ceremonies that purport to reenact Indian rituals.[75] American identity itself is thus rooted in the thinkability of genocide insofar as it was earlier defined by the disappearance of those who were all too recently referred to as the "vanishing Indian." At the close of the frontier, this idea of America celebrates its transcontinental reach with the Buffalo Bill Wild West Show, in which "civilized" Indians played the role of savages in urban arenas. These tamed savages are here no longer figured as Americans at all except through their imitation of those who now occupy their wild ancestral lands and call themselves "free."[76]

My argument in this chapter is emphatically *not* that racialized citizens of settler colonialist states are actual or would-be *génocidaires*. The settler colonialist is not always, and almost never merely, a ruthless exploiter but can also be a developer, a civilizer, an educator. To be any or all of these things, however, is entirely consistent with uneasiness about one's own status as successor to the "Native." The settler's question is, "How can we live among these savages without civilizing them?" For the colonial project of civilization and governance to get under way, however, living *without* the "savages" must always be a conceivable option. It then follows that living without the settler must also be imaginable for a nationalist liberation struggle to occur as an outcome of colonialism—a struggle that reimagines ethnic indigeneity as the foundation of a nation capable of self-rule and sees colonialism as the illegitimate rule of a race over a nation.

Democracy and Biopolitics

We have seen that colonial struggle lies at the origin, both intellectual and historical, of modern identity politics, which is all about the implicit relation of *demos* (the people as a mass), *ethnos* (peoples as nations), and *topos* (the territory to be occupied and ruled) that *precedes* the political demand for popular sovereignty over a place *and* its inhabitants—actual, virtual, and potential. In the politics of former colonial states (whether colonized or colonizing), this produces a conception of democracy in which the elimination of bodies, at least to the extent of ethnic cleansing, becomes an alternative to the conversion of minds. Genocide, as Michael Mann points out, is the "dark side" of this conception of democracy: that legitimate rule by *the people* over a territory presupposes the absence (physically or culturally) of *other peoples* occupying that territory.

Put provocatively, Mann's thesis is that all successful democracy is the product of ethnic cleansing, but this version of his claim derives its plausibility from expanding the normal meaning of ethnic cleansing to encompass a continuum of policies that begins with voluntary assimilation, runs through cultural suppression, and concludes with genocide.[77] Within this conceptual framework most Americans were ethnically cleansed by the process of immigration itself: their voluntary decision to come (and, in the case of legal immigrants, ours to admit them) implied a choice to assimilate to the creedal elements that define us as a people—something to be *for* rather than *against*—and thus to become part of the ethnic melting pot that defines us as "American." To be American is to regard ethnic cleansing through immigration as benign (and also to fear that it may not occur if immigration is illegal). The nonassimilation, cultural suppression, and killing of the indigenous peoples is ethnic cleansing of a darker, more reprehensible, type that puts the U.S. in a category with other settler democracies that wish their natives would either assimilate or be gone.

Mann's argument is that, whereas mass slaughter of those who occupy a place (such as Troy or Carthage) is as old as history, genocide, the elimination of a group identity wherever it appears, is a pathology associated with the relation between the ruling people and the nonruling occupants of a territorial space and precedes the political demand for popular sovereignty over that territory. This conception of democracy is often highly racialized: it is based on preexisting political identities that are presumed to be unchanging and upon a social memory of victimhood and oppression (or a fear of reprisal for it). What Mann calls democracy's "dark side" is a genuine part of democratic theory—the part that gives democracy its political purchase as something worth fighting for and fighting against. Stable democracy, as Mann sees it, is often the product of successful ethnic cleansing.

Until Mann's book, this conception of democracy was undertheorized in contrast to two other views that *begin* with the sovereignty of a *demos* over a *topos*. The first well-established conception of democracy views it as a *decision procedure*, generally majority rule, in which no minds are expected to change through a process that aims, rather, at achieving a legitimate finality of result. Democratic theory, according to this conception, deals with methods of interest aggregation that, *if* they could replicate the ideal results of iterative bargaining,[78] could justify allowing a majority (or perhaps a coalition of minorities) to rule, regardless of the time sequence of arrivals, departures, repressions, and removals that constitute the body politic.[79]

A second conception of democracy views it as a *truth procedure*, similar to the scientific method, in which individual minds are subject to change through a dialogue of equals engaged in rational persuasion. In this conception we are all (or might as well be) minorities for the purpose of democratic deliberation: the practical question is how to a reach finality in deliberation while valuing the deliberative process for its own sake.

These two well-theorized conceptions of democracy are often distinguished as *aggregative* and *deliberative*. Each presents itself as a qualification of the other. Both would treat historically grounded fears of victimhood as merely *limitations* on or *exceptions* to the normative forms of democratic sovereignty that aim at an appropriate balance between finality and truth in decision making.[80]

Mann's account of "the dark side of democracy" suggests that focusing not on finality or truth but on victimhood would place the addition or subtraction of bodies to the *demos* at the center of the democratic project. This addition and subtraction can take place by assimilating bodies, ignoring them, expelling them, or, in the worst case, killing them. On democracy's dark side, majority rule can become a body count before it is a vote count, and public deliberation can consist of paranoia.

There is little theoretical justification for abstract majority rule when we are no longer in the business of persuading one another—when our votes are rooted in the fear of being victimized on the basis of a preexisting identity. In these circumstances it becomes plausible to argue that, after evil, doing justice to former victims is the most basic legitimation of political power. If this is true, the historical justification for majority rule in Europe was that European history could be summarized as the victimization of large majorities by small (originally feudal) minorities. Majority rule here is a specific historical remedy and not the closest approximation of the natural right of the people to govern themselves when unanimous consent is unobtainable (because of faction, superstition, and the like). The more general case of "popular sovereignty" is indifferent as to whether "the people" happens to be a numerical majority in the territory it rules. Territorial rule is a species of property-based remedial justice (distinct, for example, from monetary reparation *inter vivos*) in which *the people* are an intergenerational community—the living, the dead, and the yet unborn—that can *imagine* itself as the victim of extermination.[81] Thus popular sovereignty is, essentially, dominion by a people over *land* as a permanent defense against racialized persecution. Peoplehood, as such, thus becomes a historical alternative to (and refuge from) the migratory trajectory of race and its contingent relation to place.[82]

The third, defensive version of democratic thinking is far more common than we might initially suppose. Much of the twentieth century, for example, was taken up with the claim that majority rule is really just a way to protect human rights when the majority legitimately fears being victimized by the minority. We might generalize from these claims a version of democratic theory that favors the principle of self-rule by potentially victimized people over abstract adherence to rule by a numerical majority. According to this argument, it is the legitimate fear of victimization on the basis of ethno-national identity—not the relative number of people in the potentially victimized group—that justifies the right of that group to the territorial rule of a "homeland."

What, then, is the meaning of democracy where a formerly ruling group, perhaps a majority, has been disgraced by its role in prior injustice? Could the arguments that normally support majority rule be used to justify specific forms of minority rule instead? These are the unanswered constitutional questions posed by an ethics of human rights that is also a politics of victimhood.

Victimhood and the Right to Rule

The core question here is about the relationship between democracy and prior injustice. In the aftermath of radical evil, what does victimhood lack, and what should it want? Can a national self-rule be the sublimation of victimhood? And is overcoming victimhood what nations want?

If we begin with a state of nature in which there are no prior relationships of victimhood, then the social contract theories of either Locke or Rousseau would imply a commitment to rule by (at least) a bare majority, if only as a best approximation of what the unanimous decision would have been under circumstances of perfect, undistorted communication.[83] Matters are otherwise, however, if majority rule is simply a typical case of rule by the formerly oppressed who seek political power as protection from a return to racialized oppression, ending, perhaps, in genocide. In the aftermath of such atrocity, so the argument goes, a guilty majority can no longer assert its own interests as before. Henceforward, and for the indefinite future, it has no right *not* to have its interests subordinated to those of surviving victims. To have one's interest subordinated to the interests of others is part of what it means to be ruled by them.[84] Accepting as legitimate the subordination of one's interests, and renouncing all pride in one's national identity, is what it means, constitutionally, to live in a state of disgrace.[85]

The problem of Tutsi minority rule in postgenocide Rwanda provides a clear illustration of the unresolved conflict between the Wilsonian theory of democratic rule and fidelity to the ethical meaning of Auschwitz. Even before becoming principal victims of genocide, Tutsis were frequently described as the Jews of Central Africa. Originally a pastoralist caste, they were dispersed throughout the region—unlike the cultivators (Hutus), who had customary roots in a tribal homeland. In the precolonial regime of Rwanda's *mwami* (king), those who intermediated between the kingdom and the tribes were considered to be Tutsis, but these same individuals might (also? rather?) have been considered Hutus if they acquired customary rights in a particular homeland. Prior to colonialism, the distinction between Hutu and Tutsi was not binary (either/or) and not totalizing in Lévinas's sense.

It was not until Belgian colonial rule that what had amounted to a caste distinction between pastoralist and cultivators was redescribed as a difference between "native" and "settler." The native's identity was based on *place* (they preceded the settlers as occupants of the territory to be settled). In contrast, the settler's identity, insofar as it is translocal, could be termed a matter of *race*.

A race, unlike a tribe, was conceived by colonial rulers to be essentially migratory.[86] The Belgian rulers of Rwanda thus described Tutsis as a race of "Hamites," "white" Negroes, who had migrated to Hutu tribal lands— thereby simultaneously racializing the Tutsi and ethnicizing the Hutu. By analogizing the Tutsi-Hutu difference to that between settlers and natives, the Belgians could conceive the Tutsis to be appropriate agents (and minor beneficiaries) of their colonial rule over Rwanda. When that rule was about to end, Belgium's initial plan to turn power over to the Tutsi race was blocked by a Hutu revolution demanding majority rule. The ideology of "Hutu Power" embraced the Belgian view of Tutsis as a stateless race of settlers and demanded that they be treated as an alien elite that had always been parasites and had become, more recently, collaborators in colonial rule. Following the emergence of Hutu Power, an individual was considered to be either Tutsi or Hutu—one could not be considered *both* Tutsi and Hutu once the distinction between them had become "political" in Schmitt's sense.[87]

The genocide committed against Rwanda's remaining Tutsis in 1994 was simultaneous with an invasion by an army of Tutsi expellees who had lived as refugees in Uganda.[88] Commentators differ about the extent to which the genocide was provoked by the Tutsi invasion and the extent to which that invasion itself was justified (at least in retrospect) by the need to rescue Tutsis still living in Rwanda from the near certainty of genocidal massacre. In hindsight it is clear that, if the army of Tutsi exiles had been held back at the Ugandan border, no one (else) would have rescued Tutsi survivors of the initial genocide who were hiding within Rwandan territory; equally clear, however, is that the initial killings would have been far fewer had no invasion of Tutsi exiles been threatened.[89]

Today the Tutsi minority rules postgenocide Rwanda as a victim state, consciously modeled on post–Holocaust Israel.[90] To grasp the meaning of this analogy, imagine that the fears that Goebbels invoked as propaganda during World War II had been descriptively correct—that Germany faced invasion by a militarized form of international Jewry seeking to reverse the historic course of German nativism.[91] This hypothetical scenario for understanding the Holocaust as a reaction by German "natives" against Jewish (and other) "settlers," already adumbrated in *Mein Kampf*,[92] resembles the actual scenario in Rwanda on the eve of genocide. Assuming that it was the invasion of Jewish exiles that had triggered "the final solution" of exterminating the interned Jewish population of German-rule Europe, and that such an invasion would have been justified under international law as a humanitarian intervention to rescue survivors, would it have also been justified to create an Israel out of a defeated Germany? Present-day Tutsi rule in Rwanda assumes that, following the Holocaust, a history of genocide (and the fear of its repetition) can justify the suspension of normal standards of majority rule in the successor state. Tutsi minority rule in Rwanda would thus be no more illegitimate (as racialized oppression) than Jewish rule of postwar Germany would have been after 1948 (the year in which the Genocide Convention was signed and Israel was created by the UN). Why? Because the basis of the minority's right to rule is not race per se but, rather, the transformation of racial identities into those of victim and perpetrator through the act of genocide itself. The rationale for Tutsi rule in postgenocide Rwanda would thus be analogous to granting Jewish survivors of the Holocaust sovereignty over a defeated and disgraced Germany while permitting returning Jewish exiles to share that rule—perhaps in the name of victims who did not survive, perhaps on behalf of rescuers.

Thus stated, the analogy between Rwanda and a post-Holocaust Israel in Germany brings out the tension between a politics of victimhood and democratic theory. Consider, for example, Daniel Jonah Goldhagen's broad description of ordinary Germans as "Hitler's willing executioners." Is this an argument against majority rule in Germany—or at least against the eventual reunification of East and West? If so, the appellation of "willing executioners" could more plausibly be applied to the surviving adult Hutu population of Rwanda, a country of six million in which an estimated three to four million Hutus directly participated in the murder of perhaps eight hundred thousand Tutsis and Hutu resisters. The trial, conviction, and execution of those responsible for mass murder, based on Nuremberg standards of individual accountability, would amount to another, even larger genocide than that which actually occurred. Is the collective disenfranchisement of those responsible a less severe, but justifiable, alternative to holding individual trials in such large numbers?

Or are trials a second-best alternative to what victimhood really wants—the right to rule? The argument for victims' rule, even as a minority, is that a state cannot live on after genocide as though the numerical distribution of bodies between majority and minority were an untainted fact. "Justice" in Rwanda today is thus the code word not for prosecution of the guilty but for Tutsi minority rule—legitimated by the disgrace of the Hutu majority. As Mahmood Mamdani explains,

> The dilemma of post-genocide Rwanda lies in the chasm that divides Hutu as a political majority from Tutsi as a political minority. While the minority demands justice, the majority calls for democracy. The two demands appear as irreconcilable, for the minority sees democracy as an agenda for completing the genocide, and the majority sees justice as a self-serving mask for fortifying minority power.[93]

In Mamdani's account, however, the deeper choice is between a presumption of forgiveness, on the one hand, and victims' rule, on the other. Rather than make this choice, postgenocide Rwanda claims to be an example of both. It is thus a prototypical state of disgrace in which a sullen majority is ruled by returning exiles in the name of victorious victims.[94] They rule, as we have seen, in the name of justice—or perhaps in its stead.

But what would it mean for former victims to rule *justly* over those who once oppressed them? This question is neither inherently unanswerable nor merely rhetorical—it is, and must be, addressed whenever courts or legislative bodies create institutions designed to remedy past injustice within a democratic framework. After radical evil it is conceivable that a dominant group, even if it is a majority, has so grossly abused its right to rule that it must legitimately subordinate its interests to those of the former victims who now rule that group. To say that this is conceivable, however, does not exempt victims' rule from requirements of justice. In this case we must ask whether forms of virtual rule, which are often attenuated cases of victims' rule, could in principle be better suited to redressing bad history without reproducing it.

The postslavery United States did not become Liberia—a country ruled by former slaves. Instead, our history of slavery resulted (eventually) in a body of antidiscrimination law. As we saw in chapter 3, the constitutional origins of antidiscrimination law lie in the rights of U.S. citizens living out of state to be treated as well under the law as the in-state majority treats itself and hence better than it is obliged to treat the federally unprotected local minority that lost out in the democratic process. Thus described, the individual protected by antidiscrimination law is *virtually* represented by the local majority—that individual has no rights that the local majority does not grant itself but can be denied no rights that the local majority grants itself. When the concepts of antidiscrimination law are extended to the descendants of slaves, this limits the extent to which a white majority in America (while there is a white majority) may take only its own interests into account when it rules a once victimized minority.[95] The limitation arises because antidiscrimination law will treat the ruling majority as a virtual representative of the now constitutionally protected groups—"discrete and insular minorities" that do not rule and yet may not be treated as ordinary electoral minorities in disregard of their particular histories of victimhood.[96]

Antidiscrimination law, a scheme that limits how majorities may rule the permanent minorities they once oppressed, is one end of a continuum of constitutional schemes that subject democratic processes to the claims of victimhood. Along this continuum lie schemes to adjust voting procedures and electoral constituencies in order to give constitutionally protected groups enhanced representation in the legislative process.[97] Consociational Democracy (separate electorates) is another step toward political autonomy,[98] which would grant groups that fear victimization the right to rule themselves (and others?) through the territorial partition of an existing state. Next there is the type of right asserted in Rwanda: a group that fears future victimization asserts the right to rule directly over those who have perpetrated atrocity in the past. Another possibility, of course, would be the expulsion (repatriation? resettlement? extermination?) of the traumatized victim group—which suggests that our spectrum of possibilities may, in fact, come full circle in making the foundational atrocity conceivable once again.

Having come full circle, why not create a *new* national homeland for the victimized group? Hannah Arendt's great work, *The Origins of Totalitarianism*, had explained how stateless peoples could subsequently be persecuted everywhere because they were sovereign nowhere.[99] In the interwar period, she argued, blacks and Jews had been the principal victims of "racism" precisely because they represented stateless diasporas rather than localizable ethnic claims to self-determination. Arendt saw clearly that describing stateless peoples (Jews/Tutsis) as "races" made genocide conceivable to movements and parties advocating the expulsion or direct elimination of natives by settlers or vice versa. Establishing Israel could thus have been viewed either as a humane Wilsonian solution to the post-Holocaust refugee problem or as a belated endorsement of the SS's prewar "Emigration Policy," the policy that preceded its "Final Solution to the Jewish Question."[100] Arendt nevertheless argued that, once victimhood becomes the dominant trope of national identity, every group claiming to be a victim could claim virtual sovereignty, at least to the extent of an immunity from being judged by its historical enemy and a special privilege to judge its own conduct toward that enemy. The whole project of building nationhood on the notion of the righteous victim was thus antithetical to the concept of democratic citizenship as a way to produce a *legitimately* ruling majority through persuasion and cooperation. In Arendt's view, Zionism, which was originally critical of the religious cult of victimhood in Diaspora Judaism, had made support for Israel the secular equivalent of that cult—a nation in which post-Holocaust survivorship was believed to transcend the democratic questions posed by Jewish-Arab relations.[101] Before departing to cover the trial of Adolf Eichmann, Arendt sadly acknowledged to Karl Jaspers that "it was for the sake of these victims that Palestine became Israel."[102]

If the creation of Israel had mooted the question I have raised of whether Jewish survivors of the Holocaust deserved to rule Germany, the Eichmann trial raised the question of whether Israel (which had not existed as a state *during* the Holocaust) was entitled to judge Germans for their crimes against Jews. It thus aimed to transform the meaning of Nuremberg retrospectively from victors' justice, which was troubling enough to liberal legalists,[103] to victims' justice, which was more troubling still to a diasporic intellectual like Arendt, whose entire adult experience after World War I had made her doubt the Wilsonian premise that nationhood could be the answer to collective fears of victimhood.[104]

Based on her critique of victims' rule, Arendt was troubled by Israel's claimed right to judge Eichmann from the standpoint of his victims themselves. As Eichmann's prosecutor, Israel represented the victim as survivor, the victim as judge, the victim as avenger, the victim as sovereign. It now stood as the "seventh million," the surviving remnant of world Jewry, speaking for the six million dead.[105] The sense of justice on which the trial was based proclaimed itself to be different from justice as impartiality, a justice neutral between alleged victims and those whom they accused. It was, rather, to be a form of justice based on the premise of "Never again." In trying Eichmann, Israel thus asserted that the consequence of overcoming victimhood with nationhood was the new state's sovereign right to prosecute the very genocide that had led to its creation. While Arendt believed that, ultimately, there was a legal and moral rationale for convicting Eichmann,[106] she saw the theory under which Israel tried him as an outgrowth of the post–World War I Wilsonian framework, laid bare in *Origins of Totalitarianism*, that had made the Holocaust thinkable.

Like most reporters, Gourevitch describes postgenocide Rwanda in much the same way that St. Paul saw the entire world—as a place where all have sinned in wish if not in deed. Genocide had been committed in Rwanda by those who imagined they might suffer it; once this happened, a genocidal punishment of perpetrators became an imaginable response. If the difference between sins committed and those of the heart was a matter of "could have" versus "would have," Rwandans seemed to face a clear choice: the demand for justice would continue the cycle of genocidal violence; the Pauline notion of universal forgiveness was an opportunity to start anew.[107] Paul's message, however, was that sinners have been forgiven by God. This is why they can safely stop sinning, confess, and be reborn. But what could it mean in a secular, constitutional context to believe that one is *already* forgiven?

Archbishop Tutu offered an answer when he visited Rwanda in 1994, immediately after the genocide.[108] Forgiveness would mean, he suggested, that Rwandans had not been judged, and may never be—but also that the resumption of useless suffering would be indefinitely postponed. Such forgiveness, he argued, was even more imperative in Rwanda than it had been in South Africa, which had avoided genocide.

Tutu's argument suggests, however, a significant difference between the secular context and the world described by Paul. Secular survivorship after Auschwitz does not make past suffering meaningful in the Pauline way, the way of theodicy, where the sinner is forgiven and the sin is redeemed (*felix culpa*). Unlike the Christian *sinner* who can be reborn as saint, the secular *survivor* of radical evil—Auschwitz, Rwanda—is simply not yet dead. The promised outcome is not (necessarily) redemption; it is simply additional time for those who survive. Can extra time be ethically significant in the aftermath of evil, even if justice does not follow?

What might it mean to live ethically in such a survivor's state? If the aftermath of sin is a state of grace, the aftermath of evil is a state of *dis*grace. The survivors' state would be one of constant wakefulness based on the awareness that humanitarian responses almost always come too late but are required nonetheless.[109] The same state of disgrace, however, can be more neutrally described as one of depressive hypervigilance in which uneasy survivors who occupy a common space spend the time that remains defending against their persecutory anxieties and well-founded fears of cohabitation. Girumuhatse's unchallenged arrival, for example, means that the time of evil is already past but the time of justice has not yet arrived.[110]

Century's End

The following chapter confronts the fact—often mentioned in earlier chapters—that the issues of transitional justice are now widely believed to be a permanent part of the human condition and an appropriately ethical response to the horrors of the twentieth century. Contemporary humanitarian practice is based on the premise that *ethics comes before politics*. The opposite of this view—putting politics before ethics—is now commonly derided as the error shared by the Right and the Left throughout the twentieth century—an era of revolution and counterrevolution in which individuals were exquisitely sensitive to the suffering of their comrades and insensitive to pain inflicted on their foes.[111] This is what politics *is*, Carl Schmitt argued—a selective antidote to humanitarian pathos that makes it ultimately possible to kill (and die) for the sake of countrymen or comrades.[112] As we have seen, the emergent literature on human rights implicitly shares Schmitt's "concept of the political" in two ways: as the "liberalism of fear" and as the theory of third-party intervention.

Chapter 5 considers what it would mean—finally and permanently—to put ethics first. Can we extract from the politics of victimhood that marked the twentieth century what some French philosophers have called the "victimary" essence of mankind as the basis of ethical imperatives that precede and transcend the claims of revolution and counterrevolution alike?

To confront this question, I contrast the works of two French philosophers who have dealt with it at its most abstract and, arguably, profound level. The first we have already discussed—Emmanuel Lévinas, a one-time student of Heidegger, refugee from Nazism, German prisoner of war, and Talmudic scholar. The second is Alain Badiou—protégé of Althusser, celebrant of May '68, one-time Maoist, and still a professed revolutionary.[113] Arguing against Lévinas's view of both the nature and primacy of ethics, Badiou believes that the task of any serious political philosophy is to define an ethical position faithful to the truth that revolution is not impossible, even today—after Evil. Badiou presents what he considers to be a deeper version of the ethics of revolution and struggle in explicit response to Lévinas's ostensibly deeper version of the ethics of humanitarianism (itself an implicit response to Heidegger's ethics as a deeper version of totalitarianism).

The contrast between Lévinas and Badiou allows us to consider more deeply the primacy of ethics and the limitations that Human Rights Discourse places on the scope of ethics itself. For Badiou, it is, specifically, the concern of ethics with bodies and languages that is commonly held to precede politics: a concern to reconcile a thin universalism (based on the fact that our animal bodies feel and die) with a thicker relativism based on the plurality and incommensurability of human languages that give meaning to our human lives and feelings.[114] Ethical discussion of languages (and cultural systems that resemble them) is now commonly expected to focus on the problem of *difference* and to prefer a baseline cultural relativism to the culturally imperialist danger of false universals. In the ethical discussion of bodies—and especially bodies that suffer—the greater danger is now widely seen to be false relativism.[115] A principled resistance to moral relativism when it comes to the suffering of bodies is thus the specific ethical view that underlies the present-day politics of human rights. That politics affirms the power of living individual bodies to express their freedom in the terms provided by cultures/languages that are to be treated as equal if and only if they condemn the intentional infliction of physical cruelty as evil and genocide as the prime evil.[116] As Badiou describes the main thesis of post-Auschwitz humanitarian ethics: "Evil is that from which the Good is derived. . . . 'Human rights' are rights to non-evil."[117] The human rights that follow from this presumed consensus on evil are "rights not to be offended or mistreated with respect to one's life (the horrors of murder and execution), one's body (the horrors of torture, cruelty and famine), or one's cultural identity (the horrors of the humiliation of women, or minorities, etc.)."[118] Any ethical responsibilities that follow from these rights are constantly vulnerable to the fragility of empathy, indifference, or outright denial when we are faced with evil itself.[119] This version of ethics also implies, of course, a politics of its own, which carries forward the counterrevolutionary version of the politics of victimhood discussed earlier insofar as it makes future revolutionary commitment unthinkable.[120]

Badiou's version of ethics is an effort to make such commitment thinkable again. The "intuitive power" of his view, according to Slavoj Žižek's sympathetic account, is that it accurately describes "the experience each of us has when he or she is subjectively fully engaged in some Cause which is 'his or her own': in those precious moments, am I not fully a subject?"[121] According to Badiou, post-Auschwitz humanitarian ethics effectively blocks the production of political subjects in precisely this sense.

This is, I think, a fair characterization of the ideology of human rights that I have criticized thus far. But is Human Rights Discourse right to link the zealous pursuit of a cause with evil? We must now consider its strengths and weaknesses as philosophy.

5

"NEVER AGAIN"

The Prime Evil

In previous chapters I have suggested that Human Rights Discourse opposes a polemical concept of the *ethical* to the twentieth-century concept of the *political*, which (as Carl Schmitt conceded) was also polemical.[1] Human Rights Discourse, I have argued, is against the ideologies of both revolution and counterrevolution that dominated much of the twentieth century even while it indirectly carries on significant parts of the counter-revolutionary project. To point this out is to criticize Human Rights Discourse for its historical specificity by calling attention to the forms of justice it excludes, often surreptitiously, in putting beneficiaries on the same footing as potential victims and allowing them to disavow their links with perpetrators.

The late twentieth century saw a renewed interest in "radical evil" defined through the paradigm of genocide, often coded simply as "Auschwitz."[2] The challenge to philosophy was famously stated by the philosopher Theodor Adorno: "A new categorical imperative has been imposed by Hitler on unfree mankind; to arrange their thoughts and actions so that Auschwitz will not repeat itself, so that nothing similar will happen."[3] "Auschwitz demonstrates," Adorno says, "that culture has failed." Describing "culture" as "what abhors stench because it stinks," he describes the need for new thinking that resists the appeal to civilizing feelings. Otherwise, "it is from the outset in the nature of the musical accompaniment with which the SS liked to drown out the screams of its victims" (pp. 366–67).

In disregard of Adorno's warning, many late-twentieth-century philosophers attempted to postpone another Auschwitz through forms of cultural persuasion that expand our conception of what "stinks." In celebrating the fin de siècle culture of respect of human rights, for example, Richard Rorty stresses its contingency on our subjective capacity to "feel for each other" and our willingness to treat as ethically fundamental the shared qualities of all *Homo sapiens* (and perhaps companion species) capable of conscious suffering.[4] If "everything turns," as Rorty says, "on who counts as a fellow human being,"[5] the boundary of ethics lies in our capacity to identify with the common humanity of other cultures—strengthened, when possible, by the belief that *they* identify with our humanity. His goal of broadening our definition of "the human" implies a view of ethics in which cultural diversity is an affirmative value.

Rorty's humanitarian project thus runs up against its limit when it intensifies our hatred of the inhumanity of cultures that reject diversity. Any reader of Schmitt knows how this new conception of the "inhuman" arises: the cultural belief that there is a single "human race" implies that "humanity" is itself a "race" that is always potentially at war with the subrace within it that rejects our common humanity.[6] The American philosopher Hilary Putnam, no Schmittian, also understands that when moralists such as Rorty rely on culture to do the work of ethics, they can at best postpone, rather than prevent, the repetition of Auschwitz: "The danger in grounding ethics in the idea that we are all 'fundamentally the same' is that a door is opened for a Holocaust. One only has to believe that some people are not 'really' the same to destroy all the force of such a grounding."[7] Putnam goes on to state Lévinas's position as follows: "My awareness of my ethical obligation must not depend on any 'gesture' of claiming (literally or figuratively) to 'comprehend' the other."[8]

Writing shortly after Auschwitz (after Evil), Lévinas had argued against the hope of founding ethics on recognition of our common humanity. The very project of incorporating the "other" into the "same," described by Lévinas as "Totalization" (a term encompassing totalitarianism), would also encompass Rorty's conceptualization of justice as a "larger" form of ordinary human identification.[9] Lévinas rejects arguments that appeal to our shared humanity and argues that ethics after Auschwitz must be based on the mere fact that we and others occupy common ground without presuming any (other) affinity or relationship. Auschwitz revealed, according to Lévinas, the ethical limits of the project of identification that teaches us to treat the other as the same.

No twentieth-century thinker went further than Lévinas in dismantling the structure of pre-Auschwitz thought to articulate Adorno's "new categorical imperative" and thus to restate the ethical a priori as the "Ethics of Ethics."[10] According to Lévinas, "the disproportion between suffering and every theodicy was shown at Auschwitz."[11] Auschwitz here stands for the proposition that we are all, even (or especially) the most civilized among us, capable of genocide and that building moral thought around this recognition changes everything: henceforward we must fear our propensity to commit genocidal violence even more than being its victims.[12] As a distinctively Jewish contribution to ethics, Lévinas turns anti-Semitism inside out by continuing to treat Jews as hostages for all mankind. The Jews really *are* responsible for the suffering of humanity, he says, but in a good way, and not because they unjustly benefit from it. Jewish ethics, thus conceived, resists idealizing relations to one's coreligionists and stresses, rather, one's nonidentification with those among whom one lives. It is only under the shadow of politics that ethics appears to be a matter of filiation (Aristotelian *philia*) and that killing the enemy for the sake of the friend becomes distinguishable from murder (and possibly even genocide) as Schmitt insisted it *is* in politics.[13]

In post-Auschwitz humanitarianism our ethical responsibility to another human arises *before* we recognize him as friend or enemy.[14] For Lévinas, this idea is not merely a post-Holocaust afterthought. His claim that ethics comes first is an argument that putting our political identity first enables us to *imagine* the absence of otherness (and ultimately the elimination of the other). By acknowledging the simultaneous presence and disavowal of murderous (eliminationist) thoughts in all of us—including those who merely look away—Lévinas sought to depoliticize the distinction between who we are and who we are *not*.[15] He understood, without using the word, that a political form of the self-other distinction is intrinsically *paranoid*—a reintrojection of our own murderous wishes toward others in the form of fearing for the self.

We first encountered the ideas of introjection and projection in our earlier discussions of Melanie Klein. It was she who originally interpreted the moralized feelings that would at first seem to connect us with fellow humans as projections outward of our feelings toward the good and bad parts of ourselves: she showed how "bad" (demonized) others are also the threatening parts of the self that we externalize and how "good" (idealized) others are also the parts of the self that we seek to protect from such internal threats of persecution. What the self-aware victim recognizes in a perpetrator or beneficiary is thus never wholly other. If it were, he could not *recognize* it.

Overcoming Paranoia

Lévinas, who was roughly Klein's contemporary, sees an ethics based on *recognition* of others as fundamentally flawed insofar as it depends upon our capacity to see others as ultimately the same as ourselves. His purely ethical critique of what he calls "Totalization"—which is really the process of projection-introjection—sheds light on the *imperative* to move beyond it (and thus on the ethics of psychoanalysis itself). From a Kleinian perspective, the phenomenology of *inter*psychic struggle—for example, the Hegelian struggle between Master and Slave—is entirely (and not just additionally) *intra*psychic. The ethical implication is that human rights idealism after Auschwitz is a symptomatic twin of human rights paranoia after Auschwitz, an overidentification with our common humanity as a defense against the fear of being persecuted as inhuman. Klein believed that psychic repair must begin with the acknowledgment of others as genuinely external to the "internal objects" that we project and introject as split-off parts of the self. What makes these proximate others exterior (we might say *extra*psychic) is that they *survive* the damage caused by our very presence.[16] This corresponds to Lévinas's call for "responsibility" experienced as the ethical imperative to *repair* what is both "proximate" and "exterior" to the self.

Klein's own writings, however, say too little about the ethical *separation* necessary to distinguish the real externality of others from the internal objects whom we fantasmatically destroy through our projective mechanisms.[17] The gap in her thought between therapy and ethics is filled by her colleague, Donald Winnicott, who argues that the internal

> object is always being destroyed. This destruction becomes the unconscious backcloth for love of a real object; that is, an object outside the area of the subject's omnipotent control. . . . The destructiveness, plus the object's survival of the destruction, places the object outside the area of objects set up by the subject's projective mental mechanisms.[18]

For Winnicott (unlike Klein) "the object that is destroyed is not repaired by the subject but, rather, because of the object's survival, it is made whole, separate and external, in the subject's perception."[19] An ethics based on the reality of *separation* (exteriority in Lévinas's sense) is arguably more stable than one that relies on mechanisms of interpersonal *identification*, which are always fantasmatic and implicitly paranoid.[20] In Winnicott's view, the infant would never leave its inner world merely to satisfy desire—the fantasy of a good object would provide satisfaction enough in the unconscious, where wishes are omnipotent.[21] But this very omnipotence makes unconscious aggression problematic. "*It is*," thus, "*aggression . . . that makes the infant need an external object*, and not merely a satisfying object."[22] His endogenous aggression creates an unbearable internal reality that he flees through fantasizing an external world that he can destroy with thoughts.

Winnicott is not the only psychoanalyst to find in Klein's concept of projective identification a gesture toward a nontotalizing approach to ethics. In their critical elaboration of Klein's concept of *projection*, Laplanche and Pontalis usefully distinguish between a type of projection that consists of the ability to recognize in others what one refuses to acknowledge in oneself and a type that discovers in outside reality the self one does not *wish* to be. They also criticize Klein for failing to distinguish "within the category of *identification*" between "modes . . . where the subject makes himself one with the other person and those where he makes the other person one with himself."[23]

To the extent that projective identification is the basis of politics, the political project of expanding our identification with humanity as a whole is riddled with ambivalence from its outset.[24] Psychoanalysis enables us to describe that ambivalence using the vocabulary of projection and introjection and to see the limitations of an ethics that merely reverses these two mechanisms—for example, the Golden Rule ("Do unto others *as* you would have them do unto you") or "Love your neighbor *as* yourself." If the self was originally another other (and that other was already another self), then the *imperative* to treat the self *as* the other (or the other *as* the self) does not capture anything distinctively ethical—it describes what we are *already* doing as something necessary and unavoidable.

Psychoanalysis, thus conceived, is an ethical project that undermines the descriptive project of psychology (the expansion of consciousness though greater self-consciousness) by *working through* the mind to arrive at *something else* that is both more and less than bodily enjoyment.[25] What begins in a critical study of mental phenomena ultimately comes out on the side of materialism. As materialist *ethics*, psychoanalysis follows an unconditional imperative to reach and surpass whatever is *not* conscious (there must always be something) because it is more real than consciousness itself—that without which there would *only* be consciousness.[26] Why is this more real? Because it functions apart from consciousness; because it is (like our animality)[27] something more deeply *inside* us than the internalized subject, and yet (like our sociality) it is more radically *outside* us than the externalized object because its operation is *other* than the intersubjective and intrasubjective processes of projection and introjection that produce the individual ego. The need to go beyond these processes—to work through the hidden paranoia of the Golden Rule—is the ethical problem to which proponents of human rights after Auschwitz must respond and generally do not.

Because Lévinas attempts such a response, his claims deserve close scrutiny. He saw Freudian mechanisms of projection, identification, and displacement as clinical descriptions of the human capacity for totalization (treating the other as an extension of the self) and the consequent disavowal of responsibility for the suffering of others whom we distinguish from the self. The human ego is *always*, according to Lévinas, the displacement of a proximate other—a fact that Auschwitz finally requires mankind to acknowledge. His ethics can thus be restated in the language of psychoanalysis as the imperative to consciously avow *everything* that the defense of projective identification enables us to disavow unconsciously. Thus, according to Lévinas, "I am [unconsciously, Klein would say] responsible for the persecutions I undergo . . . since I am responsible for the responsibility of the other."[28] His ethical response to our a priori usurpation of the place of another is what he comes to call "substitution." An ethics of substitution, says Lévinas, should take primacy over a politics of recognition on which weak, psychological notions of compassion, sympathy, and all-around fellow-feeling are based.

Why does Lévinas consider our "substitution" *for* the other to be ethical in a way that our "displacement" *of* the other is not?[29] At first, his concept of "substitution" appears to be at cross-purposes with Human Rights Discourse because it holds victims responsible for their own suffering. Substitution means, he says, that "the persecuted one is liable to answer for the persecutor" (p. 118).[30] This claim attempts to address and supersede the difficulty in Human Rights Discourse already noted: that empathetic identification with the suffering of others is also paranoid idealization of the self. Lévinas's account of substitution rejects the delusions of virtue that lead self-identified sufferers to produce victims in their turn. To avoid the snares of projective identification, Lévinas defines "substitution" as precisely *not* a "relation" between the "good" and "bad" parts of ourselves (the internal objects described by Klein). Instead, it is "the possibility of putting oneself in the place of the other" (p. 117–18). Lévinas argues that this nonrelationship with the other must be ethically presupposed before the phenomenology of distinguishing self *from* the other gets under way.

To express his idea that substitution is ethically prior to phenomenology, Lévinas invokes the concept of a "hostage." To be held hostage is to suffer *for* another (that is, in *place* of another) without suffering *as* the other or *through* the other. A hostage need not identify subjectively with an internal alter ego whose suffering he assumes—and is not necessarily either a martyr or a scapegoat.[31] He is simply in the line of fire.

For Lévinas, the hostage situation is our baseline ethical predicament because his *substitution* for the victim redeems (ransoms) the one who

would be persecuted while simultaneously alleviating the fault of the persecutor. "The self, a hostage, is already substituted for the others" (p. 118). This
means that we have a responsibility toward hostages that is not contingent
on any particular relationship that would give them just claims against us.
"The self," Lévinas says, "is under the weight of the universe, responsible for
everything" (p. 116). Thus conceived, the Responsibility to Protect human
rights victims is not an ethical evasion of responsibility for the violence that
a rescuer may inflict on perpetrators, nor for the violence committed
against him by those who consider him as simply an occupier. We have
already seen, however, that he cannot, according to Lévinas, evade responsibility for whatever happens by merely standing by. We are thus left with
the conclusion that he is ethically responsible for what happens regardless
of what he does. Does ethics require any more of him than psychoanalysis,
namely, that he *assume* responsibility for the evil he is also against?

The plausibility of Lévinas's ethical response to projection and introjection assumes that, after Auschwitz, we are all guilty of every evil—and that
our imperative *now* is to accept this responsibility and postpone the return
of evil for as long as possible. Is this what we now need from ethics or
merely a truncation of it to oppose a particular conception of politics that
would *limit* our responsibility?

Atrocity and Event

Alain Badiou rejects the humanitarian effort to ground ethics on the
"consensual self-evidence of Evil":[32]

> The upholders of ethics make the consensual identification of Evil depend
> upon the supposition [that] . . . the Nazi extermination is radical Evil in that it
> provides for our time the unique, unrivalled . . . measure of Evil pure and sim-
> ple. As a result, the extermination and the Nazis are both declared unthink-
> able, unsayable, . . . yet they are constantly invoked . . . to schematize every
> circumstance in which one wants to produce, among opinions, an effect of the
> awareness [*conscience*] of evil. (pp. 62–63)

Since Auschwitz, he argued, humanitarian ethics has put the incontrovert-
ible evil of genocide in the place once occupied by the all-too-contestable
notion of Good on which other ethical views are based.

Like Schmitt, Badiou argues that humanitarian ethics is nothing other
than a politics, but, going beyond Schmitt, he further specifies it as a *politics
of victimhood.*

[This] . . . ethics subordinates the identification of [the universal human Subject] to the universal recognition of the evil that is done to him. Ethics thus defines man as a victim. It will be objected: "No! You are forgetting the active subject, the one that intervenes against barbarism!" So let us be precise: man *is the being who is capable of recognizing himself as a victim.* (p. 10)

Recognizing oneself as a potential victim is the form of persecutory anxiety on which Schmitt's own concept of the politics itself is based—a diagnosis that he failed to make of Nazism. Badiou's new critique of the politics of victimhood applies equally to humanitarian ethics and the rarely acknowledged Schmittian politics to which it leads.

Badiou's first criticism of present-day Human Rights Discourse is, nevertheless, much the same as Schmitt's critique of the Treaty of Versailles: that it implicitly reproduces the evils of imperialism in a humanitarian guise.[33] Two further objections follow: one is that an ethics grounded in our direct recognition of evil (epitomized by atrocity stories) tends to dismiss any positive conception of the Good as merely desensitizing us to the cruelties committed in its name; the other is that, by attributing Evil to our general insensitivity to the pain of others, humanitarian ethics "prevents itself from thinking the singularity of situations as such" (pp. 13–14).

Behind such Schmittian claims, however, lies a more profound point that goes to the heart of the Lévinasian view: Badiou argues that humanitarian ethics is "nihilist because its underlying conviction is that the only thing that can really happen to someone is death" (p. 35). Humanitarian ethics thus oscillates, according to Badiou, between the implicit squeamishness of Western beliefs about "the victimary essence of man" and a nearly pornographic fascination with the power to decide which otherwise exotic victims will die and which will not because "we" can always intervene to save them based on our common humanity (pp. 34–39).

Slavoj Žižek sympathetically characterizes Badiou's view as a critique of "the fundamental lesson of postmodernist politics . . . that *there is no Event,* that 'nothing really happens'" except for fleeting moments of collective identification that must be "dispelled . . . in order to avoid catastrophic 'totalitarian' consequences."[34] To refute this view, Badiou attempts to capture in purely formal terms what it would mean to be subjectively seized by a new "truth," revealed by an "event" that could not have been anticipated.[35] Such a "truth-event" (whether in politics, science, love, or art) is, for Badiou, the real object of "an ethics" because it interrupts the preexisting structure of our situation and retroactively reveals what was previously unthinkable within it.[36] For Badiou, an event is always a supplement to a situation ("the evental site") that is in retrospect only a *condition* of the event, its place. The actual event (what happened) does not exist in the simple past of its conditions but only in the future anterior—it is what it *will have been* for those who believe in it. An "Ethics of Politics," according to Badiou, requires its subject to name the event that changed everything and to make the new truth that was revealed appear as the logic of a future world.[37] He does not hesitate to describe the political event as a "miracle" for those who believe.

Badiou's account of the political event as *ethically* transformative subtracts all historical content from the twentieth-century concept of revolution, including any reason for believing that it is likely to succeed. Fidelity to the event is revolution's ethical remainder, the abstract form of militancy for a truth that once set revolutionaries apart. In Badiou's *finale* to the twentieth century,[38] the revolution as an "event" is always and inevitably something that the revolutionaries *miss* because it "vanishes as soon as it appears."[39] The revolutionary, as a "militant for truth," must believe only that a revolution *then* was "not impossible" and that it changed everything. This is, for Badiou, the fin de siècle trace of the twentieth-century faith that a revolution is possible *again*.[40]

Badiou here transposes revolutionary politics from the realm of strategy to that of faith. Any profound transformations that could have been foreseen as a possibility inherent in the given situation would also be preventable by means of the always excessive powers of those who rule. For this reason a true event, such as Lenin's October Revolution, would not have seemed possible within the situation that produced it (Czarist Russia in the midst of World War I) and was therefore unthinkable to contemporaneous analysts (even to Marxists of the Second International) until it had already happened.[41] And yet it happened. As a militant philosopher whose works span the fin de siècle collapse of Marxist-Leninism, Badiou can no longer say that Lenin's genius was strategic—that he saw revolutionary preconditions in Russia that others missed, the view taken by mid-century Marxist historians such as Isaac Deutscher.[42] Badiou's concept of "fidelity" should be read as an answer to this ethical objection to twentieth-century Marxist philosophy—it is an argument that deciding to believe "a truth" can have the same ethical relation to knowledge that the concept of "truthfulness" does.[43]

What if, Badiou asks, the militant does not believe in a Leninist *analysis* of the present situation (which is likely to be false) but rather in the "evental" status of October 1917 itself? Fidelity to 1917 can be lived thereafter as what Badiou calls a "truth process" that makes visible the "void" (subjectivities that have yet to "count"), the "gap" (excessive power of the state to repress the social elements on which it is based), and the lag (although Badiou does not call it this) between what is already present and the future it defers.[44] These *ethical* "truths" can be asserted as the subjective traces of an event, even though such assertions may appear fanatical to those who do not believe that the event took place.[45]

Such denials of the event are always possible, according to Badiou. They take the form of reducing what happens to its context and then arguing that, because it was antecedently possible, and not something altogether new, there was no real change. Whatever succeeds, according to this argument, must be reducible to what Badiou calls "ordinary becoming"; nothing truly revolutionary could succeed insofar as success itself is explainable by context. But this is a purely formal argument that can always be made, regardless of whether there was an event; it is really a general denial that anything new could ever have happened. As such it must be false. The very need for such a formal denial presupposes that something truly new would not be reducible to its context but would, instead, take the *form* of an "intense singularity." It will rupture what Badiou calls the "logic" (order) in which "what there is" can appear as a coherent world, revealing, as a "truth," that in the context of that world there is *also* "what there is not."[46] If the truth left by an event is never something possible within the logical structure of a situation ("world"), then it *must* be denied by subjects for whom the world goes on unchanged: for them a miracle is defined as what will not have happened; a revolution as what will have failed. The event will thus have *dis*appeared, *except* for its effects on faithful subjects for whom the world has already changed, and who thus believe that something new was "not impossible."[47]

Badiou's formal proposition that revolutionary change is "not impossible" is, of course, a thin reed on which to rest a political alternative to the post-Auschwitz ethics of non-evil.[48] He thinks, as we have seen, that revolutionary change happens only when it is not believed to be possible by anyone, including the revolutionaries, who must act in accordance with the universal truth of its nonimpossibility alone. This reduces fidelity to the revolutionary project to its vanishing point—the absence of any political analysis that would justify revolutionary hopes. Badiou's materialist dialectic lies outside Marx's historical materialism in which revolutionary change is a structural possibility in the objective situation. Such an argument would not persuade anyone who is not already engaged in revolutionary politics, but, as a philosopher, Badiou is not attempting political persuasion. He is, rather, emphasizing the very point that those who do *not* believe that revolution is possible find *incomprehensible* about those who nevertheless persist in a revolutionary cause, namely, their *persistence* itself.[49] Because there are *truths*, Badiou argues, ethics opens the possibility of fidelity to something more real than our present situation, and constitutively outside it. This, of course, assumes that both ontology and politics precede ethics—that "what there is" is *affected* by "what happens" through the hope that there can be something *else*.

Badiou objects to humanitarian ethics because it limits itself to what there is: bodies (that suffer) and languages (that mean). If ethics were concerned only with pain and meaning, then it would be entirely a matter of rescuing bodies and understanding minds, and an ethics of non-evil would take the form of saying that no language could make suffering meaningful (except the language of rescue itself). But ethics is also concerned with truths such as, for example, the truth that revolution is not impossible. Because such truths are *exceptions* to what already is, a politics that reduces the event to its situation is, according to Badiou, "rotten" and "pessimistic."[50] He thus defends as "ethical" modes of political engagement that might seem heroic or futile to those who do not feel subject to its demands—and quintessentially *un*ethical when they lead down paths of violence.[51] This conception of ethics is "infinitely demanding" in part because it is not limited by pragmatic analysis of likely outcomes.[52]

Denying the Event

We are now in a better position to understand the issue between Badiou and Lévinas. Lévinas's claim that the suffering of others cannot be justified is an ethical argument against violence performed in fidelity to the truth of an event such as October 1917 or May 1968. For Lévinas, it would be unethical to place the truth of what happened *then* ahead of the suffering of others *now*. Badiou's belief in "truths" of this (or any other) kind would, according to Lévinas, once again permit ontology to make the claim on ethics that suffering is meaningful[53] and that violence can be ethically justified by fidelity to a truth.[54] Badiou argues that *what is not* can have "truth effects" that are (in Lévinas's sense) "otherwise than being." His *event* thus occupies the place of the *other* (*autrui*) in Lévinas's philosophy, giving politics the kind of primacy over ontology that Lévinas accords to ethics.

But what can count as an event that generates new truths? Writing in the 1980s, Badiou acknowledged that his definition of an event was "circular,"[55] because its *definitive* effect is to produce the subject who is faithful to it. Fidelity is thus retroactively constitutive of the event itself: it becomes an event, through the subjective "intervention" *of being named as what it will have been.*[56] By conceding this point, he undermines the polemical force of his objection to humanitarianism on the grounds that atrocity and mass death are *not* events.[57] The post-Holocaust "politics of memory" calls for fidelity to Auschwitz *as* an event that changed everything: Human Rights Discourse now claims for it "universal" meaning embodied in the 1948 Genocide Convention, which mandates that genocide shall never again occur.[58] This seems a prima facie rebuttal to Badiou's claim that an ethics based on Auschwitz could never be universal in *form.*

Restating his view in 2006, Badiou acknowledged that positing a Holocaust event was among the ways that the twentieth century "thought its own thought" as something "previously unthought—or even unthinkable."[59] There were others. Some saw it as a "century of crime"—a "totalitarian century" encompassing the atrocities of Nazism and communism"; others (like Badiou) saw it as "a century of revolution and counter-revolution—the Soviet Century" that also ended in 1989. (There is also what Badiou calls the "rump century," a "liberal century" that *begins* with the apparent triumph of capitalist democracy in 1989 and ends on 9/11.) Each of these conceptions of "the century" was grounded on a new subjectivity called into being by a previously unexpected event that changed everything (Lenin's Revolution, the Holocaust, Hiroshima, and the Fall of Communism). There was, moreover, a tendency among twentieth-century intellectuals to continue speaking in the language of fidelity to an event when their allegiance migrates from one conception of the century to the next. Thus,

> renegades of the leftism of the seventies, . . . who remain inconsolable that "Revolution" has ceased to be the name of every authentic event . . . [are] busy turning the extermination of the Jews by the Nazis into the single and sacred Event of the twentieth century; identifying anti-Semitism as the destinal content of the history of Europe; turning the word "Jew" into the victimizing designation of a surrogate absolute; and the word "Arab," barely hidden behind the word "Islamist," into the designation of the barbarian. (p. 165)

In *Logics of Worlds*, his most recent major work, Badiou completes his philosophical lexicon by developing a new theory of the "body" to supplement his earlier "theory of the subject." His mature view is, in a nutshell, that events have the ontological status of a truth—they are ruptures/voids in being itself—that produce "fidelity" in "subjects" (they *subjectivate* these subjects) and leave "traces" on "bodies."[60] These "evental traces" transform the "logics" of "worlds"—that is, how being appears (is experienced). As a philosopher, Badiou's central question is how "change" can be "thought."[61] By "change" he means what is not reducible to the "continuous becoming" of its contextual site; and by "thought" he means the formal properties of a subjectivity that *thinks* such change.

Badiou thus attempts to peel off "subjectivation," what Marxists used to call "consciousness," as the affective layer between the logic of appearance (the becoming of a world that seems increasingly coherent) and the true contingency of being as revealed by an event through which the "inexistent" appears. The subjectivity that comes after an event then splits into "four subjective destinations"—the "faithful" (which is presupposed by the others), the "reactive," the "obscure," and, finally, the "resurrected" (for example, a "new Spartacus," such as Karl Liebnecht, appearing in a "new world").[62] These "destinations" differ with respect to the "traces" left by the event (contemporaneous to all) on what Badiou calls the "subjectivizable body." He now acknowledges that his theory of the "body" was an "enigma" of his earlier work, which did not explain that the body is "anything but bio-subjective."[63] In his latest work the "subject" and the "body" are intrinsically social ("transhuman," rather than collectivities made up of individuals). Such subjectivizable bodies do not exist in Human Rights Discourse, which recognizes humans only in biology and culture.[64] Here is more of what he says.

> What does the subject subjectivate? (p. 51) . . . A body [that] becomes something like the trace of the event (p. 53).[65]
>
> From this point of view every reactive disposition is the contemporary of the present to which it reacts (p. 54). . . . So it is really the "no" to the event (p. 55). . . . The form of the faithful subject . . . remains the unconscious of the reactive subject (p. 56). . . . His own contemporaneousness is dictated to him by what he rejects and fights (p. 57). The Good as a resistance to Evil [is] the pure form of the reactive subject (p. 58).

The *reactive* subject, according to Badiou, does not continue living in the pre-evental past. His reaction consists of extinguishing the traces of the event itself by arguing that "reasonable" ameliorations in the present have "no relation, not even a mental one," to events such as the French and Russian revolutions, which produced only disastrous consequences that must be repudiated.[66] The "pure form of the reactive subject," according to Badiou, appears in the thesis "that every willing of the Good leads to disaster and that the correct line is always that of resistance against Evil" (p. 58).

Things stand differently for the obscure subject . . . because it is the present which is directly its unconscious. . . . Thus, what bears this body is directly linked to the past even if . . . [its] only demand is that one serve it by nurturing everywhere and at all times the hatred of every living thought, every transparent language and every uncertain becoming" (p. 61).[67]

We will call [the] destination [that] reactivates a subject . . . *resurrection*. . . . [A] resurrection presupposes a new world, which generates the context for a new event, a new trace, a new body . . . [after] a truth procedure [has] been extracted from its occultation (p. 65).

Badiou's new conceptual framework draws directly on Lacan's account of ethics as a "subjectivation" by "the real" object of desire—which is here treated as an embodied *event*. The faithful subject's *real* desire is thus to embody something *new*. The object/cause of that desire is the "event" itself, which is here described as "a subversion of appearing by being, which . . . unfolds within appearing itself" (p. 378). Unlike modes of mere becoming (such as a trend), an "event" (such as the Paris Commune) exists "maximally for the duration of its appearance/disappearance and confers on the site the power of a [strong] singularity" (p. 374). This means that, for Badiou, *naming* an event is no longer a matter of a definition but of degree—an ascription of "maximal intensity" to the existence of an otherwise transitory happening.[68] "We could say," according to Badiou, "that the event extracts from one time the possibility of another time . . . [that] deserves the name of a new present. The event is [thus] neither past nor future. It presents us with the present" (p. 384). The event here is an *outside*, ethically speaking, to the logic of the situation (world) in which it happens to appear; it is more real than what appears precisely in the sense (common to Lacan and Kant) that for anyone called by it an ethical imperative is more *urgent* than its context. Badiou's new terminology reframes the question of whether Auschwitz *is* an event as a question, rather, about which the four kinds of subjectivation is produced by claiming it as such. Does the conviction that there is nothing worse than what happened there *produce* a new present—or does it block all thought of the present as something new?[69] Does the now transcendent image of the starved and genocided body *obscure* through spectacle the ethical choice between revolution and reaction?

Badiou's account of subjective "fidelity" to the event is a major contribution to the *ethics* of revolutionary thought, linking Marx to Lacan. Fidelity is typically dismissed by secular humanists as the virtue that a convert (or "true believer") claims *instead* of personal empathy or compassion. Badiou, however, sees questions of fidelity, perseverance, and betrayal as the core concerns of ethics,[70] and the rest as (mostly) social pressure to be "conformed" to this world.[71] In the conclusion to *Logics of Worlds* Badiou says,

> I am sometimes told that I see in philosophy only a means to re-establish, against the contemporary apologia of the futile and the everyday, the rights of heroism. Why not? Having said that, ancient heroism claimed to justify life through sacrifice. My wish is to make heroism exist through the affirmative joy which is universally generated by following consequences through. We could say that the epic heroism of the one who gives his life is supplanted by the mathematical heroism of the one who creates life, point by point. (p. 514)

There is something odd, however, about a "heroism" that does not capture the will to physical violence that distinguishes political revolutions from, for example, scientific revolutions. For Badiou, epistemic paradigm shifts in science, mathematics, art—and even love affairs—also reveal revolutionary truths hidden in the present situation as it appears.[72] His purely formal account of being faithful to all such truths reduces militancy itself to perseverance—and misses the difference between having *an* ethics of this or that and *the* ethics that Aristotle saw as the foundation of politics.

Badiou would not view the foregoing comment as an ethical objection to his view. "Faith," he says in his book on St. Paul, "allows one to have hope in justice."[73] But this hope, as it turns out, "is not the imaginary of an ideal justice dispensed at last" (p. 96); it is "not hope in an objective victory"(which is *why* it "does not disappoint" [Rom. 5:2]), but, rather, in "a subjective victory . . . the subjectivity of a victorious fidelity" (p. 95).[74] To reach such a conclusion, Badiou must argue that for "Paul himself . . . the event is not death, it is resurrection. . . . Suffering plays no role" (p. 66).[75] He must likewise eliminate "from the subjective field [of politics] . . . the whole 'leftist' tradition which believes that a progressive politics 'fights against oppression.'"[76] He may be right that progressive politics can no longer "disappoint" if one no longer expects the victims of oppression to *win*.[77] But what's left when the victim's story (such as the Crucifixion) is subtracted from faith in an event (such as the Resurrection)? What's left, according to Badiou, is that we can hope for the second coming of the truth we missed when it was first revealed.

How, then, could *fidelity* to "the event," which has always already happened, give exigent meaning to the present? There is clearly a tension between the messianic belief that everything necessary for salvation (the Christ event) has already happened and the equally messianic belief that salvation itself is yet to come. So what about now? This question was addressed by Walter Benjamin, who said that the "revolutionary thinker" sees the "chance offered by every historical moment" to connect with "a quite distinct chamber of the past ... which up to that point has been closed and locked. "It is by means of such entry," says Benjamin, "that political action, however destructive, reveals itself as messianic."[78] Badiou's concept of the "event" allows us to describe Benjamin's messianism as "*inter*-evental: at messianic moments we stop "the locomotive of history" and "leap" into a "moment of the past charged with now-time."[79] Benjamin, too, explicitly distinguishes his version of messianism from a politics of humanitarian compassion that gives past suffering a "false aliveness" by making it seem a homogeneous extension of the present.[80]

But Benjamin is still in favor of a *redemptive* politics that would make meaningful the suffering of past victims and, figuratively, rescue even the dead.[81] To regard the working class (or any revolutionary subject) as merely "the redeemer of future generations" would deny the messianic potency of "hatred and the spirit of sacrifice" which is "nourished by the image of enslaved ancestors rather than by the ideal of liberated grandchildren."[82] Benjamin thus proclaims that "every concept of the present participates in the concept of the Judgment Day" by rendering "'summary justice' ... concerning some moments that preceded it." Here it would seem that unjust suffering comes before the revolution, which must always claim to be remedial and redemptive with respect to victimary history.[83]

Badiou says just the opposite: "it is not because there is reaction that there is revolution; it is because there is revolution that there is reaction." Here atrocity stories (past massacres, and the like) are part of reactionary history, whether or not the victims themselves were faithful subjects. The essential question for Badiou is what happened first, the revolution itself or the atrocities committed in order to defeat the revolutionaries. Those who focus on the defeat, rather than the event, inhabit what Badiou calls the "subjective destination" of the reactionary who denies that there ever was a revolutionary event worth suppressing and believes that amelioration would have come regardless. Once we *all* arrive at this reactionary conclusion, historical victims can be rehabilitated (as nonrevolutionaries they were innocent), and the excesses committed against them will seem, in retrospect, unnecessary and regrettable. *Logics of Worlds* is a powerful argument against the view that revolutionary thought is *about* the persecution of revolutionaries and that it is kept alive through a cultural history of past defeat and victimization.[84] How could it become true, Badiou asks, that revolutionary militancy is justified *now* because those persecuted earlier were *not* revolutionaries? To assimilate them to ordinary victims, who also suffered, would be to deny that they wanted something new. The alternative is Badiou's fourth "subjective destination," *resurrection*, which consists of embodying once again what he calls the universal truth of militant ideas.

Trauma, Agony, and the Value of Suffering

Badiou's most recent argument against Human Rights Discourse is that it limits ethics to what already exists (animal bodies and languages) and denies that truths are the "exception" to this limitation. An ethics of human rights, which foregrounds respect for bodies and languages, "knows individuals and communities, that is to say passive bodies, but it knows no [faithful] subjects" in Badiou's sense.[85] He thus argues that ethical humanism concerned with survival as such (ecology, bioethics, and interpersonal respect) treats man as a domesticated animal living only in his own present:

> If I wished to scandalize, I would say that my conviction is that this domestication, which subtends the project-less humanism that is inflicted upon us, is already at work in the promotion, as spectacle and norm, of the victimized body.
>
> Why is it . . . that today it is never really a question of man except in the form of the tortured, the massacred, the famished, the genocided? . . .
>
> We could say that what contemporary "democracies" wish to impose upon the planet is an animal humanism. In it man only exists as worthy of pity. Man is *a pitiable animal.*
>
> . . . [Pity], when it is not the subjective instance of propaganda for humanitarian interventions, is nothing but the confirmation of . . . the deep animality . . . to which man is reduced by contemporary humanism.[86]

Part of Badiou's originality is to recognize "animal humanism" as an exception to the cultural pluralism that is also required by Human Rights Discourse (a discourse of the human, as such), which insists that, as bodies (*not* as minds), all humans are the same. Because of cultural pluralism, the difference between minds is to be *respected*—it is a theorem of linguistics that no "language" is superior to another. But because of "animal humanism," cultural diversity is no longer considered an excuse for physical cruelty. If cultures are to be respected, bodies must be *saved*. This animal humanism is, nevertheless, what Badiou calls a "violent and warmongering ideology" that "seeks to destroy what is external to it": it condemns as "inhuman" that which "commands humanity to exceed its being" so as to "maintain a purely animal pragmatic notion of the human species."[87] In this "'postmodern'" reduction of "humanity" to bodies,

> "Human rights" are the same as the rights of the living. The humanist protection of all living bodies . . . is essentially a *democratic materialism* . . . because . . . [it] culminates in the identification of the human animal with the diversity of its sub-species. . . . Having said that, democratic materialism does stipulate a global halting point for its multiform tolerance. . . . A language that aims to regulate all other languages and to govern all bodies will be called dictatorial and totalitarian. What it then requires is not tolerance, but a "right to intervention" legal, international, and, if needs be, military. Bodies will have to pay for their excess language.[88]

Badiou objects to both "animal humanism" and cultural pluralism because their "fundamental imperative is: 'Live without Ideas.'" A humanitarian ethics of no-evil, according to Badiou, aims to make us less politically militant in order to be more compassionate, until we eventually regard militancy itself as a sign of the unethical and antihuman—a mark of the enemy. Humanitarian ethics thus excludes from those deserving of compassion all whose militant belief makes them capable of cruelty. Why? Because *their* conception of good is indistinguishable from humanitarianism's conception of evil.

Badiou's counterargument is that the figure of man's animal body does not call forth any universal thought of the *human* that could have supreme ethical value. What animal humanism wants, according to Badiou, is to "abolish discussion" of the "man who must come" (p. 177). But Badiou goes further than to stress that Human Rights Discourse ("animal humanism") has this limitation. He also treats the "debris of bodies" that is now an icon of the Holocaust as both a reaction against the twentieth-century cruelties driven by the politics of ideas and an occultation of any aspect of the present that might portend a new "uncertain becoming."[89] Elsewhere he states that "if philosophy serves any purpose, it is to take away the chalice of sad passions . . . to teach us that pity it not a loyal affect . . . and that victimhood is not the starting point for thought."[90]

In making his attack on humanitarian ethics, Badiou deliberately opens himself to the charge that a politics of fidelity to truth, which became common to both Left and Right, was responsible for the cruelties of the twentieth century. His principal expositor, Peter Hallward, presents this as a virtue: "Badiou is one of the very few contemporary thinkers prepared to accept the certainty of violence and the risk of disaster implicit in all genuine thought. . . . Since evil is something that happens to a truth or in proximity to truth, there can be no fail-safe defense against evil that does not foreclose the possibility of truth."[91]

The essence of Badiou's present position is that, even after Auschwitz, there *can* be genuine events, revolutionary openings—perhaps expressed by ethical violence—and that serious political thought must allow for this possibility by placing the virtues associated with political militancy ahead of all (other) ethical claims that the event calls forth.[92] Yet his formal definition of an "event" makes him no less dependent on subjective consensus than his humanitarian opponents, who ground ethics on our ability to know an atrocity when we see it. To keep on acting in fidelity to an event (as Badiou urges) is indistinguishable from conforming oneself to the possibility that revolutions can occur and thus militantly *opposing* the forces of reaction and occultation by *naming* them as such.[93]

The political anthropologist Talal Asad directly challenges the claim that, after Auschwitz, our primary ethical responsibility must be to alleviate pain and avoid causing it. This notion, Asad argues, denies agency to those who suffer pain—it assumes they do not suffer willingly—and invests agency in those who aid them. It thus denies the intelligibility and efficacy of a moral view in which pain (of certain kinds and at certain times) is actively sought as a way of achieving or displaying some supremely important moral virtues that involve self-knowledge under stress: "Christian and Islamic traditions have, in their different way, regarded suffering as the working through of worldly evil. For the suffering subject, not *all* pain is to be avoided; *some* pain must be actively endured if evil is to be transcended."[94]

Asad's point brings us back to the moral imperative of "Never again." The humanitarian ethics that took root a half-century after Auschwitz established an apparent consensus that human suffering always has a negative moral value (that there is, indeed, nothing worse). Asad means to question this consensus. Moral agency, he suggests, is psychosomatic in potentially good ways—it can induce states of bodily agony that saints, martyrs, and their acolytes regard as valuable achievements and that witnesses might find admirable.

There is nothing unintelligible about ascribing value to human suffering. The British analytical philosopher Derek Parfit calls attention to our time bias in favor of *pain in the past* and against *pain in the future*. This bias, taken to extremes, is the essence of the modern view that cruelty (avoidable human suffering) is the greatest evil, and no-cruelty the ultimate moral good.[95] Asad's argument shows that this modern time bias is parochial, even within Western Christendom, and that other time biases are morally plausible.[96] One *counter*bias, perhaps more nuanced than ours, could regard specific types of future pain not as useless suffering but as a valuable element in the moral transformation necessary to achieve states of happiness that are at once mental and physical in a strong Socratic sense that removes our fear of death.[97]

Thus stated, the time bias embodied in the ethic of "Never again" seems unduly limiting. Even Lévinas acknowledges, as we have seen, the distinction between useless suffering and morally valuable suffering—between pain that is inflicted and pain that is actively sought on behalf of others or as a way to improve or expiate one's soul. The former can be understood through the post-Freudian concept of psychic *trauma*—pain that may or may not be conscious when first suffered and that is reexperienced endogenously (as fright, panic, phobia, anxiety, helplessness) in a "second scene" to which it gives enhanced affective meaning. What is "traumatic" in the second occurrence of danger is that, here, the ego is "attacked from within . . . *just as* it is attacked from without"[98] and thus recognizes the danger as part of a cycle that may be interrupted but never fully escaped.[99] Trauma is pain that is consciously experienced as happening *again* and, because of its inherent tendency to repetition, becomes the implicit target of the imperative "Never again."

Morally desirable pain—the pain of love, sacrifice, and even martyrdom—is better designated by the word "agony." Agony may be no less intense than trauma, but it is never suffered unconsciously and may well be morally significant for the sufferer while it occurs. Agony, moreover, is not generally experienced by the sufferer or bystanders to be happening *again*; it is, rather, something to be remembered and even honored as a moral singularity, unrepeatable except in the form of ritual emulation. Suffering agony (or religious passion) can be considered morally transformative and may therefore be actively sought. For this reason stories of agony, such as the Passion of Christ, *can* be considered exemplary and universal (as it is in *The Imitation of Christ*),[100] notwithstanding Badiou's argument to the contrary.[101]

We can now see more clearly the limitations that the imperative "Never again" has placed upon us. Humanitarian ethics after Auschwitz epitomizes a recent tendency to respond to all agony (whether moral or not) as though it were psychological trauma that becomes worse through the experience of repetition. Auschwitz did not, according to this view, have the moral character of agony—a meaningful experience of suffering for those who underwent it at the time; it was, rather, trauma, a horror that cannot be consciously experienced *except* as repetition and that consequently *must not* be repeated. In treating future atrocity as the repetition of Auschwitz, we thus greatly truncate the moral vocabulary available for expressing feelings toward those whom we do and do not aid and for comprehending those who become capable of killing and dying for reasons of fidelity to a truth. To grasp this point, it is enough to say that physical suffering, the body in pain, is not an ethical absolute that renders moot political analysis and politically motivated action in the future.

The ethics of "Never again" does not merely limit the ethical vocabulary available in politics; it also limits us grammatically to a concern with what the past *will have been*. Note, that this is not the same as a counterfactual concern with what the past *would have been* if, for example, we had known then what we know now. Neither is political ethics directly concerned with what the future *is to be*. The major pronouncements of Human Rights Discourse have a grammar in which "'narration,' 'event,' and 'past' are of equal importance," and the time of the narrator is "prospective."[102] In its syntagmatic form, the ethics of "Never again" relies heavily on a prospective narration of a past trauma that elides usage of the present tense by the historian-witness.

But a trauma for whom? In psychoanalysis, a meaningless death is not traumatic for the person who undergoes it (and will not reexperience the loss) but rather for the one who survives the death of another and is unable to go through what Freud calls "the work of mourning." The trauma of Auschwitz thus belongs not to the dead but to the survivors—and ultimately to us. It is *our* trauma—the "unthinkable" event of the twentieth century—and not the suffering of the Holocaust's unnamed victims that is addressed by the fin de siècle ethics of "Never again." Thus the *value* of our subsequent, and self-inflicted, suffering from Holocaust "remembrance" lies in the fact that it is a repetition of something that has already happened as though it has become meaningful only now. The point is to be *reminded* of the Holocaust before it happens *again*.[103]

The Trauma of the Witness

When described in Badiou's vocabulary, the Holocaust has become an "event" that has the universal significance of "genocide"—a crime invented after the fact to describe what had already occurred. Subsequent genocides are to be experienced as repetitions of the Holocaust by *us*, the no longer innocent bystanders who should never again have allowed such things to occur.

Friedrich Wetter, Cardinal Ratzinger's successor as Archbishop of Munich, puts this point clearly speaking at Dachau (which falls within his See): "We as Germans," he says, "do not carry the responsibility for that which happened then, but we do carry the responsibility that such a thing can never happen again."[104] Wetter's statement can be read as drawing a straightforward distinction between the guilt of those Germans who carried out the Holocaust and the rather different responsibility of Germans born after the evils of Nazism were fully known. Before Germany's defeat in 1945, Wetter might be arguing, there was no collective responsibility on the part of Germans like that imputed under Article 231 of the Treaty of Versailles—there was only the individual responsibility prosecuted at the Nuremberg trials and their successors. It would seem to follow that Germany's collective responsibility for Hitler comes *after* Nuremberg and is the *product* of the atrocities revealed there. This responsibility does not take the form of accepting guilt for what happened in the past but, instead, of upholding the *truth*, which from now on is always *about* the past.

Cardinal Wetter's apparently straightforward distinction between "before and after" evokes a more subtle conception of historically created time that lies at the core of Human Rights Discourse. For its victims, Nazi genocide was a singular event—being murdered could happen to them only once; they could never experience it as happening *again*. From this it follows that those responsible for Nazi murders when they occurred must be considered guilty; but those who were not responsible were *not* guilty. So whose responsibility does Cardinal Wetter have in mind? It is neither as victims nor as perpetrators but rather as *witnesses* to an established historical truth that Germans can be told that they were not responsible for the Holocaust before it happened but would be responsible were it to happen again.

The witness who refigures his former self as having been *shocked* by the first disaster can thus be said to experience the next disaster as *repeating* that which he originally experienced only in hindsight. *Bearing* witness is *like* first-party trauma insofar as it consists of reexperiencing something that could not have been understood when it happened for the first time. *Un*like the original victim, however, the witness did not experience the injury itself—merely the shock of discovering it. It is the unanalyzed trauma of perception itself that the witness experiences as its *repetition*. By feeling (morally) good about feeling bad again, the witness defends against the paranoid or depressive anxiety produced by initial feelings without affecting indifference to the suffering before his eyes.[105]

In postwar German theology, witnessing (confessing) the Holocaust becomes an act of Pauline fidelity that frees Germany from its evil past. Postwar Germans are thus expected to "believe in" the Holocaust and to regard "Holocaust Denial," as an offense against truth itself.[106] Cardinal Wetter is thus reminding postwar German Catholics of their special responsibility to *bear witness* to the truth of the Holocaust; having seen it once, he warns, the trauma of its repetition would be experienced as something happening to *them*. From Wetter's Christian perspective, Germany's defeat in 1945 becomes the moment when *belief* in the Holocaust is equated with a commitment to a truth that did not exist under Nazism. A new Germany's commitment to the Holocaust-as-truth creates a temporal distance between those Germans responsible for preventing another Holocaust and those who could not have known what happened under its evental name.[107]

It is worth noting here that the "The Holocaust" was *named* by taking what survivors *witnessed* and demanding that bystanders also attest to it.[108] As a Holocaust survivor, Elie Wiesel speaks primarily in the voice of a traumatized onlooker. His trauma is that of any helpless bystander during an atrocity—and he claims to reexperience that trauma when he sees another Holocaust.[109] It is, of course, the misery of the onlooker—the repression of annoyance or disgust that must have occurred before his compassion can well up—that is the dark underside of post-Holocaust humanism. The ethics of witnessing heightens our sensitivity to the suffering of the victim we introject while allowing us to remember, rather than feel, the suffering we project onto others but do not experience as our own.[110] Humanism's project of redirecting unease into aestheticized compassion is not cathartic in the sense that Aristotle found tragedy to be; it is, rather, traumatic in a Freudian sense.[111] For the philosopher Jean-François Lyotard, "Auschwitz" marks the end point of all historical narratives that give past suffering an agonistic meaning. If Wiesel wants to make the whole world a witness, Lyotard's response is that *forgetting* trauma is necessary to the act of witnessing, but it is also a cause of anxiety for the self-identified witness who must thereafter remember *not* to forget.[112]

The foregoing point illustrates the value of psychoanalysis in ferreting out the narcissistic aspect of our fascination with images that identify us both *with* and *as* the victim and the psychic costs of such fellow feeling in the repression or disavowal of possibly hostile feelings *about* the victim that might have been conscious but are not. The trauma experienced by those who bear witness to the Holocaust as *truth* is, as we have seen, empathetic trauma—trauma at one remove. This is what we now mean by ethics after Auschwitz, an ethics of compassion that regards human cruelty, and the indifference that allows it to happen, as the worst thing of all. The paradigmatic object of our compassion is the victim who does not see *us* as a source of help and who sees *himself* as helpless. Because we see him as *virtually* depressed—because we treat him as though he cannot feel his pain for himself—we can feel his pain *for* him. Instead of feeling bad about ourselves, as in depression, by identifying with those whom we would otherwise reproach, we come to feel *good* about ourselves by identifying with the suffering of others who might otherwise reproach us.

But what conception of the victim's subjectivity makes us feel good when it becomes the object of our compassion? It cannot be the reproach or rancor of the victim who sees us as a perpetrator or beneficiary of his suffering. The victim as object of compassion is a potential witness to his own suffering—already an observer of his feelings—who enables us, as fellow witnesses, to identify ourselves as potential victims. It is the victim-as-witness/witness-as-victim who experiences the trauma of helplessness as happening yet again. Compassion thus occupies the moral space that would otherwise be filled by either guilt or indifference—we feel bad (when we do) for the suffering of others despite the fact that we are helpless (not guilty), and we feel good by feeling bad because our helplessness is not indifference toward pain with which we identify, even though we do not feel it. If those who feel compassion identify most of all with the *helplessness* of victims, this may explain why it is in the nature of compassionate aid to be postponed—why it almost always comes too late.

The aura of futility that surrounds humanitarian projects is thus a reflection not only of the immensity of the task but also of the way in which the object of compassion is, finally, the helplessness of the compassionate witness himself. This helplessness is "trauma" in the precise Freudian sense that an exogenously caused pain is thereafter endogenously reproduced. Since Auschwitz, a self-inflicted feeling of helplessness is triggered whenever we see another Holocaust.[113]

If helplessness is the feeling the witness introjects from genocide victims, what feelings does he in turn project onto them? Wiesel describes the murder by hanging of a Jewish child, "dying in slow agony under my eyes":

> Behind me. I heard the . . . man asking:
>   "Where is God now?"
>   And I hear a voice within me answer him:
>   "Where is He? Here He is—He is hanging here on the gallows."[114]

Wiesel thus chooses not to entertain the proposition that the near extermination of European Jewry, or indeed any single death, could be a fulfillment of God's will. He would rather say God died at Auschwitz than consider what happened there to be God's will.[115] As a witness, Wiesel thus projects onto the genocided victim a death wish toward any God who would demand human sacrifice as a collective atonement for sin (the very God of Deuteronomy 28). Like Lévinas, he sees the Holocaust as an end point to the Western project of theodicy—the justification of divinely permitted evil to fulfill God's higher purpose.

Wiesel's assertion that the Nazis murdered God parallels, perhaps intentionally, Christian accounts of the Crucifixion as the death of God that changes everything. The idea that God is on the side of victims, and against their persecutors, is a core humanistic creed of Holocaust Judeo-Christian theology.[116] As such, it claims to *come after* a more primitive religious morality in which those singled out for persecution are stereotypically guilty and in which the application of a stereotype is *not* a basis for questioning their guilt.[117]

The anthropologist-cum-theologian René Girard has shed considerable light on the assumed prehistory of our present-day equation of victimhood with innocence. He distinguishes the moral logic of victim*hood*, thus described, from a preexisting "mechanism" that he believes to be common to all pagan religions. In this mechanism the victim (scapegoat) is always the one to blame for collective catastrophe—his sacrifice cleanses the community of its fault.[118] Because only the victim is to blame, the perpetrator (whether mob or priest) is not guilty; and, because the perpetrator is not guilty, the group that benefits does not share in perpetrator guilt as it might if the victim were innocent.

Whether or not Girard is correct about the universality of scapegoating, it is clearly the precursor needed by the Judeo-Christian morality that he avows. The historical achievement of Judeo-Christianity, according to Girard, has been to transform the antecedent terminology of religious sacrifice into that of universal humanitarianism[119]—the language of victim, perpetrator, beneficiary, and bystander set forth in chapter 1 of this volume.[120] For Christians since the Crucifixion, for Jews since Auschwitz, the new question is whether the beneficiaries of persecution share the guilt of perpetrators or whether, instead, they will bear witness to the innocence of victims.[121] "When we understand that victims are scapegoats . . . we simply mean that victims are innocent, that they are picked arbitrarily by the persecutors, who manage to convince themselves that they are guilty."[122]

Wiesel's project makes sense within Girard's theological framework. By describing Holocaust survivors as *witnesses* to the innocence of those who died, Wiesel brings the remnant of surviving Jews into the kind of messianic age that Christians entered, according to Girard, with Christ's Crucifixion.[123] Wiesel thus provides good Christian reasons to end the persecution of the Jews and embrace a newly hyphenated Judeo-Christianity based on the shared conviction that cruelty is the worst thing humanly possible in this godforsaken world. As the self-conscious vanguard of Human Rights Discourse, Wiesel's post-Holocaust Judaism is closer to Pauline Christianity than rabbinic Judaism had been.[124]

But what is the relation between Jew-as-witness and Jew-as-victim in Wiesel's post-Holocaust revision of Judaism? He expects us to recognize the unconscious trauma of his witnessing—its traumatic aspect—whenever he reports on genocides in Cambodia, Bosnia, Rwanda, and Darfur.[125] Even when the information he provides is general knowledge, we are meant to see his need to tell us as a form of (non-neurotic) compulsive behavior *caused* by his transformative experience at Auschwitz. It was Wiesel's presence at *another* Holocaust that makes his observation of *this* one disturbing to those on whom he calls to bear witness to his witnessing.[126]

The traumatic aspect of witnessing—and the secondary transmission of that trauma—is a secular counterpart to the bodily charisma that marked a biblical prophet as someone who had been changed, against his will, by what he has seen and heard.[127] Prophets, according to the cultural critic Philip Rieff, "do not 'predict' the future; they seek to transform the present, of which the future is all too likely, otherwise, to be a continuation."[128] Wiesel places himself in this tradition. There is, he insists, a duty *never to forget* his revelations about Auschwitz in much the way that Moses warned his people never to forget the revelations at Sinai."[129] But the content of Wiesel's prophecy is distinctively post-Jewish. He finds salvation, and offers it, through his faith that human suffering is the prime evil and that those who look away become complicit in it.[130]

Even after centuries of Judeo-Christian thought, however, the ethical standpoint of the humanitarian witness remains underanalyzed. What is being witnessed? The victim's suffering? The victim's innocence? The *uselessness* of human sacrifice? If there is no moral value attached to the victim's suffering in itself, what makes it morally valuable for the *witness*?

The conventional narrative of witnessing the Holocaust (in Wiesel and others) falls outside the traditional discourse of religious martyrdom.[131] No one now suggests, for example, that those who die in later genocides are martyrs to their belief in the innocence of those who died in earlier genocides or, perhaps, the innocence of all the victims of mass atrocity. If the vast majority of atrocity victims die for nothing, they are, in Agamben's sense, *homini sacri*, bare life, whose killing was *neither* prohibited as murder nor celebrated as sacrifice. We thus bear witness to their deaths not in order to enlist as martyrs in their cause but rather to disavow any connection between bystander and beneficiary.[132] It is in that disavowal that our own trauma lies.

Trauma, Truth, and the Event

The third-party trauma undergone by those who bear witness to the Holocaust as *truth* is trauma at one remove. By accepting the imperative "Never again be a bystander," they are expected to treat the spectacle of human suffering, which did not pain them the first time, as traumatic when they see it *again*. We must thus take up the question of trauma (*delayed pain*) as it affects third-party spectators who would otherwise be considered beneficiaries of and/or bystanders to the victimization of others.

Let us first consider the modern usage of "trauma" itself, which originated, as we saw in chapter 2, as a medical term used to describe injuries that can cause recurring and intermittent pain. This term allowed doctors to distinguish still experienced pain from a prior injury (such as a train wreck) from new pain as well as from pain that is merely remembered. As a medical description, trauma could easily be extended from injuries that *still* caused pain long after they occurred to injuries that did not cause pain when they occurred but did so *only afterward*. Based on this medical usage, early psychoanalysts were able to describe as "trauma" mental injuries that have recurring effects even (and especially) when these are not consciously recognized.

Trauma, in its psychoanalytic usage, is strikingly ambiguous between that of the witness to a disaster or atrocity and the trauma projected by the witness onto those whose suffering is observed but not felt. Behind this ambiguity, however, lies the insight that witnessing another's trauma is a form of repressed identification that *substitutes* for feeling the trauma of the witness himself, such as the experience of being assaulted or violated by an intrusive image. Living as a conscious witness to the trauma of others thus makes us *un*conscious of certain related feelings toward victims (such as disgust, anger, and resentment) that they might reasonably recognize in us and that we might find in ourselves if we did not, instead, repress them in order to heighten our sensitivity to suffering that is *not* our own.

We must thus ask what continuing ethical significance an injury that is repressed gives to the experience that originally caused it: what *attaches* the witness to the image of atrocity in a way that makes him feel (morally) better about himself through future self-reproach? How can such witnessing, and the knowledge it produces, make the once passive spectator feel singled out, special, and morally outraged when new images bring these original feelings back to mind?

As we saw in chapters 2 and 3, nothing in the image of human atrocity itself requires us to feel outraged or compassionate rather than, say, embarrassed, irritated, or titillated when we see it.[133] All these feelings are forms of self-identification that heighten our sensitivity to whatever we observe, but the identificatory process itself places us on a razor's edge between any one of these and each of the others.

To understand the ethical appeal of Human Rights Discourse, we thus need to look beyond identification per se to the moralized feeling (good or bad) that we project onto the internalized victim with whom we consequently identify. If we invest the victim inside us with our own feelings of abjection, then the self we become in witnessing him will feel superiority; if we instead offload onto the victimary object our own feelings of shame, then we, as witnessing subjects, will feel embarrassment—and if we also regard him as our enemy, we may feel triumph, or at least satisfaction, at his downfall. Only when we imbue the victim's suffering with our own sense of moral worth do we *equate* feeling good about ourselves with feeling bad about him.

We have now reached the ethical kernel that distinguishes post-Holocaust Human Rights Discourse from the other, and equally specific, processes of political identification that we no longer consider benign. By ascribing negative moral worth to the victim's suffering, these other forms of politics put the witness/bystander in a position of intellectual and moral superiority to the torments of others. Human Rights Discourse, however, views the unimaginable suffering of victims as a source of intensified moral worth that witnesses at first understand themselves to lack but believe that they may eventually acquire through feelings of compassion. Compassion, as the affective imitation of another's suffering, is the way that witnesses can pursue such moral equality with victims. This appeals to Judeo-Christians in a way that other forms of attachment to the pain of others—the sadistic, the prurient, the triumphant—do not.[134]

Judeo-Christian ethics after Auschwitz thus distinguishes two types of trauma and two corresponding forms of victimhood. On the one side, trauma becomes morally meaningful when it is transformed into self-conscious agony, a singular event that makes a martyr of the victim and leads the onlooker to revere him as a kind of saint. There is also, since Auschwitz, another way to express the moral significance of trauma—to insist that suffering is essentially useless, not a path to higher good, and that its repetition is even worse for the witness than the original occurrence because it is experienced to be happening *again*. Here the projection of positive moral worth onto the victim's presumed suffering appears as a self-conscious choice on the part of *onlookers* to become more virtuous in their own eyes. These two views of trauma reflect two versions of the politics of victimhood. The former treats the suffering of victims as an analogue to that of martyrs who die for God, the latter as an analogue to that of Auschwitz victims who were abandoned by God. In the first model, victimhood is reduced to an aspect (precursor) of resistance; in the second, the memory of past victimhood is infused with the kind of self-satisfaction characteristic of voyeurs.

As a challenge to both views of suffering, however, we must still ask whether trauma could possibly be a truth event that valorizes victimhood as a form of fidelity to it. Badiou's great merit is to pose this question. He argues that an event must contain a universal truth and that, inasmuch as a trauma does not, acting in fidelity to it is ethically impossible. To him, this means that St. Paul's claim that Christ's Passion saved mankind from sin could not be an object of faith for Christian militants, but that Christ's Resurrection must be.

Despite Badiou's claim, however, most believing Christians venerate symbols of a Cross rather than an empty tomb, and many regard Christ's Passion as placing more serious ethical demands upon them than his missing body. The Cross means to believers that Christ's *passion* was both his own bodily pain and also *com*passion—moralized pain that was suffered for others. In his post-Holocaust version of the Theology of the Cross, Jürgen Moltmann goes so far as to describe Christianity as the worship of a savior who could still feel love for humanity even after believing, as some Holocaust victims would later believe, that he had been abandoned by God.[135] Christ's trauma on the Cross here models not the pain that drives us more deeply into ourselves but, rather, the valorized suffering that substitutes itself for the pain of others.[136] Such suffering has, for many believing Christians, the essential qualities that Badiou finds in the "event"—it would not have been thought possible until it happened, and, for those who believe it happened, nothing will be the same thereafter. Here what divides believers from nonbelievers is more than a chasm of faith: part of what believers believe is that the event has changed nonbelievers as well—and that *non*belief is now a reaction against new truth that often takes the form of denying its effects (they would have happened anyway) or obscuring the reality of the present through bodily spectacle.

Restated in Badiou's terms, Human Rights Discourse is the philosophical position that the Holocaust *could* have the universality of a truth and that ethics thereafter has been a struggle between those who are subjects of that truth and those who would deny it.[137] The "truth effect" shared by Judeo-Christianity and Human Rights Discourse is that, by internalizing the suffering victim, we substitute his suffering for our own. In such an ethics, the real sin is *self-centeredness,* feeling *only* our own pain, which is equivalent to *apathy,* an inability or unwillingness to suffer another's pain. Apathy here presents itself as a commonsense belief in the impossibility of feeling any pain but one's own; the struggle against apathy requires faith that this is *not* impossible. I find more problematic the further claim that *by* substituting another's suffering for our own we identify ourselves as a compassionate *subject* who now suffers *for* another. This form of subjective identification (*imitatio Christi*) is rejected by Lévinas and could be rightly criticized by Badiou as the "occultation" of truth by a transcendent body.

What, then, shall we conclude about ethics after Auschwitz? An ethics of no-evil is indeed possible. Compassion (true feeling) is an ethical choice to imagine the pain of others as though it were our own while at the same time regarding their pain morally valuable in a way that our own would not be until it, *too,* is felt by others.[138] I disagree with the premise that human suffering is worse than injustice and that compassion for suffering is the wellspring of moral value. This premise assumes that bodies suffer pain and that reciprocity of feeling is the only way to overcome the bad effects of mimetic rivalry.[139] The very absurdity of this thought—that pain, which has no value when felt directly, has infinite value when felt at one remove—merely indicates that one cannot simply believe it without also believing *in* it.[140] Such faith implies that moral value lies not in the superiority of the other but in the otherness of his pain and challenges us to combat through imagination (and ultimately through culture) the limitations of our ability to feel compassion for, much less pay attention to, the full scope of suffering on earth.[141] The inherent limits to our human empathy mean that this project is destined to fail, prompting us to feel bad, but in a good way, because acknowledging these limits is the element in the human that would lead it toward the realization that the human is *not all.*

Badiou may be wrong in his specific conclusions about Christ's Passion and the Holocaust, but he is right to pose the question as to whether they were *traumas* or *events.* A trauma cannot be *both* repeated and remembered. By entering conscious memory, the pain becomes something past—the point here is conceptual. A conscious attempt to reenact or recover it would be something other than repetition, perhaps imitation or recollection, because its *unconscious* would be different. Unlike a trauma, which conceals a truth, an event reveals a truth that would have otherwise been hidden. Could that truth itself have been a trauma or, perhaps, the fact that we were traumatized? If so, the distinction between fidelity and memory collapses. The affective *trace* of revealed trauma is the subjectivity of bearing compassionate witness to what must have happened before one knew and must not happen again. Badiou's legitimate question is whether the *truth* to which we must be faithful is something more than a memory that guarantees the pastness of our pain. For there to be such "a truth," he argues, something genuinely new would need to have happened—something that would have seemed impossible had it not actually occurred. This conceptual argument, thin as it is, may still be enough to establish that nontraumatic truths in politics are not *im*possible—a claim that Human Rights Discourse has taught us to resist. That something new is not impossible could then become the formal foundation of what Badiou would call an "*Ethics of Politics*" that could challenge Lévinas's evocation of an "Ethics of Ethics" that ends the cyclicity of violence.

The distinction between trauma and event brings us to the specific problem posed by the centrality of Auschwitz for Human Rights Discourse— what is the ethical meaning of Jewish suffering for a world of onlookers that wants to universalize it? And what is its consequent meaning for Jewish identity itself? This is the form in which the Jewish Question was originally posed by Pauline Christianity. In chapter 6 I take up the ways in which, after Auschwitz, that question is still with us.

6

STILL THE JEWISH QUESTION?

Human Rights as Anti–Anti-Semitism

The global politics of human rights after Auschwitz is still about the Jews. Today oppressed groups can qualify themselves as bearers of human rights by recognizing what happened to Jews during the Holocaust and asserting that another holocaust might happen to them; they are often said to *dis*qualify themselves as bearers of human rights by denying the Holocaust and declaring themselves enemies of the Jews.

The figure of the Jew enters into today's Human Rights Discourse at two distinct levels. Most obviously Human Rights Discourse has treated the commitment to protect the remnant of world Jewry that survived the Holocaust as a litmus test of one's commitment to human rights. To be indifferent to the survival of Jews today would be to deny the evental status of the Holocaust in Human Rights Discourse.

But there is also a second, and more complicated, level at which present-day Human Rights Discourse takes up the figure of the Jew—through the doctrine of "anti–anti-Semitism," which is much more ambivalent about the survival of Jews as such than the first discursive level.[1] The anti–anti-Semite is one who, having seen the Holocaust, now sees its possible recurrence everywhere and is *against* it.

As a second-level position, anti–anti-Semitism is thus the latest Christian assimilation of Judaism—one that regards Christianity's acceptance of Jewish religious survival as a test of its post-Holocaust commitment to human rights.[2] Human Rights Discourse (the secular form of Judeo-Christianity) is not limited to the protection of the Jews. It bases its claim to universality on the premise that what happened to Jews in the Holocaust should never again happen to *anyone*.

Today's Human Rights Discourse, as anti–anti-Semitism, thus consists of denying that support for human rights is still about the Jews, while reminding itself that Human Rights Discourse is not yet truly universal because there are still anti-Semites. It thereby puts itself, much like earlier versions of Christianity, in a position to criticize *some* Jews, *as* Jews, without thereby repeating the earlier forms of anti-Semitism to which it is vehemently opposed. The new criticism is that some Jews still refuse to universalize their own group experience in order to become witnesses to *all* human suffering as true humanitarians (Judeo-Christians) have now done. If Jews want to occupy the standpoint of the prototypical witnesses, they must, it is argued, give up the sacrosanct status of being *exceptional* as victims.[3] In a world that has learned to feel good about itself by feeling bad about the Jews, one can take special umbrage at Jews who refuse to apply the Holocaust's lessons to their own treatment of Palestinians. These Jews are to be criticized for thinking that they are the only real Jews, and that the Holocaust confers special privilege on actions they take to protect themselves from those who, as enemies of the Jews, become the moral equivalent of Nazis who would bring about the Holocaust again. This attitude has become a seemingly new offense that Jews, and Jews alone, can commit now that their victimary identity has been universalized. But is this reason for resenting Jews really new?

Why Are There Still Jews?

Universalizing Judaism is nothing new in Western culture; neither are complaints against the Jews for singling themselves out within a broader community that identifies with them. The notion that there were Jews was, as we shall see, essential to a Pauline Christianity that proclaimed its new, more universal values as a repudiation of past prejudice against Jews by the Greco-Roman world.

Like other early followers of Christ, St. Paul saw him through the lens of Jewish history. For Paul, Christ was, at least, the Jewish Messiah, but his death on the Cross had fulfilled God's promise to the Jews in an unexpected way—by allowing them to put their sins in the past and become reconciled to God through *believing* that their historical suffering had now acquired universal meaning. Paul writes explicitly as a Jew when he explains this to "the Romans."[4] But he also writes *against* those whom he now considers *bad* Jews because they do not accept this new truth about themselves.[5] *Refusing* to believe in the universal significance of their own history was, for Paul, an offense against God that only Jews could commit.

What did the new *offense* of being Jewish mean for the Jews who remained? The fact that there *had been* Jews, Paul thought, was necessary to establish that, although God had created all, his promise to Abraham was not originally extended to everyone. Now that the Jewish Messiah had come, however, everyone had the choice of *becoming* a Jew. The direct implication was that *remaining* a Jew was also a choice, for which Jews in particular would now be held accountable in the eyes of God. For Paul, that there are *still* Jews posed a direct challenge to his argument that after Christ we can all be Jews. Paul's Jewish Question was not about the value and significance of Judaism as such but rather about its temporality now that what had happened to the Jews could be meaningful for everyone.

Paul thus presents the generic form of the Jewish Question throughout Western history: "Why are there still Jews?" The Jewish version of the Jewish Question was originally posed by Hebrew prophets in response to complaints against a God who engages in collective punishment. The prophetic answer would eventually become Jewish messianism, the tradition of Deuteronomy, Jeremiah, and Deutero-Isaiah, which foretells the extermination of many Jews, and the eventual exile of most, so that a few (the remnant) can return to Zion and rule the world in peace according to God's unfolding plan.[6] It is not clear whether the fulfillment of this prophecy would mean that everyone would finally come under Jewish law or that difference between Jew and non-Jew would cease to matter *for the Jews* (who might then finally embrace Christianity as Judaism for everyone).[7] The prophecy that *not all* Jews will be saved *as* Jews is extended and complicated by Paul's message that some *non*-Jews are the *real* Jews—that gentiles can now choose to accept the suffering of the Jews, and their Messiah, as the basis of their own redemption.[8]

Paul's answer to the Jewish Question thus becomes the basis of its best-known version as a complaint, not *by* Jews but rather *about* them. Here, as well, the question takes a temporal form—it asks why there are *still* Jews, but it now imagines a final answer that is in some sense post-Jewish. Paul rejects the message of God's choice of Abraham that Judaism, as such, is *not* for everyone. He then argues that those who are capable of making Abraham's leap of faith can be the *next* Jews, but that *not all* Jews can recognize that God's promise, revealed to the prophets, has already been fulfilled in Christ (Rom. 4). A Judaism that persists despite Christ would henceforth include an element of *unbelief*—a *subtraction* of trust in God's word that leaves prophetic religion with a remainder of mere obedience to God's commandments. Paul explicitly *trusts* the Jewish God to have fulfilled his promise and then proclaims that Jewish prophecy is relevant to the Romans, and the world, in a way that transcends Jewish law. This would be a Judaism that *is* for everyone—except, perhaps, for those Jews who insist on being the only real Jews. It thus becomes possible, or even imperative, for those who claim to be the next Jews to denounce those who still think they are the only Jews.

The irony of Paul's effort to universalize his own Judaism lies in its potential to exclude those Jews who do not get the message. The specific form of universalization proposed by Paul consists of identification with a victimary identity that was *originally* Jewish—so much so that some knowledge of the particularity of Jewish history is required for the identification to occur.[9] But it also calls attention to the continuing history of those who remain Jews and whose persistence can seem increasingly offensive even as their numbers shrink.[10]

Paul's vision of a post-Jewish world was not, as some have charged,[11] a decisive first step toward the Holocaust. As he conceived it, a future world without Jews could eventually result from voluntary assimilation or conversion rather than persecution, ethnic cleansing, or extermination. Paul thus regards Judaism itself as inherently transitional. His Jewish Question concerns *how long* Jews can remain Jews, and in his final account (Rom. 15) he concludes that they will do so until just before the Second Coming, putting them among the last converts to grasp the universal meaning of their own message. His conception of Judeo-Christianity here models, perhaps for the first time, what it would mean for two religions to be *different*, for them both to be still regarded as *religions*, and for one to *supersede* another without immediately abolishing it.

The Holocaust, however, posed an even larger theological problem for Christians than the problem Paul originally addressed. For Christians, to confess the Holocaust was to acknowledge that European Christendom killed (or let die) most of its remaining Jews. To reject such an interpretation of Paul, post-Holocaust Christianity had to disavow the Deuteronomic prophecy that the Jews must first be nearly destroyed in order to be saved. After the Jews *had* been nearly destroyed, Christianity would fully commit itself to saving them in a different sense. The consequence of this commitment was to defer the expectation of a post-Jewish world indefinitely but perhaps not eternally. For postwar Christians, the embrace of Judeo-Christianity meant that whether the Messiah has already come (or not) would be much less important than agreement among Jews and Christians that the messianic moment is not now. On the Jewish side of the hyphen, a parallel convergence took place. Postwar Judaism became (at long last) more like Christianity in finally believing that everything necessary for messianic redemption has already happened, because, after the Holocaust, a surviving remnant of Jews returned to Zion in apparent fulfillment of the Deuteronomic promise.

Today the notion that Human Rights Discourse is still about the Jews takes the form of a taboo against saying so. To criticize Jews explicitly in the context, for example, of U.S. and European support for Israel is now to implicitly identify oneself with the enemies of Human Rights Discourse.[12]

The foregoing discussion suggests that the creation of a twentieth-century culture of human rights after the Holocaust has a strong conceptual similarity to St. Paul's creation of Christianity after the Crucifixion of the man he regarded as the *Jewish* Messiah. In both instances, the response was to give redemptive meaning to the suffering of the Jew by universalizing it and, in both instances, the primary technique of universalization was hyphenation—the redescription of Christianity itself as a Judeo-Christianity that both continues and supersedes the distinctive features of Jewish suffering by allowing everyone to claim them. Assimilation through hyphenation constructs the present moment as a step toward a world without Jews and provides an always new basis for criticizing those who come to see their Judaism, reactively, as what resists supersession.

Human Rights and Judeo-Christianity

We can now list the principal points of similarity between Paul's creation of Judeo-Christianity and the postwar use of Judeo-Christianity as the paradigm of human rights:

- *Universalism.* Paul sees Christianity as a universal form of Jewish identity. All gentiles, whether circumcised or not, can now receive the favor God promised to the Jews by confessing that the death of the Jewish Messiah now has meaning for them. Human Rights Discourse universalizes the position of Jewish victims of the Holocaust. It preaches that everyone can assert the rights that Holocaust victims should have been accorded, but only after confessing that the Jewish Holocaust now has meaning for them.
- *Particularism.* The problem with universalizing Judaism in both cases is that the Jews seem to be the only ones who did not get the message. For Paul it is a problem that there are still Jews who set themselves apart through *lack* of faith in Christ after Christ has universalized their identity as suffering subjects for whom divine compassion was felt. In Human Rights Discourse it is equally problematic that Jews set themselves apart by arguing that their history of persecution, culminating in the Holocaust itself, makes them specially exempt from criticism of their conduct based on universal human rights (and even more problematic that Israeli security

is the *constitutive exception* to observing human rights law, its very reason for being).

- *Transcendence.* For Paul, confessing the link between Christ's Crucifixion and his Resurrection is a leap of faith that recasts Christian belief not simply as a variant of Judaism alongside others but as a transcendence of it. After accepting the Christian *truth*, the sins that one commits will take the form of *denials* of that truth and thus be essentially unlike the sins one could have committed before knowing it. Confessing the Holocaust as a paradigm of *truth* has a similar redemptive significance for those who come to believe that nothing like it should ever happen again. The next such event will then have to be experienced as *another* Holocaust and allowing it to happen as a consequence of Holocaust-*forgetting*, a new sin that could not have been committed before.

Human Rights Discourse thus requires those living outside the hyphen of Judeo-Christianity to acknowledge the universal significance of modern Jewish history. Islam bears a special burden in this regard.[13] Although the Qur'an itself contains extensive, and respectful, readings of the two Abrahamic religions that it claims to supersede, Islam is now expected to censor those supersessionist claims if it wishes to fit into the specifically Judeo-Christian form that secularism takes in Europe and the U.S.[14] Having renounced the Christian forms of anti-Semitism, our tolerant secular culture now challenges Islam *not* to be anti-Semitic and describes as Islam*ism* the face of Islam that refuses the terms of this challenge.

In the demonology of Judeo-Christians, Islamism is now itself subject to forms of hyphenation—Islamo-Fascist, Islamo-Terrorist, and so forth—that place it firmly in the camp of historical enemies of Judaism that no longer deserve to exist. This makes it tempting for some Islamists to declare their opposition to the Judeo-Christian character of our secularism by being provoked into Holocaust denial and equally tempting for too many on the Left to blame the Jews and Israel, specifically, for Islamist attacks on the Judeo-Christian culture that was built around the figure of the Holocaust. In its effort to save the Jews, Judeo-Christianity may thus have placed Jews in greater danger than at any time since the Holocaust itself.

Anti–anti-Semitism is the secular form in which Judaism itself has survived the Holocaust—a double-hyphenated form that presupposes and reproduces its own enemies in order to survive. The Jew-as-survivor turns his own Judaism into a sacralization of the Holocaust—the Jewish equivalent of the postwar Christian "Theology of the Cross."[15] And so anti-Semitism becomes, paradoxically, the form in which Jews can be attacked for practicing the politics of victimhood by those who reject the globally dominant form of Human Rights Discourse.

The Jew as Human: Secularization

The post-Auschwitz supersession of Jewish victimary identity is not the first conception of a democracy based on human rights to present itself as a final answer to the Jewish Question. Twenty-first-century humanitarianism is part of a long line of cultural imperialism that rests "on the power to universalize particularisms linked to a singular historical tradition by causing them to be misrecognized as such."[16] The historical specificity of the Enlightenment was focused on tolerating the Jews (as distinct, perhaps, from atheists or Muslims). Proponents of greater toleration argued that, once their persecution ceased, ghettoized Jews could themselves become enlightened and reenter world history, from which they had withdrawn.[17] The Jewish contribution to this discussion, extending from Spinoza's *Tractatus Theologico-Politicus* to Moses Mendelssohn, an admirer and peer of Lessing and Kant, was to assert a convergence between the divine revelation first given to the Jews and worship of a universal God who ruled through reason that had become directly accessible to an enlightened mankind. The prototype of political emancipation for *all* inhabitants of a secular state would be the secularized "citizen" who had overcome (from either side) the Judeo-Christian divide by identifying faith with reason. "The French Revolution," according to historian Lynn Hunt,

> revealed that human rights have an inner logic. . . . As soon as a highly conceivable group came up for discussion . . . those in the same kind of category but located lower on the conceivability scale . . . would inevitably appear on the agenda. . . . Protestants were the first identity group to come up [in Revolutionary France] . . . In less than two years, Jews . . . got equal rights, in part because the explicit discussion of their rights had made granting equal rights to Jews more imaginable.[18]

Hunt points out that the effect of full political emancipation for French Jews had been the relinquishment of their communal rights (especially in Alsace) to govern themselves as a separate "nation" (pp. 156–59).

In the 1840s the "Left Hegelian" Bruno Bauer argued that universal political emancipation (based on the 1789 Rights of Man) was best understood as a universalization of the position that Jews had occupied in Christian society: all Germans were to have the rights demanded by the German Jew. Because this new definition of citizenship was to be a reversal of the pariah position that Jews had once occupied, Bauer called upon Jews *in particular* to renounce their Judaism once universal emancipation has been achieved. Jews, he thought, had evolved over two millennia as a persecuted identity—what we might now call a cult of victimhood—that had given their emancipation as prototypical victims a special significance.[19] Bauer's post-1789 conception of political emancipation saw an eventual world without Jews as a postreligious world in which Christians gave up their prejudices so that Jews could give up their Judaism without having to convert.[20] He concluded that the liberal commitment to treating *Jewish* rights as a paradigm for *human* rights placed a legitimate duty of secular assimilation on actually existing Jews whose once intractable particularity had brought Christians to universalize the concept of citizenship.[21]

German Jews were not fully emancipated until the founding of the Wilhelmine Empire in 1871. (The unhyphenated political identity of the "German Citizen" was born at the same moment as the final emancipation of the German Jew.) In 1879 the Prussian historian Heinrich von Treitschke attacked Jewish influence in the new German state, and the word "anti-Semitism" was coined by a German nationalist (Wilhelm Marr) to combat the allegedly pernicious role of assimilated (and often converted) Jews in German culture, business, and politics. Anti-Semitism differed from theological anti-Judaism by treating "The Jew" as essentially a racial, rather than religious, identity, which was not changeable through religious conversion or cultural assimilation.[22] Even after one no longer had to be Christian to be German, the Jews were *still* Jews.

It was also in the 1870s that the rabbinically trained Hermann Cohen became the first and only nonbaptized Jew to attain a chair at a major German university, the Professor of Philosophy chair at Marburg.[23] He suggested that Jewish demands had led the way to general emancipation by giving particular content to the civil and political rights that the Rechtstaat now recognized for all German citizens.[24]

Cohen began to write explicitly at the end of his life about what it means to remain a Jew in a world suffused with Kantian rationality. He argued that the Jewish presence, always and everywhere, as *another* religion would make it necessary for the modern nation-states to ground their laws on universal principles that granted respect to religion as such, independent of its truth.[25] Because it was the universal exemplar of a *particular* religion (as distinguished from the *true* religion), Judaism was becoming, implicitly, the "religion of mankind" whose universal message was to connect the ideas of religion and tolerance. Cohen thus argued that Jews, who lived everywhere while seeking no state of their own, would always have a deparochializing effect on the nations (*goyim*) among whom they were dispersed.[26] In presenting secularization as the universal form of Judaism, Cohen proclaimed that "our modern Judaism represents this religion of mankind. And the awareness of this religio-cultural goal prevents us from feeling any possible conflict between our Judaism and our Germanism."[27]

Writing in 1915, Cohen urged American coreligionists to oppose U.S. involvement in the European war, arguing that a German victory in the East would free the great mass of unemancipated Jews from oppression under the tsar and advance the internal reformation of the Jewish religion itself as a vanguard of secular humanism. Progressive Jewish Americans, moreover, had reason to identify with the German-Protestant alliance that had produced *Deutschtum* (what Derrida's English translator calls "Germanity").[28] Cohen thus argued, "The Reform of Judaism was a German Reform, reaching you from Germany and through Germans."[29] What about the rise in anti-Semitism in Germany that seemed to accompany German-Jewish emancipation? Helping nations to overcome their tendency to persecution is, said Cohen, the "world historical idea" of Judaism.[30] Cohen concluded that the true spiritual homeland of *modern* Jewry was "not Israel but Germany" and urged American Jews to recognize that Germany was already more "Jewish" than the U.S. was destined to become. Only Germany, he had argued, could defeat the tsar and liberate the Jews. (France had abandoned this Napoleonic mission, betraying the ideals of its own revolution, by allying with the tsar against Germany.)[31]

The terms of debate changed in 1917, when the tsar was overthrown by a Communist revolution. From this point on it became possible to argue that communism had emancipated Russian Jewry, that the Soviet Union was its new spiritual homeland, and that the Communist *Internationale* had become the universal form of the Jewish messianic mission.[32] The historian Yuri Slezkine describes the choice of *shtetl* Jews between the *three* Promised Lands (the U.S., the USSR, and Israel) as the definitive experience of twentieth-century modernity. It was also, however, a distinctively Jewish choice because of the role that capitalism, communism, and Zionism had played in the modernization of Jewish identity.[33] I would add, however, that capitalism, communism, and even nationalism were often described as Jewish ideas (universalizations of Judaism) and that twentieth-century attacks on each of these ideas could sometimes take the form of anti-Semitism. To this extent the central ideological debates of the twentieth century were also about what the secularization and universalization of Judaism would mean for Jews and for the world. It would thus seem, once again, that the Jews are not merely themselves but are also exemplary, as they had been for St. Paul.

What, however, is the significance of this story for Germany, the "spiritual homeland" of Jewish communism, Jewish capitalism, and Zionism itself? In a sense, the answer is obvious: Hitler and the Holocaust. But Hitler's anti-Semitism—not merely anti-Judaism—was understood by the Germans of his era as a response to an "International Jewry" that had been politicized as the Communist *Internationale* and financialized as international capitalism. Therefore, according to Nazi propaganda, "the Jews are guilty of everything."[34]

In retrospect, the willingness of anyone to entertain such ideas is rightly seen as grotesque and reprehensible: yet nearly two centuries of German-Jewish convergence on the topic of Enlightenment had made it a conceivable reaction to Cohen's view of Wilhelmine Germany as a Judeo-Protestant hybrid to advocate purifying both its Germanic and Jewish elements in the form of separate political monocultures.[35] It thus seemed natural in the 1920s for anti-Hitler German nationalists, such as Ernst Jünger, to argue that the German-Jewish synthesis should be undone,[36] and conceivable for academic critics of Enlightenment thought, including Heidegger and Schmitt, to join the Nazi Party in the 1930s.

Cohen's view of German-Jewish assimilation was rejected on different grounds by Gershom Scholem,[37] an emigrant from Germany to Palestine, who traced the genealogy of assimilationism itself to a Jewish heresy, Sabbatianism, which took hold after the catastrophic expulsion of the Marranos from Spain. Here the supposed messiah, Sabbatai Zevi, outdid the scandal of the crucifixion with an even greater scandal, that of converting to Islam while a prisoner in the Turkish Sultan's court.[38] Sabbatianism had appeal, according to Scholem, because it implied that through *concealment* of one's Jewish identity in the exilic world (*galuth*) one could become *more deeply* Jewish.[39] If assimilation was understood as this kind of hyper-Judaism, then Zionism would actually present the *secular* alternative to it—a recognition that from the standpoint of the nations (*goyim*) Jews can never cease to be Jews, even if they convert, and that they must move to Israel in order to escape their messianic illusions about Germany, especially after its defeat in World War I.[40] The German-Jewish synthesis that survived as Weimar culture[41] would be scapegoated for that defeat by Hitler, who proclaimed that Jews were being their *most* Jewish when they seemed most German.[42]

There is thus a chilling sense in which the "Jewish Question" to which Hitler's "Final Solution" was addressed is the same question that Hermann

Cohen proposed to answer: Are emancipated Jews still Jews?[43] Nazi ideology was based on the assumption that, ultimately, the Jews cannot be converted—that they will always remain Jews, regardless of behavior and professed beliefs, because they regard themselves as *secretly* different. This is, as we saw in chapter 4, the originary form of the racism that believes itself to be antiracism—here the hatred of a racism ascribed to Jews themselves.

What, then, did it mean for Israel to become a state *because of* Hitler? Before Hitler, a Jewish state in Palestine might have been based on the principle of self-determination of settler colonies; a Jewish "homeland" within a Palestine "protectorate" was consistent with the then prevailing practice of creating tribal homelands to buttress British colonial rule.[44] The Holocaust, however, superimposed Hitler's specifically racial conception of Judaism onto the nationalist and tribal models of Zionism as it originally developed within the conceptual framework of late-nineteenth-century imperialism. For post-Holocaust Zionism, the *land* of Israel (Eretz Yisrael) would become a site of racial origin and destination, and the *preservation* of "Israel" would become the object of *religious* commitment.[45] If the Holocaust now functions for assimilated Jews as the Crucifixion did for early Christians, the site of messianic disappointment, the return to Zion functions as the Resurrection: an impossibility becoming real. The pre-Holocaust argument that a Jewish state that was pariah among its neighbors could not survive was replaced by a new argument: that *because* the Jewish state *is* a pariah among its neighbors it *must* survive. The alternative would be another Holocaust or, rather, an "extension of the first one."[46]

Anti–anti-Semitism now meant that Israel would henceforth be conceived neither as a nation like any other nor as a remnant of colonialism. It was, instead, the principal exception to the postcolonial condemnation of racialized states, because an attack against Israel (whether ideological or military) would amount to an attack on the Jews. The result is a discourse of human rights that, like Pauline Christianity, gives what once happened to the Jews a universal significance that the whole world is expected to embrace. Once again the Jewish-Christian difference produces "the Jew" as the figure of a "race" within a universal. The problem with this conception of the role of Jews in universalizing human rights is that once again, as with Pauline Christianity, the Jews do not get it: they still think they are the *only* Jews. This allows Jews to be considered a race that can be accused of racism, and thus hated, by any victim group that considers itself to be the *real* Jews.[47]

The result has been a no-win situation for the Jews that remain. Twentieth-century Jewish cosmopolitanism took two major forms—capitalist and communist—both of which were attacked as being secretly (or really) Jewish. Jews who did not engage in these two forms of globalized aspiration could be said to have chosen particularism and thus attacked or stigmatized for being closed off. And Jews who found themselves persecuted for either universalism or separatism could then be attacked for practicing a politics of victimhood and thus reducing their ancient religion to a form of martyrology in which all Jewish victims become heroes who died *for* Judaism. Yet Jews who reject the politics of victimhood and commit acts of violence will be accused of being perpetrators who are worse than everyone else—"Judeo-Nazis."[48] Among these options, there is no good choice for Jews. Despite (perhaps because of) global anti–anti-Semitism, a resurgence of anti-Semitism has never been a greater danger since the Holocaust itself.

It is thus necessary in the remainder of this chapter to consider the role that Holocaust thinking plays in the political theology of three nations to which it has become central: Germany, Israel, and the United States. We will then consider the transformation of this thinking in the context of the present-day equation between terrorists and enemies of the Jews and, finally, the extent to which the global politics of human rights is modeled on the Christian commitment to the survival of Judaism in its secular, post-Holocaust form.

Germany's Holocaust

If in earlier chapters I toyed with the idea that a Germany, disgraced and humiliated by the revelations of the Holocaust, might have *become* Israel, we can now see that for some pre-Holocaust German Jews it was *already* an Israel—the bicultural Israel that might have been in which Jews had a spiritual homeland without needing sovereignty. This casts light on what I have (following Frank Stern) called postwar German *philosemitism*—Germany's strong identification with its missing Jews as the foundation of what was best in its own (German) culture.[49] I am not speaking here simply of the cultural status Germany's few remaining or returning Jews presently enjoy[50] but, rather, about the centrality of *Yiddishkeit* itself as a source of German pride and a culture that Germany has a special responsibility to preserve now that Hebrew has become the language of modern Israel.

Just as the "rise of modern Israel from the ashes of the Holocaust" is often called "miraculous," so, too, is the postwar European "miracle" in which West Germany can portray itself as a legitimate successor to its missing Jewish culture. Instead of *simply* burying its twelve-year history of genocide and collaboration, Western Europe, and especially West Germany, rebuilt itself on the archeology of a cosmopolitan Jewish civilization that had been destroyed in the two great wars of nationalist excess. If the Judaism celebrated by Hermann Cohen, Jewish rationalism, was supposed to bring about a postnationalist cosmopolitanism in Europe, a "virtually Jewish" postwar Europe could celebrate itself as the resurrection of the dream to which Cohen's generation had given voice. Western Europe's "cities without Jews" would now commemorate and celebrate their Jewish heritage and represent themselves as its cultural continuation.[51] And post-Holocaust scholars of German-speaking culture would come to describe it in terms Cohen had foreseen as the likely consequence of a German-Jewish triumph in World War I.[52]

If postwar Western Europe internalized its missing Jews without speaking directly about the past, it is equally important to understand the alternative form of German-Jewish identification practiced by the German '68ers who, as children of the Nazi generation, repudiated their parents' silence.[53] The German New Left thus saw itself as engaging in the resistance that its parents (the Good Germans) *should* have mounted against the original Nazis.[54] This time, however, the resistance would be against Good Germans themselves—its slogan, "We are all German Jews." The German Jews invoked by this chant were not, however, the patriotic Germans of Hermann Cohen's World War I tract with whom the newly philosemitic Good Germans now identified. The student protesters of 1968, rather, identified with Jews who became the principal object of German persecution while Good Germans looked away. "What was New Leftism then?" asks Paul Berman: "It was—it pictured itself as—Nazism's opposite and nemesis: the enemy of the *real* Nazism, the Nazism that had survived Nazism" (p. 39).

In Berman's telling, everything changed by 1969, when Germany's small radical student movement, evolving toward support of the Red Army Fraction, found an outlet for its desire to resist Nazism by resisting the support of their parents' (ex-Nazi) generation for Zionism.[55] By attacking the ex-Nazi generation's sheepish support of Israel and all things Jewish, those who had claimed to be acting on behalf of *true* Jews (the dead ones) against the good Germans had been transformed, according to Berman, into classic anti-Semites.[56]

One need not agree with Berman's caricature of the German New Left, or with his view of the centrality of the Red Army Faction within it, to see how deeply his argument is bound up in the questions of universalizing and particularizing Jewish identity. Was Germany's postwar embrace of philosemitism nothing other than a continuation of the same conformity and respect for authority that had led Germans to embrace or condone Nazism? Was it, rather, full acknowledgment, at last, that Germanity and Judaism were one after all—that the two cultures were inextricably connected? Was postwar German support for Zionism in Israel the new form that Nazism took—yet another final solution to the Jewish Question? Or was German opposition to Zionism (and especially *German* opposition) the face that Nazism took a full generation after the Holocaust? Surely the underlying question Berman raises is the old one: Can one claim to supersede the Jewish Question without also claiming to be the next Jews?

A further question, closer to the surface, is whether Germany can claim to supersede Nazism without coming to terms with the centrality of the Jewish Question in its own culture. Is the culture of conformity that led Germans to accept Hitler the most likely catapult of German recovery or its greatest obstacle in overcoming its Nazi past? This question is addressed extensively in *Germany's Second Chance* by the political scientist Anne Sa'adah.[57]

Sa'adah describes two distinct strategies of political transition: an "institutional" approach, on the one hand, and a "cultural approach," on the other. The institutional approach says that any transition from a bad regime to a liberal, democratic, human rights–oriented regime must begin with the people one has—those who lived under the old regime and will continue to live under the new one. If this is so, then many, if not most, of these people will have been compromised, perhaps severely, by their lives in the previous regime. To make them loyal to the new order, the architects of transition must thus persuade them that it was the old institutions that were to blame for the way they were then and that they will be better people under new and better institutions. When the institutional approach succeeds, those who were compromised under the old regime will actively support the new institutions because they see them as bulwarks against returning to the old institutions that they now blame for making them what they were (pp. 3–4, 26–46). The institutional approach thus creates what Shklar calls a "liberalism of fear" as a way of turning the page of history.[58] It is the conformists in the old regime who are the real constituency of this approach, which tries to make it easy for them to conform in the new regime as well.[59]

Such moral objections to the institutional approach are the basis for what Sa'adah calls a "cultural" approach.[60] Here those who conformed to or benefited from the old regime must themselves undergo an inner moral change. Such a moral transformation cannot simply be a matter of distinguishing "the way we were then" from "the way we are now," as the institutional approach enables them to do. Instead, it requires postwar Germans to actively rebut the presumption that they retain the attitudes they held under Nazi rule.[61] But artistic and political statements that confront citizens of the new regime with existential questions about the past have substantial costs (p. 56). The most important is cultural: there is no end to the past if the new regime must act as though it is never really over. There is also a political cost: the cultural approach excludes from the new order too many whom it needs, most of whom are merely conformists and will be conformists no matter what the regime happens to be (pp. 24–58, 277–81).

Sa'adah concludes that the approach she calls "institutional" is generally sufficient to bring about what we have been calling cultural change and opposes the cultural approach because it can lead too many citizens to mistrust democratic institutions that produce culture wars (chaps. 3, 6). Her argument here is largely consistent with the New Left analysis of Germany's *successful* transition as one that made the political base of postwar Germany largely overlap with that of Hitler's Third Reich.[62] Sa'adah herself recognizes that the very success of the institutional strategy in the immediate post-Nazi period led directly to the cultural strategy of the generation of '68, in much the way that Berman describes, and hopes that future transitions from dictatorship will use a "hybrid" model that encourages reflection on the past.[63]

But "how does a state recite, much less commemorate, the litany of its misdeeds, making them part of its reason for being?"[64] The foregoing words were written by the cultural theorist James E. Young, who points out that the U.S. does not allow its public spaces to be polluted or obstructed by "countermonuments" to its crimes against American Indians and enslaved Africans.[65] (The only monument to atrocity on the Washington, D.C. Mall is the museum commemorating *Germany's* Holocaust victims.)[66] For the first half-century after World War II, getting over it was precisely what the victors of World War II wanted Germans *not* to be able to do. The Western and Soviet victors in the war both expected their respective Germanys to suffer loss in a form of self-reproach, rather than to sublimate their crimes in the form of cultural monuments and move on.[67] No mainstream German public figure in the forty-five years after the war dared to protest the government's decision not to build monuments to the German military and civilian war dead.[68] The issue finally came to a head when, at the tail end of the cold war, U.S. President Ronald Reagan, over widespread protest, joined West German Chancellor Helmut Kohl in the town of Bitburg to dedicate the first commemorative cemetery for the Nazi war dead.[69]

On October 4, 1990, the Parliament of a reunited Germany held its first ceremonial meeting in the Reichstag building in Berlin where no parliament had met since the 1933 elections that brought the death of the Weimar democracy and the birth of the Third Reich. The speaker of the Parliament, Rita Süssmuth, "thanked all those who had made German unity possible and paid her respects to the only surviving member from the last free session at the Reichstag, who stood up to acknowledge the applause. In 1933 he had stood up to be counted among the minority who opposed Hitler's takeover after a fire had partially damaged the buildings."[70] The speaker then went on to say, "We remember all the victims of the Nazis and we remember the victims of the SED regime [East Germany's ousted Communists], the victims of the Berlin Wall and barbed wire."[71] These victims, here equated with one another in national memory, are then conjoined through common sacrifice in the project of redeeming a new Germany no longer divided by the Berlin Wall, no longer separated as East and West, no longer scarred by the past.

The forty-five years of political partition and communist oppression are figuratively represented in the reunification ceremony as Germany's penance, or purgatory, for Nazism. At the end of this history reunified Germany becomes, if not the greatest victim of Nazism, certainly the most long-suffering. It finally recognizes itself in the mirror of Robert Jackson's Nuremberg Opening Statement, which argued that a "ring of evil men" had perpetrated a "Common Plan or Conspiracy" of which Germany itself had *also* been a victim.[72] This criminal conspiracy, Jackson argued, had left Germany divided and in ruins. It meant, according to Jackson, that "the German, no less than the non-German world, has accounts to settle with these defendants." The reunification ceremony marked the end of Germany's long period of penance and its achievement of full status among the victims of World War II that had been originally promised by Jackson at Nuremberg.

German Chancellor Kohl concluded the 1990 Reichstag celebration by reassuring the world that a reunited Germany was no longer a danger: "We must never forget, suppress or play down," he said, "the crimes committed in this century by Germans. . . . Above all we owe this to the victims of the Holocaust, the unparalleled genocide of European Jews."[73] German recognition of the unique victimary position of Jews was the implicit condition of allowing them in 1990 to include themselves among the Nazi victims, and finally to mourn Nazism's destruction of Germany along with the loss of its Jewish culture.

There was, however, a troubling aspect to Kohl's identification of Germany's victimized Jews with its own postwar victimhood at the hands of the communist (but not the Western) victors in World War II. Was this act of identification a reburial *without* mourning of Germany's own victims? Could Germany's newfound entitlement to feel self-pity for the war also be a way to evade self-reproach? Following the Reichstag ceremony, Chancellor Kohl, an academically trained historian, concluded that the newly reunified Germany could commemorate *all* the victims of Nazism, Jewish and German alike. He thus commissioned a monument to the Holocaust at the site of its former division and disgrace, Berlin. That commission, eventually won by the Jewish-American architect Peter Eisenman, occasioned a new discussion of the universality and particularity of the Jewish Question in defining German identity.

The journalist Jane Kramer's account of the construction of the Berlin Holocaust Memorial describes a process through which Germany admits itself to the global family of Holocaust victims and thus to the global politics of victimhood that I have called secular Judeo-Christianity.[74] Does Germany now see itself in the mirror of the monument as archeologist and mourner rather than as beneficiary and murderer? Is the truth commemorated at Berlin Holocaust Memorial that *killing* all those Jews was bad *for* Germany (its culture, science, economy) and no longer just a bad thing Germany *did*? If so, what does Germany's symbolic identification with its missing Jewish victims say about the real Jews whom Germans demonized and killed? The underlying question raised by Kramer's analysis is whether Germany should still consider itself guilty and, if so, whether the guilty can appropriately mourn their *own* losses rather than, for example, repenting and atoning.

We have thus far traced the metamorphoses of the German-Jewish/Jewish-German relationship, to the point where Germany comes to see *itself* as the burial monument of its missing Jews. Was the German Jew the true German of the twentieth century? Was he the true Jew? Many argue that the historical fate of Jews who believed they were the most authentic Germans made it necessary to pass the torch of Jewish secular redemption from Germany to an Israel that has learned the lesson of the Holocaust and become a state where Jews are always welcome. Others argue that an independent Palestine should have embodied the bicultural Enlightenment ethic that Jews once found in Germany and that Israel has disgraced in the name of Jewish sovereignty and security.[75] Has the Jewish Diaspora ethic of the *Haskalah* found its true home in North America, an*other* Promised Land in which Jews live freely as a permanent minority—the historical alternative to Israel? If so, why do most North American Jews (and almost all Israelis who choose to live in North America) still see Israel as the privileged interpreter of the Holocaust's meaning? Do they regard it as a nation that must exist for the sake of those Jews whom they do not wish to be? Is this why atrocities committed by *those* Jews never seem to surprise or disappoint Israel's supporters or to significantly diminish their support?[76]

In the following section we take up the relation of Israel's Holocaust to the experience of German and American Jewry and ask in the context of the Jewish Question how Israel is able to regard its security as a matter of universal significance because of its willingness to fight for those relatively few Israelis who still think they are the *only* Jews and whose right to exist as such must *Never again* be threatened.

Israel's Holocaust

In 1987 the Israeli-born military hero Itzhak Rabin, then serving as the defense minister, asked his fellow Israeli general, Yossi Peled, a Polish-born Holocaust survivor, "to go with him on an official visit to West Germany"; they visited Dachau, where Rabin made a speech. "I wish to tell you here that we won," Rabin said. As he spoke, General Peled turned his head and cried.

Visiting Auschwitz in 1992, General Ehud Barak (then Israeli chief of staff and later the assassinated Rabin's successor as prime minister) likewise equated his arrival with that of a victorious Jewish army. As Barak acknowledged, however, "We, the soldiers of the Israeli Defense Forces, have come to this place fifty year later, perhaps fifty years too late."[77]

Despite such expressions of continuity between resistance to the Holocaust and fighting *for* Israel, official Zionism's relation to the Holocaust was ambivalent while it was occurring and immediately afterward. Many in the Jewish settlement in British-administered Palestine (the *Yishuv*)[78] attributed the fate of Jews in Europe to their refusal to immigrate while there was still time.[79] Its leaders did little more than the rest of the world to rescue Jewish victims while the Holocaust was taking place.[80] According to the Israeli historian Idith Zertal, the Jewish Agency in Palestine "never deviated from the sphere of realism" in its limited efforts to make contact with Jews *left behind* in Europe.[81]

Before the Holocaust, many in the Jewish Agency—David Ben-Gurion chief among them—had presented Zionism as the strongest possible critique of the Jewish *religion* that was consistent with the continuation of Jewish *identity*.[82] They argued that Judaism had become, in its exilic, liturgical form, a cult of persecution and victimhood that secular Zio*nism* would bring to an end.[83] This openly postreligious form of Judaism presented Europe's Jewish Question as a problem of diaspora, where Judaism is merely a religion and not a nationality. In Israel, many Zionist believed, emancipated Jews would be truly free to leave their archaic religion behind—something no longer possible for their soon-to-be de-emancipated brethren in Germany. Before it became the land of "Never again," Israel was expected to become the land of "I Told You So."

As the catastrophe of European Jewry became apparent, the Zionist argument changed, but only as a matter of degree. By 1943 Ben-Gurion would call for the creation of "the Jewish state . . . [as] an atonement, however partial and belated, for the annihilation of the Jewish people," thereby endowing "the death of millions with meaning" (p. 32). But his 1948 proclamation of that state "dismissed the history of two millennia of Jewish life outside of the Land of Israel."[84] The Zionist "pioneers" initially responded to the Holocaust survivors who eventually arrived as a "wrecked people" with a "Diaspora mentality."[85]

Yet a few years later, when Ben-Gurion wished to mobilize world support for Israel against the Arabs, he defined the "murdered millions . . . post factum (and unverifiably) as potential Zionists, retroactive future citizens of a State of Israel that did not exist at the time of their death" (p. 61). By the end of its first decade, Israel would find ways to commemorate the Holocaust as "an era of heroism, of triumph over past passivity . . . that *made possible the continuation of the Jewish people even in the inferno . . . and thereby helped the creation of the State of Israel*" (pp. 213–14).

Ben-Gurion's was not the only voice of Zionism, and the link he eventually forged between Israel and the Holocaust was not inevitable.[86] The *Yishuv* itself had been sharply divided on the question of whether independence from Britain should take the form of an explicitly Jewish state until "awareness of the scope of Holocaust" led them to "adopt an explicitly statist approach" in 1942.[87] Today the Israeli theologian David Hartman argues against the messianic view of Israeli statehood.[88] But Israel is nevertheless supported by Jews, such as Hartman, for the sake of *saving* (at least rescuing) the Jews they do not wish to be. And so we return to the Jewish Question once again, in the form of what the Israeli historian Idith Zertal calls "wholesale and out-of context use of the Holocaust" to render "Israel . . . itself immune to criticism."[89]

The eventual consensus of Israel's founders was that it owed its independence to the Holocaust and, more directly, to the newfound support of Allied governments that had failed to prevent the Holocaust from occurring.[90] But while newly independent Israel was "ingathering" diaspora Jews as settlers, the rest of the world was both decolonizing and dispersing, through immigration, to states like Britain and France that were once their colonial masters. Israel could thus appear as either the last gasp of settler colonialism in the Middle East—or as something else, a homeland to the Seventh Million, those who had survived the Holocaust.

Transforming support for Israel into the lesson of the Holocaust became Prime Minister David Ben-Gurion's "last great national undertaking" (p. 90). Idith Zertal's *Israel's Holocaust* provides a masterful account of his accomplishment and its costs. Her story begins with his equation of the heroism of Holocaust *resisters* in the Warsaw Ghetto with that of fighters for the Jewish state;[91] the second building block in the Zionist self-transformation was the "Exodus 1947" affair, which equated the fate of Holocaust *refugees* with the establishment of Israel itself.[92]

A third building block in Zertal's narrative was the identification of Israel as the voice of the Holocaust *dead* through the Eichmann trial. The prosecution took place under the Nazis and Nazi Collaborators (Punishment) Law that had been enacted in the early 1950s, so that Holocaust survivors could bring charges against fellow refugees, "concentration camp block supervisors" and the like, who would now become subject to prosecution merely because, as Jews, they had also ended up in Israel (p. 64). "During the 1950s and early 1960s," says Zertal, "some forty trials were held under that law" (p. 66).[93] The forward-looking significance of these trials was that Israel was not merely a place of refuge and amnesty for all Jews who suffered in the Holocaust, regardless of how they had managed to survive. It was also (in some cases) a living accuser of those who were complicit in the extermination of Jews who did *not* survive (pp. 64–65). The State of Israel had thus potentially identified itself as a legitimate plaintiff on behalf of the six million Jewish dead.

It would still be a giant leap, however, for Israel to prosecute Eichmann in the name of the Seventh Million. Ben-Gurion's decision to take this leap arose from his disastrous alliance with the British and French in their 1956 takeover of the Suez Canal—the last gasp of a dying colonialism that was immediately repudiated by the U.S. president Dwight Eisenhower. In an attempt to reverse this setback in Israel's vital relationship with the U.S., Ben-Gurion authorized the abduction of Eichmann, whose whereabouts in Argentina was already known to Israel's intelligence force, the Mossad. Eichmann was to be the first and only true Nazi to be tried under the Nazis and Nazi Collaborators (Punishment) Law. The aim of convicting him was not, however, to establish Israel as the venue of choice for all future prosecutions of German war criminals.[94] Rather, according to Zertal,

> Ben-Gurion's nationalism needed now to forge new memories according to its own specific profile and goals. . . . The total helplessness of European Jewry

in World War II could now directly serve as the "counter-metaphor" to the discourse of Israeli omnipotence and also as its ultimate justification. (p. 95)

But forging new memories of the Holocaust itself was not Ben-Gurion's only goal. "Right from the outset," according to Zertal, he "added another dimension to the planned trial. Ben-Gurion announced that it would not merely educate the world about what happened to the Jews of Europe but would also 'expose the facts regarding Israel's Arab neighbors'" (p. 97).[95] His explicit goal was thus to "present the local enemy as the reincarnation of the Nazis." By equating Arabs with Nazis, he began "the process of . . . explicit mobilization of the Holocaust in the service of Israeli politics and state policy, especially in the context of the Israeli-Arab conflict" (pp. 98–99).[96]

The Nazi-Arab equation, which was heavily stressed throughout the Eichmann trial, was, in Zertal's view, almost entirely conceived, planned, and implemented by Ben-Gurion himself.[97] She sums up Ben-Gurion's self-conscious transformation of Zionist political consciousness as follows: "The Holocaust, along with its victims, was not to be remembered for itself but rather as a metaphor, a terrible, sublime lesson to . . . the world that Jewish blood would never be abandoned or defenseless again" (p. 96). This "sublime lesson" would be the basis for "an Israeli nuclear bomb" (p. 99), the civic religion instilled in all succeeding generations of Israeli youth.[98] The Eichmann trial thus became, in retrospect, the moment in Israeli history when it fully redefined the dead victims of the Holocaust,[99] not as people who missed the point of Zionism but rather as martyrs in the struggle for an Israel that was yet to be created (and where many Holocaust survivors would not choose to go). From this point forward, Israeli monuments would show Holocaust victims and Israeli soldiers joining hands: the trial had made Israel a nation of surviving victims who were still unreconciled victims.[100]

Thus the consequence of the Eichmann trial was that Israel no longer wanted to be a nation "like any other" and claimed, instead, to be based on an exceptional form of victimhood. The secular religion of "Israeliness" so created would reproduce the sense of singular oppression, which many earlier Zionists had deplored in European Judaism, as an identity that could be shared by an emerging majority of immigrants from the Middle East.[101] The transformation in Israeli political culture that followed the Eichmann trial would lead directly to the sense of providence that accompanied Israel's territorial expansion following the 1967 war (pp. 164–208). Israel's "overwhelming victory," resulting in the occupation of all of biblical Judea and Samaria, "was frequently presented in terms of divine intervention in Jew-

ish history, the antithesis of the Holocaust and continuation of the "miraculous" victory in the 1948 war."[102]

The apparent military and political triumph of Ben-Gurion's conception
of "Israeliness," however, was also the beginning of the end of its brief hegemony within Israel itself. The lesson of the Eichmann trial, "Never again,"
was to become the manifesto of Meir Kahane's Jewish Defense League and
then a focal point of post-Occupation Israeli political identity as new immigrants, first from the U.S. and later from the USSR, created permanent Jewish settlements in the Occupied Territories.[103] Substantial numbers of these
settlers linked the onset of the messianic age "with the miraculous incorporation of Greater Israel (i.e., the territories occupied in the 1967 war) into
the Israeli state," thereby transforming "Jewish Israeli society into a holy
moral community":[104] they created a neo-Orthodox counterculture that
fused the biblical and Holocaust-based sense of providence. This development led to a growing division within Israel between religious and nonreligious Jews and also between *Ashkenazim* and *Mizrahim* (the latter being
Jews from the Middle East and North Africa) over the rationale for holding onto the territory occupied in the 1967 war that "shattered both the
hegemony of secular Zionism and *Ashkenazi* ethnic dominance" of Ben-
Gurion's Labor Party.[105]

To many *Mizrahim*, for whom neither the Holocaust nor the Jewish
Enlightenment was a formative experience, the irredentism of a God-given
right of Jews to occupy *all* of the Promised Land was no less plausible than
the absolute right of European Jews, as Holocaust escapees, to security
against the repetition of that disaster. Did Israel's control of these lands
have a different justification than its occupation of the territory that would
have been Palestine following the 1948 war? And was it also different from
the justification for creating a Jewish State in *part* of colonial Palestine
rather than giving the *entire* British Mandate area independence with
majority rule?[106] A large and stable minority of Israelis see Israel's (re)estab-
lishment of its biblical borders through its own military strength as having
greater legitimacy than the territorial compromise brokered by the UN in
1948.

In opposition to the providential view of Israel's 1967 war,[107] the "Never
again" of Human Rights Discourse (protection of bare life) became the *lib-
eral/secular* position in Israeli politics—the cultural alternative within
Israel to Kahane's interpretation of that slogan as implying "They [the
Arabs] Must Go."[108] Israel's government quickly outlawed Kahane's Kach
movement. But the notion that Israel, as a state, is *not* Kahanist, and seeks
only the military security of post-Holocaust Jewry, presents Israel's *security*

itself as having a redemptive (messianic?) significance for the post-Holocaust *world*. A Holocaust-based commitment to Israel's security thus presents itself as the principal reason for Western powers to regard Israel as the exception, within Human Rights Discourse, to the norms of human rights and to look away when it bombs civilians in Hebron, Jenin, and Lebanon and detains large numbers of Palestinians without trial. The idea that Zionism is *not* Kahanist but merely interested in providing security for Jews is the foundational paradox of Human Rights Discourse itself—the reason that Israel *must*, ultimately, be supported, even by its humanitarian critics, no matter what it does.

To its secular defenders, Israel thus represents a cultural commitment in world politics to defend the human rights of a victimized people who will always, henceforward, be quintessentially Jewish. Their default position (and the more or less explicit position of many U.S. Jews) is that Israel always needs more time to do apartheid (separate development) right so as to be spared the moral damage of Kahanism (ethnic cleansing). Were Israel's friends to "abandon" it merely because of something it *did*, so the argument goes, it would be *forced* to become Kahanist in order to prevent another Holocaust.[109] Once again, we see secular Jews of Israel claiming support of the "world community" as the only people who can block the success of a Kahanism or Sharonism or both, the continuing possibilities of which they are also committed to defending as essential to the survival of Israel as a Jewish state.[110] (This is a variant of the claim, already mentioned, that many Jews defend Israel as a necessary homeland for *other* Jews whom they do not wish to be.)

The moral landscape in which Israel had operated since the Eichmann trial seemed to change, however, at the end of the cold war in 1989. Until then Israel had claimed to be fighting for the "survival" of the Jewish people because "Arabs = Nazis";[111] the collapse of Eastern bloc support for Palestinian armed struggle produced a brief moment in which Israelis, like Rabin, would say "we won" and embrace the Oslo Accords as the final undertaking of the Palestinian Liberation Organization (PLO) to do everything that Israel thought necessary to prove they were *not* Nazis. That the Palestinian Authority was not fascistic *enough* to suppress a second Intifada brought an end to the Israeli illusion of peace through final victory. The result has been a qualification, and sharpening, of the hypothesis that "Arabs = Nazis."

Today a pro-Zionist version of Human Rights Discourse makes a distinction *among* Arabs. It no longer says that "*all* Arabs = Nazis"; rather, it says that "not all Arabs = Nazis." Those who *are* Nazis, however (the "*not-all*"), are even *more* Arab than the Arabs themselves—they are Islam*ists*, not necessarily Arab, who hate *all* Jews and not merely Israelis. In the post–cold war version of Holocaust-based Human Rights Discourse, Islamism has been described as the *next* Nazism and, sometimes, as the prototypical form of totalitarian thinking as such.[112] Here we are not here dealing with an ordinary politics of victimhood but with its virtualization in the form of a globalized identity politics. To engage in this identity politics is to act out a fantasy of potential victimhood that always seems to be *about* the Jews and also potentially *against* the Jews.

The Holocaust has thus become increasingly, not decreasingly, important in global politics as the twentieth century recedes into the past—the final victory declared by Rabin at Dachau and Barak at Auschwitz was premature. Today the definition of the Holocaust as prime evil seems to put every transnational group identity that claims victimhood into conflict with Jews who seem to stand for privileged access to such claims.[113]

In the world today there is thus a terrible repoliticization of the Jewish Question in which Jews and other groups implicitly charge one another with stealing their own identities. As Paul Berman suggests, there is a dark side to empathetic identification with the victimhood of others: the accusation that they are *not* what they pretend to be because we *are* what they pretend to be.[114] At the level of moral psychology, Berman writes, the struggle between Israelis and Palestinians (and some of the tensions in the U.S. between Jews and blacks) concerns who the real "Jews" are in a universal (ethical) sense and who are the usurpers of the Jewish claim to stand for all victims everywhere.

We have thus reached a moment in which everyone who claims political high ground is also claiming to be either the authentic claimants to the grievances traditionally raised by Jews or the rescuers of those legitimate claimants. This is why, among all the states that have bad practices, Israel is singled out as the one state that *should not* have them.[115]

Because the Holocaust is the primal murder that founds contemporary Human Rights Discourse, the essence of that discourse is to prohibit *another* Holocaust by creating a Holocaust taboo. Israel has claimed, as we have seen, a special vulnerability to violations of this taboo and thus argues that whatever it takes to defend *itself* constitutes a legitimate *exception* to the universality of Human Rights Discourse, which is based on the idea that the Jews must not be exterminated again.[116] From this perspective the 1948 Genocide Convention, which aims to prevent another Holocaust, implicitly requires that any subsequent genocide must be *compared* to the Holocaust and that the "world community" must consider whether recognizing the occurrence of *another* Holocaust strengthens or weakens its commitment to protect the Jews. (Would finding variants on the Jewish "case" detract from the uniqueness of the Holocaust or reaffirm its broader meaning?)[117]

I have already suggested that the metaphorical identification of Israel's security with a Holocaust taboo perversely gives rise to the thought it prohibits—a new anti-Semitism that singles out Western protection of the Jews as the prime cause of a wide variety of world problems. This is not, moreover, the only anti-Semitic use of Israel's equation of itself with the Holocaust metaphor. Just as it is possible to criticize Israel for wrapping itself in the politics of victimhood, and claiming it is uniquely entitled to do so, it is also possible to criticize the politics of victimhood for taking the protection of Jews as its foundational example. In this respect Israel now bears the brunt of arguments traditionally made against diasporic Judaism by critics such as Nietzsche, who felt contempt for victimary moralities of *ressentiment*. And so all too many protest movements in the West, and many *against* the West, end up being against the Jews or Israel or both because they seem to represent the moral pathology of victimhood in an extreme form.

It would be easy to say that we should ignore metaphors, abjure anti-Semitism, and treat Jews as a people like any other. We cannot do this, however, without first recognizing the role that anti-Semitism and its denial play in the politics of Israel/Palestine—and the role that the politics of Israel/Palestine have come to play in Jewish identity throughout the world. The terrorist attack on 9/11, for example, succeeded in making U.S. support for Israel—and not global terrorism—the foreground political issue in almost every country *but* the U.S. and Israel. It thus becomes increasingly possible to blame pro-Israeli American Jews for claiming a monopoly on victimhood in a way that makes the fear of anti-Semitism itself increasingly plausible.

America's Holocaust

The idea of Israel has always been part of American political thought. Long before Palestine became present-day Israel, an earlier Israel had been established in the New World by Puritan settlers who regarded themselves as God's Holy People, displacing the Canaanites who inhabited their Promised Land.[118]

We Americans the peculiar, chosen people—the Israel of our time; we bear the ark of the liberties of the world . . . and, besides our first birth-right—embracing one continent of the earth—God has given to us, for a future inheritance the broad domains of the political pagans, that shall yet come and lie down under our ark. . . . We are the pioneers of the world; the advance-guard sent on through the wilderness of untried things, to bread a path in the New World that is ours. . . . Long enough have we . . . doubted whether, indeed, the political Messiah had come. But he has come in *us*, if we would but give utterance to his prompting. And let us always remember that with our-selves, almost for the first time in the history of the earth, national selfishness is unbounded philanthropy; for we can not do a good to America, but we give alms to the world.[119]

The idea of America-as-Israel (a "light unto the nations") made it possi-ble for diasporic Jews elsewhere to conceive of immigration to America as the *end* of their diaspora rather than a continuation of it. America, like bib-lical Canaan, was not the permanent homeland of its native inhabitants but an empty space (virtually a wilderness) in which freedom-loving people everywhere (else) could *make* their home. By 1903 Solomon Schecter, con-sidered the founder of Conservative Judaism (which adapted "orthodoxy" to American conditions), could proclaim to the newly created Jewish Theo-logical Seminary: "The history of the United States does not begin with the Red Indian. . . . This country is, as everybody knows, a creation of the Bible, particularly the Old Testament."[120]

Schecter's point was that, if all who accepted America's promise were in this sense "Israelite," there need be no contradiction between remaining a Jew and becoming fully American. America, like Pauline Christianity, represents an "Israel" that is open to all—a providential site in which the grandchildren of immigrant Americans become "one blood" because of intermarriage based on a shared belief in freedom.[121] Based on such reason-ing, the nineteenth- and twentieth-century narratives of *Jewish* immi-gration to America could be read backward as normative stories of Americanism itself: in such stories there is always a moment of secular con-version—and also an anticipated conversion to secularism itself (which Schecter tried to stave off by relaxing many of the observances that made assimilation difficult for practicing Jews).[122] His invocation of the originally Jewish idea behind America is that the *true* Americans are not those who happened to have been there first but those who were called (chosen) by its promise of freedom.

Such arguments contributed to the twentieth-century reinterpretation of *both* American settlers and biblical Jews as refugees from religious perse-cution rather than seekers of a theocratic monoculture. By 1947 (just after the Holocaust), the U.S. Supreme Court could describe an American conception of religious freedom that explicitly transcended the distinction between Christian and Jew and for the first time forbade state governments from giving legal effect to the predominance of Christianity as such. In the words of Justice Black,

> The early settlers of this country came here from Europe to escape the bondage of laws which compelled them to support and attend government-favored churches. The centuries immediately before and contemporaneous with the colonization of America had been filled with turmoil, civil strife, and persecutions. . . . With the power of government supporting them, at various times and places, Catholics had persecuted Protestants, Protestants had persecuted Catholics, Protestant sects had persecuted other Protestant sects . . . and all of these had from time to time persecuted Jews. In efforts to force loyalty to whatever religious group happened to be in league with the government . . . men and women had been fined, cast in jail, cruelly tortured, and killed.[123]

Black's invocation of on America based on freedom from religious persecution makes its creation only accidentally similar to other colonizations that merely seized land. Written on the eve of Israel's creation, he says that the U.S. is another Israel—or would have been had its early settlers been Jews rather than Puritans. Black here redescribes the U.S. as a place of refuge for *all* who first conceive of themselves to *be* Americans before becoming so—just as modern Israel represents itself as an ingathering of all who are already Israelis because they have never "forgotten" Jerusalem after two millennia of exile. The predestined and transformative role that immigration (*aliyah*) plays in both America and Israel allows both to describe themselves as ethnic "melting pots."[124]

As I suggested in chapter 4, the American equation of racial purity, not with biological inheritance but rather with an inner love of freedom, makes it easy to take special umbrage at the charge of racism—for example, the charge that Americanism (or U.S. identification with Israel) is a form of racism. This sensitivity does not mean that we believe we are immune to criticism. Americans find it perfectly intelligible that outsiders criticize us for acting as if we are the *only* Americans, while also criticizing us for not acting like *true* Americans. Americans do not think this is unfair but, rather, that it is the price of being *special*. We are thus puzzled (as are Israelis) by the charge of fundamental hypocrisy that underlies persisting objections to our exceptional role in the world.[125] Are Americans being accused of wanting every other nation to become America—and thus something more than it already is? For America to accomplish this universalizing mission, there needed to have been Jews who *became* Americans, no longer regarding themselves as the only Jews—an argument that resonates with St. Paul's own answer to the Jewish Question and also with Hermann Cohen's argument about the assimilated, Judeo-German character of global *kultur*. In the U.S., as the argument goes, the global mass culture that is instantly identified as "American" is largely based on the Jewish immigrant experience of becoming American.[126] And once the unmarked character of Jewish assimilation had become the face of Americanism to the postwar world, America's anti–anti-Semitism, partly a response to the Holocaust, made it ignominious to suggest that Jewish assimilation had subverted, or even changed, earlier American values, as the Nazis had said about German values.[127] Post–World War II "American*ism*" has thus been far more immune to the charge of being *ersatz* than Wilhelmine "German*ity*" was. The most obvious reason is that America won its world war; another is that a political culture built around the contrast between *Jewish* experience in the New World and the Old had contributed to mass mobilization for the war effort as well as to its moral legitimacy as Nazi crimes against the Jews of Europe became a reason to fight. In the cultural narrative produced by their children, *shtetl* Jews resisted assimilation before *arriving* in America so that the eventual fusion of Judaism and Americanism would serve to deparochialize the nations and make *every* freedom-loving person a lover of America as well. The providential result was that America became capable, both morally and materially, of freeing the Old World from the worst evil known to human history.

During the second half of the twentieth century globalized Americans looked back on the years between 1920 and 1950 as a second American Renaissance based on a newly hyphenated Judeo-Christian culture.[128] Postwar Jewish Americans no longer had to choose between passing as Christians and demanding accommodation.[129] And, for many Jewish intellectuals, the Holocaust was to become the basis of a new secular discourse of human rights in which what happened to Jews made solidarity with victims everywhere a sufficient secular substitute for Judaism as a religion.[130] Jewish American assimilation after the 1960s took the form of a Holocaust-based politics of victimhood that was paradigmatic of a shift toward identity politics in America at large. The end point of this reasoning, however, makes the acceptance (or not) of any victimary claim as, in the final analysis, a question of *Jewish* survival—and thus a contemporary version of the age-old Jewish Question. America's post–cold war vulnerability to terrorist attack is thus linked by supporters and opponents alike to its moral commitment to Israel as well as to growing ideological similarities between the U.S. and Israel.

Mine is emphatically *not* an argument that U.S. foreign policy is *influenced* (perhaps excessively) by Jewish American intellectuals; instead, it is an argument concerning the internal convergence of thought about what it means to be a Jew in America and what it means to be American in the world. Thus my argument is directed at the *Israeliness* of the way the U.S. expresses itself on matters of human rights. Through Human Rights Discourse, I contend, the U.S. has *appropriated* Jewish American victimary identity to describe its *own* global hegemony—that we have *always* been an Israel is now taken to explain why the U.S. is hated by anti-Semites throughout the world.[131]

The late-twentieth-century appropriation of a putatively "Jewish" identity by the U.S. could not have occurred without the help of many U.S. Jews. For assimilated American Jews after the Holocaust, the immediate question was, quite simply, whether "it *could* happen here."[132] If not, it might no longer be necessary to remain Jewish. If so, those Jews who were most assimilated would be most vulnerable to an American Hitler. We here encounter the Jewish Question once again. But in the first twenty years after the Holocaust, *it* was largely unmentioned (if not unmentionable) by a generation of American Jewish leaders who had not known, and perhaps would not have believed, the full extent of the catastrophe in Europe while it was occurring.[133] Rabbi Arthur Hertzberg observes that teaching the Holocaust in Jewish religious schools during this period was virtually taboo—the Holocaust was not yet the "usable past for the American Jewish community" that it would become.[134] In hindsight, he suggests, there may have been embarrassment on the part of Jews safely in America at having done too little to help European to immigrate while there was still time.[135] Although there may also have been a vicarious sense of shame that more of the victims had not died as heroes, there was certainly no *pride* in the extent of Jewish suffering, as such. In the secular Judaism of my childhood (the 1950s), the questions of whether a Holocaust could happen in America, whether anyone would help us, and whether *we* would have resisted far eclipsed any spiritual significance that the Jewish religion may still have had.[136]

The historical puzzle is the two-decade *latency* period between the revelation of the Holocaust and the development of a strong political ideology based upon it.[137] This latency period was not only the result of indifference, combined, perhaps, with the fear occasioned by postwar McCarthyism, which targeted many Jews as potentially disloyal leftists,[138] thus heightening Jewish fears that "*it* could happen here." There was also a strong affirmative sense among Jewish Americans that their own experience in the New Promised Land was something novel and valuable in world history.[139] The prominent role of American Jews in the New Deal, the war effort, and the popular culture that celebrated both had made it "unthinkable for most American Jews" to proclaim "the primacy of Jewish over American loyalty."[140] It took some time for the argument that "Hitler knows you're a Jew" to become a defining element of American Jewish identity politics—indeed, the principal reason for *still* being Jewish.[141]

The main catalyst for developing a Holocaust-based Jewish identity in America, as in Israel, was the trial of Adolf Eichmann, discussed earlier in this chapter in relation to Israel. The trial enabled American Jews, as Ben-Gurion intended, to identify themselves—not through their *rejection* of Israel as a place to emigrate but, rather, by regarding *both* Israel and America as witnesses to (and havens from) the destruction of European Jewry. Commemorating and mourning a European Jewry that most American and Israeli Jews did not actually remember would thus become a common basis of secular Jewish identity in both countries following the Eichmann trial. This substitution of commemoration for memory has allowed the Holocaust to become more, not less, important to American and Israeli Jews, even as it becomes more distant in time.[142]

Along with a growing identification of Jewish Americans with Israelis beginning in the 1960s came an increased use of the Holocaust analogy to define political identity in America, whether one is Jewish or not. The historian Peter Novick argues that the coincidence between the Eichmann trial in Jerusalem and a rising civil rights movement in the U.S. transformed the New Deal politics of "Americans All" into a politics of victimary identity that dominated the 1970s and beyond.

Novick's history of the Jewish side of the story allows me to supplement my earlier account of the U.S. civil rights movement: in chapter 3 I showed how Martin Luther King Jr. reframed the Exodus story (originally Jewish) as though the demand of Moses had been to "let my people stay." He thereby claimed that black Americans were the kinds of victims that biblical Jews *would have been* had they remained in Egypt after their emancipation and taken on the task of liberating the Egyptians as well. We can now see that this blurred what had seemed a clear analogy between blacks and Jews as diasporic peoples in America: King was not only the Moses who liberates his *own* people but an alternative Moses—*also* an Egyptian!—whose message was addressed to Egypt as a whole. Under King's leadership, blacks were claiming to be the *other* Jews and, in the context of U.S. history, perhaps the *real* Jews because the message of their emancipation might be even *more* universal. Precisely at this moment, however, Israel's trial of Eichmann showed what it meant for *Jews* to be the real Jews—both in Germany and Israel. Thereafter Jewish Americans began to accuse blacks of "Holocaust envy,"[143] and blacks responded by accusing Jews (yet again) of thinking that they are the *only* Jews at a time when Israel itself is practicing apartheid.[144] And so a new era in U.S. identity politics was born out of the black-Jewish debate over who holds rights to the Holocaust analogy within the politics of victimhood.[145]

The result, according to Novick, is "a change in the attitude toward victimhood from a status all but universally shunned and despised to one often eagerly embraced. . . . The greatest victory is to wring an acknowledgment of superior victimization from another contender" (pp. 8–9). Novick does not argue that this cultural change is "the cause of American Jewry's focusing on the Holocaust in recent decades" (p. 8), nor does he assert, as some have, that the Jewish American Holocaust industry explains U.S. support for Israel (pp. 166–67).[146] His more subtle claim is that, as Israeli conduct and policy became more controversial, the Holocaust was a point of unity for American Jews in much the way that Avraham Burg would later describe it as a unifying identity for Israeli *Ashkenazim* and *Mizrahim*.[147]

Novick's book explains how Jews, such as Elie Wiesel, who believed that God died (or turned his face) at Auschwitz, could still portray the Holocaust as a sacred event, "equal to the revelation at Sinai" (p. 201).[148] As a new cornerstone of both secular and religious Judaism, the Holocaust would function more clearly than any biblically stated prohibition as "the archetype and yardstick of evil" (p. 197). It might even function as a revelation to God himself. The God who had promised at Sinai to protect the Jews looked bad after the Holocaust; but Israel's territorial expansions in 1948 and 1967 made it seem to some Jews that "He was back on the job" (p. 150). Perhaps God, too, had gotten the message that Jews in danger should "Never again" be "abandoned."[149]

Whether the lesson of the Holocaust was news to God, its meaning to secular Jewish leaders was clear: commemorating the dead of Europe and the future unthinkability of Israeli military defeat were as one. As American Jews commemorated, increasingly, their own *lack* of memory of what the Holocaust destroyed,[150] the moral imperative "to remember" would thus inevitably produce a double sense of loss—the loss of any continuation of that world and the absence of any memory of having lost it. The Jewish scholar Yosef Hayim Yerushalmi gives a concise account of this mentality: "my terror of forgetting is greater than my terror of having too much to remember."[151]

But what is there to remember? American Jews were not there when European Jewry was annihilated and will not be there if Israel is ever militarily defeated. As *Americans*, Jews are urged to remember precisely that they were not there, and only thus were they spared. This is what Holocaust promoters, such as Elie Wiesel, warn *never to forget*, ominously suggesting that those who were once spared might once *again* be victimized (deservedly?) for *not* remembering.[152]

From a post–9/11 perspective, however, the significance of Novick's 1999 book is that the United States has embarked upon its "war on terror" with a victimary consciousness that has learned the lesson of the Holocaust—we are another Israel fighting Islamist "Nazis" who hate us for what we are, rather than for anything we have done. At this point the Holocaust is invoked not merely as a particular historical occurrence but also as the figuration of evil that prefigures all future evils; it is thus no longer the exclusive property of Jews and other Nazi victims. The United States, by identifying *itself* as a potential victim if it *forgets* the Holocaust, invites the rest of the world to equate anti-Americanism with anti-Semitism and thus turns its own enemies into enemies of Jews.[153] It is, ironically, in the universal form of Human Rights Discourse itself that Americanism has become a Judaism and Judaism an Americanism (with Israel functioning as a conscious enabler and, perhaps, also an unwitting victim of U.S. policies in the Middle East).

The moral logic of Human Rights Discourse invokes the Holocaust as a figure of the absolute evil to which war is the only appropriate response. Within this logic, Israel becomes the paradigm of a righteous country, and other countries cloak themselves in virtue by emulating Israel's righteousness and also through support of Israel itself. As the only global movement opposing these actions, Islamist jihad is understood as a struggle *against* the Western world's commitment to the survival of Israel and thus directs its violence against the U.S. and Europe and not just against Israel itself. By identifying itself as *another Israel*, the United States has embarked upon a "war" with no discernable geopolitical strategy or objective. The U.S., as the world's sole military hegemon, now portrays itself not only as the would-be rescuer of Jews but as itself a Jew among the nations.[154] We are back once again to the Jewish Question.

The War on Terror

The present "War on Terrorism" takes America's Holocaust beyond the duty to bear witness and toward a stronger identification with the victimary position itself. Our enemy is no longer merely the "totalitarianism" that we defeated in its Nazi form in World War II and in its Stalinist form in the cold war. Those appear in retrospect to have been wars of rescue in which "captive nations" (as they were once called) would be delivered from persecution into freedom. A war in which the enemy is "Terror" is something else; it is war against an *affect* that is typically accompanied by feelings of subjection to a power that hates us for no reason and with no limit, merely because of what we *are*. Terror is precisely the feeling that totalitarian regimes were once said to inflict on those over whom they exercised what Arendt called "total domination."[155] It was this feeling from which we aimed to liberate them and it is now the feeling from which we fight to free ourselves in the new century of human rights.[156]

What could it mean for Human Rights Discourse to regard "terror" as its enemy? To answer this question we must first consider the meaning of enmity itself. In a world full of dangers that are all too real, enmity itself is a product of projection. The enemy is always and everywhere *whom* we fight. To fight is to have an enemy; having an enemy is *why* we fight.

But having an enemy is not enough to make one fight. On the contrary, terror of one's enemy is typically a reason to submit—it is, at an affective level, already surrender. We fight (struggle) partly to *overcome* our terror and we are *able* to fight only to the extent that we have already done so. If terror is what we must battle in ourselves in order to fight, fighting is a substitute for feeling terror—a way to keep that feeling at bay. In this sense, we always war against our terror and we win that war by fighting our enemy instead.

Enmity is thus an externalization of terror. We overcome our inner terror by refusing to surrender to the outer enemy. It is a truism (how could it not be true?) that a war against the enemy must continue for as long as terror lasts. But terror is also the internalized enemy; it is our affective surrender to the enemy's presumed wish.[157]

When Jesus says, "love your enemies,"[158] he expresses the unconscious fantasy that comes just before fearing them—a fantasy of *being* what they desire. As *terrorized* beings we (still) unconsciously satisfy the desire of others, who, as our enemies, hate us for our love and would destroy us through this very vulnerability. Hating *them* protects us from the self-destructive effects of satisfying their desire to destroy us—which is why their hatred *of* us makes them worthy of being hated *by* us. Hence we could not hate the enemy if we did not fear that our capacity to love him would transform into terror. This may be Jesus's point in saying that we should love them *nevertheless* (despite their hatred of our love)—that we should not give up on the real desire underlying enmity itself, which is to love one's enemy.[159]

The foregoing is merely an elaboration of what it means to war against a generic enemy: what must be felt and disavowed for enmity to exist. Terror (fearful submission, submissive fear) is our general name for this introjection and displacement of feeling, a substitute for the names of more specific fears produced by more specific enemies. Whenever we name the enemy, we come to fear something more specific than "fear itself." To continue to identify our known enemies as "terrorists" would then be to reduce them to how they make us feel—and our feeling to a transmission of their authentic affect in the form of induced paralysis or helplessness. When President George W. Bush declared that "we will never surrender to terror," he was in fact disavowing the very feeling of terror through which surrender is normally induced.

I belabor the obvious here in order to bring out the peculiarity of replacing the idea of a war on enmity (the very idea of war itself) with a war on terror*ism*. If terror is whatever we try *not* to feel by making war, what does it mean to regard our global enemy as the terror*ist*?[160]

"Terrorism" primarily refers not to state policy that aims to brutally suppress resistance (and can be used to *fight* terrorism) but, rather, to a method of resisting state power through violent action aimed at making the state itself ungovernable Terrorism in this sense is not the name of an enemy but refers, instead, to a range of highly visible destructive acts that are indiscriminate in their effects and political in motivation.[161] It is normal for states to make such actions crimes, if they are not already so designated, and to deter, intercept, and punish them. Criminalizing these actions implicitly depoliticizes them by making their political motives cease to matter.

But, by calling terrorism our *enemy*, such actions are wholly identified with *their* political motive, which is itself portrayed as an indiscriminate and limitless hatred of *us*. We thereby disavow whatever political feelings we may have that *made* them enemies and render our own presence in the situation wholly *innocent*. If they are *essentially* "terrorists"—if that is their political identity—then "we" are constituted by a refusal to become their victims in order to assert the innocence that we already take for granted. To give our enemy the political subjectivity of "terrorist" is thus to assign our-selves the political subjectivity of innocence: moral self-doubt is the precise feeling we disavow in doing so.

The late-twentieth-century invention of "terrorism" as a singular enemy should have required as much theoretical heavy lifting as the mid-century argument of Hannah Arendt and others that our real enemies were not the dueling ideologies of "communism" and "fascism" but something called "totalitarianism," which was no one's ideology (although the term was invented by Mussolini, based on the Lukacsian notion of "totality"). That theoretical discovery was inseparable from the political project of identify-ing a commitment to human rights with anti–anti-Semitism and identify-ing "the Jew" as paradigmatic victim of politically motivated *inhumanity*.[162] But, now that "terrorism" has succeeded "totalitarianism" as the enemy of "human rights," political theory has taken refuge in the assumption that political ideologies have been replaced by a more primal religious fanati-cism that denies the evental status of the Holocaust in order to rationalize the murder of innocents.

No one has taken up this charge with a greater passion than Paul Ber-man,[163] who finds in the "terrorist's" fascination with murder and suicide the kernel of totalitarianism itself—a contempt for what the Islamist theo-logian Sayyid Qutb calls the originally "Jewish" wish to cherish and cling to life, which Berman takes to be the basis of secular humanitarianism (p. 68). As Qutb described it, the post–World War II creation of a Zionist state in Palestine was a catastrophic consequence of the post-Ottoman effort to treat Islam as *a* religion among others, according to Judeo-Christianity's own understanding of "religion," which is based on a "separation of Church and State" (p. 90).[164] He saw this as a threat to the monotheistic basis of Islam—not merely its belief that God is the only God but also that the reli-gious vanguard of Islamism should submit to nothing *other* than God.[165] Berman professes great intellectual respect for Islamism, believing it to be a far more worthy moral adversary than Nazism because Qutb does not quarrel with Western hypocrisy about its ideals but rather with those ideals themselves (p. 89). By rejecting the core of Judeo-Christianity, Qutb places his ideas outside Human Rights Discourse; Berman is correct about this. Also striking, however, is the way in which Berman's argument *for fighting* Islamism reproduces the logic of twentieth-century anti–anti-Semitism.

Qutb's doctrine was wonderfully original and deeply Muslim, looked at from one angle; and from another angle, merely one more version of the European totalitarian idea. And if his doctrine was recognizable, its consequence was certainly going to be predictable. Qutb's vanguard . . . was going to inaugurate a rebellion—this time a rebellion in the name of Islam, against the liberal values of the West. (Totalitarian movements always, but always, rise up in rebellion against the liberal values of the West. That is their purpose.) And rebellion was bound to end in a cult of death. (p. 99)

Here Berman provides an updated answer to the Jewish Question: Why are there still Jews? That answer implicitly endorses St. Paul's view of Christianity as establishing the importance to all mankind of the history of Jewish persecution. The supersession of Judaism by Judeo-Christianity once again becomes an argument for its secular preservation—Paul had explicitly argued in Romans that Israel (his name for the Jewish people) must continue to exist until the end of time.[166] Paul Berman adds to Paul (the Saint) a theological argument that belief in hastening the end of time—millenarianism—is ultimately about the destruction of the Jews as such, and thus the Holocaust. Qutb is, for Berman, the world-historical theologian who argues that there is no time left for Jews, except for those willing to live on as *dhimmies* (unbelievers) in a restored caliphate.

Berman devotes the bulk of *Terror and Liberalism* to showing that Islamism provides a more powerful, and intellectually respectable, foundation for totalitarian politics (and anti-Semitism) than either communism or fascism once did. For Berman the Islamist suicide bomber is not merely *like* a Nazi—rather, Islam*ism* is the purest theological tincture of Nazism, the site where the essence of absolute evil can be seen most clearly. The post-9/11 reasons for fighting Islamism are thus the *same* as the twentieth-century reasons for fighting fascism and communism—not *realpolitik*, not self-interest, but the "deepest Western" ideals of liberal humanism that accord human life the highest possible value.

Berman thus supports a moralized version of the "class of civilizations" thesis associated with Samuel P. Huntington and Bernard Lewis (pp. 14–20).[167] Defending the Jews and Israel, he believes, is nothing less than a defense of the Western ideal of liberated humanity, and the Jews, as such, continue to be a force for deparochializing, and then secularizing, whatever local culture they inhabit. As Berman's theological enemy, Qutb stands for the position that diasporic Judaism's gradual abandonment of theocracy betrayed monotheism's original message that God alone should rule.[168] From this perspective, the eventual apostasy of secular Judaism was prefigured by the founder of Judeo-Christianity, St. Paul, who distinguished the secular authority of imperial Rome from religious authority.[169] That secularism is now defended on humanitarian grounds shows the extent to which twenty-first-century discourse on human rights continues a two-thousand-year debate about what it means to universalize the Jewish experience as *human*.[170]

A further point concerns the role of the Jewish-Christian difference (and its preservation) in defining the secular as a period of time, an *era*. Berman implies that Qutb saw something like a secular era in the period between the Judeo-Christian abandonment of God (by God?) under a Christianized Rome and Romanized Christianity. The secular era, thus defined, would have come to an end with God's revelation of the Qur'an to Muhammad, after which belief in the continuation of secular time perpetuates human ignorance (*jāhiliyya*) of a truth already revealed.[171] For Berman, the struggle against Islamism is nothing less than the defense of a secularity in which there is *still* time for Jews. In his political theology, the Islamist enemy says that *time is up*.[172]

Human Rights Discourse, the humanitarian face of Judeo-Christianity, is an effort to prolong the secular era as a time in which truth is still debatable. In this respect, secular liberalism is no less *religious* in its conception of world history than Qutb's Islamism—it endeavors to put hate in the past by spreading the belief that the final truth is yet to be revealed. As a latter-day Paul, Berman proclaims this and calls upon us to become witnesses for liberalism. Now, however, the message is not exclusively Christian but rather Judeo-Christian—spreading the message of the Holocaust and treating those who deny it as enemies of all humanity.[173] In chapter 7 I explore the moral psychology of compassion and consider its specificity and limits as a politics.

7

BYSTANDERS AND VICTIMS

The World as Bystander

Since the Holocaust the mainstream literature on human rights has addressed a world of onlookers: those who are neither victim nor perpetrator of an evil and who might imagine afterward that they had a choice about whether to stand by or intervene. The story, repeated time and again, is that the onlookers did not care or simply looked away and that such indifference or willful ignorance is no longer excusable now that the term "Good German" has entered our political vocabulary as a reproof.

Human Rights Discourse calls into being a "world" of onlookers by challenging them to refuse to be mere bystanders. At a psychic level, this refusal comes through their engagement with the multiform cultural practices of Human Rights Discourse. The ethical transformation of indifferent bystanders into compassionate witnesses is a promise inherent in the cultural approach to human rights that begins by assuming an audience of onlookers who might avert their gaze rather than of beneficiaries who would have been perpetrators. The progression from bystander to witness—a story of advancing moral responsibility—implicitly blocks the charge that observers, like survivors, are potential beneficiaries who could easily have been perpetrators had their position been threatened. This chapter explores Human Rights Discourse as both a psychic and material defense against that underlying charge and considers the degree to which the bystander/witness story has, as its unconscious, the beneficiary/perpetrator story discussed in earlier chapters.

That Human Rights Discourse addresses us as bystanders, and not beneficiaries, is indicative of the transposition of human rights itself from the register of political mobilization to that of global popular culture.[1] In this culture, apathy—our natural response to the pain of others—is to be replaced by empathy, the morally induced ability to feel the pain of others as our own. If consumers of our popular culture only felt less apathy toward (and thus more empathy for) victims, the argument goes, they would *hold* themselves responsible for what they *allow* to happen. The culture also assures them, however, that they were not really responsible—that their true failing did not arise in any particular relation to perpetrators or victims but rather from a simple *lack* of compassionate feelings combined, perhaps, with willful inattention to the facts.[2] To overcome this *natural* failing, "we" (the *potential* bystanders) should henceforward equate ourselves with "them" (the victims) because the true victim of human rights violations is our "common humanity." The fin de siècle discourse on human rights, thus, "replaces the victim/perpetrator dyad with a fantasmic 'we' of common humanity figured variously as powerless, numbed, or passively complicit witnesses to suffering they did not themselves directly cause."[3]

The moral identification of bystanders with victims is accomplished through the act of witnessing itself, which can be predicated alike of the survivor who was *present* and an audience that, but for the choice to witness, would have been entirely *absent*. As a cultural act, the real work of witnessing is not visual but grammatical: it resequences the temporal order of other verbs into a "realistic" narrative in which the meaning of the past will be fulfilled in the time of the witness himself.

> This work affirms human solidarity *retrospectively* in a lesson about the consequences of human frailty; this is what happened, this is what was not done to prevent it, and this is what "we," frail humanity, must make sure does not happen again. The historiography on bystanders . . . mostly defers redemption to a future when lessons will have been learned.[4]

These lessons apply not only to neighbors but also to strangers—and, ultimately, to the world community at large. The potential bystander here, no matter how proximate or remote, is someone in a position to choose to look the other way, but who is given a chance to redeem the past by engaging with human rights culture itself.

That culture is first and foremost what forces potential bystanders to *look*. Its rhetoric presupposes mass media, especially visual, that both create and problematize the global awareness of human degradation while it is still occurring. Once we have chosen to see the obscene images of atrocity through the "graphic" (implicitly pornographic) visuals of which we are routinely warned, we are already implicated as *voyeurs*.[5] Our next choice, according to the narrative conventions of human rights, is whether to feel something and, then, whether to project those feelings onto the victim and thus identify with him. These essentially dramatistic conventions proactively structure the onlooker's choice as that of an audience before a *scene* of suffering that might titillate him, annoy him, or cleanse him (make him innocent) through heightened feelings *for* (cathartic identification *with*) the victim.[6]

As a fertile ground of popular culture, Human Rights Discourse is a necessary supplement to politics-as-usual: this discourse *itself* counteracts the natural indifference of bystanders on which tyrannies rely. When "the CNN effect" works, the bystander sees *himself* (his common humanity) in the image of victimary identity presented on the screen.[7] This identification does not, of course, always occur; the viewer may, literally, look away from visuals that are too assaultive, a response human rights documentarians take pains to avoid. What the Human Rights Discourse portrays as empathy for today's victim is, according to its own script, a retrospective identification with a *past* bystander who "might have done something differently if not constrained by natural human inclinations that *we* recognize as regrettable and condemn."[8]

For us, refusing to be a bystander now means identifying with that other bystander while experiencing feelings we believe he did not have when the atrocity occurred. This act of identification *consists* of a counterfactual fantasy in which that other bystander would have been an opponent of the regime *because* he had the feelings we have now on his behalf. The "fantasmic 'we'" in this case is the transtemporal union of the consumers of today's visual culture of human rights and the past bystanders whom they are *not*.[9]

The figure of the indifferent bystander evoked by Human Rights Discourse is a moralized composite of past and present—an allegory rather than a diagnosis of real individuals who might inhabit any fixed moment in time. As the *hypothetical* opponent of past evil with whom we presently identify, the indifferent bystander whom we are *not* merely lacked the compassion that Human Rights Discourse has taught *us* to feel. This means, in effect, that we experience our own compassion at one remove—attributing to ourselves subjective feelings that we imagine *former* bystanders could now share by embracing the culture of human rights. There is, however, no historical moment in which bystanders really would have become active resisters if only they had felt more concern for victims.

How, then, does Human Rights Discourse represent the value of *having been* a contemporaneous opponent of the old regime? Its account is consistent with the moral psychology it ascribes to those who *would have been* opponents had they known then what they know now. But, in this account, whatever made some resist *without* knowing how history would judge them either fades from view or becomes inexplicable. Those who actually resisted the old regime are thus retrospectively honored for being early adopters of feelings that are central to the culture of the new, thereby assimilating what they did with what former bystanders are capable of wishing. (Treating resisters as compassionate bystanders downplays the messier aspects of their opposition, including violence and any actions they took at the time to confront bystanders with their status as beneficiaries.)

The point of Human Rights Discourse is not, however, to draw sharp lines between those beneficiaries who opposed the regime in time, those whose complaisance was the result of affective indifference to the suffering of others (a common human failing), and those who were relatively active in their complicity with the regime. Human Rights Discourse, as we saw in chapter 1, focuses rather on the line between beneficiaries and bystanders, redrawing it so that beneficiaries can identify themselves as bystanders who would have been opponents if only they had known. Its desired effect is to embrace the cultural transformation of all former bystanders by cleansing their present condemnation of the past of any taint arising from the benefits they still enjoy.

But where does this leave victims?

Feeling Bad, Feeling Better

As humanitarian witnesses, we expect victims to feel *bad*. But bad in what sense? Does victimization make them feel bad, or at least worse, in a moral sense? In the sense of being psychologically *depressed*? Emotionally *wounded*? Do they feel bad in the sense of being personally *aggrieved* toward others? If so, is it also appropriate for them to feel *enraged*? Do angry victims feel specially *entitled not to suffer more*, because even ordinary misfortune would be too much for those who have already suffered undeservedly and to excess?[10]

There are other possible ways in which we might expect victims to feel bad. We might say, for example, that victims are supposed to feel the kind of *rancor* appropriate to those who are unjustly punished.[11] But many victims of injustice continue to see themselves as *unlucky* compared to other potential victims, without feeling any particular resentment toward perpetrators and beneficiaries. Some victims feel *lost*. Being lost, having losses, *losing*—as negative states, these are all ways of feeling bad. So, too, are forms of *trauma* associated with the infliction of violence, pain, or both of which the victim seems presently unaware. Thus victims who do not yet *feel* bad are often said to *be* traumatized.[12]

As compassionate witnesses, we do not merely recognize that victims feel bad; we also want them to feel better. What new moral feelings (good feelings) are supposed to overcome the victim's bad feelings when the evil from which they suffer is gone? Obviously the emotional antidote to victimhood varies with the specific bad feelings that accompany it. A victim who previously felt depressed is now supposed to feel *elated*—a celebratory mood of triumph (like a baseball team that comes from behind to win in the bottom of the ninth). If the victim felt wounded, he is now supposed to feel *healthy* (perhaps no longer hobbled by the past). Those victims who felt morally damaged may now be entitled to feel morally *superior*—perhaps because their past suffering tested and ennobled them, perhaps because their ability to forgive is what counts as virtue in one who overcomes the experience of moral corruption (sin).

But what of the victim who felt aggrieved? For him feeling better might mean restitution—a sense of having been made whole for his injury or insult. And what if, in addition to feeling aggrieved, he also felt enraged? Feeling better might then require him to let go of his anger, to calm himself whether or not restitution has been made.

But there are also other possibilities. If victimhood makes future suffering seem too much to bear, overcoming it might consist of feeling *ordinary* once again. The successor emotion for victims who feel unjustly punished (treated as being *bad* when they were not) might be to feel vindicated or exonerated—and thus *good*. What of the victim who merely felt unlucky? He might overcome this specific way of feeling bad through a reversal of fortune or, perhaps, even a broadened perspective that makes him feel lucky after all. And what about those victims who feel lost? Such victims might recover by being *found* or *saved*. Redemption, whether deserved or not, is the feeling we associate with past suffering that has been valorized and made meaningful. But is it redemption that lost victims always want? Not necessarily. The saved victim can be ungrateful to his redeemer—a problem lying at the heart of Judeo-Christian theology.

We, as moral witnesses to victimhood, can project many different ways of feeling bad onto victims—the list is not exhaustive. But, when we are done, there may still be a surviving victim who exists apart from the internal object of our compassion. How bad does *he* feel? And *how* does he feel bad?[13]

The Drowned and the Saved

The problematic relation between compassionate witnessing and victimhood is Primo Levi's special topic within the vast Holocaust literature. The victim who survived speaks *instead of* those who died (as a "proxy," Levi says), and yet the survivor could not have had the same experience. Speaking out of what he calls "a strong and durable impulse,"[14] Levi claims to "have deliberately assumed the calm, sober language of the witness, neither the lamenting tones of the victim nor the irate voice of someone who seeks revenge."[15] His feelings are, nevertheless, different from those of an unvictimized onlooker who might be called *as* a witness; they are, moreover, presumptively inaccessible to a reader who accepts the truth of what he says and chooses to *bear* witness. But witness to what?

If Levi were the survivor of a shipwreck, his reader could be expected to think about how bad he felt when it happened and how much better he would feel now that he is back on shore. Yet no one reading Levi's testimony would think to ask him (in the manner of a TV talk show host) how great it must feel to have survived. The whole point of his story is to distinguish surviving Auschwitz from the standard narrative surrounding shipwrecks: there was no value in the suffering of those who "drowned" and no elation in being "saved." His words are worth quoting at length:

The "saved" of the *Lager* were not the best, those destined to do good, the bearers of a message. Preferably, the worst survived, the selfish, the violent, the insensitive, the collaborators of the "gray zone," the spies. It was not a certain rule . . ., but it was nevertheless a rule. . . . The worst survived, that is the fittest; the best all died.[16]

. . . I must repeat: we, the survivors, are not the true witnesses. This is an uncomfortable notion of which I have become conscious little by little, reading the memoirs of others and reading mine at a distance of years. We survivors are . . . an anomalous minority . . . who by their prevarications or abilities or luck did not touch bottom. Those who did so, those who saw the Gorgon, have not returned to tell about it . . . but they are . . . the submerged, the complete witnesses, the ones whose deposition would have a general significance. They are the rule, we are the exception. . . . We . . . tried . . . to recount not only our own fate but also that of the drowned; but . . . no one ever returned to describe his own death.[17]

Levi's survivors were thus "saved" only in the limited sense suggested by his title: they were not "drowned."[18] Their release from Auschwitz did not generally heal the moral damage they suffered there. "For the majority," Levi says, "liberation was neither joyful nor lighthearted" (p. 70), He further observes that it was liberation, not camp life, that led to many suicides.[19] Those prisoners who found victory in survival were, for Levi, the lucky exceptions, mostly political prisoners who could sustain feelings of struggle and defiance while in captivity (pp. 71, 73).[20]

Levi's account of Auschwitz challenges the assumption that victimhood wants to survive—that becoming a "survivor" satisfies the victim's desire.[21] By showing the ways in which victims felt bad, Levi shows how he came to feel even worse as a survivor. Was his desire at that point to have been *simply* the victim he could never again be?

The Desire of the Victim

In his first book Levi describes what it was like to walk out of the camps and face the now defeated Germans. "I felt as though I was moving among throngs of insolvent debtors, as if everybody owed me something and refused to pay." But what could he now desire of a defeated and disgraced Germany? It had already suffered; it could never have suffered enough; and yet from now on any additional suffering would appear to be *too much*. The postwar victors thus avoided suggesting that Germany should suffer more while demanding that it "remember"—the form self-punishment often takes. But Levi did not want to be remembered: he wanted to be heard. What were his interlocutors to make of his *still* being there? He had found no moral value in salvation. Should he therefore be counted as a victim, despite having been saved? Or was he now just another witness who remembered the past? His story was already over for Germans whose devastating defeat was considered equivalent to whatever collective punishment might have been deserved.[22]

What, then, did Levi really want? His problem as a survivor was at once ethical and ontological: that the desire of the victim and of the witness cannot coexist at one time in a single subjectivity. Insofar as he described himself as *having been* victim, he wrote as someone who *will have* survived. He is therefore not (no longer) the victim at the moment he writes but, rather, one who witnessed close at hand the atrocities at Auschwitz. But he also writes with the authority of someone who *would have* died, even though his testimony presupposes his survival.

How could Levi make demands of justice on his listener, especially a German listener, if he spoke from no political position that was temporally intelligible? This is not a who/whom question, but rather a now/then question.[23] It concerns what the *Lager* will have been in the context of the postwar understanding of Germany's defeat and disgrace. How then shall we describe Levi's seemingly impossible desire for intertemporal justice?

As a preliminary approach, we might say that he really wanted to be a ghost, neither living nor dead, and for Germans to be *haunted*. The historian Inga Clendinnen describes him as follows: "He recognized himself as an Ancient Mariner button-holing the wedding guests on the way to the feast, darkening their unshadowed celebrations with his doleful tales: an importunate, isolated revenant from an irrelevant, macabre Elsewhere."[24] For such a ghost, haunting is a moral protest against the presumption that the mere passage of time expiates past crimes.[25] He thus expresses a virtual morality that seems orthogonal in time to justice among the living, and sometimes violently at odds with it. (Consider the demands of Hamlet's father.)[26] But what of the haunted? They sometimes feel sympathy for their ghosts but are also persecuted and accused by them.[27] If they do not quite blame the ghost for tormenting them, neither can they entirely forgive his reproaches for a past they cannot change.[28] The haunted are witnesses to past victimhood but without the comfort that Human Rights Discourse affords to those who respond compassionately.

"Haunting" has thus become in recent literature a common trope for conjuring the co-presence of what cannot exist together at the same time—for example, the living and the dead; the present and the past, and (in Levi's case) victim and survivor.[29] As a metaphor, the ghost is the figure of impossible desire because his spatial existence as a being out of time is at odds with a realistic view of the relation between ontology and ethics.[30] The spatiotemporal continuum, described by Kant, excludes a priori the spatial presence of the past except in memory (and in *places* of memory that can be visited).[31] Modern ethics, especially that of Kant, presupposes the nonexistence of spirits and systematically excludes demands that purport to emanate from the dead. For us to take the *standpoint* of justice is to treat past and future only as present *positions*, effectively reducing time to its spatial traces.[32] But past and future can be localized in space only if there could *be* no outstanding grievance that would have prevented the present from coming to be, no claim on behalf of the future under which the present *ceases* to be.[33]

Kantian ethics thus has difficulty with the desire of a revenant like Primo Levi. When we say that we do not believe in ghosts, what we *do* believe is that they exist only in our minds. And yet they demand to be seen. Visibility is a willed assault by the ghost upon the haunted who do not regard it as unjust to wish that the ghost would *dis*appear. But ghosts do something more than forcibly appear: they also command those they haunt with unfinished business. Memory is a refusal to be *commanded* by a ghost. We lay our ghosts to rest by distinguishing the historical truth they tell from justice *inter vivos*.[34]

From Grief to Grievance and Back Again

But what does it mean for Levi to *be* a ghost in whose existence the rest of us do not entirely believe? How is *he* supposed to internalize our wish that he disappear? What is he to do with his excess grief if the rest of us think that truthful memory is the only kind of presence that the past could really have in matters of justice? These *extra* (and ongoing) feelings of grief distinguish the victim who remains external from the internalized victim to whom compassionate witnesses relate.[35] The literary scholar Anne Anlin Cheng describes grievance as essentially political and grief as its ethical remainder.[36] But her point is not that literary portrayals of victimhood—she focuses on race—are too politicized but, rather, that our literature on racial victimhood enables the intended audience to imagine its own depression as what satisfies the victim's desire. The effect is to leave the audience saddened but oddly unthreatened, because there is no further question of justice for the victim himself. Melancholics feel sad, Cheng says, not because they are unable to reverse the victim's loss but because they no longer desire to do so (p. 9).[37]

Cheng's view of what attaches a literary audience to its sadness is consistent with my account of how the beneficiaries of structural injustice find security in *self*-reproach. Cheng thus identifies the melancholic element in compassion—its unconscious *embodiment* of victimhood—as an exclusion of the surplus grief of the external victim whose loss remains.[38] This "exclusion . . . is," she says, "the real stake of melancholic retention" (p. 9). By containing the other within himself, the melancholic feels sadder but also safer than he otherwise would—sadder because the hostility he would have felt toward an external victim (scapegoat) is redirected toward an internalized victim who is his substitute and safer because the internalized victim, kept alive through the melancholic's apparent self-reproach, is never psychically lost.

But neither is such a victim *really* dangerous. By enabling us to identify with an *internalized* victim who is similarly depressed, our culture of humanitarian compassion makes the *external* victim seem more accepting of the permanence of loss and thus less threatening. Fantasizing the existence of such a victim may be essential to the psychic gain of melancholia, but this does not mean that the external victim *is* "self-hating," "self-shamed," and altogether too depressed to be capable of effective action (p. 187). As a psychic compromise between sacrificing and rescuing a now internalized victim, cultural melancholia has little to do with justice toward the victim who remains external to us, which is why it provides such a powerful defense against anxiety for those who occupy a beneficiary position.

But what of the external victim whose surplus grief is supposedly absorbed, if not canceled, by a post hoc culture of compassion? Levi's testimony (unlike Wiesel's) must be read as a protest against an audience that needs him to be depressed so that it can imagine its indifference as the cause of that depression and its empathy as the fulfilled meaning of his life. When those who read him thus imagine their own melancholia as satisfying his desire, they are also imagining a victim (Levi) who has already internalized the witness position through which they have come to identify *with* him. For Levi himself, suicidal wishes could have been a way to fulfill the desire of those depressed by his presence to *finally* disappear into memory.[39] Perhaps, but we should avoid leaping to conclusions about how victims truly feel: those whose loss depresses *us* (the Lost themselves) do not necessarily suffer from depression, even if they suffered in other ways.[40] The main point is that cultural practices that make us feel bad about the past do not necessarily lead to interpersonal justice and are often an intrapsychic substitute for it. Can we say more?

I have pointed throughout this book to a *relation* between the beneficiary and bystander positions. By this I mean that ascribing one position instead of the other is a matter of interpretation and argument and also that each position may conceal the unconscious reality reflected by the other. People can be made anxious about their bystander position, for example, by suggesting that henceforth they will be beneficiaries of continuing *in*action, that they will no longer be considered mere witnesses to the present situation *now that they know* its true character. (Al Gore's argument about global warming sometimes suggests that considering yourself a bystander is a matter of willful ignorance.) To be *accused* of being a beneficiary is, as we know from earlier chapters, also to be accused of harboring aggressive wishes toward the victim that could have made one a perpetrator. Beneficiaries can defend against this paranoia—we can call it perpetrator anxiety—by separating feelings that can transcend time and space from their link to any action that must occur here and now. A beneficiary who cannot act, perhaps because the bad history is *over*, becomes a bystander, separated by time, who can look back, perhaps with sorrow but without fear. He then becomes a mere *successor* to those who went before. This is, of course, the future that Human Rights Discourse promises beneficiaries after evil and how it helps them to repress their anxieties about having to pay because the evil persists. Compassion is thus both an affective symptom of such repressed anxieties and a mechanism of their repression through distancing in space and time.[41]

My model for understanding the beneficiary's unconscious is Freud's paradigm of melancholia as the symptom of a surviving child's unconscious ambivalence toward a dead parent whose heir and successor he both wishes and does not wish to be. Here the melancholic's inescapable sense of *loss* would be a defense against the child's anxiety that he has *gained* through the fulfillment of whatever unconsciously hostile wishes he may have had toward the dead missing parent. In depression generally, according to Freud, the potentially guilty beneficiary transforms the suffering he might have wished on someone else into his *own* loss and identifies *himself* as the loser. By redirecting that hostility inward, he thus transforms himself from beneficiary to witness, deriving a perverse sense of worth and satisfaction from the merciless criticism that he—and he *alone*—directs against himself.[42] Viewed as a defense, his sadness consists of redirecting hostile feelings inward, toward himself, so that his mental *image* of his body substitutes itself for the loss his unconscious would have inflicted on another. The self-inflicted suffering of Freud's melancholic makes him feel bad, but in a reassuring way, because the real objects of his hostile feelings are others whom he no longer fears.

My view of posttraumatic politics throughout this book is similar to Freud's view of how depression overcomes paranoia. The paranoia of the dependent child in Freud's theory corresponds to the position of a beneficiary who discovers his unacknowledged desire to *have* a victim. Depression defends against paranoia by repressing both the survivor's hatred of his would-have-been victim and the fact that his internalized victim is destroyed by hostile wishes in the unconscious, where wishes are omnipotent. For me, the Freudian unconscious corresponds to a realm in which wishes that are not morally avowable remain, nevertheless, politically intelligible. What Freud describes as symptoms of depression correspond, in my view, to the obsessive self-reproach of beneficiaries who try to *imagine* the suffering of others by (now consciously) projecting their own body image into the (now fully historicized) picture of victimary identity.[43] In the politics of historical memory, the original loss is now ongoing and irreparable, but only because, in the beneficiary's mind, it has become his own loss. He reminds himself to feel bad, but in a good way, because he suffers *as though* he were someone else. Freud's theory of melancholia models the somaticization of ethics that I have criticized throughout this book as a barrier to justice.

But the *injustice* of melancholia to the still external victim is obscured in Freud's writing on the topic, which is concerned only with his patient, the melancholic, who is unable to mourn his internalized victim and move on. Identifying with and *as* the victim of the loss represses and perpetuates that patient's ambivalence about being, rather, a perpetrator or beneficiary. But the object of those negative feelings is nothing outside the beneficiary's unconscious mind.[44] So we are not asked to consider *whose* primary loss the melancholic internalizes as his own loss or how this might affect ongoing relations with the real (external) loser.[45]

When Freud writes generally about the clinical situation, however, his account is less one-sided. Here the position of the surviving victim—the object of aggression who lives on—is occupied by the analyst, toward whom the patient's feelings are alternately paranoid (an unconscious perpetrator) and depressed (an unconscious beneficiary). Freudian therapy uses the feelings of victimization ("countertransference") produced in the *analyst* to enable patients to overcome the paranoia of would-be perpetrators and live on as depressive, but otherwise accepting, beneficiaries of their given situation.

What does it mean to *be* the surviving victim of a patient who is ambivalently both beneficiary and perpetrator?[46] As a psychoanalyst of children, Donald Winnicott understood that he was the victim of their projected aggression in much the way a mother is. As the prototypical victim, the mother/analyst is, originally, an *internal* object that needs to become external ("not-me") so that the child/patient can be reconciled to dependency as the prototypical beneficiary without feeling subject to retaliation as a prototypical perpetrator.[47] To become separate in this way, the object that is "not-me" must be identified with whatever in the child's mind can survive the aggression that would otherwise destroy "me."[48] By surviving his destructive wishes, the mother/analyst teaches the child/patient that he is not omnipotent and can *use* others without necessarily destroying them. This lesson can be an essential step in separating without guilt: "in some patients, the inability to use people leaves them trapped in a narcissistic lock."[49] The ability to use people is also essential to the psychic development of the reasonably secure beneficiaries described in earlier chapters. They, too, learn to regard their would-have-been victims as figures in their own *transition* to ethical maturity. There is thus a similarity between Winnicott's description of "transitional objects" (such as blankets or teddy bears, which were once both "cuddled" and "mutilated") and the former victims described in theories of transitional justice that allow beneficiaries to achieve a supposedly healthy separation from their past (p. 53). By *allowing* themselves to be used, Winnicott's ethical victims create trust where there might otherwise have been anxiety about destructive (and ultimately self-destructive) wishes (p. 61). In this model of "using people" as "trusting people" (p. 61), the victim is relatively powerful (an adult/analyst) and the beneficiary is dependent (a child/patient). Here the beneficiary's hostile feelings are transferred (through projection) to the victim, whose role is to "hold" them safely and thus build confidence in a robustly external reality.[50] Winnicott's central thesis is succinctly stated by his biographer Adam Phillips: "It is destructiveness, paradoxically, that creates reality, not reality that creates destructiveness."[51]

But what is the victim-as-fiduciary to do with the hostile feelings that he or she holds in trust? In the special case of psychoanalysis (and perhaps also of parenthood) the victim of hostility protects the beneficiary from perpetrator anxiety. Successful treatment would not be possible if the analyst (in this case Winnicott) becomes so depressed by the process as to be incapable of expressing back the hostile feelings that are transferred to him as well as those that he generates on his own. But, as a victim, the good-enough analyst must know when to transmit that transferred hatred back to the patient/beneficiary who must also learn how to "go on being" without paranoia.[52]

Do such concepts shed light on what is right and wrong in Human Rights Discourse? The paranoia of beneficiaries is no less an obstacle to achieving social justice than it is to achieving reconciliation. To overcome it the victim must be good enough. But how "good" must the victim be? How much hatred can be transferred back? And in what ways must the beneficiary be allowed to "go on being" without also being made to change? These are, of course, the questions that might distinguish the projects of justice and reconciliation during transitional periods, even if they were to converge in the end.[53]

In the meantime, however, we must ask in what ways the paranoia of beneficiaries should be treated differently in political analysis than it is in psychoanalysis, which is a special case because the only goal is to help the beneficiary. Comparing most victim/beneficiary situations with this special case goes some way toward explaining the political difficulties arising because the victims who exist outside the beneficiary's mind are *not* acting mainly for his sake. We have earlier discussed "mock reparation" as a "manic defense" (a "light-headedness" or "elation") that comes when one's split-off negative feelings are not held in trust by the victim but are merely *disavowed* in the self.[54] But must affective disavowal always be a substitute for genuine reparative action toward the victim who exists outside one's mind? Surely genuine reparation—assuming there can be such a thing—would require an affective change of some kind before—and certainly after—a material change occurs. What is that affective change, and must it occur on both sides?

According to Human Rights Discourse, the upwelling of compassion in beneficiaries—their choice to be witnesses rather than bystanders—is *itself* a redistribution of affect. Many experts on transitional justice say that compassion breaks the cycle of grievance begetting grievance and suggest that material redistribution is morally valuable if and when it is grounded in compassion rather than fear.[55] We must ask, however, whether cultivating feelings of compassion is still in the realm of therapy for beneficiaries rather than of justice for victims. How good could this be, even as therapy, if the effect of compassion is to stop being paranoid and become depressed?

Melancholia and Compassion

There are, of course, significant differences between Freud's theory of depression, as discussed earlier in this chapter, and the concept of compassion that underlies a culture of human rights. In compassion the depressive stops feeling sorry for himself and instead feels pity for the victimary object whom he now regards as a substitute for himself. Because this substitution is desirable, we consider compassion, unlike depression, to be a virtue—it makes feeling bad a good thing for us. But it does not necessarily benefit the victim who exists outside our projected feelings of pity, especially if these disguise an underlying contempt or disgust. The latter feelings are, of course. antithetical to compassion—the compassionate witness of Human Rights Discourse would disavow them and reproach himself were they to arise. But my argument is strengthened, not undermined, by the fact that compassion is asserted to deny uglier feelings. It is this element of implicit self-reproach that *links* compassion back to melancholia and to the paranoia that precedes it.[56]

Once we understand that compassion takes a critical standpoint toward prior feelings of depression and superiority, we can see why it so easily unravels in times of stress. The compassionate witness is more than a mere bystander—his compassion gives him a claim to be trusted by surviving victims whom he might otherwise fear. But that very compassion also makes him hyperaware of "bad" victims who make him feel *suddenly unsafe* by rejecting the melancholic incapacity for political action projected onto them. When the external victim presents himself as sufficiently aggrieved to pose a threat (for example, when the panhandler shows the face of the mugger), there is an immediate regression to paranoia. Here *loss* of compassion (and with it the "witness" position) presents itself as a *new* basis for fearing victims who *no longer* seem to be innocent. It should therefore come as no surprise how fragile a human rights culture can be nor how suddenly a beneficiary who is convinced of his own compassion can become a born-again persecutor.

Thoughtful advocates of human rights are aware that the link between compassion and social justice is easily broken. To protect the "true feelings" of compassion from such vicissitudes, they generally restrict it to physical, rather than social, forms of injury. It is with somaticized victimhood that the compassionate witness of Human Rights Discourse identifies. *Somaticization* (the concern with innocent bodies) is to modern victimology what *symbolization* was to the ancient practice of sacrificing scapegoats to expiate collective sins.[57] In Human Rights Discourse we, as compassionate witnesses, resist seeing the sufferer as a vicarious surrogate for ourselves, a human sacrifice from which we benefit. Instead, we project ourselves back into the image of starved, mutilated, genocided bodies whose suffering is fantasmatically our own. The *compassionate* bystander is no longer a beneficiary who *has* a victim; rather, he is the witness that his imaginary victim wants.[58]

Virtuous Victims?

What would it mean to become the victim of (or as conceived by) a compassionate witness? Levi's writing on Auschwitz, a masterpiece of postwar political thought, strongly opposes the two contrasting accounts of victimhood as a source of virtue discussed in previous chapters: the first locates that virtue in *resistance*, the second in *innocence*.

The ethical virtue of victims who resist was most fully developed in Jean-Paul Sartre's *Being and Nothingness*.[59] That work, written in occupied France, portrayed passivity as a type of collaboration that refuses to recognize itself as such. If passive collaboration is not innocent, according to Sartre, neither is passive victimhood: we cannot be victimized *against* our will without also being victimized *through* it. There is thus no such thing as a surviving *victim*. When survivors consider themselves to be victims, they do so by denying that they made a choice to collaborate rather than resist. But the choice to resist is not something *given* by the historical context. For Sartre, it is, rather, a negation of context and would thus be no less available in Auschwitz than in any other situation.

Levi agreed with Sartre's conceptual point that victims collaborate in their subjugation, but he did not find the kind of moral value in resistance to Auschwitz that Sartre found in resistance to the Occupation or to fascism in general. For Levi, Sartre's conception of moral liberation was itself an outcome of the war and was thus inapplicable to the camps. "The deeply rooted consciousness that one must not consent to oppression but resist it," he says, "was not widespread in Fascist Europe."[60] Levi believed, moreover, that Auschwitz must be viewed, sui generis, as a political regime because its essential injustice was to demoralize its subjects and rulers alike. His picture of Auschwitz is best compared to classical paradigms of unjust rule[61] that contrast with paradigms of just rule: it is the polar opposite of the twentieth-century welfare state,[62] aiming to make its inhabitants *un*happy in every possible way—even those unnecessary to its utilitarian purposes, such as using their labor for war production.[63] No moral victory can be gained here by refusing to be defined by one's context.

But if Levi finds Auschwitz to have been an exception to the Sartrean claim that victims cleanse themselves through resistance, he stands more strongly against the alternative view that Holocaust victims should be absolved of any moral damage arising from the victimary context. Proclamations of victimary innocence have become an article of faith for post-Holocaust Judeo-Christianity—a truth to which Holocaust martyrs testified by their death and survivors (like Wiesel) testify as living witnesses.[64] Pope John Paul II embraced this view in 1979, praying before the cross erected at Auschwitz to commemorate the two Catholic saints who were martyred there.[65] His view was controversial. Why, some asked, were these two deaths considered Christ-like, while the death of a *million* Jews at Auschwitz *because* they were Jews was not. Does it take a Christian saint to die *for* the Jews? Some criticized the pope from the opposite perspective, arguing that his equation of Golgotha and Auschwitz meant that the Jews were no longer *merely* Jews and thus no longer needed to convert.

For Levi, however, Auschwitz undermined the central assumption of postwar Judeo-Christianity: that the moral innocence of victims retroactively glorifies the compassion of any would-have-been savior who now bears witness to it. This is why he describes passive salvation—what Christians call "grace"—as a source of shame for the passive victim whose suffering becomes the basis of a former bystander's newfound moral worth. Only by ignoring shame could the witnessing world believe that its compassion satisfies the victim's desire to be *found* innocent (blameless). But to whom does this *found* innocence accrue—the victim or the witness? Compassionate witnessing appropriates a surplus value (grief) produced by suffering that would otherwise have been wasted. If the witness (as would-be savior) did not find innocence, he would merely be a bystander.

Notwithstanding Primo Levi, the visual iconography of human rights turns bystanders into witnesses by calling upon them to become retroactive opponents of what they see. In the retrospective role of witness, the beneficiary typically refuses responsibility for past evil. We didn't do it, he insists. We *wouldn't* do it, and reminders of it would make us paranoid except in times delimited as "transitional"—times set aside for compassion. Merely by surviving the victim thus provides involuntary therapy for beneficiaries, who become depressive rather than paranoid. But should they be depressed?

Just Lucky

I have suggested throughout this book that beneficiaries of a now repudiated evil *ought* to question the continuing advantages they retain. Does their doing so mean that the evil lives on? My account of justice-as-struggle presupposes that undeserved benefits derived from evil could be legitimately reappropriated to offset or remove the negative aftereffects of that evil itself.

Having argued this, however, it is past time to concede that it is good, prima facie, to be a beneficiary; that is, benefits from the past, even from an evil past, must be counted as presumptively *positive* aftereffects. To be sure, this presumption can be rebutted by invoking the equitable principle that no one should profit from his or her own wrongdoing. But situations of transitional justice are constructed, as we have seen, by distinguishing the beneficiaries of past evil from the perpetrators, those who *did* something wrong. Are continuing beneficiaries who remained bystanders just lucky that they did not become perpetrators? Is this why it is morally acceptable for them to keep their now admittedly undeserved gains? Is this why there should be no cost *to them* in acknowledging that their gains are undeserved? The time after evil (and before justice) is, I have argued, a time when beneficiaries feel *lucky*.

By definition, there is nothing *wrong* with benefiting from *luck*. The benefits of luck are always undeserved—that's what being lucky *means*. Being lucky implies that one has no ethical need to ascribe one's good fortune to skill or virtue. It is therefore unbecoming for the lucky to act as though they had somehow *earned* the benefits they enjoy. The lucky should, perhaps, be modest, but they should not be depressed. They are additionally lucky that, although their benefits are undeserved, there is *nothing* wrong with this. "Luck" is what we call those undeserved benefits that we get to keep without guilt.

To say that benefits are, prima facie, good luck is to admit that that the existence of a baseline for historical justice is a matter of chance. We speak of "moral luck," for example, when someone by chance avoids a disaster (perhaps a car crash) for which he would have been at fault and hence liable. If the accident did not occur, there would be nothing wrong per se about his retaining the benefits that he would have lost but for chance. We call this *moral luck* because it *could have been* wrong for him to retain those benefits under different circumstances in which his own conduct was exactly the same.[66]

Is birth a matter of moral luck in the sense that successor generations receive a windfall benefit that might have resulted from their own wrongdoing, but that through sheer good fortune did not? Those who categorically oppose historical justice across generations usually assume that it would be *un*just to penalize a new generation that was lucky to have avoided guilt. The lucky winners of nonrevolutionary transitions (such as that of South Africa or the U.S.) might also claim that the miracle of national rebirth spared them from becoming perpetrators of injustice and thus removed the taint of wrongdoing from their retention of benefits. If being *born* is the basis of claiming to start with a clean slate,[67] to be *re*born is to claim that atonement has occurred—that one has recovered this moral innocence of birth without shedding the weight of memory. Is the reality of luck what Kleinian psychotherapy teaches children, its undeserving beneficiaries, to accept and what the practices of transitional justice teach the rest of us?

This book is meant to challenge the assumption that generational change or spiritual conversion wipes the slate clean, transforming historical injustice into mere good fortune. Ascribing good fortune to "fate" has always been the way societies separate the realm of moral luck from that of justice.[68] This would seem to be a fallback position of beneficiaries of past injustice who no longer defend the systems that produced their gains but who believe that they are still lucky enough to retain them. Why should they be expected to disgorge their gains as aftereffects of past evil *merely* so that the evil will have no such aftereffects? Primo Levi would have asked himself this general question when haunting a supposedly reborn Germany. My answers in this book have not been general. I argue that traces of injustice are embedded in the structures of society and of unconscious desire.

But I must also state explicitly my assumption that such specific arguments must be made—*that a beneficiary position does not automatically raise questions of justice*. There is a sense in which good fortune is just life as it would be in the absence of such arguments—and only the greatest good fortune would allow a new generation to benefit from past injustice without being tainted by it. Is "just lucky" a plausible claim by survivors of a past catastrophe, whether natural or moral, who expect to keep the gains that resulted from it? I do not think this is a general rebuttal to claims of historical injustice—it is merely the default position in the event that no such claims are made. Historical beneficiaries would be lucky indeed, however, if it turned out that all such claims could be successfully rebutted.

The conception of justice adumbrated in this book is not merely about redistribution among groups existing at a single time or of a single generation. It is also, following Walter Benjamin (and perhaps Proust), a recovery of lost time. I argue in chapter 9 that the linkage between any two discontinuous moments is optional—that it is in this respect a matter of chance. This means, however, that, as there are moments when beneficiaries who did nothing wrong are lucky, so, too, are there moments, perhaps of danger, when *another* moment flashes up as a time that has never really passed.

My answer to a happy-go-lucky view of history must not deny the moral importance of chance and discontinuity. It, rather, asserts the intertemporal—or, more precisely, interevental—dimension of justice itself as an outgrowth of the beneficiary position and the anxieties arising from it. My argument in this chapter is that humanitarian compassion defends against the beneficiary's anxieties by constructing him as a viewer who can choose to insert himself into the picture viewed. Twenty-first-century humanitarianism *calls* the beneficiary a bystander in order to *recall* him as a witness who will *no longer* look away from those who still suffer. The new, affective bond to be created between them is made possible by an act of memory that makes compassion in the present *discontinuous* with the past.

Historical memory thus conceived is more than a cautionary reminder—like the warning label ("Poison") on a bottle or a sign that says "Danger of Electrical Shock." Here the danger is not that something bad might happen unless we are careful but that what has already happened might still be going on *unless we remember*. But, *if* we remember, what happens will be different—the point is conceptual, not instrumental—the memory itself would *make* it different because we would be conscious of it happening *again*. Repressed *by* memory is the experience that it never stopped happening—that the past is unconsciously repeated.

The idea that one time is the *real* (or unconscious) of another time is, of course, central to psychoanalysis; it is no less central to the intertemporal conception of justice that underlies this book. I believe that historical disasters heighten the salience of otherwise latent moments in the past and that, at these times, beneficiaries who considered themselves immune from liability are no longer so lucky. There is, instead, a moral imperative—perhaps a *new* generational imperative—to restore justice while there is *still* time. Ascribing urgency to the time that remains is, I think, the moral meaning of disaster.

To the extent that the twentieth century was a disaster, how should its survivors behave? Although the ship of state is a common metaphor in political theory, few political theorists have started with the shipwreck.[69] Yet shipwrecks are a legal metaphor for disasters occurring outside the scope of political sovereignty and salvage is the form of *justice* that follows such disasters, even as piracy is the paradigm of *unjust* salvage by those responsible for the shipwreck.[70] Levi's metaphor of "saved" and "drowned" puts him in the position of an "ancient mariner" interrupting the celebrants of Europe's postwar feast. Are they legitimate salvors of the wreckage left by Nazi piracy? We cannot take this metaphor too far.[71] Although the Allied powers prosecuted Nazi leaders as pirates, the postwar Occupation regime struck a balance between what lawyers would call rights of restitution and rights based on "adverse possession" that allow beneficiaries of unjust acts to keep their gains.

8

ADVERSE POSSESSION

Beneficiaries as Survivors

I have argued throughout this book that something more should be expected of surviving beneficiaries whose unjustly acquired gains continue to appreciate in value after the perpetrators of past evil have been defeated. The time has come to ask whether we have, or can develop, the conceptual tools required to redistribute accumulated wealth for reasons of historical redress.

Most legal theorists who have difficulty imagining a feasible scheme of reparative justice assume that its goal must be to compensate victims for their loss. It is one thing, they say, to compensate the victim of an accident for financial and physical injuries; it is quite another to figure out the loss resulting from near-term failure to compensate if a lawsuit were to be brought several generations later. On the one hand, there would be too many intervening causal variables to know how well off the plaintiff and defendant would be *but for* the accident; on the other hand, the experience of being wronged (and wronging) vitiates over time and vanishes between generations. This is why the law generally cuts off tort-based remedies with statutes sharply limiting the time in which they can be claimed.[1]

If and when there are political reasons to recognize historical injustice through something called "reparations," most writers on the subject urge that these be seen as minimal and symbolic rather than as compensation for continuing loss.[2] In many such cases, they suggest, the decay of memory would normally count against reparative justice and only counts in favor when historical "memories" are stirred up to *remind* people of what they would otherwise no longer remember. The political mobilization of victimary identities tends to give *claims* to reparation a legitimacy that trumps their illegality under statutes of limitations. But accommodating such claims, however necessary, should never be confused with compensation for past injury, much less with a broader restoration of social justice going forward. The first reason to avoid such confusion is that, with the passage of time, many intervening causal factors would explain today's social outcomes—and thus many paths to the present could have led to different distributions of advantage and disadvantage. Second, there is the question of what would have happened had full compensation been paid on the spot: Would it have been wasted by the recipients or lost in the *next* historical catastrophe rather than invested safely in a risk-free debt instrument on which interest has continued to compound until this very moment? Finally, there is the problem posed by the concept of compound interest itself, which (according to the formula) accumulates exponentially over time. *How* could the resulting "debts" ever be paid as the time gap increases from acknowledged injuries due to the Holocaust, North American slavery, the Spanish *Conquista*, or the sack of Carthage? And *why* should they be paid at any given moment if they become increasingly valuable to those who hold them as time goes on? Such potentially irresolvable problems are intrinsic to a loss-based model of reparative justice.

But we need not stumble on such problems if we begin with a *gain*-based model of reparative justice. Here, the primary burden would be to figure out *who should pay* and *how much*; only then would we need to find someone with an arguable right to *get paid*. Only then would we ask under what contingencies, and at what price, the right to retake unjustly held gains could actually be *exercised*.

Law students typically learn to address such questions in classes on "property," rather than on "torts" or "contracts." Many property law textbooks start with cases on "adverse possession," which are really about the occupation of *someone else's* space—how de facto possession, perhaps by force or fraud, becomes de jure entitlement. (These cases are often about squatters, but they might just as well be about colonial conquest and settlement.)[3] The question typically posed in such cases is whether "property law" allows a remedy against the unjust occupant or cuts it off. In the latter instance, the occupant is said to have acquired ownership *constructively* (by operation of the law), rather, for example, than contractually (by transfer from the previous owner). Students thus learn that, although much property is acquired contractually (through the operation of contract law), the specific province of property law is to address that which is *not*. Such property is typically acquired through cutting off remedies (cases of adverse possession, right of conquest, etc.) or through granting them (for example, by ejecting an illegitimate occupant or possessor and returning the lost property along with any gains to its "rightful" owner).[4]

One way of understanding the creation of market societies (at least of free markets in land) is thus to say that their establishment cuts off legal claims based on the feudal "estates in land" and that doing so appears justified, retrospectively, as a politically necessary *remedy* for the injustice of feudalism itself. The historical development of common law property could thus be conceived as a way for English courts to treat feudalism as something that was historically *past* while recognizing its continuing effects on wealth. I do not claim here that fully marketable freehold land titles came about in this way. I contend, instead, that one reason for their presumed sanctity in market societies is that the legal creation of bourgeois land titles *could have been remedial* (and was so interpreted once feudalism was *gone*). Property law is thus the precontractual foundation of market societies (their account of how unowned things come to be owned) and is thus distinguishable from contract and tort law (how owned things can be transferred or damaged) insofar as it retains the possibility of "restitution," which is a nonpossessory right created through the operation of law as a remedy for past injustice.[5]

By the early twentieth century, property law—as the historically grounded part of legal education—treated three types of backward-looking justice as "restitution." The first is an *undoing* of the past that sets things right, for example, returning something zwrongfully or mistakenly taken to its rightful owner, fully restoring the status quo before the injustice occurred. A second type of legal restitution is compensating the victim for his economic loss, much like a tort remedy (which is generally incorporated into the teaching of property as a way of *limiting* restitutionary damages).[6] The third type of restitution occurs when it is *unjust* for beneficiaries of wrongdoing to keep the portion of their accumulated gains that exceeds the damages their surviving victims might claim. Here the legal remedy is disgorgement of ill-gotten gains whether or not victims of the wrong survive and even if successors to their claims could not directly prove individual losses in an equal or greater amount.

For the purpose of this book, a gain-based approach to reparative justice is central because it directly addresses the circumstances in which the benefits of past injustice have been cumulative, in which an ever decreasing number of the direct victims survive, and in which individual victims would have difficulty proving losses on the scale of the cumulative gains that were thereby produced. In this respect, gain-based remedies differ from loss-based remedies, which typically require proof of direct causation to establish liability—my action (whether gainful or not) must be shown to have caused your loss.[7] Freed of this constraint, a gain-based approach to restitution would allow recovery from the *beneficiaries* of past injustice long after the perpetrators are gone, sometimes even generations later.[8] The underlying theory is that a component of present-day social advantage is attributable to a past wrong and that this component can be continuously valued, up or down, under changing historical circumstances.

From the gain-based perspective of "unjust enrichment" remedies, it is always worth asking whether systemic versions of reparative justice are appropriate, even if only as partial steps toward distributive justice, and also whether claims for reparations could be justified, even beyond those necessary to achieve equality. I think that economic equality (socialism) might set an effective limit on the value of claims to historical reparation and will explain why at the end of this chapter. First, however, I argue that restitutionary remedies are central to the functioning of property-based societies, and that we have ample conceptual tools for providing them. Most remarkable is how infrequently these tools are used to address the kinds of issues discussed in this book. The reason, I think, is that beneficiaries of past injustice tend to undervalue such claims and that their potential owners—the successors in interest to victimary identities—do not understand that their value fluctuates over time.

Property and Restitution

The law of property defines, as we have seen, the side constraints that the justice or injustice of a past, such as feudalism, will place on present and future distributions of wealth.[9] In postfeudal societies, as we have seen, the property rights of present asset holders are often used to cut off restitutionary claims against current possessors who are well settled in their use.[10] There is thus a presumption in favor of leaving possession of property undisturbed when the possessor has committed no (new) offense and is using the property productively. In the exceptional cases in which the repose of the possessor is disturbed in the interests of historical redress, restitution takes the form of returning an asset presently possessed by another or by creating a new asset considered its equivalent.[11] All property regimes strike a balance between a forward-looking interest in *repose* and a backward-looking interest in *redress*.

In functioning markets, property rules also determine who must pay or be paid for future benefits or harms that result from the mutual interaction of endowment holders. The economist Armen Alchian explains that "property rights are not private"; rather, they determine "the divergence between social costs and private costs." The "ability to 'use' *other* people's resources, and thereby remove their options, enables one to make other people bear part of the costs of one's decisions." Behind Alchian's free market individualism lies an implicitly collectivist assumption that costs and benefits are always jointly caused, and that property rules determine how these "costs are divided between the decision-maker and outsiders."[12] Property rules thus determine who must pay or be paid to avoid *collective* costs or to produce *collective* benefits, or both, and thus determine the degree to which the "external" (social) effects of his resource use will be "internalized" and thus "*made* private" (my emphasis).[13] In this sense free market economics is founded on projection and introjection (the self as other, the other as self) under conditions that presuppose an underlying "jointness of beneficiaries." Although most economists refrain from characterizing the "invisible hand" in psychoanalytic terms, they assume that

> the use everyone makes of his own marketable goods depends on the preferences and desires of other people. When one uses goods, he must reckon with the gains he otherwise could have. Sometimes this inducement feedback is called "internalizing the external effect." In essence, much of economic theory concerns the allocation of the uses of economic goods by *internalizing* external effects.[14]

In determining the *degree* to which externalities must be internalized, property rules are both the foundation of free markets and the *theoretical* exception to the claim that markets minimize the social costs of individual decisions. Property rules thus function within market theory (like property law in legal theory) to establish the continuing effect of the past in limiting the otherwise most efficient use of resources—which, if there were no bad history, would be a bad thing, but could be a good thing if property rights were originally created as a matter of remedial justice that could not be accomplished all at once or even in a single generation.

Here, as elsewhere in this book, we can see the interaction of normal and countervailing conceptions of how fundamental institutions operate. The ostensibly normal principle of the market is that endowment transfers occur through bargaining that leaves both sides better off. But a counter-principle is required to cover cases of noncontractual (involuntary) transfers. The rules governing those transfers are of two basic kinds. Rules of the first kind, *liability rules*, require the taker to pay just compensation for the loss suffered by the initial endowment holder. This effectively allows the taker to keep whatever incremental gains are left over, implicitly rewarding nonconsensual transfers that create new wealth and penalizing those that do not. Rules of the second kind, now generally called *property rules*, give the endowment holder the choice of refusing the transaction even *with* compensation.[15] As a purely legal institution, the market is thus constituted by an initial set of endowments governed by property and liability rules that determine when one must pay to impose external diseconomies and when one must be paid *not* to do so. The present answers to these legal questions largely determine the social distribution of wealth—which can, in principle, be changed, according to market theory, without raising "social cost" through inefficiency.[16]

My suggestion in this chapter is that historical injustice should be viewed, primarily, as a form of property—the creation of an asset—rather than as personal liability for a harm, but, in order to explain this, I must next distinguish between property as a right and as a remedy. The legal effect of asserting a *right* to property is generally to limit the remedies available to others for the harms one causes through the otherwise beneficial use of that property. What if another benefits by violating one's property right? The *remedy* might be either property reducing or property creating. In a property-reducing remedy, damages are limited to the plaintiff's *loss*, and any surplus benefit from this involuntary "transaction" will remain with the violator. But if such a forced transaction would have been *unjust* and not merely illegal (even the *law* makes this distinction!), then the surplus is awarded to the plaintiff through the creation of rights in *rem*, essentially a new asset, that can appreciate in value and be claimed by and against successors in interest.

Whether or not new property could have been justly created in a Lockean State of Nature,[17] we know that it can be legally imputed as a consequence of wrongdoing. The notion that existing property might *already* be remedial explains its significance in market societies as the fundamental constraint that past history places on the present. Because the property holder is (or might as well be) a survivor of past injustice to whom restitution was granted, infringing on his claims could be like reopening a healed wound. There are many sectors of society in which heritable property rights provide their present holders with revenue streams traceable to some long past injury or usurpation. The supposed legitimacy of such rights is historical, and the political arguments for respecting them are not intrinsically stronger than the arguments for creating new property to reverse a historical injustice.[18] This *is why* policies of restitution are consistent with the moral framework of respecting property and why successors in interest to those who were dispossessed of land or labor by force or fraud *could be* endowed with assets held by interlopers and their successors in interest. Property owners are often in a position to force others to deal with them so as not to repeat bad history. So why *not* counteract the ongoing wealth effects of historical injustice by creating legal estates in property for disadvantaged groups? The present possessors of revenue streams, however innocent of personal wrongdoing, would have to give way when restitution is required.

There are often plausible counterarguments to be made against granting the remedy of restitution. The first is that those endowed with remedially created property would seek economic rents from present asset holders, and could thus, like feudal lords, enjoy windfall (undeserved) gains that have nothing to do with distributive justice in its ordinary sense. A further objection is that remedies such as tribal reservations of land or of places in university)[19] would lead to market inefficiencies unless, for example, a Native American woman were allowed to sell back her own remedial rights to preferential treatment (and even those of future generations) to a beneficiary of past injustice at a price he could afford to pay. The long-term effectiveness of the remedy would then depend on how much the first generation is paid for giving it up and what is done with the proceeds.

Both these potential objections to remedially created property apply to property in general—their kernel of truth is simply that market efficiency sometimes disfavors enforcing property rights that reduce the opportunities and incentives to bargain, as entailed feudal property once did.[20] This point is echoed by some liberal theorists, such as John Rawls, who assume that the normal path of distributive justice in a democracy is to weaken (by interpreting it as minimal) the veto power of *all* claimants to property and that the large-scale creation or transfer of property would occur only during changes in what he calls "the basic structure" (the legal framework of the state and economy) that are typical of democratic revolutions.[21]

Property creation is not, however, limited to revolutionary situations. It is also available as a partial remedy for historical injustices that cannot or will not be reversed. At a time when the British Crown was giving land grants to the colonizers of North America, indigenous occupants sometimes requested and received *in the form of property* a portion of the land that had been taken in the name of the Crown.[22] Had such property grants been more extensive, and more scrupulously honored, their cumulative proceeds might have curtailed the differential benefits accrued by settlers and, at least conceivably, left indigenous property holders better off than they would have been had there been *neither* conquest *nor* the economic development that followed. But this opportunity for justice was not forever lost. A similar result could be replicated today by creating a fund that models retroactively the hypothetical present value of the endowments of which indigenous peoples were unjustly deprived and which have subsequently enriched the present holders as a direct consequence of indigenous impoverishment. We should therefore consider more closely the mechanisms other than constitutional change through which the benefits of past injustice might be disgorged.[23]

The textbook wrongs that call for restitution include unjust enrichment through coercion, conversion of property, dispossession of or trespass to land, negligence, mistake induced by fraud, fraudulent misrepresentation, breach of trust, usurpation of office, and so forth. Restitution may be awarded to plaintiffs even in the absence of defendant wrongdoing in cases, for example, of innocent misrepresentation, benefits voluntarily conferred by mistake (whether or not upon request), gratuitous transfers (whether or not made in reliance on a relation), innocent conversion of chattels, mingling one's funds with a wrongdoer (or withdrawing commingled funds), mistaken gifts, mistakes about a legal duty, mistaken payments, and even *plaintiff's* accounting errors. Claims for restitution in *quantum meruit* allow recovery of unjust benefits from another's labor or service[24]—a broad category that includes outright enslavement, false imprisonment, failure to pay for improvements to property and noncompensation for unrequested, but beneficial, interventions (such as acts of rescue, provision of medical care to the unconscious, and sometimes even the unsolicited rendering of legal services).[25] Although the core legal meaning of restitution is disgorgement of *unjust* gains,[26] this remedy is not limited to gains acquired by *unlawful* means.[27]

What, then, counts as restitution? It could be merely a return of what was lost, such as specific property, or a recovery of costs that were incurred as in a rescue, The core idea, however, is to do an explicit or implicit *accounting* that connects the gains of the defendant to the losses of the plaintiff in a way that supplements the separate accounts maintained by each. The ability of the law to "trace" assets means that restitutional remedies that do not simply *return* property can, instead, create a beneficial interest in an asset or fund that has grown in value owing to the original injustice or in close correlation with it.[28] Once this has been done, disputes about the remedy depend upon proving a counterfactual proposition (that the enrichment of the defendant would not have occurred but for the impoverishment of the plaintiff) or a factual proposition (that the enrichment of the defendant occurred *through* impoverishing the plaintiff—or both).[29]

Although there are many forms in which the surviving body of an injustice can be recovered,[30] the most general is as the *corpus* of a constructive trust in which the wrongdoer is treated as a fiduciary holding assets on behalf of the plaintiff.[31] According to Judge Benjamin Cardozo,

> A constructive trust is the formula through which the conscience of equity finds expression. When property has been acquired in such circumstances that the holder of the legal title may not in good conscience retain the beneficial interest, equity converts him into a trustee. . . . Constructive trust is then the remedial device through which preference of self is made subordinate to loyalty to others.[32]

Cardozo's description of constructive trusts is presented here as a necessary element in the legal underpinning of market economies as such.[33] We have already seen that markets do not require that *all* injuries to property must lie where they fall as, for example, competitive injuries do—*some* injuries must be compensated.[34] The possibility of a constructive trust completes the picture by creating a double view of the present—seeing it simultaneously as it is and as it might have been. Although courts are reluctant to award restitution in a wide range of cases where the law encourages parties to bargain,[35] it is an available remedy in cases of exceptional culpability, and for wrongs that might be profitable *because* the victim was not at the table to bargain.[36]

The possibility of restitution, therefore, provides an effective counterprinciple within market theory itself through which *a duty to have bargained* with one's victims can be retroactively enforced. Unlike *in personam* remedies in tort or contract, a cause of action for unjust enrichment allows a plaintiff to proceed even when the original wrongdoer can no longer be named as a party and even when the proceeds of the original asset are collectible only in a different form. Because restitutionary remedies create rights *in rem*, the effect is to make what was already someone's property legally available for redistribution, but only according to criteria that are themselves property based.

The legal effect of tracing assets into a constructive trust is a double (parallax) view of the separate accounts, and thus the economic positions of the gainer and the loser,[37] which become reversible, first potentially (in order to consider the case) and then actually if the plaintiff prevails. This is not merely a reversal of fortune—one windfall undone so that another can occur; it is a form of justice that can come only after *in*justice and is thus more reflexively, and deeply, just than the prior status quo, which can now be seen both as it is and as it might have been.

Restorative Justice and Reparations

Can a conceptual understanding of property-creating remedies in private law help clarify what "mass restitution" might mean as a component of large-scale social transformation in the direction of justice? A number of legal scholars have debated the analogy between micro- and macro-applications of the concept of "unjust enrichment."[38] The obvious problem is that imputing a "constructive trust" directly addresses the question of "who benefits" from an ongoing injustice without necessarily considering whether the injustice would, or even should, continue were its beneficiaries to change. By commodifying past injustice, restitutionary remedies may give successful plaintiffs (former victims) a beneficial interest in continuing a harmful practice.[39] Would such harmful practices cease, or change for the better, if they had different beneficiaries? Or would a change in beneficiaries be sufficient to render them just?

Such questions recapitulate venerable debates in the history of socialism, conceived as a *remedy* for the injustice of capitalism. One strand of socialism argues that the moral problem with capitalist relations of production is, quite simply, that the wrong people benefit. A variant of this view suggests that, if the revenues flowing from capitalist production were collectively, or publicly, *owned*, the system itself would change through voluntary action of its new owners. The socialist countertradition, no less venerable, is that the *benefits* produced by capitalism are *intrinsic* to the unjust relations of differential wealth and power that it reproduces. A variant of this view is that many of these benefits are in fact "relational" goods—forms of social advantage that would cease to *be* benefits if everyone possessed them equally.[40]

Parallel issues arise at a lower level of social analysis—for example, in recent litigation against tobacco companies. Is the problem that tobacco use is both harmful and addictive or that the *wrong people* profit from it? Suppose that successful plaintiffs, smokers and their heirs, end up with a share of the companies' profits. Does this imply that tobacco companies could have avoided wrongdoing by issuing stock options to dying smokers that could eventually be exercised by their heirs? If so, a tobacco industry run as a consumer cooperative[41] with extra shares for heavy smokers could do no wrong no matter how dangerous its products.[42] Those who argue that the *wrong* consists of producing addiction and disease might conclude that *no one* should profit from such a product, and regard it as perverse to give those profits to the very smokers who should, rather, be deterred.

But, if *anyone* is going to profit from societal harm, why should it be the survivors of those who *smoked*? Tobacco is a product for which society already pays a high cost, and which it might well have prohibited if large markets for it did not already exist. If such concededly harmful products are allowed to exist, why not confer the benefits from selling them on descendants of slaves or remnants of aboriginal peoples They could then benefit from society's willingness to *indulge*, rather than *reward*, those sins it considers venial, namely, the addictive behavior of smokers themselves. By extension of this reasoning, we might also deal with the issue of presently prohibited products, such as marijuana, not by legalizing it outright but, rather, by giving "First Peoples" a regulated monopoly to grow and sell it.[43] If we are going to have a marijuana "problem" anyway, why not suffer it for the benefit of First Peoples?

Such thinking is not new. In medieval Europe, as we have seen, the Catholic Church was largely funded by selling absolution from guilt at a near-monopoly price—there was little expectation that sinners would compensate those adversely affected by their conduct. Our present discussion suggests that there may be something *right* about recapturing the windfall gains from presently harmful activities (such as manufacturing cigarettes or causing pollution) as a *penance* paid by society as a whole for past injustice—a form of purgatorial practice, like the medieval sale of indulgences. Today a similar approach to *repairing* past evil is reflected in the idea that gaming licenses should be granted as a quasi-monopoly from which dispossessed indigenous peoples, and *only* such groups, should be allowed to profit. If *anyone* should be allowed to throw off externalities without compensation, so the argument goes, it should be those who have suffered ongoing impoverishment as a result of some originary injustice. Their restitution would consist of the *license* to impose certain costs on society that would in legal parlance "lie where they fall." The reparative effect of the license thus allows its victimary possessor the excess profit that comes from not paying for costs that they impose on others (Alchian's "external diseconomies").

Gaming is not the only social nuisance that can be swept into a program for correcting past injustice. Suppose that, by way of reparation, a successor state conferred on indigenous peoples an exclusive license to *pollute* land that was unjustly taken from them. The result is that all present polluters would henceforth have to pay *them* at the going price for permission to continue. Perhaps the total amount of pollution would then be less because the price would be higher, because it would be a monopoly price. But the price would not necessarily be higher, and, adjusted for price, the total social cost of pollution (or other nuisances) could remain *unchanged* by reparative justice—the only necessary difference would be in *who pays* and *who gets paid* for changes in the *amount* of pollution.

What would have changed if pollution levels remain the same? After reparative justice, one might argue, we would live in the purgatorial state of a *deservedly* bad environment. By this I mean that we have an environment worse than we would legislate for ourselves if no one could claim residual rights traceable to that injustice. Such arguments are often made, but rarely at the level of generality I have suggested. Sometimes they focus on traditional Native American practices, such as hunting now endangered species or using drugs that are now prohibited (peyote or cannabis). But is the point of exempting First Peoples from environmental regulation we apply to ourselves that we want them to go on as far as possible as though we settlers were not here?[44] Such claims could be stated as a limited license to harm our environment without paying for the external diseconomies that they cause.[45] When we let the ongoing victims of historical injustice internalize economic externalities of the kind described by Alchian, we implicitly concede that remedial justice itself is the strongest property-based rationale for continuing such harmful activities. In a well-ordered society, with no bad history, we would normally assume that no one has a privilege to ride roughshod, either literally or metaphorically, over the interests of others. Proponents of retroactive justice must thus argue, in effect, that First Peoples have a *legitimate* right to destroy our commons in much the same way that, for example, French aristocrats *illegitimately* (claiming *droit de seigneur*) rode roughshod over the crops of peasants while on foxhunts.

Although such purgatorial practices provide a way for the living to pay for past sins, they do not fully address what victimary identity wants. It could add insult to injury, for example, if present-day Turkey were to address the Armenian genocide by granting individual Armenians (or Armenian organizations) exclusive licenses to operate casinos at resorts in a society that generally disfavors gambling on religious grounds. Would it be equally insulting to give Jewish organizations exclusive rights to all commercial uses of the Swastika and the right to license what might be considered the Nazi (and Holocaust) "brands"? Economic windfalls that treat genocide as conferring a more or less exclusive right to *profit* from genocide are not redress *themselves*. The wrong of slavery is not redressed by treating it retroactively as wage labor—just as the wrong of rape would not be redressed by considering it as involuntary prostitution that should, at least, have been paid. There must also be, as we have seen throughout this book, an element of moral victory for victims—a *judgment* in their favor—without which redress would merely make "forced transactions" in the past a little more *acceptable* going forward. A gesture of acknowledgment is essential for reparative justice to occur.

But reparative justice would be impossible if it could be *entirely* gestural. No one has suggested, for example, that the U.S. government's 1988 payment of $20,000 to individual Japanese Americans who had been illegitimately interned forty-six years earlier constituted compensation for their loss; nor was there an attempt at restitution of their forcibly abandoned property or disgorgement of the unjust gains that were later accrued from it. The token lump sum payments were, primarily, a way of *touching* those still marked by that injustice with an act of apology. Their *admitted* insufficiency was said to strengthen that message on the grounds that paying *more* than token reparation would have focused attention on the amount rather than the gesture. But in most cases a reparative gesture would not come off if clearly identifiable windfall gains from the underlying injustice were left undisturbed. For a wrong to be redressed, any windfall benefits traceable to it must be expropriated, which makes unavoidable the question of how, and to whom, the proceeds should be redistributed so that justice will be served.

Is there anything to be learned from other attempts at reparative justice that have occurred in recent years? Although such reparation schemes are metaphorically based on private law concepts, they are generally created and paid for by governments in contexts where litigation is likely to be barred by statutes of limitations, sovereign immunity, and judicial doubts about the standing of named plaintiffs to claim the proceeds of past wrongs and about the liability of named defendants to pay. Comparisons among these schemes tend to treat them as policy and to stress issues affecting policy design. Scholars thus ask whether the historical wrongs (or harms) are discrete or continuing, whether the payout should be lump sum or ongoing, and whether finality is either a desirable or attainable goal in such matters.[46]

A further question is whether and how to regulate the social consequences that follow from clarity can be achieved by considering broader forms of social remediation as forms of restitutionally created property. If, for example, remedial rights of access to elite higher education (such as preferential admission) could be sold on the market by members of the restituted group, the price of an elite education would go up for those who are willing and able to pay. Would this be better for *all* members of the previously disadvantaged group than allowing only *some* (perhaps the least disadvantaged) preferential access to the most highly valued opportunities? Or would it perpetuate the *kinds* of inequality that were to be remedied by *increasing*, rather than reducing, the wealth gap attributable to elite higher education? There is a tension here: on the one hand, remedially created property rights must be marketable if they are to be valued within a single generation; yet, as claims to historical redress, they must also be *descendible* across generations. It would seem that the *feudal* ideas of "reversionary" claims and "life estates," still central to the law of trusts, are also applicable to questions of restitution for historical injustice.

My purpose in this chapter is to bring these core doctrines of property law into greater coherence by arguing against the grain that historical justice—justice across time—is entirely *conceivable* to market societies that, nevertheless, resist it.

Compounding Damages

The most heavily studied examples of reparations and restitution are those involving Holocaust victims,[47] where the harms were historically discrete and the victims, perpetrators, and beneficiaries clearly identifiable. The Holocaust example is invoked by some to demonstrate the limited conditions under which reparations programs are feasible; others cite the Holocaust to establish precedents for similar measures to make reparations for atrocities, such as U.S. slavery, that were responsible for even more deaths, suffering, and accumulated wealth over a much longer period. From the perspective of this chapter, we can see that these otherwise valuable studies presuppose a damages-based, and not a property-creating, remedy; they then deal with the history that comes after by calculating compound interest on what the original damages should have been.

The best-known proponent of such an approach is Randall Robinson, who argues that the legal standards rightly established to provide restitution in Holocaust slave labor cases make it inexcusable to ignore the bill run up during 246 years of U.S. slavery.[48] In presenting that bill, Robinson relies heavily on the earlier work of Robert Westley, who itemizes the original, recurring, and compounding costs of that history to African Americans based on the same formulas used to compensate Holocaust survivors.[49] "Let me try to drive the point home here," says Robinson:

> Through keloids of suffering, through coarse veils of damaged self-belief, lost direction, misplaced compass, shit-faced resignation, racial transmutation, black people worked long, hard, killing days, years, centuries—and they were never *paid*. The value of their labor went into others' pockets—plantation owners, northern entrepreneurs, state treasuries, the United States government.
> Where was the money?
> Where *is* the money?
> There is a debt here.[50]

Developing Robinson's theme of white hypocrisy, Westley reflects in a more recent article on why U.S. courts have dismissed lawsuits seeking restitution for black slavery, despite allowing recovery for the forced labor of deceased Nazi victims. According to Westley, black slavery in the U.S. is still considered under a simple tort model in which injuries and liabilities are nondescendible. The reason for this difference, he argues, is the "implicit devaluation of people of African descent" and not, he suggests, the oft-cited inability of courts and legislatures to evaluate much larger claims over much longer periods.[51]

There may be hypocrisy, and worse, in allowing Holocaust reparations to extend in the form of pension benefits to children of survivors in ways that were not considered for the immediate descendants of slaves, most of whom never even got their "Forty Acres and a Mule." But in focusing on white racism, Westley ignores the deeper question of whether a *modified* "damages" model (extending to offspring) is a more appropriate remedy for historical slavery than the construction of a financial asset that indexes the resulting inequality. Should Holocaust survivors and their heirs have been given a major financial interest in Europe's (or at least Germany's) postwar industrial growth? Should surviving Jews in Eastern Europe have been allowed to *profit* from communism by running enclaves of capitalism within it? The particular history of European anti-Semitism, leading to the Holocaust, would have precluded discussion of capitalism and profiteering as *remedies* for Jewish suffering, even though a significant part of the *moral* entitlement that accompanies *newly established* capitalism is rooted in a sharp sense of grievance over the oppression that came before.

But, as suggested earlier in this chapter, remedially created property tends to bring out some of the less morally appealing characteristics of capitalism. This underscores the ways in which greater *license* (in the moral sense) is an often plausible remedy *within* capitalism for its past inability to regulate itself. Later in this chapter I consider whether alternative, socialist, remedies can be crafted that reduce inequality rather than increasing license, but first I must elaborate another difficulty with the damages approach, mentioned earlier in this chapter—that the passage of time makes proof of damages more tenuous.

We have already seen that Robinson and Westley deal with the passage of time by first assuming that damages for slavery were entirely backward looking and that, if these damages could have been calculated on the spot, this amount could be treated as the principal on which compound interest is still accruing. "Each year," Westley argues, that "the government fails to pass Black reparations legislation the debt increases rather than diminishes and the obligation to redress wrongs inflicted on the Black community becomes more difficult to satisfy."[52] This claim—that there is still a running debt—assumes that the horrible price of Civil War itself did not, as Lincoln said in his Second Inaugural, spend down "the wealth piled up by the bondsman's two hundred and fifty years of unrequited toil."[53] Lincoln here raised a general question about the measure of damages for historical injustice: Should the cost paid by beneficiaries to *end* it offset, perhaps fully, the recompense still owed to victims? Westley, and other proponents of black reparation, need not answer Lincoln's point by claiming that the Civil War did not cost *enough*. Instead, they could rightly reject Lincoln's idea of *charging* the cost of ending slavery to the slaves, so that cumulative harm caused by slavery would be *net of* the harm resulting from the Civil War.

A more difficult problem for a damages-based view, mentioned earlier in this chapter, is whether the *ongoing* harm of U.S. slavery (postabolition) is properly measured by compound interest on unpaid damages for the backward-looking wrong. Because interest increases exponentially with the passage of time, older injustices will eventually become much more valuable than newer ones, even if their original magnitude and ongoing effects are much less. The present value of the damages to the Carthaginians or the Albigensians could, for example, be much higher than the damages to Jews under Nazism, merely because the debt was incurred longer ago and has yet to be repaid. For the same reason, the biblical enslavement of the Jews in Egypt could be worth more from the standpoint of reparative justice than the Holocaust. This reductio ad absurdum of the argument for urgent redress does not advance the project of liquidating historical claims to victimhood, but rather serves to rationalize their persistent illiquidity: Why would a society that did not provide immediate and complete compensation for historical injustice before the cumulative bill ran up ever voluntarily retire such a debt?

The real challenge is to develop a financial model that explains how the constructive value of unjust enrichment *fluctuates* over time as the political, social, and economic relations of the affected groups also change. This poses (in a very different register) Walter Benjamin's question of when to seize the present moment to *redeem* the past. Here, however, redemption would, arguably, take the financial form of a preference on the part of both victims and beneficiaries for liquidity rather than a running debt. We must thus develop a new conception of transitional justice (liquidation of past claims) that occurs at a historical moment when beneficiaries seek redemption, victims demand it, and a price can be assigned that reflects the implied risk of not redeeming *now*.

A proper description of our task is to understand why historical injustice is rarely *redeemed*, and yet must remain *redeemable*—and then to describe, as Walter Benjamin tried to do, the exceptional (miraculous) status of a "now-time" in which another time is also made present and thus redeemed. This intertemporality of justice is, I suggest, not merely a matter of occluding the experience of history's apparent losers but of the proper *valuation* of the present claims that can be made *through* them—and of seizing a moment when that value is finite and calculable. My claim is that the value of closing out (settling) slave history *changes* over time, rather than compounding.

How might the present value of unjust collective enrichment, considered as a constructive trust, vary historically? An unexpected, dramatic, and rapid change in political volatility might, for example, raise the present value of a historical claim or grievance that has been latent for decades or even centuries—and thus create a new opportunity to mitigate or profit from political risk. Dramatic changes in socioeconomic inequality—or, more significant, in the *rate* at which it changes—could also affect the present valuation of past injustice. The kernel of truth in Robinson and Westley does not lie in their specific method for determining the liquidation value of the unjust enrichment—the constructive trust arising from slavery; it is, rather, that justice has an intergenerational dimension that already affects the flows of revenue *inter vivos* and that is thus, *in principle*, subject to rectification. Once we recognize that justice is inherently both *inter*temporal and *intra*temporal, we must ask what form of asset makes up the *corpus* of the constructive trust such that it can be continuously valued over time. My suggested answer, developed later in this chapter, is that the trust might contain *options* rather than zero-coupon bonds, but first I must take up a question that arises if the value of such trust would be very large, as Robinson and Westley contend.

That question is political: How would the likely existence of very large constructive trust, arising from grave historical injustice, be optimally *managed* by a real (rather than constructive) trustee, such as a state consciously committed to achieving historical justice. Neither Robinson nor Westley advocates a lump sum payment of liquidated damages to the present generation; they suggest, instead, that the existence of the "debt" would justify collecting *taxes* sufficient to fund permanent social and educational *programs* designed to offset the permanent damage done by slavery.[54] Their view thus converges with the argument that in a system of forward-looking, tax-supported justice the greatest burden of taxes could legitimately fall on the continuing beneficiaries of past injustice simply because the past has made them rich, and, in turn, the greatest benefit from public expenditure could legitimately flow to those who are poor simply because the past has made them poor.

We are here entering the realm in which state fiscal and regulatory policies could affect the *value* of historical grievances without purporting to liquidate them once and for all. Suppose, for example, that the net effect of past injustice (such as a history of slavery) on income amounted to an annual difference of $10,000. Government might respond by making transfer payments of $10,000 per year until such time as the statistical difference no longer appears. As an alternative, however, it might provide each eligible person with a one-time capital endowment (for example, $200,000) sufficient to yield $10,000 in perpetual annual income if a recipient chooses to purchase an annuity. The endowment-based approach would give each recipient the right to make other choices, such as investing in education or in a business, and to leverage their endowment by investing it in options that give them contingent claims on the future value of their present opportunities.[55] This policy, like other fiscal policies, could be debt financed. The notion that a public debt might be appropriately *incurred* to correct social injustice is, of course, different from the idea that an unpaid debt is already *owed* as reparation to its victims, who may spend it as they like. If a penitent nation were seriously sorry about its past, the "national *debt*" (both real and metaphorical) would seem a suitable vehicle for expressing that sorrow.

But the very idea of *swapping* claims based on past injustice for government bonds casts further doubt on the assumption that historical grievances can *themselves* be valued as though they were that debt. Suppose the net effect of redistributive fiscal policies were both to reduce the ongoing economic gap attributable to past historical injustice and also to dampen differential effects of economic volatility on the revenue flows to, say, the top and bottom 20 percent of all incomes, as the economist Simon Kuznets proposed.[56] The effect of such a change might be to lower the *present value* to historical victims of gain-based claims for restitution, which might give historical beneficiaries a greater incentive to fully liquidate historically based claims against their future income. Would victimary groups then have reason to embrace or resist opportunities to close the books at a moment when the value of their historical grievance is low? Such questions cannot be asked, or answered, using the conceptual model of compound interest on a debt that underlies most discussion of historical restitution.

The biggest obstacle to valuing unjust enrichment as something other than a debt is the absence of a putatively just starting point from which ill-gotten gains can be traced. How well-off would U.S. blacks have been had there been no slavery? (Is the real question, how well-off would Africa have been?) How well-off would indigenous peoples have been had there been no conquests? (Is the real question, how well-off would Europe have been?) Some of the barriers to imagining a just starting point are conceptual. It is impossible to ask where the proletariat would stand had there been no capitalism, for, without capitalism, there would have been no proletariat. There remains, however, a problem common to both models: their apparent reliance on the construction of counterfactual histories. The reparations literature discussed in this chapter regards present-day African Americans as victims of a less equal distribution of wealth than would have occurred if their ancestors not been slaves. Such a counterfactual argument attempts to isolate imported forced labor itself from other causal factors explaining wealth disparities and takes paid labor (supported by voluntary immigration) as a baseline norm in imagining the U.S. without a history of slavery. Could we then subtract from U.S. economic history the unjust inequality that arises from paid labor? Counterfactual history is here impossible because we cannot conceive of capitalism without the exploitation of wage workers, nor can we conceive of a historical remedy, such as socialism, by imagining what would have happened without capitalism. But neither should a remedy for slavery require us to imagine a world in which it never happened. It is the actual history of unjust inequality that makes its remediation an *option*. If so, then we should be able to evaluate that option without relying upon counterfactual causal claims.[57] How could this be done?

Justice as Optional

This chapter lays a foundation for my still tentative hypothesis, implicit throughout this book, that historical grievances in market economies can be conceived as options held in a constructive trust.

Options are contingent claims that can be priced based on the *volatility* of an underlying phenomenon.[58] The *underlier* of an option is in the simplest case the price of an asset such as a stock or commodity; it can also be an index such as a stock index or, just as conceivable, an index of income inequality or political stability. A *put* is the *option to sell* an underlying asset at a set price (the *exercise price*); a *call* is the *option to buy* the asset at the exercise price. But the put or call is *itself* a commodity that can be bought (in which case one is *long* the option) or sold (in which case one is *short* the option). The put/call distinction would thus determine *what* the property right is and the long/short distinction would determine *who* has it. The *buyer of the put* acquires a *right to sell* the underlier at the exercise price (which is also called the *strike* price); the *seller of the put* gets cash up front in return for giving up his *right not to buy* the asset at the strike price when the market price is lower. Being long or short a call is just the opposite. Thus the buyer of a call is entitled to purchase the underlying asset at its strike price when its market price is higher. Put and call options typically expire as of a certain date; some can be exercised only on their date of expiration, others at any time before. All options can, in theory, be valued (have a price), and are tradable even when they cannot be exercised because the strike price or the expiration date has not been reached.

For the purpose of this book, a central point is that unexpired options, like running debt instruments, can be continuously valued, but their value fluctuates with the utility of an underlier rather than increasing exponentially over time as unpaid compound interest on debt would. This is highly relevant to the questions of intertemporal justice because it directs attention to moments when historical claims might be liquidated through bargaining and when their settlement can be legitimately *enforced* at a price that has not been directly bargained.

There is thus a further dimension of options theory that is relevant to my argument: that what is being bought and sold in the options market is the right to *force* a transaction (purchase or sale) on a counterparty at a price that would be unfavorable to him at the time the forced transaction takes place. According to the legal theorist Ian Ayres:

> The option holder can force a sale at the exercise price even if the seller does not want to sell. While call options give the option holder the choice of whether *to pay* a non-negotiated amount (the exercise price), put options give the option holder the choice of whether *to be paid* a non-negotiated amount. Call options when exercised give rise to "forced sales"; put options give rise to "forced purchases."[59]

He concludes that, although call options are well understood as an economic rationale for tort remedies requiring compensation for a *loss*, "put options have been embedded in the common law for a long time without our noticing them. . . . This entire legal realm of benefits conferred (which is the analytic doppelganger of tort call options) established the circumstances where people have the option to be paid, the option to force a purchase."[60]

Ayres's reason for stressing the importance of puts along with calls can be elaborated to address the issue of gain-based remedies discussed in this chapter. The strike price of a put defines the value at which the holders of the underlying asset can be *forced* to buy it back at a loss, which could be as large as the total value of the asset itself. This free fall could begin at the moment the asset value falls below the strike price. But whether or not the strike price is reached, the holders of the asset (or anyone else) could voluntarily buy back the put itself at its present value.

What is the present value? For an out-of-the-money (nonexercisable) option, it depends in a linear progression upon how long it has to run, how well or badly the underlying asset would do under the assumption of maximum stability (its risk-free rate of return), and (exponentially) on the changing volatility of the underlying asset.[61] What is this asset? In the case of the macro-level injustice, it could be a (yet to be constructed) composite index connecting some measure of economic growth with some measure of inequality, such as the Gini Coefficient, and perhaps some measure of political stability.

What is volatility? It is simply a measure of how *probable* any given change in the underlying index is, independent of the direction of that change. But if the index of unjust advantage in fact trends upward, then volatility will increase much more sharply in the *less probable* event that the index of advantage *falls* than it would if the index were to rise by the same amount, which is more probable. As already mentioned, the effect of a change in volatility on the option price is exponential (a square).[62]

The exponential effect of increased volatilities on the value of a put helps explain the common observation, beginning with Tocqueville, that historical grievances (regardless of duration) tend to be pressed at times of rapid change, whether that change is for better or worse, but are more likely to be expressed at moments when the value of an unjust advantage has suddenly declined. When this occurs, those to whom the grievance can be put will have a greater interest in social settlement in order to protect what they have. For the same reason, the value of the victims' put will typically be higher when questions of revolution and counterrevolution are salient. Redistributive class compromises, such as the welfare state, are often responses to situations in which questions of revolution and counterrevolution become salient.[63]

My suggestion here is that in nonrevolutionary situations, justice would be optional in the sense that, even when historical grievances that have no intrinsic value—and thus cannot be *put*—their price would depend on the volatility of the underlying index (uncertainty about the future) and how long one's time line is. The question for historical victims in these situations is not whether to exercise their put but whether to liquidate it now or to be patient and allow it to run longer. If my suggestion bears fruit, a victimary group's ability to price both present options on the future and past options on the present would make it possible to speak of restitution as something possible at every moment without relying on counterfactual assumptions about a history in which *ceteris* is never *paribus*. So, viewing the grievance as an involuntarily bought put option captures the fact that the beneficiaries of unjust advantage who begin to lose that advantage can justly fear losing much more, perhaps everything, after the strike price has been reached.

Why do I view historical grievances as in their simplest form a long put, which exposes beneficiaries' gains to risk of seizure in a falling market, rather than as a long *call*, which would, instead, cap beneficiaries' *gains* in a rising market? I believe that such a cap could be justified on forward-looking grounds of distributive justice: John Rawls might have argued, for example, that in hypothetical bargaining over the permissible *extent* of socioeconomic inequality, it could be rational for the less talented and ambitious to purchase a call on the social benefits produced by the more talented and ambitious. The resulting range of income dispersion would then be limited to plus-or-minus effect of the *premium* paid by some and bought by other for calls at-the-money. Thus, in forward-looking arguments for economic redistribution the relatively *worse off* could be considered to be a long call. My point, however, is that in *backward*-looking arguments for rectifying injustice the historical *victim* could be considered to be long a put.

Much empirical and conceptual work would need to be done in order to develop a composite index of sociopolitical volatility expressing the factors that make questions of revolution and counterrevolution salient. My goal here is not to specify when a revolutionary option can be exercised but merely to underscore the point that at all other times the put (grievance) itself could still have a calculable value. Here the idea of revolution itself is necessary to express the contingency of every nonrevolutionary moment, so that it is possible to value that contingency as such. Introducing contingency is, I think, the role that historical injustice—an evil origin—plays in the self-understanding of every political moment.

There are many questions raised by my options-based approach to backward-looking and forward-looking justice that I cannot adequately address in this chapter. An obvious objection is that a multigenerational option would be hugely, perhaps incalculably, expensive. An equally obvious response is that victims of historical atrocities actually paid a huge, involuntary price and that such atrocities acquire historical significance when, and because, successors in interest *continue* to make forced purchases through ongoing or cumulative oppression. (The challenge, of course, is to operationalize this metaphor.) It could also be said that the *repetition* of a past grievance is important because it effectively *renews* a historical option that might otherwise expire. But perhaps we should conceptualize it, rather, as the *repurchase* of an option that did expire, but at a discounted price owing to past history—or, perhaps, as a more complicated embedded call entitling them to repurchase their put for less than its current market value. Further research might enable us to describe and test such chaining effects using some of the advanced techniques that Ayres develops to deal with "multiple takers."[64]

There is, however, another line of response to the objection that very long term options, even if we posit their existence, would be far too expensive to be traded. The response is that "perpetual options" can be written on a macroeconomic index such as GDP growth, income inequality, or any composite index that measures the spread, covariance, and so forth of other macro indexes. Perpetual options could not be settled by delivery of the underlier, but there are already perpetual options on microeconomic indexes of asset and commodity prices that can be cash settled for as long as the relevant index can be measured. Options on macro indexes could be settled in the same way and, if such options were widely held, the effect of continuous cash settlement could be continuous adjustment of the distribution of social wealth. Robert Shiller, the main proponent of this approach, sees such readjustments as politically and economically stabilizing because the cash settlement mechanism would forestall the need for victimary groups to "put" their grievance by demanding "delivery" in the form of economic or political control. Such options would operate, he thinks, as a form of insurance rather than speculation by bringing presently uncompensated bearers of historical injustice to the table and allows beneficiaries to pay a price that both reflects and offsets the risk that unliquidated claims against them will be exercised.[65] What neoclassical economics describes as the *free market* (no forced sales or purchases) is describable in this options-based model as the special case in which all destabilizing historical grievances are already fully hedged and correctly valued.

My options-based approach to historical grievances does not, however, assume that historical options are correctly valued in market societies. We can observe, for example, that beneficiaries of past injustice will ignore or undervalue the option that past history gives victims to demand restitution (payback) under conditions that have yet to occur. Because of this cognitive bias, such beneficiaries will be unwilling to pay what it should cost to preserve the status quo. Conversely, the victims of past injustice sometimes overvalue their grievances and will often miss present opportunities for a historical settlement during times when the option to "put" bad history cannot be exercised. We know from options theory that the "time value" of an unexercisable option largely depends on how /volatile/ the present situation is and that in politics there is rarely agreement on the value of more time. A negotiated sellout/buyback of the victims' unexpired put is thus unlikely. The important point, however, is that options pricing theory makes the liquidation of historical grievances conceivable even in at nonrevolutionary moments when they have only time value. To assess the value of the time that remains for them, victimized groups must consider not only their directional risk (the likelihood of becoming better or worse off) but also their volatility risk—the likelihood that more rapid or wider swings in relevant social indexes will make beneficiaries of continuing injustice willing to pay more or less to induce victimary groups to liquidate a running option. The intent of a negotiated settlement (historical compromise) is to make the ongoing effects of bad history (adverse possession) fade away. But these effects can also fade away without negotiated settlement. This possibility is analytically equivalent to saying that a just settlement would be valueless under the circumstances. Options-pricing theory does not tell us whether this means that it is too soon or too late to settle; it merely helps to specify what it might mean for victims and beneficiaries to evaluate their historical options, correctly or incorrectly, at any given historical conjuncture.

I thus argue that the modern theory of options pricing makes the liquidation of historical grievances conceivable at any moment when they still have what economists call "time value," even if they have no intrinsic value. This means that historically victimized groups must consider not only their directional risk (the likelihood of becoming better or worse off) but also their volatility risk—the likelihood that more rapid or wider swings in relevant social indexes will make beneficiaries of continuing injustice willing to pay more or less to induce victimary groups to liquidate a running option. When an option is "out of the money," its value depends not on how high the spot price of a settlement would be if paid as a lump sum by current beneficiaries but rather on how *speculative* that price is—that is, its variance over the relevant time period. Negotiated settlements (historical compromises) might thus be expected to occur in periods when volatilities change rapidly, facilitating a historical sellout/buyback of the victims' unexpired put.

The option of final justice—its optionality as well as its conceivability—is the ongoing question to be addressed by everyday politics. Although the gap between what one side would demand and the other would pay to close out bad history might widen or narrow over time, we should expect convergence to be relatively rare. Thus the still necessary concept that there could be *a right time* to exercise any given option is inseparable from the broader idea of optionality itself in which the time to strike is *not now.*[66]

The kernel of truth in revolutionary justice is that sometimes a resolution must be *forced* in order to overcome "the cognitive effects of endowments" (wanting to keep what one has) that lead those who are *short* the historical put to undervalue it and the countervailing cognitive bias that leads the restitutionary plaintiff to overvalue its put option.[67] The idea of justice as optional—a central concern throughout this book—means that the liquidation value of an option for historical redress rises and falls under different economic, political, and social conditions.

There has, I think, been a growing recognition that, even when the revolutionary option is not exercisable, the legal theory of free markets places few intrinsic barriers on restitutionary claims. Advocates of free markets once commonly assumed that any one-time redistribution of property endowments would inevitably create allocative inefficiencies by creating future uncertainty. Recent experience of transitional justice—especially the transition to *capitalism* in former communist countries—has made this assumption less common. In the Eastern European political transition, market theorists thus supported some restitutionary claims on the grounds that granting them would *reduce* the uncertainty that exists as long as they were still outstanding. This change in perspective was not merely opportunistic; it was consistent with the widespread view of legal theorists that endowments would have *no* effect on allocative efficiency if newly created rights are fully marketable and the new system is perceived to be *more* stable than its predecessor. It follows that a well-designed redistribution of entitlements to correct for past inequity will not necessarily reduce *total* wealth in a society and would affect with certainty only its *distribution.*[68] There would thus be "no reason to think that the status quo distribution of property rights (real or implicit) in an inefficient communist or quasi-communist economy is stable. Regardless of how property rights are distributed during the transition, property holders will continue to divide and combine them in response to market forces."[69]

A similar argument could support the equitable redistribution of wealth in circumstances where political volatility has already either increased or decreased for other reasons. This argument would have two parts: first, that greater distributive justice would advance political stability and, second, that political stability would itself become more desirable in the aftermath of achieving greater distributive justice, because, once the *gains* attributable to the *impoverishment* of historical victims are eliminated, the option to "put" those grievances to historical beneficiaries would have little remaining time value. According to proponents of this view, "there is no reason to treat transitional justice measures as presumptively suspect on either moral or institutional grounds, unless we are to treat the justice systems of consolidated liberal democracies as suspect as well."[70]

Among the many questions I cannot address in this chapter is the period over which volatility is measured. Critics of capitalism sometimes distinguish between three levels of periodicity: epochal changes in the mode of production, long waves within capitalism, and periodic crises.[71] An options-based approach to historical restitution would be of greatest political interest to the extent that the option price is sensitive to changes occurring within shorter periodicities. How short these can be is a topic for detailed empirical analysis; the price points at which a past injustice can be put to its present beneficiaries may occur more frequently than complacent beneficiaries now think, but we should still expect their occurrence to be infrequent.

We cannot leave this topic without recognizing that the *language* of liquidating historical options is often used in settler colonial contexts to rationalize the official termination of a victimized people that is on the verge of "dying out." The U.S. government, for example, has (more or less unilaterally) attempted to liquidate the options of Native Americans several times, each time imposing what is, in effect, a new defeat on its formerly conquered victims. What followed, successively, were the "allotment" of reservation lands as individual private property that could be lost in a single generation, the planned elimination of tribal autonomy as a basis for collective rights, and the gradual restoration of some tribal rights—especially those based on treaties that had been illegitimately abrogated by the U.S. government or its colonial predecessors.[72] Taken as whole, this is not a story in which indigenous peoples received a settlement that would legitimately terminate their historical claims in perpetuity; it is, rather, a story of their political "termination" as peoples with *standing* to make restitutionary claims.[73] The relation between the termination of claims and the extermination of peoples will be taken up in chapter 10.

Toward Equality?

Proponents of liberal democracy who feel politically safe tend to reject economic redistribution based on historical claims of victimhood. Their argument goes roughly as follows: when we look at the histories of

injustice—histories of usurpation, coercion, and exploitation—there is ultimately no temporal stopping point, no moment of past injustice to which
we can return for the purpose of setting things right. Therefore we cannot
make backward-looking restitution to victims the basis for future justice
but, instead, must develop a conception of forward-looking justice that
treats the past as consistently and irremediably horrible. Liberal democracy, they conclude, is the appropriate response to finding a history of
injustice as far back as we can go. If we recognize that everything is unjust,
and has been always and everywhere, then what is the point of trying to
rectify past horrors? This objection to backward-looking justice is based on
its impossibility and not its undesirability.[74]

For many liberal democrats, the time of rectifying past wrongs is never
now. This permanent delay in the day of reckoning would here be seen not
as a *bug* in the liberal program of justice but as a desirable *feature*. Advocates of "transitional" forms of justice thus typically reject Walter Benjamin's view that politics can produce a privileged connection between two
historical moments. Injustice, they say, is always compounded, rather than
eliminated, whenever the pursuit of justice is primarily backward looking.

The liberal argument against reversing any particular moment in a
whole history of injustice contains a kernel of truth. If abstract sociometric
remedies could be applied to *any* form of inequality in the present, then
there is no obvious way to limit remediation by making the arbitrary choice
of some *single* injustice that must now be set right. But the absence of a
nonarbitrary baseline for restorative justice does not necessarily mean that
arguments about justice must disregard *all* past history. We might as easily
conclude that equality, as such, is a remedy for the cumulative injustices
that are the *sum* of all past history.

The remedial equality I have in mind does not rest on an ethical defense
of egalitarianism as an ideal.[75] It simply assumes that most inequality is a
result of history and that *most* of history was bad. But once we start to correct for particular moments of historical injustice, we will find no stopping
point—liberals may be right about this. If so, we should ask whether there
is a form of backward-looking justice that does not require a stopping
point. Perhaps we could eliminate all the effects of bad history by eradicat-
ing inequality altogether, if not forever then at least for a while? Were we to
treat material equality as both an approximation and a cap on remedial
justice, then the most a disadvantaged group can legitimately desire is that
its ongoing disadvantage be wiped out.

Once we recognize that the many unequal advantages in society could
not be justified starting now, an obvious question arises: "Why not social-

ism?" Transitional justice, as the normal state of the late twentieth century, presents itself as a historically specific terminus for what used to be called the "transition to socialism"—an argument that *nothing* should follow doing just enough to achieve political stability.[76] Much more could be done. The techniques for creating financial derivatives—new property rights— could be used to describe the redirection of social revenue flows as contingent claims to be triggered by future events. The actual use of such financial instruments has already resulted in massive, previously inconceivable transfers of wealth with no pretense of justice, backward looking or otherwise. Why shouldn't greater justice be an option too?

9

STATES OF "EMERGENCY"

Nuremberg

Building on the previous focus on victims, bystanders, and ongoing beneficiaries, this chapter begins with the obvious questions about perpetrators: How is a society that is moving beyond past evil supposed to feel about the guilty, and how are those who condoned such conduct supposed to feel about their past? An obvious answer is that a transitional regime should prosecute perpetrators in a way that makes those who silently stood by feel remorse. *Their* repentance and conversion is now considered a major goal of trials conducted with the stated purpose of convicting and punishing the guilty. This idea is a creation of Nuremberg. Nuremberg itself, however, has been interpreted and reinterpreted as the linchpin of every post-Holocaust view of human rights considered in this book. The present chapter shows how Nuremberg has been misread to support the cultural interpretation of human rights that I criticize and, more recently, to protect human rights violators. In my own account of Nuremberg, there *are* human rights violators, but the victim of their violation is *not* the future entity that frames itself as human rights culture. That culture, which identifies itself with the innocence of past victims, is, in fact, an ideology of continuing beneficiaries whose complicity in the former violation is now masked.

Since Nuremberg, trying major human rights violators for their crimes has become the default response to radical evil after it has been defeated. Such trials are held in order to achieve something *real* and as the established alternative to doing something *merely* symbolic. But human rights trials are *also* symbolic: they link a real result—conviction of the guilty—to establishing a moral truth about the past in the minds of those who previously looked away.

Nuremberg has become the prototype of the human rights trial, but this is not how it was conceived by those who planned it. Their original goal had been to find each defendant vicariously liable for a Nazi conspiracy to take over Germany for the purpose of violating international law with respect to aggressive war and war crimes. According to the conspiracy theory, Nazi leaders could have been guilty of an inchoate crime (conspiracy) even if no other crime had occurred, and they could each have been found vicariously liable for any crimes committed to further the organization's criminal intent.[1] This legal approach was the basis of the London Agreement establishing the Nuremberg Tribunal and was a core element in the indictments of those charged.[2] In its final judgment, however, the tribunal had difficulty with the concept of convicting Nazi leaders for conspiracy—a crime unknown in continental jurisprudence—and did not find sufficient evidence of coordination among them except on the charge of planning a war of aggression.[3] Yet the unexpected bonanza of evidence, both documentary and visual, made it possible to convict German leaders as individuals for crimes against humanity and war crimes. This outcome was a triumph for the Allied prosecutors, arguably even better than achieving their original goal.

There was, however, a downside when the Nuremberg Tribunal did not *also* convict those defendants who were found guilty of "a common plan or conspiracy" (as the charge against them read). Conspiracy was a common law crime (illegal "combination") that had been adapted in the 1890s to prosecute restraint of trade. It became the U.S. government's preferred technique for prosecuting alleged subversives during World War II and the cold war. Under the Smith Act (1940), individual members of the Nazi and Communist parties (and also "front" groups) were tried for combining in an organization that intended to overthrow the government. Prosecution, based on organizational (rather than individual) *intent*, was considered by many New Dealers to be more protective of First Amendment values than the prosecutions of dissidents during World War I, which had been based either on the *content* of an individual's speech or the likely *consequences* of the speech.[4] The original U.S. approach to political trials at Nuremberg followed the theory of the Smith Act: Nazism was to be treated as a criminal conspiracy of a kind that could have been legitimately prosecuted even before it took power.

The defendants would be tried not just as individuals accused of specific crimes but as representatives of the organizations in the Nazi state to which they belonged and which were allegedly criminal. As leaders and organizations were tried at the same time, evidence against an individual could be held against his organization and vice versa. . . . The Nazi regime, its leaders and its institutions would be seen as plotting from the very beginning all the crimes of which they were now accused.[5]

Although conspiracy is a concept peculiar to Anglo-American law, the Soviets strongly supported the U.S. plan to prove that the SS, the Gestapo, and the Leadership Corps of the Nazi Party had been criminal organizations from their inception—a view that was consistent with the Allies' approach to denazifying the areas they controlled.[6] Convicting the Nazi leaders tried at Nuremberg for conspiracy would have set the stage for prosecuting all Nazis (and many active collaborators) for combining in an organization that had collective criminal intent. Under this legal theory, all *other* Germans—both bystanders and opponents—could then be counted among the victims of Nazism.[7]

But the American theory of collective responsibility—not of Germany as a whole but only of Nazis—did not prevail in the tribunal's judgment, which, instead, decollectivized responsibility by holding defendants individually responsible for Nazi crimes.[8] The guilty verdicts achieved at Nuremberg set a strong, and unexpected, precedent for prosecuting bureaucratic underlings—not for their Nazi associations but only for what they did or authorized. It also opened, unexpectedly, a broader question that the original conspiracy charge against the defendants would have foreclosed—whether individual Germans were *morally* responsible for what they condoned, even if they were not active Nazis. Despite its origin as a judicial compromise, the Nuremberg Tribunal's rejection of the conspiracy charge is now widely celebrated as a principled decision that is central to its legacy in holding officials *individually* responsible for authorizing *collective* crimes.[9]

Because of Nuremberg, the subsequent literature on human rights trials focuses on the need to link the legal accountability of officials for acts of genocide to the moral accountability of ordinary citizens for their indifference.[10] One would therefore have expected that, as more perpetrators were convicted for what they did, more bystanders and conformists would have been led to confront what they knew (or should have known) while human rights offenses were still occurring. By this standard, however, Nuremberg could not have been considered an immediate success. Prosecutors had expected that their initial conviction of the major war criminals would lead to the trials of thousands—perhaps tens of thousands—of individual perpetrators; a decade later the number convicted was only in the hundreds, and most of these individuals had already been pardoned or released.[11] There was, moreover, little political will to resume prosecutions once the onset of the cold war had made the rehabilitation of former Nazis seem more desirable than it had been in 1945, when the Soviets were still considered allies.[12] During the cold war years the Nuremberg precedent remained a dead letter, and the problem of genocide committed with impunity remained unaddressed until the late 1990s, when the UN created special courts to address it in the former Yugoslavia and Rwanda.[13] These would be the first serious attempts to prosecute genocide since Nuremberg.

Prosecuting genocide, however, had not even been the focus of Nuremberg as originally conceived—the intent was rather to bolster the legitimacy of an Allied occupation and reconstruction of postwar Germany by convicting its wartime leaders of crimes which included Germany itself among the victims.[14] Henry Stimson (Roosevelt's secretary of war) and Supreme Court Justice Robert Jackson (a Roosevelt adviser and future chief prosecutor at Nuremberg) saw Hitler as another Napoleon and believed that the victorious power made a mistake in 1815 by failing to try, and possibly execute, Napoleon for leading France into criminal wars of aggression and war crimes.[15] Aware of Hitler's immense popularity among Germans, the World War II Allies feared that he might also emulate Napoleon's quick return from exile in Elba, and that, like Napoleonic France, Nazi Germany would have to be defeated a second time. Determined to avoid a similar mistake in 1945, the soon-to-be-victorious Allies resolved to try discrediting the Nazi regime as a criminal conspiracy to take over Germany and lead it into a ruinous war.[16]

During the trials themselves, the massive evidence of extermination camps, both documentary and visual, did more to discredit Nazi rule of Germany than the alleged conspiracy to violate international conventions, which had been the original rationale for prosecution.[17] The legal definition of "crimes against humanity" remained vague throughout the trials,[18] and convictions for such crimes were limited to those that occurred after the commencement of war—for example, the Final Solution, but not prewar Nazi persecution and the internment of Jews, among many other crimes.[19] Only in 1948, with the drafting of the Genocide Convention, did "genocide" and other forms of gross persecution based on ethnicity, race, ideology, and religion receive a clear name and status as triable offenses under international law.[20] The recently ended Nuremberg trials became, in retrospect, the first instance in which crimes against humanity (such as genocide) had been prosecuted as offenses *distinguishable* from war crimes. Despite this anachronism, however, since the 1960s "Nuremberg" has been the dominant political metaphor for doing something real about genocide as such— so much so that the history of unprosecuted genocide since Hitler is typically recited not as a story of Nuremberg's failure to take hold but, rather, as a story of the failure of the international community to honor Nuremberg.

The event that fixed in place Nuremberg's larger, metaphorical meaning was the trial and execution of Adolf Eichmann by the State of Israel. In the words of the legal historian Lawrence Douglas, "The Eichmann trial served to *create* the Holocaust" by retrospectively interpreting Nuremberg as the world's response to it.[21] Here, for the first time, crimes against humanity were to be prosecuted separately from war crimes. The latter, Israel implicitly conceded, were best prosecuted before presumptively impartial international tribunals. With respect to crimes against humanity, however, Israel asserted the then novel legal doctrine of universal jurisdiction.[22] These crimes, it said, may be prosecuted with equal legitimacy by any state with custody of the alleged perpetrator, even if, like Israel, it had not existed when the crimes were committed.

Israel claimed, moreover, to be doing something more than standing in for any other state as a potential judge of crimes against humanity. The concept of crimes *against* humanity suggested that humanity was both the victim and the judge and that in such cases the prosecution should be brought, whenever possible, by a state that speaks in the name of victims themselves.

The Eichmann trial thus aimed to transform, retrospectively, the generally accepted meaning of Nuremberg from victors' justice (which had been troubling enough to many liberal legalists) to victims' justice,[23] which thinkers such as Hannah Arendt would find more troubling still.[24] Truly at issue, she well knew, was not the legality of Eichmann's conviction according to established legal norms but a new legitimation of Israel as a state that could lay a universal claim on the world's conscience by speaking for humanity in the voice of the victim. Through the Eichmann trial the Nuremberg precedent, originally a rationale for the Allied occupation of Germany, had become a rationale for the Israeli state in Palestine.[25]

The Purpose of Human Rights Trials

For Jews of my generation, born immediately after World War II, Nuremberg stood for the proposition that, no matter how unspeakable the crime, there are always individuals who are responsible for it. If individuals *are* responsible, Nuremberg told us, they must be *held* responsible so that the crime will never happen again. From this postwar perspective, Nuremberg could easily be seen as a historic failure insofar as it did not result in mass prosecutions of the hundreds of thousands of "good Germans" who were Hitler's "willing executioners."[26] The standard of individual responsibility set forth at Nuremberg thus stood as a challenge that the postwar world had yet to meet. During the Vietnam War, many protesters read Nuremberg through the lens of the Eichmann trial as an argument that individual bureaucrats and ordinary soldiers should be held to account for the crimes of their government—and that U.S. citizens must make an existential choice between resistance and complicity.

In 1968 Jean-Paul Sartre himself interpreted Vietnam via Nuremberg in a way that aimed to produce a new generation of existential choosers. Writing for the unofficial War Crimes Tribunal convened by Bertrand Russell, Sartre argued that ordinary war crimes had risen to the level of genocide in Vietnam because this war was being fought *by means of* imposing civilian casualties (raising the "kill ratio") to levels at which popular support for the guerrillas would cease.[27] If the U.S. military strategy in Vietnam amounted to a strategically staged genocide, then the task of my generation, the '68ers, was to bring the lesson of Nuremberg home: we must refuse to be like Germans who looked away while their government committed crimes against humanity in their name.

The relevance of Nuremberg to Vietnam would be strikingly affirmed by Telford Taylor (Robert Jackson's successor as chief prosecutor) in his 1970 book on that topic.[28] Taylor measured the success of Nuremberg by the extent to which its precedents were followed in ordinary prosecutions, not merely of those vanquished in war but also of those whose human rights abuses were committed on behalf of still powerful states.[29] Nuremberg will have finally taken hold, he believed, when victorious powers subject their own leaders and soldiers to the jurisdiction of international tribunals with the power to convict them of war crimes and crimes against humanity. I literally came of age on the assumption that, if Nuremberg was right, more trials should have followed and that such trials would be justified in the aftermath of Vietnam.[30]

The literature on transitional justice that began to appear in the 1990s took a very different perspective on Nuremberg than I had taken in 1968.[31] Nuremburg was no longer about complicity and existential choice but, rather, about the cultural effect of trials on an amorphous social whole. In the transitology literature, Nuremberg is not considered to have been a failure because a large number of guilty individuals avoided prosecution but, instead, is seen as a success because German public opinion has repudiated the entire Nazi era. That this success was achieved after very few trials leads scholars of transitional justice to the conclusion that more trials might have been counterproductive. From their perspective, the movie *Judgment at Nuremberg* may have been a more effective element in the successful transition to a human rights culture than the judgments actually rendered—and Telford Taylor, who acted as consultant on the film, should have viewed his legal and historical work as mere source material—the factual premise of the drama we now know. By the late 1990s a newly reunified Germany was widely described as a country that blessedly had the Nuremberg experience but not too much of it.

But why must *any* prosecutions occur in order to produce the desired cultural effect? The clear implication of the fin de siècle view of Nuremberg is that, if trials are important as cultural symbols of justice after evil, their *possibility* is something we could not do without while evildoers, such as Slobodan Milosevic or Saddam Hussein, remain in power.[32] But going forward with the trials of tyrants who have been deposed is now considered a discretionary decision for the victors—something that may or may not occur depending on how well it fits into the overall plan for transitional justice. Perhaps this open embrace of the discretionary nature of postwar prosecutions (a fact that Robert Jackson deplored)[33] is what finally turned the trials of Milosevic (who escaped through natural death) and Hussein (who was grotesquely executed) into failures of transitology because they did *not* produce the desired cultural effects.

Postwar human rights trials are generally described in the vast fin de siècle literature on transitional justice as (at least) show trials—not an extension of ordinary law enforcement but cultural events that are justified (or not) by their effectiveness in educating the public about its collective past. Among mainstream human rights scholars today, there is a broad consensus that for this purpose it is better to prosecute too few of the guilty than too many. The trials will have gone on for too long, they argue, if most of those compromised by the old regime come to feel that they could be subject (perhaps legitimately) to human rights prosecutions. If they face serious jeopardy, these former functionaries and collaborators will not see individual prosecution of exemplary defendants as their own second chance.

Human rights trials do not only decide the guilt or innocence of the defendants; more important, they demonstrate that, after evil, power still lies in the hands of those who were spared justice and exposure despite sharing a measure of responsibility with those prosecuted. *They* are the true audience of the trials that actually occur. The successful human rights trial provides them with broad assurance that the individual defendant will be punished, if at all, for the respects in which he differs from the many who shared his fears and wishes, and that collective guilt will go unpunished. Such trials do not produce a nation of existential choosers, responsible for everything; the trials, rather, enable the conformists of the old order to conform in the new.[34]

Techniques of Closure

In post–cold war writings on comparative "transitology,"[35] the principal functions performed by the Nuremberg trials in West Germany's successful transition from Nazism are now widely seen to be distinguishable and separately achievable (with or without trials):

- *Deterring future perpetrators.* The Nuremberg trials created a precedent for prosecuting future perpetrators. Such potential liability has arguably deterred some human rights violations and reduced the severity of others.
- *Recognizing past victims.* The Nuremberg trials provided an opportunity for victims to come forward as witnesses and accusers and thus recognized their suffering as worthy of investigation and prosecution.
- *Denouncing wrongdoers.* The Nuremberg trials resulted in guilty verdicts. Regardless of the sentence, such verdicts condemned human rights violators to live and die in a state of disgrace.
- *Creating a factual record.* Like ordinary trials, those at Nuremberg focused on evidence presented, and contested, in court. They thus produced a judicially authenticated archive of past human rights violations that made it harder for future apologists to deny their occurrence or diminish their magnitude.
- *Strengthening the rule of law.* Defendants before the Nuremberg Tribunal were accorded due process of law. Providing defeated Nazi leaders with a real possibility of acquittal established a fundamental difference between the legal system put in place by Germany's occupiers and that of the Nazis themselves.
- *Presuming the innocence of those who were not tried.* The guilty who remained unprosecuted were never said to be beyond the law, as they would

have been had a blanket amnesty been declared. This spared most of them continuing recrimination insofar as the unconvicted must be presumed innocent by newly created adherents to the rule of law.[36]

If these were the separate purposes served in retrospect by holding trials at Nuremberg, each of them might be served as well, sometimes better, by other techniques such as truth commissions, open archives, commemorative monuments, therapeutic interventions, dramatizations, literature, roots tourism, and even theme parks. In the literature of transitology, a history of human rights trials is simply one of many possible narratives about past perpetrators that could legitimate (or not) the new regime. The real addressees of these narratives are, as we have seen, the passively unjust in the old regime whom the transitologist hopes to make passively just in the new regime.

By the 1990s the Nuremberg example had been assimilated to other techniques of culture production and mythmaking in the overarching project of transitional justice. The question was no longer how many evildoers could be identified and disgraced but rather how few we would need to single out in this way to produce the best cultural result. In this context trials, and the alternatives to them, could be weighed aesthetically—recognizing that the alternatives are no *less* likely to do justice than trials that in the long run will inevitably disappoint those who are seeking justice rather than closure.

Closure was the stated goal of both the amnesty in South Africa and the prosecution of Argentine and Brazilian generals. Although the connection of closure to forgiveness is obvious, the link between punishment and closure is equally strong, especially in contexts of transitional justice. Here the point of actually punishing someone would be to counter the idea that nothing in the past can ever truly be finished. In the literature of transitology a crucial property that they are now seen to share is what I call the "alreadyness" of both punishment and forgiveness. The foregoing argument presupposes an analysis of the meanings of punishment and pardon as concepts *implying* closure, because, when somebody is *already* punished, doing something more to him is inappropriate excess that may be difficult to distinguish from vengeance or ordinary sadism. What would be the point of a punishment, this argument goes, if there is double jeopardy? It would then never be over. And what would be the point of forgiveness if we can later *un*forgive? It could then always be reconsidered.[37] Being already punished is similar, from the standpoint of closure, to being pardoned—a perpetrator who has been either punished or pardoned can no longer be accused and tried (both are better off in this respect than one who is falsely accused).

The field of comparative transitology thus treats evil as a *cycle* of recrimination and its replacement by a juridical (or other) process as a way to *close* that cycle. If closure does not come, it will be because people do not think that the sanctioning of perpetrators was a *real* punishment or that their pardon was *real* forgiveness. Yet the vast literature on transitology focuses mainly on the techniques for making a nominal punishment or pardon part of a culture of human rights in which it is already too late to do more. Writers on transitional justice thus make an essentially procedural point when they say that either punishment or pardon can break "the cycle of vengeance."[38] *Procedurally* both punishment and pardon would take historical redress of grievance off the table and thus stop the hideous process of victims becoming perpetrators in their turn. This concern with the cyclicity of grievance has become so predominant in fin de siècle Human Rights Discourse that it all but swallows up any concern for righting any particular grievance or restoring justice more generally.[39]

The recent literature on transitology accepts as axiomatic Arendt's criticism of the Eichmann trial, namely, that crimes so massive as to be unforgiveable are also inherently unpunishable.[40] If *neither* true punishment nor true pardon is possible for the perpetrators of twentieth-century atrocity—a Hitler, Stalin, or Pol Pot—then we cannot consider *either* the trials or amnesties of such individuals to bring the kind of closure that they would in ordinary cases. This literature assumes that trials conducted after radical evil could not possibly be required as a matter of justice per se, and that the reasons for conducting them are wholly cultural. Based on this assumption, such trials should be pursued exactly to the degree necessary to produce the desired cultural effects, no more and no less.

Overcoming the "Culture of Impunity"

The cultural argument for holding human rights trials pervades the literature on transitional justice of the 1990s.[41] A culture of impunity is said to exist when crimes are committed under the imprimatur of law by public officials who have low expectations of future accountability. Human rights advocates do not generally argue that holding a few procedurally legitimate trials convicting officials of ordinary crimes would deter future tyrants; indeed, they acknowledge that the precedent of such trials might even increase the ruthlessness with which the next dictator hangs on to power once his hands become bloody.[42] The hope of those who advocate human rights trials is, rather, that civil society would somehow *prevent* future seizures of power once it expects accountability from its public officials. Such "prevention" differs from "deterrence," according to the Argentine legal theorist Carlos Nino, because it operates through the cultural expectations of those on whose acquiescence future violations depend.[43] In making this claim, however, he is careful not to argue that cultural change on the part of officials prevents them from violating human rights. If tyrants who expect to be summarily shot by successor regimes (*á la* Ceausescu) may become more ruthless in holding on to power, so, too, may officials who expect to be tried—especially if negotiated amnesties and Latin American "self-amnesties" become less reliable.[44] The implicit point of Nino's distinction between deterrence and prevention is to shift the addressee of the cultural interpretation of Nuremberg from officials who will refuse to commit human rights violations to the general population who will now intervene to prevent them. This argument assumes that ordinary citizens *condoned* past evil because human rights trials were inconceivable within their prior political culture.

What makes the prior era of citizen passivity a "culture of impunity"? As a cultural rather than legal phenomenon, "impunity" names the void that could be filled (according to Nino) by holding human rights trials that result in conviction and at least some punishment.[45] But a "culture of impunity" has no coherent temporality of its own: it is always portrayed as a past culture that lacks what we now have and sometimes as a future culture in which we will have lost it once again. There is no ruling constellation of political forces that understands *itself* to be a "culture of impunity."

What, then, does it mean to explain the replacement of dictatorship by democracy in cultural rather than political terms? If we take for granted that the winners in society must remain largely the same under both regimes, then a change in *their* attitude toward governmental accountability would be all that is necessary for regime change. Explaining this change as *cultural* implies a willingness to leave the beneficiaries of dictatorship untouched after the dictators are gone. Human rights culture, when seen as the successor to that "culture of impunity," is thus a *past* future rather than a present in which human rights could actually prevail.[46]

Once we acknowledge that the culture to be created by human rights trials is an alternative to struggling for historical justice, it becomes necessary to state coherently what that alternative is. Presumably the facts revealed in these trials are meant to make past conformists feel good about having changed with the times. They might for a while and, on commemorative occasions, tell one another stories about what they would have done had they known *then* whatever truths they *now* accept. But if a new emergency, perhaps following a terrorist attack, once again persuades them that there is no time for ordinary justice, they could revert to their previous attitude of deference to the government's claims. Next time, however, they are more likely to *anticipate regret* if future scrutiny discredits what their leaders said in support of measures taken. They will thus have learned to draw *analogies* between their present feelings about the past and their likely future feelings about the present. This is what it means to treat the Nuremberg experience as primarily cultural.

In a culture that anticipates regret based on human rights, a concern with what present action *will have been* becomes central to the rationale of conformity itself: one now condones apparent human rights violations out of provisional deference to factual claims that may be proven wrong in hindsight.[47] If and when this happens, conformists can once again feel that they would have resisted had they known. But for them it is always either too soon or too late—there is nothing in human rights culture that demands resistance *now*, while the public still believes a danger is real. A culture of human rights serves, rather, to remind the public that emergencies do not go on forever and that they often end in a climate of regret for the excesses that took place.

Is the creation of such a culture an advance because it will make the expression of historical remorse easier next time? A culture that makes it easy to go back to respecting human rights also makes it easier to violate them; such a two-way ratchet would not be much of a safeguard.[48] To avoid this objection, the cultural argument for conducting Nuremberg-type trials assumes that they create a one-way ratchet—that citizens who have come to deplore the previous legal impunity of public officials are likely to oppose (by force, if necessary) future *declarations* of emergency power. A citizenry that is vigilant, armed, and organized might resist in this way. In such circumstances, however, it is also likely that the government will mobilize support for its repression based on the threat of revolution by armed, militant organizations. It is, moreover, no part of Nino's argument that the shift from a culture of impunity to one of accountability produces a revolutionary consciousness in citizens.

We must therefore return to the effect of a culture of accountability on officials themselves. As we have seen, the cultural possibility of being held to account would not necessarily deter them from violating human rights. It could, however, create standard cultural practices through which future human rights violators can subsequently account for what they have done. The point of adhering to such practices is not to prevent those individuals from committing human rights violations but rather to protect them from human rights *prosecutions* by allowing them to document, in retrospect, that they never had a culture of impunity and always showed respect for law.

In liberal democracies human rights violations are often based on executive declarations of emergency power that are supported by the legislature. This point is directly relevant to Nuremberg. Hitler declared his extraordinary powers following an election, and these powers were authorized by a democratically elected Reichstag, which had the formal power to rescind them but never had the opportunity to do so. Even if the Reichstag had not acted, Hitler could have employed jurists, such as Carl Schmitt, to argue that an executive has inherent power to grant himself exceptional authority in times of emergency. Schmitt himself would surely have obliged—in 1937 he wrote that at moments of "total war" the state executive's declaration of a "total enemy" supersedes the constitutional distinction between foreign (military) and domestic (political) threats.[49] In hindsight some Nuremberg defendants might have regretted not having gotten contemporaneous legal opinions from Hitler's Ministry of Justice that would cover them in the event of future regime change. For this reason, government lawyers now advise officials to seek and rely on assurances of the forward-looking legality of acts that might subsequently seem to have been violations of human rights. Is *this* the main difference between a pre-Nuremberg "culture of impunity" and a post-Nuremberg culture of official accountability?

My question is not hypothetical. After 9/11 the Bush Justice Department (with notable dissenters) paid its respects to the post-Nuremberg accountability by issuing opinions from the Office of Legal Council (OLC) that violations of international law (such as authorizing the torture of military detainees) are within the inherent powers of the executive branch in time of emergency and are judicially unchallengeable if Congress is silent or consents. These legal opinions are questionable on their merits and might not provide a successful defense if human rights trials were to be held. But they were not written for the purpose of trial advocacy; indeed, their very existence is meant to preclude a Nuremberg-type trial from being held. Should one be held?

The view that an OLC opinion letter should block later prosecution for human rights offenses presupposes a cultural interpretation of Nuremberg in which officials who anticipate the possibility of Nuremberg-type prosecutions can seek, and receive, prospective immunity from them. Here the very fact that officials seek and obtain assurance of the legality of their conduct means that there is no *culture* of impunity to be overcome by holding trials. But this argument also gives officials a clear path back to *legal* impunity by establishing a paper trail of reliance on the advice of the OLC and their own good-faith belief that the emergency was real.[50] Such reasoning implies, however, that an OLC opinion, whatever its substantive merits, should have the same effect as an anticipatory presidential pardon, which, once granted, would almost certainly be upheld by the courts even if shifts in the legal climate discredit the president who issued it.[51] A pardon can, of course, be issued for any reason or none at all—it simply means that there will be no trial in the country issuing it.[52] If this is also the effect of an OLC opinion, then the OLC can tell officials whatever it takes to get their compliance—the validity of its opinion will never be adjudicated. But a government that will say anything to officials who are all too willing to believe what they are told is hardly an example of the rule of law and should raise doubts about whether a liability-averse bureaucracy will be a bulwark of human rights, as Nino and others assume. Further, the OLC opinions are on their face different from presidential pardons—a U.S. president who pardoned public officials in advance for any crimes they commit would do something even worse than declaring *himself* to be above the law—he would do the same for all covered members of the government and largely relinquish his legal power to control them.

The Bush administration's OLC opinions are both a consequence of Nino's cultural interpretation of Nuremberg and its reductio ad absurdum. In a culture of accountability, human rights violators could (and would) prospectively establish their concern for being held retrospectively liable for actions taken during an emergency, thereby avoiding liability. Such officials would, of course, need to document their concerns—and could remain open to liability if they go beyond what the documentation allows. But this assumes that the original Nuremberg defendants did not seek adequate documentation because they lived in a culture of impunity and that a culture of accountability could have given them sufficient basis to avoid prosecution for acts that were, in retrospect, prima facie violations of human rights. Thus, under the cultural interpretation of Nuremberg, we can have human rights violators who are shielded from prosecution by a human rights culture. This is not adherence human rights as such but rather their replacement by a cultural simulacrum.

A cultural interpretation of Nuremberg deflects attention from the central legal question it posed—whether the individual responsibility of officials for crimes against international law is diminished or enhanced when the domestic rule of law is suspended. The question is not whether an emergency existed at the time; not whether officials happened to believe the factual claims of the government; and not whether there is contemporaneous documentation of their good faith. A regime such as Hitler's is likely to face illegal resistance (e.g., bombing, arson, and assassination) before it consolidates power. Many of its officials will thus plausibly believe that emergency conditions justify summary process—and to believe this even more strongly if there is a threat of armed resistance to their repressive measures. That human rights violations occur in such circumstances is not an exception to the lesson of Nuremberg; it *is* the lesson of Nuremberg.

The Lesson of Nuremberg

I do not see Nuremberg as a symbolic moment in a cultural transition but rather as a legal precedent about the relation between states of emergency and ordinary justice. To better understand that precedent we need to focus on the legal rationale for Nazi human rights violations between Hitler's rise to power in 1933 and Germany's defeat in 1945: the state of emergency declared under Article 48 of the Weimar Constitution following the Reichstag fire, which allowed Hitler's government dictatorial powers that it never relinquished.

The aftermath of the Reichstag fire was not the first time that Article 48 had been invoked. Since 1919, when the Weimar Constitution was adopted, previous German governments had used it to deal with civil unrest, especially when instigated by Communists. Hitler's immediate predecessor as chancellor, Franz von Papen, had recently used Article 48 to suspend civil liberties and the rule of law in Prussia, Germany's dominant state, in order to counteract a possible alliance between Communists and Social Democrats in the forthcoming election.[53] On January 30, 1933, Hitler, the leader of the largest party in the Reichstag, was invited to form a coalition government, and he immediately requested a new election to be held on March 5. The Reichstag fire took place on February 27, and the Reichstag Fire Decree was enacted immediately thereafter, suspending the civil liberties protected by the Weimar Constitution and vastly increasing the executive powers of the Reich government over the *länder*. Although the Nazis did not gain a majority of the Reichstag in the March 5 election, on March 23 the newly elected legislature passed an Enabling Act (the Law to Remedy the Distress of the People and the Reich) that allowed Hitler, as chancellor, to enact legislation on his own, whether or not it deviated from the Constitution. The basis of this action was the emergency created by the Reichstag fire itself. In the run-up to the March election, Göring (who was already both president of the Reichstag and minister in charge of Prussia's state police) conducted police raids of Communist Party headquarters in Berlin, which yielded "secret" evidence (never produced) of a Communist plot for a coup d'état, following planned terrorist attacks on property and a mass uprising. When the Reichstag fire occurred, Göring described it within minutes as "the signal" for that coup.[54] To counteract such claims, Ernst Torgler, the Communist Party leader in the Reichstag, immediately surrendered to the police so that he could establish his innocence in court. His judicial exoneration at the Leipzig trial, however, had no direct effect: he was not released from custody, nor was the "State of Emergency" lifted on the grounds that its factual basis had not been proved.[55] Thereafter German courts simply ceased to question the state's claim that a danger of Communist violence had justified the measures taken.[56]

In a postwar memoir, written after his Nuremberg acquittal, Papen would recall,

> Göring presented some . . . documents which had allegedly been found during a raid on the Communist headquarters. . . . They included plans for the liquidation of a number of political leaders, among them most of the Cabinet ministers and myself. I must confess that it did not occur to me that the Nazis, now a responsible government party, would find it necessary to forge such documents in order to bolster . . . their case. We were all convinced that the Communists had planned an armed uprising and represented a menace to the security of the state.[57]

Later historians do not believe such documents existed, much less that Göring would have bothered to forge them in order to persuade Hitler's cabinet. He had kept his alleged evidence "secret," even during Torgler's trial, where no link to the Reichstag fire or any other "treason" was proven. Yet it was not until Germany's defeat that lack of public evidence destroyed the domestic credibility of the factual claim on which Hitler took absolute power—that the Communists had a clandestine plan to resist him.[58] We now believe that the Reichstag fire was not a true emergency that might have resulted in an anti-Nazi *putsch* because no mainstream postwar German politician would argue otherwise today.

But this postwar perspective on Nazi crimes obscures the fact that the Nuremberg defendants were not allowed to raise an Article 48 defense based on their prewar knowledge. The trial could then have turned on whether they as individuals should have accepted, uncritically, the factual basis on which the emergency was declared and the extraordinary powers that their government asserted as a consequence. Should German officials (*even* Nazis) have questioned the government's claim to have information (perhaps secret) that the fire was set by Communists (aka politicized Jewry) who hated the German way of life and that foreign countries (not only the USSR but also Britain, France, and the U.S.) were harboring these anti-Nazi terrorists because of domestic Jewish influence. Would the plausibility of these allegations going forward have justified measures that might *otherwise* be seen as violations of human rights? Had the issues at Nuremberg been framed in this way, each individual defendant could have addressed what he knew or believed about the reality of the alleged Jewish-Bolshevik threat that Hitler faced when he took power.

A trial allowing Nazis to defend themselves on Hitler's own terms would have had a different meaning than Nuremberg now has. It is highly plausible that, when Hitler became chancellor in 1933, his enemies, including Jews and Communists, would (and arguably should) have responded with a campaign of direct action before it became too late to resist. The Reichstag fire could well have been the beginning of such a campaign. Even if it wasn't, a strong right-wing reaction to it could have provoked left terrorism. The German Communist Party clearly believed that a large part of Hitler's appeal lay in his ability to crack down on left terrorism to come, and that he was the only electable leader capable of also cracking down on the extremists to his *right*.[59]

Were the Nuremberg prosecutions successful because the Nazi government's allegations about the Reichstag fire were probably trumped up? Or because Göring, at the height of his power, boasted of having personally planned it?[60] None of these questions is relevant to the Nuremberg precedent we now have, which denies accused officials an individual defense based on good-faith acceptance of their government's position that Germany faced a collective threat. Had the Nuremberg trials allowed such a defense, a future court could distinguish the false emergency of the Reichstag fire (for which Jews and Communists were scapegoated as the pretext for a vast expansion of state powers) from a true emergency (perhaps the attack on the Twin Towers, the Pentagon, and, potentially, the U.S. Capitol), which would justify mass detentions without trial, suspending free speech, and the like. Based on the Bush administration's view, at least, some convictions at Nuremberg were, essentially, for failure to procure legal opinions granting future immunity from prosecution. If this view were correct, invocations of Nuremberg would teach nothing to German citizens who believed their government in 1933 and perceived the foreign and domestic threat to be *increasing* thereafter; it would teach nothing to German officials who, during that emergency, accepted without proof the government's factual allegations about who posed a credible threat; and it would teach nothing to citizens and officials deciding, thereafter whether to question, or simply obey, otherwise improper orders.

Yet Nuremberg now stands for such lessons. Germany's declared emergencies of 1933 (following the Reichstag fire) and 1934 (following the Röhm Purge) had been central to the prosecution's case that there was a *conspiracy*. By allowing the defendants to be prosecuted for creating the kind of danger anticipated by the emergency provisions of Article 48, the tribunal denied them a defense based on their individual belief that the German government was *responding* to such an emergency. Because of Nuremberg, a national danger—even when recognized by domestic courts—does not create blanket immunity from prosecution for crimes committed in accordance with a *führerprinzip* (leader principle). Nor can individual immunity be created by a legal opinion conditioning it on the official's good-faith belief in the truth of what he had been told. Hitler's arbitrariness and lack of consultation were a basis for the tribunal's finding of insufficient evidence that most defendants joined with him in a "conspiracy or common plan," but it did not consider the possibility that their offenses could be *mitigated* by trusting that Hitler had sound reasons for his decisions. Its finding of no conspiracy (with respect to human rights offenses) meant simply that a defendant's Nazi beliefs and associations were not an *aggravating* element in the individual crimes of which he was convicted.

In concluding that there may have been *no conspiracy* to fake a national emergency, the tribunal did not go on to require the prosecution to prove that the individual defendants knew (or should have known) there was *no emergency* as a necessary mental element of each crime. Its compromise ruling, crafted by Judge Biddle with the help of Herbert Wechsler, was that most defendants were to be found guilty of war crimes and crimes against humanity even though individual guilt had not been charged as part of the indictment. The overall result would gut the legal theory on which the trials themselves were based and replace it with a new approach to the individual liability of officials that it has been the subsequent task of international criminal law to interpret.

How, then, should the Nuremberg Tribunal's judgment now be read? It *cannot* be read as an internally well-reasoned decision; it *must* be understood as a rejection of the conceptual basis of the indictment, and it *could* be seen as a precedential ground for future prosecutions of individual officials for human rights violations. There are several possibilities:

- The tribunal's decision was *ill*egitimate and self-discrediting, and should not be followed in future cases where the existence of a state of emergency must be allowed as a defense.
- The tribunal's decision was *self*-legitimating in the sense that it rejected the victor's justice of Versailles (collective liability) and set the stage for the international tribunals for Yugoslavia and Rwanda, and later for the International Criminal Court, to find individual officials criminally liable but only for what they actually did.
- In convicting the Nazi leaders *anyway*, the tribunal implicitly upheld a form of guilt by association that would set a precedent for Eastern European purges and show trials during the cold war.
- *Because* the Tribunal rejected in advance the Soviet-bloc's interpretation of Nuremberg, we can now regard that wrong interpretation as a paradigm of *injustice* that retrospectively vindicates the post–cold war equation of Nazism and Stalinism.

My interpretation is preferable to all these alternatives insofar as it treats the tribunal's narrow *holding* in the case as implicitly denying *both* the conspiracy charge *and* the emergency defense. I thus concede that the entire *Nuremberg* trial would have been a gross miscarriage of justice *if* a defendant's good-faith belief that the emergency existed had been grounds for acquittal. I base this on the fact that the conspiracy charge in the indictment had precluded individual defendant from claiming, as Papen did in later memoirs, that they *believed* there was a danger of a *putsch* from the left (Communists) or the right (the SA) and were themselves unknowing victims of whatever conspiracy there might have been to conceal the truth. But the trial and its result were *not* a miscarriage of justice. *Therefore* its holding must have been that neither an actual emergency nor good-faith belief in its existence can be *allowed* as a defense in cases that bring individual criminal charges against officials for war crimes and crimes against humanity. Allowing this defense would be tantamount to allowing "reason of state" as a defense. But the rules of the Nuremberg tribunal going forward explicitly *prohibited* this defense.

Before Nuremberg, the doctrine of reason of state was widely thought to preclude criminal prosecution of heads of state and high officials for how they dealt with the state's enemies. To call an enemy attack, a domestic putsch, a subversive plot, and so forth, a political "emergency" was to say that someone acting with sovereign authority to defend the state could not later be called before a court.[61] The doctrine of reason of state had essentially blocked the creation of international criminal law, as the textbooks now describe it, because, as a knock-down argument denying all courts, foreign and domestic, jurisdiction over political leaders, it precluded the need for them to make a criminal defense. Nazi leaders could not have been criminally prosecuted at all if reason of state—that is, a good-faith belief that the state was threatened by an emergency—had been admissible as a defense against a charge of violating human rights.[62]

My argument is buttressed by the fact that the London Charter creating the Nuremberg Tribunal specifically disallowed a defense based on reason of state (Articles 7 and 8). This clearly meant that "following orders" was inadmissible as an excuse for committing war crimes and crimes against humanity. But what does it say about "following the law"? In my view, the Nazi suspension of law under the emergency made this distinction moot by turning law into orders—the *führerprinzip* itself.[63] The lack of distinction between law and orders strips away the (still limited) immunity that officials can legitimately claim when *following the law* leads them to a bad (sometimes very bad) result. That German law itself required them to follow orders *and* lend the authority of their office to governmental violations of human rights made them individually liable for such violations under international criminal law.

It was thus the Article 48 emergency itself that stripped the Nuremberg defendants of the protections normally afforded to officials who act in good faith under a rule of law. The *legal* significance of Nuremberg is that the individual liability of human rights violators cannot be easily shed in an emergency and that those who give contrary assurances (whether based on the *führerprinzip* or today's opinion letters on "the unitary executive") may assume an additional measure of liability on themselves.[64] Jurists were successfully tried at Nuremberg for creating the legal carapace under which human rights violations occurred—the message of *Judgment at Nuremberg* is that they should have known better.[65] Because of Nuremberg, government lawyers cannot create future immunity by saying whatever it takes to persuade officials *now* to go along.[66]

The Nuremberg Tribunal's verdict, though clearly the outcome of a compromise among the judges,[67] was thus fundamentally correct. By refusing to convict the guilty defendants on the conspiracy charge it stumbled upon a doctrine of individual liability that applies to public officials, regardless of political affiliation, who rubber-stamp the factual claims of their superiors by disregarding previously existing safeguards. Nuremberg means that, when a government suspends ordinary procedures, it also sweeps away the immunity from prosecution under *international* law of those who could normally claim immunity by *adhering* to ordinary procedures. This outcome, which could not have been anticipated by Nuremberg prosecutors, became the kernel of legal truth established by the case.

In the present chapter I have suggested that the history of Nuremberg interpretation has gone through the following distinct phases:

1. The forward-looking view of the original prosecutors (1943–1945) focuses on a Nazi conspiracy as a middle ground between German responsibility and individual responsibility; this view is reflected in the Nuremberg indictments.

2. The tribunal's final judgment (1946) finds sufficient evidence for the nonvicarious criminal liability of individual leaders. (Subsequent trials are held at Nuremberg through 1948, but large-scale denazification does not occur. The Geneva Genocide Convention is signed.)

3. There follows a period of latency in the West (1948–1960) in which neither Nazi associations nor individual human rights violations are prosecuted.

4. Beginning with the Eichmann Trial (1960) through the end of the cold war, some Holocaust perpetrators, including Auschwitz guards, are successfully prosecuted (1963–65, 1977). The fall of Latin American dictators occasions a debate about whether Nuremberg created a duty to prosecute human rights violators or merely made *both* prosecution and its deliberate forbearance available as strategic options for transitional regimes.[68]

5. The democratic "transitions" that accompany the end of the cold war (1989) adopt the view that Nuremberg itself was a success because of its cultural effect, which can be replicated with or without trials. Under this interpretation, prosecutions occur (e.g., for the former Yugoslavia and Rwanda), but they are openly described as optional and selective.

6. A corollary of the cultural interpretation allows officials fighting the War on Terror (post-2001) to anticipate and block prosecution for human rights violations by obtaining legal opinions from superiors that actions based on good faith to combat terrorism under emergency conditions are on the side of human rights.

My view (let us number this 7) is that the real meaning of the tribunal's final judgment (2) is based on the rationale for rejecting the theory of collective, vicarious liability contained in the indictments (1). By proposing (7), I mean to block the anticipatory defense attempted by (6) in which the treatment of "terrorism" as a human rights violation, combined with a good-faith belief that terrorism is a threat, protects government officials from prosecution for acts, such as torturing prisoners and attacking civilians, that otherwise could themselves be considered human rights violations.

If I am correct that (7) supersedes (1) through (6), then the cultural interpretation of Nuremberg is a perversion of its meaning. The tribunal's judgment struck a blow against the Nazi *culture* of official impunity: it removed the *legal* obstacle to enforcing international criminal law against official violators who rationalized their acts based on emergency conditions—a point no less important than the tribunal's groundbreaking interpretation of international criminal law as applying to such acts.[69] This is precisely what compliant U.S. officials have feared since 9/11—and their fears have become *more* justified as a consequence of the very legal opinions through which they sought protection.[70] The Nuremberg precedent assumes that, from the perspective of government officials, it is always an emergency, whether declared or not, that starts them down the path to human rights violations. The legal status of the emergency itself must thus be rethought if we are to understand the meaning of human rights at the beginning of the twenty-first century.

Emergencies

With the fall of the Twin Towers we come full circle to the Reichstag fire—the very emergency that the judgment at Nuremberg did not allow as a defense. It is thus more important than ever that we understand what the Nuremberg precedent was and what it could mean today. Does the relevance of Nuremberg today relate to whether the U.S. public has been given false information about the relation between 9/11, Iraq, and politicized Islam?[71]

As interpreted, the Nuremberg principle has continuing relevance not because the Nazi leaders made the right *kind* of argument about the wrong factual situation but because they drew incorrect legal conclusions from the kind of argument they made: they assumed that an emergency made them less responsible rather than more so. Political conformity in the absence of due process is an individual choice that officials are *asked* to make and may have a duty under international law to refuse. Those who act as a rubber stamp have effectively *taken* responsibility for the conduct they approved.

My claim that a state of emergency, whether genuine or not, *intensifies* the legal responsibility of individual officials for state action is novel only from the parochial standpoint of the U.S., where it is presumed that constitutional government is never suspended. This presumption, sustainable in wartime only by bending the Constitution,[72] partially explains U.S. unwillingness to subject its officials to human rights tribunals, such as the new International Criminal Court. Because *dictator* remains a dirty word in the U.S., we do not recognize that enhanced responsibilities follow from exercising dictatorial powers.[73]

The office of dictator is, however, as old as Roman law, where it was understood to carry personal liabilities when the dictatorship lapsed with the emergency's end. In Roman law countries with histories of dictatorship (and sometimes constitutions, like those of Germany and France, that expressly allow it), constitutional thinkers commonly understand that political opponents of the regime are likely to be rounded up and thrown in jail during a dictatorship but that, afterward, the officeholders of that regime are legally answerable for their acts. This is not to say that potential legal liability in these countries should lead to conviction rather than vindication or amnesty; it is to say, however, that the willingness of officials, while in power, to tell (and to accept) lies about the dangers that justified human rights violations is subject to subsequent judicial review. The Nuremberg precedent is centrally applicable to the Bush administration officials who sought and gave assurances that the post-9/11 emergency turned war crimes and crimes against humanity into a means of human rights enforcement against terrorists; it is much less centrally applicable to Guantánamo detainees, such as Salim Hamdan, who have been tried for war crimes by the first U.S. military tribunal convened since the aftermath of World War II.

Nuremberg's recent co-optation into the project of fighting terrorist threats has been a profound moral mistake that ignores the context in which regimes claim emergency powers. Most such regimes do not rely on popular indifference or the atmosphere of fear created by repressing their most serious opponents. They also seek to mobilize popular support by persuading sympathizers that there is a real danger of suffering serious (perhaps worse) violence and that time is running out.[74] A context of rising popular violence and mob hysteria can strengthen a potential dictator's political base, while allowing moderates to rationalize heightened state powers as a better protection for human rights than their own heightened vigilance would be.[75]

Would a history of human rights trials make it easier to argue in such circumstances that the state of emergency should be postponed because *there is still time* to rely on the mechanisms of ordinary justice? Perhaps it would if the dictator comes to power because of general indifference and in the absence of an internal or external threat. But, if popular apathy is not the problem, it hardly matters whether a political culture that includes successful human rights trials could be invoked to make the public less apathetic. Such a culture would also include a history of human rights *violations* that were later proven and condemned. This further fact could reassure conformists in the next emergency that they will have the opportunity to change with the times, as conformists in the past have always done. It is *their* "transition" that the cultural interpretation tries to ease.[76] This is why the rhetoric of successor regimes shifts so quickly from achieving *justice* to promoting a culture that can bring nearly everyone from the old regime on board when an apparent danger has passed or been discredited.

But, insofar as human rights *violations* are still official policy, Nuremberg-based principles can, and should, slow progress toward a forward-looking *culture* of human rights that would enable officials to avoid individual liability as *violators*. This is a simple, procedural reason to resist dubious efforts to recast Nuremberg as the global link between fighting terrorists and promoting transitional justice. A deeper reason concerns the substance of the human rights culture itself. To the extent that such a culture is *what comes after* a past, and largely discredited, emergency, it tends to substitute *itself* for the true victim of future human rights violations. At this point our belief in human rights can become an ideological rationale for committing the kind of violations (including group-based violence, preemptive war, and the physical abuse of detainees) prosecuted at Nuremberg. Can such conduct be justified to defend a culture of human rights in a time of mass insecurity? The subject of human rights is *not* a culture—and certainly not a culture that regards its own permanent endangerment as the *true* emergency that must always be cited as a decisive reason for setting aside the human rights of its purported enemies.

Faced with the reality of the Holocaust, a previously unthinkable truth, Karl Jaspers famously confronted his fellow postwar Germans with the ethical imperative to consider their guilt for things beyond their control and perhaps outside their knowledge—an imperative of self-reflection that comes before deciding on "the guilt of others" for their acts and omissions.[77] My effort to link the central meaning of Nuremberg to the concept of "emergency" preserves Jaspers's insight by arguing that there was a *right time* for those condoning an evil regime to oppose it. The cultural interpretation of Nuremberg as an instrument of transitional justice is concerned, rather, with what they would have done if they believed something else. It suggests that their failure then was not to consider what the present moment *will have* been when new facts later appear. But for a *would-have-been* opponent of past evil, *now* is never the time to renounce one's present gains. There is, at any given moment, some knowledge he will have lacked—some revelation yet to come or that now appears to have come too soon. The temporal displacements produced by post hoc perpetrator trials always give beneficiaries and mere conformists more time to be against what *was*.

"Change Has Come"

Should the Obama administration refrain from prosecuting Bush-era human rights violations now that change has come? The recent literature on "transitology" suggests that, *if* the German people had somehow managed to overthrow Hitler (or, better yet, voted him out of office), the Nuremberg trials would have been superfluous as an instrument of cultural change. A similar argument is made about the relevance of Barack Obama's election. Why prosecute now that "change has come" and the whole world knows what happened? If human rights is primarily a "culture," then the fact that the U.S. already *has* such a culture, or has now returned to it, would become a reason *not* to prosecute those who believed in good faith that extralegal measures were justified after 9/11. The only reason to prosecute the guilty, according to this argument, is to prove that we can do so—that ours is *not* a "culture of impunity." But, if we can, then we shouldn't—so the real culture of impunity arrives when human rights are once again believed to be secure.

I have argued in this chapter that such a view is wrong if Nuremberg was right. Former Attorney General Gonzales has claimed that he, and other Bush administration officials, should not be prosecuted because they believed in good faith that a true emergency was present and thus did not *intend* to undermine the rule of law as such. But the tribunal's final judgment at Nuremberg makes the existence of an emergency inadmissible as a defense—otherwise there should have been a new trial allowing it. If the defendants are not allowed to plead that there really *was* an emergency, what is the relevance of their *believing* that one existed at the time? Honorable intent would, of course, be relevant to pleas in mitigation at the time of sentencing—and could also count in favor of a pardon following conviction. But it is no less true that a *lack* of good-faith belief that the emergency was real would *aggravate* the offense of anyone convicted of human rights violations, as it might have done in the case of Nazis who were hanged for their intentional abuses of power. To reach such conclusions about any given official a trial would be needed, or at least a pretrial investigation that would recommend prosecution or pardon based on publicly disclosed facts.[78] I see little basis for the legal view that *no* U.S. officials could be convicted of a human rights violation unless they were *also* part of a conspiracy to undermine democracy that was arguably similar to German Nazism.[79] This is precisely the prosecution theory that the Nuremberg tribunal rejected in holding defendants criminally responsible as individuals. Even if Bush administration officials were allowed by U.S. courts, based on standard domestic practice, to raise advice of counsel as a defense, this would, at most, be a legal theory that, to be tested, would probably require waiver of attorney-client privilege.

What about the lawyers who gave such advice? There is, of course, precedent under Nuremberg for trying lawyers: the "Lawyers' Trial" followed that of the "Major War Criminals." These Nazi jurists did not get a free pass at Nuremberg by invoking their good-faith professional opinion that Article 48 permitted the government and its *Führer* to exercise unlimited powers. But the post-9/11 OLC did not even *claim* to be following orders issued under an emergency—it purported to give its independent legal opinion that Bush administration officials could not be prosecuted for the acts about which its advice was sought. OLC attorneys would be liable for malpractice if they did not advise their clients that whether an opinion letter from *them* could defeat Nuremberg-based prosecutions in U.S. (and especially non-U.S.) courts was merely an untested legal theory, which presupposed that there would otherwise be liability. If the purpose of giving bad (or incomplete) advice was to induce its recipients to do as they were told, then the lawyers could be charged as accessories to whatever violations of human rights were subsequently committed.[80]

The core meaning of Nuremberg is that officials, top to bottom, can be held responsible for failure to question orders that are prima facie violations of international criminal law. Encouraging underlings to document and question illegal orders (as FBI officials actually did) is perhaps the strongest reason in favor of prosecuting those above. Those who take it as reason *not* to prosecute do not, ultimately, want a human rights culture that would make violations more difficult in the next emergency and future prosecutions less necessary. In such a culture people would do the right thing when it matters.

10

SURVIVING CATASTROPHE

Religion and Counterreligion

Before concluding this book we must ask why victims, whether individual or collective, should not be sacrificed for the good of the collectivity that survives. The simple answer is justice. Justice as we know it begins with the idea that sacrificial victims can be innocent and that, if so, their suffering is undeserved. This idea creates a strong presumption against being the perpetrators of such suffering, especially through violence, and also against being its beneficiaries. All theories of justice take victimization of the innocent—human sacrfice broadly conceived—as their paradigm of injustice. They use the dyad of victim/perpetrator to ask who does what to whom and that of victim/beneficiary to ask for whose sake and at whose cost it is done.

But human sacrifice was not always thought to raise questions of justice. A moral world (*our* moral world) in which victims are innocent by definition was built upon rejection of an earlier moral world in which scapegoating was the central mechanism of collective *expiation* rather than the originary source of collective *guilt*. René Girard reminds us that the original meaning of "victim" was scapegoat, and that scapegoating works (when it does) by singling out *as* a victim the one who is to be blamed for a catastrophe.[1] In his account the singling out of sacrificial victims by the mob prevents something worse—contagious violence in which the community destroys itself. Such violence is contained because the sacrificial victim is subsequently worshiped by the surviving community, creating a taboo on repetition of the foundational murder. "The peoples of the world do not invent their gods," Girard says, "they deify their victims."[2]

In considering this primal mechanism of the scapegoat we must constantly remind ourselves that it comes *before* whatever conception of justice we normally apply. Because the victim, and only the victim, is to blame, the mob or priest that slaughters him is *not* considered guilty of anything, and, since there is no perpetrator guilt, the surviving community that witnesses and benefits from the victim's sacrifice does not ask whether its collective gain is undeserved. Victimization was thus understood to be a form of group repair—a cleansing to be celebrated in ritual and myth—before it was understood to be a historical injustice that can stain the group forever after. "Archaic religions have little to do with gods and a lot to do with two institutions: sacrifices and prohibitions . . . [that] are indispensable to the survival of mankind. . . . Their survival value justifies, for a while, their compromises with human violence. If you look at the history of religion you can always see that . . . all religions are victories of a sort over violence."[3]

What has changed? The *question* of justice is originally posed, according to Girard, as a challenge to gods who demand human sacrifice. As this challenge develops, the scapegoat mechanism, which is still necessary to contain evil (because *not all* must die) also becomes a paradigm of evil (because the *innocent* must die). To question whether the gods are just is therefore to apply to them a standard that is both singular and universal. A singular idea of justice demanding that gods forsake sacrifice coheres with an idea of one universal God who demands that one forsake all *other* gods.[4]

A *just* God, according to Girard, is thus one who would put human sacrifice in the past—and refuse to be considered the cause of it. For Christians (from Augustine through the twentieth-century's "Theology of the Cross"), the justification of the ways of such a God to Man is that he identifies himself vicariously *with* the victim of human hatred and also directly as the victim of human hatred. This is because our idea of justice implies that ultimately God himself is being questioned.[5] The *question* of justice (Milton's theodicy) thus presupposes the standpoint of innocent victim*hood* toward a preexisting practice that Girard (or his translator) calls "victimage."

The definitive questions raised by victimhood (but not victimage) are why the innocent suffer and whether God himself is the perpetrator. This means that two concepts of the victim (victimage and victimhood) underlie justice—and that these are dialectically related. In the now dominant concept, the victim is presumed innocent, the perpetrator is therefore guilty and the beneficiary/onlooker must avoid association with perpetrator guilt in order to justify his ongoing gains. But in the originary conception the victim is always the one to be blamed and is appropriately made to suffer for the group's catastrophe. Being a victim thus meant being sacrificed long before the subjectivity of the innocent victim became the baseline for universal justice.

But both these concepts of the victim still exist. Today those who can be *justly* made to suffer are called perpetrators/sinners; we do not *also* call them "scapegoats" (victims) because that word now *connotes* innocence. But we still *use* the victimage mechanism to sacrifice those we call "perpetrators" in order to curb contagious violence and reunite the group. The main difference is that both our language and our social process generally presuppose that victimizing the innocent has *already* been criticized and superseded. This explains both the genesis and the inherent limitation of a humanitarian conception of justice (including Human Rights Discourse), which assumes Girard's victimage mechanism is a past to be overcome and also claims to *be* that overcoming. For us the last sacrifice should have been sufficient to ward off the next catastrophe ("Never again," we say). This distinguishes us from supposedly primitive cultures in which another sacrifice must come whenever another catastrophe seems imminent.

The idea that justice comes *after* victimary history assumes that the present justification of suffering depends on its pastness: that *un*justifiable suffering (the bad kind) is that which lies ahead. But when it happens again (the Holocaust, Darfur) we also tend to see this as an anachronistic *reversion* to the same old pattern of cyclical violence and discover once again a version of this throwback to paganism as the thing to be against—and ended once and for all. ("This time will be the last," we say, and then say, when it happens again, "When will we learn?"). The real anachronism here is not merely a return to pagan scapegoating (ritual sacrifice) but also a reversion to the monotheistic critique of paganism that always sees the answer as the *re*conversion of what the Egyptologist Jan Assmann calls "the pagan within" who would, otherwise, be once again capable of sacrificing the innocent: "converts must not," according to Assmann, "forget their past. They must remain aware of their old form of existence in order to retain their new identity . . . and to steer clear of any form of relapse."[6] Human Rights Discourse thus fits the ideal type of what Assmann calls a "counterreligion" that is based on rejecting, remembering, and continuing to struggle with a false religion that preceded it.[7]

As a counterreligion, the humanitarian conception of justice is limited by the very genealogy that Girard helps us to see. He claims that the *question* of justice (is the victim innocent?) subverts the effectiveness of the victimage mechanism, which only works because (when) it is not exposed as an ongoing basis of *in*justice to the victim. (When this occurs the victim needs to be redeemed rather than mythologized.) It seems to me, however, that he has really shown something else: that *both* victimage and victimhood exist as alternative conceptions of the moral relevance of suffering in societies where the question of justice has arisen. We must therefore ask whether human sacrifice (or innocent suffering) is problematic only because *not everyone* who survives benefits from it. If everyone benefits, could we say that victimhood reverts to victimage—as we do in discussing the supersession of Cro-Magnon man by *Homo sapiens*? Yet taking the place (or living on the ruins) of a vanished civilization could also be considered an injustice to any survivors. Why should *anyone* benefit?

There is in religious anthropology a distinction, apparently unnoticed by Girard, between being *sacrificed* and being *used*. This point carries forward to the distinction, in my introduction to this volume, between the death camp that *destroys* human life and the work camp that instrumentally *exploits* it. Many secular philosophers, such as Kant, Habermas, and Rawls, regard destruction and instrumentalization as morally continuous, if not equivalent; they see *violence* against others as a special case of treating separate individuals as a means only and not as ends in themselves.[8] Nietzscheans, however, regard sacrificial violence as a refusal to use the victim instrumentally. As *purifying* violence, sacrifice is thus distinguishable from *use*; it makes the victim what he is—an end in himself, indeed a god.[9] The mythical violence of a sacrifice thus presents itself as the opposite of continuing exploitation.

Why Not Sacrifice?

Recent Israeli debates over the justice of Palestinian claims show real confusion about whether victimage is *always* really victimhood (as Girard thinks) or whether there are forms of sacrificial violence that are not ongoing exploitation and thus need not be repented. The historian Benny Morris's evidence that Palestinian residents were deliberately expelled by Israel during the 1948 War has been widely cited to support present-day Palestinian claims to victimhood.[10] But it now seems that Morris was talking about victimage instead. He argues that the sacrifice of Palestinians, like that of North American Indians, was necessary for Israel's creation and survival and is no more to be regretted than if they had died out. His clear implication is that Israelis, like North Americans, can deplore what happened to prior inhabitants without wishing that it hadn't. But, in Girardian terms, this means that it is *acceptable* to benefit from victimage if one does not do it again right away—there must be a taboo on further violence that lasts until one *has* to do it again to avoid the next catastrophe; in more Nietzschean terms, the spontaneity of such violence distinguishes it from a utilitarian policy toward Palestinians.[11]

Morris does not present a utilitarian argument that Israeli gains exceed Palestinian losses (although he sometimes suggests that a complete ethnic cleansing would have been more humane than what actually happened).

His main point is that Israeli acknowledgment of the Palestinian expulsion does not necessarily support a Palestinian politics of victimhood; it might equally support a national history that treats vanished Palestinians as *mythic* predecessors whose sacrifice was part of Israel's foundation in much the way that many present-day Americans mythologize First Peoples without really wishing to be ruled by them or share the land. Morris's comparison with the U.S. might have been strengthened by pointing out that Israel's failure to *complete* its supersession of the not yet "vanished" Palestinians has led it to demonize, rather than divinize, them and that, consequently, it has produced in *them* a militant subjectivity of victim*hood*. But this would undermine his polemic against the Palestinian's present claim. So perhaps Morris merely *wishes* that Palestinian victimhood were victimage—a past sacrifice that could be celebrated (and made taboo) without giving rise to grievance. This happens, he suggests, in states that had *successful* ethnic cleansings: it is *failed* attempts at ethnic cleansing that give rise to the politics of victimhood.

Morris's suggestion that archaeology could supplant historical justice bears chilling similarity to Himmler's 1943 Posen Speech, telling senior SS officers how Europe's Jewish past would be commemorated in museums after the messy business of eliminating Jews was done,[12] but in the case of Israel it is more disingenuous than sinister. He could not mean, for example, that the Palestinians' grievance would be less valid if Israel's removal of them had been more frank and thorough, their loss more total. Morris also knows that his argument will appeal only to supporters of Israel who think the Palestinians' loss is no more remediable than the claim of any other vanished civilization, while treating the Holocaust as a grievance that continues.[13] Before dismissing Morris's argument as a mere provocation, however, we should note that his principal critic, the Israeli philosopher Adi Ophir, implicitly reverses it by treating the 1948 catastrophe as the source of a negotiable grievance by present-day Palestinians and the destruction of European Jewry as a truly irremediable loss and not a basis for claims to victimhood by Israel (or present-day Jews). Is this the sacrifice that Israel should celebrate in its museums and rituals, rather than making instrumental use of it against the Palestinians?

Both Morris and Ophir rely on an implicit distinction between the forms of victimization that give birth to ongoing injustice (a politics of victimhood) and those that purify and expiate those who come after. When historical catastrophes are viewed as cleansing, it does not matter to the successor society whether the catastrophe itself was natural (disease, volcano, or meteor) or man-made (extermination)—just as it would not matter to Morris that the Palestinian "catastrophe" was the result of deliberate expulsion. No matter how the catastrophe occurred, its result is a new civilization built on the *ruins* of the old.[14]

Why then are *moral* catastrophes (such as U.S. slavery, apartheid, colonialism, and the Holocaust) commonly seen to compromise the justice of successor societies? The ethical underpinning of settler colonialism assumes that they would *not*—that there is no ethical difference between a Europe built upon the ruins of the Roman Empire (or *Homo sapiens* that survive earlier hominids) and a British Empire that merely *happened* to overlap with Mughal rule of India. Now that settler colonialism has been discredited, we no longer assume that occupying another's space is analogous to the temporal succession of "civilizations" in human history.

But what is the ethical difference? Should the construction of the great Aztec pyramids, and the massive human sacrifices carried out upon them, now be discussed in the same moral register as the Holocaust? Is it a failure of empathy on our part that it has not been?[15]

What Comes After Sacrifice?

The time has come to dig deeper. What is the logic of violence that our humanitarian conception of justice purports to end once and for all, and what new logic of violence does it perpetuate? We must, I think, reconsider this question in order to understand what comes after the horror of the twentieth century. The new century began with two competing answers: the Judeo-Christian response (post-Holocaust Human Rights Discourse) that is a successor to the counterrevolutionary project and the Islamist response that fills the vacuum left by the demise of revolutionary messianism.

Both sides originate in the monotheistic rejection of prior religions in which the periodic sacrifice of victims (through killing or expulsion) expiated collective fault for divinely imposed catastrophes such as floods and famines. Such sacrificial practices are the *past* of monotheistic religions— by putting them to an end, monotheism claims to connect the worship of a singular god with the promise of justice in human affairs. But what is the logic of violence that our two dominant forms of monotheism purport to end once and for all, and what new logic of violence does monotheism bring?

The Aztec cult of a mad, self-devouring divinity, Huitzilopochtli, was not yet two hundred years old when the Spanish conquistadors arrived. The purpose of that cult, originally described by Spanish priests, was to separate the creative and destructive sides of the divinity by feeding him with human blood. The Mexican writer Octavio Paz thus describes a pre-*Conquista* "Aztec peace" in which the "subject nations constituted a reserve of sacred sustenance . . . the blood bank."[16] The injustice of this system was not lost on those who fed the sacrifice. Oppressed tributaries allied with Cortés in the hundreds of thousands to overthrow the rulers of Tenochtitlán, who initially saw his strategy of conquest through alliance and subsequent massacre as similar to the Aztecs' relatively recent creation of empire. The Spaniards, however, saw it differently. Many explained their rule as the substitution of a Christian Empire that saved souls for one based on the ritual killings of defeated enemies according to a fixed calendar, even though 90 percent of the indigenous population died, mostly (we now know) of diseases brought by the Spaniards.[17]

Were the European conquests of the New World the beginning of the end of empires based on human sacrifice, such as those on the Aztec pyramids? Paz emphatically refuses to say so. "The critique of Mexico begins," he says, "with the critique of the pyramid" (p. 308). For Paz, the rest of Mexican history, including its revolutionary celebrations of its Aztec past, is essentially a prolongation of pre-*Conquista* pagan cruelty. His critique of the pyramid implicitly suggests that Girard's Christian project of putting human victimage in the past has barely begun and bears a marked affinity to Daniel Goldhagen's description of the Holocaust as (what one critic calls) "orgiastic 'super-*pogrom*,'" differing from previous, less ideological episodes of scapegoating mainly in scale and ambition.[18] Such arguments are at odds with more recent reconsiderations of the European conquest of the Americas on its five hundredth anniversary as a prolonged "Holocaust" inflicted on native inhabitants[19]—an extension of the holy war fought to bring the more primitive violence of the Aztec pyramids to an end.[20] But if colonialism was a prolonged Holocaust, what was the Holocaust?

Those who see the Holocaust as an extension of the Spanish *Conquista*, and not of the human sacrifices on the Aztec pyramids, tend to focus on Nazi *ideology* as a super*crusade* rather than a super*pogrom*. This view, advanced by many exiled German intellectuals such as Arendt, Horkheimer, and Adorno and later developed by Holocaust scholars like Zygmunt Bauman, sees Nazism, and "totalitarianism" thought more broadly, as universal social engineering run amok, a perverse consequence of *de*mythologization rather than a return to myth.[21]

What of the contrary view? Those who call the Holocaust a return to primitive scapegoating (or to the Aztec pyramids) are often unclear about whether they are offering an explanation of why it worked or why it failed.[22] The ambiguity in their claim runs deep. Is their point that, if Nazi Germany had won World War II, Jews would not be considered innocent because Hitler's use of the scapegoating mechanism would have worked in uniting his people? Or, rather, are they arguing that Hitler's persecution of the Jews was doomed to fail because it revived the ancient technique of scapegoating in a modern context where it had already been discredited?

If the scapegoating mechanism cannot work under conditions of modernity, then it does not explain the Holocaust.[23] Those who interpret the Holocaust through this mechanism ignore the fact—both political and theological—that what comes after the pagan sacrifice of victims (scapegoats) is a pathology of monotheism that cloaks its violence not with the virtue previously ascribed to heroes but instead with the innocence now ascribed to victims. It is, I think, the particular blindness of humanitarians to regard their opponents as *reverting* to pagan cruelty (suicide bombing and the like), as though once we have arrived at humanitarianism nothing can come *next*.

Monotheistic violence is what comes next—a violence that claims to break the cycle of violence when one must do what it takes to defeat the enemy once and for all.[24] Monotheistic violence thus involves an *intensification* of enmity, which is no longer a matter of expressing and containing what Girard calls "mimetic rivalry" but becomes, instead, a matter of defending a God who is now revealed to have always been on the side of victims. Monotheistic violence is not necessarily committed *by* the victim, but it is always committed *for* victims who must be saved/rescued. When Paul's Lord says "Vengeance is mine, *I* will repay,"[25] he repudiates ordinary vengeance while also elevating and infinitizing his own vengeance as divine justice. This higher form of vengeance (combining its critique and supersession) becomes the humanistic version of God's work—it is defined as *not*-vengeance but rather violence directed against the false gods who demand vengeance.

The violence that kills off false gods (that establishes their non*existence*) is thus a vengeance that belongs exclusively to the one true God ("Vengeance is *mine*"). Such righteous violence intensifies enmity by making it both political and theological—and in all instances a matter of final struggle "in which the enemy must be 'annihilated' (cease to exist) rather than merely 'defeated.'"[26] The cruelty of the monotheistic religion that claims to supersede the violence of "earlier" religions (as it categorized them) was sharply criticized by Montaigne in the immediate aftermath of the Spanish conquest of the Aztecs.[27] From its own perspective, however, monotheism triumphs over religions based on human sacrifice because it splits off the creative and destructive sides of divinity: it glorifies God as the Creator rather than appeasing Him as the Destroyer.

Creation and Destruction

It is worth pausing to consider what it means for a creature to conceive of the Creator as having split off its destructive wishes. A natural being, unlike a creature, carries its essence or purpose within itself; it seeks to know *itself* (perhaps in the Socratic mode) in order to pursue its own good. In contrast, a created being has no good of its own but, rather, a purpose external to it—that of its Creator. It therefore cannot know through introspection its reason for being and needs to be told through signs or direct revelation.[28] To think of one's reason for being as coming from *outside* poses a problem beyond the need to get God's message. A self-conscious creature can conceive of its own destruction if the Creator becomes dissatisfied or simply changes his mind.

A more or less well-founded fear of the Creator fills the space of absent nature in creaturely existence. Fearing God would be a reason to hate Him if we were not afraid that this very feeling would justify His wrath. This is why loving God, in the Abrahamic religions, is a *commandment*, and why obedience to that commandment generally takes the form of *prayer*. The collective "we" that is expressed through prayer both loves and fears a God who is always sparing us an extermination that we would otherwise deserve and that would surely come if we hated Him rather than blaming ourselves for misfortune. Our professions of faith in God's unconditional beneficence disavow the link between fearing God and hating Him, and defend against the anxiety caused by an unavowed hatred that God alone knows. The prayers commanded by monotheism thus repress (and *unthink*) the wish to commit deicide[29] by restating fear of God as a love that constantly doubts itself.[30] The monotheist's split-off hatred of God must then be projected onto others so that it can be reexperienced as hatred of those who hate God. What we now call genocide is imaginable within the Abraham religions as a collective punishment for the wish to commit deicide, and the redemptive stories that constitute a people are all about being *spared* this punishment,[31] as in, for example, Exodus 20:4: "for I the Lord your God am a jealous God, visiting the iniquity of the fathers upon the children . . . of those who hate me."

Monotheistic religions abound with histories and prophecies of the extermination that occurs when a collectivity falls out of favor with its Creator by forsaking, disobeying, hating, or betraying him—the destruction from on high ("shock and awe") that generals and journalists now call "biblical."[32] The first such event in the Bible was the Flood—described as a near-total biocide of terrestrial animals—"Never again" is first uttered by God as a postdiluvian promise to Noah. (It was, however, a qualified promise—never again by *water*.) Moses' Great Sermon at the end of Deuteronomy prophesizes future genocides directed against the Jews for turning away from God, and the Old Testament thereafter describes divinely ordained mass slaughter (both by and against Jews) that would fit the description of genocide in the 1948 Geneva Convention. The New Testament conceptions of Armageddon and the Last Judgment are future genocidal moments that many proponents of human rights devoutly hope will never come. Against this background, it was important to the post-1945 survival of Judaism to describe the Holocaust as something that God did *not* will and that is not a reason for survivors to hate Him.

Judeo-Christianity, viewed as a singular, post-Holocaust religion, worships a God for whom cruelty is the worst evil of all. This God makes *genocide* (typified by the destruction of the Jews) taboo for man in much the way that earlier theology unthinks *deicide*. The biblical idea that such genocide/deicide is God's prerogative alone is a foundation for the modern idea that humanly inflicted mass murder is the ultimate sacrilege and that anyone committing it is the devil incarnate, a usurper (and would-be murderer) of God Himself, the originary *génocidaire*. This suggests that the taboos on genocide and deicide share both a common biblical genealogy and a common psychological root in the wish to transgress.

Atonement for the wish to kill God (and to *play* God) is the time-honored recipe of prophetic politics for avoiding the fate of the peoples that have perished by God's will. It also suggests, however, that love of neighbor—as God's commandment—is nothing so simple or direct as the *fact* of loving one's neighbor (or not). It is rather the atonement for hatred of God and the anxiety that one's hatred may have killed Him. Thus we are commanded (in relevant part): "You shall fear your God; I am the Lord" and "you shall love your neighbor as yourself; I am the Lord."[33] Love of neighbor (nonextermination) and a fear of hating God are here conjoined at the very highest level of Judeo-Christian doctrine. That Human Rights Discourse is also a religion that preserves in secular form the biblical fear of genocide should make it unsurprising that the repudiation of Human Rights Discourse today takes the theological form of attacking its Judeo-Christian specificity.

The Uneasy Religion of Humanity

I have argued throughout this book that late-twentieth-century Human Rights Discourse has the particularity of world religion—that of Judeo-Christianity, which misunderstands itself to be the *last* monotheism because it claims to be the religion of humanity as such. It thus justifies its own particular violence as a continuation of the struggle against barbaric human sacrifice (the pyramid) in its horrifyingly modern incarnation (the Holocaust). As a religion that describes God's *own* beliefs as ultimately humanitarian, Judeo-Christianity sees sacrificial victims as innocent, the perpetrators as guilty, and continuing beneficiaries as unjustified until they, too, repent under the tutelage of experts in transitional justice.

There remains, however, a question of whether the religion of humanity is still a religion of *God*, and this is the question Islam poses. How does humanity confront its hatred of a deity who once demanded or condoned the sacrifice of some in the community, the victims, for the benefit of the rest? The question of justice originates in a question about God's purpose. If monotheism is a way to overcome the cruel gods we hate, Islam charges earlier monotheisms with failing to root out the temptation to hate God whenever cruelty appears.

But is such a temptation inherent in the monotheistic project of replacing "sacrifice" with "justice"? According to Jan Assmann, "Obliterating the distinction between 'sacrifice' and 'justice' . . . is linked to another distinction . . . the one between true and untrue in the sphere of religion."[34] The Mosaic worship of an unseen god thus introduces a distinctive concept of believing as fidelity that is distinguishable from seeing—the extra element being the truth revealed to Moses himself.[35] Believe *me* (God's representative), says Moses, and not the evidence of false gods that appears before your eyes.[36] Islam's further revelation claims to remove the hatred of God, and the wish to kill him, that leads from monotheism to Judeo-Christian humanism. It results in a conception of justice not as a standard for judging God from the standpoint of suffering victims but rather as a reason for beneficiaries to obey with inner zeal.

What does it mean for a community to *cease* worshipping gods that *it* believes to be both false and cruel and to *remember* the One True God who remains invisible? To turn away from false gods is the prototype for rejecting a past cyclicity of violence based on a new understanding of the "human." As a matter of cultural memory, rejecting false gods presupposes a human capacity to kill them off (iconoclasm as "theoclasm").[37] Assmann's point is that one's conscious *dis*belief in self-destructive gods requires a further *belief* that disbelief was strong enough to kill them. This combination of conscious disbelief and unacknowledged belief is necessary to transform sacrificial cults into *religions* in which people must remember (and constantly be reminded of) a god who is external, just, and nondestructive. The central characteristic of the monotheistic religions that come after human sacrifice is what Assmann calls a collective "traumatization of the perpetrator."[38] This traumatization is, according to Assmann, typical of religions that regard pagan sacrifice as part of their past—and the distinctive marker of a monotheistic, rather than pagan, form of violence.[39]

The fundamental difference between the sacrificial violence committed to *appease* the gods of pagan religion and the "civilized" violence of monotheism is that the latter violence is directed *against* the old (false) gods that one has the power to kill through disbelief.[40] But this is the very deicidal power that humans must henceforth deny themselves (repress) in order to accept their newly revealed position as the beneficiaries of a divinely *created* nature. Monotheistic violence redirects the deicidal wish inward, replacing human sacrifice with repression.

My point is not that monotheistic violence is less self-limiting than pagan violence is (the populations of Troy and Carthage were exterminated by pagans); rather, it is that by demonizing its victim monotheistic violence leaves its murderous feelings toward its own dead gods repressed and potentially inexpiable. Unlike the sacks of Troy and Carthage, which were later mythologized by the triumphal civilizations of Greece and Rome, the genocide committed *in God's name* against the Amalekites is a guilty violence that presents perpetrators (such as King Saul, who was a conscientious objector) the choice between exterminating a people to kill its gods or confronting one's potential hatred of one's own God. This hatred is itself the inner crime for which a just and all-knowing god *could* justly accuse a true believer.[41] Monotheistic violence is thus, unconsciously, violence against a former god that is repressed and redirected against an enemy of the one true God.[42] To be at war with God's enemy is to deny that we are no less capable of hating God than of loving him.

What comes after human sacrifice is a political unconscious in which beneficiaries have latent perpetrator guilt that can either be denounced by a prophet or forgiven by a messiah. Pauline messianism is, as we have seen, a template of the transitional justice that I describe as Human Rights Discourse—a mode of argument that pushes evil back into the past by postponing justice for the future. The Islamic counterargument, inherently prophetic, accuses beneficiaries who do not change their ways of hating God. In monotheistic religion, the distinctive role of prophets, rather than messiahs, is to argue that something *more* must be done for the present time to end. Prophecy thus rejects the view that the necessary moral transformation has already occurred—that change has come—and that beneficiaries of past evil need more time, a secular time, to realize this. The conflict between these perspectives is paradigmatically religious.

Messianic and Prophetic Time

Once we understand that Human Rights Discourse is secular religion (our own version of universal truth), it lies open to criticism on religious grounds. The most serious is still the charge made by Jewish prophets of creeping infidelity—putting humans ahead of God. This path begins with the Judeo-Christian revelation, embraced by Girard, that cruelty to humans is the worst thing possible and leads to a natural worship of (addiction to) whatever eases human pain. The danger of mistaking revealed religion for analgesia (an "opiate of the people") is that it leads believers to be *suspicious* of God's will. They may not acknowledge their suspicion directly as a humanist article of faith, but they do believe that, *if* the one true God were capable of cruelty, he could be justly hated for being *in*human. The prophetic tradition calls upon those who judge God's will by human standards to turn away from a path that will lead to hatred of God. Hating *us* for hating God is the theological position that Judeo-Christianity projects onto its Islamist "other."[43] To address these issues at the level of political theology we must describe what is claimed in a prophetic politics, and the claim of Pauline messianism, to both fulfill and supersede these claims. Prophets typically proclaim that the present cannot continue and that its beneficiaries must "turn aside from the direction given by the otherwise unalterable thrust of power."[44] The tendency of secular humanists to view these elements in Islam as the enemy of Human Rights Discourse—and to challenge contemporary Muslims to repudiate them—blinds us to the ethical limitations of our own secular humanitarian*ism* as the ideology of self-professing *humans*.[45]

In lectures delivered shortly after the Iranian Revolution, Norman O. Brown interpreted the Qur'an as a revelation of the limits of humanitarian ethics that derive from its origins in St. Paul's Theology of the Cross.[46] He began by rejecting "the time honored prejudice that treats Koranic theology as a confused echo of half-understood Jewish or Christian traditions, selected and polemically distorted to construct a newfangled monotheism."[47] Brown approached Islam not as an *oriental* religion but as an alternative answer to the Athens-Jerusalem question that Tertullian also asked at the outer regions of the Roman world: how to synthesize neoplatonism and biblical revelation. The answer, according to Brown was *not* incarnation—the idea that past prophecy has been fulfilled, before we were ready, by a man who was God. What if, Brown, asked, the answer is *one last* revelation that did *not* come before humans were ready for it? When framed as a reopening of the prophetic tradition that Pauline thinking foreclosed, the Qur'an's message is that justice has *already* been realized on earth. Once this is revealed, according to Brown, our still Pauline deferral of justice would be based on mere ignorance.[48]

Brown thus describes what is "new" in Islam as an "evolutionary mutation in the prophetic tradition in response to the limitations built into the structure of orthodox Christianity by its historic compromise with Roman imperialism,"[49] and he calls Muhammad a "prophet against empire," whose message marks a

> return to the original Mosaic theocratic or theopolitical idea. The kingdom of God is a real kingdom on earth. The dualism between temporal and spiritual regimen is rejected; the concessions to Caesar (or Constantine) are abrogated. Prophetic revelation has to replace Roman law with its own law. . . . The prophetic movement then has to be a political revolution. Muhammad is the prophet armed; Islam is committed . . . to the seizure of power. At the same time the Mosaic theocratic idea is freed from its national (ethnic) limitations and given new and revolutionary content as a program for instituting theocratic world government.[50]

For Islamic theopolitics, secular rule violates "the principle that there is no God besides God"—it is a form of "idolatry or atheism" that must be overcome by transferring to God "the power that was in the ancient oriental urban king" who sought to spread his empire.[51] Here Brown interprets Muhammad as not merely a prophet against empire (Caesaro-Papism in all its forms) but also a prophet against Leviathan, the man-god of the state,[52] and all forms of human "lordship," except that of God alone.[53]

Islam's decision "to take responsibility, to seize power" marks a break, according to Brown, in the "stalemated confrontation between prophet and king in the Old Testament and between Caesar and Christ in the New."[54] As the anti-Paul, Muhammad rejected the prophetic path from Moses to Isaiah's "Suffering Servant" (and thence to the Messiah); he resumed the path that leads from Moses to Elijah. Elijah's prophecy had preempted the impulse toward messianic deferral (passivity toward the Caesarism of one's day) by rejecting any interval of secular history that would come between the end of evil and the coming of justice.[55] It had been Paul (via Deutero-Isaiah) who reintroduced such an interval. This allowed him to describe Jesus not as another prophetic messenger demanding immediate justice but as the embodiment of a now *absent* God for whom justice was interrupted by compassion. In Paul's theology the experience of hiatus between Christ's Resurrection and return allows a still waiting community to believe in justice to come, with varying degrees of urgency.[56] Qur'anic justice is, according to Brown, a challenge to secular rule that is always to be proclaimed in the present instant. "In fully developed Islamic theology," according to Brown, "only the moment is real."[57]

Thus conceived, the Qur'anic revelation deliberately blocks the path, described by Max Weber,[58] that leads from monotheistic revelation to a this-worldly realism about human suffering. The monotheistic rejection of myth recasts *all* potential victims of human sacrifice (Isaac, Joseph, Daniel, etc.) as innocent, entirely historical figures whose suffering is not desired by the one true God.[59]

But what comes after this demythologization of this world? The Christian doctrine of incarnation is one answer: it presents the self-sacrifice of the one true God *within* history as the *end* of Jewish prophecy. By viewing Christ's Crucifixion and Resurrection as history (not myth), it turns the Jewish Bible into allegory and seems to lead, inexorably, to a universal politics of human rights based on a realistic and compassionate account of past Jewish suffering that abstracts from the prophetic elements that were constitutive of Judaism itself. The development of monotheistic thought, from *demythologization* to *realism*, corresponds to Weber's earlier account of secularization as a "disenchantment" of the world.[60] That disenchantment is the cost that must by paid by Girard's God, who humanizes himself by identifying with the pain of sacrificial victims.

Islam is another answer to the question of what comes after demythologization. The Qur'anic revelation puts a stop to the secularizing tendency of monotheism by refusing Incarnationism—and all secular versions of the move from prophecy to allegory and on to realism. Islamic philosophy does not see the present as historical in the sense of being a figural representation of some other time: it is not "realistic" in this sense. If history is *not* the actual reality, there is no time *like* the present—and perhaps no time *but* the present for achieving God's justice: it is never too soon and never too late. In attributing this version of prophetic politics to Islam, Brown presents the Qur'an as a "poetic" alternative to the "narrative" history (as a time between two times) based on St. Paul. For believers, it thus provides another route to the twenty-first century, revoking the Pauline view that the present is to be understood historically. Brown notes that its allusions to biblical stories (of, for example, Moses or Jesus) present themselves as coming *after* the project of narrative, often leaving open just when, in a known plot line, a Qur'anic episode occurs.[61] As an alternative route to the twenty-first century, the Qur'anic thought revokes the view that the present time is incomplete. Its dominant syntagma of justice is the present imperative (action) that follows revelation of a previously invisible truth.

The Beneficiary

The urgency of justice in prophetic thought contrasts sharply with forms of postmessianic secular thought in which the beneficiaries of injustice become self-conscious by opposing the *completion* of time.[62] Judeo-Christian thinkers do not want the time *after* their conversion to stop. They want *more* time to argue that nothing is forever, that there is *still time* to change. They thus profess faith in a future in which the past will have been different because of increased awareness of the unjustified suffering that occurred. Increasing such awareness is the form of therapeutic action that Human Rights Discourse promises to provide.[63] It is also the culmination of a strand of monotheistic thought (the Judeo-Christian strand) in which demythologizing past sacrifice—*all* of it—is a precondition for the redemption of mankind. In the meantime—after evil but before justice—the newly self-aware beneficiary of past sacrifice wants *not* to be identified as a would-be (or would-have-been) perpetrator and thus acknowledges the innocence of all historical victims.

What does the convert want in the prophetic tradition? He wants a *benefactor* whose beneficence is finally *revealed*. If his ultimate benefactor, God, is not the perpetrator of his human suffering, then his subjective position would consist of fidelity to that revealed truth. Subjection to God *alone* is the literal meaning of "Islam," a state of self-renunciation that could be achieved in the instant. From the perspective of prophetic anti-messianism, any view of compassion that is *not* renunciatory is merely therapeutic.[64] And Qur'anic prophecy is militantly antitherapeutic.[65] In Islam there is no angry God ("the . . . All-Powerful of our rational theodicies") who shows his compassion by first provoking and then forgiving the human desire for his death. Islamic revelation takes aim at the very site of deicidal wishes by making God's compassion integral to the original purpose of creation itself.[66] Allah's compassion is creation itself,[67] a restriction/renunciation of possibility that God has imposed upon himself in order to become known.[68] The Arabic name (*Al'-Lāh*) expresses "the nostalgia of the revealed God (i.e., revealed *for man*) yearning to be once more *beyond* his revealed being"—and which we experience as identical with the sadness of the unknown god "yearning to be *known*."[69]

What does Qur'anic prophesy demand? The "transmissive compassion" of Islam is described by Corbin's mentor, Massignon, not directly as a wish to relieve human suffering but as "a psychosomatic shock."[70] The soul, according to Corbin, "is not the [compassionate] witness of an external event but the medium in which the event takes place."[71] This is *not*, as in Christianity, compassion for the victims of evil, beginning with Adam's Fall, and an implicit questioning of the divine purpose that would allow creaturely suffering to happen. Nor is it compassion for the God who dies a human death to vicariously atone for mankind's sin and thus lay to rest man's fear of His motives. In the Qur'an, compassion is for God as Creator and is felt by humans not *for* his possibly innocent victims but *as* his undeserving beneficiaries.

The Qur'an thus completes monotheism's critique of sacrificial religion by rejecting outright, as a relapse into idolatry, the doctrine that God Himself must die on the Cross (*Agnus Dei, qui tollis peccata mundi*) to vicariously atone for human sin and make mankind worthy of his Creation.[72] In Islam the universal beneficiary does not begin as an unreconciled victim who overcomes the corrosive effects of hating God for human sin but as a creature whose ability to imagine himself as an instrument of Allah's purpose is integral to the ongoing process of creation itself. Greater equality among humans is produced here not by *reconciling* themselves with God; rather, it is a direct consequence of obedience to God's purpose as expressed through His commands. Such militant obedience to an externally revealed truth is, in the prophetic tradition, a form of struggle-as-justice (*itjihâd*) that rivals the model of justice-as-reconciliation in the Judeo-Christian tradition that claims to bring the era of prophecies to an end.

Thus described, prophetic justice suspends the victim/beneficiary dialectic set forth in chapter 1. Here there is no founding crime (Adam? Cain?) from which the surviving community benefits, no victim position with which the beneficiary must identify in order to achieve vicarious atonement. The beneficiary's struggle (*itjihâd*) is, rather, to discover the true purpose of his benefactor and to obey it.[73]

Because such obedience is open to everyone, prophetic politics has the potential of universalizing the beneficiary position, just as messianic politics potentially universalizes the victimary position. But the justice that follows from compassion for the benefactor is not necessarily equivalent to that which follows from compassion for the victim. In the latter conception, equalization is inherent in justice—"the last shall be first," according to Christ[74]—and the distribution of advantage shall be for the sake of the *worst-off*, according to Rawls. In Islam the universal beneficiary does not begin as an unreconciled victim who overcomes the corrosive effects of hating God for human sin but begins as a creature whose ability to imagine himself as an instrument of Allah's purpose is integral to the ongoing process of Creation itself. Here greater equality among humans is not produced by *reconciling* themselves with God; instead, it is an indirect consequence of obedience to God's purpose, which requires the believer to be against the self-worship of all (including victims) who believe that true thoughts must be their own rather than Allah's. Is struggle-as-justice the only viable twenty-first-century alternative to the counterrevolutionary politics of justice-as-reconciliation? Putting my overarching theme in this way foregrounds the choice between militancy and reconciliation as spiritual paradigms—but what about justice itself? Are *either* militancy or reconciliationadequate proxies for it? Becoming a militant for truth—perhaps an "inconvenient truth" such as global warming—might unbind a beneficiary from present gains that do not truly belong to him. But it would not require him to confront the unjust origin of those gains or his fear of those who presently suffer because of them. Even if beneficiaries of injustice have faith in an all-compassionate Benefactor, they also have victims whose continuing presence reveals the truth that their apparent blessings are *not* universally shared in the given situation. In a struggle for *justice*, moreover, no situation is merely given: there is always a *question* of what has been unjustly taken and what the takers are allowed to keep.

My conclusion to this volume asks in what voice (or voices) can such a call for justice be heard. I argue that this question originates in political theology and I address the need for a theory of justice in time that Human Rights Discourse obscures.

CONCLUSION

JUSTICE IN TIME

The Grammar of Injustice

In this book I have contrasted two paradigms of historical injustice. The first is based on class struggle and revolves around the triad of perpetrator/victim/beneficiary; the second, based on anticolonial struggle, revolves around the dyad of native/settler.

Viewed grammatically, these paradigms of justice (the answers to who/whom questions) involve the person and declension of nouns.[1] A noun's person consists of its number (singular or plural) and its relation to the sentence uttered as a communicative act (performance). In the first and second person, the English pronouns "I" (we) and "you" are shifters: "I" always refers to "the one who speaks"; you are the discursive other, "the one who is addressed." The third person stands outside the act of enunciation. He, she, or it appears (or, in the third-person plural, *they* appear) within the enunciated sentence as "the one (or those) who is (are) absent."[2] The declension of a noun indicates how its form varies depending on its use *within* the enunciated sentence as the subject or object of a verb.[3] A noun can be the subject of a verb (the nominative case),[4] the direct object (accusative case), or the indirect object (dative case). The noun as direct object is the thing or person to or toward which the act or motion is directed; the indirect object is the thing or person for whose sake, at whose expense, with whom, within which, and so on, the act or motion occurs.

Most accounts of justice in political philosophy concern the relation of person (position of enunciation) to paradigm (declension). The most familiar is the Golden Rule, which consists of a simple first- and second-person reversal of subject and a direct object ("Do as you would be done to"). More complex views of distributive justice step beyond the second person (victim/perpetrator) to consider for whose sake, at whose expense, and through whose acquiescence or complicity the act is done. They typically propose reversals of direct and indirect object in third-person utterances about the relationship of perpetrator, victim, and beneficiary. The class-based paradigm of justice associated with Marx would focus on the gains to beneficiaries that come *at the expense of* historical victims and suggest that society should henceforth be governed as though history had occurred *for the victims' sake*. In the human rights paradigm the beneficiary carries an awareness that past injustice has occurred *for him*—but also that it was done *to* someone else *by* someone else. By acknowledging this in time, he hopes to resist the claim that remedies must come *at his expense*—or so I argue in this book.

I also argue, however, that the grammatical form through which the beneficiary expresses such resistance allows him to achieve a *temporal* distancing from the perpetrators of past injustice, even as he becomes socially closer to the victims. Our syntagmas of injustice—in contrast to our paradigms—allow us to speak, for example, of what has occurred *previously* that does not have to be corrected until *later*.

In grammar, syntagmatic analysis (the answers to "before/after" questions) involves the conjugation of verbs. Conjugating a verb shows how its form varies with time, aspect, and mood.[5] The grammatical *time* of a verb is past, present, or future; the *sequencing* of verb times in a sentence establishes a relation between the "time considered" and the present of narration: Are we considering, for example, the past of the past—or perhaps the past of the future? The *aspect* of a verb concerns whether the action/motion is simple, complete, progressive, or repeated. A verb's *mood* can be indicative, subjunctive, optative, or imperative, and the sequencing of verb moods in a sentence makes it possible to speak of what would have, should have, could have, or might have happened in ways that are distinguishable from indicative assertions of fact.

The linguist Emile Benveniste describes the relationship of tense, aspect, and mood among the verbs in a sentence as "intralinguistic" rather than strictly "chronological."[6] Grammatical time is thus more varied and specific than the astronomical conception of time we use to *date* events.[7] The narrative use of the sequencing of tenses, aspects, and moods creates distance or tension or both between a *before* and *after* from the standpoint of the *now* of narration itself. In a narrative of oppression, for example, grammatical time can make the present of enunciation an interruption or deferral of an ongoing (or underlying) justice that will resume; in a narrative of redemption, it can make the present a completion of repetitive events that are now to be placed entirely in the past.

My argument throughout this book treats our syntagmas of justice as no less important than our paradigms. It is through syntagmatic variation that our paradigms of justice become utopian, messianic, prophetic, or realistic.[8] Advocates of transitional justice, for example, typically rely on realistic narratives to show that justice takes time. Such realism presents itself as a prosaic, but unexceptionable, response to twentieth-century horrors based on utopian or messianic promises. My counterclaim is that the narrative of physical cruelty (human rights abuse) is not the natural cry of a humanity burned out on the poetics of justice; rather, it takes the form of a story already told. The narrative "realism" of transitional justice thus tells each atrocity as the repetition of an earlier atrocity—a lesson still to be learned— that should caution against thinking we are ready to change.

Realism as Figuration

Representing "reality realistically," according to philosopher of history Hayden White, has the "plot structure of redemption." It makes the historical present understandable as the "fulfillment" of some past figure, such as Adam, who is narratively re-presented (made present once again) in a successor-figure such as Jesus.[9] Here the "fulfillment of a figure over the course of a given period of time or narrative diachrony is not predictable on the basis of whatever might be known about the figure itself apart from its fulfilled form." What will become our "prosaic" conception of history originates, according to White, in the "long process of expropriation of the Hebrew Bible by its Christian interpreters since the time of St. Paul himself." Here there is a tendency to place

> the principal weight of meaning on the act of retrospective appropriation of an earlier event by the treatment of it as a figure of a later one. It is not a matter of factuality: the facts of the earlier event remain the same even after appropriation. What has changed is the relationship that agents of a later time retrospectively establish with the earlier event as an element in their own past.[10]

"Figural realism" as a way of reasoning backward from a present singularity to its past *figurae* is different from a causal claim, which is repeatable going forward. It also differs from myth and epic, in which the events told lie outside the time of their telling. Figural realism, rather, has the underlying poetic (syntagmatic) structure of allegory that has been developed, beyond mere symbolic comparison, into a narrative of before and after.[11]

White recognizes, however, that we no longer assume historical narratives must present themselves as allegories of salvation. Our imperative to "'view the present as history'"[12] often commits us to make our narratives "realistic"—often "brutally" so. This commitment gives us an ethical stake in the distinction between history and narrative fiction, which White's stress on their shared poetic roots in allegory would seem to undermine. But a narrative always *tells* a story: there is a time of the telling that comprehends the time told. The latter is a past that lacked sufficient time to fulfill its meaning; a past that *needs* the present of narration to become more fully what it was. In seeing realistic history as hard-won truth about the past, we may be no more aware of writing *postallegorically* than we are of writing prose.[13]

An example of White's point is the historical narrative of the twentieth-century atrocities that prefigure our present understanding of human rights. Here the narrative performance of bearing witness overcomes an insufficiency in past time.[14] But the moral lesson of such an allegory is *knowingly* anachronistic—a past atrocity represents the failure of a justice that always lies outside the historical narrative—belonging, perhaps, to an original baseline or an ultimate end state that may correspond to no realistically describable time. Ethical realists believe that paradigms of justice are not *always* operative, as they might be if we lived in an eternal (i.e., continuous) present. They see justice as, rather, a property of another time—perhaps another *kind* of time—that would have been or will have been sufficient for justice to be done. Their "realistic" approach to historical justice is thus not grounded in the ontological view that they are describing reality as such: it is realistic, however, in the more limited sense of being antiutopian.

The poetics of historical suffering on which Human Rights Discourse relies is consistent with its poetic origin in St. Paul's figural realism. For Paul, realism was a consequence of messianism—an argument for the faithful to be patient in the time it takes for time to end. Now, however, religious messianism appears to be the limit case of historical realism: the case in which the times themselves have changed.[15] This belief in a future *sufficiency* of time is, of course, what makes messianic action seem politically *un*realistic at all other times; this is only to say, however, that most political realism assumes that the present is *not* a messianic moment. In realistic narratives of justice, White remarks, "redemption takes the form, less of a fulfillment of a promise than of an ever-renewed promise of fulfillment."[16] This is a secular shell of messianism to which redemption *never comes*.

Are there ways to speak of justice that avoid both a messianic and a realistic voice? To explore this question we must recover elements in the political theology of *justification* (how good comes from evil) that are *both* interpersonal and intertemporal—and thus encompass the relation between *who* suffers and *when* that suffering occurs.[17]

Time and the Other

The British analytical philosopher Derek Parfit describes his task as a postreligious version of the project of theodicy, which was to provide historical justification for suffering in the world.[18] Why should suffering matter if it is *not now*? Why should it matter if it is *not mine*? And (in the absence of God and an afterlife) why should suffering matter if it is *not mine now*? To find moral meaning in *our own suffering here and now* (within secular, historical time) Parfit argues that we must formulate answers to these questions that do not depend on either God or an afterlife.[19]

Parfit begins by rejecting the common assumption among secular thinkers "that a difference in *who* feels a pain has a great rational significance, while there cannot be rational significance in *when* a pain is felt." These are, rather, Parfit says, "*different* differences. Time is not the same as personal identity. By itself this fact cannot show that time is less significant" (pp. 164–65). He thus treats the difference between *self* and *other*, and the related difference between *now* and *then*, as contingent and in flux (pp. 453–54). In taking this position, Parfit agrees with the utilitarians' repudiation of personal bias in the justification of suffering—it should not matter if the suffering is mine—but questions their implicit assumption of a time bias in the justification of suffering. If the explicit goal of utilitarian ethics is to minimize future suffering, then it must assume that past suffering is better, *morally* better—that I could rationally desire to maximize the *proportion* of suffering in my life that lies in my past while being morally indifferent to *how much* suffering that was. This means that I would prefer, hypothetically, to *have had* ten hours of pain yesterday (whether I remember it or not) rather than to expect to have one hour of pain tomorrow even if I will immediately forget about it (pp. 165–86). But why does the moral significance of a single moment depend on its location in a continuous time sequence?

Parfit's question shows that utilitarianism (despite its apparent allergy to metaphysics) implicitly assumes that there is such a thing as "*time's passage* . . . or the *objectivity of temporal becoming*" (p. 178), which does the work of justifying suffering through pastness. As a metaphor, however, "time's passage" presupposes what Parfit terms a strict analogy between "now" and "here," suggesting that both are ultimately perspectival—contingent on the experience of a thinking subject who can move "through time" in much the way that time itself allows him to move through space. But what could it mean for the subject to move *through* time? How *fast* could he go? How *long* could he linger in the moment? Parfit concludes that the metaphorical analogy between *here* and *now* is misleading and that motion through time may be "indefensible . . . an illusion," along with the utilitarians' time bias (pp. 178–79).[20] But he has even stronger criticisms of nonutilitarians who regard the "when" of human suffering as having little, if any, moral relevance in comparison with the "who."[21]

For Parfit, the ethical issue of overcoming interpersonal bias cannot be addressed without reference to time. In this regard he is true to the project of postreligious theodicy—the justification of human suffering—in a way that most secular philosophers are not. For classical utilitarians, morality consists of being unbiased between my suffering and yours—the question is not *whose* but *how much*. For many antiutilitarians, my natural bias against you must be directly reversed by morality—I must *not* justify your suffering as a means to my own good.[22] Secular philosophy's focus on interpersonal bias presupposes what Parfit calls a further fact (and Kant calls *noumenal* essence) that gives each person's life a unity over time and thus makes time itself (the *when* of suffering) less central to justice. But this, according to Parfit, ignores intertemporal changes in personal identity itself: "We may regard some events within a person's life as, in certain ways, like birth or death."[23] Here he recognizes the claims that might be made about conversions and other moral ruptures and denies "that a person's continued existence is a deep further fact, that must be all-or-nothing" (p. 341) for the purpose of ascribing moral value.

From Parfit's perspective, moral value inheres in thoughts and experiences themselves rather than in their attribution to separate selves *or* to continuing selves at separate times. He thus rejects two ideas that form the core of postreligious ethics, including Human Rights Discourse: the moral "separateness of persons" and their moral continuity across time (p. 329).[24] Parfit's conclusion, which places ethics *before* the ontological identification of either a self or a moment, is uncannily similar to that of Lévinas, for whom the "alterity" and "diachrony" of suffering present a singular challenge. Unlike Lévinas, however, Parfit denies that there is any redemptive significance in substituting the self's suffering for the other's *or* to putting the other's suffering in the past. For Parfit, it is always the *experience* of suffering that matters morally; it simply does not matter *whose* it is or *when* it was. He thus rejects privileging both the self and the present and finds ethical value in the separateness of meaningful moments.

Parfit's revival of secular theodicy shows that there are ethical limits to the project of minimizing future suffering by trying to maximize the past suffering that we acknowledge and regret. This project, as I have argued, devalues the present as a time for justice—and produces a messianic politics of reconciliation detached from its prophetic roots. Is a return to prophetic politics the answer?

Holy Terror and Human Rights

It is too easy, perhaps, for unbelievers to see the defects in a prophetic view of justice as an alternative to secular humanitarianism. From a man-centered perspective, obedience to God can easily be a pretext for injustice, as it has been throughout history. Our ideas of secular justice arise from and presuppose a critical perspective toward obedience—especially on the part of victims—no less fundamental to ethics than the relation of gratitude between beneficiary and benefactor that is one model of the relation between humans and God.

For the Qur'anic philosopher Tariq Ramadan, such reasoning reflects the grounding of pre-Islamic monotheism in a "skepticism and doubt" about God's goodness. Its common thread is a suspicion that the victim is innocent (an absolute respect for human life) and concern that God himself may be the ultimate perpetrator (in demanding, for example, the sacrifice of Isaac). According to Ramadan, Islam's departure from other Abrahamic religions begins with Abraham's readiness to kill Isaac in obedience to God's command and Isaac's willingness to submit out of absolute faith in God's beneficence.[25] The essence of Islam's teaching is that religion is *all*, which is expressed in its conception of *Tawhid*—totality—according to which "There is no God but Allah"[26] and thus no room for Promethean figures who would bring to humans benefits that they suspect God has denied them.[27]

Ramadan stresses that the Western *mix* of pagan Hellenism and Hebrew monotheism introduced the idea of Promethean rebellion against God into the Adamic myth of Creation and thus led from authentic monotheism to an eventual disenchantment of the created world. He thus presents the Qur'an as an *answer* to the "West's" deep-seated suspicion of God's goodness, which reflects its incomplete supersession of the pagan ideas that produce rebels like Prometheus and lead secular humanists to conclude that cruelty toward man is an ultimate evil for which God Himself could be justly hated.[28]

Norman O. Brown provides further context for Ramadan's (all but explicit) claim that a monotheism lacking the Qur'anic revelation is a path toward secular humanism. The Adam of Islam is not, according to Brown, like Shelley's Prometheus, "exempt from awe."[29] Islam's Adam is, rather, the first Prophet, whose message, like that of later prophets, is "Fear the Lord."[30] Islam would seem to provide a more deeply monotheistic response to the conceivability of hating God than that of Trinitarian Christianity, in which a once transcendent God voluntarily relinquishes omnipotence by dying on the Cross in order to show his love for mankind.[31] The Islamic belief that "God is greater" implies, according to Brown, that infidelity, a betrayal of God's name, is even worse than cruelty.

There are, of course, forms of both Judaism and Christianity that also hold that militancy in the name of God is more important than compassion. These views typically reject the hyphenated Judeo-Christianity that claims to supersede and reject Christian anti-Semitism. We have seen, for example, that Badiou's account of Paul's *Epistle to the Romans* repudiates the Theology of the Cross—as universal victimhood—and celebrates, instead, the *formal* subjection of a convert to a revelatory event.[32] Badiou's paradigm of such a truth event is Christ's Resurrection—Paul's faith that it *happened* and his consequent proclamation that *all* humans are immortal as a new, and universal, truth. Like Brown, Badiou endorses a subjective militancy that can reveal the otherwise hidden truth of a present situation, and he invokes the terms "insurgency" and "uprising" to describe the emergence of such truth from radical action.[33]

My point in stressing the formal similarity between Badiou's ethic of subjective fidelity and the prophetic politics Brown finds in Islam is that they share on openness to forms of subjectivity that Human Rights Discourse opposes as fanatical. They would both regard the humanitarian ethic of "no evil" (compassion plus tolerance) as largely reactive against the imperative demands of conversion to a truth. In contrast, advocates of human rights who claim to transcend exclusively Western values say that militants of any stripe are atavistic, a throwback to tribal warfare and religious superstition that are part of the West's own evil past.[34]

The liberal social theorist Paul Berman, for example, sees our secular commitment to human rights as the outcome of an *anti*prophetic strand of monotheism that evolved into what he regards as the true religion of mankind. Here Creation *without* Revelation leads inevitably to doubt and rebellion—and ultimately a willingness to war against religious warfare in the name of human reconciliation. In criticizing Islam's core religious doctrine of *Tawhid*, Berman elevates Human Rights Discourse (globalized liberalism) to the level of a political theology that opposes all forms the prophetic tradition (including its secular forms) as Holy Terror. Berman would thus make equally strong objections to any form of submission to a higher truth that seems to justify cruelty. For believers, according to Berman, there is nothing worse than infidelity; for Berman, there is nothing worse than submission, even (perhaps especially) to a revealed truth.

In equating the human capacity for absolute evil (cruelty) with fidelity to truth, Berman explicitly identifies the element in Islam that many Western intellectuals cannot stomach with the originary kernel of twentieth-century totalitarianism.[35] The conceptual root of both, he argues, is a view of human freedom as submission to a true and absolute master. For Berman, freedom consists of subjective resistance to mastery as such and is finally a rebellion against the dominion of death and any cults that glorify it.[36] He thus rejects any religion (or theology) that tries to eliminate the temptation to rebel against God and portrays submission to an unseen (and purely spiritual) God as no less servile than submission to the human gods or idols that monotheism originally rejected.[37] Like all humanists—both secular and religious—Berman would refuse to worship any God who would create us for his own benefit (the world as work camp) or destroy us with his own wrath (the world as death camp). A God worth worshipping would have to be human (Become Man) or humanitarian (on man's side). He would run the world as a refugee camp and see rescue of humans from each other as the sole remaining Godlike power.

Berman's core assumption is that *no* new truths will ever be revealed that would justify human victimization—and that the claims of true believers are always a guise for a return to age-old cruelty. Such humanistic ideas, which Ramadan rejects, make Western monotheism "a religion for departing from religion"—a phrase he takes over from the French political theologian Marcel Gauchet as a criticism of Judeo-Christianity, which Berman regards as its principal virtue.[38] According to Berman, the Islamism of Qutb and Ramadan attacks Judeo-Christianity for its absolute respect for human life—a "Western" value that Berman thinks is worth defending at all costs and that these thinkers find unacceptable insofar as it provides a basis for human rebellion against God, which they seem to regard as (even) worse than human cruelty. In Berman's defense of Human Rights Discourse, cruelty is always worse—and *worst* of all is to refuse compassion to cruelty's victims in the service of either politics or revealed religion.

The obvious appeal of Berman's argument should not blind us, as unbelievers, to the limitations of the Human Rights Discourse that regards the prophetic tradition, especially in Islam, as its enemy. Its principal defect, as we have seen, lies in its view that justice (heaven?) can wait—that what beneficiaries have received is not an *imperative* to change but more time.[39] This is, of course, the view that writers on the idea of Christian Empire since Eusebius and Augustine have taken of the providential meaning of Romanity for the world. Despite their otherwise opposing views, both believed imperial violence to be justified not as divine justice—God's rule on earth—but, rather, in the Pauline sense of allowing more time for pagans to be converted while holding off the return of godless rulers (anti-Christs). As a *protector* of the faith, a Christian emperor rules so that humanity will not fall under the deception that "the day of the Lord is already here." (2 Thess. 3–10).[40] In its claim that God's rule *is* already here, Islam reinterprets world history in a way that rejects every providential justification of "Rome," especially its later offshoot in Byzantium (*al rūm*). Unlike a secular Christian ruler, the rightly instructed caliph was supposed to rule as God's vicar, a successor to Muhammad and not merely someone who postpones the apocalypse until God's kingdom comes.[41] For this reason, some present-day Islamist thinkers (especially Qutb) focus heavily on the world-historical significance of Islam's initial triumph, its corruption under the Ottoman Empire (which formally abolished the caliphate), and its late-twentieth-century resurgence as the only truly global force against empire.[42]

This book demonstrates that Human Rights Discourse depends upon a highly particular and contestable view of what really happened in the twentieth century and, above all, of whether it was the beneficiaries of past injustice who (mostly) won. Today's provisional winners always want more time: the time they have is never sufficient for justice to be done. Their professed compassion for victims is a distinctive ethical attitude that refuses apathy but that can also substitute for justice insofar as they consider it to be an intrinsically valuable state of mind in a way that outrage, for example, would not be. In monotheistic religion the distinctive role of prophets, rather than messiahs, is to argue that something *more* must be done for the present time to end.

What would it mean for that time to run out? The conceptual alternatives are presently clearer as theology than as politics. There is, I have suggested, a strand of prophetic thought—certainly in Islam, but not only there—that would proclaim a different terminus to the twentieth century than Human Rights Discourse—a different view of what that century meant or might yet come to mean. It questions the effort of humanitarian politics to carve out a realistic historical narrative of past suffering that is redeemable only in the future. The prophetic call for "justice now" is in this sense unrealistic, and even antirealistic—it considers the present an illusion that cannot last and claims to be *recalling* those addressed to a hidden reality, already revealed.

My conclusion points to broader questions about justice and time, prophecy and messianism that would require further study of religion. But this entire book has concerned the underlying grammar of pastness in expressions about justice—the pastness of human sacrifice, the need to stop repeating it, and the way such expressions situate their utterance in a grammatically constructed present. It has tried to give specificity to the early-twenty-first-century discourse of human rights—both ideologically (as a continuation of the counterrevolutionary project) and theologically (as a culmination of Paul's Judeo-Christianity). In the discursive project of putting evil in the past, human rights claims to leave prophetic politics behind and suggests that anyone persisting in it is a throwback to a time when cruelty was condoned and even celebrated. The construct of an Islamist "enemy" represents an outside to this argument—asserting prophecy as the sole remaining successor to both revolution and its humanitarian alternative. The mere possibility of prophetic politics may be enough to demonstrate that Human Rights Discourse has an *outside*, that it is not the last word, that something will come after its proclaimed final struggle against political Islam and all forms of militancy. I cannot say what this will be. But urgency—a *growing* urgency—is required, I believe, for any conception of justice to be morally intelligible. Judeo-Christian compassion is not enough.

Moral Urgency

Human Rights Discourse generally functions in twenty-first-century politics as a strategy for making justice *less* urgent. Its stated goal is to prevent peoples and their governments from acting on bad wishes by holding them responsible for what they do rather than what they may wish. A central lesson of the discourse of human rights that gradually took hold after Nuremberg was to decollectivize responsibility for gross violations of human rights by teaching the world to distinguish between the acts that individuate perpetrators and the thoughts that do not—to hold individuals responsible for what was actually done rather than holding groups responsible for their hopes and fears.[43] It thus insists on upholding the moral difference between committing an atrocity in reality and in fantasy.

I believe, however, that the moral concerns relevant to twenty-first-century politics should not be limited to responsibility and guilt but must also encompass the disavowals of feeling that make them morally intelligible to us as desires belonging to others whom we are *not*. The intelligibility of feelings attributed to others is a precondition for believing them to be unjustified and disavowing them as our own.[44]

My claim throughout this book is that the often honorable insistence on the individual *responsibility* of perpetrators prevents Human Rights Discourse from confronting its own political demons. Politics, after all, is not merely about what people do but also about what they support, wish, and condone—all of which engage us at the level of fantasy, where wishes and deeds are the same and where our freedom has as much to do with imagination as with will. The unconscious site where collective fantasies do their work is precisely where we are not so clearly distinguishable from one another and from the demons that lie within.

Less secular approaches to overcoming evil were all about confronting one's demons and thus focused equally on both the imagination and the will. Martin Luther, for example, suggested that, in condemning the sins directly willed by others, one simultaneously commits those very sins in one's own imagination. The one who refuses to commit the sins actually committed by others, Luther says, "always remains among them, even though he does not see it. He is always doing the same things that he is condemning even if he does not believe that to be true." Luther concludes that sin is not escapable merely by imagining that it is another, and not oneself, who wills it. On the contrary, sin itself is still "in" those who are "doing in their minds what others are doing through their actions."[45] Luther's central point, derived from Paul, is that in consciously disavowing evil we may still unconsciously embody it: we might thus continue to *do* what we no longer *will*, often by conceiving of a self that is incapable of consciously willing it.

Unconscious wishes are not directly moral in the Kantian sense that we avow responsibility for them as our own, but they are indirectly moral in the sense of being motivationally intelligible as the affect felt *by* others—and especially *toward* ourselves. The gap between moral responsibility and moral intelligibility (a morality at one remove) is filled throughout this book by psychoanalysis and political analysis,[46] both of which assume a difference between consciousness and something more material (or "real") that constrains our choices, whether from the inside or the outside.

The fin de siècle discourse on human rights resists the question of moral intelligibility and forecloses the type of argument I have made throughout this book. I have suggested, for example, that our capacity to fear genocide involves the projection onto (some specific) others of our capacity to commit it; I have also claimed that among the worst moral effects of suffering injustice is to become capable of inflicting it. The underlying reversibility of our moral concepts of active/passive, being/having, self/other have been central to my analysis, and are, I believe, the foundation of an ethical standpoint toward global politics today. From my perspective, Human Rights Discourse is a set of cultural techniques that allows individuals to disavow the collective wishes on which past struggles were based in much the way that missionaries get pagans to renounce their violent gods. This book has taken a critical look at what such disavowals mean. Does the present *unthinkability* of a past wish (for example, to exterminate a perceived enemy) mean that it is gone? Where did it go? In whom do we believe it now resides?

Twenty-first-century Human Rights Discourse does not welcome such questions. Its most positive achievement has been to insist that someone is to *blame* for human rights violations and to reject excuses that deflect blame onto the victim. This technique of keeping the paranoid anxieties of beneficiaries at bay leaves little psychic energy available for a turn toward greater justice. If Human Rights Discourse is what comes after evil, something must come next.

ACKNOWLEDGMENTS

When I presented my previous book, *Political Identity: Thinking Through Marx*, to my friend Norman O. Brown (who had read every draft) he made three criticisms: there was no discussion of identification; there was not enough death; and my book had not come to terms with religion, and, more specifically, with Judaism. This book is my answer to Nobby, whose conversation I have missed while writing it. I dedicate the finished product to my mother, who has become in her retirement a student of political philosophy, and to my late father, who after Suez carried on a brief correspondence with Gamel Abdel Nasser on what I now understand to be the Jewish Question.

I am grateful to the following individuals for comments on previous versions of this manuscript: Mahmood Mamdani, Wendy Brown, Rei Terada, Jerry Neu, Eleanor Kaufman, Dana Cuff, Ellen Hawkes, Janice Meister, Paul Held, Benjamin Lozano, Gabriel Brahm, Alok Rai, Sara Kendall, and Masumi Matsumoto. In revising particular chapters, I have received valued comments from, Sampie Terreblanche, Robert Post, Marianne Constable, Jane Curry, Michael MacDonald, Adam Hefty, Val Hartouni, Alan Schrift, Danielle Celermajer, Jeffrie Murphy, René Girard, Tracy Strong, Bob Hammerton-Kelly, Ritu Meister, Helene Moglen, Sheila Namir, Manuel Schwab, Bernie Richter, Tom Meister, and Gopal Balakrishnan. Research and editorial assistance came at points along the way from Will Hull, Kimberly Geiger, Sara Kendall, Kristin Mattern, Ellen Hawkes, Janice Meister, and Andrew Meister. The late Steve Kaye proofread the entire manuscript with fondly remembered comments. I am grateful to my copyeditor Rita Bernhard for being meticulous, prompt, and also patient. Susan Pensak, at the Press, improved the final manuscript. Robert Swanson and Bernie Richter created the index.

This book might not have appeared without the vision and support of Peter Dimock, my original editor at Columbia University Press. Peter immediately grasped my overarching project and emboldened me to do it all. Wendy Lochner took up the project later on and gave me a prompt and thorough reading of the penultimate text. Peter and Wendy each asked me to write additional sections that clarified the overall shape of the book as I meant it to be.

Finally, I must thank the undergraduate students in several successive versions of my lecture course, "After Evil," and of my senior seminar, "The Political Theology of Paul." Their interest in this project kept me going.

* * *

Progress on the book was advanced by a residential fellowship at the University of California (UC) Humanities Research Institute at UC Irvine in 2004. At other points along the way UC Santa Cruz provided me with leave and sabbatical.

Earlier versions of some chapters were published in the following form: "Sojourners and Survivors: Two Logics of Non-Discrimination," *Studies in American Political Development* 9, no. 2 (Fall 1995): 225–28; *University of Chicago Law School Roundtable* 3, no. 1 (1996): 121–84; "Forgiving and Forgetting: Lincoln and the Politics of National Recovery" in *Human Rights in Political Transitions: Gettysburg to Bosnia*, eds. Carla Hesse and Robert Post (New York: Zone, 1999), 135–76; "Human Rights and the Politics of Victimhood." *Ethics and International Affairs* 16, no. 2 (2002): 91–108; "The Liberalism of Fear and the Counterrevolutionary Project." *Ethics and International Affairs* 16, no. 2 (2002): 118–25; "Ways of Winning: The Costs of Moral Victory in Transitional Regimes," in *Modernity and the Problem of Evil*, ed. Alan D. Schrift (Bloomington: Indiana University Press, 2005), 81–111; "'Never Again': The Ethics of the Neighbor and the Logic of Genocide," *Postmodern Culture* 15, no. 2 (2005); "Anticipatory Regret: Can Free Speech Be Protected When It Matters?" *boundary 2* 32, no. 3 (2005): 169–97; "Athens, Jerusalem, and Rome after Auschwitz: Still the Jewish Question?" *Thesis* 11, no. 102 (August 2010).

Portions of this book were first presented as talks at UC Santa Cruz, UC San Diego, UC Irvine, the University of Cape Town, Columbia University, Columbia Law School, The University of Seattle Law School, Arizona State University Law School, the Tanner Center at the University of Utah, the Townsend Center at UC Berkeley, the Comparative Literature Department at UC Irvine, the Modern Language Association, and Colloquium on Violence and Religion meetings at Stanford University and UC Riverside. I am grateful to those who invited me and for audience responses.

NOTES

Preface: My Task

1. Were "we" right to resist the U.S. government for its strategy of increasing the civil-ian kill-rate in Vietnam? Or should "we" rather have regarded U.S. military occupa-tion of Southeast Asia as necessary to forestall the kind of genocide that occurred in Cambodia following U.S. withdrawal?

2. For a strikingly personal account of my generation's experience, see Gareth Evans, "Crimes against Humanity and the Responsibility to Protect," International Crisis Group, http://www.crisisgroup.org/home/index.cfm?id=6140&l=1 (accessed Janu-ary 30, 2010).

Introduction

1. A fin de siècle "mainstreaming" of human rights is anticipated in Michael Ignatieff, "Human Rights: The Midlife Crisis," *New York Review of Books*, May 20, 1999, p. 235; it is proclaimed in Ignatieff, *Human Rights as Politics and Idolatry*, ed. Amy Gut-mann (Princeton: Princeton University Press, 2001).

2. These earlier versions have present-day defenders. See, e.g., Thomas Pogge, *World Poverty and Human Rights: Cosmopolitan Responsibilities and Reforms* (Cambridge: Polity, 2002), chap. 2.

3. John C. Torpey, *Making Whole What Has Been Smashed: On Reparation Politics* (Cambridge: Harvard University Press, 2006), introduction and chap. 1. Cf. Janna Thompson, *Taking Responsibility for the Past: Reparation and Historical Injustice* (Cambridge: Polity, 2002).

4. According to one estimate, seventy million people were intentionally murdered by their own governments. R. J. Rummel, *Death by Government* (New Brunswick, N.J.: Transaction, 1994); Robert Gellately and Ben Kiernan, eds., *The Specter of Genocide: Mass Murder in Historical Perspective* (New York: Cambridge University Press, 2003); Eric D. Weitz, *A Century of Genocide: Utopias of Race and Nation* (Princeton:

Princeton University Press, 2003); Yehuda Bauer, "Comparisons with Other Genocides," in Bauer, *Rethinking the Holocaust* (New Haven: Yale University Press, 2001); David Rieff, "An Age of Genocide," in Rieff, *At the Point of a Gun: Democratic Dreams and Armed Intervention* (New York: Simon and Schuster, 2005); Tzvetan Todorov, "What Went Wrong in the Twentieth Century," in Todorov, *Hope and Memory: Lessons from the Twentieth Century*, trans. David Bellos (Princeton: Princeton University Press, 2003). See also Samantha Power, *"A Problem From Hell": America and the Age of Genocide* (New York: Basic Books, 2002); Jonathan Glover, *Humanity: A Moral History of the Twentieth Century* (New Haven: Yale University Press, 2000).

5. Claudia Card, *The Atrocity Paradigm: A Theory of Evil* (Oxford: Oxford University Press, 2002); Susan Neiman, *Evil in Modern Thought: An Alternative History of Philosophy* (Princeton: Princeton University Press, 2002).

6. "Helsinki became . . . a legal and moral trap [for the Soviet leadership]. Having pressed the United States and its allies to commit themselves in writing to recognizing existing boundaries in Eastern Europe, Brezhnev could hardly repudiate what *he* had agreed to in the same document—also in writing—with respect to human rights." John Lewis Gaddis, *The Cold War: A New History* (New York: Penguin Press, 2005), p. 190; see, generally, pp. 186–91. Gaddis's well-known view of cold war history, summed up in this book, was an element of the post-9/11 U.S. doctrine of humanitarian "pre-emption," which Gaddis himself initially endorsed.

7. See, e.g., Samantha Power, "Bystanders to Genocide," *Atlantic Monthly* 288, no. 2 (2001); Power, *"A Problem From Hell,"* chap. 10.The failures of the UN mission are described by its commander on the ground in Roméo Dallaire and Brent Beardsley, *Shake Hands with the Devil: The Failure of Humanity in Rwanda* (New York: Carroll and Graf, 2004).

8. For the defense of a strong, but rebuttable, presumption in favor of international rescue, see Michael Walzer, "The Duty to Rescue," in *Arguing about War* (New Haven: Yale University Press, 2004).

9. In present-day Human Rights Discourse the dangers posed, for example, by U.S. imperialism ("empire lite") are far from the worst thing imaginable in comparison with, for example, another Holocaust. See Michael Ignatieff, *Empire Lite: Nation Building in Bosnia, Kosovo, and Afghanistan* (London: Vintage, 2003); Ignatieff, *The Lesser Evil: Political Ethics in an Age of Terror* (Princeton: Princeton University Press, 2004); Samantha Power, "Never Again: The World's Most Unfulfilled Promise," PBS *Frontline*, http://www.pbs.org/wgbh/pages/frontline/shows/karadzic/genocide/neveragain.html (accessed January 30, 2010). .

10. David Rieff, *Slaughterhouse: Bosnia and the Failure of the West* (New York: Simon and Schuster, 1995), p. 27.

11. Paul Berman, *Power and the Idealists; or, the Passion of Joschka Fischer and Its Aftermath* (Brooklyn: Soft Skull, 2005), pp. 203–4.

12. Ibid., pp. 233–34. The passage above refers to Bernard Kouchner, founder of Doctors Without Borders (and now French Foreign Minister), but Berman ascribes similar views to other 68'ers supporting U.S. intervention in Iraq on ethical grounds, including Joschka Fisher, Régis Debray, and Daniel Cohn-Bendit.

13. International Commission on Intervention and State Sovereignty, *The Responsibility to Protect* (Ottawa: International Development Research Center, 2001).This report, commissioned by Canada, was presented to the UN Secretary General in September 2001. Its foreword, written on September 30, 2001, suggests that "the issue of intervention for human protection purposes" had become less "controversial" as a result of "the horrifying event of 11 September, 2001" and the subsequent Security Council Resolutions authorizing international intervention in states unable or unwilling to stop Al Qaeda terrorism (pp. vii–ix). The report's "Responsibility to Protect" doctrine was subsequently endorsed by the UN's 2005 World Summit and invoked as the basis for various Security Council Resolutions on Darfur. For a broad statement of the doctrine, see Gareth Evans, "The Responsibility to Protect and the Use of Military Force," International Crisis Group, http://www.crisisgroup.org/home/index.cfm?id=5209&l=1 (accessed January 30, 2010). For a fuller development, see Gareth Evans, *The Responsibility to Protect: Ending Mass Atrocity Crimes Once and for All* (Washington, D.C.: Brookings Institution: 2009).

14. Berman, *Power and the Idealists*, p. 254 (quoting Wolf Biermann).

15. The phrase "international community" has become "a post-Cold-War nom de guerre for the Western powers" when called upon to intervene. See Mahmood Mamdani, *Saviors and Survivors: Darfur, Politics, and the War on Terror* (New York: Pantheon, 2009), p. 12.

16. Such humanitarian interventions need not involve violence committed at a distance, although it generally does. Thus the intervention to prevent the proximate violence by Kosovar Serbs against their Albanian neighbors consisted largely of the NATO bombing of Serbian cities. Both the ethnic cleansing of neighbors and the aerial bombardment of cities are prima facie violations of modern humanitarian law, and both are the subject of separate trials now under way in The Hague. These trials demonstrate the twentieth-century paradox that bombing is both the quintessential means of intervention to stop barbarity at a local level and the paradigm of barbarity inflicted at a distance. See Sven Lindqvist, *A History of Bombing* (New York: New Press, 2001).

17. Étienne Balibar, "What Is a Politics of the Rights of Man?" in Balibar, *Masses, Classes, Ideas: Studies on Politics and Philosophy before and after Marx*, trans. James Swenson (New York: Routledge, 1994); "'Rights of Man' and 'Rights of the Citizen': The Modern Dialectic of Equality and Freedom," in Balibar, *Masses, Classes, Ideas*.

18. Putting evil in the past often takes the form of turning a *place* of genocide (Auschwitz, Rwanda, the Cambodian Killing Fields, etc.) into the name of a *time* to which we must not return. See Adi Ophir, *The Order of Evils: Toward an Ontology of Morals* (Cambridge: Zone, 2005), p. 519.

19. "The Declaration of the Rights of Man and the Citizen transformed everyone's language virtually overnight." Lynn Avery Hunt, *Inventing Human Rights: A History* (New York: Norton, 2007), p. 133.

20. "By fixing the ideas of 1789 to the top of their bayonets, the Napoleonic armies may be said to have *externalized* the French Revolution's founding violence in the form of a 'war of liberation.' . . . Of course, this would-be crusade for human rights turned into a bid for the mastery of Europe which consumed several million lives, among

them those of one million French soldiers." Arno J. Mayer, *The Furies: Violence and Terror in the French and Russian Revolutions* (Princeton: Princeton University Press, 2000), pp. 13–14.

21. For a multidimensional argument that the Rooseveltian conception of human rights is different from the post–cold war approach, see Elizabeth Borgwardt, *A New Deal for the World: America's Vision for Human Rights* (Cambridge: Belknap Press of Harvard University Press, 2005).

22. A related point is that appeals to "human rights" now function differently than they once did within the structure of specifically *legal* ideas—Human Rights are now more frequently raised as the obstacle that globalization places in the path of social reform than as a basis for local resistance to the world economy. For development of the latter point, see David Kennedy, "The 'Rule of Law,' Political Choices, and Development Common Sense," in *The New Law and Economic Development: A Critical Appraisal*, ed. David Trubek and Alvaro Santos (New York: Cambridge University Press, 2006); Duncan Kennedy, "Three Globalizations of Law and Legal Thought: 1850–2000," in *The New Law and Economic Development: A Critical Appraisal*, ed. David Trubek and Alvaro Santos (New York: Cambridge University Press, 2006).

23. "The term 'human right,'" according to historian Lynn Hunt, "appeared in French for the first time in 1763" (with the publication of Rousseau's *Social Contract*) and coincided with the rise of the eighteenth-century epistolary novel, which stressed that all selves have an inner core of feeling that are the same. What is new in Rousseau and Condorcet is the link between natural rights and humanitarianism—the notion that there are rights all humans have in virtue of being human (having human *bodies*) regardless of their culture or political regime. See Hunt, *Inventing Human Rights*, pp. 22–26.

    Hunt goes on to argue that this humanitarian idea was detoured by the nineteenth-century equation of human rights with movements for popular sovereignty—a process that began well enough when the French Revolution *declared* human rights as the only legitimate basis for ruling the nation but ended badly when the nation-state invented biological racism to distinguish those humans who have rights from those who do not (ibid., p. 186, and, more generally, pp. 177–96). In rejecting this path, Hunt believes, recent human rights advocates have now returned to its historical origin as a compassionate concern for bodily suffering (ibid., pp. 57f–58, 206–14.)

24. Costas Douzinas, *Human Rights and Empire: The Political Philosophy of Cosmopolitanism* (New York: Routledge-Cavendish, 2007), p. 4 (and, generally, chaps. 1, 8); *The End of Human Rights: Critical Legal Thought at the Turn of the Century* (Oxford: Hart, 2000), p. 445, and, generally, chaps. 1, 5, 14). Douzinas suggests that the humanitarian strand in the natural rights tradition is the beginning of its end, because it delinks rights from the political project of overthrowing oppressors and substitutes a psychological project of sympathetic identification with their victims. He would thus regard the humanitarian turn that Hunt celebrates as antithetical to the revolutionary potential of the natural rights tradition.

25. For a thoughtful discussion of these issues, see Jeffrie G. Murphy, *Getting Even:*

Forgiveness and Its Limits (Oxford: Oxford University Press, 2003); Jeffrie G. Murphy and Jean Hampton, *Forgiveness and Mercy* (Cambridge: Cambridge University Press, 1988).

26. "The role of memory in constituting who we are and what agents we are is in tension with the ideal of successful forgiveness as that which ends in forgetting the wrong done to us." Avishai Margalit, *The Ethics of Memory* (Cambridge: Harvard University Press, 2002), p. 208; see, generally, chap.. 6.

27. Hannah Arendt, "The Tradition of Political Thought," in Arendt, *The Promise of Politics*, ed. Jerome Kohn (New York: Schocken, 2005), pp. 58f–59. A brief version of the argument of this recently published essay appeared as "Irreversibility and the Power to Forgive," in Arendt, *The Human Condition* (Chicago: University of Chicago Press, 1998).

28. Martha Minow's book, *Between Forgiveness and Vengeance*, explicitly states the standard view in her title: that there is something to be said for both forgiveness and vengeance but that the optimal position is a middle ground between them. See Minow, *Between Vengeance and Forgiveness: Facing History after Genocide and Mass Violence* (Boston: Beacon, 1998). For a subsequent version of her argument, see *Breaking the Cycles of Hatred: Memory, Law, and Repair*, ed. Nancy L. Rosenblum (Princeton: Princeton University Press, 2002).

29. When considered from such a political perspective, Minow's discussion takes it for granted that the victims never win and that the real point of reconciliation is to reach a moral compromise less harmful to them than any of the alternatives. For this reason, she believes that victims should be encouraged to embrace the metaphor of "healing" as a substitute for transitional justice.

30. Cf., e.g., Ruti Teitel, "Transitional Justice Genealogy," *Harvard Human Rights Journal* 19 (2003); Eric A. Posner and Adrian Vermeule, "Transitional Justice as Ordinary Justice," *Harvard Law Review* 117 (2003).

31. Giorgio Agamben, *The Time That Remains: A Commentary on the Letter to the Romans*, trans. Patricia Dailey (Stanford: Stanford University Press, 2005), p. 67. On the "compression" of messianic time, see, generally, pp. 59–78. Agamben earlier discusses the "as if" as an aestheticization of the messianic—"the enunciation of redemption in exchange for the appearance of redemption"—as reflecting Adorno's view (especially in *Minima Moralia*) that the moment for its realization had been missed (pp. 35–39). Cf. Jacob Taubes, *The Political Theology of Paul*, ed. Aleida Assmann and Jan Assmann, trans. Dana Hollander (Stanford: Stanford University Press, 2004), p. 75.

32. Agamben, *Time That Remains*, pp. 41–42.

33. Ibid., p. 63.

34. See Talal Asad, *Formations of the Secular: Christianity, Islam, Modernity* (Stanford: Stanford University Press, 2003).

35. This view is held by many believing Christians. See, e.g., Reinhold Niebuhr, *Moral Man and Immoral Society: A Study in Ethics and Politics*, Library of Theological Ethics (Louisville: Westminster John Knox, 2001).

36. Hans Blumenberg, *The Legitimacy of the Modern Age*, trans. Robert M. Wallace (Cambridge: MIT Press, 1985).

37. See, e.g., Reinhart Koselleck, *The Practice of Conceptual History: Timing History, Spacing Concepts*, trans. Todd Samuel Presner et al. (Stanford: Stanford University Press, 2002), esp. chaps. 6–7; Koselleck, *Futures Past: On the Semantics of Historical Time*, trans. Keith Tribe (New York: Columbia University Press, 2004), pt. 2.

38. Mamdani, *Saviors and Survivors*, pp. 273–82.

1. The Ideology and Ethics of Human Rights

1. Cf. Samuel P. Huntington, *The Third Wave: Democratization in the Late Twentieth Century* (Norman: University of Oklahoma Press, 1991); Robert Roswell Palmer, *The Age of the Democratic Revolution*, 2 vols. (Princeton: Princeton University Press, 1959).

2. See, e.g., Hunt, *Inventing Human Rights*; Gary Jonathan Bass, *Freedom's Battle: The Origins of Humanitarian Intervention* (New York: Knopf, 2008).

3. See, e.g., Richard Rorty, "Human Rights, Rationality, and Sentimentality," in Rorty, *On Human Rights: The Oxford Amnesty Lectures, 1993*, ed. Stephen Shute and Susan. L. Hurley (New York: Basic Books, 1993).

4. Douzinas, *The End of Human Rights*, p. 380.

5. The revolutionary notion of "winning" is well exemplified in William Hinton's *Fanshen: A Documentary of Revolution in a Chinese Village* (New York: Monthly Review Press, 1967). There Hinton describes the Maoist effort to root out the effects of centuries of oppression, both cultural and material, through a systematic program of economic redistribution and political reeducation that treated even the most minor beneficiaries of past oppression as would-be perpetrators. In the process of "settling accounts" with such persons, the revolution was able to enlist former victims as retroactive combatants against an evil that has already lost.

6. Revolutionaries (such as Trotsky) who question the use of terror or who (like Allende) refuse to consider it are later celebrated as moral martyrs. Because of them, future revolutionaries can claim that terror is not essential to the revolutionary project and would not be necessary but for the ruthlessness of their enemies.

7. Mayer, *The Furies*, chaps. 3–4.

8. Reinhart Koselleck, "The Modern Concept of Revolution," in Koselleck, *Futures Past: On the Semantics of Historical Time*, trans. Keith Tribe (New York: Columbia University Press, 2004), p. 56. See also Étienne Balibar, "'Rights of Man' and 'Rights of the Citizen': The Modern Dialectic of Equality and Freedom," in Balibar, *Masses, Classes, Ideas: Studies on Politics and Philosophy before and after Marx*, trans. James Swenson (New York: Routledge, 1994).

9. To defeat a revolution that has taken power, beneficiaries of the old regime need a popular base for their counterrevolutionary ideology. "Counterrevolution, which originates with the classes, remains lame and ineffectual unless it connects with the anti-revolution, which is a matter of the masses. Evidently counterrevolution, not unlike revolution, can be made only *with* the masses, which is not to say that either the one or the other is made *for* them." Mayer, *The Furies*, p. 57.

10. See, e.g., Alex Boraine, *A Country Unmasked: Inside South Africa's Truth and Reconciliation Commission* (New York: Oxford University Press, 2000), esp. chap. 11; Pris-

cilla Hayner, *Unspeakable Truths: Facing the Challenge of Truth Commissions* (New York: Routledge, 2002); Carlos Santiago Nino, *Radical Evil on Trial* (New Haven: Yale University Press, 1996); and, generally, Minow, *Between Vengeance and Forgiveness*. For a retrospective account of this literature, see Naomi Roht-Arriaza and Javier Mariezcurrena, eds., *Transitional Justice in the Twenty-First Century: Beyond Truth versus Justice* (Cambridge: Cambridge University Press, 2006).

11. See chapter 2 in this volume.

12. *Truth and Reconciliation Commission Report* (Cape Town: Juta, 1998), vol. 5, chap. 5.

13. See, e.g., Glover, *Humanity*. Cf. George Kateb, "On Political Evil," in Kateb, *The Inner Ocean: Individualism and Contemporary Culture* (Ithaca: Cornell University Press, 1992), pp. 199–221; Judith N. Shklar, "The Liberalism of Fear," in *Liberalism and the Moral Life*, ed. Nancy L. Rosenblum (Cambridge: Harvard University Press, 1989), pp. 21–38. For an update on the case for liberalism as a war on terror, see George Kateb, "A Life of Fear," in Kateb, *Patriotism and Other Mistakes* (New Haven: Yale University Press, 2006), pp. 60–92.

14. For a valuable discussion of this point, see also Judith N. Shklar, *The Faces of Injustice* (New Haven: Yale University Press, 1990), pp. 40–50.

15. See, e.g., Nino, *Radical Evil*, and Hayner, *Unspeakable Truths*.

16. For a useful discussion of this and related questions, see Herbert Morris, "Shared Guilt," in Morris, *On Guilt and Innocence: Essays in Legal Philosophy and Moral Psychology* (Berkeley: University of California Press, 1976).

17. Ruti Teitel, *Transitional Justice* (Oxford: Oxford University Press, 2000), pp. 132–42.

18. Anne Sa'adah, *Germany's Second Chance: Trust, Justice, and Democratization* (Cambridge: Harvard University Press, 1998), p. 1. Andrei Markovits called my attention to this book.

    For the argument that Hitler used wealth confiscated from his victims to create economic benefits for his ordinary Germans (while also providing windfalls to the Nazi elite), see Götz Aly, *Hitler's Beneficiaries: Plunder, Racial War, and the Nazi Welfare State*, trans. Jefferson Chase (New York: Metropolitan, 2007).

19. The Argentine jurist Carlos Nino, for example, argued that the function of human rights trials is less to punish the guilty than to change the political culture through widespread publicity and discussion. See Nino, *Radical Evil*. See also Mark Osiel, *Mass Atrocity, Collective Memory, and the Law* (New Brunswick, N.J.: Transaction, 1997). These issues are addressed more fully in chapter 7, this volume.

20. Osiel, *Mass Atrocity*.

21. See, e.g., Carla Hesse and Robert Post, eds., *Human Rights in Political Transitions: Gettysburg to Bosnia* (New York: Zone, 1999); Neil J. Kritz, ed., *Transitional Justice: How Emerging Democracies Reckon with Former Regimes*, 3 vols. (Washington, D.C.: United States Institute of Peace Press, 1995), vol. 1.

22. See, e.g., *Nunca Más (Never Again): A Report by Argentina's National Commission on Disappeared People,* (London: Faber, 1986); *Guatemala, Never Again!,* (Maryknoll, N.Y.: Orbis, 1999).

23. Although it expressly labels apartheid a "crime against humanity," the *TRC Report* generally treats it as the "context" for the "gross abuses of human rights" (killing,

torture, etc.) that were committed to defend, and sometimes to oppose, it. Mahmood Mamdani, "Amnesty or Impunity: A Preliminary Critique of the Report of the Truth and Reconciliation Commission of South Africa," in *Identities, Affiliations, and Allegiances*, ed. Seyla Benhabib, Ian Shapiro, and Danilo Petranovich (New York: Cambridge University Press, 2007); "The Politics and Political Uses of Human Rights Discourse," conference at Columbia University, November 8–9, 2001. See also *TRC Report*, vol. 1, chap. 4, and vol. 5, chaps. 1–2.

24. See, e.g., Kateb "On Political Evil," pp. 206–212; Nino, *Radical Evil*, chaps. 1–4. See also Harold Hongju Koh and Ronald Slye, eds., *Deliberative Democracy and Human Rights* (New Haven: Yale University Press, 1999).

25. See, e.g., Wynand Malan, "Statement by Mr. Wynand Malan, Deputy Chair of the Human Rights Violations Committee of the Truth and Reconciliation Commission, 16 May 1997," http://www.justice.gov.za/trc/media/pr/1997/p970516a.htm (accessed January 30, 2010).

26. The *TRC Report* addresses this issue as follows: "A pertinent question is the extent to which individual South Africans can be regarded as responsible for the premises and presuppositions which gave rise to apartheid. The kindest answer consists of a reminder that history suggests that most citizens are inclined to lemming-like behaviour—thoughtless submission rather than thoughtful accountability. This is a tendency that needs to be addressed in ensuring that the future is different from the past and serves as a reminder that the most penetrating enquiry into the past involves more than a witch-hunt. It involves, rather, laying a foundation against which the present and all future governments will be judged" (vol. 1, chap. 4, §105.) For the TRC's "findings" on civil society's responsibility for the crimes of apartheid, see vol. 5, chap. 6, §§151–58.

27. It is notoriously difficult to make principled moral distinctions among the passively unjust. See, e.g., Shklar, *The Faces of Injustice,* pp. 40–50; Morris, "Shared Guilt," pp. 111–17, 132–35.

28. The *TRC Report*, for example, concludes by displacing onto "other structures" the redistributive project that might have been a consequence of its findings: "The primary task of the Commission was to address the moral, political, and legal consequences of the apartheid years. The socio-economic implications are left to other structures. . . . Ultimately, however, because the work of the Commission includes reconciliation, it needs to unleash a process that contributes to economic developments that redress past wrongs as a basis for promoting lasting reconciliation. This requires *all those who benefited* from apartheid (not only those whom the Act defines as perpetrators) to commit themselves to the reconciliation process" (vol. 5, chap. 6, §165).

29. For an attempt to make Rawls consistent with the transitional justice project that I describe above as post-Rawlsian, see Allan Gibbard, *Reconciling Our Aims: In Search of Bases for Ethics*, ed. Barry Stroud (Oxford: Oxford University Press, 2008), lec. II; Gibbard, *Wise Choices, Apt Feelings: A Theory of Normative Judgment* (Cambridge: Harvard University Press, 1990).

30. See chapter 3, this volume.

31. Robert Nozick gives a hypothetical argument that capitalist inequality *could have*

developed from a situation of initial equality of resources with no illegitimate acts. But what if the actual history of capitalism perpetuates the effects of illegitimate acts? Nozick's likely response is that offsetting these effects would be a matter of remedial justice (in which it is crucial that *only* traceable beneficiaries be made to pay) and not a matter of distributive justice (in which it would not matter who pays provided that cumulative differences between the best-off and the worst-off are reduced.) Thus described, Nozick's view would seem to support claims to historical justice (the restitution of illegitimately accumulated gains) against versions of *transitional* justice in which the present is described as a new beginning regardless of the legitimacy of the past. Capitalism itself is just, in such a view, if its entire history is just or if it begins *as* an act of just restitution. See Robert Nozick, *Anarchy, State, and Utopia* (New York: Basic Books, 1974), esp. pp. 161–64.

32. For a discussion of how class might be reconceptualized along these lines, see Robert Meister, *Political Identity: Thinking Through Marx* (Cambridge: Blackwell, 1991), pt. 2.

33. Torpey, *Making Whole What Has Been Smashed*, p. 56.

34. Edmund S. Morgan, "The Big American Crime," review of *Many Thousands Gone* by Ira Berlin; Slave Counterpoint, by Philip D. Morgan; and other works, *New York Review of Books*, December 3, 1998, p. 16. For a tendentious argument that "white guilt" and "black rage" are mutually manipulative responses to the *end* of racialized oppression, see Shelby Steele, *White Guilt: How Blacks and Whites Together Destroyed the Promise of the Civil Rights Era* (New York: HarperCollins, 2006).

35. For useful discussions of this point, see Shklar, "The Liberalism of Fear" and *The Faces of Injustice*.

36. See, e.g., Kritz, *Transitional Justice*; Aryeh Neier, *War Crimes: Brutality, Genocide, Terror, and the Struggle for Justice* (New York: Times Books/Random House, 1998). Ruti Teitel, "Transitional Jurisprudence: The Role of Law in Political Transformation," *Yale Law Journal* 106, no. 7 (1997); Teitel, *Transitional Justice*; José Zalaquett, "Balancing Ethical Imperatives and Political Constraints: The Dilemma of New Democracies Confronting Past Human Rights Abuses," *Hastings Law Journal* 43 (1992); Naomi Roht-Arriaza, *Impunity and Human Rights in International Law and Practice* (New York: Oxford University Press, 1995); Neier, *War Crimes*; Osiel, *Mass Atrocity*. For neoliberal second thoughts on the project of democratization, see Fareed Zakaria, *The Future of Freedom: Illiberal Democracy at Home and Abroad*, 1st ed. (New York: Norton, 2003); Gary Rosen, ed., *The Right War? The Conservative Debate on Iraq* (New York: Cambridge University Press, 2005).

37. Walter Benjamin, "On the Concept of History," in *Selected Writings (1929–1940)*, ed. Howard Eiland and Michael William Jennings, trans. Edmund Jephcott et al. (Cambridge: Belknap Press of Harvard University Press, 2003), p. 395; on "redemption," see, esp., pp. 389–90.

38. "Even the dead will not be safe from the enemy if he wins. And this enemy has not ceased to be victorious." Ibid., p. 391.

39. Paul Ricoeur, *The Symbolism of Evil*, trans. Emerson Buchanan (New York: Harper and Row, 1967), p. 147.

40. Martin Luther, *Lectures on Romans: Glosses and Scholia*, ed. Hilton C. Oswald, vol.

25, *Luther's Works* (St. Louis: Concordia, 1972), p. 205. In Stendahl's interpretation, the effect of Christ's sacrifice is the *acquittal*, rather than forgiveness, of sinners. Krister Stendahl, *Paul among Jews and Gentiles, and Other Essays* (Philadelphia: Fortress, 1976), 23–40.

41. Carl Schmitt, *The Concept of the Political*, trans. George Schwab (Chicago: University of Chicago Press, 1996), p. 51. Page references that follow are to this text.

42. See, e.g., Shklar, *The Faces of Injustice*, pp. 1–14.

43. Benjamin, "On the Concept of History," p. 392. Benjamin acknowledged Schmitt's influence. See, e.g., Walter Benjamin, *Selected Writings, Vol. 2 (1927–34)*, ed. Michael William Jennings, 4 vols. (Cambridge: Belknap Press of Harvard University Press, 1999), p. 389; Horst Bredekamp, "From Walter Benjamin to Carl Schmitt, via Thomas Hobbes," *Critical Inquiry* 25, no. 2 (1999). For a recent, if implicit, development of the Schmitt-Benjamin line of argument in relation to the former Yugoslavia, see Michel Feher, *Powerless by Design: The Age of the International Community* (Durham: Duke University Press, 2000).

44. Counterrevolutionary thought continues (with a twist) the old Socratic idea that the physical and material suffering of victims of injustice is nothing compared to the moral harm that makes them capable of committing injustice in their turn. For a perceptive discussion of whether the true victims of injustice are the unjust or their prey, see Shklar, *The Faces of Injustice*, pp. 28–40.

45. C. Fred Alford, *Melanie Klein and Critical Social Theory: An Account of Politics, Art, and Reason Based on Her Psychoanalytic Theory* (New Haven: Yale University Press, 1989), pp. 80–87. See also Robert Meister, "Two Concepts of Victimhood in Transitional Regimes," in *TRC: Commissioning the Past* (Johannesburg, South Africa: University of the Witwatersrand, 1999).

46. Although Klein refers to these internal subjectivities as "objects" (a term derived from Freud's instinct/object distinction), her account of them cuts across the uses of the subject/object distinction in philosophy. "*Internal* objects" are thus used in Kleinian theory to express the psychic *reversibility* of two distinct processes: first, the process of internalization/externalization (Klein's projection and introjection); second, the reversibility of active/passive (Klein's splitting of the ego through identification/disidentification). Kleinian theory focuses on how we dissociate from the inner feelings that we project onto others in order to feel the affect that we introject from others as our own. See, e.g., R. D. Hinshelwood, *A Dictionary of Kleinian Thought*, 2nd ed. (Northvale, N.J.: Aronson, 1991), pp. 68–83, 362–67.

47. Teresa Brennan, *The Transmission of Affect* (Ithaca: Cornell University Press, 2004), p. 29. Cf. D. W. Winnicott, "Hate in Counter-Transference," in Winnicott, *Through Pediatrics to Psycho-Analysis* (New York: Brunner/Mazel, 1992).

48. For the uses of Kleinian theory in group analysis, see Donald Meltzer, *The Kleinian Development*, Roland Harris Trust Library, No. 8 (Pitlochry, Scotland: Clunie Press for the Roland Harris Trust Library, 1985), pt. 3; Wilfred R. Bion, *Attention and Interpretation: A Scientific Approach to Insight in Psycho-Analysis and Groups* (New York: Basic Books, 1970).

49. See Jean Laplanche and J. B. Pontalis, *The Language of Psycho-Analysis*, trans. Don-

ald Nicholson-Smith (New York: Norton, 1974), entries on "Projection" and "Projective Identification."

50. Lacan famously states that all "desire is the desire of the other." Michael Bracher explains this statement as a claim about the reversibility of Freud's distinction between narcissistic and anaclitic desires (the desires to be and to have) and also between the active and passive aims of the desires (the desire to do to/for, or be done to/for). See Mark Bracher, "On the Psychological and Social Functions of Language: Lacan's Theory of the Four Discourses," in *Lacanian Theory of Discourse: Subject, Structure, and Society*, ed. Mark Bracher (New York: New York University Press, 1994), pp. 19–80. René Girard expresses a similar, but cruder, view in arguing that all human desire is mimetic rivalry—that human desire is both imitative and competitive. In Girard's view we, as humans, want to acquire what the other has in order to be what he is, and to be what he is in order to acquire what he has. See, e.g., René Girard, "Mimesis and Violence," in *The Girard Reader*, ed. James G. Williams (New York: Crossroad, 1996); see also René Girard, Jean-Michel Oughourlian, and Guy Lefort, *Things Hidden Since the Foundation of the World*, trans. Stephen Bann (books 2 and 3) and Michael Metteer (book 1) (Stanford: Stanford University Press, 1987), bk. 1, chap. 1, and bk. 2 (Interindividual Psychology).

51. For a discussion of this point at the level of poetics, see Emile Benveniste, "The Linguistic Functions of 'to Be' and 'to Have,'" in *Problems in General Linguistics*, trans. Mary Elizabeth Meek (Coral Gables: University of Miami Press, 1971).

52. Rawlsian justice is not in its underlying conception a way of winning. In Rawlsian liberalism, all social good is regarded as a collective product—the product of a moral consensus on the principles of justice itself. (But see Nozick, *Anarchy, State, and Utopia*, p. 198.) Achieving that consensus would require that individuals abstract from their present and past social positions in order to debate the degree of inequality that would be justified in the *future*. Like Rawlsian liberalism, transitional liberalism regards all social good as the product of a hard-won political consensus, but here the consensus will be on the illegitimate inequality of the *past* rather than on principles of redistribution for the future.

53. Klein's theory of the distribution of affect would remain relevant to the critique of group thought even if psychoanalytic techniques are supplanted in individual therapy by advances in neuroscience. This insight makes it possible to think of groups, whether they define themselves as instrumental (interest groups) or cultural (identity groups), as having features in common with therapy groups: here the stated purpose is to figure out what internalized objects we are addressing when we think we are talking to another member of the group. Nontherapeutic groups have other purposes but reveal similar links between their intrapsychic and interpsychic dimensions. See Adam Phillips, "Superiorities," in Phillips, *Equals* (New York: Basic Books, 2002); Wilfred R. Bion, "Group Dynamics: A Re-View," in *New Directions in Psycho-Analysis: The Significance of Infant Conflict in the Pattern of Adult Behaviour*, ed. Melanie Klein, Paula Heimann, and Roger Ernle Money-Kyrle (New York: Basic Books, 1957); Bracher, "On the Psychological and Social Functions of Language."

54. Frank Stern, *The Whitewashing of the Yellow Badge: Antisemitism and Philosemitism*

in Postwar Germany, trans. William Templer (Oxford: Oxford University Press, 1992); "German-Jewish Relations in the Postwar Period: The Ambiguities of Antisemitic and Philosemitic Discourse," in *Jews, Germans, Memory: Reconstructions of Jewish Life in Germany*, ed. Y. Michal Bodemann, *Social History, Popular Culture, and Politics in Germany* (Ann Arbor: University of Michigan Press, 1996). See also Jane Kramer, *The Politics of Memory: Looking for Germany in the New Germany* (New York: Random House, 1996).

55. The discussion of South Africa's Truth and Reconciliation Commission in chapter 2 illustrates the role that fantasies of guilt and forgiveness can play in national recovery alongside (or in place of) a more realistic insistence on truth and justice.

56. Freud's argument about guilt and repression, developed most fully in *Civilization and Its Discontents*, is complemented by his argument about grief and grievance in "Mourning and Melancholia," *Standard Edition of the Complete Psychological Works of Sigmund Freud,* ed. James Strachey and Anna Freud, vol. 14 (London: Hogarth, 1957). See also "Paper on Metapsychology," ibid., vol. 14; "The Economic Problem of Masochism," ibid., vol. 19; and *"Civilization and Its Discontents,"* ibid., vol. 21.

57. Freud, "Mourning and Melancholia," pp. 250–52; Eric L. Santner, *Stranded Objects: Mourning, Memory, and Film in Postwar Germany* (Ithaca: Cornell University Press, 1990), chaps. 1–2.

58. Rose argues that this "link between mourning and ethics" virtually guarantees that the nation must remain haunted by its past as a consequence of the cultural and psychological devices through which it attempts to break free of its past. Jacqueline Rose, *States of Fantasy* (New York: Oxford University Press, 1996), pp. 3–5. The intertemporal metaphor of haunting appears frequently in discussions of transitional justice. See, e.g., Tina Rosenberg, *The Haunted Land: Facing Europe's Ghosts after Communism* (New York: Random House, 1995). See also chapter 7 in this volume.

59. Judith Shklar makes this clear in "The Liberalism of Fear."

60. See Judith N Shklar, "A Life of Learning," in *Liberalism without Illusions: Essays on Liberal Theory and the Political Vision of Judith N. Shklar*, ed. Bernard Yack (Chicago: University of Chicago Press, 1996). She directly criticizes Schmitt in Judith N. Shklar, *Legalism: An Essay on Law, Morals, and Politics* (Cambridge: Harvard University Press, 1964), p. 125.

61. Shklar's dissertation adviser, Carl Friedrich, was a leader in this movement. See, e.g., Carl J. Friedrich, *Totalitarianism: Proceedings of a Conference Held at the American Academy of Arts and Sciences, March 1953* (New York: Grosset and Dunlap, 1964); and Carl J. Friedrich and Zbigniew Brzezinski, *Totalitarian Dictatorship and Autocracy* (Cambridge: Harvard University Press, 1956). The younger generation of Shklar's colleagues when she joined the Harvard faculty contributed to this line of thought. See, e.g., Adam Ulam, *The New Face of Soviet Totalitarianism* (Cambridge: Harvard University Press, 1963); Zbigniew Brzezinski and Samuel P. Huntington, *Political Power: USA/USSR* (New York: Viking, 1964).

62. See Judith N. Shklar, *American Citizenship: The Quest for Inclusion* (Cambridge: Harvard University Press, 1991).

63. Shklar explicitly condemned violence committed in the name of "victims" as no less "cruel" than the violence of their oppressors, in "Putting Cruelty First," in *Ordinary*

Vices (Cambridge: Belknap Press of Harvard University Press, 1984), pp. 15–23, esp. p. 21.

64. For an alternative view, see Bruce A. Ackerman, *The Future of Liberal Revolution* (New Haven: Yale University Press, 1992). Ackerman has elsewhere acknowledged the influence of Shklar, with whom he studied as an undergraduate. Cf. John Rawls, *The Law of Peoples; with, the Idea of Public Reason Revisited* (Cambridge: Harvard University Press, 1999), esp. §10.

65. Shklar, "The Liberalism of Fear," p. 21.

66. Schmitt, *The Concept of the Political*, p. 71.

67. Shklar, *Ordinary Vices*, introduction and chap. 2. See also Bernard A. O. Williams, "The Liberalism of Fear," in *In the Beginning Was the Deed: Realism and Moralism in Political Argument*, ed. Geoffrey Hawthorn (Princeton: Princeton University Press, 2005).

68. Kateb, "On Political Evil," pp. 212–213. Kateb goes on to make explicit the counter-revolutionary implications of his view. Revolutionary violence is permissible, he says, only against genuine evil, represented by Hitler, Stalin, Mao, and Pol Pot. It is just another form of cruelty when used to resist oppression, such as blacks suffered under apartheid or peasants suffer throughout the world. Mere injustice, for example, British rule of the American colonies, would never justify political violence, according to Kateb (p. 202).

69. The concept of "genocide" was invented by legal scholar Raphaël Lemkin immediately after World War II based on his seminal study of Nazi policies toward the populations of occupied countries. Raphaël Lemkin, *Axis Rule in Occupied Europe: Laws of Occupation, Analysis of Government, Proposals for Redress* (Washington, D.C.: Carnegie Endowment for International Peace, Division of International Law, 1944).

70. Slavoj Žižek, in *Welcome to the Desert of the Real* (London: Verso, 2002), discusses 9/11 in the context of such films as *Independence Day* and *The Matrix*, which prepared us at the level of fantasy to experience ourselves as the objects of destructive desire when the attacks actually occurred. He claims that, if "terror" was what we already *expected* to feel in these circumstances, it must rather be a fantasmatic symptom of *another* trauma—and not our real trauma itself.

71. For an exploration of these conventions, see Susan Sontag, *Regarding the Pain of Others* (New York: Farrar, Straus and Giroux, 2003). Cf. Carolyn J. Dean, "Indifference and the Language of Victimization," in Dean, *The Fragility of Empathy after the Holocaust* (Ithaca: Cornell University Press, 2004). This theme is discussed extensively in chapter 7 of this volume.

72. On "isolation" as a defense mechanism, see Sigmund Freud, "Inhibitions, Symptoms, and Anxiety," in Strachey and A. Freud, *Standard Edition of the Complete Psychological Works of Sigmund Freud*, 20:119–23.

73. For a dissection of press accounts of the former Yugoslavia in the 1990s, see Feher, *Powerless by Design*; Charles King, "Trouble in the Balkans," review of *Explaining Yugoslavia* by John B. Allcock, *Times Literary Supplement*, July 20, 2001.

74. The heretofore implicit link between genocide and the democratic rule of a *topos* by an *ethnos* is spelled out in Michael Mann, *The Dark Side of Democracy: Explaining*

Ethnic Cleansing (New York: Cambridge University Press, 2005). For further discussion, see chapter 4 in this volume.

75. For discussions of this view, see Deen K. Chatterjee, ed. *The Ethics of Assistance: Morality and the Distant Needy* (Cambridge: Cambridge University Press, 2004); Deen K. Chatterjee and Don E. Scheid, eds., *Ethics and Foreign Intervention* (Cambridge: Cambridge University Press, 2003).

76. International Commission on Intervention and State Sovereignty, *The Responsibility to Protect*. For further developments, see "The Responsibility to Protect Coalition," http://r2pcoalition.org/; and "Responsibility to Protect: Engaging Civil Society," http://www.responsibilitytoprotect.org/ (accessed January 31, 2010).

77. See David Miller, *National Responsibility and Global Justice* (Oxford: Oxford University Press, 2007), pp. 27ff.

78. See, e.g., Minow, *Breaking the Cycles of Hatred*. Cf. Octavio Paz, "Critique of the Pyramid," in Paz, *The Labyrinth of Solitude: Life and Thought in Mexico*, trans. Lysander Kemp (New York: Viking Penguin, 1985); René Girard, *I See Satan Fall Like Lightning*, trans. James G. Williams (Maryknoll, N.Y.: Orbis, 2001), esp. chaps. 12–14 and the conclusion.

79. For a discussion of the impact of Hiroshima on the philosophy of history, see Paul van Dijk, "Final Time and the End of Time: The Philosophy of History under Nuclear Threat" in Van Dijk, *Anthropology in the Age of Technology: The Philosophical Contribution of Günther Anders* (Amsterdam: Rodopi, 2000.)

80. Carl Schmitt, *The Nomos of the Earth in the International Law of the Jus Publicum Europaeum,* trans. G. L. Ulmen (New York: Telos, 2003).

81. Giorgio Agamben, *Homo Sacer: Sovereign Power and Bare Life*, trans. Daniel Heller-Roazen (Stanford: Stanford University Press, 1998), pt. 3; Agamben, *State of Exception* (Chicago: University of Chicago Press, 2005).

    Agamben says, "The sacredness of life, which is invoked today as an absolutely fundamental right in opposition to sovereign power, in fact originally expresses precisely both life's subjection to a power over death and life's irreparable exposure in the relation of abandonment. . . . Life is sacred only insofar as it is taken into the . . . originary exception in which human life is included in the political order in being exposed to an unconditional capacity to be killed" (*Homo Sacer*, pp. 82–85). Cf. Jacques Rancière, "Who Is the Subject of the Rights of Man?" *South Atlantic Quarterly* 103, no. 2–3 (2004).

82. René Girard, *The Scapegoat*, trans. Yvonne Freccero (Baltimore: Johns Hopkins University Press, 1986); Girard, Oughourlian, and Lefort, *Things Hidden*; Raymund Schwager, *Must There Be Scapegoats? Violence and Redemption in the Bible* (San Francisco: Harper and Row, 1987).

83. Tomaž Mastnak, *Crusading Peace: Christendom, the Muslim World, and Western Political Order* (Berkeley: University of California Press, 2002).

84. Carl Schmitt, *Political Theology II: The Myth of the Closure of Any Political Theology*, trans. Michael Hoelzl and Graham Ward (Cambridge: Polity, 2008), chap. 2.

85. Cf. Lévinas, *Totality and Infinity*, p. 239. Lévinas took the primacy of ethics to its extreme by putting it ahead even of ontology and God (the world itself and its Creator).

86. Ibid., p. 238.

87. Emmanuel Lévinas, "Useless Suffering," in Lévinas, *Entre Nous: On Thinking-of-the-Other*, trans. Michael B. Smith and Barbara Harshav (New York: Columbia University Press, 1998), pp. 98–99.

88. David Kennedy, *The Dark Sides of Virtue: Reassessing International Humanitarianism* (Princeton: Princeton University Press, 2004), sec. 1.

89. For a moral history of medical analgesia, see Thomas Dormandy, *The Worst of Evils: The Fight Against Pain* (New Haven: Yale University Press, 2006).

90. The priority of ethics arises, Lévinas says, "from the fear of occupying someone's place." Leaving no doubt about the conceptual relation between genocide and colonialism, he quotes Pascal: "My place in the sun [is] the beginning and prototype of the usurpation of the whole earth." Lévinas elaborates Pascal as follows: "My . . . 'place in the sun,' my home—have they not been a usurpation of places which belong to the others already oppressed or . . . expelled by me into a third world." Emmanuel Lévinas, "From the One to the Other: Transcendence and Time," in Lévinas, *Entre Nous*, pp. 144–45.

91. Ethics thus arises "without the remembered present of any past commitment." "Diachrony and Representation," in Lévinas, *Entre Nous*, p. 170; Lévinas, "Useless Suffering," p. 93.

92. Lévinas claims that his post-Auschwitz ethics is "without theodicy." It can survive the loss of faith and hope in God's justice, and is meant in their absence to remind me that I, too, am responsible for saving the world. Emmanuel Lévinas and France Guwy, "What No One Else Can Do in My Place: A Conversation with Emmanuel Levinas," in *Religion: Beyond a Concept*, ed. Hent de Vries (New York: Fordham University Press, 2008), pp. 302–4. Lévinas here implicitly rejects Walter Benjamin's concept of our "weak messianic power" as a "secret agreement between past generations and the present one." Benjamin, "On the Concept of History," p. 390.

93. Emmanuel Lévinas, *Totality and Infinity: An Essay on Exteriority*, trans. Alphonso Lingis (The Hague: M. Nijhoff, 1979). In an earlier set of lectures, he explained that "proximity as exteriority is not reducible to spatial contiguity" and is better understood as a form of "non-oincidence"—a concept that he models on the separation between different moments of *time*. "Time signifies this *always* of non-coincidence, but also the *always* of the *relationship* . . . It is a distance that is also a proximity." Lévinas, *Time and the Other and Additional Essays*, trans. Richard A. Cohen (Pittsburgh: Duquesne University Press, 1987), p. 30. This point is developed in the conclusion to this volume.

94. For the distinction between spatializing and temporalizing discourses, see Jonathan Boyarin, "Space, Time, and the Politics of Memory," in *Remapping Memory: The Politics of Timespace*, ed. Jonathan Boyarin (Minneapolis: University of Minnesota Press, 1994), p. 20.

95. "The face of the other in its precariousness and defenselessness is for me at once the temptation to kill and the call to peace, the 'You shall not kill.' The face which already accuses me makes me suspicious but already claims me and demands me" (ibid., p. 167). Because no group has derived ongoing benefit from the Rwandan genocide, the beneficiary problem discussed here does not present itself. In the ab-

sence of that problem, Mamdani proposes (on something like Lincolnian grounds) a humanitarian ethic for Rwanda, based on common survivorship. See Mamdani, *When Victims Become Killers*, pp. 270–82.

96. Although Lévinas himself was not opposed to economic (or any other kind) of aid that may relieve useless suffering, he insisted that the duty to rescue comes first. The intrinsic rationale for intervention would thus be independent of whatever redistribution follows.

97. Philip Gourevitch, "The Return: With a Million Exiles Coming Home, Killers and Genocide Survivors Are Being Forced to Live Together. (Letter from Rwanda)," *New Yorker* 72, no. 43 (1997); Gourevitch, *We Wish to Inform You That Tomorrow We Will Be Killed with Our Families: Stories from Rwanda* (New York: Farrar, Straus, and Giroux, 1998), p. 308.

98. Lévinas saw this threesome as primarily Jewish. "The direct encounter with God, *this* is a Christian concept. As Jews, we are always a threesome. I and you and the Third who is in our midst. And only as a Third does He reveal Himself." Emmanuel Lévinas, "Ideology and Idealism," in *The Levinas Reader*, ed. and trans. Seán Hand (Oxford: Blackwell, 1989), p. 247.

99. As an apparent exception to his broader view, Lévinas affirms "the nonalterity of the enemy" *from* whom we rescue, and thus "seems to grant Schmitt the political— rather than ethical—dimension of the enemy." Gil Anidjar, *The Jew, the Arab: A History of the Enemy* (Stanford: Stanford University Press, 2003), p. 172. See also Jacques Derrida, *Adieu to Emmanuel Levinas*, trans. Pascale-Anne Brault and Michael Naas (Stanford: Stanford University Press, 1999), p. 147 n. 95.

100. Emmanuel Lévinas, "Ethics and Politics," in Hand, *The Levinas Reader*, p. 294.

101. In presenting sovereign violence as an exception to the violence it claims to stop, Schmitt famously declares that the sovereign is not bound by his own laws: "Sovereign is he who decides on the exception." Carl Schmitt, *Political Theology: Four Chapters on the Concept of Sovereignty*, trans. George Schwab (Cambridge: MIT Press, 1985), p. 5.

102. Lévinas here rationalizes Israeli complicity in the Sabra and Chatila massacres using the same vocabulary as Schmitt: "There is certainly a place for defence," he says, "for it is not always a question of 'me,' but *of those close to me* who are my neighbours. I'd call such a defence a *politics*, but a politics that is ethically necessary." Lévinas, "Ethics and Politics," pp. 292, 294 (emphasis added). These passages are from an interview conducted with Lévinas by Shlomo Malka and Alain Finkielkraut and are usefully discussed in Howard Caygill, *Levinas and the Political* (London: Routledge, 2002), esp. pp. 191–94. Israel is, according to Lévinas, "the most fragile, the most vulnerable thing in the world." Emmanuel Lévinas, "Politics After," in Lévinas, *Beyond the Verse: Talmudic Readings and Lectures*, trans. Gary D. Mole (Bloomington: Indiana University Press, 1994), p. 187.

103. This also describes the father's position in Freud's Oedipal triangle. See, e.g., D. W. Winnicott, "The Use of an Object in the Context of *Moses and Monotheism*," in *Psycho-Analytic Explorations*, ed. Clare Winnicott, Ray Shepherd, and Madeleine Davis (Cambridge: Harvard University Press, 1989).

104. Emmanuel Lévinas, "Peace and Proximity," in *Emmanuel Levinas: Basic Philosophi-*

cal Writings, ed. Adriaan Theodoor Peperzak, Simon Critchley, and Robert Bernasconi, trans. Simon Critchley, Tina Chanter, and Nicholas Walker, *Studies in Continental Thought* (Bloomington: Indiana University Press, 1996), p. 168.

105. Lévinas, like Schmitt, rejects the Hegelian starting point of an originary struggle between Two for mastery (the "struggle for recognition"). For elaboration of the Hegelian concept, see, e.g., Axel Honneth, *The Struggle for Recognition: The Moral Grammar of Social Conflicts*, trans. Joel Anderson (Cambridge: Polity, 1995).

106. See, e.g., Mahmood Mamdani, *Citizen and Subject: Contemporary Africa and the Legacy of Late Colonialism* (Princeton: Princeton University Press, 1996).

107. See, e.g., Ignatieff, *The Lesser Evil*; Lévinas, "Useless Suffering," p. 94.

108. Lévinas goes on to say, "The just suffering in me for the unjustifiable suffering of the other, opens suffering to the ethical perspective of the inter-human. In this perspective . . . the suffering in the other, where it is unforgivable to me, solicits . . . suffering in me" ("Useless Suffering," p. 94). It is not entirely clear by the following page whether Lévinas is endorsing or caricaturing this view of the moral pain of third parties. (The two interpretations, perhaps, are not mutually exclusive.) In a footnote he explains: "This suffering *in me* is so radically mine that it cannot become the subject of any preaching. It is as suffering *in me* and not as suffering in general that *welcome suffering*—attested to in the spiritual tradition of humanity—can signify a true idea: the expiatory suffering of the just who suffers for others."

109. "This ultimate passivity which nonetheless turns into action and into hope, is patience—the passivity of undergoing, and yet mastery itself. In patience disengagement within engagement is effected. . . . Extreme passivity becomes extreme mastery. . . . thus alone does violence remain endurable in patience. It is produced only in a world where I can die as a result of someone and for someone" (*Totality and Infinity*, p. 238–39).

110. Ibid., p. 240.

111. Schmitt stressed the constitutive role of enmity in creating friendship, but he did not go on to address the responsibilities that friends have to one another and whether these are ethical or political. His younger contemporary, Hannah Arendt, developed her own concept of "the political" around the *polis*, considered as a relation among friends, rather than the *pólemos*, a relation of hostility. It is arguable that Arendt's concept of the ethical, developed in her later writings, addresses our a priori responsibility to those excluded (as noncitizens) from the circle of political friendship—a category that would include our "enemies" in Schmitt's sense. See, e.g., Hannah Arendt, *The Human Condition* (Chicago: University of Chicago Press, 1958), pp. 28–59; "Some Questions of Moral Philosophy," in *Responsibility and Judgment*, ed. Jerome Kohn (New York: Schocken, 2003); "Thinking and Moral Considerations," in *Responsibility and Judgment*, ed. Jerome Kohn (New York: Schocken, 2003). For an elaboration of the "friend" side of Schmitt's friend-enemy distinction, see Jacques Derrida, *The Politics of Friendship*, trans. George Collins (London: Verso, 2005), chaps. 4–6.

112. International Commission on Intervention and State Sovereignty, *The Responsibility to Protect*. Bernard Kouchner, as French foreign minister, has suggested invoking the "Responsibility to Protect" doctrine to force international assistance on the

military regime in Burma. Seth Mydans, "Myanmar Faces Pressure to Allow Major Aid Effort," *New York Times*, May 8, 2008.

113. "The proximity of the neighbor—the peace of proximity—is the responsibility of the ego for an other" (Lévinas, "Peace and Proximity," p. 167). See also Lévinas, *Totality and Infinity*, pp. 220–53, 281–85. In this respect, Lévinas anticipates the recent thought of Giorgio Agamben, who asks us to "imagine two political communities insisting on the same region and in a condition of mutual exodus from each other." In such an "aterritorial . . . space," "the being-in-exodus of the citizen" would oppose itself to the limitations of the nation-state. "The political survival of humankind is today thinkable," Agamben goes on to say, "only in a world in which the spaces of states have been thus perforated and topologically deformed and in which the citizen has been able to recognize the refugee that he or she is." Giorgio Agamben, "Beyond Human Rights," in Agamben, *Means Without End: Notes on Politics*, trans. Vincenzo Binetti and Cesare Casarino (Minneapolis: University of Minnesota Press, 2000), pp. 24–26. Cf. Lévinas, *Totality and Infinity*, pp. 232–37.

114. Lévinas and Guwy, "What No One Else Can Do in My Place," p. 304–5.

115. Lévinas, *Totality and Infinity*, III.C.

116. Ibid., p. 235 (emphasis added).

117. "It is the decision that replaces the condition of disorder and insecurity of the state-of-nature with the order and security of the stately condition that makes him sovereign and makes everything else possible, including law and order. For Hobbes . . . the sovereign decision creates the state dictatorship of law and order in and over the anarchistic insecurity of a pre- and substately natural existence." Carl Schmitt, *On the Three Types of Juristic Thought*, trans. Joseph W. Bendersky (Westport, Conn.: Praeger, 2004), p. 62.

118. Talal Asad, "Redeeming the 'Human' through Human Rights," in Asad, *Formations of the Secular: Christianity, Islam, Modernity*, (Stanford: Stanford University Press, 2003), p. 12.

119. Michael Walzer, *Regicide and Revolution: Speeches at the Trial of Louis XVI* (New York: Cambridge University Press, 1974).

120. Sigmund Freud, "Totem and Taboo," in *The Standard Edition of the Complete Psychological Works of Sigmund Freud*, vol. 19; Freud, "*Civilization and Its Discontents*"; Freud, "*Group Psychology and the Analysis of the Ego*," ibid., vol. 21; Freud, *Moses and Monotheism*, ibid., vol. 23.

121. Norman O. Brown, *Love's Body* (New York: Random House, 1966), pp. 3–31.

122. As a relatively recent moral trope for the murderous encounter with the Other, Auschwitz is now commonly read backward into the entire history of colonialism, which has become describable as a prolonged Holocaust. See, e.g., Ward Churchill, *A Little Matter of Genocide: Holocaust and Denial in the Americas, 1492 to the Present* (San Francisco: City Lights, 1997); David E. Stannard, *American Holocaust: Columbus and the Conquest of the New World* (New York: Oxford University Press, 1992).

123. C. L. R. James, *The Black Jacobins: Toussaint L'Ouverture and the San Domingo Revolution*, 2d ed. (New York: Vintage, 1989).

124. The interstate system still exists, supported by a UN Charter that prohibits unilat-

eral invasions of one state by another, but this is now considered a surmountable obstacle, making it advisable (but not essential) for any state intervening in another to get the support of a multilateral coalition as a proxy for the world community itself.

125. Mahmood Mamdani, "The Politics of Naming: Genocide, Civil War, Insurgency," *London Review of Books*, March 8, 2007; Mamdani, "The New Humanitarian Order: Is the ICC's 'Responsibility to Protect' Really Just an Assertion of Neocolonial Domination?" *Nation*, September 29, 2008.

126. See Bass, *Freedom's Battle*.

2. Ways of Winning

1. Many ANC activists continued to believe that there would eventually be a full disclosure of what was done to them and their dead comrades. See, e.g., Kader Asmal, Louise Asmal, and Ronald Suresh Roberts, *Reconciliation through Truth: A Reckoning of Apartheid's Criminal Governance*, 2nd ed. (Cape Town: David Philip, 1997). Cf. Neier, *War Crimes*, pp. 104–5.

2. Dullah Omar, "Justice in Transition," http://www.doj.gov.za/trc/legal/justice.htm (accessed January 30, 2010).

3. See, e.g., Asmal et al., *Reconciliation*.

4. George M. Fredrickson, "Reform and Revolution in American and South African Freedom Struggles," in Fredrickson, *The Comparative Imagination: On the History of Racism, Nationalism, and Social Movements* (Berkeley: University of California Press, 1997), pp. 147–48. Jakes Gerwel, "National Reconciliation: Holy Grail or Secular Pact?" in *Looking Back, Reaching Forward: Reflections on the Truth and Reconciliation Commission of South Africa*, ed. Charles Villa-Vicencio and Wilhelm Verwoerd (Cape Town: University of Cape Town Press, 2000).

5. *The Promotion of National Unity and Reconciliation Act. No. 34 of 1995, Amended in 1997 and 1998.* (An amendment extended the original eighteen-month term of the TRC to two years.)

6. See chapter 3 in this volume.

7. Charles Villa-Vicencio, "Getting on with Life: A Move toward Reconciliation," in Villa-Vicencio and Verwoerd, *Looking Back, Reaching Forward*.

8. Gandhi, *Hind Swaraj* (Ahmedabad: Navajivan, 1946), pp. 72–75. The philosopher Bernard Williams makes a similar point when he explains that shame internalizes the figure of the watcher. "The root of shame," he says, "lies in . . . being at a disadvantage in what I shall call, in a very general phrase, a loss of power. The sense of shame is a reaction of the subject to the consciousness of that loss." Bernard A. O. Williams, *Shame and Necessity* (Berkeley: University of California Press, 1993), pp. 219–20. For biographical context, see Erik H. Erikson, *Gandhi's Truth: On the Origins of Militant Nonviolence* (New York: Norton, 1969); Mohandas K. Gandhi, *An Autobiography: The Story of My Experiments with Truth*, trans. Mahadev Desai (London: Jonathan Cape, 1966).

9. As a parable of Indian independence, Gandhi's story was meant to illustrate the difference between the tactics of nonviolence and its two alternatives: armed struggle,

on the one hand, and the cowardice of passive acceptance of British rule, on the other. This reading is supported by histories of Gandhi's actions during the "Quit India" movement of 1942. See, e.g., Francis G. Hutchins, *Spontaneous Revolution: The Quit India Movement* (Delhi: Manohar, 1971), chaps. 5–6, 9.

10. Alok Rai, "Afterword," in Premchand, *Nirmala*, trans. Alok Rai (Delhi: Oxford University Press, 1999).

11. *TRC Report*, vol. 2, chap. 6; vol. 5, §138; Desmond Tutu, *No Future without Forgiveness* (New York: Doubleday, 1999), pp. 167–75; Martin Meredith and Tina Rosenberg, *Coming to Terms: South Africa's Search for Truth* (New York: Public Affairs, 1999), chap. 14. Boraine, *A Country Unmasked*, chap. 7. On the Mandela United Football Club Hearings, see *TRC Report*, vol. 2, chap. 6; vol. 5, chap. 6, §138.

12. Mandela made this view explicit in his description of the TRC's charge: "All of us, as a nation that has newly found itself, share in the shame at the capacity of human beings of any race or language group to be inhumane to other human beings. We should all share in the commitment to a South Africa in which this will never recur. Nelson Mandela, "Speech in National Assembly, 15 April, 1997," http://www.doj.gov.za/trc/media/1997/9704/s970415e.htm (accessed January 30, 2010).

13. See, e.g., Sampie Terreblanche, "The Production of the Past" (paper read at a Sawyer Seminar held at the Institute of African Studies, Columbia University, April 1, 2000); Terreblanche, "Dealing with Systematic Economic Injustice," in Villa-Vicencio and Verwoerd, *Looking Back, Reaching Forward*; Bob Myers, *Is This Really What We Fought For? White Rule Ends, Black Poverty Goes On* (London: Index, 1997).

14. For a perspective from authors on the *TRC Report*, see Charles Villa-Vicencio and Wilhelm Vervoerd, "Constructing a Report: Writing up the 'Truth'," in *Truth v. Justice: The Morality of Truth Commissions*, ed. Robert I. Rotberg and Dennis F. Thompson (Princeton: Princeton University Press, 2000).

15. *TRC Report*: vol. 1, chap. 1, §§71–72.

16. Desmond Tutu, *The Rainbow People of God: The Making of a Peaceful Revolution* (New York: Doubleday, 1994).

17. The "noble human being . . . helps the unfortunate, but not, or almost not, from pity, but prompted more by an urge begotten by an excess of power." Friedrich Wilhelm Nietzsche, *Beyond Good and Evil: Prelude to a Philosophy of the Future*, trans. Walter A. Kaufmann (New York: Vintage, 1989), p. 205.

18. *TRC Report*, vol. 1, chap. 1 ("Chairperson's Foreword").

19. *TRC Report*, vol. 5, "Minority Position Submitted by Commissioner Wynand Malan," pp. 436–56.

20. See, e.g., Dave Beresford, "TRC Slams ANC, PAC and Winnie," *Electronic Mail & Guardian*, October 27, 1998; Steven Laufer et al., "ANC in Court Bid to Block Truth Report," *Business Day (SA)*, October 29, 1998; Suzannne Daley, "South African Panel's Report Arrives in Swirl of Bitterness," *New York Times*, October 30, 1998; Maureen Isaacson and Jean Le May, "Human-Rights Group Slams ANC," *Sunday Independent (SA)*, November 1, 1998. These events are recounted in Meredith and Rosenberg, *Coming to Terms*, pp. 303–7.

21. For a somewhat more detailed discussion of the *Report*, see Robert Meister, "Ways of Winning: The Costs of Moral Victory in Transitional Regimes," in *Modernity and*

the Problem of Evil, ed. Alan D. Schrift (Bloomington: Indiana University Press, 2005).

22. For an explanation of its approach, see Charles Villa-Vicencio, "Restorative Justice: Dealing with the Past Differently," in Villa-Vicencio and Verwoerd, *Looking Back, Reaching Forward*; André du Toit, "The Moral Foundations of the South African TRC: Truth as Acknowledgement and Justice as Recognition," in Rotberg and Thompson, *Truth v. Justice.*

23. But only the dissenting commissioner (an Afrikaner) insists that true reconciliation would require *"all those who benefited* from apartheid" to engage fully with the need to make costly amends Cf. *TRC Report*, vol. 1, p. 124; vol. 5, p. 258.

24. For a thoughtful discussion of the tension between psychic and material aspects of reconciliation (and of the above-referenced quotes), see Jacqueline Rose, "Apathy and Accountability: The Challenge of South Africa's Truth and Reconciliation Commision to the Intellectual in the Modern World," in Rose, *On Not Being Able to Sleep: Psychoanalysis and the Modern World* (Princeton: Princeton University Press, 2003), pp. 227–31.

25. Shklar, *The Faces of Injustice*, p. 101.

26. For a description of the lessons learned from past truth commissions, see *TRC Report*, vol. 1, §§24–30; Timothy Garton Ash, "True Confessions," *New York Review of Books* 44, no. 12 (1997); "The Truth about Dictatorship," review of *Transitional Justice*, 3 vols., ed. Neil J. Kritz, and other works, *New York Review of Books* 45, no. 3 (1998). See also Tina Rosenberg, "Afterword: Confronting the Painful Past," in Rosenberg, *Coming to Terms: South Africa's Search for Truth* (New York: Public Affairs, 1999); Ruti Teitel, "From Dictatorship to Democracy: The Role of Transitional Justice," in *Deliberative Democracy and Human Rights*, ed. Harold Hongju Koh and Ronald Slye (New Haven: Yale University Press, 1999); Teitel, "Bringing the Messiah through Law," in *Human Rights in Political Transitions: Gettysburg to Bosnia*, ed. Carla Hesse and Robert Post (New York: Zone Books, 1999). For a comprehensive selection of the theoretical literature through 1995, see Kritz, *Transitional Justice*, vol. 1.

27. See Terreblanche, "Production of the Past," pt. 3; Mamdani, "Amnesty or Impunity"; Mahmood Mamdani, "Reconciliation Without Justice," *Southern African Review of Books* 46 (1996); "When Does Reconciliation Turn into a Denial of Justice?" Pretoria: Human Sciences Research Council, February 18, 1998. See also Truth and Reconciliation Commission, *Public Discussion: Transforming Society through Reconciliation: Myth or Reality*, March 12, 1998. For a discussion of the impact of these interventions on the Commission, see Antjie Krog, *Country of My Skull* (Johannesburg: Random House, 1998), chap. 10. For a detailed account of the ways in which the TRC was diverted from fulfilling its mandate, see Terry Bell and Dumisa Buhle Ntsebeza, *Unfinished Business: South Africa, Apartheid, and Truth* (London: Verso, 2003).

28. See, e.g., *TRC Report*, vol. 2, chap. 3, §§42–45, on the increase in police shootings during the mid-1980s.

29. By the late 1970s South Africa's State Security Council (SSC) had, as part of its "total strategy," embraced the same extra-legal tactics of state terrorism, torture, and mur-

der that were practiced by other U.S.-supported authoritarian regimes toward the end of the cold war. These were the techniques that were later condemned as "gross" violations of human rights by truth commissions set up to promote democratic transitions in Latin America and elsewhere. Priscilla Hayner, "Same Species, Different Animal: How South Africa Compares to Truth Commissions Worldwide," in Villa-Vicencio and Verwoerd, *Looking Back, Reaching Forward*. See also Hayner "Fifteen Truth Commissions, Impunity, and the Inter-American Human Rights System," *Boston University International Law Journal* 12 (1994); and Hayner, *Unspeakable Truths*.

30. See, e.g., *TRC Report*, vol. 5, chap. 7, §§61–85.

31. Jeremy Cronin, "Á Luta Dis-Continua: The TRC Final Report and the Nation Building Project," paper delivered at the conference "TRC: Commissioning the Past," University of the Witwatersrand, June 11–14, 1999."

32. DeKlerk's initial decision to abandon apartheid was a direct of the loss of Thatcher's support after the cold war ended in 1989, along with military aid from the Soviet bloc for the ANC's armed struggle (Sampie Terreblanche, personal communication).

33. Rian Malan, *My Traitor's Heart: A South African Exile Returns to Face His Country, His Tribe, and His Conscience* (New York: Atlantic Monthly Press, 1990).

34. Malan drives home this point about projective identification by playing with the English word "blank," which is also Afrikaans for "white": "To most whites, blacks are . . . blank screens onto which whites project their own fears and preconceptions" (p. 155). See Wilfred R. Bion, *Experiences in Groups, and Other Papers* (London: Tavistock/Routledge, 1989), pp. 141–91; Bion, *Second Thoughts: Selected Papers on Psycho-Analysis* (London: Heinemann Medical, 1967), esp.chaps. 3–4, 7; Meltzer, *The Kleinian Development*, pt. 3; Malcolm Pines, "Bion and Group Psychotherapy," in Pines, *International Library of Group Psychotherapy and Group Process* (London: Routledge and Kegan Paul, 1985). Hinshelwood, *Dictionary*, entry on "Wilfrid Bion."

35. Cf. Breyten Breytenbach, *The True Confessions of an Albino Terrorist* (San Diego: Harcourt Brace, 1994). Breytenbach, one of the great South African literary figures in both Afrikaans and English, served seven years in prison for committing terrorist acts against the apartheid regime.

36. Malan, *My Traitor's Heart*, p. 346.

37. In the words of Klein's disciple, Hanna Segal: "Manic reparation is a defence in that its aim is to repair the object in such a way that guilt and loss are never experienced. . . . [T]he object in relation to which the reparation is done must never be experienced as having been damaged by oneself." Hanna Segal, *Introduction to the Work of Melanie Klein* (London: Hogarth, 1973), pp. 95–96. For further elaboration, see D. W. Winnicott, "The Manic Defense," in Winnicott, *Through Pediatrics to Psycho-Analysis* (New York: Brunner/Mazel, 1992).

38. There is a Christian message in his view that passive beneficiaries were saved (often without deserving it) by the hidden moral qualities of victims.

39. "We that come from the old order—or the majority of us—are horrified by the stories that victims of gross human rights violations have told over the past year. We

are horrified and feel betrayed. We feel done in. We feel our dignity impaired. That things like these were possible, right under our noses. How could this have happened? We are victims of the cruelest fraud committed against us! . . . But the experience of those who come from the struggle, those who were on the receiving end of these things, the things that horrify us . . . this pain can help us soften in our own indignity at the betrayal." Wynand Malan, "Statement by Mr. Wynand Malan, Deputy Chair of the Human Rights Violations Committee of the Truth and Reconciliation Commission, May 16, 1997," http://www.justice.gov.za/trc/media/pr/1997/p970516a.htm (accessed January 30, 2010).

40. *TRC Report*, vol. 5, chap. 9, "Reconciliation." See also, Krog, *Country of My Skull*.

41. As we saw in chapter 1, the new culture of human rights aims to replace a politics of cruelty, and the mutual fear it inspires, with a fear of fear itself.

42. This argument resonates with the commonplace fin de siècle understanding that those who opposed violations of human rights while they occurred will merely have anticipated the future regret that most continuing beneficiaries *will* have felt for being apathetic about such violations. For a critique of such views, see Robert Meister, "Anticipatory Regret: Can Free Speech Be Protected When It Matters?" review of *Perilous Times* by Geoffrey R. Stone, *boundary 2* 32, no. 3 (2005).

43. As "Americans," we should have little difficulty understanding the conflicted forms of projection and introjection through which Afrikaners have rationalized keeping their conquered territory. Throughout U.S. history, "playing Indian" and fearing Indians has been part of what it means to be an "American." The Indians were (in our national fantasy) "split" into idealized objects with whom we identified and persecutory objects whom we eliminated or controlled. See, for example, Philip Joseph Deloria, *Playing Indian* (New Haven: Yale University Press, 1998). I am grateful to Adam Hefty for calling my attention to the slogan "U.S. out of North America."

By the end of the twentieth century most U.S. citizens would at least disavow the worst excesses of the North American genocide, and would probably acknowledge that they are tangible beneficiaries of the fact that it was far more effective than South Africa's. Yet few who take this view regret that European settlers were not exterminated or expelled, and even fewer would argue that the world would be a better place if European immigration to North America had never occurred. What, then, is the function within our political culture of condemning its foundational atrocities? This question is addressed in chapter 10 in this volume.

44. Such manic fantasies of omnipotence were, for Freud, the other face of depression and not a form of reparation (even of the damaged internal object). Neither is the phenomenon Freud and his followers describe as a "refusal to mourn" a way of "swallowing loss" by incorporating and entombing the lost object within ourselves where we can punish it interminably without addressing our own feelings of guilt and aggression. In addition to Freud's "Mourning and Melancholia," see Melanie Klein, "A Contribution to the Psycho-Genesis of Manic-Depressive States," in Klein, *Love, Guilt, and Reparation and Other Works, 1921–1945* (New York: Delacorte/S. Lawrence, 1975); Klein, "Mourning and Its Relation to Manic-Depressive States," in Klein, *Love, Guilt, and Reparation*; Nicolas Abraham and Maria Torok, "Mourning

or Melancholia: Introjection *versus* Incorporation," in Abraham and Torok, *The Shell and the Kernel: Renewals of Psychoanalysis*, trans. Nicholas T. Rand (Chicago: University of Chicago Press, 1994).

45. John Bowlby, "Pathological Mourning and Childhood Mourning," *JAPA* (1963).

46. See also Alexander Mitscherlich and Margarete Mitscherlich, *The Inability to Mourn: Principles of Collective Behavior*, trans. Beverley R. Placzek (New York: Grove, 1975); Stern, *The Whitewashing of the Yellow Badge.*

47. Many former combatants did not have to choose between moral victory and material reward; they rose to power in the new regime (Thabo Mbeki, Frank Chikane) or in the new economy (Moletsi Mbeki, Cyril Ramaphosa).

48. See, for example, Heribert Adam, F. van Zyl Slabbert, and Kogila Moodley, *Comrades in Business: Post-Liberation Politics in South Africa* (Cape Town: Tafelberg, 1997). Mahmood Mamdani, "Now Who Will Bell the Fat Black Cat," review of *Comrades in Business* by Heribert Adam et al., *Electronic Mail and Guardian*, October 17, 1997.

49. Sampie Terreblanche, "Testimony before the TRC during the Special Hearing on the Rule of the Business Sector," Carlton Hotel, Johannesberg, November 11, 1997. See, more generally, Terreblanche, *A History of Inequality in South Africa, 1652–2002* (Pietermaritzburg: University of Natal Press, 2002); Pule Molebeledi, "SA Still Needs Economic Liberation," *Business Day*, March 23, 2003; John Battersby, "Academic Slams Mbeki for Neglecting the Poor," *Sunday Independent*, December 12, 2002; "The ANC Is Not a Socialist Movement," *Mercury*, December 12, 2002.

50. To be precise, the TRC does not put forward either struggle or reconciliation as a model of justice. It employs, instead, the term "restorative justice," which is its English translation of *ubuntu*, and provides a long list of examples of "reconciliation through truth" to illustrate "restorative justice" as a type of moral triumph over pain. *TRC Report*, vol. 1, §§80–100; vol. 5, chap. 9, esp. §§62–152.

51. Peter Brooks, *The Melodramatic Imagination: Balzac, Henry James, Melodrama, and the Mode of Excess* (New Haven: Yale University Press, 1976), pp. 11–12.

52. Krog, *Country of My Skull*, chaps. 1–8, 13–17; Tutu, *No Future Without Forgiveness*, chaps. 5–8.

53. Impatience with structural injustice is a feature of both revolutionary and reformist thought. See, e.g., Antonio Negri, *Insurgencies: Constituent Power and the Modern State*, trans. Maurizia Boscagli (Minneapolis: University of Minnesota Press, 1999); John Rawls, *A Theory of Justice* (Cambridge, Mass.: Belknap Press of Harvard University Press, 1971).

54. Elaine Scarry, *The Body in Pain: The Making and Unmaking of the World* (New York: Oxford University Press, 1985), pp. 3–11.

55. Ibid., pp. 161–62.

56. Emily Dickinson, *The Complete Poems of Emily Dickinson*, ed. Thomas H. Johnson (Boston: Little, Brown, 1960), p. 323.

57. One might argue that historical injustices are thus less easily put in the past than physical pain, for contingent reasons: we know more about physiology than sociology, and our techniques of physical palliation are vastly more effective than the

forms of memory-politics on which transitional justice relies to put social injuries in the past.

58. Derek Parfit questions what he calls a "time-bias" in our *beliefs* about pain (even our own pain) that are largely independent of our memory of pain. Thus he claims that we would prefer ten hours of past pain to one hour of future pain. This bias seems to exist, according to Parfit, even if we remember the past pain intensely and are told that we will not remember the future pain at all (e.g., because it will occur at the moment of our death). See Derek Parfit, *Reasons and Persons* (Oxford: Clarendon, 1984), pp. 165–68, and the conclusion to this volume.

59. See Ian Hacking, *Rewriting the Soul: Multiple Personality and the Sciences of Memory* (Princeton: Princeton University Press, 1995), chaps. chaps.13, 15.

60. For a relatively nuanced defense of this view of torture, see, e.g., Ignatieff, *Human Rights as Politics and Ideology*. For a trenchant critique with respect to "torture," see Talal Asad, "Reflections on Cruelty and Torture," in Asad, *Formations of the Secular: Christianity, Islam, Modernity* (Stanford: Stanford University Press, 2003). For a discussion of recent attempts to abolish and legalize torture itself, see Sanford Levinson, ed., *Torture: A Collection* (Oxford: Oxford University Press, 2004).

61. Jan Assmann, "Remembering in Order to Belong: Writing, Memory, and Identity," in Assmann, *Religion and Cultural Memory: Ten Studies*, trans. Rodney Livingstone (Stanford: Stanford University Press, 2006). See also Jacques Derrida, *Archive Fever: A Freudian Impression*, trans. Eric Prenowitz (Chicago: University of Chicago Press, 1996).

62. Lauren Berlant, "The Subject of True Feeling: Pain, Privacy, and Politics," in *Cultural Pluralism, Identity Politics, and the Law*, ed. Austin Sarat and Thomas R. Kearns (Ann Arbor: University of Michigan Press, 1999), pp. 72–73. Page numbers in the text refer to this article.

63. Berlant concludes, "The desire to use trauma as the model of the pain of subordination that gets congealed into identities forgets the difference between trauma and adversity: trauma takes you out of your life shockingly and places you into another one, whereas structural subordination is not a surprise to the subjects who experience it, and the pain of subordination is ordinary life. . . . The reparation of pain does not bring into being a just life" (pp. 76, 78).

64. There is indeed a genre of Holocaust pornography that collects images and memorabilia very similar to those preserved by the genre of Holocaust melodrama. For further discussions of the pornography of self-exploitation, see Robert Meister, "Beyond Satisfaction: Desire, Consumption, and the Future of Socialism," *Topoi* 15 (1996); and Meister, "Vigilante Action against Pornography: The Symbolic Destruction of Symbols," *Social Text* 12 (fall 1985).

65. St. Augustine's description of Heaven includes enjoyment of the deserved suffering of sinners without fearing for the state of one's own soul. Saint Augustine, *The City of God against the Pagans*, trans. R. W. Dyson (Cambridge: Cambridge University Press, 1998), p. 1181; see also pp. 1020–21.

66. This dialectical play of motives across a change of scene is the type of symbolic action described in Kenneth Burke, *A Grammar of Motives, and a Rhetoric of Motives*

(Cleveland: World, 1962). For further development, see Hayden V. White, *Metahistory: The Historical Imagination in Nineteenth-Century Europe* (Baltimore, Md.: Johns Hopkins University Press, 1973). The classic development of genre theory is in Northrop Frye, *Anatomy of Criticism; Four Essays* (Princeton: Princeton University Press, 1957), 4th essay.

67. See, for example, Eugene de Kock, *A Long Night's Damage: Working for the Apartheid State* (Saxonwold: Contra, 1998). For an account of the torturers' testimony before the TRC, see, e.g., Krog, *Country of My Skull*, chap. 6; and Meredith, *Coming to Terms*, chaps. chaps. 3–4.

68. Peter Brooks, *Troubling Confessions: Speaking Guilt in Law and Literature* (Chicago: University of Chicago Press, 2000), p. 55.

69. The TRC's final list of the victims of politically inflicted violence was published in volume 8 of its *Report* (2003). For a comprehensive accounting of the victim/beneficiary side of apartheid, see Sampie. Terreblanche, *Labour Patterns and Power Relations in South African History (1652–2000)* (Cape Town: African Institute of Policy Analysis and Economic Integration, 2000). He criticizes the *TRC Report* in "Production of the Past." The *TRC Report* itself addresses the issue of its limited mandate with respect to the history of racialized oppression (vol. 1 chaps. 2, 4–5).

70. "Those who have benefited and are still benefiting from a range of unearned privileges under apartheid have a crucial role to play. Although this was not part of the Commission's mandate, it was recognised as a vital dimension of national reconciliation. This means that a great deal of attention must be given to an altered sense of responsibility; namely the duty or obligation of those who have benefited so much (through racially privileged education, unfair access to land, business opportunities and so on) to contribute to the present and future reconstruction of our society" (*TRC Report*, vol. 1, chap. 5, §111).

71. Jacques Derrida, *Specters of Marx: The State of the Debt, the Work of Mourning, and the New International*, trans. Peggy Kamuf (New York: Routledge, 1994).

72. The psychoanalyst Melanie Klein takes the *Oresteia* as a model of psychic reparation. Klein's account of the taming of the Furies, however, is concerned only with the ways in which it repairs our internal world; it provides no account of how the tragic resolution produces anything more than symbolic reparation in our relations with others. It does not provide a viable alternative to the pursuit of social justice. Melanie Klein, "Some Reflections on the *Oresteia*," in *Envy and Gratitude, and Other Works, 1946–1963* (New York: Free Press, 1984). For a more favorable appraisal of this article, see Alford, *Melanie Klein and Critical Social Theory*, p. 107.

73. Cf. Jacques Derrida, *On Cosmopolitanism and Forgiveness*, ed. Simon Critchley and Richard Kearney (London: Routledge, 2001), pt. 2; Vladimir Jankélévitch, "Should We Pardon Them?" *Critical Inquiry* 22, no. 3 (1996); Paul Ricoeur, *Memory, History, Forgetting* (Chicago: University of Chicago Press, 2004), epilogue ("Difficult Forgiveness"), esp. pp. 483–86.

74. Meredith and Rosenberg, *Coming to Terms*, p. 3.

75. *TRC Report*, vol. 6, chap. 1, §1.

76. Charles Phalane, "Victims Have Waited Too Long, Says Tutu," *Independent On Line* March 21, 2003.

77. See Institute for Justice and Reconciliation, "Statement: Actions Required to Ensure the TRC Success," paper presented at the conference "The TRC: Ten Years On," Iziko South African History Museum, April 20–21, 2006); Charles Villa-Vicencio, "The Complex Legacy of the TRC: Unfinished Business Needs to Be Addressed," *Cape Times*, April 5, 2006. For further materials, see *Truth & Reconciliation in South Africa: 10 Years On* (Cape Town: Institute for Justice and Reconciliation, 2006).

78. See Christelle Terreblanche, "Apartheid Victims and State Clash," *Independent On Line* January 22, 2006. For Ntsebeza's account of the TRC's shortcomings, see Bell and Ntsebeza, *Unfinished Business*, chaps. 11–14.

79. Boraine became head of the International Center for Transitional Justice in New York. For a summary of his view, see Alex Boraine, "Truth and Reconciliation Commission in South Africa: The Price of Peace," in *Retribution and Reparation in the Transition to Democracy*, ed. Jon Elster (Cambridge: Cambridge University Press, 2006).

80. Blumenberg, *The Legitimacy of the Modern Age*, pt. 1. Following World War II Blumenberg himself described this space as "no longer . . . one of hope for the final events but . . . one of fear of judgment and the destruction of the world" (p. 44).

81. Alister E. McGrath, *Iustitia Dei: A History of the Christian Doctrine of Justification* (Cambridge: Cambridge University Press, 1986).

82. Ricoeur calls this the "sin of sins." It is, he goes on to say, "no longer transgression, but a . . . desperate will to shut oneself up in the circle of interdiction and desire" (*The Symbolism of Evil*, pp. 146–47).

83. Blumenberg, *The Legitimacy of the Modern Age*, pp. 134–35.

84. The TRC offered the victims of racialized oppression something more complicated. While it was telling whites to blame *themselves* for their indifference to apartheid, it encouraged black victims to blame the *system* (and the times) for white attitudes.

85. When Coetzee's protagonist, David Lurie, is asked, "What does God want from you, besides being sorry?" he answers, "I am sunk into a state of disgrace from which it will not be easy to lift myself. It is not a punishment I have refused. I do not murmur against it. On the contrary, I am living it out from day to day, trying to accept disgrace as my state of being." J. M. Coetzee, *Disgrace* (New York: Penguin, 2000), p. 172.

86. Ibid.

87. Cassian, quoting Paul (2Cor.7:10), distinguishes between the detestable sadness that leads to indolent despair and that which "works repentance unto lasting salvation."

88. See, e.g., St. Gregory of Nyssa, "Sermon 3" ("Blessed are they that mourn, for they shall be comforted)," in Gregory of Nyssa, *The Lord's Prayer. The Beatitudes*, trans. Hilda C. Graef (Mahwah, N.J.: Paulist, 1954). In his manual on monastic discipline St. John Cassian describes virtuous sorrow as "obedient, courteous, humble, mild, gracious and patient . . . It stretches itself out tirelessly, in its desire for perfection, to every bodily pain and to contrition of spirit." John Cassian, *John Cassian, the Institutes*, trans. Boniface Ramsey, O. P. (New York: Newman, 2000), p. 213.

89. St. Gregory of Nyssa, "Sermon 3," pp. 106–7.

90. Ibid., p. 214.

91. Cassian, *John Cassian: The Institutes*, pp. 209–38; Evagrius, *Evagrius of Pontus: The*

Greek Ascetic Corpus, trans. Robert E. Sinkewicz (New York: Oxford University Press, 2003). See also Siegfried Wenzel, *The Sin of Sloth; Acedia in Medieval Thought and Literature* (Chapel Hill: University of North Carolina Press, 1967), chap. 1. For a contemporary reinterpretation of acedia and a compendium of modern and medieval references, see Kathleen Norris, *Acedia & Me: A Marriage, Monks, and a Writer's Life* (New York: Riverhead, 2008).

92. Notably Walter Benjamin associates the medieval sin of acedia with nineteenth- and twentieth-century "historicism," which he tellingly describes as an attempt to "relive an era"—to bring the past into the present—through a "process of empathy" that denies the possibility of redemption. "Its origin is indolence of the heart, that *acedia* which despairs of appropriating the genuine historical image as it briefly flashes up. . . . The nature of this sadness becomes clearer if we ask: With whom does historicism actually sympathize? The answer is inevitable: with the victor." Benjamin goes on to distinguish this "historicism" from (what he calls) a "historical materialism" that "knows what this means. Whoever has emerged victorious participates to this day in the triumphal procession in which the current rulers step over those who are lying prostrate" ("On the Concept of History," VII, p. 391).

93. The hermetic tradition in Egypt included St. Anthony, and St. Evagrius, and Cassian. See, e.g., Athanasius, *The Life of Antony*, trans. Tim Vivian, Apostolos N. Athanassakis, and Rowan A. Greer (Kalamazoo: Cistercian, 2003). After spending some years among the desert monks in Egypt, Cassian described in detail the cardinal sins to which the penitents were subject and how the Desert Fathers combated them. His works traveled with him to Europe and eventually became the core texts of medieval monasticism. See, e.g., Morton W. Bloomfield, *The Seven Deadly Sins; an Introduction to the History of a Religious Concept, with Special Reference to Medieval English Literature* (East Lansing: Michigan State College Press, 1952), chaps. 2–3; Philip Rousseau, *Ascetics, Authority, and the Church in the Age of Jerome and Cassian* (Oxford: Oxford University Press, 1978), pt. 5.

94. Bloomfield, *Seven Deadly Sins*, pp. 109–10; Norris, *Acedia & Me*, chaps. 1–3, 7–8, 15.

95. See Cassian, John *Cassian, the Institutes*, "Tenth Book."

96. In *acedia*, the monk who renounces pleasure suffers from inappetence, the lack of desire or restlessness—the "noonday demon." Stanley W. Jackson, "Acedia the Sin and Its Relationship to Sorrow and Melancholia," in *Culture and Depression: Studies in the Anthropology and Cross-Cultural Psychiatry of Affect and Disorder*, ed. Arthur Kleinman and Byron Good, Comparative Studies of Health Systems and Medical Care series (Berkeley: University of California Press, 1985), pp. 53–54.

97. Benjamin, "On the Concept of History," VII. For a Benjaminian interpretation of "apocalypse" as the revelation of "hidden truth," see Malcolm Bull, *Seeing Things Hidden: Apocalypse, Vision, and Totality* (London: Verso, 1999), esp. chap. 4.

98. Today the specific characteristics of *acedia* as a diversion from penitential work are buried under the mountain of academic literature on mourning and melancholia—the two forms of sadness on which modernity has staked a claim. Like modern melancholia, monastic *acedia* is an unproductive state of dejection and despair—but, unlike melancholia, *acedia* was not primarily a psychological condition consisting of excessive and pathological forms of self-reproach. It was itself a *sin* for

which one should *be reproached*. Stanley W. Jackson, *Melancholia and Depression: From Hippocratic Times to Modern Times* (New Haven: Yale University Press, 1986), pts. 3–5.

99. Cf. John Milbank, *Being Reconciled: Ontology and Pardon* (London: Routledge, 2003).

100. In the monastic disciplines the vice of acedia was often cured by music (a theme in *Disgrace*) and by keeping busy with manual labor (another theme), which is also understood in the monastic tradition as a form of penitence itself. If today we can scarcely conceive of true penitents whistling while they work, this is because we conflate acedia with melancholia. For an argument that acedia is, instead, the sin of "not caring," see Norris, *Acedia & Me*.

101. The imperative of undergoing sorrow is difficult to express in a culture where saying "sorry" is a polite substitute for being sorry. In contrast, the sorrow of the other calls forth different emotions that still reflect the genealogical connection between sorrow and disgrace. It is because of this linkage that observing another's sorrow can feel like witnessing his shame—which, as we shall see in our discussion of Lincoln (chapter 3), elicits embarrassment followed by compassion. For other accounts of sorrow/apology, see Charles L. Griswold, *Forgiveness: A Philosophical Exploration* (Cambridge: Cambridge University Press, 2007); Nicholas Tavuchis, *Mea Culpa: A Sociology of Apology and Reconciliation* (Stanford: Stanford University Press, 1991); Elazar Barkan, *The Guilt of Nations: Restitution and Negotiating Historical Injustices* (New York: Norton, 2000); Thompson, *Taking Responsibility for the Past*.

102. J. M. Coetzee, *Elizabeth Costello* (New York: Viking, 2003), pp. 64–65.

103. Assuming that refusing to avert one's gaze is the inescapable lesson of the Holocaust, Coetzee's alter ego concludes that we must make ourselves capable of *feelings* for the suffering of animals dying all around us while recognizing that our neighbors "are participants in a crime of stupefying proportions?" (ibid., pp. 79, 115). See also Coetzee, "Lesson 6: The Problem of Evil." The Israeli philosopher Adi Ophir makes a similar point: "People kill in a systematic, industrialized way as a matter of routine, every day—killing animals for food (one should take into consideration the possibility, at the moment seemingly absurd, cynical, horrifying or insane, that one day the three and a half years of Auschwitz will pale in the face of centuries of industrialized slaughter, the endless and superfluous taking of lives by human beings" (*Order of Evils*, p. 530).

Coetzee's point here bears on the general relation between Human Rights Discourse (the lessons of Auschwitz) and the view of ethics that the French philosopher criticizes as "animal humanism (discussed in chapter 3 in this volume,). If the post-Holocaust ethics means, above all, refusing to condone physical pain, then "in relation to [animals], all people are Nazis; for the animals, it is an eternal Treblinka." Isaac Bashevis Singer, "The Letter Writer," in *The Séance and Other Stories*, trans. Aliza Shevrin and Elizabeth Shub (New York: Farrar, 1968), p. 270. In response to the argument that animals are killed for food, Singer's grandson, Stephen R. Dujack, asks: "If the victims of the Holocaust had been eaten, would that have justified the abuse and murder? Did the fact that lampshades, soaps, and other "useful" products were made from their bodies excuse the Holocaust? No. Pain is pain." Dujack, "Holocaust on Your Plate," quoted in Karen Dawn, "Moving the Media," in *In Defense of Animals: The Second Wave*, ed. Peter Singer (Malden, Mass.: Blackwell, 2006), p. 201. Cf. Omer Bartov, *Murder in Our Midst: The Holocaust, Industrial Killing, and Representation* (New York: Oxford University Press, 1996); Charles Patterson, *Eternal Treblinka: Our Treatment of Animals and the Holocaust* (New York: Lantern, 2002); Stephen Dujack, "Animals Suffer a Perpetual 'Holocaust,'" *Los Angeles Times*, April 21, 2003.

104. The link between post-Holocaust ethics and compassion for purely physical suffering has been made by many writers. See, e.g., Scarry, "The Difficulty of Imagining Other Persons."

105. See, e.g., Susan D. Moeller, *Compassion Fatigue: How the Media Sell Disease, Famine, War, and Death* (New York: Routledge, 1999).

106. For a striking discussion of this point (based on the use of *Uncle Tom's Cabin* to cultivate "true feelings" of compassion in rulers preparing for modernity in the Rodgers and Hammerstein musical *The King and I*), see Lauren Berlant, "Poor Eliza," in *The Female Complaint: The Unfinished Business of Sentimentality in American Culture* (Durham: Duke University Press, 2008).

107. For fin de siècle studies in the media's promotion of Human Rights Discourse, see, e.g., Robert I. Rotberg and Thomas George Weiss, eds., *From Massacres to Genocide: The Media, Public Policy, and Humanitarian Crises* (Washington, D.C.: Brookings Institution, 1996).

108. John Cassian, *John Cassian, the Conferences*, trans. Boniface Ramsey, O.P. (New York: Paulist, 1997).

109. Columba Stewart, *Cassian the Monk* (New York: Oxford University Press, 1998), p. 123. Stewart makes clear that, for monks, the coming of tears during prayers of repentance encompass "both keen sorrow and deep joy" because they are also a sign of grace. A recent monastic text on tears compunction stresses their central role in consoling the penitent: "My listlessness is broken because I have used tears, and the Lord's word has promised that those who weep shall be consoled." "Listlessness" here is defined as the modern meaning of "acedia," which the daily practice of tearful confession overcomes. The goal of such prayer is a state of "unspeakable joy" which is "close to passionlessness or *apatheia*." Jeremy Driscoll, *Steps to Spiritual Perfection: Studies on Spiritual Progress in Evagrius Ponticus* (New York: Newman, 2005), pp. 58, 61; see, generally, chap. 3. For an earlier-twentieth-century treatment of this subject, see Irénée Hausherr, *Penthos: The Doctrine of Compunction in the Christian East* (Kalamazoo: Cistercian, 1982).

110. Cassian, *John Cassian, the Conferences*, XVIII–XXIV.

111. Mary C. Mansfield, *The Humiliation of Sinners: Public Penance in Thirteenth-Century France* (Ithaca: Cornell University Press, 1995). For a modern Catholic interpretation of the separate need for communal reconciliation in penitential practice, see James Dallen, *The Reconciling Community: The Rite of Penance* (New York: Pueblo, 1986).

112. Mansfield, *Humiliation of Sinners*, p. 22. The medieval practice of public self-abasement as a conventional form of rehabilitation has more in common with what celebrities now do on talk shows than with recent issues of transitional justice. Such

public displays of penance, which became a cliché by the late Middle Ages, were a *profession* of sin to satisfy a social demand.

113. For this reason, Bloomfield objects to the post-fourteen-century designation of the original list of seven cardinal sins that could be remedied through confession and penitence as "deadly sins" and thus worthy of Hell. See Bloomfield, *Seven Deadly Sins*, pp. 43–44, 157ff.

114. Jacques Le Goff, *The Birth of Purgatory*, trans. Arthur Goldhammer (Chicago: University of Chicago Press, 1984), p. 290.

115. Ibid., p. 213.

116. How (and where) the souls of the dead must suffer corporeally is a central question addressed by the medieval literature on Purgatory and, more generally, on haunting. See, e.g., Stephen Greenblatt, *Hamlet in Purgatory* (Princeton: Princeton University Press, 2001), chap. 2.

117. According to Le Goff, Purgatory is "an intermediary other world in which the trial to be endured by the dead may be abridged by the intercessory prayers, the 'suffrages' of the living" (*Birth of Purgatory*, p. 11). Hence persons who were anticipating Purgatory provided in their wills not only for almsgiving but also for the purchase of indulgences and the endowment of prayers (p. 211). To promote such practices, the Church institutionalized prayer for souls in Purgatory through the creation of new liturgies for the dead, chantries to sing them, and ecclesiastical orders to receive alms. The medieval historian Jean-Claude Schmitt summarizes these developments as follows: "Henceforth all Christians could hope to be saved, but only on condition that after death, they would undergo salutary punishments—the duration and intensity of which depended both on personal merits (good and bad acts and repentance for the latter at the time of death) and on the suffrages (masses, prayers, and almsgiving) undertaken by relatives and friends for the dead's salvation." Jean-Claude Schmitt, *Ghosts in the Middle Ages: The Living and the Dead in Medieval Society*, trans. Teresa Lavender Fagan (Chicago: University of Chicago Press, 1998), p. 4; see also Greenblatt, *Hamlet in Purgatory*, chap. 3.

118. Greenblatt, *Hamlet in Purgatory*, chap. 2. Work itself came to be associated with penance—the corporeal suffering inflicted on those in Purgatory as well as the pain of their own prescribed tasks. Conversely, however, penance also required work(s). Monasticism (and other ascetic disciplines) reflected a choice to undergo Purgatory in this life so as to reduce one's burdens in the next. As Greenblatt puts it, "The faithful could elect penance or ardently hope for suffering in this life as a way to lessen the reckoning that would ultimately and inevitably have to be paid. . . . Heavy penance, and for that matter ordinary suffering, in this life could in effect do the beneficial work of purgatorial fire at a much reduced level of pain" (p. 70).

The Protestant Reformation was grounded in a rejection of Purgatory and the corrupt ecclesiastical practices to which it gave rise. Both Luther and Calvin argued that salvation is through faith alone, that faith itself is a gift from God not accorded to everyone, and that working without cease is a way to cope with one's anxiety about whether one is already saved. Cf. Max Weber, who famously discusses the forms of asceticism grounded in this nonpurgatorial notion of work, in *The Protestant Ethic and the Spirit of Capitalism*, trans. Talcott Parsons (New York: Scribner's, 1958).

119. For a secular version of this idea, see Stanley Cohen, *States of Denial: Knowing About Atrocities and Suffering* (Malden, Mass.: Blackwell, 2001).

120. See, e.g., Tertullian, "On Penance," in *Treatises on Penance: On Penitence and on Purity*, trans. William P. Le Saint (Westminster, Md.: Newman, 1959). For a historian's view, see Mansfield, *Humiliation of Sinners*, chaps. 1–5, 9.

121. Jackson, "Acedia the Sin," esp. p. 50.

122. See ibid., pp. 43–62. The sale of work (in the above sense) to support the institutions of the Church was also a medieval invention, giving rise to the Lutheran question of whether work could ever be sufficient to save one's own soul or that of others.

123. Historically the monasticism of the Desert Fathers anticipated the medieval invention of Purgatory; theologically it was a form of early admission to Purgatory, allowing the repentant sinner to graduate more rapidly to Paradise. The postmodern substitution of secular compassion for religious rites of penance has not left behind its purgatorial logic—but, rather, has demonasticized it.

124. Rian Malan ends *My Traitor's Heart* on a similar note, describing the works of Neil and Creina Alcock as an alternative to "phony forgiveness" (bk. 3, "A Root in Arid Ground").

125. Dante Alighieri, *The Divine Comedy*, trans. Mark Musa (New York: Penguin, 1984): *Purgatory*, Canto XXI, l. 66.

126. As Le Goff remarks, "The souls in Purgatory are destined to be saved in Heaven . . . they are suffering, but God's justice which is perfect and mingled here with mercy and hope alleviates their suffering and decreases it by degrees as they rise toward Heaven" (*Birth of Purgatory*, p. 340).

127. Thus the portals to Hell are inscribed, "Abandon every hope, all you who enter." Dante, *Divine Comedy: Inferno*, Canto III, l. 9. The portals of Purgatory are narrower, but, for those who enter, the guilt-ridden relationship to the past is not yet one of closure. Dante, *Divine Comedy: Purgatory*, Canto IX, ll. 75–76; see Le Goff, *Birth of Purgatory*, pp. 346–47.

128. Blumenberg, *The Legitimacy of the Modern Age*, p. 135.

129. The earthly *victims* of sin do not have much moral standing in Dante's account. As intercessors, they stand below saints and family members in the hierarchy of those whose suffrage counts toward a sinner's redemption. Because souls in Purgatory are already dead and the victims of their sins, if truly innocent, would have gone straight to Heaven, there is no expectation that works of penance will eliminate the negative aftereffect of the past sin on those among the living who still suffer from it.

130. Greenblatt, *Hamlet in Purgatory*, p. 149. It is a measure of our modernity that More's view seems today more like a quaint carryover of medieval superstitions about the afterlife than a shocking expression of disregard for those still alive.

131. Bentham considered the concept of rights *against* the state as a vestige of feudal law and did not think that recasting such rights as universal could be the final step in undermining the legitimacy of feudalism itself. Instead, he sought to overcome claims based on ancestral privilege or historical injury by appealing to forward-looking interests, which he called "utility." Jeremy Bentham, "Anarchical Fallacies: Being an Examination of the Declarations of Rights Issued during the French Revo-

lution," in *The Works of Jeremy Bentham*, ed. William Tait and John Bowring (Edinburgh: Simpkin, Marshall, 1843; reprint, Elibron Classics Replica Edition, 2005); Jeremy Waldron, ed., "*Nonsense upon Stilts*": *Bentham, Burke, and Marx on the Rights of Man* (London: Methuen, 1987).

132. John Rawls based his theory of justice on a hypothetical "original position" in which individuals address one another as though they were not yet born. Having only a future, and not yet a past, they would be in a position to discuss what interests should attach to each historical identity without knowing which one will be their own. If the interest differentials between identity groups fall within the (relatively narrow) limits that would be accepted in the original position, Rawls argues, then we can no longer treat the better-off as beneficiaries of *injustice* (in the sense that their gains were *caused* by unjustified losses inflicted on the worst-off). Historical redress would thus be off the table (*Theory of Justice*, chap. 3).

133. Having no future interest in the outcome of our hypothetical dialogue about justice would be entirely concerned with establishing a final truth about the past. But would that truth lock us into an eternal struggle with our enemies because we lack forward-looking reasons to make peace? Or, rather, would it lead us to perpetual reconciliation because we have no forward-looking reasons to make war? Cf. John Evan Seery, *Political Theory for Mortals: Shades of Justice, Images of Death* (Ithaca: Cornell University Press, 1996), chap. 5.

134. For assessments of the ongoing effects of apartheid, see Michael MacDonald, *Why Race Matters in South Africa* (Cambridge, Mass.: Harvard University Press, 2006); R. W. Johnson, "False Start in South Africa," *New Left Review* 58 (2009); Patrick Bond, "Reply to Johnson," *New Left Review* 58 (2009).

135. June Jordan, "Poem for South African Women," in *Passion: New Poems, 1977–1980* (Boston: Beacon, 1980). President Obama used this line throughout the 2008 campaign.

136. Schmitt, *Political Theology II*, pp. 120–21.

137. R. W. Johnson, *South Africa's Brave New World: The Beloved Country since the End of Apartheid* (London: Allen Lane, 2009).

3. Living On

1. Some of this recent scholarship suggests that the total abolition of slavery under the Thirteenth Amendment might have meant something more than manumission—the form of "freedom" possible under the law of slavery itself. For a development of the idea that "manumission is not abolition," see Guyora Binder, "Did the Slaves Author the Thirteenth Amendment? An Essay in Redemptive History," *Yale Journal of Law and Humanities* 5 (1993); and Binder, "The Slavery of Emancipation," *Cardozo Law Review* 17 (1996).

2. Through them, Savage tells us, "The conquering nation sought in the means of law to construct some tangible proofs that the war had achieved a moral reformation justifying its cataclysmic violence." Kirk Savage, "The Politics of Memory: Black Emancipation and the Civil War Monument," in *Commemorations: The Politics of National Identity*, ed. John Gillis (Princeton.: Princeton University Press, 1994),

p. 127. See also Kirk Savage, *Standing Soldiers, Kneeling Slaves: Race, War, and Monument in Nineteenth-Century America* (Princeton: Princeton University Press, 1997). For further reflections on this theme, see Sanford Levinson, "They Whisper: Reflections on Flags, Monuments, and State Holidays, and the Construction of Social Meaning in a Multicultural Society," *Chicago-Kent Law Review* (1995); and, more generally, Levinson, *Written in Stone: Public Monuments in Changing Societies*, Public Planet Books series (Durham: Duke University Press, 1998).

3. See Owen Fiss, "Human Rights as a Social Ideal," in *Human Rights in Political Transitions: Gettysburg to Bosnia*, ed. Carla Hesse and Robert Post (New York: Zone, 1999).

4. Walter Benjamin, "Paralipomena to 'On the Concept of History,'" in *Selected Writings (1929–1940)*, ed. Howard Eiland and Michael William Jennings, trans. Edmund Jephcott et al. (Cambridge: Belknap Press of Harvard University Press, 2003), p. 407; Benjamin, "On the Concept of History," pp. 390–91. Benjamin goes on to say that "a critique of the concept of . . . progression must underlie any criticism of the concept of progress itself" and that revolution "cannot do without a notion of the present that is *not* a transition" (pp. 395, 396; my emphasis).

5. Koselleck, "The Modern Concept of Revolution."pp. 54–56.

6. See Hannah Arendt, *On Revolution* (New York: Viking, 1963), chap. 5. Arendt (quoting Clinton Rossiter) contrasts the ancient conception of a cyclical return of periods with "an 'absolutely new beginning,'" analogous to God's self-legitimating act of creation *ex nihilo* (p. 212). For a discussion of the American overthrow of British rule from a legal perspective, see Duncan Kennedy, "The Structure of Blackstone's *Commentaries*," *Buffalo Law Review* 28 (1978); and Robert Meister, "The Logic and Legacy of *Dred Scott*: Marshall, Taney, and the Sublimation of Republican Thought," *Studies in American Political Development* 3 (1989).

7. James M. McPherson, *Abraham Lincoln and the Second American Revolution* (New York: Oxford University Press, 1990).

8. Whether its sign is + or – depends on whether the revolution has been postponed or missed.

9. Eric Foner, *Reconstruction: America's Unfinished Revolution, 1863–1877* (New York: Harper and Row, 1988).

10. "Reconstruction was . . . the basic issue of the Civil War . . . In the fullest sense, secession was the South's effort to avoid . . . reconstruction." William Best Hesseltine, *Lincoln's Plan of Reconstruction* (Chicago: Quadrangle, 1967), p. 12.

11. For a favorable depiction of the KKK as an anti-Reconstruction terrorist organization, see D. W. Griffith, *The Birth of a Nation*" (silent film, 1915).

12. "The name ["Redeemers"] implied a divine sanction for the retaking of the authority the whites had lost in the Civil War and a heavenly quality to the reestablishment of white supremacy in the post-Reconstruction South. "Reconstruction," the North's word, was sturdy, purposeful, and optimistic. "Redemption," the South's, was empyrean." Nicholas Lemann, *Redemption: The Last Battle of the Civil War* (New York: Farrar, Straus and Giroux, 2006), p. 185. This book provides an account of the Redeemers' success in undermining and reversing Reconstruction. The dominant view of U.S. Civil War history between the end of Reconstruction in 1876 and the beginning of the Second Reconstruction in 1954 was, roughly speaking, that of the

Redeemers. Its description of the Southern past as more good than evil appears in "Gone with the Wind," a depression-era romance that defended Southern values from any lingering national contempt for the ethic of the slaveholder.

13. Between 1976 and 1996 the U.S. used Redeemer-like movements to "roll back" communist revolutions that had come to power in Nicaragua, Angola, Mozambique, and Afghanistan following the Vietnam War. The Contras, RENAMO, UNITA, the Taliban, and Al Qaeda resisted communist reconstruction of social life by making their societies "ungovernable." The prototype of these anticommunist insurgencies were the *Gladio* organizations that the postwar OSS (and later CIA) had organized as "stay-behind" armies that were prepared to function as "a resistance" in the event of a communist "takeover" (electoral or military) of Western Europe. These organizations, uncovered by the Church Committee in the 1970s, were never activated, although the Italian *Gladio* (incorporating elements of both the Mafia and the Catholic Church) played an important role in preventing the Italian Communists from gaining power. It was, however, the *Gladio* model that was successfully implemented after 1976, when communist governments took over in Asia, Africa, Central America, and Afghanistan. For discussion of this phase of the cold war, see Chalmers A. Johnson, *Blowback: The Costs and Consequences of American Empire* (New York: Metropolitan, 2000); Mahmood Mamdani, *Good Muslim, Bad Muslim: America, the Cold War, and the Roots of Terror* (New York: Pantheon, 2004).

14. Ezekiel's characterization of birth as moral cleansing also implicitly rejects the predominantly Hindu notion of reincarnation as a form of inter-temporal justice in which one body is punished or rewarded for the sins of the past body thought to incarnate the same soul but without the same memories.

15. Hermann Cohen, *Religion of Reason out of the Sources of Judaism*, trans. Simon Kaplan (Atlanta: Scholars, 1995), chap. 11; Franz Rosenzweig, *The Star of Redemption*, trans. Barbara E. Galli (Madison: University of Wisconsin Press, 2005), bk. 2, chap. 3.

16. The "Lincoln myth" and the debate over his true motives are well discussed in J. David Greenstone, *The Lincoln Persuasion: Remaking American Liberalism* (Princeton: Princeton University Press, 1993), chap. 1.

17. During the war a considerable amount of reconstruction was carried out in the Union-occupied portions of the Confederacy (as well as in some of the border states that never seceded). The conditions imposed upon reconquered areas raised issues of constitutional significance for both sides. Sometimes these conditions were more, and sometimes less, stringent than Lincoln might have imposed once total victory was assured. For the evolution of Lincoln's war aims, see Hesseltine, *Lincoln's Plan of Reconstruction*, pp. 35–36; and McPherson, *Abraham Lincoln and the Second American Revolution*, pp. viii–ix, and chap. 4. See also Herman Belz, *Reconstructing the Union; Theory and Policy during the Civil War* (Ithaca: Cornell University Press, 1969); Eben Greenough Scott, *Reconstruction during the Civil War in the United States of America* (Boston: Houghton, Mifflin, 1895).

18. See Abraham Lincoln, "Address Delivered at the Dedication of the Cemetery at Gettysburg, November 19, 1863," in *Abraham Lincoln, His Speeches and Writings*, ed. Roy P. Basler (New York: Da Capo, 1990).

19. Abraham Lincoln, "Peoria Speech," October 16, 1854, quoted in Mark E. Neely, *The*

Last Best Hope of Earth: Abraham Lincoln and the Promise of America (Cambridge: Harvard University Press, 1993), pp. 37–38.

20. This event had led many prominent refugees to immigrate to the United States. Lincoln was highly aware that the influx of immigrants had precipitated the crisis of the party system of the 1850s, although, as Tyler Anbinder points out, the bulk of the immigration from Germany in the 1850s was probably caused by potato blight rather than political defeat. See Tyler Anbinder, *Nativism and Slavery: The Northern Know Nothings and the Politics of the 1850s* (New York: Oxford University Press, 1992).

21. On Lincoln's view of Southern secession as being counterrevolutionary from a global perspective, see James M. McPherson, *Abraham Lincoln and the Second American Revolution*, pp. 28–29. Although I do not closely follow their interpretations of Lincoln, I am also indebted to Greenstone, *The Lincoln Persuasion*; and Garry Wills, *Lincoln at Gettysburg: The Words That Remade America* (New York: Simon and Schuster, 1992).

22. He embraced for a time the plan of the American Colonization Society to resettle freed slaves in Africa. Fortunately for Lincoln's future reputation, only one of his speeches on this subject survives, although until his death he apparently viewed the colonization of emancipated slaves as a legitimate postwar outcome. See Hesseltine, *Lincoln's Plan of Reconstruction*, pp. 92–94; for less conclusive, but more disturbing, evidence, see Belz, *Reconstructing the Union*, p. 282. Neely also comments on the pre-presidential Lincoln's "inability to imagine a biracial future for America if the black race were free" (*The Last Best Hope*, pp. 40–41).

23. Lincoln was well aware that Pauline Christianity uses slavery as a metaphor for sin itself. Orlando Patterson points out that Paul's mission to the Gentiles was largely carried out among the community of freed slaves who owed the expansion of their personal liberty to the growing sovereignal liberty of the Emperor, Caesar Augustus, and his successors. Ordinary slaves who were redeemed or ransomed "for a price" would have been indentured to their redeemer until the lien could be repaid. (This was the institution of the *postliminium*). They would be expected to glorify the master who freed them and to become slaves to no other man. See Orlando Patterson, *Freedom* (New York: Basic Books, 1991). Perhaps this is what Paul has in mind when he says, "Whoever was called in the Lord as a slave is a freed person belonging to the Lord, just as whoever was free when called is a slave of Christ" (I *Corinthians* 7:22).

24. See Phillip Shaw Paludan, *A Covenant with Death: The Constitution, Law, and Equality in the Civil War Era* (Urbana: University of Illinois Press, 1975), pp. 79–84.

25. For a useful comparison between Lincoln and such figures as Bismarck and Cavour, see Carl N. Degler, "One among Many: The Civil War in Comparative Perspective," in *Lincoln the War President* ed. Gabor S. Boritt (New York: Oxford University Press, 1992). For historical treatments of Bismarck and Cavour, see Otto Pflanze, *Bismarck and the Development of Germany: the Period of Unification, 1815–1871*, vol. 2 (Princeton: Princeton University Press, 1963); Denis Mack Smith, *Cavour* (New York: Knopf, 1985); Massimo Salvadori, *Cavour and the Unification of Italy* (Princeton: Van Nostrand, 1961).

26. As England's principal suppliers of cotton, the Confederate states hoped for military support from the foreign powers that depended on it. Their strategy was in some ways similar to that of Kuwait in gaining foreign support against Sadaam Hussein's effort to reunify Iraq by force. Lincoln's decision to free the slaves, however, effectively eliminated whatever sentiment there was in England for interfering with his efforts to reunify the United States by force. For a brief account of the role of foreign recognition in the Confederate war plan, see, e.g., Stephen John Stedman, "The End of the American Civil War," in *Stopping the Killing: How Civil Wars End*, ed. Roy E. Licklider (New York: New York University Press, 1993).

27. For stimulating reflections on this theme, see Rose, *States of Fantasy*. According to the *Diagnostic and Statistical Manual of Mental Disorders*, vol. 3, the inability to acknowledge traumatic suffering typically results in depression, psychic numbing, anxiety, isolation, and hypervigilance—a syndrome now known as "traumatic stress disorder." See, e.g., John P. Wilson and Beverley Raphael, *International Handbook of Traumatic Stress Syndromes* (New York: Plenum, 1993); Tom Williams, "Diagnosis and Treatment of Survivor Guilt: The Bad Penny Syndrome," in *Human Adaptation to Extreme Stress: From the Holocaust to Vietnam*, ed. John P. Wilson, Zev Harel, and Boaz Kahana (New York: Plenum, 1988).

28. Abraham Lincoln, "Second Inaugural Address, March 4, 1865," in Basler, *Abraham Lincoln, His Speeches and Writings*.

29. Lincoln's Second Inaugural Address is consistent with the abolitionist view, represented by Julia Ward Howe's "Battle Hymn of the Republic," that the Civil War as an inevitable act of divine judgment that redeemed the American nation from its sin of slavery and allowed it to resume its millennial mission of saving the world. Ernest Lee Tuveson, *Redeemer Nation; the Idea of America's Millennial Role* (Chicago: University of Chicago Press, 1968), chap. 5, esp. pp. 197–207. A contrary view is that "Lincoln's distinctive mark . . . was his refusal to indulge in triumphalism, righteousness, or vilification of the foe. . . . Nothing could be farther from the crusading righteousness of Julia Ward Howe in her 'Battle Hymn of the Republic'" (Wills, *Lincoln at Gettysburg*, pp. 183–84). For further discussion of Lincoln's distinctive use of biblical imagery, see Garry Wills, *Under God: Religion and American Politics* (New York: Simon and Schuster, 1990), pp. 207–21.

30. For a discussion of the vicarious sacrifice of Christ in pre–Civil War American theology, see Ann Douglas, *The Feminization of American Culture* (New York: Knopf, 1977), chap. 4.

31. This was, in fact, the view that many Southerners took of their impending defeat. See, e.g., Richard E. Beringer, et al., *Why the South Lost the Civil War* (Athens: University of Georgia Press, 1986), chap. 15, esp. p. 393.

32. Abraham Lincoln, Second Inaugural Address.

33. For differing perspectives, see Kenneth M. Stampp, "The Southern Road to Appomattox," in Stampp, *The Imperiled Union: Essays on the Background of the Civil War* (New York: Oxford University Press, 1980); Beringer et al., *Why the South Lost the Civil War*; and Stedman, "The End of the American Civil War."

34. The range of conceivable outcomes are a fight to the death, a negotiated partition backed by the power to resume fighting, and de facto secession through continuing

military stalemate between rebel and government forces. See Roy E. Licklider, "Ending Civil Wars: The Implementation of Peace Agreements," *Journal of Democracy* 14, no. 3 (2003); and Licklider, "The Consequences of Negotiated Settlements in Civil Wars, 1945–1993," *American Political Science Review* 89, no. 3 (1995).

35. This argument has been used in wars of empire, as well as in civil wars, and by leaders as diverse as Pericles and Hitler. See Wills, *Lincoln at Gettysburg*, pp. 182–83.

36. Quoted in Jonathan Truman Dorris, *Pardon and Amnesty under Lincoln and Johnson: The Restoration of the Confederates to Their Rights and Privileges, 1861–1898* (Chapel Hill: University of North Carolina Press, 1953), p. 37.

37. The discussion in this section draws on Licklider, "The Consequences of Negotiated Settlements in Civil Wars"; and Fred Charles Iklé, *Every War Must End* (New York: Columbia University Press, 1971). See also Paul Kecskemeti, *Strategic Surrender: The Politics of Victory and Defeat* (Stanford: Stanford University Press, 1959).

38. On post–Civil War amnesties, see Dorris, *Pardon and Amnesty*; and Charles Fairman and the Oliver Wendell Holmes Devise, *Reconstruction and Reunion, 1864–88*, History of the Supreme Court of the United States series, vols. 6–7 (New York: Macmillan, 1971), chaps. 3, 15.

39. The issue of lustration was heavily debated during the democratic transitions of the early 1990s See Rosenberg, *The Haunted Land*. See also George Weigel, "Their Lustration—and Ours," *Commentary* 94, no. 4 (1992); Anthony D'Amato, "Peace vs. Accountability in Bosnia," *American Journal of International Law* 88 (1994). Jeri Laber, "Witch Hunt in Prague," *New York Review of Books* 39, no. 8 (1992); John Moore Jr., "Problems with Forgiveness: Granting Amnesty under the Arias Plan in Nicaragua and El Salvador," *Stanford Law Review* 43, no. 3 (1991). Diane F. Orentlicher, "Settling Accounts: The Duty to Prosecute Human Rights Violations of a Prior Regime," *Yale Law Journal* 100, no. 8 (1991): esp. pt. 3 (on "mitigating the burden" in "transitional societies").

40. The specific features of Lincoln's policy changed over time with military and political exigencies, and at war's end Lincoln may even have condoned General Sherman's policy of working through existing rebel governments, a policy embodied in the Sherman-Johnston peace convention signed a mere three days after Lincoln's death. See, generally, Belz, *Reconstructing the Union*, chaps. 6, 10 (the evolution of Lincoln's view is summarized on pp. 291–304; Lincoln's probable attitude toward the Sherman-Johnston peace convention is discussed on pp. 278–79).

41. For analysis of Lincoln's legal position on secession, see Akhil Reed Amar, "Abraham Lincoln and the American Union," 2001 *University of Illinois Law Review* 1109.

42. Lincoln's wartime policy was that a number of citizens equal to 10 percent of the 1860 electorate must be granted amnesty in order for self-government to be restored. See Belz, *Reconstructing the Union*, pp. 154–66; and Hesseltine, *Lincoln's Plan of Reconstruction*, pp. 70–71.

43. Dorris, *Pardon and Amnesty under Lincoln and Johnson*, pp. 34–35.

44. For an example, see Robert H. Kellogg, *Life and Death in Rebel Prisons: Giving a Complete History of the Inhuman and Barbarous Treatment of Our Brave Soldiers by Rebel Authorities, Principally at Andersonville, Ga., and Florence, S. C.* (Hartford: Stebbins, 1866).

45. His trial and eventual execution did not accomplish the intended purpose of establishing a definitive moral truth about Andersonville. Instead, the singularity of the prosecution, and the irregularities that occurred in the presentation of evidence, convinced some Southerners that Wirz had become a martyr of the Confederacy. The Wirz trial and its context are discussed in Ovid L. Futch, *History of Andersonville Prison* (Gainesville: University of Florida Press, 1968), chap. 8. For an account of the evidence by one of the presiding officers at the trial, and a response to the charge, inscribed on a monument erected to Wirz, that he was "judicially murdered," see N. P. Chipman, *The Tragedy of Andersonville; Trial of Captain Henry Wirz, the Prison Keeper* (Sacramento: Author, 1911).

46. The charge against Davis was motivated partly by a desire to prove that secession, and waging war to defend it, were themselves treasonous acts under the Constitution and partly by the allegation (never substantiated) that Davis was somehow complicit in Lincoln's murder. Chase, however, had to preside over the impeachment trial of President Johnson, and for this and other reasons the Davis trial was delayed.

47. It did not apply to the suspicion of conspiring to commit murder under which Davis was first arrested. That apparently false accusation, on which he was never indicted, reinforced Davis's lifelong refusal to seek or accept the individual clemencies that had earlier been accorded to other Confederate leaders. See Dorris, *Pardon and Amnesty under Lincoln and Johnson*, pp. 302–5.

48. For discussion of the entire matter, see Roy Franklin Nichols, "United States vs. Jefferson Davis, 1865–1869," *American Historical Review* (January 1926); Dorris, *Pardon and Amnesty under Lincoln and Johnson*, chap. 8; and J. G.. Randall, *Constitutional Problems under Lincoln*, rev. ed. (Urbana: University of Illinois Press, 1951), chap. 5; see also chap. 4 for a discussion of the prosecutions for treason during the Civil War).

49. On the issue of postwar treason indictments, see Randall, *Constitutional Problems under Lincoln*, pp. 96–102.

50. Between 1868 and 1898 Congress restored the right to hold office of almost all former Confederate officials by two-thirds vote, using a procedure specifically provided for this purpose in the Fourteenth Amendment itself. The two notable exceptions were Jefferson Davis and Robert E. Lee, whose disloyalty had special symbolic weight for Northern politicians. Lee's right to hold office had already been posthumously restored by President Ford to reaffirm the Republicans' "Southern Strategy" in the aftermath of Watergate (p. 129). But arguments on behalf of Lee and Davis for a full restoration of the rights of citizenship took on new life during the debate over granting amnesty to Americans accused of draft evasion or military desertion following the Vietnam War. Politicians opposed to amnesty, many from the South, argued that it was inappropriate for individuals who had been disloyal to their country in wartime, especially if the amnesty were not accompanied by an obligation of national service.

It remained for Jimmy Carter—a century after the first Reconstruction ended—to articulate the now settled meaning of the Lincolnian vision of national recovery. In restoring full citizenship to Jefferson Davis, he called upon Americans "to clear away the guilts and enmities and recriminations of the past, to finally set at rest the divisions that threatened to destroy our Nation and to discredit the great principles on which it was founded." This message applied equally to the amnesty President Carter granted to those who disagreed with their government about Vietnam: "I have a historical perspective about this question. I come from the South. I know at the end of the War Between the States there was a sense of forgiveness for those who had not been loyal to our country in the past." See Francis MacDonnell, "Reconstruction in the Wake of Vietnam: The Pardoning of Robert E. Lee and Jefferson Davis," *Civil War History* 40, no. 2 (1994): 129–32.

51. Don Edward Fehrenbacher, *The Slaveholding Republic: An Account of the United States Government's Relations to Slavery*, ed. Ward McAfee (New York: Oxford University Press, 2001).

52. Akhil Reed Amar, "The Bill of Rights and the Fourteenth Amendment," *Yale Law Journal* 101, no. 6 (1992); and Amar, *The Bill of Rights: Creation and Reconstruction* (New Haven, Conn.: Yale University Press, 1998). See, more generally, Bruce A. Ackerman, *We the People*, vol. 2 (Cambridge: Belknap Press of Harvard University Press, 1991); Akhil Reed Amar, *America's Constitution: A Biography* (New York: Random House, 2005).

53. Binder, "Did the Slaves Author the Thirteenth Amendment?"

54. Woodrow Wilson, *A History of the American People*, documentary ed. (New York: Harper, 1918), vols. 4–5.

55. See John Hart Ely, *Democracy and Distrust: A Theory of Judicial Review* (Cambridge: Harvard University Press, 1980).

56. James McPherson has recently suggested that Americans tend to underestimate the magnitude of the social revolution that was actually accomplished in the years immediately following the Civil War because this progress was halted and partially reversed by the "counterrevolution" of 1877. See McPherson, *Abraham Lincoln and the Second American Revolution*, chaps. 1, 7.

57. For more on the persistence of the legal logic of slavery, see Binder, "The Slavery of Emancipation"; Meister, "The Logic and Legacy of *Dred Scott*"; Robert Meister, "Sojourners and Survivors: Two Logics of Non-Discrimination," *University of Chicago Law School Roundtable* 3, no. 1 (1996).

    The idea that descendants of slaves are *not slaves* as a matter of constitutional definition has made it difficult for African Americans to claim protection under the Thirteenth Amendment against, for example, hate speech and what some call the "prison-industrial complex." There is, however, a body of U.S. constitutional law that applies the Thirteenth outside the area of race, for example, to wife abuse, child abuse, and so on. For discussion of these developments, see Akhil Reed Amar, "The Case of the Missing Amendments: R.A.V. v. City of St. Paul," *Harvard Law Review* 106, no. 1 (1992); Akhil Reed Amar and Daniel Widawsky, "Child Abuse as Slavery: A Thirteenth Amendment Response to Deshaney," *Harvard Law Review* 105 (1992); Akhil Reed Amar, "Remember the Thirteenth," *Constitutional Law Commentary* (1993).

58. Nationwide emancipation might not have happened if the North had settled for anything less than total victory. George McClellan, who had been fired as Lincoln's

top general, ran against Lincoln in 1864 on the platform of a compromise on slavery to bring about reunion. Until late in that year there was no large-scale Northern support for Lincoln's strategy of total victory and little thought of abolishing slavery in the three border states that remained in the Union. See, e.g., James M. McPherson, *Battle Cry of Freedom: The Civil War Era* (New York: Oxford University Press, 1988), chaps. 25–26.

Union military success in late 1864 led the Confederacy to consider emancipating plantation workers to replenish its faltering armies. In early 1865 Jefferson Davis presented to the Confederate Congress an emancipation proclamation that would have freed slaves who were willing to take up arms. Bruce Levine, *Confederate Emancipation: Southern Plans to Free and Arm Slaves During the Civil War* (New York: Oxford University Press, 2007).

59. For philosophers such as Aristotle and Hegel the concept of slavery appears as a "coward's bargain," whereby the defeated enemy at sword's point agrees to become the slave so that his vanquisher will spare his life. Such a bargain would not explain the institution of hereditary enslavement.

60. For an account of this tradition, see Sacvan Bercovitch, *The American Jeremiad* (Madison: University of Wisconsin Press, 1978). For a continuation of the "jeremiad" tradition, see, generally, Derrick A. Bell, *And We Are Not Saved: The Elusive Quest for Racial Justice* (New York: Basic Books, 1987). An example of Reconstruction-based interpretation of the Fourteenth and First Amendments is Amar, "The Bill of Rights and the Fourteenth Amendment."

61. Scholars who stress his links to the Radical Republicans have attributed such a view to Lincoln. See, e.g., Hans Louis Trefousse, *The Radical Republicans: Lincoln's Vanguard for Racial Justice* (New York: Knopf, 1969).

62. Rancière, "Who Is the Subject of the Rights of Man?"

63. A constitutional right to nondiscrimination means that a majority may not exclude protected minorities from whatever benefits it chooses to create, but it does not in itself determine what those benefits must be.

64. See Meister, "The Logic and Legacy of *Dred Scott*."

65. John Harrison, "Reconstructing the Privileges and Immunities Clause," *Yale Law Journal* 101 (1992): secs. II and III.

66. The constitutional text itself does not expressly deny the states power to naturalize foreigners in the event that Congress fails to legislate a "uniform rule." In 1817, however, the Marshall Court determined that the federal power of naturalization was preemptive, thereby allowing Congress to expand the category of constitutionally protected sojourners to include naturalized federal citizens. *Chirac v. Chirac*, 2 Wheat. 259, at 269 (1817).

67. Joseph Story, *Commentaries on the Conflict of Laws, Foreign and Domestic, in Regard to Contracts, Rights, and Remedies, and Especially in Regard to Marriages, Divorces, Wills, Successions, and Judgments* (Clark, N.J.: Lawbook Exchange, 2007). As a matter of federal law, these questions were highly salient within federally administered territories in which the inhabitants consisted of U.S. citizens living out of state, immigrants from sovereign states, descendants of indigenous peoples that may or may not have claims based on treaty, and descendants of slaves who may be

subject both to federal law governing extension of slavery into that territory and the state law on which their individual slave status was based. The latter issue would become central in the Dred Scott Decision. See Meister, "The Logic and Legacy of *Dred Scott*."

68. Nor were tribally identified Americans accorded protection under international law. The tribal "remnants" that came to inhabit many states were, rather, treated as "denizens" (a status in traditional English law falling between citizenship and alienage) until 1924, when all native-born Americans who descended from indigenous tribes were "naturalized" by an act of Congress. Almost a third of those covered by this Act had not previously been considered to be full citizens, even after a half-century of genocide had brought their population to an all-time low. See James H. Kettner, *The Development of American Citizenship* (Chapel Hill: University of North Carolina Press, 1978), pp. 287–300. Cf. Perry Dane, "The Maps of Sovereignty: A Meditation," *Cardozo Law Review* 12 (1991); and Judith Resnik, "Dependent Sovereigns: Indian Tribes, States, and the Federal Courts," *University of Chicago Law Review* 56 (1989). For a comprehensive history of federal-tribal relations, see Francis Paul Prucha, *The Great Father: The United States Government and the American Indians*, 2 vols. (Lincoln: University of Nebraska Press, 1984).

69. His treatise was thus an indirect answer to Lincoln's "house divided" speech and also to Taney's unfounded assumption in *Dred Scott* that, to exist anywhere in the United States, slavery must be enforced everywhere in the United States. Hurd argued, instead, that Negroes had *not* originally entered American territory as chattel under local law but, rather, as stateless persons who lacked standing in imperial courts to assert extraterritorial claims against those of slave-ship masters. It followed that American colonists, who had no legal basis for freshly enslaving anyone, nevertheless had the discretion under existing doctrines of private international law to presume that Africans were *already* slaves at the time of their original purchase by Europeans. This argument eliminated the need for Hurd to ground North American slavery on either purchase or conquest—the trick could be turned by the simple extension of comity in private international law to the presumed notice that Portuguese or Dutch law took of possibly repugnant local customs in Africa.

Hurd's precise claim is that under imperial law it was a matter of local discretion whether to presume the validity of the original sale of Africans to the Portuguese and Dutch slavers, a point that was developed in the administration of formerly Portuguese and Dutch colonies subsequently acquired by Britain. Under the prevailing doctrine of comity in private international law, there was thus no recognized body of positive law under which enslaved Africans arriving in North America could obtain federal judicial review of their claim to have been stolen property that may not be legally resold. John Codman Hurd, *The Law of Freedom and Bondage in the United States*, 2 vols. (Boston: Little, Brown, 1858, 1862). (See §§165–66,170, 243 [especially p. 321 n. 1]), and 286ff.). For a general discussion, see Meister, "The Logic and Legacy of *Dred Scott*, pp. 234–39.

70. Meister, "The Logic and Legacy of *Dred Scott*."

71. *The Slaughter-House Cases*, 83 U.S. 36, at 73 (1873) (Miller, J.). The Fourteenth Amendment also gave constitutional legitimacy to those portions of the Civil Rights

Act of 1866 (potentially challengeable under *Dred Scott*) that struck down the provisions of the Black Codes (enacted in 1865 by almost all the ex-Confederate states), specifically denying Negroes the freedom of contract, property rights, judicial protection, and ordinary rights of mobility afforded under state law to free laborers who were white. (The exception was Texas, which delayed enactment. In several states the effect of the Black Codes would have been to apply harsh vagrancy laws to those Negroes whose conditions of labor no longer resembled those of slavery.) Fairman, *Reconstruction and Reunion,* pp. 110–17; Harrison, "Reconstructing the Privileges and Immunities Clause," pp. 1388–89.

72. The Fourteenth Amendment thus reversed the holding of *Dred Scott* while preserving its structure. To grasp this point fully we must recognize that *Dred Scott* did not foreshadow the arguments based on states' rights that southerners made to defend segregation a century later. Taney's reasoning, instead, was understood (and even welcomed by writers such as Hurd) as an expansion of the *federal* power to equalize among states, a power that might have eventually been used to subject all state laws conferring rights on Negroes to a strict standard of federal judicial review of their adverse impact on the sovereign power of some states to preserve the institution of slavery.

Thus, in 1860, the U.S. Congress passed legislation introduced by Mississippi Senator Jefferson Davis that would have implemented *Dred Scott*'s promise of nondiscrimination against out-of-state slaveholders in much the way that the Civil Rights Act of 1964 implements the Warren Court's promise of nondiscrimination against the descendants of slaves. This view of *Dred Scott*'s implications was partly shared by Abraham Lincoln, who predicted, in his debates with Douglas, that "the next *Dred Scott*" case (*Lemmon* v. *The People*) would explicitly allow slaveholders to claim some of the benefits of Southern law while in the North.

For pre–Civil War Americans like Jefferson Davis, who anticipated a future based on *Dred Scott* (and not the Fourteenth Amendment), the constitutional commitment to the equality of slave and free states would no longer be protected only by the veto power of the Senate over future legislative efforts to abolish slavery. The Court's opinion in *Dred Scott* meant that the laws of free states and federal territories could henceforth have been subject to federal judicial review on the issue of whether they discriminated against an interstate diaspora of slaveholders.

73. Although he specifically mentions the existence of customary slavery among the African tribes, Hurd does not rest his argument on the comity owed to sovereign African states that recognized slavery. Neither does he argue that statelessness, as such, is what made Africans subject to enslavement when they arrived on these shores.

74. The defeated Southern states were, in fact, the first beneficiaries of this interpretation of the Fourteenth Amendment, which effectively allowed them to restore large elements of the prewar power structure. Scholars who stress Lincoln's fundamental conservatism and his ongoing quarrel with the Radicals in his own party tend to attribute to Lincoln this version of a lenient and magnanimous peace. From this perspective, the post–Civil War Constitution requires that we address the past only indirectly, through the neutral principle of nondiscrimination—a preexisting con-

stitutional doctrine that was adapted to address the national trauma of the mid-nineteenth century and the need to remedy the aftereffects of slavery and war. John G. Randall, *Lincoln, the President* (New York: Dodd, Mead, 1945). On Lincoln's wartime disagreements with the Radicals, see Belz, *Reconstructing the Union*.

75. For the extent of slavery's embeddedness in national institutions, see Fehrenbacher, *The Slaveholding Republic*.

76. Herbert Wechsler, "Toward Neutral Principles of Constitutional Law," *Harvard Law Review* 73 (1959).

77. And also state antimiscegenation laws that were later struck down in *Loving v. Virginia*, 388 U.S. 1(1967).

78. Akhil Reed Amar uses a similar argument to ground the constitutionality of some limited restrictions on hate speech in the Thirteenth Amendment's ban on slavery: "the intentional trapping of a captive audience of blacks in order to subject them to face-to-face degradation" might be proscribed as "temporary involuntary servitude, a sliver of slavery" (Amar, "The Case of the Missing Amendments," p. 158). My argument in the text, however, is not based on extending the metaphor of captivity to justify the regulation of speech addressed to "captive audiences" consisting of blacks. I argue only that the symbolic reinforcement of past patterns of enslavement can increase the harm of discrimination. From this it does not necessarily follow that otherwise protected speech could be legitimately restricted merely because it echoes a traumatic historical pattern.

79. James, *Black Jacobins*; David Scott, *Conscripts of Modernity: The Tragedy of Colonial Enlightenment* (Durham: Duke University Press, 2004).

80. Just as the Marshall-Wilson model of nondiscrimination can be expanded to include many forms of virtual nationhood, the Lincolnian reading of the Fourteenth Amendment has been expanded to support women, the disabled, the elderly, and gays in the moral logic of national recovery. Shklar, *American Citizenship*.

81. As we shall see in chapter 8, there is no possibility of restorative/reparative justice for crimes against past generations if there is no present generation of survivors to whom meaningful compensation can be made. This point raises two important questions: (1) Do claims for reparative justice end with the extinction of the victimized group? and (2) Should reparative justice always promote greater distributive justice (equality) among the living? For discussion of these points, see Thompson, *Taking Responsibility for the Past*; Miller, *National Responsibility and Global Justice*, chap. 6, esp. pp. 143–46.

82. This paradigmatic shift was a serious blow to our own indigenous peoples who fared particularly badly under Lincoln and his Republican successors, and who were subject to genocidal policies carried out by Civil War heroes including Sherman, Sheridan, Hancock, and Custer. They brought new zeal to the "savage wars" on the frontier that had been interrupted by secession. Richard Slotkin, *The Fatal Environment: The Myth of the Frontier in the Age of Industrialization, 1800–1890* (New York: Atheneum, 1985), esp. chaps. 4, 8, 14, 17.

83. Kit Carson, for example, was a federally sponsored *génocidaire* against the Navajos. See Clifford E. Trafzer, *The Kit Carson Campaign: The Last Great Navajo War* (Norman: University of Oklahoma Press, 1982).For a concise account of the historical

debates surrounding this episode, see Thomas Powers, "The Nestor of the Rockies," *New York Review of Books* 48, no. 17. The significance of Kit Carson in nineteenth- and twentieth-century popular myths of the "frontiersman" is summarized in Slotkin, *The Fatal Environment*, pp. 200–207.

84. For discussion of these issues outside the North American context, see Richard Mulgan, "Should Indigenous Peoples Have Special Rights?" *Orbis* 33 (1989); J. Morton, "The Cunning of Recognition: Indigenous Alterities and the Making of Australian Multiculturalism; Taking Responsibility for the Past: Reparation and Historical Justice," *Thesis Eleven* 85, no. 1 (2006); John Danley, "Liberalism, Aboriginal Rights, and Cultural Minorities," *Philosophy and Public Affairs* 20, no. 2 (1991); Patrick Macklem, *Normative Dimensions of Aboriginal Self-Government* (Ottawa: Royal Commission on Aboriginal Peoples, 1994); Thompson, *Taking Responsibility for the Past*, chaps. 3–4.

85. See, e.g., Anthony J. Hall, *The American Empire and the Fourth World* (Montreal: McGill-Queen's University Press, 2003); V. G. Kiernan, *America, the New Imperialism: From White Settlement to World Hegemony* (London: Verso, 2005). For a discussion of wars of extermination followed by "the guilt of dispossession", see Slotkin, *The Fatal Environment*, chap. 4.

86. For how many generations should collective guilt and reparation continue? This question is addressed in Berel Lang, *The Future of the Holocaust: Between History and Memory* (Ithaca: Cornell University Press, 1999), chap. 11.

87. One critic sees these programs as largely, if not entirely, a way for guilty whites to avoid the stereotypical imputation of racism. See Steele, *White Guilt*, p. 27.

88. Freud, "Inhibitions, Symptoms, and Anxiety."

89. *Adarand v. Peña*, 515 U.S. 200, at 239 (1995) (Scalia, concurring).

90. Scalia's liberalism is an example of Shklar's "liberalism of fear." To be an "American" in Justice Scalia's sense is to see an idealized version of oneself as, at least potentially, an innocent victim of racism. In this way, the politics of redistribution is dismissed as a return to racism. Behind the politics of affirmative action lie fantasies of racial war—of genocide and the collective punishment for genocide, which itself is potentially genocidal.

91. *Grutter v. Bollinger*, 539 U.S. 306 (2003). Parenthetical page citations above are to this opinion.

92. See Sigmund Freud, "Analysis Terminable and Interminable," in *The Standard Edition of the Complete Psychological Works of Sigmund Freud*, vol. 23.

93. *Brown v. Board of Education*, 349 U.S. 294 (1955) (Brown II).

94. Ronald Dworkin, *Sovereign Virtue: The Theory and Practice of Equality* (Cambridge: Harvard University Press, 2000), chaps. 4–5; Douglas W. Rae and Douglas Yates, *Equalities* (Cambridge: Harvard University Press, 1981). For a conceptual discussion of this model, see James S. Coleman, *Equality of Educational Opportunity* (Washington, D.C.: U.S. Department of Health, Education, and Welfare, Office of Education., 1966); Coleman, "The Concept of Equality of Education Opportunity," *Harvard Educational Review* (1968); and Coleman, "Equality of Educational Opportunity—Reply," *Journal of Human Resources* 3, no. 2 (1968). For applications, see, Frederick Mosteller and Daniel P. Moynihan, eds., *On Equality of Educational Op-*

portunity (New York: Random House, 1972); Christopher Jencks, *Inequality: A Reassessment of the Effect of Family and Schooling in America* (New York: Basic Books, 1972). For a contrary argument using similar methods, see Richard J. Herrnstein and Charles A. Murray, *The Bell Curve: Intelligence and Class Structure in American Life* (New York: Simon and Schuster, 1996).

95. Beneficiaries could, in principle, eliminate the ongoing disadvantages attached to victimhood by simply calculating and offsetting them. From this perspective, the continuing effect of victimhood is presumed to be the difference between the median outcome of the population of former victims with respect to primary goods (wealth, income, health, education, and so forth). For an extended discussion of this theme, see Dworkin, *Sovereign Virtue*, esp. chaps. 1–2, 9.

96. For an elaboration of this argument, see Michael Walzer, *Spheres of Justice: A Defense of Pluralism and Equality* (New York: Basic Books, 1983).

97. Dworkin, *Sovereign Virtue*, pt. 1.

98. In the U.S. we seem to have reached consensus that gender differences do not matter, and so we routinely (and without public debate) renorm standardized tests in which the median raw score of boys is lower than that of girls. The reason for this is that boys eventually "catch up." But would they if the tests used to determine their advancement were not renormed? That we do not routinely renorm tests in which median raw scores show statistically measurable racial bias suggests that we have not reached consensus on whether (or to what extent) racial differences are *natural* and thus validly measured by the test, and whether they need to be corrected, through renorming, so that the test itself will not be *historically* biased.

99. "The past is never dead. It's not even past." William Faulkner, "Requiem for a Nun," in *Novels, 1942–1954* (New York: Library of America, 1994), p. 535.

100. Michael Walzer, *Exodus and Revolution* (New York: Basic Books, 1985). For further discussion of the multiple, and conflicting, analogies between blacks and Jews (and also between America and Israel), see chapter 6 in this volume.

101. George M. Fredrickson, *Black Liberation: A Comparative History of Black Ideologies in the United States and South Africa* (New York: Oxford University Press, 1995).

102. The U.S. Civil Rights movement belongs to the *post*-Exodus rabbinic tradition adumbrated in Deuteronomy 23:8 and Psalm 17 that sees the messianic age as coming after Jews *return* to Egypt and are reconciled to the nation that once enslaved them but that also gave them shelter in the time of Joseph. Jews, here, are not described as a nation, like others, that seeks a land, but rather as a people whose mission is to bring universal reconciliation between the oppressed and their former oppressors. This tradition is interpreted in Emmanuel Lévinas, "The Nations and the Presence of Israel," in *In the Time of the Nations*, trans. Michael B. Smith (Bloomington: Indiana University Press, 1994). On the analogy between King's career and that of Moses, see the following works by Taylor Branch: *Parting the Waters: America in the King Years, 1954–63* (New York: Simon and Schuster, 1988); *Pillar of Fire: America in the King Years, 1963–65* (New York: Simon and Schuster, 1998); and *At Canaan's Edge: America in the King Years, 1965–68* (New York: Simon and Schuster, 2006).

103. Martin Luther King Jr., *Strength to Love* (New York: Walker, 1996), chap. 14 ("Paul's Letter to American Christians").

104. Ibid., p. 40. In his initial campaign for civil rights, the Montgomery Bus Boycott, King declared: "We are not struggling merely for the rights of Negroes but for all the people of Montgomery, black and white. We are determined to make America a better place for all people." Quoted in Stewart Burns, *To the Mountaintop: Martin Luther King, Jr.'s Sacred Mission to Save America, 1955–1968* (San Francisco: Harper, 2004).

105. Cf. my discussion of Étienne Balibar's view of "racism as a universalism" in chapter 4 of this volume.

106. If the messianic mission of blacks was to liberate all Americans from sin, this was a reason for patience, as well as commitment. King did not believe that justice was "the highest good" but rather "love in calculation. Justice is love correcting that which revolts against love" (Burns, *To the Mountaintop*, p. 126).

107. Mallory Olin, "The Political Theology of the Civil Rights Movement: Martin Luther King, Jr. & St. Paul," undergraduate seminar paper, 2006.

108. For a discussion of the dialectic between civil rights and human rights (MLK vs. Malcolm X), see Asad, "Redeeming the 'Human' through Human Rights," pp. 140–48.

109. The threat of violence was entirely on the surface of the white politics opposed to King; its existence had always been the main reason stated by self-declared southern "moderates" for slowing the pace of change. By the 1970s "white backlash" (both southern and northern), would come to be accepted, even by northern liberals, as an objective constraint on the politics of racial equality.

110. King's political theology, like Paul's, focused on the time between two messianic moments which might have come at once but did not—the end of evil (in this case American slavery) and the final redemption of past suffering, when whites too would be freed from the nation's slaveholding past. "To cooperate passively with an unjust system makes the oppressed as evil as the oppressor" (King, *Strength to Love*, p. 19).

111. Wallace understood, as did King before his death, that the initial success of the Civil Rights movement precluded a possible class alliance between blacks and poorer whites. It was this weakness on the class question that King was trying to address when he joined forces with the Memphis sanitation workers' strike in the days before his murder. King's change in strategy was a direct response to the national challenge posed by George Wallace in 1968 on the class issue, described in the press as "white backlash."

    Before his 1972 campaign was cut short by a would-be assassin's bullet, Wallace had won over many of the Democratic voters who would become Nixon's "Silent Majority" and, later, "Reagan Democrats." Wallace had thus effectively blocked the coalition between the civil rights and labor movements that the Democratic presidential candidates Hubert Humphrey, Walter Mondale, and George McGovern were trying to forge as a post–New Deal national majority.

112. The Wilsonian antidote to a history of political victimization was nationhood—the right to be sovereign somewhere, even if it was somewhere else. His internationalism describes a system for protecting the sovereign coequality of self-determining "peoples." "All peoples and nationalities" have a right, he said, "to live on equal

terms of liberty and safety with one another, whether they be strong or weak." Woodrow Wilson, "The Fourteen Points," in *The Political Thought of Woodrow Wilson*, ed. Edmund David Cronon (Indianapolis: Bobbs-Merrill, 1965).

113. Wilson's view of the protection of minority rights in the international system is (as we shall see in the next chapter) a variant of Marshallian federalism in which the local majority in a state becomes the virtual representatives of resident out-of-state minorities, thereby respecting on an equal basis their right to rule, albeit elsewhere. In Wilsonian internationalism, as distinct from Marshallian federalism, the main mechanisms for protecting individual human rights are political rather than judicial. Therefore the principle of virtual representation has to be reversed. Instead of saying that foreign minorities are to be treated as well as the local majority treats itself, the implicit standard is the treatment that foreign majorities accord to their minorities. See also Meister, "The Logic and Legacy of *Dred Scott*."

114. At the level of political psychology, however, the virtual "ingathering" of the nation as a victimary identity is not merely fictitious; it is a necessary form of self-idealization that can be an effective defense against well-founded fears of persecution. "Well-founded fear of persecution" is the threshold condition for claims to political asylum under international law. For a discussion of the implementation of these ideas in the interwar period, see Inis L. Claude, *National Minorities: An International Problem* (Cambridge: Harvard University Press, 1955); and Charles S. Maier, "Unsafe Haven: Why Minorities-Treaties Fail," *New Republic* 207, no. 16 (1992).

115. See, e.g., Hannah Arendt, *The Origins of Totalitarianism* (New York: Harcourt Brace Jovanovich, 1973), chap. 9.

116. Claude, *National Minorities*, p. 9.

117. The philosopher Bernard Williams explains this problem in implicitly Wilsonian terms: "What the breakaway group claimed, after all, was the right to set up a culturally homogeneous state. This may commit the breakaway state to accepting the right of some minority to do the same thing, if they can; but if the minority cannot do that, it does not necessarily commit the new state to respect their rights to cultural self-expression, in the middle of what was precisely intended to be a culturally unitary state." Bernard A. O. Williams, "Left-Wing Wittgenstein, Right-Wing Marx," *Common Knowledge* I 1, no. 1 (1992).

118. See Meister, "Beyond Satisfaction"; Wendy Brown, "Wounded Attachments," in Brown, *States of Injury: Power and Freedom in Late Modernity* (Princeton: Princeton University Press, 1995).

119. Not surprisingly the Bible is the source of both models. In the Old Testament the Children of Israel are sojourners who forge a new identity as survivors under the leadership of Moses. Having lived in bondage in a strange land, they make the transition from cult to nation to covenantal state where their survival becomes the basis of another story. This transformation is both a journey and a return. The survivorship and national renewal of the Jews enable them to conquer the indigenous Canaanites who must live like sojourners in the land of their birth. Cf. Walzer, *Exodus and Revolution*; Edward Said, "Michael Walzer's 'Exodus and Revolution': A Canaanite Reading," *Arab Studies* 8, no. 3 (1986); and Jonathan Boyarin, "Reading Exodus into History," *New Literary History* 23, no. 3 (1992). Exodus is not, however, our only canonical text of survivorship. The *Aeneid* is an effort to portray the founding

of Rome as a survivor story. On the dialectical relation between the two models, see Meister, "Sojourners and Survivors."

4. The Dialectic of Race and Place

1. See, e.g., Mann, *The Dark Side of Democracy*, chap. 2.
2. N.B. The claim is not that genocide arises only in periods of colonialism but rather that the framework in which genocide becomes thinkable derives from the moral logic of colonialism.
3. For discussion of the genealogy of "race war" as countering earlier historiographies of power, see Michel Foucault, *"Society Must Be Defended": Lectures at the Collège de France, 1975–76*, ed. Mauro Bertani and Alessandro Fontana, trans. David Macey (New York: Picador, 2003), Lecs. 3–4.
4. For the relation between these two points of origin, see, e.g., Patricia Seed, *Ceremonies of Possession in Europe's Conquest of the New World, 1492–1640* (Cambridge: Cambridge University Press, 1995); Tzvetan Todorov, *The Conquest of America: The Question of the Other*, trans. Richard Howard (New York: Harper and Row, 1984). See also Hall, *The American Empire and the Fourth World*, pt. 1.
5. Schmitt, *The Nomos of the Earth*, pt. 1. Schmitt defines *nomos* as "the first measure of all subsequent measures, the primeval division and distribution" of land (p. 67); it is "the radical title . . . that turns part of the earth's surface into the force-field of a particular order . . . visible in the appropriation of land in the founding of a city or colony" (p. 70). "Thus, for us, *nomos* is a matter of the fundamental process of appropriating space that is essential to every historical epoch—a matter of the structure-determining convergence of order and orientation in the cohabitation of peoples on this now scientifically surveyed planet. . . . Every . . . new epoch in the coexistence of peoples, empires, countries . . . and power formations of every sort, is founded on . . . new spatial orders of the earth" (pp. 78–79). On "tyranny" and "piracy" as the twin enemies of the "sovereign" in the early modern *nomos* of the earth, see Gil Anidjar, "Terror Right (Carl Schmitt)," *CR-the New Centennial Review* 4, no. 3 (2004).
6. Foucault, *"Society Must Be Defended,"* pp. 95–111. Douzinas describes "the main trope of European nationalism" as follows: "At the origin of the nation we find a story of the nation's origin." Costas Douzinas, "Theses on Law, History and Time (the Cultures of Human Rights)," *Melbourne Journal of International Law* 7, no. 1 (2006): 15.
7. Étienne Balibar, "Racism and Universalism," in Balibar, *Masses, Classes, Ideas: Studies on Politics and Philosophy Before and After Marx*, trans. James Swenson (New York: Routledge, 1994). Cf. Tzvetan Todorov, *On Human Diversity: Nationalism, Racism, and Exoticism in French Thought*, trans. Catherine Porter (Cambridge: Harvard University Press, 1995).
8. The "discovery" of the Americas by Chinese voyagers in 1421 had an opposite nomothetic effect—that of *de*globalizing the Chinese Empire, which remained the center of its own world for centuries thereafter. Gavin Menzies, *1421: The Year China Discovered America* (New York: Perennial, 2004).
9. The argument that follows is based on Mamdani, *Citizen and Subject*; Mahmood

Mamdani, *When Victims Become Killers: Colonialism, Nativism, and the Genocide in Rwanda* (Princeton: Princeton University Press, 2001). For a brief summary, see Mamdani, "Race and Ethnicity as Political Identities in the African Context," in *Identity: For a Different Kind of Globalization*, ed. Nadia Tazi, Keywords series (New York: Other, 2004).

10.   Ancient Jews did not have to believe that they were biologically distinct (they probably did not) in order to conceive of their divinely willed extermination as a collective punishment that would prevent (or delay) them from reaching their divinely promised destiny. Race here relates not to lineage but to "chosenness"—the notion that one *has* a collective destiny that is not tied to the present time and space, and that links successive generations. (Genocide would be considered a *racialized* killing—something more than mass murder—to the extent that it wipes out the collective *future* of the present generation's *past*, whether or not this is conceived as biological descent, confessional faith, cultural continuity, linguistic preservation, and so on. Mere occupancy of the same place is what could *not* be considered racial continuity—hence the relation between racialized thinking and the conceivability of extermination.)

      The political/theological conception of race developed in this chapter differs from narrower conceptions that treat race as a biological (or pseudo-biological) trait. Ivan Hannaford, for example, writes an intellectual history of race as "the notion that human beings are descended from common material origins and are possessed of recognizable physical, mental, and cultural traits that are *transmitted biologically* [my emphasis] and are used more often than not to group and classify people into four, five, twelve, or thirty-eight divisions, usually in some arbitrary hierarchical order." Ivan Hannaford, *Race: The History of an Idea in the West* (Baltimore, Md.: Johns Hopkins University Press, 1996), pp. 3–4; cf. Todorov, *On Human Diversity*. For a genealogy of the race/biology connection, see Vanita Seth, *Indians of Europe: Producing Racial Difference 1500-1900* (Durham: Duke University Press, 2010), chap. 5.

11.   For an account of this mentality, see Thomas Pakenham, *The Scramble for Africa, 1876–1912* (New York: Random House, 1991).

12.   For a discussion in the North American context, see Hall, *The American Empire and the Fourth World*, chaps. 1, 6.

13.   Jason D. Hill, "Forgetting Where We Come From: The Moral Imperative of Every Cosmopolitan," in Hill, *Becoming a Cosmopolitan: What It Means to Be a Human Being in the New Millennium* (Lanham, Md.: Rowman and Littlefield, 2000). Cf. David Held, *Democracy and the Global Order: From the Modern State to Cosmopolitan Governance* (Stanford: Stanford University Press, 1995), esp. chaps. 6, 10.

14.   At the onset of European colonialism, racialized thinking was not limited to the pseudo-biological concept of race that took over in the nineteenth century; it could encompass (what we would consider) linguistic, cultural, religious, and even psychological characteristics that persisted across generations and locations. Then, as today, the term "race" could be used to assert or deny something about descent, language, culture, ethnic background, physiognomy, and so forth—and to distinguish these from one another. It has thus been intelligible, for example, to base nationhood on a demand for racial purification and to assert (as Americans now do)

that the "nation" is made up of multiple races. My use of the term "race" is always situated in politics—I am interested in racialization—and this chapter specifically concerns European colonialism as a dynamic political relations between the earth and its various populations, divided into settler races and first occupants (natives). On the dynamic and fluid uses of "race" and "ethnicity" in pre- and postmodernity, see Robert Bartlett, "Medieval and Modern Concepts of Race and Ethnicity," *Journal of Medieval and Early Modern Studies* 2, no. 1 (2001).

15. Solnit's phrase, "becoming native," implies (in my terminology) the re-ethnicization of a diasporic racial identity. See also Stephen Sedley, "Settlers v. Natives," *London Review of Books*, March 8, 2001.

16. Rebecca Solnit, *A Book of Migrations: Some Passages in Ireland* (London: Verso, 1997), pp. 114–15. On the Zionist resonances of this point, see also, e.g., Ze'ev Sternhell, *The Founding Myths of Israel: Nationalism, Socialism, and the Making of the Jewish State*, trans. David Maisel (Princeton: Princeton University Press, 1998); Michael Berkowitz, *Zionist Culture and West European Jewry before the First World War* (Cambridge: Cambridge University Press, 1993).

17. Brian Barry and Robert E. Goodin, *Free Movement: Ethical Issues in the Transnational Migration of People and Money* (University Park: Pennsylvania State University Press, 1992); Henry G. Schermers et al., *Free Movement of Persons in Europe: Legal Problems and Experiences* (Dordrecht: Martinous Nijhoff, 1993).

18. See Mamdani, *Citizen and Subject*, pt. 3.

19. On the U.S. "myth of the frontier" (and consequent "savage wars") as superseding narratives of class struggles in the settler metropolis, see Slotkin, *The Fatal Environment*, chaps. 1, 3–4, 8, 12–14.

20. "Before the rise of the word "ethnicity," [in America] the word 'race' was widely used to refer to larger and smaller groupings of mankind: for example, the Irish race or the Jewish race. In fact, the National Socialist genocide in the name of 'race' is what gave the word a bad name and supported the substitution of 'ethnicity.'" Werner Sollors, *Beyond Ethnicity: Consent and Descent in American Culture* (New York: Oxford University Press, 1986), p. 38.

21. Werner Sollors, *The Invention of Ethnicity* (New York: Oxford University Press, 1989); Sollors, ed., *Theories of Ethnicity: A Classical Reader* (New York: New York University Press, 1996).

22. The etymological root of "ethnic" is the same as "heathen," reflecting the encounter of early Christian missionaries with indigenous religious practice (Sollors, *Theories of Ethnicity*, pp. 2–12).

23. See, e.g., Louis Hartz, *The Liberal Tradition in America: An Interpretation of American Political Thought Since the Revolution* (New York: Harcourt, 1955).

24. See chapter 6 in this volume for an extended discussion of this point in relation to the "Jewish Question" in America.

25. The "myth of the frontier," as Slotkin tells us, resulted in a chronic underestimation of the number of natives coexisting with settlers at any given time (*The Fatal Environment*, p. 52).

26. For further discussion of "freedom" in America as a simultaneous dilution and intensification of racial self-definition, see chapter 6 in this volume.

27. See Hartz, *The Liberal Tradition in America*; Louis Hartz, *The Founding of New So-*

cieties: Studies in the History of the United States, Latin America, South Africa, Canada, and Australia (New York: Harcourt, 1964).

28. Étienne Balibar, "Racism and Nationalism," in Balibar, *Race, Nation, Class: Ambiguous Identities*, trans. Chris Turner (London: Verso, 1991), p. 49.

29. Étienne Balibar, "Is There a Neo-Racism?" in Balibar, *Race, Nation, Class*, pp. 18–19. Here Balibar defines "theory" as an "intellectual posture" that satisfies the popular desire to know why societal violence is sometimes unavoidable unless it is controlled by state power.

30. Balibar, "Racism and Nationalism," pp. 54–55.

31. Ibid., pp. 37–67; and Balibar, "Racism and Universalism." Cf. Foucault, *"Society Must Be Defended."*

32. "When outsiders speak about Israel the phrase is always 'the Jews.'" Krister Stendahl, "Paul and Israel," in *Final Account: Paul's Letter to the Romans* (Minneapolis: Fortress, 1995), p. 4.

33. Taubes, *The Political Theology of Paul*, chap. 1, esp. pp. 26–38.

34. Agamben, *The Time That Remains*, Day 3. See also chapter 6 in this volume.

35. The relation of race to Paul's view of the "Jewish Question" is pursued in chapter 6 in this volume.

36. Balibar uses the pejorative term "racism" to link the theories under which mass democracies claimed to rule colonized peoples with those they later use to resist the democratic claims that immigrants from former colonies make in the metropole. On this point I agree, however, with Foucault that "we should reserve the expression 'racism' or 'racist discourse' for something that was basically no more than a particular and localized episode in the great discourse or race war or race struggle. It was a reworking of that old discourse, which at that point was already hundreds of years old, in sociobiological terms, and it was reworked for purposes of social conservatism and, at least in a certain number of cases, colonial domination" (Foucault, *"Society Must Be Defended,"* p. 65).

37. Balibar, "Racism as Universalism," pp. 200–201, 203.

38. Ibid., pp. 59, 61.

39. Ibid., p. 203.

40. Balibar, "Is There a Neo-Racism?" p. 22. The quotations in the text above are from this article.

41. For development of a similar point in the context of modern anti-Semitism, see Moishe Postone, "The Holocaust and the Trajectory of the Twentieth Century," in *Catastrophe and Meaning: The Holocaust and the Twentieth Century*, ed. Moishe Postone and Eric L. Santner (Chicago: University of Chicago Press, 2003), p. 89.

42. See Mastnak, *Crusading Peace*, chaps. 1–3, 6; Anidjar, *The Jew, the Arab*; Anidjar, "Terror Right (Carl Schmitt)."

43. Aimé Césaire, *Discourse on Colonialism*, ed. Robin D. G. Kelley, trans. Joan Pinkham (New York: Monthly Review Press, 2000), pp. 35–36. I am grateful to Sara Kendall for calling this passage to my attention.

44. One might argue, in fact, that the state form itself originated in Europe out of the collapse of the Roman Empire, when the original distinction between Romans (i.e., cosmopolitans) and barbarians turns into a distinction between translocal peoples

(*gens*), which become races and then nations, and local identities, which become pre-national tribes. This framework of thought, which took shape between the ninth and twelfth centuries in Europe, acquired new life when European nation-states (based on peoplehood) reinvented the idea of imperialism in the eighteenth and nineteenth centuries by conquering local tribes. See, e.g., Robert Bartlett, *The Making of Europe: Conquest, Colonization, and Cultural Change, 950–1350* (Princeton: Princeton University Press, 1993), chaps. 8–9, 11; See also Patrick J. Geary, *The Myth of Nations: The Medieval Origins of Europe* (Princeton: Princeton University Press, 2002); Robert Bartlett, review of *The Myth of Nations: The Medieval Origins of Europe* by Patrick J. Geary, *Journal of Modern History* 75, no. 4 (2003).

45. Joseph Ruane and Jennifer Todd, *The Dynamics of Conflict in Northern Ireland: Power, Conflict, and Emancipation* (Cambridge: Cambridge University Press, 1996), pp. 21–25; Michael MacDonald, *Children of Wrath: Political Violence in Northern Ireland* (Cambridge: Polity, Blackwell, 1986).

46. Solnit, *Migrations*, p. 99.

47. Indeed, some of the same individuals (including Francis Drake, Humphrey Gilbert, Richard Grenville, and Walter Raleigh) were originally involved in both schemes, and many of the same families were granted landed estates in both colonies. David Beers Quinn, *The Elizabethans and the Irish* (Ithaca: Cornell University Press for the Folger Shakespeare Library, 1966), esp. chap. 9.

48. For a detailed, comprehensive treatment of this period, see Nicholas P. Canny, *Making Ireland British, 1580–1650* (Oxford: Oxford University Press, 2001); Canny, "The Permissive Frontier: The Problem of Social Control in English Settlements in Ireland and Virginia, 1550–1650," in *The Westward Enterprise: English Activities in Ireland, the Atlantic, and America, 1480–1650*, ed. Kenneth R. Andrews et al. (Detroit: Wayne State University Press, 1979). The colonization of the British is placed in comparative historical perspective by Michael Hechter, *Internal Colonialism: The Celtic Fringe in British National Development* (New Brunswick, N.J.: Transaction, 1999), chaps. 3–4, 9, 11. Ireland is discussed within the framework of postcolonial studies by David Lloyd, *Ireland after History* (Notre Dame: University of Notre Dame Press, 1999); see, esp., Lloyd's introduction, which treats mass emigration as the distinguishing anomaly of the Irish colonial experience.

49. A gripping narrative of the global significance of Irish colonization can be found in Angus Calder, *Revolutionary Empire: The Rise of the English-Speaking Empires from the Fifteenth Century to the 1780s* (New York: Dutton, 1981), pp. 17–110. See also Nicholas P. Canny, "The Theory and Practice of Acculturation: Ireland in a Colonial Context," in *Kingdom and Colony: Ireland in the Atlantic World, 1560–1800* ed. Nicholas P. Canny and Anthony Pagden (Princeton: Princeton University Press, 1988).

50. On the origins of the Anglo-Irish ascendancy, which lasted well into the twentieth century, see Nicholas P. Canny, "Identity Formation in Ireland: The Emergence of the Anglo-Irish," in *Colonial Identity in the Atlantic World, 1500–1800*, ed. Nicholas P. Canny and Anthony Pagden (Princeton: Princeton University Press, 1987); and Canny, "Migration and Opportunity: Britain, Ireland," in Canny and Pagden, *Kingdom and Colony*.

51. "The settler-native distinction was interwoven with the religious and ethnic one but

is not reducible to it. . . . In practice many of those who made up the 'settler' population were descended from people who came simply as immigrants, just as many eighteenth- and nineteenth-century Protestants were of native stock. But they were part of a society defined in terms of 'settlers' and 'natives' and took their appointed place within it. . . . The descendants of the settlers soon identified with Ireland and regarded themselves as "Irish" but they did not forget their origins or their difference from those they saw as the native Irish—nor were they permitted to do so" (Ruane and Todd, *The Dynamics of Conflict in Northern Ireland*, pp. 25–26.)

See also Thomas Bartlett, "'What Ish My Nation?'" in *Irish Studies: A General Introduction*, ed. Bartlett et al., pp. 44–59 (Dublin: Gill and Macmillan, 1988).

52. Among the new Anglo-Irish *colons* of the Tudor and Stuart era were the poets Edmund Spenser (who arrived as a colonial administrator) and Sir Philip Sidney, son of the Lord Deputy of Ireland, who, along with Spenser, was prominent in the deforestation and resettlement that stirred native rebellion. The pastoral verse of Spenser and the younger Sidney, constructing a mythology of Arcadian origins for the Elizabethan age, contrasts sharply with their writings on Ireland that depict the native pastoralists, whose land they had confiscated, as savage barbarians. Recent literary scholarship describes the lengths to which Spenser went in comparing the pastoralist practices of native Irish herders (who drank the blood of their cattle, as well as the milk) to the cannibalistic and bestial customs attributed in myth to ancient Scythians and by explorers to Amerindians. See Solnit, *Migrations*, chap. 10, esp. pp. 106f–7.; Patricia Coughlan, *Spenser and Ireland: An Interdisciplinary Perspective* (Cork: Cork University Press, 1989); Joan Fitzpatrick, *Irish Demons: English Writings on Ireland, the Irish, and Gender by Spenser and His Contemporaries* (Lanham, Md.: University Press of America, 2000).

53. Bartlett, "'What Ish My Nation?'" p. 45. This Home Rule movement by the Anglo-Irish was an outgrowth of earlier connections between the "Commonwealthmen" of Ireland and North America. See, e.g., Nicholas P. Canny, "The Passage to Maturity: Colonial Ireland and Colonial America, 1650–1790," in Canny and Pagden, *Kingdom and Colony*.

54. "The Negro analogy seems to have taken over (though never completely) from the Amerindian as Africans came to replace Indians, in European imaginations, as the principal exemplars of cannibalism and savagery." See Rawson, *God, Gulliver*, pp. 219–20 (and references cited). Swift draws extensively on this physiological stereotype in his description of the Yahoos in *Gulliver's Travels*. On Swift's use of the analogies between the Indians and Irish and the Hottentots and Irish, see Rawson, pp. 79–91, 108–13. See also Quinn, *The Elizabethans and the Irish*, pp. 23–27.

55. For a discussion of the later history of "black Celts" in nineteenth-century England and America, see, e.g., L. Perry Curtis, *Anglo-Saxons and Celts: A Study of Anti-Irish Prejudice in Victorian England* (New York: New York University Press, 1968), chaps. 2, 4, esp. p. 72.

56. Noel Ignatiev, *How the Irish Became White* (New York: Routledge, 1995). Well into the twentieth century, however, there are also positive references to "black" (or pure, native) Irish in the writings of Anglo Irish nationalists. See, e.g., Edward Said's famous argument that Yeats, Césaire, and Fanon are all examples of *négritude*—

black cultural resurgences against the white settlers. Edward W. Said, *Culture and Imperialism* (New York: Vintage Books, 1994), pp. 220–38. See also Curtis, *Anglo-Saxons and Celts.*, chap. 9; Hechter, *Internal Colonialism*, chaps. 9, 11, esp. pp. 268–69, 342–43.

57. James H. Webb, *Born Fighting: How the Scots-Irish Shaped America* (New York: Broadway, 2004).

58. Walter Scott, *Ivanhoe: A Romance* (New York: Modern Library, 2001).

59. On the general topic of European "myths of ethnogenesis," see Geary, *The Myth of Nations*. For a partial defense of such myths, see Rogers M. Smith, *Stories of Peoplehood: The Politics and Morals of Political Membership*, Contemporary Political Theory series (Cambridge: Cambridge University Press, 2003), chap. 2. As Solnit reminds us, "Origins nest within each other, each obliterating the one it succeeds" (*Migrations*, p. 114).

60. Mamdani, "Race and Ethnicity as Political Identities in the African Context"; Mahmood Mamdani, "When Does a Settler Become a Native? Reflections on the Colonial Roots of Citizenship in Equatorial and South Africa," in *Inaugural Lecture, University of Cape Town*, new series no. 208 (May 13, 1998).

61. The detribalization and extermination of indigenous Americans immediately following the Civil War is described in chapter 3 in this volume. For discussion of the first instance in which North American settlers came to regard themselves as native Americans, see Jill Lepore, *The Name of War: King Philip's War and the Origins of American Identity* (New York: Knopf, 1998). A broader history of this process is presented in Patricia Seed, *American Pentimento: The Invention of Indians and the Pursuit of Riches* (Minneapolis: University of Minnesota Press, 2001). For more polemical accounts of the racialization of ethnicity in the Americas and Africa, see Churchill, *A Little Matter of Genocide*; Sven Lindqvist, *Exterminate All the Brutes*, trans. Joan Tate (New York: New Press, 1996). On "eliminationism" as both a policy and a fantasy, see Daniel Jonah Goldhagen, *Hitler's Willing Executioners: Ordinary Germans and the Holocaust* (New York: Knopf, 1996), pt. 1.

62. For the *locus classicus* of this argument, see Arendt, *The Origins of Totalitarianism*, pt. 2 ("Imperialism").

63. Uday Singh Mehta, *The Anxiety of Freedom: Imagination and Individuality in Locke's Political Thought* (Ithaca: Cornell University Press, 1992); Seed, *American Pentimento*.

64. For a compelling discussion of the latter topic, see Anthony F. C. Wallace, *Jefferson and the Indians: The Tragic Fate of the First Americans* (Cambridge: Belknap Press of Harvard University Press, 1999).

65. Mamdani, "Race and Ethnicity as Political Identities" pp. 4–8.

66. Melanie Klein, "Notes on Some Schizoid Mechanisms," in Klein, *Envy and Gratitude, and Other Works, 1946–1963* (New York: Free Press, 1984); Klein, "A Contribution to the Psycho-Genesis of Manic-Depressive States." See also Hinshelwood, *A Dictionary of Kleinian Thought*, entries 9, 11, and 13.

67. Frantz Fanon, *The Wretched of the Earth*, trans. Constance Farrington (Harmondsworth: Penguin, 1967).

68. Jean-Paul Sartre, "Introduction," in Fanon, *The Wretched of the Earth*.

69. Frantz Fanon, *Black Skin, White Masks*, trans. Charles Lam Markmann (London: Paladin, 1970), p. 157 n.

70. For recent examples of this backward-looking view of Kantian ethics as the *end* of Hegelian struggle, see Jürgen Habermas, *The Inclusion of the Other: Studies in Political Theory*, trans. Ciaran Cronin and Pablo De Greiff (Cambridge: MIT Press, 1998); and Honneth, *The Struggle for Recognition*.

71. Emmanuel Lévinas, *Totality and Infinity: An Essay on Exteriority*, trans. Alphonso Lingis (Pittsburgh: Duquesne University Press, 1969), preface.

72. See, e.g., Patricia Seed, "Imagining a Waste Land, or Why Indians Vanish," in Seed, *American Pentimento*, chap. 2.

73. The settlers in a colony typically include *subjugated* races, such as blacks in the United States or Indians in East Africa, who act as intermediaries between the *colons* and indigenous peoples. Their subsequent struggle for nonracialized citizenship within the postcolony eventually complicates the anticolonial struggle of the native. See Mahmood Mamdani, *From Citizen to Refugee: Uganda Asians Come to Britain* (London: Frances Pinter, 1973); Mamdani, "When Does a Settler Become a Native?"

74. The foregoing account is based on Lepore, *In the Name of War*. See also Stephen Saunders Webb, ed., *1676, the End of American Independence* (Syracuse: Syacuse University Press, 1995); Richard Slotkin and James K. Folsom, eds., *So Dreadfull a Judgment: Puritan Responses to King Philip's War, 1676–1677* (Middletown: Wesleyan University Press, 1978).

75. Deloria, *Playing Indian*. See also Shari M. Huhndorf, *Going Native: Indians in the American Cultural Imagination* (Ithaca: Cornell University Press, 2001).

76. Gary Frank Reed, "Freedom as the End of Civilization: Studies in the Troubled Relationship between the Ideas of Liberty and Civility," Ph.D. dissertation, University of California, Santa Cruz, 1977.

77. Mann, *The Dark Side of Democracy*, chap. 1, esp. p. 12. See also Norman M. Naimark, *Fires of Hatred: Ethnic Cleansing in Twentieth-Century Europe* (Cambridge: Harvard University Press, 2001); Gellately and Kiernan, *The Specter of Genocide*.

78. These include, minimally, "Pareto Optimality."

79. A range of arguments for majority rule are surveyed and summarized in Elaine Spitz, *Majority Rule*, (Chatham, N.J.: Chatham House, 1984). See also Willmoore Kendall, *John Locke and the Doctrine of Majority-Rule* (Urbana: University of Illinois Press, 1940); John Stuart Mill, *Considerations on Representative Government* (London: Routledge, 1905); Giovanni Sartori, *Democratic Theory* (Westport, Conn.: Greenwood, 1973). For recent discussions, see Jon Elster, "Majority Rule and Individual Rights," in *On Human Rights: The Oxford Amnesty Lectures, 1993*, ed. Stephen Shute and Susan. L. Hurley (New York: Basic Books, 1993). The standard rationale for majority rule as a technique of aggregative democracy is given in Amartya Sen, *Collective Choice and Social Welfare* (San Francisco: Holden-Day, 1970). For an argument that democratic procedures are always imperfect for the purpose of interest aggregation, see Kenneth J. Arrow, *Social Choice and Individual Values*, 2nd ed. (New York: Wiley, 1963).

80. See, e.g., Amy Gutmann and Dennis F. Thompson, *Democracy and Disagreement* (Cambridge: Belknap Press of Harvard University Press, 1996); Amy Gutmann, *Why Deliberative Democracy?* (Princeton: Princeton University Press, 2004); Koh and Slye, *Deliberative Democracy and Human Rights*. For a balanced critique of both aggregative and deliberative conceptions of the common good, see Ian Shapiro, *The State of Democratic Theory* (Princeton: Princeton University Press, 2003), chaps. 1–2.

81. Twentieth-century political thought was marked by heightened apocalyptic imagery of one's own destruction *as a people*. See, e.g., Omer Bartov, *Mirrors of Destruction: War, Genocide, and Modern Identity* (Oxford: Oxford University Press, 2000).

82. Smith, *Stories of Peoplehood*. Cf. Saskia Sassen, *Territory, Authority, Rights: From Medieval to Global Assemblages* (Princeton: Princeton University Press, 2006); Benedict R. O'G Anderson, *Imagined Communities: Reflections on the Origin and Spread of Nationalism* (London: Verso, 1983).

83. Brian M. Barry, "The Public Interest," *Proceedings of the Aristotelian Society,* supplementary volume 38, no. 1964; *Justice as Impartiality*, Oxford Political Theory series (Oxford: Oxford University Press, 1995), §23; Power, "Bystanders to Genocide"; Power, "*A Problem From Hell*"; Cf. Jürgen Habermas, "Citizenship and National Identity: Some Reflections on the Future of Europe," *Praxis International* 12, no. 1 (1992); Habermas, "Struggles for Recognition in Constitutional States," *European Journal of Philosophy* 1, no. 2 (1993).

84. Cf. Jon Elster, "Majority Rule and Individual Rights."

85. Theodore Dalrymple, "The Specters Haunting Dresden," *City Journal* (winter 2005).

86. See Mamdani, "Race and Ethnicity"; Solnit, *Migrations*, pp. 114–15.

87. My account of Rwanda follows Mamdani, *When Victims Become Killers*, chaps. 2–5. For a schematic version of his argument, see his "Race and Ethnicity."

88. Mamdani, *When Victims Become Killers*, chaps. 6–7.

89. For a discussion of the Clinton administration's failure to act, see, e.g., Power, "Bystanders to Genocide" and "*A Problem from Hell*," chap. 10. The failures of the UN mission are described by its commander on the ground in Dallaire and Beardsley, *Shake Hands with the Devil*.

90. Mamdani, *When Victims Become Killers*, chap. 8.

91. See Jeffrey Herf, *The Jewish Enemy: Nazi Propaganda During World War II and the Holocaust* (Cambridge: Belknap Press of Harvard University Press, 2006), chaps. 4–7. Goebbels based some of his propaganda on a leaked version of the proposal by Roosevelt's treasury secretary Henry Morgenthau to force poverty on a soon to be defeated Germany. See, e.g., Borgwardt, *A New Deal for the World*, pp. 209, 349 n.40.

92. Adolf Hitler, *Mein Kampf*, trans. Ralph Manheim (London: Hutchinson, 1969), chap. 11 (esp. pp. 300–320). In the end Hitler's policy of extermination did not involve popular mobilization. In the context of our overall argument, we should note that the techniques and concepts of the Holocaust were originally developed by German settler colonialism in Southwest Africa to exterminate the Herero natives. See Mamdani, *When Victims Become Killers*, pp. 10–13, and the sources cited therein.

93. Mamdani, *When Victims Become Killers*, pp. 273–74.

94. Was this outcome forestalled in South Africa just in the nick of time? In the 1980s a dystopic literature was produced by liberal white South Africans imagining what it would be like for disgraced whites to live in a postrevolutionary, black-ruled country. See, e.g., Nadine Gordimer, *July's People* (New York: Viking, 1981). For a parable that confronts the possibility of confession without atonement in the post-apartheid 1990s, see Coetzee, *Disgrace*, which is discussed in chapter 2 of this volume.

95. For further development of these points, see chapter 8 in this volume.

96. Ely, *Democracy and Distrust*. See also Shapiro, *The State of Democratic Theory*; Lea A. Brilmayer, "Carolene, Conflicts, and the Fate of the "Inside Outsider," *University of Pennsylvania Law Review* 134 (1986); Brilmayer, "Shaping and Sharing in Democratic Theory: Towards a Political Philosophy of Interstate Equality," *Florida State Law Review* 15 (1987); and Brilmayer, "Consent, Contract, and Territory," *Minnesota Law Review* 39 (1990).

97. See, e.g., Lani Guinier, *The Tyranny of the Majority: Fundamental Fairness in Representative Democracy* (New York: Free Press, 1994).

98. Arend Lijphart, *Democracy in Plural Societies: A Comparative Exploration* (New Haven: Yale University Press, 1977).

99. Arendt, *The Origins of Totalitarianism*, pt. 2.

100. In 1937, in Berlin, Adolf Eichmann met a Haganah agent named Polkes on the topic of Jewish emigration to Palestine. Eichmann accepted "Polkes' invitation to Palestine" for a follow-up meeting, but the two had to meet in Cairo after Arab uprisings had "forced the Mandatory Powers to declare a state of siege and close the frontiers of Palestine." From these meetings both Eichmann and his superior, Heydrich, understood that in some "Jewish nationalist circles people were pleased with the radical German Jewish policy" insofar as it could potentially accelerate Jewish emigration to Palestine and hasten the day when Jewish settlers would outnumber Arabs. Heinz Höhne, *The Order of the Death's Head: The Story of Hitler's SS*, trans. Richard Barry (New York: Penguin, 2001), pp. 334–38. This period in Eichmann's life is well described in Hannah Arendt, *Eichmann in Jerusalem: A Report on the Banality of Evil*, rev. and enl. ed. (New York: Penguin 1994), pp. 58–64.

101. For the transformation of her view of Zionism during the 1940s, See Hannah Arendt, *The Jewish Writings*, ed. Jerome Kohn and Ron H. Feldman (New York: Schocken, 2007), pp. 343–401.

102. Ibid., p. 415.

103. Shklar, *Legalism*, pp. 143–79; Yosal Rogat, *The Eichmann Trial and the Rule of Law* (Santa Barbara: Center for the Study of Democratic Institutions, 1961), pp. 28–43; Otto Kirchheimer, *Political Justice: The Use of Legal Procedure for Political Ends* (Princeton: Princeton University Press, 1961); Lawrence Douglas, *The Memory of Judgment: Making Law and History in the Trials of the Holocaust* (New Haven: Yale University Press, 2001); Gary Jonathan Bass, *Stay the Hand of Vengeance: The Politics of War Crimes Tribunals* (Princeton: Princeton University Press, 2000), chaps. 1, 5.

104. The concerns are directly and clearly expressed in Arendt's correspondence with Jaspers before, during, and after the trial. See Hannah. Arendt, *Hannah Arendt/Karl*

Jaspers Correspondence, 1926–1969 (New York: Harcourt Brace Jovanovich, 1992), pp. 400–500.

105. These were the words of Eichmann's prosecutor, Gideon Hausner. See Tom Segev, *The Seventh Million: The Israelis and the Holocaust*, trans. Haim Watzman (New York: Hill and Wang, 1993), pt. 6. For an account of how the trial and Arendt's critique of it were received by Diaspora Jewry, see Peter Novick, *The Holocaust in American Life* (Boston: Houghton Mifflin, 1999), chap. 7.

106. Arendt, *Eichmann in Jerusalem*, pp. 278–79.

107. Tutu, *No Future without Forgiveness*, chap. 11. For a comparison of Tutsis and South African whites, see Mamdani, "When Does a Settler Become a Native?"

108. This was also the year of South Africa's first free elections.

109. Josh Cohen, *Interrupting Auschwitz: Art, Religion, Philosophy* (New York: Continuum, 2003), chap. 3.

110. Giorgio Agamben notes "the paradoxical tension between an *already* and a *not yet* . . . implicit in the concept itself of transitional time" (*The Time That Remains*, see, esp., "Day Four").

111. See, e.g., Glover, *Humanity*; Rummel, *Death by Government*.

112. Schmitt, *The Concept of the Political*, p. 71.

113. See, e.g., Alain Badiou, "The Cultural Revolution: The Last Revolution?"; "Selections from 'Theorie Du Sujet' on the Cultural Revolution"; and "Further Selections from 'Theorie Du Sujet' on the Cultural Revolution," all in *positions: east asia cultures critique* 13, no. 3 (2005).

114. Alain Badiou, "Democratic Materialism and the Materialist Dialectic," *Radical Philosophy* 130 (2005). (This article is excerpted from the preface to *Logics of Worlds*, cited below.) For an example of the view Badiou criticizes, see Michael Walzer, "Nation and Universe," in *The Tanner Lectures on Human Values, XI*, ed. Grethe B. Peterson (Salt Lake City: University of Utah Press, 1990); Walzer, *Thick and Thin: Moral Argument at Home and Abroad* (Notre Dame: University of Notre Dame Press, 1994).

115. Lévinas, "Useless Suffering," p. 99.

116. Badiou, "Democratic Materialism"; Asad, "Redeeming the 'Human' Through Human Rights."

117. Alain Badiou, *Ethics: An Essay on the Understanding of Evil*, trans. Peter Hallward (London: Verso, 2001), p. 9; see, generally, chap. 1.

118. Ibid., p. 9.

119. For contrasting perspectives, see Cohen, *States of Denial*; Carolyn J. Dean, *The Fragility of Empathy after the Holocaust* (Ithaca: Cornell University Press, 2004).

120. Cf. Badiou, *Ethics*, pp. 10ff.

121. Slavoj Žižek, *The Ticklish Subject: The Absent Centre of Political Ontology* (London: Verso, 1999), p. 48.

5. "Never Again"

1. To employ "the polemical sense of the political" is to ask what any given set of concepts is *against*. Jacques Derrida, "On Absolute Hostility: The Cause of Philosophy

and the Spectre of the Political," in *The Politics of Friendship*, trans. George Collins (London: Verso, 2005), p. 117.

2. Previously cited examples include Card, *The Atrocity Paradigm*, pp. 250ff.; Neiman, *Evil*; Glover, *Humanity*; and Nino, *Radical Evil*. See also Joan Copjec, ed., *Radical Evil* (London: Verso, 1996); Giorgio Agamben, *Remnants of Auschwitz: The Witness and the Archive*, trans. Daniel Heller-Roazen (New York: Zone, 2000). The mid-century *locus classicus* for this line of thought is Theodor W. Adorno, *Negative Dialectics*, trans. E. B. Ashton. (New York: Seabury, 1973), esp. pp. 361–408.

3. Adorno, *Negative Dialectics*, p. 365. Parenthetical references above are to this text. (See also Cohen, *Interrupting Auschwitz*, pp. 4ff.)

4. Rorty, "On Human Rights," p. 122. See, also Richard Rorty, "Justice as a Larger Loyalty," in *Cosmopolitics: Thinking and Feeling beyond the Nation*, ed. Pheng Cheah and Bruce Robbins (Minneapolis: University of Minnesota Press, 1998). Habermas, *Inclusion of the Other*, pt. 4.

5. Rorty, "On Human Rights," p. 124.

6. For further development of this point in another context, see Foucault, *"Society Must Be Defended,"* pp. 60–62.

7. Hilary Putnam, "Lévinas and Judaism," in *The Cambridge Companion to Levinas*, ed. Simon Critchley and Robert Bernasconi (Cambridge: Cambridge University Press, 2002), p. 35.

8. Ibid., p. 55. See also pp. 41, 54.

9. Rorty, "Justice as a Larger Loyalty."

10. The "Ethics of Ethics" is Derrida's description of the Lévinasian project. See Jacques Derrida, "Violence and Metaphysics: An Essay on the Thought of Emannuel Levinas," in Derrida, *Writing and Difference*, trans. Alan Bass (Chicago: University of Chicago Press, 1978), p. 111.

11. Ibid., p. 97.

12. "It is . . . attention to the suffering of the other that, through the cruelties of our century (despite these cruelties, because of these cruelties), can be affirmed as the very nexus of human subjectivity, to the point of being raised to the level of supreme ethical principle—the only one it is impossible to question" (Lévinas, "Useless Suffering," p. 94).

13. Derrida, *The Politics of Friendship*, foreword, chaps. 4–6.

14. The literary critic Eric Santner describes this version of a distinctively Jewish ethic as one in which "the very opposition between 'neighbor' and 'stranger' begins to lose its force." According to Santner, "my *answerability to my-neighbor-with-an-unconscious*" who is thus "a *stranger* not only to me but also to him- or herself" (*On the Psychotheology of Everyday Life*, p. 9; see also pp. 23, 82).

15. For a defense of this formulation, see Richard Rorty, "Human Rights, Rationality, and Sentimentality," p. 128.

16. See, e.g., Melanie Klein, "Love, Guilt, and Reparation," in Klein *Love, Guilt, and Reparation and Other Works, 1921–1945*, The Writings of Melanie Klein, vol. 1 (New York: Delacorte Press/S. Lawrence, 1975); Klein, "Mourning and Its Relation to Manic-Depressive States"; Klein, "Notes on Some Schizoid Mechanisms; Hinshelwood, *Dictionary*, entry 10.

17. D. W. Winnicott, "The Use of an Object and Relating through Identifications," in Winnicott, *Playing and Reality* (London: Tavistock, 1980), p. 90.

18. Ibid., p. 94.

19. Jan Abram, *The Language of Winnicott: A Dictionary and Guide to Understand His Work*, ed. Harry. Karnac (Northvale, N.J.: Aronson, 1997). Abram goes on to quote Winnicott: "Here it is the destructive drive that creates the quality of externality. . . . There is no anger in the destruction of the object . . . though there could be said to be joy in the object's survival" ("The Use of an Object," p. 93).

20. Winnicott formulates the difference between ethical separation and projective identification as follows: "Projective mechanisms assist in the act of *noticing what is there*, but they are not the *reason why the object is there*. In my opinion this is a departure from theory which tends to a conception of external reality only in terms of the individual's projective mechanisms" ("The Use of an Object," p. 90).

21. Winnicott, "The Manic Defense," pp. 130–36.

22. D. W. Winnicott, "Aggression in Relation to Emotional Development," in Winnicott, *Through Pediatrics to Psycho-Analysis* (New York: Brunner/Mazel, 1992), p. 217.

23. "Projection" and "Projective Identification," in Laplanche and Pontalis, *The Language of Psychoanalysis*. In his own subsequent work, Laplanche makes a further distinction: first, projective identification can refer to a direction outward of one's own aggression toward the other, which is consequently reexperienced as though it were the other's aggression against oneself; second, projective identification can refer to "deflection" of unacceptable self-destructive impulses that are reexperienced in the form of hatred of the other—a defense mechanism that Laplanche believes to be primary. Jean Laplanche and Serge Leclaire, *The Ego and the Id: A Volume of Laplanche's Problematiques*, trans. Luke Thurston and Lindsey Watson (New York: Other, 1999), pp. 209–11.

24. This is nowhere more apparent than in the evident link between the techniques of European colonialism and the occurrence of "an Auschwitz" in the heart of "civilized" Europe. See, e.g., Adam Hochschild, *King Leopold's Ghost: A Story of Greed, Terror, and Heroism in Colonial Africa* (Boston: Houghton Mifflin, 1998); Lindqvist, *Exterminate All the Brutes*; Césaire, *Discourse on Colonialism*.

25. The imperative is not "Enjoy yourself!" because the self is what can neither enjoy nor be enjoyed. See Brown, *Love's Body*. Cf. the Spinozist account of "freedom of mind" in Hampshire, *Spinoza and Spinozism*.

26. Alenka Zupančič, "When Surplus Enjoyment Meets Surplus Value," in Zupančič, *Jacques Lacan and the Other Side of Psychoanalysis: Reflections on Seminar XVII*, ed. Justin Clemens and Russell Grigg (Durham: Duke University Press, 2006); Zupančič, *Ethics of the Real: Kant, Lacan* (London: Verso, 2000); Jacques Lacan, *My Teaching*, trans. David Macey (London: Verso, 2009).

27. For a discussion of consciousness as a loss of intimacy with our inner animality (a way of being in the world "like water in water"), see Georges Bataille, *Theory of Religion*, trans. Robert Hurley (New York: Zone, 1989). Cf. Brown, *Life Against Death*, pt 1.

28. Emmanuel Lévinas, "Responsibility for the Other" in Lévinas, *Ethics and Infinity:*

Conversations with Philippe Nemo, trans. Richard A. Cohen (Pittsburgh: Duquesne University Press, 1985), p. 99.

29. "The ego is a substitution" (Lévinas, "Substitution," in *Otherwise Than Being*, p. 127). References in the text above are to this work.

30. Earlier in this chapter, and more obscurely, he says: "I have not done anything and I have always been under accusation—persecuted. . . . I am, answering for everything and everyone. . . . Responsibility . . . is responsibility . . . for what the ego has not wished . . . What can it be but a substitution of me for the others? . . . In this substitution . . . identity is inverted . . . the self is absolved of itself. Is this freedom? It is a different freedom from that of an initiative. Through substitution for others, the oneself escapes relations" (pp. 114–15).

31. For the contrast between sacrifice (the expiation of sin) and martyrdom, see Girard's *I See Satan Fall Like Lightning* and *The Scapegoat*. Girard's view is discussed more extensively below.

32. Badiou, *Ethics*, p. 58. Page references in the paragraphs that follow refer to this text.

33. "Who cannot see that this ethics which rests on the misery of the world hides, behind its victim-Man, the good-Man, the white-Man? Since the barbarity of the situation is considered only in terms of 'human rights'—whereas in fact we are always dealing with a political situation. . . . Every intervention in the name of civilization *requires* an initial contempt for the situation as a whole, including its victims. And this is why the reign of 'ethics' coincides, after decades of courageous critiques of colonialism and imperialism, with today's sordid self-satisfaction in the 'West,' with the insistent argument according to which the misery of the Third World is the result of its own incompetence, its own inanity—in short, of its *subhumanity*" (p. 13).

34. Žižek, *The Ticklish Subject*, p. 135.

35. This standpoint, which Badiou calls the "Ethics of Politics," opposes Lévinas's search for an "Ethics of Ethics." See Alain Badiou, "Politics as a Truth Procedure," in Badiou, *Metapolitics*, trans. Jason Barker (London: Verso, 2005).

36. Badiou, *Being and Event*, trans. Oliver Feltham (London: Continuum, 2005), Meditations 4–5, 7–9, 16–18, 20–23. Cf. Alain Badiou, *Logics of Worlds: Being and Event II*, trans. Alberto Toscano (London: Continuum, 2009), bks. 2, 5.

37. Badiou, *Being and Event*, Meditations 4–5, 7.

38. Badiou places his thought as an endpoint to twentieth-century post-Marxism, and his task (in the spirit of Hegelian hindsight) as extracting the philosophical kernel of Marxist-Leninism (and the Communist Party representing it) that had seized French philosophy from Sartre and Merleau-Ponty through Deleuze. Alain Badiou, "The Adventure of French Philosophy," *New Left Review* 35 (2005); Badiou, "A Speculative Disquisition on the Concept of Democracy," in *Metapolitics*, trans. Jason Barker (London: Verso, 2005), pp. xxxi–xxxviii. For a flavor of the party-inflected debates evoked by Badiou's ethic of fidelity, see Maurice Merleau-Ponty, *Humanism and Terror: An Essay on the Communist Problem* (Boston: Beacon, 1969); Jean-Paul Sartre, "Merleau-Ponty *Vivant*," in *The Debate Between Sartre and Merleau-Ponty*, ed. Jon Stewart (Evanston: Northwestern University Press, 1998).

39. Badiou, *Ethics*, p. 67.

40. Badiou readily concedes that investing some moment in the past with the ethical

status of a "truth event" is not formally decidable as either true or false. The occurrence of such an event *depends*, according to Badiou, on a faithful subject's retroactive decision to "nominate" it as such (the French Revolution, May '68, etc.), and to conform future thought about the past to the universal "truth" that follows from that name.

41. For discussion of this point, see Slavoj Žižek, "Afterword: Lenin's Choice," in Žižek, *Revolution at the Gates: Žižek on Lenin (the 1917 Writings)* (London: Verso, 2002), e.g., p. 177.

42. See, e.g., Isaac Deutscher, *The Prophet Armed: Trotsky, 1879–1921* (New York: Oxford University Press, 1954). For Badiou, keeping faith with the Party must now appear as self-deception or outright dishonesty if *what* French *marxisant* intellectuals professed to believe was a set of historical predictions, based on a Marxist-Leninist analysis that now seems to have been wildly implausible. This phenomenon is described in Tony Judt, *Past Imperfect: French Intellectuals, 1944–1956* (Berkeley: University of California Press, 1992).

43. The idea that a Marxist philosopher could *decide* to believe what he *knows* to be false would be a betrayal of the ethical virtue that philosopher Bernard Williams calls "truthfulness" in one's assertions. For an ethical objection to political fidelity in this sense, see Bernard A. O. Williams, "Deciding to Believe," in Willliams, *Problems of the Self: Philosophical Papers 1956–1972* (Cambridge: Cambridge University Press, 1973); Williams, *Truth and Truthfulness: An Essay in Genealogy* (Princeton: Princeton University Press, 2002); Williams, "Truth, Politics, and Self-Deception," in *In the Beginning Was the Deed: Realism and Moralism in Political Argument*, ed. Geoffrey Hawthorn (Princeton: Princeton University Press, 2005).

44. Badiou, *Being and Event*, Meditations 8–9; Badiou, "Politics as a Truth Procedure."

45. The most serious arguments Badiou gives for the existence of "truths" are not ethical but, rather, mathematical—based on how set theory represents the null set ("what there is not") within the ontological set ("what there is"). Stated trivially, Badiou's point is that the mathematical truth of Incompleteness (the theorem that every set contains the null set as a member) is good news for revolution. Why? Because every "situation" can be formalized as a set in which something "counts" as *not* counting ("inexistent"). If the "truth" of a situation is that which its logic renders inexistent (incapable of appearance), then its evanescent, and impossible, appearance is a breakthrough of something with a higher degree of reality than the situation itself. This suggests that what was not possible within the situation is also not *im*possible precisely because its actual appearance would *change everything*.

46. "Truth exists as an exception to what there is. . . . There isn't only what there is. And 'truths' is the (philosophical) name of what thus comes to interpolate itself in the continuity of the 'there is'. . . . Yes, there are only bodies and languages. . . . But in another sense . . . 'There is what there is not.'" (Badiou, "Democratic Materialism and the Materialist Dialectic," p. 22; see also Badiou, *Logics of Worlds*, pp. 1–9).

47. Badiou, *Logics of Worlds*, pp. 363–80 ("Simple Becoming and Real Change").

48. Cf. Badiou's discussion of "non-Boolean algebras." Badiou, *Logics of Worlds*, pp. 187–88, 571–73, 437, 581–82.

49. Badiou thus rejects the commonsense dismissal of revolutionary perseverance by

reminding us that, as a matter of mathematical ontology, you do not have to believe that revolution is possible to believe that it is not *im*possible. Demonstrating truths of this kind is all that is required of philosophy by politics, according to Badiou, and all that such a philosophy can offer. Badiou, "Truth: Forcing and the Unnameable," in Alain Badiou, *Conditions*, trans. Steven Corcoran (London: Continuum, 2008).

50. Alain Badiou and Bruno Bosteels, "Can Change Be Thought? A Dialogue with Alain Badiou," in *Alain Badiou: Philosophy and Its Conditions*, ed. Gabriel Riera (Albany: State University of New York Press, 2005), pp. 243, 247. See also Alain Badiou, "Philosophy and Mathematics," in Badiou, *Conditions*.

51. Badiou's counter to the Hegelian view of philosophy as afterthought is "that the major problem for the philosopher is to arrive early enough. . . . It is truly a race against time" (p. 254). The event in a situation is not its culmination (the realization of inherent possibilities) but the beginning of something *new*.

52. Simon Critchley, *Infinitely Demanding: Ethics of Commitment, Politics of Resistance* (London: Verso, 2007), chaps. 2–3, esp. pp. 42–49.

53. Lévinas claims that our responsibility *for* God comes before His existence and derives, rather, from His absolute alterity. Such a view denies that God's existence is of ethical importance; what matters in Lévinas's atheology is *not being God*.

54. This implication of Badiou's theory is drawn out in Slavoj Žižek, "Neighbors and Other Monsters: A Plea for Ethical Violence," in *The Neighbor: Three Inquiries in Political Theology*, ed. Slavoj Žižek, Eric L. Santner, and Kenneth Reinhard, Religion and Postmodernism series (Chicago: University of Chicago Press, 2005); and Žižek "A Plea for Ethical Violence," *Umbr(a)* (2004).

55. "If there exists an event, its belonging to the situation of its site is undecidable from the standpoint of the situation itself" (Badiou, *Being and Event*, p. 181). See also pp. 508, 524–25 (on "Forcing" and "Undecidability"); and Alain Badiou, "Eight Theses on the Universal," in Alain Badiou, *Theoretical Writings*, ed. Ray Brassier and Alberto Toscano, trans. Ray Brassier and Alberto Toscano (London: Continuum, 2004), esp. p. 150.

56. Badiou further acknowledges that once this "operation" takes place, the originary site of the event becomes superfluous for new truths to emerge (*Being and Event*, pp. 238–39).

57. His argument is further undermined by a failure to explain the functional distinction between what could not have been an "event" even though it happened (for example, Christ's death on the Cross) and what must have been an event for believers even if it did not happen (for example, Christ's Resurrection). Badiou's point about the subjective meaning of death is, of course, partially correct under any definition insofar as one's death is not an event in one's life. There is no good reason, however, why my own intense suffering, or my exposure to the suffering or mass murder of others, may not be ethically transformative of my life or that of witnesses in the purely operational sense that a Badiouian event would be. For elaboration of this point with respect to Badiou's earlier work, see Robert Meister, "'Never Again:' The Ethics of the Neighbor and the Logic of Genocide," *Postmodern Culture* 15, no. 2 (2005).

58. See Lemkin, *Axis Rule in Occupied Europe*; and Power, "*A Problem from Hell*," chaps. 1–4.

59. Alain Badiou, *The Century*, trans. Alberto Toscano (Cambridge, Mass.: Polity, 2007), pp. 1–3. Page citations that follow are to this text.

60. Peter Hallward, "Order and Event: On Badiou's *Logics of Worlds*," *New Left Review* 53 (2008).

61. Badiou, *Logics of Worlds*, bk. 5; Badiou and Bosteels, "Can Change Be Thought?"

62. Badiou, *Logics of Worlds*, pp. 63–65.

63. Ibid., bk. 1, secs. 5–6.

64. Badiou's transhuman "body" is different insofar as it "avers itself capable of producing effects that exceed the bodies-languages system (and [insofar as] such effects are called truths)" (ibid., p. 45). He goes on to say that "truths are required to appear bodily [*en-corps*] and do so over again [*encore*] (p. 46). . . . The subject is what fixes in the body the secret of the effects it produces. . . . [A militant/faithful] subject is ultimately nothing more than a local agent of truth (p. 47). The appearing of the subject, which is its logic, is the fundamental stake of . . . *Logics of Worlds*. . . . This comes down to saying that we are speaking here, under the name of 'subject,' of the forms of formalism. . . . What is difficult is not the subject but the body (pp. 49–50).

    What does Badiou mean by a "formalism"? Subjectivation consists, he says, of four "formal operations" performed by an "event" on a body. His four formal "operators" are the "bar" (of subordination), "consequence," "erasure" and "negation." bk. 1, pp. 599–600.

65. Badiou's *faithful* subject "engenders the broadening of the present . . . The work of this fidelity is the new present that welcomes, point by point, the new truth" (*Logics of Worlds*, bk. 1, secs. 2, 5–8).

66. Ibid., bk. 1, secs. 3, 5–8.

67. Those attracted to such obscurantism include "veterans of lost wars, failed artists, intellectuals perverted by bitterness, dried-up matrons, illiterate muscle-bound youths, shopkeepers ruined by Capital, desperate unemployed workers, rancid couples, bachelor informants, academicians envious of the success of poets, atrabilious professors, xenophobes of all stripes, Mafiosi greedy for decorations, vicious priests and cuckolded husbands" (ibid., p. 61). The *obscure* subject, according to Badiou, seeks erasure, not of the evental trace but of the new present produced by faithful subjects. As a third type of subjective relation to a truth event "obscurantism" invokes the "full and pure" existence of "a transcendent Body," such as a "City, God, [and] Race" that whatever was emancipatory behind the spectacle of its being overcome. The collective body produced by "occultation" is imaginary (in the Lacanian sense) rather than being either symbolic or real—one example is the spectacular crucifixion of rebels along the Appian Way shown in the movie *Spartacus*; another is Hitler's Nuremberg Rally, shown in *The Triumph of the Will*. Both occultation and reaction are, according to Badiou, inaugurated, by the work of the faithful subject that they, respectively, deny and hide (ibid., pp. 58–78).

68. "We now have at our disposal three distinct degrees of change," according to Ba-

diou. These are the "modification" (which is "ontologically neutral"); the "fact" (which is "ontologically weak"); and the "singularity"—the existence (appearance) of which has "maximal" intensity. An "event" is a *strong singularity* (p. 372, cf. p. 374). "A singularity is . . . a being the thought of which cannot be reduced to that of its worldly context" (p. 357).

69. We might ask, for example, why Hiroshima—and the consequent thinkability of the previously impossible destruction of humanity—is not the most revolutionary "truth event" of the twentieth century. Within Badiou's framework, Hiroshima might be seen as the historical site for a new possibility—nuclear annihilation—that changed everything. (Tyler Corelitz called my attention to this question.) See Van Dijk, "Final Time and the End of Time."

70. "The only thing of which one can be guilty is having given ground relative to one's desire." Jacques Lacan, *The Ethics of Psychoanalysis, 1959–1960*, ed. Jacques-Alain Miller, trans. Dennis Porter, Seminar of Jacques Lacan, bk. 7 (New York: Norton, 1988), p. 319.

71. "And do not be conformed to this world, but be transformed by the renewal of your mind" (Rom. 12:2).

72. Thomas S. Kuhn, *The Structure of Scientific Revolutions* (Chicago: University of Chicago Press, 1962).

73. Alain Badiou, *Saint Paul: The Foundation of Universalism*, trans. Ray Brassier (Stanford: Stanford University Press, 2003), p. 91. Parenthetical page references that follow are to this text

74. "How is the idea of judgment, of justice, finally rendered, connected to that of perseverance, to that of the imperative 'You must go on'? If perseverance is privileged, one obtains a subjective figure that is entirely disinterested, except for its being a coworker for a truth" (ibid., p. 94).

75. "Paul's preaching includes no masochistic propaganda extolling the virtues of suffering, no pathos of the crown of thorns, flagellations, oozing blood, or the gall-soaked sponged. . . . What constitutes the event in Christ is exclusively the Resurrection" (ibid., p. 68).

76. Badiou, *Logics of Worlds*, p. 62.

77. In defending Paul, Badiou says, "It is inappropriate to make distributive justice the referent for hope. . . . The subjective dimension named 'hope' is the ordeal that has been overcome, not that in the name of which it has been overcome" (ibid., p. 95).

78. Benjamin, "Paralipomena to 'on the Concept of History,'" p. 402.

79. Benjamin, "On the Concept of History," p. 395. He later quotes Turgot in saying that "politics is obliged to foresee the present." (Benjamin, "'Paralipomena to 'On the Concept of History,'" p. 405.)

80. "Paralipomena to 'On the Concept of History,'" p. 401.

81. "The only historian capable of fanning the spark of hope in the past is the one who is firmly convinced that *even the dead* will not be safe from the enemy if he is victorious. And this enemy has never ceased to be victorious" (Benjamin, "On the Concept of History," p. 391).

82. Ibid., p. 394.

83. Benjamin, "Paralipomena to 'On the Concept of History,'" p. 407. The phrase "sum-

mary justice" is quoted from Kafka. Cf. Žižek, *The Ticklish Subject*, pp. 145–51. (Žižek sees Badiou's version of messianic politics as continuous with that of Benjamin.) See also Agamben, *The Time That Remains*, pp. 35–42.

84. For an exemplary defense of class-consciousness as counterhistory and counterculture, see E. P. Thompson, *The Making of the English Working Class* (Harmondsworth: Penguin, 1968).

85. Badiou, *Logics of Worlds*, p. 50.

86. Badiou, *The Century*, pp. 174–76.

87. Badiou, *Logics of Worlds*, p. 511.

88. Ibid., pp. 2–3.

89. Badiou sees contemporary political Islam as "simply one of the subjectivated names of today's obscurantism." It is, he says, "absolutely contemporary" and "exists for the purpose of occulting the post-socialist present and countering the fragmentary attempts through which emancipation is being reinvented by means of a full tradition or Law"—a "new manipulation of religion" that "gives fictional shape to the atemporal filling of the abolished present." As an occultation of radical thought, Islamism is not a remnant of traditional religious culture, but, rather, "absolutely contemporaneous, both to the faithful subjects that produce the present of political experimentation, and to the reactive subjects . . . [who deny] that ruptures are necessary in order to invent a humanity worthy of the name" (*Logics of Worlds*, p. 59).

Badiou's near embrace of the term "Islamofascism"—for him a form of antileftism—embarrasses his English translator, Alberto Toscano, who notes that this concept "has recently allowed members of the so-called left [e.g., Christopher Hitchens] to sign up to the propaganda wing of the 'war on terror' as if they were joining the International Brigades" (pp. 30–31). Toscano points out, however, that "if we leave aside the not exactly representative figure of Bin Laden, with his anarchoid propaganda of the deed and kitsch fantasies of the caliphate, the relation between Islamism and emancipatory politics appears far more ambiguous," and he would like Badiou to have recognized some versions of Islamism, such as that of Shar'iati, that represent an "autochthonous universalism" that is post-imperialist and post-capitalist (p. 32). See Alberto Toscano, "The Bourgeois and the Islamist; or, the Other Subjects of Politics," *Cosmos and History: The Journal of Natural and Social Philosophy* 2, no. 1–2 (2006): 27–28. Toscano does not, however, discuss Badiou's favorable comment on the Islamic philosophies expounded by Henry Corbin and his student, Christian Jambet. (Cf. *Logics of Worlds*, p. 544; and my conclusion in this volume.)

90. Alain Badiou, *Pocket Pantheon: Figures of Postwar Philosophy*, trans. David Macey (London: Verso, 2009), p. x.

91. Hallward, *Badiou: A Subject to Truth*, pp. 257, 264.

92. See Žižek, "A Plea for Ethical Violence."

93. Daniel Bensaïd, "Alain Badiou and the Miracle of the Event," in *Think Again: Alain Badiou and the Future of Philosophy*, ed. Peter Hallward (London: Continuum, 2004).

94. Talal Asad, "Thinking About Agency and Pain," in *Formations of the Secular: Christianity, Islam, Modernity* (Stanford: Stanford University Press, 2003), p. 92.

95. See Parfit, *Reasons and Persons*, pp. 165–67, and, more generally, chaps. 8, 12–13.

96. Parfit sees in Buddhism the absence of a time bias because it is morally indifferent to whether suffering occurs in the past or in the future (see, pp. 273, 280, 502–3).

97. See, e.g., Gregory Vlastos, *Socrates, Ironist and Moral Philosopher* (Ithaca: Cornell University Press, 1991), pp. 200–35.

98. "Trauma (Psychical)," in Laplanche and Pontalis, *The Language of Psychoanalysis*, pp. 467–69. Freud elaborates this point as follows: "A danger-situation is a recognized, remembered, expected situation of helplessness. Anxiety is the original reaction to helplessness in the trauma and is reproduced later on in the danger-situation as a signal for help. The ego, which experience[s?] the trauma passively, now repeats it actively in a weakened version, in the hope of being able itself to direct its course. . . . But what is of decisive importance is the first displacement of the anxiety-reaction from its origin in the situation of helplessness to an expectation of that situation. . . . The reason why there seems to be a specially close connection between anxiety and neurosis is that the ego defends itself against an instinctual danger with the help of the anxiety-reaction just as it does against an external real danger. . . . The external (real) danger must have managed to become internalized if it is to be significant for the ego. It must have been recognized as related to some situation of helplessness that has been experienced" (Freud, "Inhibitions, Symptoms, and Anxiety," pp. 166–68).

99. "In . . . the traumatic situation, in which the subject is helpless, external and internal dangers, real dangers and instinctual demands converge" (ibid., p. 168).

100. Thomas á Kempis, *The Imitation of Christ in Four Books*, trans. Joseph N. Tylenda (New York: Vintage, 1998).

101. For an account of the classical genre of spiritual biography in which the Gospels were written, see Moses Hadas and Morton Smith, *Heroes and Gods; Spiritual Biographies in Antiquity* (New York: Harper and Row, 1965); cf. Daniel Boyarin, *Dying for God: Martyrdom and the Making of Christianity and Judaism* (Stanford: Stanford University Press, 1999).

102. I adapt this formulation from Emile Benveniste, "Tense in the French Verb," in *Problems in General Linguistics*, trans. Mary Elizabeth Meek, (Coral Gables, Fla.: University of Miami Press, 1971), pp. 206–7; cf., Lang, *The Future of the Holocaust*, chaps. 2, 9–11, introduction and afterword.

103. Novick, *The Holocaust in American Life*, pp. 240–41.

104. Timothy W. Ryback, "Forgiveness: Annals of Religion," *New Yorker*, February 6, 2006. I owe this reference to Rei Terada.

105. The position of "compassionate witness" is thus both a substitute for depression and a refusal of stoicism on the part of onlookers who might otherwise be considered beneficiaries of the disasters befalling others. Until the nineteenth century the morally appropriate response of an onlooker to disaster was thought to be stoic rather than sentimental (and ultimately compassionate). See Hans Blumenberg, *Shipwreck with Spectator: Paradigm of a Metaphor for Existence*, trans. Steven Rendall (Cambridge: MIT Press, 1997).

106. Recognizing the exceptional character of 1933–45 *as* the Holocaust now occupies the role once played by the "state of emergency" in Carl Schmitt's contemporaneous

description of that time. See, e.g., Carl Schmitt, *Four Articles, 1931–1938*, trans. Simona Draghici (Washington, D.C.: Plutarch, 1999).

107. See Koselleck, *The Practice of Conceptual History*, chaps. 5–7; *Futures Past*, chap. 14.

108. For a history of the gradual adoption of the word "Holocaust," see Novick, *The Holocaust in American Life*, pp. 133–34, and pt. 4. See also Lang, *The Future of the Holocaust*, chap. 5; Norman G. Finkelstein, *The Holocaust Industry: Reflection on the Exploitation of Jewish Suffering* (London: Verso, 2000), chap. 1.

109. The trauma that the "culture of Holocaust "remembrance" inflicts on witnesses is also the topic of Jean-François Lyotard's various works on the erasure of "the jews." For Lyotard, the newly hyphenated religion of Judaeo-Christianity survives the Holocaust by both literally and figuratively *crossing out* the space that separated Judaism and Christianity before World War II. See Jean-François Lyotard, "'the jews,'" in *Heidegger and "'the jews,'"* trans. Andreas Michel and Mark S. Roberts (Minneapolis: University of Minnesota Press, 1990); Jean-François Lyotard and Eberhard Gruber, *The Hyphen: Between Judaism and Christianity*, trans. Pascale-Anne Brault and Michael Naas (Atlantic Highlands, N.J.: Humanity, 1999).

Judaeo-Christianity is, according to Lyotard, a new, more humanistic, religion that consists of being against atrocity itself. When faced with another Auschwitz, "One will say, It was a great massacre, how horrible! Of course there have been others . . . Finally, one will appeal to human rights, one cries out 'never again' and that's it! It is taken care of. Humanism takes care of this adjustment because it is of the order of secondary repression. One cannot form an idea of a human being as a value unless one projects one's misery to the outside as caused by causes that one only needs to get down to transforming." Jean-François Lyotard, *The Differend: Phrases in Dispute*, trans. Georges Van Den Abbeele (Minneapolis.: University of Minnesota Press, 1988), pp. 26–27.

110. Agamben, *Homo Sacer*, p. 114.

111. Lyotard puts the difference well: "Anxiety, unconscious affect does not give rise to tragedy. 'The jews' are not tragic. They are not heroes. (It is not by chance that Wiesel's 'testimony' is that of a child.) . . . One cannot wage war on the Jews; one makes them disappear, annihilates them. They are not the enemy in the ordinary senses. They have no claim to the spotlight of confrontation on stage. The 'politics' of extermination cannot be represented on the political scene. It must be forgotten. . . . So that no one can remember it as anything but the end put to a nightmare. . . . Now that the elimination of the forgotten must be forgotten . . . testifies to the fact that the forgotten is always there . . . and its forgetting is forgotten" (Lyotard, "'the jews,'" pp. 28–29).

For a range of provocative views on the narrative emplotment of "Holocaust," see the essays by Hayden White, Perry Anderson, Amos Funkenstein, and Martin Jay in Saul Friedländer, ed., *Probing the Limits of Representation: Nazism and the "Final Solution"* (Cambridge: Harvard University Press, 1992).

112. Substituting the trauma of witnesses for that of victims is nowhere more apparent than in Samantha Power's much acclaimed indictment of late-twentieth-century failures to enforce the 1948 Genocide Convention (*"A Problem from Hell"*). Her argument is that we, the "world community," should reproach ourselves each time

that we witness another Holocaust that was not stopped. The very terms of this self-reproach—that what truly horrifies *us* is that genocide has been *repeated*—makes it harder to think politically about the atrocity that is being inflicted on its present victims for the first and only time.

113. See Mark Mazower, "The G-Word," *London Review of Books* 23, no. 3 (2001).

114. Elie Wiesel, *Night*, trans. Stella Rodway (New York: Bantam, 1989), p. 62.

115. "Never shall I forget that nocturnal silence which deprives me, for all eternity, of the desire to live. Never shall I forget those moments which murder my God" (ibid., p. 32). In effect, Wiesel sacrifices his belief in God so that a godforsaken world can renounce cruelty as something to "never again" condone in God's name.

116. The theologian Jürgen Moltmann, for example, describes the "Crucified God" as having been "godforsaken" (forsaken by himself) in order to identify with victims whose suffering he would otherwise seem to have willed. The mid-twentieth-century "Theology of the Cross" calls upon man to bear witness both to God's physical mortification and to the innocence of his victimhood. Jürgen Moltmann, *The Crucified God: The Cross of Christ as the Foundation and Criticism of Christian Theology* (Minneapolis: Fortress, 1993), pp. 145–59; see also chaps. 6–8, esp. pp. 273–74.

117. The victimary "scapegoat," whether human or animal, was "marked for persecution" by stereotypical signs of deviancy (such as a limp, speech impediment, or unusual circumstance of birth) which corresponded to some sign of divine disfavor found in myth. Girard, *The Scapegoat*, chap. 2 ("Stereotypes of Persecution"); Girard, Oughourlian, and Lefort, *Things Hidden*, bk. 1, chaps. 1, 5.

118. What occurs next, according to Girard, is a double substitution that aims to trick the gods. First, the ills of the collectivity are blamed on the scapegoat for whose deviancy the community as a whole now suffers divine retribution; next, however, the community's sacrifice of the scapegoat (through death or expulsion) is seen to expiate the collective sins for which divine retribution has *really* occurred. Because the scapegoat is considered to be guilty of the sins of all, Girard says, "only one must die" to cleanse the group. His interpretation attributes to the community an incoherent set of beliefs: it first deceives itself into believing that the victim is guilty, and then deceives the gods into treating the victim's transgression as a surrogate for its own. Girard points out that "the sacrificial process requires a certain degree of misunderstanding," which the "theological basis of the sacrifice" fosters: "It is the god who supposedly demands the victims; he alone, in principle, who savors the smoke from the altars and requisitions the slaughtered flesh. It is to appease his anger that the slaughter goes on and the victims multiply" (*Violence and the Sacred*, p. 7).

119. "The Psalms are the revelation of what is going on. . . . The narrator is a scapegoat in the making who, for the first time in history, is permitted to denounce his own fate. . . . Therefore, it is a reversal of myth completely in the same way that the Gospels will be. And the victim at the center is complaining about being lynched. . . . I define the Psalms as the first text in which the victim speaks instead of the mob." René Girard, "The Bloody Skin of the Victim," in *The New Visibility of Religion Studies in Religion and Cultural Hermeneutics*, ed. Michael Hoelzl and Graham Ward (London: Continuum, 2008), pp. 61–62.

120. As a professing Christian, Girard believes that the Crucifixion is the sacrifice that

will eventually bring human sacrifice to an end by redefining victimization as persecution of the innocent. Cf. Nietzsche: "From now on there is the ridiculous problem of 'how *could* God have let this happen!' The unbalanced reason of the small community found a horribly absurd answer: . . . the sacrifice of the *innocent* for the sins of the guilty! What gruesome paganism!" Friedrich Wilhelm Nietzsche, *The Anti-Christ, Ecce Homo, Twilight of the Idols, and Other Writings*, ed. Aaron Ridley, trans. Judith Norman (New York: Cambridge University Press, 2005), p. 37.

121. Note that the original Greek meaning of "martyrdom" is "bearing witness." By bearing witness to innocent suffering, onlookers refuse the role of beneficiaries and become themselves potential martyrs to a faith. On the etymology of witnessing, see Emile Benveniste, *Indo-European Language and Society*, trans. Elizabeth Palmer (Coral Gables: University of Miami Press, 1973), esp. pp. 396ff. and 525ff.

122. René Girard, "The Myth of Oedipus, the Truth of Joseph," in *Oedipus Unbound: Selected Writings on Rivalry and Desire*, ed. Mark Rogin Anspach (Stanford: Stanford University Press, 2004), p. 110.

123. Girard, *Things Hidden*, bk. 2; Girard, *I See Satan Fall Like Lightning*. Cf. Freud, "Moses and Monotheism," pp. 86–89, 135; Taubes, *The Political Theology of Paul*, pp. 80–95.

124. "Holocaust" may not, however, have been the best word to use for Wiesel's purpose: the original Greek was the Septuagint's rendering of the Hebrew term for a religious offering of flesh that is slaughtered and burnt to atone for human sin—an instance of victimage in Girard's sense. Giorgio Agamben thus criticizes Wiesel's use of "Holocaust" because it wrongly implies that death in the camps had sacrificial meaning for the victims themselves. "The wish to lend a sacrificial aura to the extermination of the Jew by means of the term 'Holocaust' was, from this perspective, an irresponsible historiographical blindness. The Jew living under Nazism is . . . a flagrant case of a *homo sacer* in the sense of a life that may be killed but not sacrificed. . . . The truth—which is difficult for victims to face but which we must have the courage not to cover with sacrificial veils—is that the Jews were exterminated not in a mad and giant holocaust but exactly as Hitler had announced, 'as lice,' which is to say, as bare life" (*Homo Sacer*, p. 114).

125. Elie Wiesel, *Against Silence: The Voice and Vision of Elie Wiesel*, ed. Irving Abrahamson, 3 vols. (New York: Holocaust Library, 1985).

126. Derrida, *Sovereignties*, pp. 76–80.

127. "The penetration of God's new word meant that the entire structure of the body was affected. Ezekiel's visions of God were literally hair-raising (Ezek. 8:3)." Philip Rieff, *Charisma: The Gift of Grace, and How It Has Been Taken Away from Us* (New York: Pantheon, 2007), p. 41.

128. Ibid.

129. Geoffrey Hartman, "Holocaust and Hope," in *Catastrophe and Meaning: The Holocaust and the Twentieth Century*, ed. Moishe Postone and Eric L. Santner (Chicago: University of Chicago Press, 2003), p. 233.

130. Jacques Derrida, *Sovereignties in Question: The Poetics of Paul Celan*, ed. Thomas Dutoit and Outi Pasanen (New York: Fordham University Press, 2005), pp. 72–73; Lyotard, *The Differend*, pp. 3–5.

131. Dying for God (sometimes by burning) figured heavily in the development of both Judaism and Christianity within the Roman Empire. Such martyrdoms were violent public murders believed to result in "posthumous recognition and immediate reward." Glenn W. Bowersock, *Martyrdom and Rome* (Cambridge: Cambridge University Press, 1995). According to the Talmudic scholar Daniel Boyarin, three conventional elements were added to the Roman "discourse of martyrdom" by Jews and Christians (such as Akiva and Justin) who died for God: (1) a public declaration of religious belief ("Hear O Israel" or "I am a Christian"); (2) the martyr's choice of violent death over adherence to untruth; and (3) the introduction of visionary and masochistic elements that Boyarin calls "erotic" (*Dying for God*, pp. 21, 93–96).

132. Trials and truth commission are important instruments of such disavowal. See chapter 2 and 9 in this volume.

133. Sianne Ngai, "Irritation," in Ngai, *Ugly Feelings* (Cambridge: Harvard University Press, 2005).

134. For reflections on these concepts in Lacanian and Kleinian psychoanalysis, see Adam Phillips, "Superiorities," in *Equals* (New York: Basic Books, 2002).

135. Moltmann, *The Crucified God*.

136. Cf. the discussion above of Lévinas's distinction between useless suffering and suffering that is morally valuable. The latter type of suffering is what Christians have called the "Imitation of Christ." See Thomas á Kempis, *The Imitation of Christ*.

137. Although Badiou would reject this use of his terminology, the Holocaust can be considered "a truth effect" left by the Germany of 1933–45 (the era between its "before" and "after").

138. For an elaboration of this view, see Scarry, *The Body in Pain*; Elaine Scarry, "The Difficulty of Imagining Other Persons," in *Human Rights in Political Transitions: Gettysburg to Bosnia*, ed. Carla Hesse and Robert Post (New York: Zone, 1999).

139. On mimetic rivalry, see Girard citations earlier in this chapter's notes; on the ontological limits of ethical reciprocity, see John Milbank, "The Soul of Reciprocity Part One: Reciprocity Refused," *Modern Theology* 17, no. 3 (2001); and Milbank, "The Soul of Reciprocity Part Two: Reciprocity Granted," *Modern Theology* 17, no. 4 (2001).

140. A mark of faith, Tertullian is supposed to have said, is that one believes *because* it is absurd. Charles Norris Cochrane, *Christianity and Classical Culture* (New York: Oxford University Press, 1957), pp. 222–24. Tertullian's *De Carne Christi* 5.4 does not, however, say "Credo quia absurdum" but, rather, "Credibile est, quia ineptum est." For a rationalist/empiricist interpretation, see Robert D. Sider, "Credo Quia Absurdum?" in *Classical World* 73, no. 7 (1980).

141. I adapt this formulation of Christian doctrine from Marcel Gauchet, *The Disenchantment of the World: A Political History of Religion*, trans. Oscar Burge (Princeton: Princeton University Press, 1997), pp. 118–20.

6. Still the Jewish Question?

1. "Today's anti-Semitism . . . is no longer the old ethnic anti-Semitism; its focus is displaced from the Jews as an ethnic group to the State of Israel . . . In this way, today's

anti-Semitism can present itself as anti–anti-Semitism, full of solidarity with the victims of the Holocaust; the reproach is just that, in our era of the . . . fluidization of all traditions, the Jews wanted to built [*sic*] their own clearly delimited Nation-State." Slavoj Žižek, *The Parallax View*, Short Circuits (Cambridge: MIT Press, 2006), pp. 253–54. Žižek is here characterizing the position of Jean-Claude Milner. See also Norman G. Finkelstein, *Beyond Chutzpah: On the Misuse of Anti-Semitism and the Abuse of History* (Berkeley: University of California Press, 2005), pt. 1.

2. In *witnessing* anti-Semitism, anti–anti-Semitism no longer *feels* its own annoyance with the Jew whose role is now to constantly call attention to it.

3. "The Jews are now doing to others what was done to them, so they no longer have any right to complain about the Holocaust. And there actually is a paradox in that the very Jews who preach the universal 'melting pot' are all the more insistent on their own ethnic identity . . . [and] an unfortunate tendency among some Zionists to transform *shoah* into *holocaust*, the sacrificial offering which guarantees the Jewish special status" (Žižek, *The Parallax View*, p. 259).

4. Taubes, *The Political Theology of Paul*, pt. 1.

5. Lyotard and Gruber, *The Hyphen*, p. 22.

6. Donald H. Akenson, *Surpassing Wonder: The Invention of the Bible and the Talmuds* (Chicago: University of Chicago Press, 2001), chaps. 5–7, 12.

7. Israel Knohl, *The Messiah Before Jesus: The Suffering Servant of the Dead Sea Scrolls*, trans. David Maisel (Berkeley: University of California Press, 2000); Gershom Scholem, *The Messianic Idea in Judaism and Other Essays on Jewish Spirituality*, trans. Michael A. Meyer and Hillel Halkin (New York: Schocken, 1971).

8. Agamben, *The Time That Remains*, Day Three; Rémi Brague, "The Political Theology of Paul: Schmitt, Benjamin, Nietzsche, and Freud," *Critique* 56, no. 634 (2000).

9. Balibar, "Racism and Nationalism;" cf. Lyotard, *The Differend*. For further discussion of the relation of nationhood to ethnicization and racialization, see chapter 4 in this volume. See also Etiénne Balibar, "The Nation Form: History and Ideology," in Balibar and Wallerstein, *Race, Nation, Class*, pp. 86–106; and Shlomo Sand, *The Invention of the Jewish People* (London: Verso, 2009).

10. For a detailed discussion of this phenomenon, see Arjun Appadurai, *Fear of Small Numbers: An Essay on the Geography of Anger* (Durham: Duke University Press, 2006). The literary critic George Steiner points out that the persistence of Judaism is a theological "scandal" for Pauline Christianity, which holds that Jewish recalcitrance has delayed Christ's Second Coming (Rom. 11). George Steiner, "Zion," in *My Unwritten Books* (London: Weidenfeld and Nicholson, 2008), pp. 111–14.

11. Daniel Boyarin notes that "much of the horror inflicted on the Jews in this century can be traced at least partially to theologically informed . . . contempt for the Jews . . . based on a particular reading of Paul's texts." Daniel Boyarin, *A Radical Jew: Paul and the Politics of Identity* (Berkeley: University of California Press, 1997), p. 40; see, generally, chaps. 2, 6). The radical critique of Paul is forcefully expressed in Rosemary Radford Ruether, *Faith and Fratricide: The Theological Roots of Anti-Semitism* (New York: Seabury, 1974). For a historical study of the development of anti-Judaism from Paul's letters, see John G. Gager, *The Origins of Anti-Semitism: Attitudes Toward Judaism in Pagan and Christian Antiquity* (New York: Oxford Univer-

sity Press, 1983); Jeremy Cohen, *Living Letters of the Law: Ideas of the Jew in Medieval Christianity* (Berkeley: University of California Press, 1999).

12. And so my critique of anti–anti-Semitism opens me to the charge of anti-Semitism. I believe, however, that it is, rather, a protest against the latent anti-Semitism that underlies Human Rights Discourse—and an expression of concern about the blatant anti-Semitism that Human Rights Discourse provokes.

13. Jacques Derrida, *Rogues: Two Essays on Reason*, trans. Pascale-Anne Brault and Michaell Nass (Stanford: Stanford University Press, 2005), pt. 1.

14. Although European Christendom often viewed Islamic power as a threat, it never seriously entertained the possibility that Islam itself is *post*-Christian in the sense that it believed Judaism to be *pre*-Christian. See, e.g., Mastnak, *Crusading Peace*; Anidjar, *The Jew, the Arab*; Jacob Taubes, "The Price of Messianism," *Journal of Jewish Studies* 33, no. 1–2 (1982).

15. See, e.g., Moltmann, *The Crucified God*. "The exemplary figure," according to Žižek, "is Elie Wiesel, who sees . . . attempts to 'desanctify' or 'demystify' the Holocaust [as] a subtle form of anti-Semitism" (Žižek, *The Parallax View*, p. 259).

16. Pierre Bourdieu and Loïc Wacquant, "On the Cunning of Imperial Reason," *Theory, Culture and Society* 16, no. 1 (1999): 41.

17. Among the many accounts of the centrality of the Jewish Question to the Enlightenment's prehistory, see Jonathan Israel, *Enlightenment Contested: Philosophy, Modernity, and the Emancipation of Man, 1670–1752* (Oxford: Oxford University Press, 2006); *Radical Enlightenment: Philosophy and the Making of Modernity, 1650–1750* (Oxford: Oxford University Press, 2001). Israel stresses the clandestine circulation of banned Spinozist texts as the source of Enlightenment materialism on the Jewish side. For a recent intellectual history of toleration, see Perez Zagorin, *How the Idea of Religious Toleration Came to the West* (Princeton: Princeton University Press, 2003). On the Jewish side, see Jacob Katz, *Out of the Ghetto: The Social Background of Jewish Emancipation, 1770–1870* (Cambridge: Harvard University Press, 1973); Pierre Birnbaum and Ira Katznelson, *Paths of Emancipation: Jews, States, and Citizenship* (Princeton: Princeton University Press, 1995). See also David Vital, *A People Apart: The Jews in Europe, 1789–1939* (Oxford: Oxford University Press, 1999). For analysis of the role that the Jewish Question has played in the specifically Western genealogy of toleration, see Wendy Brown, *Regulating Aversion: Tolerance in the Age of Identity and Empire* (Princeton: Princeton University Press, 2006).

18. Hunt, *Inventing Human Rights*, p. 150.

19. Thus the advocates of emancipation, "complain about the oppression under which the Jews lived in the Christian world . . . [and] make that oppression appear even more hateful by asserting that it also was the cause of . . . [Jewish] characteristics. . . . To defend the Jews in this manner is really to do them a great disservice . . . Of the Jews it will at least be admitted that they suffered for their Law, for their way of life, and for their nationality, that they were martyrs. They were thus themselves to blame for the oppression they suffered . . . A nothing cannot be oppressed. . . . Therefore, give the Jews the honor that . . . the hardening of their character caused by this oppression was their own fault." Bruno Bauer, "The Jewish Problem," in *The*

Young Hegelians, an Anthology, ed. Lawrence S. Stepelevich (Cambridge: Cambridge University Press, 1983), pp. 189–90.

20. Ibid. pp. 188–89.

21. There were two immediate responses to Bauer's argument. The first, by Karl Marx, pointed out that states with universal citizenship based on human rights had not abolished religious identities but rather strengthened them as the political organization of civil society. A second response, by the socialist Moses Hess, noted the threat to Jews that was implicit in Bauer's conception of secularized universal citizenship, which Hess otherwise supported. Hess concluded that Jews could successfully secularize themselves and move on to socialism only if they modeled themselves on other nations and had their own state. Karl Marx, "On the Jewish Question," in *Karl Marx, Frederick Engels: Collected Works*, Vols. 3, 5, trans. Richard Dixon et al. (New York: International, 1975–2001). Cf. Moses Hess, *The Holy History of Mankind and Other Writings*, ed. Shlomo Avineri, trans. Shlomo Avineri (Cambridge: Cambridge University Press, 2004), pt. 2; *The Revival of Israel: Rome and Jerusalem, the Last Nationalist Question*, ed. Melvin I. Urofsky, trans. Meyer Waxman (Lincoln: University of Nebraska Press, 1995); Isaiah Berlin, "The Life and Opinions of Moses Hess," in *Against the Current: Essays in the History of Ideas*, ed. Henry Hardy (New York: Viking, 1980).

22. Ritchie Robertson, *The German-Jewish Dialogue: An Anthology of Literary Texts, 1749–1993* (Oxford: Oxford University Press, 1999), p. xvii; see also Walter Laqueur, *The Changing Face of Antisemitism: From Ancient Times to the Present Day* (New York: Oxford University Press, 2006), chap. 6.

23. Cohen, the founder of German neo-Kantian philosophy, argued that the empirical foundation of the state's sovereignty must be interpreted *as if it* were normatively just—a view, he claimed, that Jews had always taken of God. This ethical conception of divine sovereignty, originating in Judaism, was given a philosophical foundation by Germany's greatest philosopher, Immanuel Kant, who demonstrated that an ethical and rational universe was a precondition for all human thought. See, e.g., Hermann Cohen, "The Transcendent God: Archetype of Morality," in *Reason and Hope; Selections from the Jewish Writings of Hermann Cohen*, trans. Eva Jospe (New York: Norton, 1971). A thoughtful discussion of Cohen's view and influence can be found in Amos Funkenstein, "Franz Rosenzweig and the End of German Jewish-Philosophy," in Funkenstein, *Perceptions of Jewish History* (Berkeley: University of California Press, 1993), pp. 270–90.

24. Cohen's theo-cosmological idea was developed by a younger Jewish neo-Kantian, Hans Kelsen, into the doctrine that positive law was grounded in a basic norm—a *grundnorm*—that makes it morally imperative to obey. Law's very existence is thus an exception to the distinction between fact and norm in modern Kantian jurisprudence in much the way that direct revelation of God's word had been an exception to the distinction between the natural and the holy in ancient Jewish law. Kelsen understood the *Rechtstaat* as providing a legal remedy for every wrong and was thus legitimated by a rule of law. In the *Rechtstaat,* law would thus legitimate the coercive state power, while also being enforced by that power. In this respect, the rule of law

was both normative and positive, a conclusion reached by Kantian transcendental deduction for the "is/ought" distinction that the rest of legal science assumes. Hans Kelsen, *Introduction to the Problems of Legal Theory: A Translation of the First Edition of the Reine Rechtslehre or Pure Theory of Law*, trans. Bonnie Litschewski Paulson and Stanley L. Paulson (Oxford: Clarendon, 1992). For a discussion of Kelsen's Kantian method, as influenced by Cohen, see Stanley L. Paulson's introduction to this work, pp. xvii–xlii, and Appendix I. Paulson notes, however, that Kelsen modified his early Kantianism after immigrating to the U.S. Cf. Kelsen, *Pure Theory of Law*, trans. Max Knight (Berkeley: University of California Press, 1967).

25. Comparing German Judaism to Alexandrian Judaism, which had flourished in the land of Egypt where Jews were once held in bondage, Cohen saw his own synthesis of Judaism and Kant as a successor to the work of Philo of Alexandria, who had merged Jewish and Platonic thought (Cohen, *Religion of Reason*, chap. 13 ["The Idea of the Messiah and Mankind"]).

26. "This is the meaning we German Jews see in the destruction of the Jewish state (already predicted by the prophets) . . . and the reason why "Jeremiah admonishes the exiled Jews to concern themselves exclusively with the welfare of the country in which they live." Hermann Cohen, "The German and the Jewish Ethos II," in *Reason and Hope; Selections from the Jewish Writings of Hermann Cohen*, trans. Eva Jospe (New York: Norton, 1971), p. 185.

27. "Religion and Zionism," in Cohen, *Reason and Hope*, pp. 167–68. For a similar argument in favor of *recognizing* Israel, cf. Lévinas, "The Nations and the Presence of Israel." Although Lévinas here avoids mention of Cohen's pre-Holocaust text, he likewise sees the scattering of Jews among the nations as necessary for their inclusion in the messianic age: "What caused Israel to be scattered among the peoples of the earth? It is the reconciliation he wanted to bring about with them" (p. 102). His Talmudic exegeses of Psalms 117 and 78 (and Deuteronomy 23:8) thus elaborate the rabbinic tradition, recovered by Cohen, in which God's plan is fulfilled through the acceptance of the Jewish settler (or wanderer) in a future Egypt (the house of bondage), Rome (a villainous version of the "distant West"), America (a later, better Rome), and Ethiopia (Cush). (Lévinas describes Cush as "a country of black men with nothing to reproach itself for, and nothing to congratulate itself for. . . . A purely geographical reference" [p. 99]).

28. Jacques Derrida, "Interpretations at War: Kant, the Jew, the German," in Derrida, *Acts of Religion*, ed. Gil Anidjar (New York: Routledge, 2002); Hermann Cohen, *Deutschtum und Judentum* (Giessen: Töpelmann, 1916).

29. He continued, "Dear brethren in America: you will now understand me when I say that any Jew of the West must, in addition to being loyal to his political fatherland, acknowledge, revere and love Germany. For Germany is the motherland of his renewed religious spirit . . . and thus the center of all that has molded him culturally." Hermann Cohen, "Thou Shalt Not Go About as a Slanderer," in Cohen, *Reason and Hope*, p. 193.

30. "The classical concept of our religion points toward the future of mankind. . . . We . . . see the entire historical world as the future abode of our religion" (Cohen, "Religion and Zionism," p. 170).

31. See Derrida, "Interpretations at War," pp. 168ff. and the passages from *Deutschtum und Judentum* quoted therein.

32. See Yuri Slezkine, *The Jewish Century* (Princeton: Princeton University Press, 2004), chap. 3 ("Babel's First Love").

33. Ibid., chap. 4 ("Hodl's Choice"). The word "Zion" (as in Zionism) is a metonym referring to Mt. Zion in Jerusalem, Jerusalem itself (the biblical capital of Judea), the lands once ruled by Jews in the Bible, and the biblical prophecy that after being scattered among the nations some Jews would return to rule those lands. For many Orthodox Jews this messianic promise would only be fulfilled at the "end of days." As a political doctrine, Zionism was the view that it should be fulfilled here and now. For secular Zionists (such as Herzl) this meant not waiting for the Messiah; for those religious Jews who embraced Zionism, however, the establishment of an Israel that ruled a large part (after 1948) or all of (after 1967) the divinely promised land would come to signify the beginning of Judaism's messianic age.

34. Herf, *The Jewish Enemy*, chap. 6. Adolf Eichmann would later testify that the Nazi leadership for a time held mildly pro-Zionist attitudes, favoring expulsion and resettlement before moving on to genocide. Both the Jewish Agency in Palestine and the Jewish Councils in Nazi-ruled Europe had cooperated with Eichmann et al. in selecting those Jews who would be allowed to immigrate to a future Jewish state. As late as 1940, "Eichmann could see himself as the future Governor of a Jewish State," perhaps in Madagascar. See Arendt, *Eichmann in Jerusalem*, pp. 58ff; Höhne, *The Order of the Death's Head*, pp. 351–52. The development of SS thinking about the "Jewish Question" and its "Final Solution" is described in chapters 24 and 25.

35. Robertson, *The "Jewish Question" in German Literature*; Elon, *The Pity of It All*, chaps. 2–4.

36. On a contemporaneous and partially successful effort to create a pure "Aryanized" version of Hindi out of Hindustani, see Alok Rai, *Hindi Nationalism* (Hyderabad: Orient Longman, 2001). A major effect of this movement was to reverse a conception of Indianness based on a Hindu-Muslim synthesis. On further parallels between the Jewish Question and the Muslim Question in pre-Independence India, see Aamir Mufti, *Enlightenment in the Colony: The Jewish Question and the Crisis of Postcolonial Culture* (Princeton: Princeton University Press, 2007).

37. For a discussion of the Scholem family's internal divisions over World War I, see Elon, *The Pity of It All*, chaps. 9–10.

38. To explain his messiah's apostasy, Nathan of Gaza (who served Sabbatianism as both its John the Baptist and Saint Paul) argued that the true Jewish Messiah must commit the worst possible sin—abandoning Judaism—in order to revoke the law and release all Jews from sin. Nathan thus deliberately echoed, and outbid, the argument Paul had used to explain why *his* Messiah, who was free of sin, nevertheless had to experience death in order to save the world from death. Scholem's thesis that any Jewish messiah must *also* be a Jewish apostate had repercussions for the debate between the Zionists and assimilationists. Gershom Scholem, "Sabbatianism and Mystical Heresy," in *Major Trends in Jewish Mysticism*, trans. George Lichtheim (New York: Schocken, 1995), esp. pp. 302–4. See also Scholem, *The Messianic Idea in Judaism*, p. 26 (and, generally, pp., 1–36, 78–141, 167–75).

39. In Scholem's view this form of messianism was also the religious foundation for the Jewish Enlightenment (*Haskalah*) and the liberalization of German Judaism in the eighteenth and nineteenth centuries that began with Moses Mendelssohn and (implicitly) culminated in Hermann Cohen. Scholem's genealogy suggests that the Jewish assimilation is a continuation of Sabbatianism, which allows an apostate to believe he is most Jewish when he appears least so, but which also opens him to the charge that Marranos have always faced—that the real Jews are those who hide their Judaism through assimilation or outright conversion (ibid., esp. pp. 302–4). See also Scholem, *The Messianic Idea in Judaism*, p. 26 (and, generally, pp. 1–36, 78–141, 167–75).

40. Scholem, who emigrated to Palestine for this reason, vigilantly opposed messianic tendencies in the Jewish Authority.

41. Émigré Weimar intellectuals made major efforts to rescue the promise of German-Jewish *kultur* from the retrospective taint of Nazism. See Anson Rabinbach, "'The Abyss That Opened Up Before Us': Thinking about Auschwitz and Modernity," in *Catastrophe and Meaning: The Holocaust and the Twentieth Century*, ed. Moishe Postone and Eric L. Santner (Chicago: University of Chicago Press, 2003). I am grateful to Bernie Richter for calling my attention to this article.

    Some anti-Zionist Israelis, such as Avraham Burg (a former speaker of the Knesset), express nostalgia for Weimar Judaism and compare many present-day Israelis to those Weimar Germans who were receptive to Hitler. According to the journalist David Remnick, "Burg warns that an increasingly large and ardent sector of Israeli society disdains political democracy. He describes the country in its current state as Holocaust-obsessed, militaristic, xenophobic, and, like Germany in the nineteen-thirties, vulnerable to an extremist minority" (David Remnick, "The Apostate: A Zionist Politician Loses Faith in the Future [Letter from Jerusalem]"). Burg endorses the diasporic flight of Israelis to the EU, which he describes in quasi-biblical terms as a fulfillment of Weimar's messianic promise. Avraham Burg, *The Holocaust Is Over, We Must Rise from Its Ashes* (New York: Palgrave Macmillan, 2008).

42. The Holocaust that began two decades after Cohen wrote was a possibility unthinkable to the generation of German Jews who had heeded his argument. We know in retrospect that Heidegger succeeded to Cohen's Chair in Marburg, that Hitler's *Mein Kampf* exploited Cohen's self-congratulatory claim by blaming Germany's wartime defeat on the Jews, and that Cohen's widow eventually died in the Theresienstadt concentration camp.

43. Anti-Semitism as a concept is different from the Christian project of converting the Jews; it is, rather, a continuation of the Spanish Inquisition's doctrine of *limpieza de sangre*, which was directed at the *conversos*. Gil Anidjar, "Lines of Blood: *Limpieza De Sangre* as Political Theology," in *Blood in History and Blood Histories*, ed. Mariacarla Gadebusch Bondio (Florence: Sismel: Edizione del Galluzzo, 2005).

44. See Mamdani, *Citizen and Subject*.

45. See Baruch Kimmerling, *The Invention and Decline of Israeliness: State, Society, and the Military* (Berkeley: University of California Press, 2001), esp. chap. 6.

46. James Edward Young, *The Texture of Memory: Holocaust Memorials and Meaning* (New Haven: Yale University Press, 1993), p. 214.

47. Paul Berman, "The Other and the Almost the Same," *New Yorker*, February 12 1994.

48. Amos Oz, "The Tender Among You and the Very Delicate," in Oz, *In the Land of Israel*, trans. Maurie Goldberg-Bartura (San Diego: Harcourt Brace Jovanovich, 1983). Oz's title is taken from Deuteronomy 28. The phrase "Judeo-Nazi" was given currency in 1981 by the Israeli scientist Yeshayahu Leibowitz (interview, *Jerusalem Post*, September 11, 1981).

49. Frank Stern, *The Whitewashing of the Yellow Badge*; Stern, "German-Jewish Relations in the Postwar Period."

50. See Sander L. Gilman, *Jews in Today's German Culture* (Bloomington: Indiana University Press, 1995).

51. See Ruth Ellen Gruber, *Virtually Jewish: Reinventing Jewish Culture in Europe* (Berkeley: University of California Press, 2002). Gruber begins with a discussion of *The City Without Jews*, a science fiction novel of the 1920s describing "what happens to Vienna, and Austria as a whole," if all Jews were to be cleared out on orders of the state (pp. 3–5).

52. "Philosophy from Kant to Wittgenstein; music from Haydn to Schoenberg; science from Alexander von Humboldt to Einstein, and literature from Goethe to Kafka. . . . The second name in each instance illustrates the crucial role of German Jews in German culture." (One might add that Kant, Humboldt, and Goethe had been staunch champions of Jewish emancipation and that Wittgenstein, Schoenberg, Einstein, and Kafka were fully emancipated, and Germanized, Jews.) See Ritchie Robertson, ed., *The German-Jewish Dialogue*, p. vii.

53. Paul Berman, "The Passion of Joschka Fischer," in Berman, *Power and the Idealists; or, The Passion of Joschka Fischer and Its Aftermath* (Brooklyn: Soft Skull, 2005), esp. pt. 2 (pp. 35–64). Parenthetical page citations that follow in the text are to this work.

54. "It was a fear that Nazism had grown into a modern system of industrial rationality geared to irrational goals . . . a Nazism declaiming in a language of democracy and freedom that had no more human content than the old-fashioned rhetoric of *Lebensraum* and Aryan superiority" (ibid., p. 37).

55. The explanation of this change, according to Berman, was Israel's victory in the 1967 War and the consequent pro-Palestinian shift of the Third World liberationist movement and their communist backers. The assumption that Communists are always on the side of the oppressed was, for Berman, a fatal illusion that soon metamorphosed into something immediately recognizable as a continuation of German anti-Semitism itself: that "the Palestinian movement turned out not to be an anti-fascist or anti-Nazi cause at all. It turned out to be an anti-Jewish cause" (ibid., p. 56).

56. The most "radical" elements of the German New Left thus supported "the terrorist actions at Munich in 1972 and at Entebbe in 1976" (60), and refused to denounce other instances in which people were murdered (or threatened) simply for being Jewish. "To have set out to fight Nazism in its sundry modern democratic disguises only to have ended up in a modern left-wing disguise, Nazi-like! That was absurd" (ibid., pp. 60–61.

57. Sa'adah, *Germany's Second Chance*. Parenthetical page citations that follow are to this text.

58. "Institutional strategies are by definition demobilizing . . . and they are especially demobilizing if, as is true of . . . Nazi Germany . . . the dictatorship was a mobilizing regime that managed to spread its nets of complicity across broad sections of the population: . . . institutional strategies choose to demobilize the population rather than try to remobilize it on democratic terms" (ibid., p. 57).

59. Sa'adah further notes that the institutional approach, when it succeeds, includes too many of the perpetrators of the old regime as functionaries in the new. For these reasons it is morally disappointing, especially to those who actively struggled against the old regime and who want to place a positive value on heroic resistance while condemning passivity.

61. Ibid., pp. 13–14, 55–58, 277–81. "Cultural strategies," Sa'adah writes, "tend to put victims first; institutional strategies tend to put order first" (p. 5). A similar distinction is made by Michel Feher, who describes the approach that Sa'adah calls "cultural" as a moral repudiation of the old regime. See Michel Feher, "Terms of Reconciliation," in *Human Rights in Political Transitions: Gettysburg to Bosnia*, ed. Carla Hesse and Robert Post (New York: Zone, 1999).

61. They must, for example, take every opportunity to resignify the Nazi swastika as an emblem of evil, along with all other symbols of "Aryanism." Any reappearance of such symbols must be seized as an occasion to comment upon how different they look now than they looked then (Sa'adah, *Germany's Second Chance*, pp. 3–6, 62–90, 144–76). Only such articulated changes in personal consciousness and public culture would make a morally complicit population resistant to the return of evil institutions (ibid., pp. 1–9).

62. Hermann Cohen's position during World War I had been to advocate the patriotic conformity of German Jews. In this respect the Germanity of Jews could have led many to conformity with Nazism had Nazis demonized another group. In the end German Jews had no choice but to be anti-Nazi. Arno J. Mayer, *Why Did the Heavens Not Darken? The "Final Solution" in History* (New York: Pantheon, 1988).

63. She concludes her book with the hope that the then unfinished TRC process would better succeed in combining the cultural and institutional approach than the German transition, which until that point had been taken as the prototype of success, and looks forward to a hybrid model of transitional justice in which "the retrospective public description of a reality that could not be openly described so long as the dictatorship lasted is supposed to serve three broad purposes: it vindicates the victims of the dictatorship (especially those who died at its hands) by restoring to light their faith and their suffering; it instructs the society that had previously succumbed to the dictatorship and willingly or unwillingly participated in its lies; and it holds a mirror up to that society in which the new image reflected is one of courage" (ibid., pp. 184–88).

64. Young, *The Texture of Memory*, pp. 21–22.

65. Ibid., p. 21.

66. For discussion of the problems faced by those who wish a similar commemoration of the victims of U.S. slavery, see James Oliver Horton and Lois E. Horton, eds., *Slavery and Public History: The Tough Stuff of American Memory* (New York: New Press, 2006).

67. For the failures of both postwar Germanys to address "The Jewish Question," see Jeffrey Herf, *Divided Memory: The Nazi Past in the Two Germanys* (Cambridge: Harvard University Press, 1997), chaps. 1, 5–9. Several commentators on the post-war period considered West Germany's inability to mourn, not only its lost Jews but also its lost leader (*Führer*) and its war dead, as the darker, depressive side of West Germany's economic miracle. See, e.g., Santner, *Stranded Objects*, chaps. 1–2; Mitscherlich and Mitscherlich, *The Inability to Mourn*; Gordon A. Craig, "An Inability to Mourn," review of *Wages of Guilt* by Ian Buruma, *New York Review of Books*, July 14, 1994.

68. The willingness of postwar Germans to regard their suffering as self-inflicted and deserved is addressed in W. G. Sebald, "Air War and Literature," in Sebald, *On the Natural History of Destruction*, trans. Anthea Bell (New York: Random House, 2003). Because of the atomic bombings of Hiroshima and Nagasaki (which, never-theless, took fewer lives than the conventional firebombing of Dresden), Japan was able to move more easily than Germany from the status of perpetrator to that of victim following World War II. See also Buruma, *The Wages of Guilt*; Dower, *Embracing Defeat*.

69. The Bitburg controversy serves as the starting point to Charles S. Maier, *The Unmasterable Past: History, Holocaust, and German National Identity* (Cambridge: Harvard University Press, 1988). See, esp. chaps. 1, 5, and epilogue.

70. Ian Murray, "Tame Day for New Boys in School of Democracy," *The Times*, October 5, 1990.

71. Serge Schmemann, "United German Parliament Assembles," *New York Times*, October 5, 1990; Deborah Seward, "Lawmakers of Unified Germany Hold First Session," *Associated Press* (1990).

72. "Their seizure of the German State, their subjugation of the German people, their terrorism and extermination of dissident elements, their planning and waging of war, their calculated and planned ruthlessness in the conduct of warfare, their de-liberate and planned criminality toward conquered peoples, all these are ends for which they acted in concert; and all these are phases of the conspiracy." "Indictment in the Major War Criminals Trials (Count I)," Yale Law School, http://avalon.law. yale.edu/imt/count1.asp (accessed January 31, 2010). Robert Jackson, "Opening Statement (Nuremberg Trials)," http://www.yale.edu/lawweb/avalon/imt/proc/11-21-45.htm (accessed January 31, 2010). See also Sa'adah, *Germany's Second Chance*, p. 157.

73. Seward, "Lawmakers."

74. Jane Kramer, "The Politics of Memory (Germany Struggles with Its Past and a Proposed Holocaust Memorial) (Letter from Germany)," *New Yorker* 71, no. 24 (1995); Kramer, *The Politics of Memory*. Her narrative implies that this form of commemo-rative identification represents for Germany the psychological equivalent of affir-mative action for the United States as described it in chapter 3 of this volume—that one must never forget to remember, whereupon one must remember to forget.

75. Burg, *The Holocaust Is Over*.

76. I owe this last suggestion to remarks by the Israeli artist and filmmaker Udi Aloni at a showing of his film, *Local Angel*. Liberal Jews, according to Aloni, regard the pres-

ence of Palestinians in Zion as a tragedy. They may believe that Palestinians who happen to be there should be treated with compassion, but, ideally, they would have preferred an Israel with no Palestinians and hence no moral problem.

77. Segev, *The Seventh Million*, pp. 512, 514.

78. Baruch Kimmerling describes the *Yishuv* as "the politically organized Jewish ethno-community in Palestine prior to sovereignty" (*Israeliness*, p. 8); see also pp. 65–67, 980–111.

79. Zionist ideology sometimes denounced the victims' conduct as "passive submission" on the part of those who had shirked the struggle to create a Jewish homeland in Palestine. Idith Zertal, *Israel's Holocaust and the Politics of Nationhood*, trans. Chaya Galai (Cambridge: Cambridge University Press, 2005), p. 26.

80. Before and during the war, Zionist leaders in Palestine worked through the Jewish Councils in Europe to select individual Jews who would be allowed by the Nazis to emigrate and on at least two occasions dealt directly with Eichmann himself (Höhne, *The Order of the Death's Head*, chaps. 13–14, esp. pp. 333–39). See also Arendt, *Eichmann in Jerusalem*, chaps. 3–5.

81. "Despite their rhetoric of lament for Diaspora Jewry, the Jews in Palestine . . . lived routinely and rather prosperously" during the years of the Jewish catastrophe. . . . [Because] Ben-Gurion considered the rescue efforts on the part of the Yishuv . . . to be hopeless . . . he avoided them" (Zertal, *Israel's Holocaust*, p. 29 and note).

82. Kimmerling, *Israeliness*, pp. 90–104, 186–205. For a comprehensive narrative of the effect of the "Judeocide" on twentieth-century Zionist thought and practice, see Arno J. Mayer, *Plowshares Into Swords: From Zionism to Israel* (London: Verso, 2008).

83. The official view of the *Yishuv* was that "dispersed Jewry [was] a dead and withered civilization . . . [to be] addressed in the past tense" (Young, *The Texture of Memory*, p. 215). "Early statists like David Ben-Gurion regarded the Holocaust as the ultimate fruit of Jewish life in exile; as such it represented a diaspora that deserved not only to be destroyed, but also forgotten. On the other hand, the state also recognized its perverse debt to the Holocaust; it had, after all, seemed to prove the Zionist dictum that without a state and the power to defend themselves, Jews in exile would always be vulnerable to just this kind of destruction" (p. 211).

84. "From the conquest by Joshua son of Nun," he said, "there never was such a formidable event." The other critical events in Jewish history, according to Ben-Gurion, were the Exodus from Egypt and the assembly at Mount Sinai. The Holocaust was not the equal of any of them, nor was any other event relating to the Jews of the Diaspora" (Zertal, *Israel's Holocaust*, p. 93).

85. Kimmerling, *Israeliness*, p. 94. There was thus a "time in Israel [extending through the early 1950s] when the bare mention of the Shoah, or the fact that one had survived it, might have been met with surly contempt. It was a time when survivors were still being shamed into silence by those claiming the foresight to have left Europe before the onslaught" (Young, *The Texture of Memory*, p. 270).

86. Jacqueline Rose points out that "Zionism was from the beginning riven by internal critique": that committed prewar Zionists, including theologian Martin Buber, scholar Judah L. Magnes, and political theorist Hannah Arendt, abhorred the con-

cept of Jewish sovereignty in Palestine and regarded its triumph following the Holocaust as catastrophic for the humanistic view of Judaism that had led them to emigrate. Their line of Zionist thought, which extends from Ahad Ha'am (who favored
cultural, but not political, autonomy for Jews in Palestine) to present-day Israeli
dissidents such as Michel Warschawski, grounds the legitimacy of Jewish settlement
in Israel not on divine promise but on the quality of relations between Jews and
their Palestinian neighbors. Jacqueline Rose, *The Question of Zion* (Princeton:
Princeton University Press, 2005), p. 13.

Rose endorses what is now a century-long tradition of antistatist dissent within
Zionism, suggesting that, "paradoxically, Jewish nationalism will come into being
only if—as a dream of seizing the land, ruling the Arabs, economically prospering—
it abolishes itself" (pp. i, 92). A representative sample of this tradition can be found in
Adam Shatz, *Prophets Outcast: A Century of Dissident Jewish Writing About Zionism
and Israel* (New York: Nation, 2004). See also Tom Segev, Roane Carey, and Jonathan
Shainin, eds., *The Other Israel: Voices of Refusal and Dissent* (New York: New Press,
2002); Michel Warschawski, *Toward an Open Tomb: The Crisis of Israeli Society*,
trans. Peter Drucker (New York: Monthly Review Press, 2004); and Warschawski,
On the Border, trans. Levi Laub (Cambridge: South End, 2005).

87.   The specific problem with statist Zionism, according to Rose, is the messianic al-
chemy of religious and political symbolism that surrounds the claim to Jewish sovereignty over a biblically defined territory, a point first raised by Gershom Scholem.
Her first chapter, "'The Apocalyptic Sting,'" takes its title from Gershom Scholem's
phrase in a 1926 letter to his friend, Franz Rosenzweig, about the replacement of
Yiddish (the language of their exile in Europe) by Hebrew (the holy language of the
Bible) within the everyday life of the *Yishuv*: "Much more sinister than the Arab
problem," wrote Scholem, "is the actualization of Hebrew. . . . Many believe that the
language has been secularized, and the apocalyptic thorn [sting] has been pulled
out. But . . . the secularization of the language is only . . . a phrase! . . . We have no
right to conjure up the old names day by day without calling forth their hidden
power. We speak in . . . a ghastly language: the names go in circles in our sentences,
one plays with them in publications and newspapers. . . . Each word which is not
newly created, but taken from the good old treasures is ready to burst. The moment
when the power stored in the language unfolds again . . . will place this holy tradition as a decisive token before our people. God will not remain silent in the language in which He has affirmed our life a thousand times and more. . . . Those who
called the Hebrew language back to life did not believe in this trial yet they created
it." Udi Aloni, *Local Angel: Theological-Political Fragments* (London: ICA, 2004), pp.
40–41. Scholem's 1926 letter to Rosenzweig is discussed in Aviezer Ravitzky, *Messianism, Zionism, and Jewish Religious Radicalism*, trans. Michael Swirsky and Jonathan Chipman (Chicago: University of Chicago Press, 1996), pp. 3–6.

88.   "I argue that justifying our national existence by claiming that we are the instruments for realizing God's messianic redemptive plan is both unnecessary and morally and politically dangerous. . . . Whether our national renaissance benefits humanity as a whole should be left for other nations to decide. . . . If there is any
positive meaning to the mission of the Jews . . . it is in showing how the universal

theme of Creation can correct the vitality of the particular without destroying it." David Hartman, "Halakhic Sobriety and Inclusiveness," in Hartman, *Israelis and the Jewish Tradition: An Ancient People Debating Its Future* (New Haven: Yale University Press, 2000), pp. 144–45.

Among these, Hartman specifically mentions the messianic Rabbi Abraham Kook, who argued for Israel's divine right to the land, and the *halakhic* Rabbi Joseph Soloveitchik who argued, rather, that Israel needed to exist so that Jews could finally distinguish their common fate as a persecuted people from their spiritual aspirations as individuals. For a political-theological critique of Kahane's *Kach* movement (based on Kook), see Leon Wieseltier, "The Demons of the Jews," *New Republic*, November 11, 1985.

89. Zertal, *Israel's Holocaust*, p. 4; see also p. 2. Parenthetical page numbers that follow are to this text.

90. My point above is about Ben-Gurion's shift in attitude. It must also be said, however, the Israel owes its success to the partial failure of the Holocaust: "More Holocaust would have equaled less chance for the Jewish State." A further point is that the Holocaust deprived Israel of millions of potential citizens and that postwar support for Israel by the Allies was driven more by opportunism than by guilt. Yehuda Bauer, "From the Holocaust to the State of Israel," in Bauer, *Rethinking the Holocaust* (New Haven: Yale University Press, 2001), pp. 258–60.

91. Lévinas himself would later describe the relation of post-1967 Israel to the Warsaw Ghetto in the following words: "Zionism, which is taken to be an imperialist endeavor . . . still carries pain and dereliction, in its depths. . . . In one respect, this struggle will always have been the struggle of the Warsaw ghetto up in arms but with no ground to which to withdraw, where each step taken in retreat counts and costs, as if it were everything. . . . Will one go so far in criticizing Israeli mistrust as to take the weapons from the defenders of the last ramparts?" (Lévinas, "Politics After," p. 187).

92. The affair was a highly publicized "clandestine" immigration to Palestine by a shipload of concentration camp survivors, "orchestrated to coincide with the presence in Palestine of the UNSCOP [United Nations Special Committee on Palestine]." Zertal goes on to say that, "as soon as the committee submitted its recommendations for the partition of Palestine on 1 September 1947, the *Exodus* refugees were 'removed from the agenda' at one fell swoop" and sent back to Germany (Zertal, *Israel's Holocaust*, pp. 50–51. (Zertal gives a fuller account of the *Exodus* episode in her *From Catastrophe to Power: Holocaust Survivors and the Emergence of Israel*, trans. Chaim Watzman and Gila Svirsky (Berkeley: University of California Press, 1998), chaps. 2, 4, 7).

Leon Uris's best-selling 1958 novel, *Exodus*, is a fictional account of a Warsaw Ghetto freedom fighter ("Dov Landau") who attempts to enter Palestine on the *Exodus* and becomes a hero of the 1948 Israeli War against the Arabs. This book played an important role in the construction of "Israel's Holocaust" for its supporters in the U.S. Leon Uris, *Exodus* (Garden City, N.Y.: Doubleday, 1958).

93. Zertal considers these initial trials little more than "purges" within Israel's refugee

populations—an illustration of Israel's "role inversion in prosecuting Holocaust victims for whom the Jewish state was supposed to have been a haven" (p. 67).

94. Zertal elaborates as follows: "All those brought to trial under that law (with one minor exception) until the 1961 trial of Adolf Eichmann, were Jewish citizens, new immigrants, miserable, pathetic individuals, themselves Holocaust survivors who, on arrival in Israel, were recognized, sometimes by chance, by other survivors and reported to the police. Israel's legal system had tried them according to the same law under which it would prosecute a decade later senior SS officer Adolf Eichmann, a Nazi who had played a central role in the logistic system of the German dictatorship, the main transporter of European Jewry to the death camps. . . . Although the court proceedings against Eichmann turned into an unprecedented, national educational project and a milestone in Holocaust discourse in western culture . . . as far as Israel was concerned the Eichmann trial was a quasi-miracle . . . unimaginable at the time the Nazis and Nazi Collaborators (Punishment) Law was passed" (pp. 66–67).

95. In response to a reporter's question, Ben-Gurion elaborated: "I was referring to Egypt where many Nazis are hiding. When I hear the speeches of the Egyptian president [Nasser] on world Jewry controlling America and the West it seems to me that Hitler is talking." In a subsequent interview with the *New York Times*, Ben-Gurion said that "the Eichmann trial will help to ferret out other Nazis—for example, the connection between Nazis and some Arab rulers" (p. 98).

96. "The transference of the Holocaust situation on to the Middle East reality . . . not only created a false sense of the imminent danger of mass destruction. It also immensely distorted the image of the Holocaust. . . . The transplanting of one situation onto the other was done by massive reference to the presence of Nazi scientists and advisers in Egypt and other Arab countries, to the ongoing connections between Arab and Nazi leaders and the Nazi-like intentions and plans of the Arabs to annihilate Israel" (Zertal, *Israel's Holocaust*, p. 100). Zertal goes on to discuss the massive effort in the trial to document a connection of former Mufti of Jerusalem Haj Amin El-Husseini "to the Nazi regime in general and Eichmann . . . in particular" (pp. 100ff.).

97. "It was his finest hour. . . . Now once again, as in the first years of statehood, he was hailed as the great, historic Zionist leader" (pp. 96–97).

98. Yitzhak Laor, "Children of the State," review of *Israel's Holocaust* by Idith Zertal, *London Review of Books*, January 26, 2006.

99. For a thorough discussion of the contemporaneous impact of the trial on Israeli society, and the subsequent reaction to Hannah Arendt's *Eichmann in Jerusalem*, see Tom Segev, *The Seventh Million*, chaps. 18–20, 24.

100. For the history of Israeli monuments, see Yael Zerubavel, *Recovered Roots: Collective Memory and the Making of Israeli National Tradition* (Chicago: University of Chicago Press, 1995).

101. See James E. Young, *The Texture of Memory*, chap. 9, for an extended discussion of Yad Vashem, Israel's Holocaust Memorial. For a discussion of the identification of Israel's Middle Eastern Jews with the Holocaust, see Burg, *The Holocaust Is Over*.

The idea that "we are all Shoah survivors," Burg argues, was a way for Israel to replace the lot of the European Jews for whom it was originally intended.

102. Kimmerling, *Israeliness*, p. 113. In her most recent book Zertal documents how the settlements have conquered Israel. Idith Zertal and Akiva Eldar, *Lords of the Land: The War for Israel's Settlements in the Occupied Territories, 1967–2007* (New York: Nation, 2007); Mayer, *Plowshares Into Swords*.

Viewed in the context of Israel's immediate past, the result is no less striking: "Since June 1967, the entire area of colonial Palestine, with considerable addition, if we take into account the Syrian (Golan) Heights, has been annexed de facto by Israel." These territorial additions mean that Israel has controlled (and may control for the indefinite future) a much larger Arab population, becoming de facto "a binational Jewish-Arab state" without, however, extending the rights of citizenship to its new Arab subjects (Kimmerling, *Israeliness*, p. 79). The Israeli government was well aware of this likely consequence in 1967. See Tom Segev, *1967: Israel, the War, and the Year That Transformed the Middle East* (New York: Metropolitan, 2007).

103. Meir Kahane, *Never Again! A Program for Survival* (Los Angeles: Nash, 1971).

104. Kimmerling, *Israeliness*, pp. 107–8 n. 57.

105. Ibid., p. 130. On the political-religious characteristics of the Gush Emunim, see, generally, pp. 110–11, 123–33, 231–32.

106. Ibid., p. 37.

107. See Segev, *1967*; Zertal and Eldar, *Lords of the Land*.

108. Meir Kahane, *They Must Go* (New York: Grosset and Dunlap, 1981).

109. For an illustration of this slippery slope, see Oz, "The Tender Among You."

110. Baruch Kimmerling, *Politicide: Ariel Sharon's Wars Against the Palestinians* (London: Verso, 2003). Diaspora Jewish organizations that had been lukewarm toward Zionism before World War II came around after revelations of the Holocaust. See also Novick, *The Holocaust in American Life*, pt. 1. It is also the case, of course, that many nonreligious Zionist leaders also attached providential significance to Israel's existence, survival, and seemingly miraculous reoccupation of the entire Holy Land after the 1967 War.

111. Zertal, *Israel's Holocaust*, p. 98.

112. For a strong statement of the post-9/11 argument that Islamism is the kernel of Nazism, see Paul Berman, "The Philosopher of Islamic Terror," *New York Times Magazine*, March 23, 2003; *Terror and Liberalism* (New York: Norton, 2003), chaps. 3–5. His view is further elaborated at the end of the present chapter.

113. "The 'Victims,' once jews, became 'Jews,' 'Jew,' that is, turned into a metonymical signifier for Humanity, and—this time, in an unreachable sky—into the very point of intersection, the obligatory point at which 'Humanity' and 'Crime' meet. 'Victim' names this connection, and 'Jew' is the Victim par excellence. So, the 'jewish State' could become the 'Jewish State.'" Cécile Winter, "The Master-Signifier of the New Aryans: What Made the Word 'Jew' into an Arm Brandished against the Multitude of 'Unpronounceable Names,'" in Alain Badiou, *Polemics*, trans. Steve Corcoran (London: Verso, 2006), p. 223.

114. Berman, "The Other and the Almost the Same."

115. Terrorists do not threaten members of the Chinese diaspora when the Beijing gov-

ernment commits a serious human rights violation. But all Jews feel vulnerable when Israel does something wrong, because Israel has made itself a metaphor for the fulfillment or desecration of the Holocaust "memory."

116. See Agamben, *State of Exception*; Girard, Oughourlian, and Lefort, *Things Hidden*.

117. Charles S. Maier, "A Holocaust Like the Others? Problems of Comparative History," in Maier, *The Unmasterable Past: History, Holocaust, and German National Identity* (Cambridge: Harvard University Press, 1988).

118. For the Puritan comparison of themselves with Ancient Israelites in Canaan, see Richard Slotkin, *Regeneration through Violence: The Mythology of the American Frontier, 1600–1860* (Norman: University of Oklahoma Press, 2000), chaps. 1–4; Perry Miller, *Errand into the Wilderness* (Cambridge: Belknap Press of Harvard University Press, 1956). For a recent effort to connect American history with that of modern Israel, see Michael B. Oren, *Power, Faith, and Fantasy: America in the Middle East, 1776 to the Present* (New York: Norton, 2007).

119. Herman Melville, *White-Jacket; or, The World in a Man-of-War*, ed. Harrison Hayford, Hershel Parker, and G. Thomas Tanselle (Evanston: Northwestern University Press, 2000), p. 135.

120. Quoted in Sollors, *Beyond Ethnicity*.

121. Ibid., chap. 3., esp. pp. 59–65; on the Pauline origins of the melting pot idea, see pp. 81–91.

122. See, e.g., Mary Antin, *The Promised Land*, ed. Werner Sollors (New York: Penguin, 1997). Early-twentieth-century debates over the Jewish-American identity were central to the emergence of a race-ethnicity distinction in the social sciences. See Hattam, *In the Shadow of Race*, chaps. 1–3.

123. *Everson v. Bd. of Educ.*, 330 U.S. 1, 8-9. (1947). This was the first case to strike down a state law as violating the Establishment Clause of the First Amendment. See, Meister, "Sojourners and Survivors."

124. This term originated in Israel Zangwill's play, *The Melting Pot*, about Jewish-Christian intermarriage in early-twentieth-century America; it has come to mean, more broadly, the cultural melding of ethnics who are destined to become a single *race* defined by its originary commitment to freedom from persecution. Jewish-Americans played a central role in developing this twentieth-century *theory* that true Americans are ethnically *diverse* but racially the *same*. The American concept of "ethnics" as non-natives who are *not*-black has allowed successive immigrant groups to regard themselves as probationary whites—and led blacks themselves to adopt the label "African American" in order to embark, belatedly, on the path from ethnic difference to racial similarity that other "hyphenated" Americans have followed. Israel Zangwill, *From the Ghetto to the Melting Pot: Israel Zangwill's Jewish Plays, Three Playscripts*, ed. Edna Nahshon (Detroit: Wayne State University Press, 2006); Michael Paul Rogin, *Blackface, White Noise: Jewish Immigrants in the Hollywood Melting Pot* (Berkeley: University of California Press, 1996), pp. 6, 64–67. See, more generally, Victoria Hattam, *In the Shadow of Race: Jews, Latinos, and Immigrant Politics in the United States* (Chicago: University of Chicago Press, 2007); David R. Roediger, *Working Toward Whiteness: How America's Immigrants Became White: The Strange Journey from Ellis Island to the Suburbs* (New York: Basic Books,

2005); For the twentieth-century development of the American conception of ethnic immigrants as a single race (and differences among proponents of this conception, such as Gans and Moynihan), see Sollors, *Theories of Ethnicity*.

125. Since 9/11 American exceptionalism has been upheld (not only by Americans) as a
sign of the U.S. government's providential mission to protect and advance human
rights throughout the world. See, e.g., Michael Ignatieff, ed., *American Exceptionalism and Human Rights* (Princeton: Princeton University Press, 2005), introduction.
For a discussion of the earlier history of this doctrine, see Robert Kagan, *Dangerous
Nation: America's Place in the World from Its Earliest Days to the Dawn of the Twentieth Century* (New York: Knopf, 2006).

126. See, e.g., Lawrence J. Epstein, *The Haunted Smile: The Story of Jewish Comedians in
America* (New York: Public Affairs, 2001). Some argue more broadly that "The
American Century" in worldwide popular culture, could also be called "The Jewish
Century" because of the role that Jewish immigrants to America played in making
that culture. See, e.g., Neal Gabler, *An Empire of Their Own: How the Jews Invented
Hollywood* (New York: Crown, 1988). There is a striking parallel between such
claims about the constitutive role of Jews and Judaism in twentieth-century "Americanism" and Hermann Cohen's argument about *Deutschtum* as a Jewish-German
synthesis.

Writing in a similar vein, jazz historian Gary Giddens claims that American
Jews "practically invented the modern pop song." Thus the hugely popular mid-
century songs of Irving Berlin (a Jewish immigrant)—"White Christmas," "Easter
Parade," and "God Bless America"—contributed to the production of American
civic religion, Judeo-Christianity, that omitted any specific mention of either Christ
or the Jews, and the Great American Songbook is filled with "standards" by George
and Ira Gershwin, Richard Rodgers, Lorenz Hart, Oscar Hammerstein, Jerome
Kern, Harold Arlen, Lerner and Loewe, Frank Loesser, and so on—all of whom
wrote music now regarded as ethnically unmarked. Gary Giddins, *Visions of Jazz:
The First Century* (New York: Oxford University Press, 1998), pp. 19, 31–45.

A more nuanced version of this argument is made by the political theorist Michael Rogin, who writes that the contribution of Jews to the creation of American
mass culture in the first half of the twentieth century distinguished them from their
German-Jewish counterparts, whose main contributions were to high culture. He
attributes this phenomenon to the fact that blacks in the U.S. filled the pariah position that Jews had occupied in Europe, as well as to consequent opportunities for
immigrant groups (first Irish and then Jews) to establish their own *whiteness* by putting on blackface in order to entertain "Americans." At the very moment when Nazis denounced both jazz and capitalism as secretly "Jewish," black music, capitalism,
and the Jewish immigrant experience were being fused into a new, mid-century
conception of the "American"—not merely as a person *from* somewhere—but as
someone with a cultural mission *to* the rest of the world (Rogin, *Blackface: White
Noise*).

127. Postwar U.S. civil rights were to be modeled on the idea that secret or originary
identities were no longer to be exposed but rather to be "covered." See Kenji Yoshi-

no, *Covering: The Hidden Assault on Our Civil Rights* (New York: Random House, 2006), pt. 3.

128. "In the mid-1930s the respectable representatives of American Jewry [generally identified as the "German Jews"] were still trying to finesse the difference between Jews and all other Americans by insisting . . . that being a Jew was like being a Methodist, that is, it meant belonging to one of the many religious denominations in America. But the mass of East Europeans and their children knew that this was not a multi-religious or multi-ethnic country: it was a Jews/Gentile country. . . . [I]n their need to 'arrive' in America, Jews kept hoping . . . [to] persuade the Gentile majority of some definition of American society that would obscure this line of cleavage." Arthur Hertzberg, *The Jews in America: Four Centuries of an Uneasy Encounter: A History* (New York: Simon and Schuster, 1989), p. 253. Cf. F. O. Matthiessen, *American Renaissance: Art and Expression in the Age of Emerson and Whitman* (New York: Oxford University Press, 1968).

129. If "Jews had remade themselves to fit the American ideal," it was no less true that the American ideal itself had been remade so that "Judaism had become one of America's 'three great faiths' . . . right next to Protestantism and Catholicism." "This was astounding . . . Fewer than 5 percent [of Americans] were Jews. . . . Perhaps Americans were more ready to recognize the Jews in their midst because they were so horrified by what had happened in the Holocaust." Hasia R. Diner, *A New Promised Land: A History of Jews in America* (New York: Oxford University Press, 2003), pp. 104–5.

130. Marx's attempt to identify and universalize the forms of victimary consciousness did not, however, regard Jews as the principal victims of world history, nor did he see his own Jewish family's struggle for political emancipation in the Rhineland as a paradigm of liberation everywhere. He focused on the transformative potential of an industrial proletariat, which was being increasingly victimized, rather than that of a persecuted minority that had been gradually emancipated. See Meister, *Political Identity*. For a different view, see Isaiah Berlin, "The Life and Opinions of Moses Hess" and "Benjamin Disraeli, Karl Marx, and the Search for Identity," both in *Against the Current: Essays in the History of Ideas*, ed., Henry Hardy (New York: Viking, 1980).

131. All major histories of twentieth-century Jewry recognize that the U.S., not Israel, was the first choice of most Jews emigrating from the ghettos and *shtetls* of Eastern Europe. See, e.g., Diner, *New Promised Land*, esp. chap. 4. Writing from the Israeli side, Baruch Kimmerling notes that Palestine was "a viable and perhaps the sole option for those Jews who did not succeed in immigrating to the United States . . . [but the] vast majority preferred the option of individual (or familial) redemption and migrated to America" (Kimmerling, *Israeliness*, p. 5).

132. This question derives from Sinclair Lewis's ironically titled prewar novel, *It Can't Happen Here* (see Hertzberg, *The Jews in America*, p. 289). Lewis wrote just before the height of sympathy for Hitler's anti-Semitism in the depression-era U.S., which reached its peak in 1944 and "dropped dramatically in 1945. Never again would it rise to the level of the Great Depression and the early 1940s" (Diner, *New Promised*

Land). In twentieth-century Jewish consciousness, America is where a Holocaust has *not* happened, where Jews have achieved the level of cultural assimilation to which emancipated German Jews aspired. It is thus in America—not Germany, not Israel—that Jews are finally safe.

133. Diner, *New Promised Land*, p. 88; Novick, *The Holocaust in American Life*, chap. 3. In *The Jews in America*, Arthur Hertzberg discusses whether the Jews who "knew" should have publicly protested Franklin D. Roosevelt's decision not to bomb the railroad tracks to Auschwitz in 1944, and debate among American Jews about the extent that relief for those in occupied Europe should include trading with the Nazi enemy for Jewish lives (pp. 291–303). Cf. David S. Wyman, *The Abandonment of the Jews: America and the Holocaust, 1941–1945* (New York: Pantheon, 1984).

134. Arthur Hertzberg and Aron Hirt-Manheimer, *Jews: The Essence and Character of a People* (San Francisco: Harper, 1998), pp. 264–65.

135. Novick, *The Holocaust in American Life*, chaps. 2–3. The above parenthetical page numbers are to this text.

136. "The only thing that all American Jews shared was the knowledge that, but for the immigration of near or distant ancestors, they would have shared the fate of European Jewry. Insofar as the Holocaust became the defining Jewish experience, all Jews had their "honorary" survivorship in common. Insofar as it attained mythic status expressing truths about an enduring Jewish condition, all were united in an essential victim identity" (ibid., pp. 190–91).

137. There was, to be sure, a political problem resulting from the presence of Holocaust survivors in the Allied Displaced Persons camps of Europe. That problem, however, was a refugee question—it was not the massive deaths that occurred in Nazi concentration camps before their liberation. Although the death camps themselves posed the legal problem of determining the individual guilt of those responsible for them, the immediate political lesson learned by liberators was that civilized countries should be more open to immigration from regimes *like* Hitler's (if these could be identified before it was too late). Even among Jewish-Americans, postwar support for Israel depended heavily on the argument that it alone made a commitment to take in the vast majority of Jewish displaced persons whom no other country wanted—and that it *would have* done the right thing while there was still time (ibid., chap. 4).

138. Diner, *New Promised Land*, p. 103; Hertzberg, *The Jews in America*, p. 306.

139. "By World War II, the peak of mass immigration was forty years in the past . . . There were few fond memories of the old country, no *Fiddler on the Roof* idylls. . . . There was a gradual but steady drift from the consciousness in which one . . . would think of oneself . . . as a Jew who happens to live in America, to the consciousness in which one was an American who 'happens to be Jewish' " (Novick, *The Holocaust in American Life*, pp. 32–33).

140. Novick ascribes Jewish-American attitudes in World War II to a well-founded "revulsion against identity (and politics) based on 'blood' or tribal loyalties" that Nazism had represented in its most vicious form: The war had been won with the slogan "Americans All" (ibid., p. 34). See also Hertzberg, *The Jews in America*, chaps. 16–17.

141. See Leo Strauss, "Why We Remain Jews," in *Jewish Philosophy and the Crisis of Modernity: Essays and Lectures in Modern Jewish Thought*, ed. Kenneth Hart Green (Albany: State University of New York Press, 1997). (I owe this reference to my Jewish mother!)

142. Novick, *The Holocaust in American Life*, esp. introduction and pt. 4.

143. Ibid., p. 192. Parenthetical page references that follow are to this text.

144. See, e.g., Jimmy Carter, *Palestine: Peace Not Apartheid* (New York: Simon and Schuster, 2006).

145. Novick writes in detail about the role of the Holocaust analogy in the emergence of a black-Jewish split. At various points in his story Jews argue that slavery was *nothing* compared to what happened to the Jews, and blacks argue (stressing its brevity) that the Holocaust was *nothing* compared to the Middle Passage. Debates ensued about whether Jewish merchants were responsible for slavery, whether blacks would have willingly sent Jews to the ovens, and so forth. Moving beyond black-Jewish relations, Novick shows ways in which the Holocaust analogy was subsequently deployed in other versions of the politics of victimhood, for example, by feminists (pornography-as-holocaust), gays (who were also victims of the Holocaust), and even the Christian Right (abortion-as-Holocaust).

146. See Finkelstein, *The Holocaust Industry*, e.g., p. 27. Finkelstein's factual claims and analysis are otherwise largely consistent with Novick's. See also John J. Mearsheimer and Stephen M. Walt, *The Israel Lobby and U.S. Foreign Policy* (New York: Farrar, Straus and Giroux, 2007).

147. "In recent years questions about Israel have divided more than they have united Jews. . . . Insofar as the Holocaust became the defining Jewish experience, all Jews had their "honorary" survivorship in common" (Novick, *The Holocaust in American Life*, p. 190) Novick concludes that "as larger numbers of American Jews no longer saw the Israeli-Palestinian conflict in black-and-white terms, the Holocaust offered a substitute of greater moral clarity. Thus, "at a discussion of the central role of the Holocaust in American Jewish life . . . at the University of Chicago, a local rabbi suggested that there was nothing surprising about this fact: 'God and Israel are too controversial'" (ibid., pp. 168–69).

148. Quoting Wiesel.

149. For a deeper and fuller discussion, see Amos Funkenstein, "Theological Responses to the Holocaust," in *Perceptions of Jewish History* (Berkeley: University of California Press, 1993).

150. See Daniel Mendelsohn, *The Lost: A Search for Six of Six Million* (New York: HarperCollins, 2006).

151. Yosef Hayim Yerushalmi, *Zakhor: Jewish History and Jewish Memory* (Seattle: University of Washington Press, 1996), p. 117.

152. The result of putting "the Holocaust at the center" of Jewish identity, Novick says, "was neither foreseen nor intended" by "most of those who set the process in motion." As Novick goes on to say, "Some of those who, from the sixties on, urged that Jews "confront" the Holocaust, when many Jews seemed ashamed of it . . . were often equally dismayed when many Jews seemed proud of it" (*The Holocaust in American Life*, pp. 202–3).

153. This is the argument of Bernard Henri Lévy, *War, Evil, and the End of History* (Hoboken, N.J.: Melville House, 2004).

154. Cf. Norman G. Finkelstein, "Israel: The 'Jew Among Nations,'" in Finkelstein, *Beyond Chutzpah: On the Misuse of Anti-Semitism and the Abuse of History* (Berkeley: University of California Press, 2005).

155. Arendt, *Origins of Totalitarianism*, chap. 12 ("Totalitarianism in Power").

156. Many mid-twentieth-century progressives believed that tactics now associated with terrorism were an appropriate weapon of the weak in guerrilla struggles against colonialism and that antiterrorist activities were frequently a cover for massive violations of human rights by oppressive regimes. Now, however, terrorism itself is defined as a human rights violation, justifying international intervention on a scale that could eventually resemble the neocolonial occupation of independent states accused of aiding or condoning the new transnational barbarians.

157. To feel terror is to project onto those who hold us in their power a desire for enmity and experience our own subjectivity as the satisfaction of that desire. See, e.g., Bracher, *Lacan, Discourse, and Social Change*.

158. Matt. 5:43–44.

159. Cf. Lacan, *Ethics of Psychoanalysis*, p. 319.

160. In answering this question, Badiou distinguishes between "a subject-effect (facing 'terrorism is a 'we'. . .); an alterity-effect (this 'terrorism is the other of Civilization . . .), and finally a periodization-effect (now commences the long 'war against terrorism')." Alain Badiou, "Philosophy and the 'War against Terrorism,'" in *Infinite Thought: Truth and the Return to Philosophy*, trans. Justin Clemens and Oliver Feltham (London: Continuum, 2003), p. 146. As Badiou points out, the "Terrorists" were members of the French revolutionary government who conceived and implemented a policy they called "The Terror." By this they meant "repressive deployment of expeditious measures without appeal, and widespread recourse to the death penalty" (p. 144).

161. "It is first and foremost . . . a spectacular, non-State action which emerges—reality or myth—from clandestine networks. Second, it is violent action aiming to kill or destroy. Lastly, it is an action which makes no distinction between civilians and non-civilians" (ibid., p. 143).

162. Arendt, for example, begins her *Origins of Totalitarianism* with a lengthy study of the history of anti-Semitism as the central pathology of antidemocratic politics in states that are, or will, become totalitarian.

163. Parenthetical page references are to Berman, *Terror and Liberalism*.

164. The initial outrage, from his perspective, was Kemal Atatürk's formal abolition of the Islamic caliphate. This act of "extermination" was the final "humiliation" needed to create a twentieth-century resurgence of Islam "as a religion for all mankind" (pp. 91ff., quoting Qutb; cf. pp. 59–60, 74–75, 86). The final outrage was the decree by Western humanitarians that a secular space should be carved out of the Islamic community so that European Jews could have a place of refuge (pp. 89–91). Underlying this claim was the expectation of the West that Islam would limit the scope of God's rule over man by reference to other, specifically humanitarian considerations. Qutb saw this as "an effort to confine Islam to emotional and ritual circles . . . and

check its complete predominance over every human secular activity" (p. 91, quoting Qutb). On the question of monotheistic violence, see, generally, Jan Assmann, "No God but God: Exclusive Monotheism and the Language of Violence," in Assmann, *Of God and Gods: Egypt, Israel, and the Rise of Monotheism* (Madison: University of Wisconsin Press, 2008).

165. Sayyid Qutb, *Milestones*, rev. ed. (Salimiah, Kuwait: International Islamic Federation of Student Organizations, 1978), e.g., p. 61.

166. See, e.g., Stendahl, *Paul and Israel*.

167. Samuel P. Huntington, "The Clash of Civilizations?" *Foreign Affairs* 72, no. 3 (1993); Huntington, *The Clash of Civilizations and the Remaking of World Order* (New York: Simon and Schuster, 1996).

168. For a comprehensive study of this idea in Islam, see Patricia Crone, *God's Rule: Government and Islam* (New York: Columbia University Press, 2004). A comparison of the notion of divine law in the three Abrahamic religions can be found in Rémi Brague, *The Law of God: The Philosophical History of an Idea* (Chicago: University of Chicago Press, 2007).

169. Berman goes to great lengths to identify the views of Ramadan (whose maternal father, Hassan al-Banna, founded the Muslim Brotherhood) with those of Qutb, its seminal theorist (Berman, "Who's Afraid of Tariq Ramadan?" pp. 47–49; Berman, *Terror and Liberalism*, pp. 70–76 [parenthetical citations above are to this work]).

170. Berman's account of the inevitable conflict between Judeo-Christianity and Islamism are parallel to the post-Holocaust arguments about the inevitable conflict between Israel and *secular* Arab nationalism, which Berman equates with fascism. Although he links these two contesting positions in Middle Eastern politics through their common hostility to Israel, his central purpose is to give those presently opposing Israel world historical significance by finding the originary kernel of both totalitarianism and terrorism in the Qur'anic idea of absolute submission to God's domination (pp. 60–120). During Europe's "five hundred years of world domination" (p. 52), Berman claims, the Islamic version of such "totalitarian" politics remained in the background of history. Its Western version, however, was exported to the Middle East where it reappeared as Arab nationalism, which was "the Muslim variation on the European idea" of fascist dictatorship (p. 60) in both its Ba'athist and Nasserite form (pp. 52–60). Arab anti-Zionism was thus, according to Berman, directly influenced by German Nazis during and after World War II (pp. 55ff., 77–78, 86–87). But Nazism itself, he thinks, was based on an idea of dying and killing for a higher authority—a "cult of death"—that comes from Islam. This was, as we have seen, the argument presented by Israel at the Eichmann trial. (For a more nuanced account of the theology of "incipient Islam," see Marshall G. S. Hodgson, *The Secret Order of Assassins: The Struggle of the Early Nizârî Ismâ`îlîs against the Islamic World* (Philadelphia: University of Pennsylvania Press, 2004).

171. After this, the fetishization of man-made law would be just that—a form of idolatry.

172. According to Berman, such an end point was preordained by Muhammad's decision to bow toward Mecca, the site of Abraham's willingness to murder Isaac at God's command, instead of Jerusalem, the site of David's Kingdom and Christ's

Crucifixion. A Mecca-oriented Islam rejects both Jewish and Christian conceptions of messianic time, and honors Abraham, Moses, Elijah, and Jesus as prophets of man's subjection to God alone—now and forever. Berman presents Muhammad's decision not merely as a turning point in world history but as a foundational choice against a conception of human rights to which the Jewish Question is central.

173. Berman's argument is based on Qutb's thirty-volume commentary, *In the Shade of the Qur'ān*, of which only a few volumes were available at the time he wrote. My reading in Qutb is also cursory, and focused on the ideas addressed by Berman. In reading both together, however, it seems possible that the construction of historical (secular) time around the question of preserving or destroying the Jews may be a mistake that is now shared by Human Rights Discourse and its Islamist "enemy."

7. Bystanders and Victims

1. The "new preeminence of 'bystanders' was first developed as a self-conscious discourse about collective social responsibility in the 1960s" (Dean, *Fragility of Empathy*, p. 77).

2. Ibid., pp. 76–79. The works of Michael Ignatieff and Samantha Power, cited above, are examples of the argument that human rights depend upon overcoming mankind's natural indifference to the suffering of the distant other.

3. Dean, *Fragility of Empathy*, pp. 79–80.

4. Ibid. For further discussion of "figural realism," see my conclusion to this volume.

5. Ibid., chap. 1 ("Empathy, Suffering, and Holocaust Pornography").

6. See Burke, *A Grammar of Motives* and *A Rhetoric of Motives*.

7. Rotberg and Weiss, eds., *From Massacres to Genocide*

8. "This retrospective identification with those who were not Nazis . . . once again 'forgets' the victims except as those 'we' could not help or against whose pain we would naturally protect ourselves. . . . The point here is not to hold bystanders responsible for the cruelty often carried out in their name, . . . but to be conscious about how 'we' may project our own fears and longing onto the past; not to deny that we are all perhaps capable of genocide, but to understand how rhetoric may be mobilized in surprising ways that facilitate if not mass murder, then a propensity to 'forget' victims, to put ourselves in their place, and thus in the end to erase the very historical memory we wish to safeguard . . . [T]hus, it is worth pondering how much the predominant construction of bystander indifference derives from a longing that 'we' would have done or will do something differently when the time comes, accompanied by an equally powerful fear that we will not" (Dean, *The Fragility of Empathy*, p. 104).

9. Ibid., pp. 104–5.

10. Freud discusses the relation between "nursing grievance" and feeling entitlement in Sigmund Freud, "Some Character Types Met with in Psychoanalytic Work," in *The Standard Edition of the Complete Psychological Works of Sigmund Freud*, 14:311–14 ("The 'Exceptions'). See also Vamik D. Volkan, Terry C. Rodgers, and George Kriegman, *Attitudes of Entitlement: Theoretical and Clinical Issues* (Charlottesville: University Press of Virginia, 1988); Sally Weintrobe, "Links between Grievance, Com-

plaint, and Different Forms of Entitlement," *International Journal of Psychoanalysis* 85 no. (2004). For discussion of the connection between victimhood and feelings of entitlement, see Adi Ophir, "The Identity of the Victims and the Victims of Identity: A Critique of Zionist Ideology for a Post-Zionist Age," in *Mapping Jewish Identities*, ed. Laurence J. Silberstein (New York: New York University Press, 2000); Lyotard, *The Differend.*

11. Unjustly punished individuals who have been exonerated (e.g., through DNA evidence) eventually may feel good—perhaps elated, perhaps merely relieved.

12. See, e.g., David L. Eng and David Kazanjian, eds., *Loss: The Politics of Mourning* (Berkeley: University of California Press, 2003).

13. I am indebted to Steve Kaye for posing this question to me.

14. Primo Levi, *The Drowned and the Saved*, trans. Raymond Rosenthal (New York: Vintage International, 1989), p. 84.

15. Primo Levi, "A Self-Interview: Afterword to *If This Is a Man*," in *The Voice of Memory: Interviews 1961–1987*, ed. Marco Belpoliti and Robert Gordon, trans. Robert Gordon (New York: New Press, 2001), p. 186. In this respect, Levi's writings contrast markedly with those of Elie Wiesel discussed in chapter 5 of this volume.

16. Levi, *The Drowned and the Saved*, p. 82.

17. Ibid., pp. 83–84.

18. Would a Christian Holocaust survivor have attached greater moral significance to being saved? A secular Jewish view of this question is explored in Jean Améry, "Resentment," in *At the Mind's Limits: Contemplations by a Survivor on Auschwitz and Its Realities*, trans. Sidney Rosenfeld and Stella P. Rosenfeld (Bloomington: Indiana University Press, 1980); W. G. Sebald, "Against the Irreversible: On Jean Améry," in *On the Natural History of Destruction*, trans. Anthea Bell (New York: Random House, 2003).

19. "Suicide is born from a feeling of guilt that no punishment has attenuated; . . . the harshness of imprisonment was perceived as punishment and the feeling of guilt (if there is punishment there must have been guilt) was relegated to the background only to re-emerge after Liberation. In other words, there was no need to punish oneself by suicide because of a (true or presumed) guilt: one was already expiating it by one's suffering" (ibid., p. 76).

20. Although Levi was captured while fighting as a partisan, he was sent to Auschwitz as a Jew and never counts himself among the political resisters there. Instead, he describes how the camp's regime enlisted the cooperation of those who happened to survive and he sees their consequent "shame" as a moral, rather than physical, sickness from which they cannot recover (ibid., pp. 71–72). On this point see Inga Clendinnin, *Reading the Holocaust*, who notes that, although "caught as a partisan, Levi was sent to Auschwitz as a Jew" (p. 34). As "a partisan . . . [he] understood something of the viciousness of Nazi ideology. In that sense he was prepared for Auschwitz" (p. 49). On the question of resistance in the camps, see Clendinnen, *Reading the Holocaust*, chap. 4.

N.B. Cancer victims may, superficially, look like concentration camp survivors, but their medical treatment, which can involve great physical suffering, does not aim to harm them morally. For a deeper discussion of the relationship between physical and moral damage and between suffering, healing, and shame, see Arthur Kleinman, *The Illness Narratives: Suffering, Healing, and the Human Condition* (New York: Basic Books, 1988), chap. 7.

21. On this point Levi is poles apart from the present-day "recovery" movements that reinforce victimary identity and describe survival as the kind of triumph that victimhood makes possible. For an early example of this view, see Ellen Bass and Laura Davis, *The Courage to Heal: A Guide for Women Survivors of Child Sexual Abuse* (New York: Perennial Library, 1988).

22. Primo Levi, *If This Is a Man / The Truce*, trans. Stuart Woolf (Harmondsworth: Penguin, 1979), p. 376.

23. See, esp., the conclusion to this volume.

24. Clendinnin, *Reading the Holocaust*, p. 34.

25. See Vladimir Jankélévitch, *Forgiveness*, trans. Andrew Kelley (Chicago: University of Chicago Press, 2005). As a voice of "the living dead," Levi's vocation in the largely celebratory climate of postwar Western Europe became what the political theorist Sheldon Wolin calls "invocation." Sheldon Wolin, "Political Theory from Vocation to Invocation," in *Vocations of Political Theory*, ed. Jason A. Frank and John Tambornino (Minneapolis: University of Minnesota Press, 2000).

26. For a discussion of the relation between spectrality and justice, see Derrida, *Specters of Marx*.

27. Eric L. Santner, *Stranded Objects*, chaps. 1–2; Dominick La Capra, "Reflections on Trauma, Absence, and Loss," in *Whose Freud? The Place of Psychoanalysis in Contemporary Culture*, ed. Peter Brooks and Alex Woloch (New Haven: Yale University Press, 2000); *History and Memory after Auschwitz* (Ithaca: Cornell University Press, 1998).

28. See Santner, *The Psychotheology of Everyday Life*, chaps. 1–2.

29. The literary critic, Bruce Robbins, notes that this use of "haunting" fits "the recent and somewhat surprising success of 'trauma' as a model for the relation between past and present. A primal, identity-bestowing injury must be endlessly repeated although (or rather because) it can never be fully or clearly or satisfyingly remembered and thus worked through, trauma offers the cultural-studies era a norm for routine scholarship . . . Beckoned by the call of some ambiguous, exigent, meaning-heavy voice from the past, we assume, perhaps hastily, that the experience can properly be described as being 'haunted.'" Bruce Robbins, "Temporizing: Time and Politics in the Humanities and Human Rights," *boundary 2* 32, no. 1 (2005): 195.

30. Modern ontology is based on the idea that space and time are interdefinable: space is the continuous dimension in which the world presently exists, and time is the continuous dimension in which what cannot coexist comes into being and passes away. Put crudely, space is the location of all possible objects that can exist at the same time; a change in time is thus required for an object to move from one point in space to another.

The idea of a spatio-temporal continuum was given its canonical formulation by Kant, but it is rooted in an earlier notion that Leibniz called "compossibility." Compossibility describes the set of everything that could exist in the same space at the same time—what Leibniz called a "possible world." In a universe of *many* possible worlds, however, "haunting" would be the form of co-presence that different times have. The idea of haunting is thus the *im*possible representation of another possible world with the present one.

Thus only in space can things or persons be seen as contemporaneously *present*. They are present in the sense that they *co*exist in relation to each other, and that each exists *now*, and not merely in the past or future. What is past does not coexist with the present. Over the course of time, it can either be remembered or forgotten, and memory itself is subject to decay. See, e.g., David K. Lewis, *On the Plurality of Worlds* (Oxford: Blackwell, 1986).

31. Burying the dead, putting them in their *place*, lets us spatialize the past so that we can move on. Another way to turn past time into a place is to create atrocity memorials and even theme parks, where the "past" can be "visited" by the living instead of haunting them at undesired moments. The rationale behind such an approach is explained in the *Lieux de memoire* series. See, e.g., Pierre Nora et al., *Rethinking France*, trans. Mary Trouille (Chicago: University of Chicago Press, 2001).

32. For a discussion of these paradoxes, see, Jankélévitch, *Forgiveness*, chap. 1 ("Temporal Decay"; cf. "Should We Pardon Them?").

33. In the present representation of other times, claims for historical redress are subject to decay and justice to future generations is deeply discounted. John Rawls recognized the latter problem as an inherent weakness of the Kantian approach in addressing duties toward the future. The problem is how to include the intertemporal other in a single communicative space in which ideal interlocutors do not know who they were or will have been. See Habermas, *Inclusion of the Other*, pt. 2 (debate with Rawls). For a discussion of the present treatment of duties emanating from past injustice, see Barkan, *The Guilt of Nations*, introduction.

34. Once the ghost is firmly in the past, there would be no present space to which he is unjustly consigned. The past is literally *nowhere*. An afterlife is, presumably, *somewhere*—a virtual location where the dead can still *be* without making claims on the living as survivors or ghosts.

35. As a generic term, "grief" encompasses both the internally and externally produced feelings of those who self-consciously suffer. We say, for example, that someone has "come to grief" when that person experiences misfortune. The word "grief," can also be used in a more limited sense to describe unusually deep or overwhelming feelings of loss—an interior wound compounding an external absence or lack. This suggests that feelings of grief can exist before, and also after, the victim associates his suffering with injustice. It is also possible, however, for anxiety about something missing to be expressed at the expense of the historical group to which blame is ascribed. "Particular forms of prejudice (such as anti-Semitism or homophobia) may involve the conversion of absence into loss with the identity-building localization of anxiety that is projected onto abjected or putatively guilty others" (La Capra, "Reflections on Trauma, Absence, and Loss," p. 187).

36. "Grief is the thing left over after grievance has had its say." It belongs "to the realm of thinking and living with loss, while grievance belongs to the realm of accountability." Anne Anlin Cheng, *The Melancholy of Race: Psychoanalysis, Assimilation, and Hidden Grief* (New York: Oxford University Press, 2001), pp. 194–95. Parenthetical page citations that follow in the text are to this work.

37. Cheng credits this point to Thomas Mann. *The Melancholy of Race*, p. 9.

38. For Cheng, the central point is that literary victimhood consists of an "imagined" relation to one's own body. This is true, of course, of the fictionalized victim who achieves self-realization by imagining that his suffering body will be found, and found innocent, by a compassionate witness such as the reader. Here, however, the witness that the fictionalized victim imagines also has an out-of-body experience, a fantasy of substituting the victim's body for his own (ibid., pp. 154–68).

39. The concept of a ghostly afterlife is relevant here as the grief of wanting to disappear (one *should* have died) in order to be remembered. For what it meant to have *been* the lost objects of post-Holocaust melancholia, see Mendelsohn, *The Lost*.

    Was Levi's own suicide a fantasmatic act of aggression against compassionate witnesses disturbed by his presence? We cannot even be sure that his death *was* a suicide. But such an interpretation would fit Freud's view that the depressive always suffers *as* someone else—an internalized victim who inhabits his body so that he can feel bad without feeling threatened. (Even in suicide, Freud claims, the depressive is fanstasmatically murdering another.)

40. Cheng thus argues that the sadness of the melancholic, which consists of living "with the ghost of the alien other within," has no necessary connection to the psychic life of the survivor who must live on "as" that ghost (ibid., p. 194).

41. For the relation of the symptomatic form of feeling to that value (the "commodity form"), see Slavoj Žižek, *The Sublime Object of Ideology* (London: Verso, 1989), chap. 1. See also Zupančič, "When Surplus Equipment Meets Surplus Value."

42. Freud's key clinical observation was that hostile wishes toward the dead (or absent) lie at the root of melancholia. Why? Because in the uncensored thought of the Freudian unconscious there can be no distinction between, for example, the death of the mother as a psychic object, and deliberate abandonment by her—between her seeming disappearance and her betrayal of an infantile trust. Here active and passive are reversible: hating the loved one is also a fear of her hatred; destroying her in fantasy is also a fantasy of being destroyed by her. Thus it is psychically unavoidable that we hate what we love, and vice versa.

43. Human Rights Discourse urges us to find our humanity by looking at pictures in much the way that an infant finds a self by seeing its body reflected in a mirror. The consequence of introjecting an image of the *body*, as Lacan points out, is that one's own conscious desires become imaginary—a fantasmatic way of putting the "body ego" back into the picture with which it first identified. Jacques Lacan, "The Mirror Stage as Formative of the *I* Function," in *Ecrits: A Selection*, trans. Bruce Fink, Heloise Fink, and Russell Grigg (New York: Norton, 2004); Bracher, *Lacan, Discourse, and Social Change*, pp. 32–45.

44. Freud's associate, Sandor Ferenczi, distinguished two types of introjection. The first, "symbolic introjection," allows us to attach psychic energy (*libido*) to mental representations produced by external stimuli. Both Freud and Ferenczi believed that introjection in this sense is simultaneously the internalization of the world and the externalization (outlet) of psychic energy, which provides release of inner tension and eventually bonds us to the external world. There is, however, a second form of introjection, which Freud and Ferenczi call "incorporation." Here, instead of internalizing the image as a symbol of something outside us, we redirect all our feelings

about the external object, both good and bad, toward our own body from which we then split off (dissociate) another version of our self. Sandor Ferenczi, *Final Contributions to the Problems and Methods of Psycho-Analysis*, ed. Michael Balint, trans. Eric Mosbacher et al. (New York: Brunner/Mazel, 1980), pp. 316–17. The significance of this text is elaborated in Nicolas Abraham and Maria Torok, "The Illness of Mourning and the Fantasy of the Exquisite Corpse," in Abraham and Torok, *The Shell and the Kernel: Renewals of Psychoanalysis*, trans. Nicholas T. Rand (Chicago: University of Chicago Press, 1994). They argue that traumatic loss can never be overcome until this somaticized type of introjection is replaced by the symbolic type, which would enable the depressive both to mourn for and separate from the lost object.

45. In Freud's paradigm of melancholia, the one who *is lost* is also dead or simply gone, and thus unaffected by the patient's ambivalence.

46. For further discussion of Winnicott, see chapters 1 and 5 in this volume.

47. Abram, *Language of Winnicott*, "Being (Continuity Of)," "Concern," "Dependence," "Holding," and "Primary Maternal Preoccupation."

48. Ibid., pp. 216–17; see also Winnicott, "The Use of an Object." Winnicott's prototype of the "good-enough mother," our first surviving victim, enables us to trust in an external reality that was not destroyed by our aggressive feelings.

49. Barbara Johnson, "Using People: Kant with Winnicott," in *The Turn to Ethics*, ed. Marjorie B. Garber, Beatrice Hanssen, and Rebecca L. Walkowitz (New York: Routledge, 2000), p. 56. Parenthetical page references above are to this text, which also appears in Johnson, *Persons and Things* (Cambridge: Harvard University Press, 2008), chap. 7.

50. Winnicott focuses on what we might consider a *normal* form of dependency—that of a child on its mother (or maternal environment), and the feelings of insecurity and aggression that result. The dependency of future generations on the past may differ significantly from the *intra*generational relations of victim and beneficiary that are central to theories of justice (like that of Rawls). Putting injustice in the *past* raises the question of whether *intra*generational dependency becomes normal when it is viewed as though it were *inter*generational. See chapter 8 and the conclusion in this volume.

51. "Winnicott makes the final, and in some ways decisive, revision of the work of Freud and Klein. If, in Winnicott's terms, the self is first made real through recognition, the object is first made real through aggressive destruction; and this, of course, makes experience of the object feel real to the self. The object, Winnicott says, is placed outside omnipotent control by being destroyed while, in fact, surviving the destruction. . . . It is the backdrop of destruction—in fantasy—that keeps the object real and so available for use. . . . It is the externality, the separate reality, of the object that makes it available for satisfaction. . . . In Winnicott's view the object was not reconstituted by the patient's reparation—as Klein believed—but is constituted by its own survival." Adam Phillips, *Winnicott* (Cambridge: Harvard University Press, 1988), pp. 131–33.

52. "In certain stages of certain analyses the analyst's hate is actually sought by the patient, and what is then needed is hate that is objective" (Winnicott, "Hate in

Counter-transference," p. 199; see also Abram, *Language of Winnicott*, pp. 172–82 ["Hate"]).

53 The convergence of social justice and mental harmony has been an end point, and sometimes a starting point, for political philosophy since Plato's *Republic*.

54. Winnicott, "The Manic Defence," pp. 132–33. Cf. chaps. 1 and 2 in this volume.

55. Minow, *Breaking the Cycles of Hatred*; Hunt, *Inventing Human Rights*; cf. Rose, "Apathy and Accountability."

56. As Cheng points out: "The path connecting injury to pity, and then to contempt, can be very brief. In short, it can be damaging to say how damaging racism has been" (*The Melancholy of Race*, p. 187).

57. René Girard's calls the latter the "victimage mechanism." See chapters 5 and 10 in this volume for further discussion of the contrast between "victimage" in Girard's sense and the present-day politics of victimhood.

58. In psychoanalytic terms the witness's desire is passive-narcissistic: its product is a body that feels helpless and depressed. See Bracher, *Lacan, Discourse, and Social Change*.

59. Jean-Paul Sartre, *Being and Nothingness; an Essay on Phenomenological Ontology*, trans. Hazel E. Barnes (New York: Philosophical Library, 1956).

60. "Reproaching . . . prisoners for . . . not rebelling represents . . . an error in historical perspective, expecting from them a political consciousness which is today an almost common heritage but which belonged at that time only to an elite" (Levi, "A Self-Interview," pp. 192–93).

61. See, e.g., Plato's *Republic* (viii–ix).

62. In the film *Life Is Beautiful* (1997) Roberto Benigni's character "translates" the tirade of a concentration camp guard to his fellow Italian inmates using the terms in which supposed beneficiaries of a welfare state believe they are competing for its prizes.

63. Giorgio Agamben discusses Levi's contribution to political theory in Agamben, *Homo Sacer*, pt. 3.

64. This view of universal victimhood, developed by postwar Lutheran theologians (such as Niemöller, Moltmann, and Stendahl), took inspiration from the life and death of Dietrich Bonhoeffer.

65. The Cross at Auschwitz was dedicated to St. Maximilian Kolbe, who volunteered for death in place of a fellow prisoner at Auschwitz (a Polish Catholic with a family). John Paul II's prayer was also directed to Edith Stein, a Carmelite nun and convert from Judaism who would be canonized in 1998 as a Catholic martyr. On the controversy over Kolbe, see James Carroll, *Constantine's Sword: The Church and the Jews, a History* (Boston: Houghton Mifflin, 2001), chaps. 1, 23, 53, 60; On Kolbe, see also Diana Dewar, *Saint of Auschwitz: The Story of Maximilian Kolbe* (San Francisco: Harper and Row, 1982); Elaine Murray Stone and Patrick Kelley, *Maximilian Kolbe: Saint of Auschwitz* (New York: Paulist, 1997). On Stein, see also Waltraud Herbstrith, *Edith Stein, a Biography*, trans. Fr. Bernard Bonowitz (San Francisco: Ignatius, 1992). I thank John Grams for calling my attention to Kolbe.

66. Bernard A. O. Williams, "Moral Luck," in Williams, *Moral Luck: Philosophical Papers, 1973–1980* (Cambridge: Cambridge University Press, 1981).

67. "A child shall not suffer for the iniquity of a parent, nor a parent suffer for the iniq-

uity of a child; the righteousness of the righteous shall be his own, and the wickedness of the wicked shall be his own" (Ezek. 18:19).

68. Williams, *Shame and Necessity*, chap. 5 ("Necessary Identities").

69. An exception is the Roman Stoic Lucretius, who saw shipwrecks as a metaphor for human existence in which the fickle winds and currents that make seafaring possible can also turn against the sailor, who should therefore lower his expectations and accept whatever fate has in store. Lucretius identified his own philosophy with the standpoint of a spectator who views the shipwreck calmly from the safety of dry land, knowing that there is nothing he can do to rescue those who will drown. His shipwreck/spectator metaphor was later used by thinkers such as Montaigne, Hegel, and Goethe to achieve perspective on the political storms of seventeenth- and nineteenth-century Europe. See Blumenberg, *Shipwreck with Spectator*.

70. Under the Law of Admiralty the beneficiaries of a shipwreck are the salvors—the antecedent rights of shippers are essentially wiped out. There are, however, terrestrial *exceptions* to the property rights of salvors up to and including a duty to return found property that was not lost at sea. (Salvors may also be entitled to compensation from survivors for the cost of rescue. The classic twentieth-century treatise is Grant Gilmore and Charles Black, *The Law of Admiralty* (Brooklyn, N.Y.: Foundation, 1957).

71. The mariner killed the albatross (his "bird of good omen") and must now bear its corpse. Samuel Taylor Coleridge, *The Rime of the Ancient Mariner*, ed. Gustave Dore (Edison, N.J.: Chartwell, 2008), pp. 18, 28–32.

8. Adverse Possession

1. On the relation of such issues to national responsibility, see, e.g., Miller, *National Responsibility and Global Justice*, chap. 4.

2. Jon Elster, ed., *Retribution and Reparation in the Transition to Democracy* (Cambridge: Cambridge University Press, 2006); Elster, *Closing the Books: Transitional Justice in Historical Perspective* (Cambridge: Cambridge University Press, 2004); Jeremy Waldron, "Superseding Historic Injustice," *Ethics* 103, no. 1 (1992); Waldron, "Redressing Historic Injustice" *University of Toronto Law Journal* 52, no. 1 (2002).

3. Joseph William Singer, "Well Settled? The Increasing Weight of History in American Indian Land Claims," *Georgia Law Review* 481 (1994); Singer, "Starting Property," *Saint Louis University Law Journal* 46 (Summer 2002).

4. If, for example, "possession is nine-tenths of the law," restitution would be the remainder.

5. Duncan Kennedy, "The Rise and Fall of Classical Legal Thought" (AFAR, 1975, 1998), http://duncankennedy.net/legal_history/essays.html#Rand&F (accessed January 31, 2010).

6. An example would be an award of damages sufficient to make the victim whole regardless of whether the amount paid in compensation is worth more or less than the benefits resulting from the wrongful act.

7. This argument can be rebutted by finding independent, and sufficient, explanations

for your loss—which is often possible when social disadvantages are overdetermined. In gain-based remedies, what must be proven is merely the counterfactual proposition that I would not have gained (or gained as much) without your loss. This, too, can be rebutted in various ways but generally not on the grounds that you would have lost anyway.

8.   Torpey, *Making Whole What Has Been Smashed*, p. 51.

9.   For development of this idea, see Nozick, *Anarchy, State, and Utopia*.

10.   The principled argument for doing this is the same as that for enforcing title based on adverse possession against an original title holder: that the role of property regimes in promoting the stability of settled expectations creates a legal bias in favor of repose.

11.   Joseph William Singer, "The Reliance Interest in Property," *Stanford Law Review* 40, no. 3 (1988).

12.   Armen A. Alchian, "Cost," in Alchian, *Choice and Cost under Uncertainty*, ed. Daniel K. Benjamin (Indianapolis: Liberty Fund, 2006), p. 296.

13.   "The problem of 'external effects' . . . [is that some] potential uses of resources can also benefit people other than the current owners. Those 'external' benefits can be made influential by paying the resource controller to adjust his use of the good. 'External effects are thus internalized, or social effects are made private.'" Armen A. Alchian and William R. Allen, *Exchange and Production: Theory in Use* (Belmont, Calif.: Wadsworth, 1969), p. 253.

14.   Ibid., p. 249. For a fuller development, see Armen A. Alchian, *Property Rights and Economic Behavior*, ed. Daniel K. Benjamin, vol. 2, *The Collected Works of Armen A. Alchian* (Indianapolis: Liberty Fund, 2006).

15.   Guido Calabresi and A. Douglas Melamed, "Property Rules, Liability Rules, and Inalienability: One View of the Cathedral," *Harvard Law Review* 85, no. 6 (1972); Harold Demsetz, "Toward a Theory of Property Rights," *American Economic Review* 57, no. 2 (1967). See, generally, Armen A. Alchian and Harold Demsetz, "The Property Rights Paradigm," *Journal of Economic History* 33, no. 1 (1973).

16.   A further attribute of property rules—essential to functioning markets—is that the initial endowment frequently carries a degree of immunity from liability to compensate others for the harms one causes them. To the extent property is a use-license that effectively cuts off the availability of legal remedies to others, it implicitly requires them to pay a negotiated price to avert harms that the property holder is otherwise at liberty to impose. John Rogers Commons, *Legal Foundations of Capitalism* (Clifton, N.J.: Kelley, 1974); Robert Lee Hale, *Freedom Through Law: Public Control of Private Governing Power* (New York: Columbia University Press, 1952); Barbara Fried, *The Progressive Assault on Laissez Faire: Robert Hale and the First Law and Economics Movement* (Cambridge: Harvard University Press, 1998); Duncan Kennedy, "The Stakes of Law, or Hale and Foucault!" in Kennedy, *Sexy Dressing, Etc.* (Cambridge: Harvard University Press, 1993); Wesley Newcomb Hohfeld and Walter Wheeler Cook, *Fundamental Legal Conceptions, as Applied in Judicial Reasoning* (New Haven: Yale University Press, 1964); Joseph William Singer, "The Legal Rights Debate in Analytical Jurisprudence from Bentham to Hohfeld," *Wisconsin Law Review* 975 (1982).

17. Nozick, *Anarchy, State and Utopia*, pp. 174–81; cf. Étienne Balibar, "My *Self* and My *Own*: One and the Same," in *Accelerating Possession: Global Futures of Property and Personhood*, ed., Bill Maurer and Gabriele Schwab (New York: Columbia University Press, 2006).

18. See, e.g., David Lyons, "The New Indian Claims and Original Rights to Land," *Social Theory and Practice* 4 (1977); Singer, "Well Settled? The Increasing Weight of History in American Indian Land Claims."

19. For a comparison of the U.S. and India in regarding reservations and reverse discrimination, see Robert Meister, "Discrimination Law Through the Looking Glass," review of *Competing Equalities* by Marc Galanter, *Wisconsin Law Review* (1985).

20. What was wrong with European feudalism from the standpoint of the market economy that eventually supplanted it? Feudal property in Europe consisted of an entitlement to collect what would now appear to have been economic rents—a distribution of the revenue from production that did not add value to the product itself. In addition to being a drag on productivity, feudal property (a system of estates in land) was encumbered by a chain of interests linking past and future estate holders. These encumbrances substantially limited the rights of any present generation to engage in transfers *inter vivos,* and thus kept valuable resources off the market. See, e.g., S. F. C. Milsom, *Historical Foundations of the Common Law* (London: Butterworths, 1969); Milsom, *The Legal Framework of English Feudalism* (Cambridge: Cambridge University Press, 1976).

21 John Rawls, *Justice as Fairness: A Restatement*, ed. Erin Kelly (Cambridge: Harvard University Press, 2001), pt. 4. Rawls does not himself use the term "revolution."

22. See, e.g., Stuart Banner, *How the Indians Lost Their Land: Law and Power on the Frontier* (Cambridge: Belknap Press of Harvard University Press, 2005).

23. Craig Rotherham, *Proprietary Remedies in Context: A Study in the Judicial Redistribution of Property Rights* (Oxford: Hart, 2002).

24. For brief summaries of the underlying case law, see Warren A. Seavey and Austin W. Scott, *Notes on Certain Important Sections of Restatement of Restitution by the Reporters* (St. Paul: American Law Institute, 1937), chaps. 1–7, 13. My understanding of the transformation of legal thought described above owes much to Kennedy, *The Rise and Fall of Classical Legal Thought.*

25. The exception to the latter is the "officious intermeddler" who intervenes inappropriately and then demands payment. See, e.g., John P. Dawson, "'Negotiorum Gestio': The Altruistic Intermeddler," *Harvard Law Review* 74, no. 5 (1961); Dawson, "The Self-Serving Intermeddler," *Harvard Law Review* 87, no. 7 (1974).

26. Douglas Laycock, "The Scope and Significance of Restitution," *Texas Law Review* 67 (1989).

27. Although culpability on the defendant's part is helpful in proving that his enrichment was unjust, justice may require defendants to relinquish assets acquired innocently. See, e.g., John P. Dawson, "Restitution without Enrichment," *Boston University Law Review* 61 (1981); Peter Birks, "Unjust Enrichment and Wrongful Enrichment," *Texas Law Review* 79 (2001).

28. "Tracing describes the process whereby a plaintiff who has been deprived of an asset elects to treat the product of an exchange transaction involving that asset as if it

were the asset of which he or she was initially deprived. An important feature of this remedy is that it often allows plaintiffs to claim specific property as their own rather than being limited to personal claims." Craig Rotherham, "Restitution and Property Rites: Reason and Ritual in the Law of Proprietary Remedies," *Theoretical Inquiries in Law* 1, no. 1 (2000): 207.

Under the law of restitution, subsequent appreciation of an asset can be recovered but subsequent depreciation (or even loss) of the asset does not necessarily reduce a plaintiff's entitlement to recover its original value (Birks, "Unjust Enrichment and Wrongful Enrichment").

29. Mark Gergen, "What Renders Enrichment Unjust?" *Texas Law Review* 79 (1999); Jennifer Nadler, *Oxford Journal of Legal Studies* 28, no. 2 (2008): 245–75; doi:10.1093/ojls/gqn011. Accessed March 23, 2010.

30. This is sometimes accomplished by an equitable lien on the sale of an asset, at times by the equitable subrogation of liabilities claimed against it, and at other times by the equitable creation of a "*quasi*" contract (a contract "implied in law") where there is no express contract—but the most general expression of the disgorgement remedy posits the existence of a "constructive" trust in which the wrongdoer is treated as a fiduciary managing assets on behalf of the plaintiff.

Subrogation is the legal doctrine through which insurers, and also governments, can recover *instead* of victims whom they have already indemnified—and is the basis for government suits having to recover ill-gotten profits from tobacco companies that had wrongfully concealed the dangers of smoking while intentionally addicting customers to their product. In their successful tobacco litigation, state governments claimed the status of subrogees on the grounds that they bore a significant portion of the health-care costs of smokers. Hanoch Dagan, *The Law and Ethics of Restitution* (Cambridge: Cambridge University Press, 2004), pp. 128–29; Hanoch Dagan and James J. White, "Governments, Citizens, and Injurious Injuries, Part I," *N.Y.U. Law Review* 76 (2001); Mark C. Weber, "Taking Subrogation Seriously: The Blue Cross-Blue Shield Tobacco Litigation Reconsidered," *Brooklyn Law Review* 67 (2002); Anthony J. Sebok, "Two Concepts of Injustice in Restitution for Slavery," *Boston University Law Review* 84 (2004): 1410–16.

31. George P. Costigan Jr., "The Classification of Trusts as Express, Resulting, and Constructive," *Harvard Law Review* 27, no. 5 (1914). See also Austin Wakeman Scott, "Constructive Trusts," *Law Quarterly Review* 71 (1955).

32. Quoted in Seavey and Scott, *Reporters' Notes*, p. 198.

In 1937 Warren Seavey and Austin Scott, Harvard Law School professors acting as reporters for the American Law Institute, consolidated the existing law of constructive trusts and quasi-contracts into a body of doctrines on unjust enrichment set forth as a *Restatement of the Law of Restitution*. Under their unified theory of restitution, benefits of past wrongs could be followed through assets that had been commingled, transferred, and even lost (perhaps to creditors in bankruptcy). American Law Institute, *Restatement of the Law of Restitution: Quasi Contracts and Constructive Trusts, as Adopted and Promulgated by the American Law Institute at Washington, D.C., May 8, 1936*, 3 vols. (St. Paul: American Law Institute, 1937). American Law Institute, *Restatement of the Law of Restitution, Quasi Contracts, and*

Constructive Trusts (St. Paul: American Law Institute, 1937), chaps. 1, 3–7, 9; Warren A. Seavey and Austin W. Scott, "Restitution," *Law Quarterly Review* 54 (1938): 29–45; John Philip Dawson, *Unjust Enrichment, a Comparative Analysis* (Boston: Little, Brown, 1951), chaps. 1, 3. For an early statement of this approach, see Austin Wakeman Scott, "The Right to Follow Money Wrongfully Mingled with Other Money," *Harvard Law Review* 27, no. 2 (1913).

Seavey and Scott began the *Restatement* with the principle that "a person who has been unjustly enriched at the expense of another is required to make restitution to the other. . . . Ordinarily, the measure of restitution is the amount of enrichment received," and go on to note that the "unjust enrichment" of "the one" and the "unjust deprivation" of the other are often "co-extensive" (Seavey and Scott, *Reporters' Notes*, pp. 12–13) Later, however, they deal with the situation of "a plaintiff who has not suffered a loss or who has not suffered a loss as great as the benefit received by the defendant. In these situations the defendant is compelled to surrender the benefit on the ground that he would be unjustly enriched if he were permitted to retain it, even though that enrichment is not at the expense or wholly at the expense of the plaintiff" (ibid., pp. 633–34).

In commenting on the *Restatement*, John P. Dawson notes that the Roman Law principle that "no one be made richer through another's loss" is also essential to common law (which needs a remedy forcing embezzlers, for example, to return any appreciation on funds they have stolen) but that both common and civil law also require "containment" of this principle (Dawson, *Unjust Enrichment*, introduction and passim). Dawson's point is directly relevant, of course, to the legal institution of the market itself, which assumes that there is no preexisting liability for a wide range of intentional or foreseeable harms to property and persons such as competitive injury. This means that legal protection from such harms must be bought from the injurer (or an insurer) if it is to be had at all.

33. Commons, *Legal Foundations of Capitalism*; Hale, *Freedom through Law*.

34. In contract actions, damages are typically limited to the amount paid out on the contract that was breached; in tort actions, damages are usually limited to the harm caused by the breach of legal duty. These are traditionally distinguished as "expectation damages" (in the case of actions for breach of contract, where the remedy is to refund the plaintiff's cost) or "consequential damages" (in the case of tort actions, where the remedy is measured by the plaintiff's loss). See, e.g., Lon L. Fuller and William R. Perdue Jr., "The Reliance Interest in Contract Damages (Parts I and II)," *Yale Law Journal* 46, no. 373 (1936, 1937). Fuller (like his Harvard Law School contemporaries, Seavey and Scott) was part of a broader movement in U.S. legal thought to restate the "rights" established under contracts, tort, and property in terms of "remedies" —that is, the measure of recovery that can be sought under each form of action. From this perspective, "restating" restitution as a right to recover unjustly gained benefits was a correlative to restating torts as the right to compensation for unjustly caused harm and restating contracts as the right to recover money paid for promises not kept (Seavey and Scott, "Restitution," pp. 31–32).

35. As Douglas Laycock points out, "We can reconcile the tension between neoclassical

law and economics and the law of restitution to a surprising extent. Economic analysts agree that actors should be required to bargain with their victims when transaction costs are not prohibitive. . . . For example, Judge Posner explains restitution of the profits from a copyright infringement on the grounds that it will deter infringers and encourage them to bargain with copyright holders" (Laycock, "The Scope and Significance of Restitution," p. 1290). For a recent discussion of these issues, see Dagan, *The Law and Ethics of Restitution*.

36. Dawson, *Unjust Enrichment*, chap. 3.

37. For further development of this idea, see Žižek, *Parallax View*, building on Kåojin Karatani, *Transcritique on Kant and Marx*, trans. Sabu Kohso (Cambridge: MIT Press, 2003).

38. Dagan, *The Law and Ethics of Restitution*, chap. 7; Hanoch Dagan, "Restitution and Slavery: On Incomplete Commodification, Intergenerational Justice, and Legal Transitions," *Boston University Law Review* 84 (2004); Dennis Kimchuk, "Unjust Enrichment and Reparations for Slavery," *Boston University Law Review* 84 (2004). See also Emily Sherwin, "Reparations and Unjust Enrichment," *Boston University Law Review* 84 (2004).

39. This concern about "mass restitution" seems to underlie the argument in Sebok, "Two Concepts of Injustice in Restitution for Slavery."

40. Some goods, such as college degrees (or even higher incomes), are valued in part because their scarcity confers relative social power over those who lack them. Would a constructive trust that effectively provided more equal access to these "relational goods" make them less valuable to their holders because they would confer less relative social power? Or would the price charged by the present owners of these goods continue to rise until the endowments provided by the trust were passed through to them? The results of such a trust could be inflationary, and inflation could substantially dilute its redistributive result. On the concept of scarcity and relational goods, see Fred Hirsch, *Social Limits to Growth* (Cambridge: Harvard University Press, 1976); Fred Hirsch and John H. Goldthorpe, eds., *The Political Economy of Inflation* (Cambridge: Harvard University Press, 1978).

41. For a conception of socialism as public ownership that implicitly substitutes for corporate liability, see Sidney Webb and Beatrice Potter Webb, *A Constitution for the Socialist Commonwealth of Great Britain* (London: London School of Economics and Political Science, 1975).

42. If such ex ante approaches would not be sufficient to eliminate the liability of the tobacco industry, ex post conversion of corporate wrongs into corporate shares would be consistent with the initial rationale for condemning a product that is harmful when used as directed. But if it is troubling to give smoking victims (and their heirs) windfall gains from tobacco stocks, this is still *less* troubling than allowing corporate wrongdoers to retain the undiluted benefit of the tobacco industry's continuing profitability.

43. This approach could easily be subverted, however, by the victimary group's lack of effective control over the state apparatus. In the hypothetical proposal about marijuana made above, for example, the aboriginal group would presumably have the

prerogative to deny a license to anyone—or perhaps to everyone, making marijuana use effectively illegal. But who would pay the cost of enforcing an aboriginal monopoly, or even prohibition, on marijuana use? Could the state expect to defray enforcement costs through a tax (or fee) paid on aboriginal profits from such licenses? Should the state use all or part of its current (tax-supported) drug enforcement budget to subsidize the marketing of rights to sub-licensees who would have an interest in enforcing their rights privately, through litigation? Could (must?) the state offer to pay the tribe directly some part of what drug enforcement now costs in return for the tribe's consent to under-enforcement? But why should the state agree to pay anything, if under-enforcement could occur even in the absence of such a bargain? An underlying question is whether aboriginals would have the right to be legally represented *by* the government in pressing such claims.

44. We sometimes tell ourselves that *their* engagement in these practices, by our standards, was socially and environmentally responsible before their land was taken, and that we therefore can trust them to self-regulate today. There is no reason to assume that indigenous American peoples avoided man-made environmental disasters before colonialism. For a more complex view of pre-Columbian history, see Charles C. Mann, *1491: New Revelations of the Americas before Columbus* (New York: Vintage, 2006).

45. In Hohfeldian terms, they would have *no duty not* to do so and are in this respect unlike the rest of us. See Hohfeld and Cook, *Fundamental Legal Conceptions*.

46. See, e.g., Eric A. Posner and Adrian Vermeule, "Reparations for Slavery and Other Historical Injustices," *Columbia Law Review* 103, no. 3 (2003).

47. Michael J. Bazyler, *Holocaust Justice: The Battle for Restitution in America's Courts* (New York: New York University Press, 2003), chap. 6; Michael J. Bazyler and Roger P. Alford, *Holocaust Restitution: Perspectives on the Litigation and Its Legacy* (New York: New York University Press, 2006); Ariel Colonomos and Andrea Armstrong, "German Reparations to the Jews After World War II: A Turning Point in the History of Reparations," in *The Handbook of Reparations*, ed. Pablo De Greiff (Oxford: Oxford University Press, 2006), chap. 10.

48. Randall Robinson, *The Debt: What America Owes to Blacks* (New York: Dutton, 2000), p. 204.

49. Westley's argument implicitly assumes that, although the revenue stream on which U.S. blacks could lay claim is very large, it is already being paid out as a return on assets (often securitized and highly liquid) presently held by people whose title *also* depends on assumptions about history. If courts were to recognize the relevant history as bad (rather than good), then those revenues could be disgorged in order to fund redistributive projects. Robert Westley, "Many Billions Gone: Is It Time to Reconsider the Case for Black Reparations?" *Boston College Law Review* 40 (1998). See also Robert S. Browne, "The Economic Case for Reparations to Black America," *American Economic Review* 62, no. 1/2 (1972).

50. Robinson, *The Debt*, p. 207.

51. Wesley states that "denial of the restitutionary rights of African slave descendants reinforces the sense of a racial double standard. . . . Persistent material inequalities

between Blacks and whites are normalized, and white privilege is entrenched as the permanent status quo." Robert Westley, "The Accursed Share: Genealogy, Temporality, and the Problem of Value in Black Reparations Discourse," *Representations* 92 (2004): pp. 105–6.

52. See Westley, "Many Billions Gone," p. 475.

53. Lincoln, "Second Inaugural." I am grateful to Paul Held for pointing out the significance of Lincoln's claim in understanding the deficiencies of the running-debt model of black reparations.

54. The justification for creating such institutions does not necessarily require the conceptual apparatus of restitution and unjust enrichment, that is, the creation of a specific *trust* to fund such programs. Even if we invoked the "trust fund" model, as we do for Social Security, we could not avoid the questions parallel to those arising about other tax-funded "entitlements": How extensively, and how rapidly, would such funds be disbursed to the present generation of beneficiaries? Should the remainder be managed so that "trust" funds are disinvested or accumulated? Does the government as fiduciary have a duty to fund the remedially established trust in perpetuity or to close the books on past injustice by spending down and eventually terminating, the trust?

55. Two legal scholars have recently proposed an endowment-based program of redistribution, and they demonstrated that it might be cheaper, more effective, and more stimulating to the economy than the current method of welfare by transfer payments. Bruce A. Ackerman and Anne Alstott, *The Stakeholder Society* (New Haven: Yale University Press, 1999).

56. Kuznets believed that the effect of democracy is to eventually dampen the inequality resulting from economic growth through redistributive taxation and social programs. Simon Kuznets, "Economic Growth and Income Inequality," *American Economic Review* 45, no. 1 (1955). A recent approach to this question, combining game theoretic models with history, can be found in Daron Acemoglu and James A. Robinson. *Economic Origins of Dictatorship and Democracy* (New York: Cambridge University Press, 2006).

57. Such an approach assumes that restitutionary arguments are causal—what philosophers of science call "postdiction" (or retrodiction), which is prediction in reverse. Under this assumption one should be able to infer a cause (e.g., past injustice) from its effect (the present distribution of wealth) or vice versa. One could then test the counterfactual causal claim—for example, by assuming away the injustice—and predict the result *ceteris paribus*. To do so, however, one would need a deductive-nomological model for making such counterfactual predictions and sound statistical methods for falsifying them. On the Hempel-Popper model of logical empiricism, see, e.g., Carl Gustav Hempel, "Deductive-Nomological Versus Statistical Explanation," in *The Philosophy of Carl G. Hempel: Studies in Science, Explanation, and Rationality*, ed. James H. Fetzer (Oxford: Oxford University Press, 2001); Imre Lakatos, "Falsification and the Methodology of Scientific Research Programs," in *Criticism and the Growth of Knowledge*, ed. Imre Lakatos and Alan Musgrave (Cambridge: Cambridge University Press, 1970).

58. Volatility is a purely statistical concept (standard deviation) that can be applied to any measurable variation of an underlier over time, for example, stock prices, climate, voting behavior, income inequality, and so forth. If the volatility of a data set is known, and its present value is also known, then it is possible to calculate the present price of an option on *any* value in the data set over any period of time. There thus need not be a market in which options are traded to arrive at a price; if there *is* a market, the options will be *liquid*, but the volatility *implied* by the price negotiated by buyer and seller can deviate from the *historical* volatility of the underlier. The idea that volatility refers to *both* a natural number, derived from an index, and the price of an option on that index that results from bargaining deepens our understanding of how the underlying market ("spot market) works. Here the actual or virtual existence of *another* market (an options market) allows traders to shed the risk that "spot prices" will go up or down (directional risk) by assuming the risk that these changes will be larger and more frequent (volatility risk). From this perspective, the "spot market" on an underlying asset is simply a synthetic derivatives position in which the options to *force* a purchase or sale at an unfavorable price would fully offset each other, so that volatility risk is fully shed and directional risk fully assumed.

    Here I cannot address the question of whether the underlying index needs to fit (or be forced into) the normal distribution assumed by current options-pricing techniques. The occurrence of "wild" patterns (in which the occurrence of extremes is far more frequent than the mathematics of randomness would predict) is debatable with respect to many underliers, including the stock market, which is the *locus classicus* for volatility pricing. If a given statistic shows a "fat-tailed" rather than a "bell-shaped" distribution, the definition of volatility as standard deviation would not hold, and options pricing would require a mathematics of chaotic discontinuity (fractal geometry) rather than the differential equations generally used by finance professionals to price options. See, e.g., Benoit B. Mandelbrot and Richard L. Hudson, *The (Mis)Behavior of Markets: A Fractal View of Risk, Ruin, and Reward* (New York: Basic Books, 2004); Donald A. MacKenzie, *An Engine, Not a Camera: How Financial Models Shape Markets*, Inside Technology series (Cambridge: MIT Press, 2006), pp. 105–18.

59. Ian Ayres, *Optional Law: The Structure of Legal Entitlements* (Chicago: University of Chicago Press, 2005), 14–15.

60. Ibid., p. 38.

61. For a nonmathematical explanation of the formula, see Richard A. Brealey and Stewart C. Myers, *Principles of Corporate Finance*, 7th ed. (Boston: McGraw-Hill/ Irwin, 2003), chap. 21, esp. pp. 570–81.

62. An option price is thus far more sensitive to higher volatilities than it is to the other variables in the option-pricing formula. When a functioning options market exists, the price at which an option actually trades can be used, as mentioned earlier, to compute the underlier's "implied volatility"—the volatility that it *would have* if the price were calculated using an option-pricing formula such as Black-Scholes. Implied volatility differs from the "historical volatility" (standard deviation) that can be used to trade options based on the formula alone, and can be used to price op-

tions in which there is no market, such as customized ("over the counter") options or "real options"—which are generally contingent claims on nonfinancial assets, i.e., those that have not yet been financialized (ibid., chap. 22). For critical views of financialization and securitization, see, e.g., Robin Blackburn, "Finance and the Fourth Dimension," *New Left Review* 39 (2006); Randy Martin, *An Empire of Indifference: American War and the Financial Logic of Risk Management* (Durham: Duke University Press, 2007).

63. See, e.g., Alexis de Tocqueville, *The Ancien Regime and the French Revolution*, trans. Stuart Gilbert (New York: Collins, 1969); Cf. Acemoglu and Robinson. *Economic Origins of Dictatorship and Democracy*; Kuznets, "Economic Growth and Income Inequality."

64. Ayres, *Optional Law*, chaps. 5–7.

65. Robert J. Shiller, "Measuring Asset Values for Cash Settlement in Derivative Markets: Hedonic Repeated Measures Indices and Perpetual Futures," *Journal of Finance* (1993): 911–31; Shiller, *Macro Markets: Creating Institutions for Managing Society's Largest Economic Risks* (New York: Oxford University Press, 1993). For further thoughts, and suggestions, on how to turn these futures into *securities*, see Shiller, *The New Financial Order: Risk in the 21st Century* (Princeton: Princeton University Press, 2003), esp. chaps. 9 and 11.

66. The medieval practice of giving alms and buying indulgences (as discussed in chapter 2 in this volume) might be considered an options market on salvation.

67. Cf. Ayres, *Optional Law*, chap. 8; Adam Przeworski, *Capitalism and Social Democracy* (Cambridge: Cambridge University Press, 1985).

68. This is a consequence of Coase's "invariance" result. R. H. Coase, "The Problem of Social Cost," *Journal of Law and Economics* 3 (1960); Harold Demsetz, "Toward a Theory of Property Rights;" Demsetz, "When Does the Rule of Liability Matter?" *Journal of Legal Studies* 1, no. 1 (1972); Demsetz, "Wealth Distribution and the Ownership of Rights," *Journal of Legal Studies* 1, no. 2 (1972). See also Ayres, *Optional Law*, p. 143.

69. Posner and Vermeule, "Transitional Justice as Ordinary Justice," p. 785.

70. Ibid., p. 764.

71. See, e.g., Ernest Mandel, *Late Capitalism*, trans. Joris De Bres, rev. ed. (Atlantic Highlands, N.J.: Humanities, 1975).

72. Hall, *The American Empire and the Fourth World*, chaps. 1, 6. This process begins by treating the *displacement* of indigenous groups by settlers *as though* it had been a treaty-based adjustment of territorial boundaries between sovereign states that were at war. It continues by shifting the paradigm of settler relations with displaced peoples from that of negotiating with independent sovereign nations to that of governing dependent sovereign nations. Once such a shift occurs, the next step is to replace the treaty-based model of settler-indigenous relations with a system of tribal "reservations"—a form of indirect rule in which displaced persons are resettled and concentrated in areas where their customary law can be said to apply. See John Codman Hurd, *The Law of Freedom and Bondage in the United States*; Story, *Commentaries on the Conflict of Laws*).

Although such systems of indirect rule claim to govern natives through their own traditional law, the "traditional" rulers are effectively agents of colonial power (see, e.g., Mamdani, *Citizen and Subject*). U.S. settler colonialism differs in this respect from versions in which inhabited territory was occupied and the inhabitants exploited. Here, almost from the beginning, there were massacres and displacements, followed by policies aimed at the re-concentration, dilution, and eventual extinction of the originally displaced persons. The bearers of an originary grievance against U.S. settlers were thus conceived to be constantly "vanishing," if not yet gone, and thus unsuitable subjects for restitution and reintegration (Prucha, *The Great Father*, esp. chaps. 26, 29, 36–37, 40–41, 45).

73. The near success of such genocidal policies has made it possible for many Americans to regard indigenous claims (albeit prematurely) as premodern history—such as the massacre of Albigensians and Huguenots—that has little relevance to the pursuit of justice among the living. In this respect, the U.S. has been unlike Mexico (and, to a lesser extent, Canada), where indigenous rights are a central focus of social justice movements. For an account of what the loss of cultural continuity might mean, see Jonathan Lear, *Radical Hope: Ethics in the Face of Cultural Devastation* (Cambridge: Harvard University Press, 2006).

74. The strongest moral arguments against payback are generally communal—that communion is itself the vicarious *assumption* of debt as an alternative to the sacrifice of one by the other. This approach rejects the assumption that the debtor occupies the sinner position—whether as perpetrator or beneficiary or both, and must pay—and that the creditor is (until being paid) his innocent victim. It might equally be said that credit-worthiness (debt-bearing capacity) is morally valuable for oneself and carries with it a god-like power to redeem (buy back) the debt of others. And, of course, it is the ultimate test of Christian virtue to allow one's debts to be redeemed (let go of sin) by trusting in the One who has the greatest debt-bearing capacity of all. If there can be a New Heaven, why not a New Earth in which the past is overcome through an act of democratic communion? The foregoing rationale presents democratic community in messianic terms—as an attempt to redeem the entire past in a single moment. See Margaret Atwood, *Payback: Debt and the Shadow Side of Wealth* (Berkeley: Anansi, 2008), chap. 2 ("Debt and Sin").

75. See, e.g., R. H. Tawney, *Equality*, 4th ed. (New York: Barnes and Noble, 1965). For a more recent account, see G. A. Cohen, *If You're an Egalitarian, How Come You're So Rich?* (Cambridge: Harvard University Press, 2000).

76. Teitel, "Transitional Justice Genealogy"; See also Teitel, *Transitional Justice*.

9. States of "Emergency"

1. When not considered as a separate ("inchoate") crime, the common law doctrine of conspiracy is a simple form of vicarious liability for other crimes—similar to the charge of "aiding and abetting" a crime or being an "accessory" to a crime which exists in most legal systems. At the International Criminal Tribunal for Yugoslavia these concepts were expanded into a still controversial doctrine of "joint criminal

enterprise," which would allow some members of an organization to be held vicariously liable for crimes committed by other members but not for membership in the organization as such. Robert Cryer et al., *An Introduction to International Criminal Law and Procedure* (Cambridge: Cambridge University Press, 2007), pp. 304–5.

2. The idea of putting Nazism itself on trial as a "common plan or conspiracy" was first proposed in a memorandum written by Lt. Col. Murray C. Bernays in 1944. It found favor with Secretary of War Henry Stimson, Attorney General Francis Biddle, and former Attorney General Robert Jackson as an alternative to Treasury Secretary Henry Morgenthau's proposal that Germany as a whole should be treated much more severely than it had been after World War I—a peace that Morgenthau's critics in the Roosevelt administration called "Carthaginian." Robert E. Conot, *Justice at Nuremberg* (New York: Harper and Row, 1983), chaps. 2, 5–6; Donald Bloxham, *Genocide on Trial: War Crimes Trials and the Formation of Holocaust History and Memory* (Oxford: Oxford University Press, 2001), chaps. 1–2; Arieh J. Kochavi, *Prelude to Nuremberg: Allied War Crimes Policy and the Question of Punishment* (Chapel Hill: University of North Carolina Press, 1998), chap. 7; Bradley F. Smith, *Reaching Judgment at Nuremberg* (New York: Basic Books, 1977), chap. 5; *The Road to Nuremberg* (New York: Basic Books, 1981), esp. chaps. 2, 6; Ann Tusa and John Tusa, *The Nuremberg Trial* (New York: Atheneum, 1984), chap. 4; Borgwardt, *A New Deal for the World*, pp. 202–30.

3. In drafting the tribunal's eventual compromise on the conspiracy charges, Francis Biddle (now the U.S. judge) had come to agree with the French judge (Donnedieu de Vabres), who argued that conspiracy was not a civil law concept, and with Herbert Wechsler, who had argued as Biddle's assistant attorney general that membership in an organization was not a sufficient basis for criminal conspiracy, and who, as Biddle's Nuremberg aide, drafted what would become the tribunal's judgment (Smith, *Reaching Judgment*, pp. 134ff.). In accepting this view, "Biddle . . . killed Bernays's central concept of the trial, supported by Secretary of War Stimson and by Jackson, that the Nazi era represented a conspiracy carried out through the medium of the organizations, and that only by a conspiracy indictment could the atrocities the Nazis had committed against their own people be brought before an international tribunal" (Conot, *Justice at Nuremberg*, p. 485). The Russians strongly disagreed with the tribunal's refusal to convict on the basis of membership in a criminal organization. See Tusa and Tusa, *The Nuremberg Trial*, chap. 17. ("The Russians could not and would not accept that . . . [the] three indicted groups did not merit declarations of criminality" [452].) One of the British judges, Norman Birkett, also resisted on the grounds that without conspiracy convictions "the Nazi regime would be acquitted" (Smith, *Reaching Judgment*, pp. 128–29). Conot concludes that "the tribunal was left with the head of one animal and the tail of another . . . a group of organizations with complicity for charges on which [it] had ruled that there had been no conspiracy" (*Justice at Nuremberg*, p. 484).

4. The Smith Act's use of conspiracy was essential to conviction and thus protected the speaker's content under the First Amendment. It also meant that innocent speech could not be prosecuted merely because of its dangerous (inflammatory) conse-

quences. Hand's approach was not upheld during World War I but was favored on speech-protective grounds by New Deal jurists such as Felix Frankfurter, Francis Biddle (who would become the U.S. judge at Nuremberg), and Robert Jackson (who would become the chief prosecutor). As an appellate judge, Hand himself would later write a key opinion in the *Dennis* case upholding the constitutionality of the Smith Act as a basis for prosecuting communist leaders. In that opinion he took "judicial notice" of the communist threat. See Geoffrey R. Stone, *Perilous Times: Free Speech in Wartime from the Sedition Act of 1798 to the War on Terrorism* (New York: Norton, 2004), chaps. 3–5; Gerald Gunther, *Learned Hand: The Man and the Judge* (New York: Knopf, 1994), pp. 151–70.

5. Tusa and Tusa, *The Nuremberg Trial*, pp. 54–55.

6. This approach prevailed in Eastern Europe, where the goal of communist-era war crimes tribunals was to prove that anti-Communists had also been Fascist. See István Rév, *Retroactive Justice: Prehistory of Post-Communism* (Stanford: Stanford University Press, 2005). In Hungary, Rév reports, Nuremberg became the prototype of show trials that occurred in Hungary following World War II (p. 237) and was not associated, as in the West, with prosecuting genocide committed against Jews. Rather, Auschwitz itself was effectively "de-Judaized" and assimilated to Nazi crimes against Communists (p. 236; see, generally, 234–39). The post-1989 rehabilitation of those prosecuted in such trials cast suspicion on Nuremberg itself at the very moment it became the foundation of post–cold war Human Rights Discourse in the West.

7. See Chief Prosecutor Robert Jackson's Opening Statement, quoted in chap. 6 in this volume.

8. Although several defendants (including Göring, Hess, Jodl, Keitel, and Ribbentrop) were convicted of conspiracy to wage aggressive war, none of the defendants convicted individually of war crimes or crimes against humanity or both was also found guilty of conspiracy to commit these crimes. A full table of charges and outcomes appears, among other places, in Norbert Ehrenfreund, *The Nuremberg Legacy: How the Nazi War Crimes Trials Changed the Course of History* (New York: Palgrave Macmillan, 2007), pp. 88–89.

9. Despite such misgivings, the Nuremberg Tribunal's apparent compromise on the conspiracy count is now celebrated as a principled decision that is central to its legacy. The U.S. Supreme Court thus notes that "the International Military Tribunal [IMT] at Nuremberg, over the prosecution's objections, pointedly refused to recognize as a violation of the law of war conspiracy to commit war crimes . . . and convicted only Hitler's most senior associates of conspiracy to wage aggressive war." Those convicted were all recorded as "present" in the notes kept by Col. Friedrich Hossbach of a rare General Staff meeting in which Hitler laid out his future plan of aggressive war in the East to provide *lebensraum* for a growing (and rearming) Germany. The IMT thus drew a strong, if implicit, distinction between rejecting all broad conspiracy counts based on Nazi associations and upholding a conspiracy conviction only against those who had been physically present at a meeting when the alleged "common plan" was announced and approved.

A Nuremberg-based *limitation* on the use of the conspiracy weapon in international criminal law is now widespread. In *Hamdan*, for example, the U.S. Supreme Court rejected prosecution claims that conspiracy to commit terrorism (in the absence of terrorism itself) was a sufficient basis to try Hamdan before a military tribunal for violating international law. The Court cites as precedent not only the Nuremberg Tribunal's judgment but also the following: Telford Taylor, *The Anatomy of the Nuremberg Trials: A Personal Memoir* (New York: Knopf, 1992), pp. 584–85, 638; Stanislaw Pomorski, "Conspiracy and Criminal Organization in the Nuremberg Trial and International Law," in *The Nuremberg Trial and International Law*, ed. George Ginsburgs and V. N. Kudriavtsev, *Law in Eastern Europe* (Dordrecht: Nijhof, 1990), pp. 213, 33–35; *Hamdan v. Rumsfeld*, 2749 S. Ct. 2006, at 2775–86 (2006).

An important point to note is that this was *not* the view of Nuremberg taken immediately thereafter by the Tokyo War Crimes Tribunal, which convicted all defendants of conspiracy (and one of *only* conspiracy). Most subsequent scholarship on international criminal law discredits the Tokyo trials for this reason. Recent examples include Ehrenfreund, *The Nuremberg Legacy*, chaps. 1–8, 11, 19; and Cryer et al., *Introduction to International Criminal Law*, chap. 6. At least one recent human rights defendant, the former prime minister of Rwanda, has pleaded guilty to genocide and also to "conspiracy, incitement and complicity in genocide" (ibid., p. 167).

10. Cf. Rose, "Apathy and Accountability."

11. John Herz, *From Dictatorship to Democracy: Coping with the Legacies of Authoritarianism and Totalitarianism* (Westport, Conn.: Greenwood, 1982).

12. See Noel Annan, *Changing Enemies: The Defeat and Regeneration of Germany* (New York: Norton, 1996). There was also a widespread sense that Germany had *already* been collectively punished for World War II by the carpet bombing of its cities such as Dresden. Punishment had been part of Churchill's stated rationale for destroying population centers, which was, prima facie, a war crime under the Hague Conventions. For a demonstration that the deliberate bombing of population centers fit the pre-Nuremberg paradigm of a war crime, see, e.g., Nicholson Baker, *Human Smoke: The Beginnings of World War II, the End of Civilization* (New York: Simon and Schuster, 2008); Lindqvist, *A History of Bombing*. For the postwar German understanding of this bombing as punishment, see, e.g., W. G. Sebald, *On the Natural History of Destruction*, trans. Anthea Bell (New York: Random House, 2003).

13. Bass, *Stay the Hand of Vengeance*, chaps. 1, 5–6; Power, *"A Problem from Hell,"* chaps. 1–8. For accounts of unpunished genocides occurring after Nuremberg, see Rummel, *Death by Government*; Glover, *Humanity*.

14. For an account of the centrality of collective security and social reconstruction in New Deal thinking about outlawing the next war, see Borgwardt, *A New Deal for the World*.

15. Bass, *Stay the Hand of Vengeance*, chap. 2.

16. Thus, to the architects of Nuremberg, it was a serious question as to whether the legitimacy of the international tribunal would require even-handed prosecution of war crimes committed by both sides (Bass, *Stay the Hand of Vengeance*, chaps. 1, 5).

17. Douglas, *The Memory of Judgment*, pt. 1.

18. Sven Lindqvist, in *A History of Bombing*, demonstrates that, before Nuremberg, crimes against humanity were typically identified with the barbarities that uncivilized people committed against their neighbors (e.g., cannibalism) and that the means employed by colonial authorities to stop such barbarities (typically the bombings, massacre, and torture of civilians) were among the war crimes banned by the Geneva and Hague Conventions in conflicts between "civilized" nations. Until Nuremberg, the concept of war crimes had not been applied to the same contexts as that of crimes against humanity.

19. In its final judgment the tribunal effectively treated crimes against humanity as a subset of war crimes. For the tribunal's legal rationale for requiring this "nexus" in order to convict for crimes against humanity, see Borgwardt, *A New Deal for the World*, pp. 228ff.

20. The central role played in this history by Raphaël Lemkin is described in Samantha Power, "*A Problem from Hell*," chaps. 1–5. "Genocide," the now accepted term for racially based mass murder, first appeared in Lemkin, *Axis Rule in Occupied Europe*.

21. Douglas, *The Memory of Judgment*, p. 6.

22. The doctrine of universal jurisdiction over crimes against humanity, proclaimed by Israel as the trier of Eichmann, is now widely accepted. It was, for example, the basis on which Augusto Pinochet was indicted in Spain and detained (for a time) in England, and also the basis on which Belgium has successfully prosecuted a few Rwandan *génocidaires*.

    As a distinctive element of contemporary human rights culture, however, universal jurisdiction can be at odds with other elements. South Africa's TRC, for example, praised the UN's declaration that apartheid was a crime against humanity while assuming that its own authority to consider and grant amnesty for such a crime trumped universal jurisdiction. (It thus suggested that F. W. de Klerk, for example, could not have been legally arrested and prosecuted while in Oslo to receive his Nobel Prize—an apparent inconsistency noted by Wynand Malan in stating his "minority position" in the TRC's *Report*, vol. 5.)

    The Chilean government raised similar objections to the proposed trial of Pinochet in the EU as undermining its own decision to grant him amnesty as part of its transition to democracy. It later moved to try him domestically for offenses arguably uncovered by the amnesty and to reverse the amnesty for other offenders. See, e.g., Naomi Roht-Arriaza, *The Pinochet Effect: Transnational Justice in the Age of Human Rights* (Philadelphia: University of Pennsylvania Press, 2005).

23. Shklar, *Legalism*, pp. 143–79; Kirchheimer, *Political Justice*, chap. 8 ("Trial by Fiat of the Successor Regime").

24. Arendt, *Eichmann in Jerusalem*, chap. 14 and epilogue.

25. See chapter 6 in this volume.

26. Goldhagen, *Hitler's Willing Executioners*.

27. Jean-Paul Sartre, "Genocide," *Ramparts*, February 1968.

28. Telford Taylor, *Nuremberg and Vietnam: An American Tragedy* (Chicago: Quadrangle, 1970).

29. Taylor, *The Anatomy of the Nuremberg Trials*. This view, suggesting that the Allied

generals could and should have been legitimately prosecuted as war criminals for bombing civilian targets in Dresden and Hiroshima, for example, is at odds with another interpretation of Nuremberg that focuses on outlawing wars of aggression. According to the latter view, wartime acts committed by the victims of aggressive war should be judged by a different standard than war crimes committed by the aggressor (Borgwardt, *A New Deal for the World*, p. 217).

30. At age twenty-one, I refused the draft on this basis. My Lai, I later learned, had occurred on my twenty-first birthday.

31. The initial literature on comparative transitions was stimulated by the "third-wave democratizations" in Latin America and Eastern Europe. See Huntington, *The Third Wave*.

32. That possibility is also essential to the rationale for human rights interventionism—attacking Serbia or Iraq can thus be seen as legitimate precursors to the arrest and trial of genocidal leaders. The clearest application of Nuremberg to Sadaam Hussein would have been a prosecution for planning and waging a war of aggression against Iran and for war crimes and crimes against humanity committed therein. Had such a trial been held before an international tribunal, U.S. government officials would almost certainly have been called as defense witnesses and, quite possibly, been charged as codefendants; cf. Milosevic's subpoena of former general Wesley Clark and his less successful effort to cross-examine former President Clinton.

33. Jackson conceded that a neutral tribunal, independent of victims and vanquished alike, would have been preferable but argued that the worldwide scope of Nazi crimes had "left but few real neutrals." To offset the inherent dangers of victors' justice, Jackson promised that the Nuremberg prosecution would seek to convict the accused "major Nazi war criminals" on the basis of their own meticulously kept documents rather than relying on the testimony of their victims. The alternative would be impunity: "Either the victors must judge the vanquished or we must leave the defeated to judge themselves." Jackson, "Opening Statement (Nuremberg Trials)."

34. This is why human rights advocates tend to be ambivalent, in retrospect, about the trials they may have initially demanded, and why today's literature on transitional justice recommends tailoring human rights trials, if any should occur, to fit local political objectives. For an example of post-hoc ambivalence about trials, see Jaime E. Malamud Goti, *Game Without End: State Terror and the Politics of Justice* (Norman: University of Oklahoma Press, 1996). An example of the tailoring approach is Roht-Arriaza and Mariezcurrena, *Transitional Justice in the Twenty-First Century*.

35. For a systematic summary of this field, see Elster, *Closing the Books*.

36. The choice, according to this nuanced view, is no longer between punishment and impunity; rather, it is among ways to legitimate the de facto impunity that is likely to occur. Given this choice, it is by no means clear that holding immediate trials is the best way to promote the long-term rule of law. Based on the Chilean example, one might argue, instead, for negotiated amnesties, which are potentially reversible under domestic law and do not require a presumption of innocence. See, e.g., Roht-Arriaza, *The Pinochet Effect*.

37. The two paragraphs above summarize Hesse and Post, "Introduction," pp. 15–20.

38. See, e.g., Minow, *Breaking the Cycle of Vengeance.* Cf. Aeschylus, *The Eumenides.*

39. This concern had its precursors in the interwar period, when many came to accept the argument of John Maynard Keynes that the failure of Versailles to provide for an adequate closure to the grievances of World War I would produce new grievances that could (and eventually did) lead to a second world war. See John Maynard Keynes, *The Economic Consequences of the Peace* (New York: Harper and Row, 1971).

40. See Arendt, *Origins of Totalitarianism,* pp. 139ff. Elsewhere Arendt argues that the possibility of forgiveness is a precondition for creating a political community, without which the cycle of vengeance begetting vengeance would be unbreakable. "Men are unable to forgive what they cannot punish and . . . are unable to punish what has turned out to be unforgiveable" ("The Irreversibility of Forgiveness," p. 241).

41. See, e.g., Osiel, *Mass Atrocity*; and the previously cited works of Minow, Teitel, Neier, and Roht-Arriaza. At the level of jurisprudence, the most rigorous statement of this view is Nino, *Radical Evil on Trial.* Nino's use of "radical evil" (p. vii) originates in Kant's *Religion with the Limits of Reason Alone.* For further discussion of this concept, see Joan Copjec, "Evil in the Time of the Finite World," in Copjec, *Radical Evil.* Jacob Rogozinski, "It Makes Us Wrong: Kant and Radical Evil," in Copjec, *Radical Evil.*

42. Neither is it evident that a history of human rights trials in one's own country—perhaps resulting in the judicial execution of previous tyrants—would deter future tyrants from seizing power. And why would the occurrence of human rights trials in one's own country be a greater deterrent than the *possibility* presented by their occurrence in other countries? Why would it be a greater deterrent than a history of extrajudicial political assassination?

43. "Trials for massive human rights violations can be justified . . . provided the trials will counter those cultural patterns and the social trends that provide fertile ground for radical evil" (Nino, *Radical Evil on Trial,* p. 146). Returning from his exile at Yale Law School to become a legal adviser to President Alfonsín, Nino saw a human rights culture that was dominant in Western Europe and North America as merely countercultural in Argentina, which had, after World War II, harbored Eichmann and twice embraced military dictatorships modeled on fascism (ibid., pp. 60ff).

   It was certainly true that liberal critics, such as Nino, were largely missing from public debate during the Latin American dictatorships. Without them, Latin American societies could be said to *lack* a culture (or even a counterculture) of accountability, but I believe it is a mistake to call that lack a *prior* culture.

44. Ibid., pp. 64–65.

45. To forestall disappointment, Nino argues that proponents of human rights trials must prepare the public to support a result in which prosecutions are few and selective—and in which punishments are calibrated to avoid a backlash of sympathy for those convicted (ibid., e.g., pp. 71, 94).

46. See Koselleck, *Futures Past.*

47. I elaborate this argument in Meister, "Anticipatory Regret," reviewing Stone, *Perilous Times: Free Speech in Wartime from the Sedition Act of 1798 to the War on Ter-*

rorism. For evidence that past emergencies have been exaggerated, see John E. Mueller, *Overblown: How Politicians and the Terrorism Industry Inflate National Security Threats, and Why We Believe Them* (New York: Free Press, 2006). Mueller's claim that such evidence is always exaggerated is itself an exaggeration, or perhaps a substitution of wishful thinking for anticipatory regret. For the argument that it is better to overestimate security threats than to underestimate them, and that democracies can restore civil liberties later, see Richard A. Posner, *Not a Suicide Pact: The Constitution in a Time of National Emergency* (New York: Oxford University Press, 2006).

48. For an argument that the U.S. Constitution provides a two-way ratchet for protecting civil liberties, see Eric A. Posner and Adrian Vermeule, *Terror in the Balance: Security, Liberty, and the Courts* (New York: Oxford University Press, 2007).

49. Carl Schmitt, "Total Enemy, Total War, and Total State," in *Four Articles, 1931–1938*, trans. Simona Draghici (Washington, D.C.: Plutarch, 1999); Heinrich Meier, *Carl Schmitt and Leo Strauss: The Hidden Dialogue*, including *Strauss's Notes on Schmitt's Concept of the Political* and *Three Letters from Strauss to Schmitt*, trans. J. Harvey Lomax (Chicago: University of Chicago Press, 1995), pp. 22–28.

50. Even within this approach, an official could be liable for going beyond good-faith reliance on the OLC opinion he receives. The protection provided by such opinions is not absolute unless the opinion itself provides absolute protection. But this is only small comfort. An OLC opinion telling officials that they proceed at their own legal risk during an emergency would not do the job of freeing them to act: they may well insist on an opinion saying that they assume *no* liability for Nuremberg-like prosecutions. This demand could be taken by OLC lawyers as reason in itself to conclude that absolute immunity from such prosecution is necessary for officials to do what it takes in a genuine emergency—and thus falls within the executive's "inherent" power. (What if, for example, national security officials threatened to go on strike at the moment of greatest threat?)

My main point is that an OLC opinion letter may more closely resemble the outcome of a labor negotiation within the executive branch than the judgment of a future court reviewing human rights violations. A further point is that, because such opinions can be rendered in secret, we might never know how absolute they had to be in order to provide the requisite level of assurance to officials aware of potential Nuremberg-based liability after the emergency ends. (After leaving office, several Bush administration officials have argued that national security officials will not do their jobs if they do not believe that they can rely on legal opinions that categorize *whatever* they did as *not* torture if it was done while relying, in "good faith," on those opinions [Dan Eggen, "Bush White House Cast Assails Obama," *Washington Post*, February 7, 2009].)

51. See Jack L. Goldsmith, *The Terror Presidency: Law and Judgment inside the Bush Administration* (New York: Norton, 2007), pp. 70–71, and chap. 3, esp. pp. 96–97. In a profile of Goldsmith, Jeffrey Rosen describes the function of the OLC as follows: "The office has two important powers: the power to put a brake on aggressive presidential action by saying no and, conversely, the power to dispense what Goldsmith

calls 'free get-out-of-jail cards' by saying yes. Its opinions, he says, are the equivalent of 'an advance pardon' for actions taken at the fuzzy edges of criminal laws." Jeffrey Rosen, "The Conscience of a Conservative," *New York Times Magazine*, September 9, 2007.

52.   The principle of universal jurisdiction over crimes against humanity makes it possible to try domestically pardoned individuals before foreign or international tribunals.

53.   Papen's suspension of the elected government in Prussia set the stage for Göring, as his appointed minister in charge of police, to exercise dictatorial powers even *before* the Reichstag fire (Conot, *Justice at Nuremberg*, pp. 114–17). For contemporaneous critiques of Weimar legality, see Carl Schmitt, *Legality and Legitimacy*, trans. Jeffrey Seitzer (Durham: Duke University Press, 2004); Otto Kirchheimer, "Weimar—and What Then? An Analysis of the Constitution," in *Politics, Law, and Social Change: Selected Essays*, ed. Frederic S. Burin and Kurt L. Shell (New York: Columbia University Press, 1969). For broader perspectives, see also Ellen Kennedy, *Constitutional Failure: Carl Schmitt in Weimar* (Durham: Duke University Press, 2004); Arthur J. Jacobson and Bernhard Schlink, eds., *Weimar: A Jurisprudence of Crisis* (Berkeley: University of California Press, 2000).

54.   See Roger Manvell and Heinrich Fraenkel, *The Hundred Days to Hitler* (London: Dent, 1974), pp. 114–49; Clinton Rossiter, *Constitutional Dictatorship: Crisis Government in the Modern Democracies* (New York: Harcourt, 1963), pt. 1 (on the uses and perversions of Article 48).

55.   Ingo Müller, *Hitler's Justice: The Courts of the Third Reich*, trans. Deborah Lucas Schneider (Cambridge: Harvard University Press, 1991), chap. 4.

56.   Ibid., chaps. 6–7.

57.   Papen's recollection is quoted in Manvell and Fraenkel, *Hundred Days*, p. 133. The reasoning behind his acquittal is described in Smith, *Reaching Judgment at Nuremberg*, pp. 284–92.

58.   "The Reichstag fire of February 27 and the events that followed proved, if proof was needed, that there was no popular front of resistance to make a stand against the preemptive counterrevolution launched and directed by Hitler, with the connivance of the traditional right" (Mayer, *Why Did the Heavens Not Darken?* p. 118–19). Mayer argues throughout chapter 5 that Hitler never faced a "clear and present danger" of resistance from the left, and that his evolving policy of de-emancipating, isolating, driving out, and eventually exterminating German Jews was a consequence of his successful repression of the domestic left, to which the Comintern responded by supporting popular fronts that would defend both bourgeois democracy and the Soviet Union against fascism. At this point Hitler linked his movement's anti-Semitism (originally a demand for racial quotas) to the argument that international "bolshevism" was a conspiracy of Jews to take over European governments (Blum = Kaganovich).

59.   Hitler's readiness to undertake the 1934 Röhm Purge ("The Night of the Long Knives") may have reassured moderate Germans that only he could take the extreme steps necessary to control more dangerous forces to his right. See Gopal Bal-

akrishnan, *The Enemy: An Intellectual Portrait of Carl Schmitt* (London: Verso, 2000), pp. 201–3; Mayer, *Why Did the Heavens Not Darken?* pp. 136–45. A day later the Röhm Purge was retroactively declared by Hitler's cabinet to have been a "national emergency," responding to the threat of an ultra-right coup (Conot, *Justice at Nuremberg*, p. 129; Manvell and Fraenkel, *Hundred Days*, pp. 150–89).

60. William Shirer, *The Rise and Fall of the Third Reich* (New York: Simon and Schuster, 1990), pp. 191ff. Göring had underground access to the Reichstag building from his headquarters as Reichstag president and, at a later Nazi gathering, insinuated that he was responsible for the fire. But, when interrogated on this matter at Nuremberg, he denied involvement in the fire and stated that his plans to arrest Communists had been made previously. Chief Prosecutor Jackson presented no direct evidence to contradict that testimony (Tusa and Tusa, *The Nuremberg Trial*, pp. 277, 280; Manvell and Fraenkel, *Hundred Days*, pp. 130ff., 220–26).

61. This idea has been somewhat alien to Anglo-American law since the Magna Carta, which is why it is usually referred to in English by a foreign-sounding name, such as *raison d'état* or *Staatsräson*. See, e.g., Friedrich Meinecke, *Machiavellism: The Doctrine of Raison d'état and Its Place in Modern History* (New Brunswick, N.J.: Transaction, 1998). "Reason of state" is closely connected with the notion that legitimate reversion to dictatorship is a possibility implicit in any constitutional regime. See, e.g., Carl Schmitt, *Constitutional Theory*, trans. Jeffrey Seitzer (Durham: Duke University Press, 2008), pp. 109ff.

62. Can the Nuremberg precedent be applied to "war crimes" committed by national leaders against their own domestic populations? The problem is that civil wars/insurgencies/antiguerrilla actions, and so on, can be *described* as war crimes insofar as they involve more or less indiscriminate use of force against civilian populations. Yet *all* governments use force in civil wars. Does merely fighting a civil war (a domestic war against civilians) open leaders to Nuremberg-based prosecution? Does it also justify (selective?) international intervention based on universal jurisdiction and the "Responsibility to Protect?" If so, we may have revived the original rationale for colonialism.

This issue was first raised to justify NATO's intervention in Bosnia, and would have been addressed by the International Criminal Tribunal for the former Yugoslavia (ICTY) in the Milosevic trial had he not died during his trial. It has been recently presented in the indictment of Sudanese President Bashir by the International Criminal Court (ICC). See Mamdani, "The New Humanitarian Order."

63. See H. L. A. Hart, *The Concept of Law* (Oxford: Clarendon, 1961), chap. 2. For a debate on the legitimacy of prosecuting Nuremberg defendants on grounds not recognized under the Nazi legal system, see Hart, "Positivism and the Separation of Law and Morals," *Harvard Law Review* 71, no. 4 (1958); Lon L Fuller, "Positivism and Fidelity to Law: A Reply to Professor Hart," *Harvard Law Review* 71, no. 4 (1958).

64. Testimony that Hitler made many decisions on his own contributed to the tribunal's finding of insufficient evidence that the Nazi hierarchy functioned as a "common plan or conspiracy." Conot, *Justice at Nuremberg*, chaps. 55–56; Tusa and Tusa, *The Nuremberg Trial*, pp. 429–32. Defending the *führerprinzip*, Göring testified that "Hitler had become Head of State, Government and the Armed forces . . . 'following

the example of the United States'" (ibid., p. 276). His interpretation of U.S. presidential power here anticipates the theory of the "unitary executive" embraced by the Bush administration.

65. For an argument that the Nuremberg precedent, and U.S. war crimes statutes, would support the prosecution of government lawyers who wrote memos supporting torture, see Philippe Sands, *Torture Team* (New York: Palgrave Macmillan, 2008).

66. A more difficult question is whether a successor regime (e.g., in South Africa or Chile) can grant immunity for crimes against humanity as part of a scheme of transitional justice. Would Nuremberg-based prosecutions of individuals be trumped by the terms of a domestic political settlement? Must courts exercising universal jurisdiction over such crimes review the legitimacy of such a settlement? (If Pinochet could still be tried in the EU for crimes against humanity, why not DeKlerk?)

67. See, e.g., Smith, *Reaching Justice at Nuremberg*, pp. 134–38.

68. José Zalaquett, "Confronting Human Rights Violations Committed by Former Governments: Principles Applicable and Political Constraints," in *State Crimes: Punishment or Pardon*, ed. Alice Henkin (Queenstown, Md. Aspen Institute, 1989); Orentlicher, "Settling Accounts." Referring to this debate, Nino concludes: "Rather than a duty to prosecute, we should think of a duty to safeguard human rights and to prevent future violations" (*Radical Evil*, p. 188).

69. The tribunal's interpretation of existing international law on crimes against humanity was clarified and superseded by the 1948 Genocide Treaty, the judicial enforceability of which presupposed that Nuremberg had effectively stripped away the ordinary legal defenses of state officials who scrupulously follow the law.

70. For specific grounds on which U.S. officials could be prosecuted for war crimes, see Jane Mayer, *Dark Side: The Inside Story of How the War on Terror Turned Into a War on American Ideals* (New York: Doubleday, 2008).

71. Following 9/11, the links were exaggerated between terrorism—which is typically invoked as the *real* emergency—and the foreign wars that the public was duped into supporting so as *not* to fight the terrorists at home. (Ahmed Chalabi misled the CIA; the *New York Times* was misled by its government sources and in turn misled the public.) My argument above is that the truth or falsity of the German emergency declared in 1933 had no bearing on whether it could be used as a defense at Nuremberg in 1945.

72. See Posner, *Not a Suicide Pact*; William H. Rehnquist, *All the Laws but One: Civil Liberties in Wartime* (New York: Knopf, 1998).

73. Although the U.S. has no singular constitutional mechanism for reverting to dictatorship during an emergency, Congress has in fact granted the executive branch many emergency powers which it can activate at its sole discretion. The U.S. government can thus assume emergency powers without suspending the Constitution. See Kim Lane Scheppele, "Terrorism and the Constitution: Civil Liberties in a New America: Law in a Time of Emergency: States of Exception and the Temptations of 9/11," *University of Pennsylvania Journal of Constitutional Law* 6 (2004); Scheppele, "Emergency Powers and the Constitution: Comment: Small Emergencies (Symposium)," *Georgia Law Review Association Georgia Law Review* 50 (2006). For a legal

approach that would both specify and limit the effect of emergency powers on otherwise protected civil liberties, see Bruce A. Ackerman, *Before the Next Attack: Preserving Civil Liberties in an Age of Terrorism* (New Haven: Yale University Press, 2006). Cf. Rossiter, *Constitutional Dictatorship*, pt. 4 (on the U.S.).

Carl Schmitt distinguishes between "commissarial" dictatorships created to save the constitution and "sovereign" dictatorships that claim the authority to permanently change it. He explicitly refers to Lincoln's eleven-month assumption of extraordinary powers to quell rebellion as an example of the former. See Carl Schmitt, *Die Diktatur, von den Anfängen des Modernen Souveränitätsgedankens Bis Zum Proletarischen Klassenkampf* (Munich: Duncker and Humblot, 1921), p. 136; see also Schmitt, *Constitutional Theory*, pt. 1, sec. 6; Otto Kirchheimer, "Decree Powers and Constitutional Law in France under the Third Republic," in *Politics, Law, and Social Change; Selected Essays*, ed. Frederic S. Burin and Kurt L. Shell (New York: Columbia University Press, 1969).

74. Rey Chow, "Sacrifice, Mimesis, and the Theorizing of Victimhood (a Speculative Essay)," *Representations* 94, no. 1 (2006).

75. In *The Furies*, Arno Mayer stresses the role of popular violence in the rise of dictators who can also claim to be the only leaders strong enough to curb it. His earlier book (*Why Did the Heavens Not Darken?*) stresses the appeal to many Germans of a Nazi government that could restore state control over the mob. Curbing mob violence against dissidents has also been an argument for reduced civil liberties in the U.S. See, e.g., Stone, *Perilous Times*.

76. *Until* a human rights trial occurs, many conformists will have been receptive to the claim that modest human rights violations were a lesser evil. To the extent that a history of trials shows that deviations from human rights have been correctible, potential conformists may become more open to "lesser evil" arguments in the future. It is also true, however, that the evidence presented at human rights trials makes violations easier to recognize when they happen again. Proponents of human rights trials can reasonably argue that this is better than nothing. For an example of the "lesser evil" argument, see, Ignatieff, *The Lesser Evil*.

77. Karl Jaspers, *The Question of German Guilt*, trans. E. B. Ashton and Philip Lamantia (New York: Capricorn, 1961).

78. Massive evidence that prosecutions are appropriate is presented in a series of articles by Mark Danner that appeared in the *New York Review of Books*: "Abu Ghraib: The Hidden Story," October 7, 2004; "Torture and Truth," June 10, 2004; "The Logic of Torture," June 24, 2004; "U.S. Torture: Voices from the Black Sites," April 9, 2009; "The Red Cross Torture Report: What It Means," April 30 2009. See, too, Danner, "We Are All Torturers Now," *New York Times*, January 6, 2005; and Scott Horton, "Justice after Bush: Prosecuting an Outlaw Administration," *Harper's*, December 2008.

79. A leading critic of Bush administration policies argues, however, that convictions under U.S. law in U.S. courts are, in practical terms, impossible because of the lack of criminal intent which U.S. prosecutors normally have the burden of proving. He thus argues for a truth commission instead of prosecutions. David Cole, "What to Do about the Torturers?" *New York Review of Books*, January 15, 2009. My sugges-

tion, above, is that the U.S. prosecutions under international criminal law (based on Nuremberg) could, and arguably should, reduce the relevance of intent up to the point of finding strict liability for particularly egregious acts of torture—and that they should, at least, shift the burden of proof on intent to the defense and probably limit its relevance to pleas in mitigation.

80. Scott Horton, "When Lawyers Are War Criminals," http://balkin.blogspot. com/2006/10/when-lawyers-are-war-criminals.html (accessed January 31, 2010); Milan Markovic, "Lawyers Aren't Special: Why It's Legitimate to Investigate the Bush Lawyers Who May Have Approved War Crimes," Slate, http://www.slate.com/ id/2206518/ (accessed January 31, 2010).

10. Surviving Catastrophe

1. What occurs next, according to Girard, is a double substitution that aims to trick the gods. First, the ills of the collectivity are blamed on the scapegoat for whose deviancy the community as a whole now suffers divine retribution; next, however, the community's sacrifice of the scapegoat (through death or expulsion) is seen to expiate the collective sins for which divine retribution has *really* occurred. Because the scapegoat is considered to be guilty of the sins of all, Girard says, "only one must die" to cleanse the group. His interpretation attributes to the community incoherent beliefs: it first deceives itself into believing that the victim is guilty, and then deceives the gods into treating the victim's transgression as a surrogate for its own. Girard points out that "the sacrificial process requires a certain degree of misunderstanding," which the "theological basis of the sacrifice" fosters: "It is the god who supposedly demands the victims; he alone, in principle, who savors the smoke from the altars and requisitions the slaughtered flesh. It is to appease his anger that the slaughter goes on and the victims multiply" (*Violence and the Sacred*, p. 7).

2. Girard, *I See Satan Fall*, p. 70.

3. Girard, "The Bloody Skin of the Victim," p. 60.

4. Cf. Assmann, "No God but God."

5. See René Girard, *Job: The Victim of His People* (Stanford: Stanford University Press, 1987), chap. 21 ("The God of Victims").

6. Assmann here explains the "anti-Canaanism" of Deuteronomic religion as a Hebrew struggle with its own pagan past. Jan Assmann, *Of God and Gods: Egypt, Israel, and the Rise of Monotheism* (Madison: University of Wisconsin Press, 2008), p. 124.

7. Ibid., pp. 7, 110.

8 For an argument that using others is more respectful of their externality than projection and introjection, see Johnson, "Using People."

9. For the distinction between sacrifice and instrumental use, see Bataille, *Theory of Religion*.

10. Benny Morris, *The Birth of the Palestinian Refugee Problem Revisited*, 2d ed. (Cambridge: Cambridge University Press, 2004); Benny Morris, *Righteous Victims: A History of the Zionist-Arab Conflict, 1881–2001* (New York: Vintage, 2001).

11. Morris's interview in *Ha'aretz* is worth quoting at length: "Ben-Gurion was right. If he had not done what he did, a state would not have come into being. . . . Without

the uprooting of the Palestinians, a Jewish state would not have arisen here. . . . There are circumstances in history that justify ethnic cleansing. I know that this term is completely negative in the discourse of the 21st Century, but when the choice is between ethnic cleansing and genocide—the annihilation of your people—I prefer ethnic cleansing. . . .

"That was the situation . . . Zionism faced. A Jewish state would not have come into being without the uprooting of 700,000 Palestinians. Therefore it was necessary to uproot them. There was no choice but to expel that population. It was necessary to cleanse the hinterland and cleanse the border areas and cleanse the main roads. It was necessary to cleanse the villages from which our convoys and our settlements were fired on. . . . Even the great American democracy could not have been created without the annihilation of the Indians. There are cases in which the overall, final good justifies harsh and cruel acts that are committed in the course of history. . . .

"If he was already engaged in expulsion, maybe he should have done a complete job. I know that this stuns the Arabs and the liberals and the politically correct types. But my feeling is that this place would be quieter and know less suffering if the matter had been resolved once and for all. If Ben-Gurion had carried out a large expulsion and cleansed the whole country—the whole Land of Israel, as far as the Jordan River. It may yet turn out that this was his fatal mistake. If he had carried out a full expulsion—rather than a partial one—he would have stabilized the State of Israel for generations."

Ari Shavit, "Survival of the Fittest? An Interview with Benny Morris," http://www.counterpunch.org/shavit01162004.html (accessed January 31, 2010); see also Adi Ophir, "A Response to Benny Morris: Genocide Hides Behind Expulsion," *Counterpunch* (2004), http://www.counterpunch.org/ophir01162004.html (accessed January 31, 2010).

12. Dominick La Capra, *Representing the Holocaust: History, Theory, Trauma* (Ithaca: Cornell University Press, 1994), pp. 106–10; Peter Haidu, "The Dialectics of Unspeakability: Language, Silence, and the Narratives of Desubjectification," in *Probing the Limits of Representation: Nazism and the "Final Solution,"* ed. Saul Friedländer (Cambridge: Harvard University Press, 1992), pp. 284–94.

13. For an argument that the Holocaust *should* be considered by Israelis as a foundational sacrifice that is past, see Burg, *The Holocaust Is Over.*

14. This view is largely consistent with how philosophers posed the "problem of evil" before the twentieth century—the problem of how destructive events (such as the Lisbon earthquake or a shipwreck) could be permitted by a deity who is no longer seen to demand human sacrifice as a matter of course.

15. Is it the Holocaust itself that now makes both Himmler's Posen speech and Morris's defense of Israel seem anachronistic, along with all previous rationales for ethnic cleansing? Both views presuppose that the problem of historical injustice arises not because there *was* human sacrifice but instead because there are still surviving victims with active claims against the collective beneficiaries of the past. This proposition is shocking as a rationale for deliberate policies of mass extermination, such as Himmler pursued. But the presence of survivors might explain why the topics ad-

dressed in this book (U.S. slavery, apartheid, colonialism, the Holocaust, etc.) are commonly seen as moral catastrophes that compromise the justice of successor societies in ways that the climatic and biological catastrophes described, for example, by Jared Diamond are not. We now commonly distinguish catastrophes inflicted through human injustice from the "collapse" of societies through natural or internal causes to which they failed to respond. According to this view, we are not compromised by what happened to Easter Islanders or Ancient Greenlanders, but we can learn and benefit from their disasters. Jared M. Diamond, *Collapse: How Societies Choose to Fail or Succeed* (New York: Viking, 2005).

16. Paz, "Critique of the Pyramid," pp. 303–4; see, generally, pp. 294–318.

17. Mann, *1491*, pp. 124–48; Miguel León-Portilla, ed. *The Broken Spears: The Aztec Account of the Conquest of Mexico*, trans. Lysander Kemp, exp. and updated ed. (Boston: Beacon, 1992). See Klor de Alva, "Preface," pp. xx–xxi.

18. Goldhagen's view is in marked contrast to the dominant interpretation by German émigré intellectuals, who saw it as distinctively Nazi and hence "a modernist event" (Rabinbach, "Thinking about Auschwitz and Modernity," esp. pp. 51–54; cf. Goldhagen, *Hitler's Willing Executioners*, e.g., chap. 3.

19. See Noam Chomsky, *Year 501: The Conquest Continues* (Boston: South End, 1993). See also Stannard, *American Holocaust*.

20. According to this view, the basis of the Spanish *elimination* of native populations and cultures was *el Requerimiento*—a demand for conversion that was read upon arrival by Spanish Christians as a basis for "holy war" (itself modeled on Islamic jihad) by an armed Christendom recoiling from its defeat by a militant Islam to its east (Seed, *Ceremonies of Possession*, chap. 5). I owe this reference to Vanita Seth.

21. The above paragraph draws heavily on Rabinbach, "Thinking About Auschwitz and Modernity." See also Zygmunt Bauman, *Modernity and the Holocaust* (Ithaca: Cornell University Press, 2000). See also Yehuda Bauer, *Rethinking the Holocaust* (New Haven: Yale University Press, 2001), chaps. 4–5.

22. The view that Nazism was a self-conscious return to premonotheistic, Teutonic mythical thinking allowed antimodern intellectuals like Heidegger to accept the intensified anti-Semitism of their time.

23. There is a conceptual problem in viewing Girard's account of the scapegoating mechanism, which he believes to be effective in containing violence, as incorporating its own critique—that it singles out the innocent as sacrificial victims. The cultural critic Rey Chow explains this problem as follows: "the victim is the means by which the community interrupts the otherwise unstoppable circle of . . . violence Girard discusses   To follow Girard's logic to its deeply unsettling conclusion, if the Jews, the Gypsies, and other exterminated groups were surrogate/ritual victims, does it mean that genocide, however reprehensible it is on ethical grounds, should nonetheless be understood as a sacrificial ritual . . . whose purpose is to forestall a worse form of disaster . . .—the disaster and horror of being victimized *themselves*, of being reduced to bare life . . . of losing *their* monopoly on violence" (Chow, "Sacrifice, Mimesis, and . . . Victimhood," pp. 144–46). (The force of Chow's argument about Girard is vitiated by her failure to observe the distinction in his work between victimhood and victimage.)

24. Assmann distinguishes between "raw" violence, legal violence, political violence, ritual violence (sacrifice), and religious violence (in which the evils of ritual violence are brought to an end). See Assmann, *Of God and Gods*, chaps. 2, 6 and pp. 142–45.

25. Rom.: 12:19 (my emphasis).

26. Mayer, *The Furies*, p. 81, commenting on Schmitt, "Total Enemy, Total War." Schmitt's own examples focus on the religious wars of the sixteenth and seventeenth centuries, but with reference to the Crusades. He specifically argues against the view that British naval warfare is less "total" (i.e., ideological, economic, and moral) than German land warfare. "The English sea warfare against Spain was a world-wide combat of the Germanic and Romance peoples, between Protestantism and Catholicism, Calvinism and Jesuitism, and there are few instances of such outbursts of enmity as intense and final as Cromwell's against the Spaniards. The English war against Napoleon likewise changes from a sea war into a 'crusade.' In the war against Germany between 1914 and 1918, the world-wide English propaganda knew how to whip up enormous moral and spiritual energies in the name of civilization and humanity, or democracy and freedom against Prussian-German militarism" (Schmitt, "Total Enemy, Total War," p. 33).

27. This is a major theme of Shklar's essay, "Putting Cruelty First," discussed in chapter 1 of this volume.

28. A self-conscious *creature* thus understands its own rationality as a form of artificial intelligence. It is not surprising that issues of intelligent design and those of *artificial* intelligence are having a simultaneous resurgence at the beginning of the twenty-first century. Cyborgs would acquire all the theological properties of humans as soon as an ambivalence of love and hate is projected onto them by a Creator who keeps their purpose hidden. At this point, to pursue the analogy, they might redirect (or reexperience) the wish to destroy their Creator by destroying one another.

29. Freud, "*Moses and Monotheism*"; Taubes, *The Political Theology of Paul*, esp. pp. 76–95.

30. Cf. Judith Butler, "Moral Sadism and Doubting One's Own Love: Klein's Reflections on Melancholia," in *Reading Melanie Klein*, ed. Lyndsey Stonebridge and John Phillips (London: Routledge, 1998).

31. Smith, *Stories of Peoplehood*.

32. For recent discussion of these issues, see, e.g., Regina M. Schwartz, *The Curse of Cain: The Violent Legacy of Monotheism* (Chicago: University of Chicago Press, 1997). Cf. Said, "Michael Walzer's 'Exodus and Revolution'"; Boyarin, "Reading Exodus into History"; Israel Finkelstein and Neil Asher Silberman, *The Bible Unearthed: Archaeology's New Vision of Ancient Israel and the Origin of Its Sacred Texts* (New York: Free Press, 2001).

33. Lev. 19:13, 19:17.

34. Assmann believes that the theologization of cultural memory becomes visible through the study of its "outer horizon" and that his own subject, Egyptology, is the outer horizon of a Europe that consciously remembers only its Hebraic and Hellenic roots. Jan Assmann, "Invisible Religion and Cultural Memory," in *Religion and Cultural Memory: Ten Studies*, trans. Rodney Livingstone (Stanford: Stanford Uni-

versity Press, 2006); Assmann, "What Is Cultural Memory?" in *Religion and Cultural Memory: Ten Studies*, trans. Rodney Livingstone (Stanford: Stanford University Press, 2006), p. 19.

N.B. We have in Assmann's Egypt (the source of the Minoan cult of Dionysus) a version of the Christ and/or Dionysus question that dominated Nietzsche's later work. Nietzsche, *The Anti-Christ, Ecce Homo, Twilight of the Idols, and Other Writings*; Walter Friedrich Otto, *Dionysus, Myth and Cult*, trans. Robert B. Palmer (Bloomington: Indiana University Press, 1965), chaps. 1, 5, 11, 17; Carl Kerényi, *Dionysos: Archetypal Image of the Indestructible Life*, trans. Ralph Manheim (Princeton: Princeton University Press, 1976), chaps. 3–5. See also Norman O. Brown, "Apocalypse: The Place of Mystery in the Life of the Mind," in Brown, *Apocalypse and/or Metamorphosis* (Berkeley: University of California Press, 1991), p. 6. Brown, "Dionysus in 1990," in ibid.

35. The dangers of worshipping false (and therefore harmless) gods do not trouble the religions that Assmann calls "primary," which are more afraid of leaving out of their sacrificial offering any powerful gods whose powers are readily observable. Their opportunism appears in retrospect as polytheism—an anachronism suggesting that converted pagans were previously committed to believing about the powers that be what monotheists claim about the one true God. From a still pagan perspective, however, the religion of a true, but unseen, god appears as "a commandment to worship no gods at all." Jan Assmann, "Monotheism, Memory, and Trauma: Reflections on Freud's Book on Moses," in Assmann, *Religion and Cultural Memory*, p. 60.

36. Ibid., pp. 49–50.

37. "The trauma of monotheism is twofold. On the one hand, it is grounded in the duty, which is never quite fulfilled, to forget one's pagan faith, which keeps surfacing (since, after all, this involves the temptation to feel at home in the world as it is.). On the other hand, it is based on the destruction of gods, who are excoriated as idols, on the deicidal power of the Mosaic distinction [between true and false gods]. . . . [In Freud's account, this] trauma has nothing to do with parricide, . . . but with the trauma of deicide" (ibid., pp. 58–59).

38. Ibid., p. 50.

39. Assmann's argument expands upon the difference between Freud's account of the origin of religion in general (*Totem and Taboo*) and his account of monotheistic religion (*Moses and Monotheism*). The replacement of the slain father by a totemic figure that can be both worshiped and ritually sacrificed was, according to Freud, the universal origin of polytheism as the religion of brothers bound by a prohibition against contagious violence, such as Girard would later describe. Assmann's account of *mono*theism adds a new element—that the father who had to be killed for polytheism (theistic pluralism) to get under way was the *one* and *only* God. *This* murder is different from Girard's founding sacrifice that is later forbidden: it has to be *repressed* because the idea of a single god is implicitly a return to the primal father from the religion of the brothers (Assmann, "Monotheism, Memory, and Trauma" and "No God but God").

40. A monotheism that believes that it can kill pagan gods through disbelief might also

be accused of blasphemously believing itself to have "invented and created" God through its belief. See Steiner, "Zion," pp. 100–101.

41. Freud's *Moses and Monotheism* digs beneath the anti-Egyptian bias of the Hebrew Torah to uncover the moment of transition from the cyclical violence of polytheism religion to the historically driven violence of monotheism. In publishing his long-term study of Judaism from his London exile, shortly before the Holocaust, Freud concluded that the persistence of anti-Semitism was an outgrowth of the peculiar admixture of monotheism and world empire (first Egypt's and later Rome's) that left Jews perennially vulnerable to persecution for alone refusing to admit, and be forgiven, for hating the very God who first revealed himself to them (pp. 86–92).

42. Assmann, "No God but God." In his earlier essay, "Monotheism, Memory and Trauma," Assmann distinguishes primary religion, based on appeasing gods through sacrifice, from the secondary religions that reject such gods. He finds evidence for his distinction in Deuteronomy, the "forgotten" fifth book of Moses, discovered centuries later (according to Kings 22–23), just before the Babylonian exile, in which Moses excoriates his adopted people and warns them of the genocidal punishments that await for forgetting his teachings. Assmann calls Deuteronomy "a traumatized text" that provides an account of "the horror of forgetting" that is also "an anticipation of Auschwitz" (ibid., p. 55, and, more generally, pp. 51–58). See also Assmann, "Remembering in Order to Belong," pp. 96–100.

43. Even such theologically oriented figures of the left as Jacques Derrida have argued that defeating Islamism can justifiably postpone electoral democracy in places with strong tendencies toward the return of anti-Semitism. This is because Islamism is the only movement in world politics today that does not claim that democracy is necessary to achieve justice on earth—obedience to God would be enough. Derrida, *Rogues*, chap. 3; cf. Anidjar, *The Jew, the Arab*, chaps. 1, 3, and Berman, *Terror and Liberalism*, pp. 110–11.

44. "Prophesizing is utterly different from prediction. It is itself an effort to induce a right decision, or correct a wrong one. Prophecy is a form of struggle for the future, in order to avoid what is otherwise inevitable" (Rieff, *Charisma*, p. 41).

45. Asad, "Redeeming the 'Human' through Human Rights."

46. Norman O. Brown, *The Challenge of Islam: The Prophetic Tradition (Lectures, 1981)*, ed. Jerome Neu (Santa Cruz: New Pacific, 2008). See also Jay Cantor, "Introduction," pp. ix–xxxi, and Robert Meister, "N. O. Brown," in *In Memoriam: Norman O. Brown*, ed. Jerome Neu (Santa Cruz: New Pacific, 2005).

47. Norman O. Brown, "The Prophetic Tradition," in Brown, *Apocalypse and/or Metamorphosis*, p. 48.

48. Paul Berman specifically mentions the anti-Pauline thrust of Islamism in *Terror and Liberalism*, pp. 73, 81, 87. The point is also implicit in Berman's contrast between the apocalyptic forms of messianism that stress Armageddon and lead to totalitarianism, and those forms of messianism, associated with Paul, that stress the deferral of justice and peaceful coexistence in the meantime with those who may not ultimately be redeemed. The latter are consistent with his view of liberalism. See, e.g., *Terror and Liberalism*, pp. 46–51.

49. Brown, "The Prophetic Tradition," p. 50.

50. Ibid., p. 51. This essay is dedicated to David Erdman. Cf. David Erdman, *Blake, Prophet Against Empire: A Poet's Interpretation of the History of His Own Times*, 2d ed. (Princeton: Princeton University Press, 1969).

51. "I think all intelligent Marxists (of which I am one) will recognize that the true religion of Karl Marx was Prometheus, that triumphant spirit of human intelligence that was going to cast off all limitations" (Brown, *The Prophetic Tradition*, p. 49).

52. Cf. Carl Schmitt, *The Leviathan in the State Theory of Thomas Hobbes: Meaning and Failure of a Political Symbol*, trans. George Schwab and Erna Hilfstein (Westport, Conn.: Greenwood, 1996), chaps. 3, 5–7.

53. This thought is developed by Sayyid Qutb, a founder of modern Islamism, for whom forms of idolatry include subservience to the market, the party, material goods, one's own emotions, and even the secular nation-state when revered as a separate source of law (Qutb, *Milestones*, p.15). Paul Berman dismisses this passage as Qutb's effort to increase the international appeal of Islamism by incorporating elements derived from Eleanor Roosevelt's Universal Declaration of Human Rights (*Terror and Liberalism*, e.g., pp. 95–98).

54. Brown, "The Prophetic Tradition," p. 51.

55. Nor does God's appearance have the character of deferral (and also *deference* and *difference*) that Derrida describes throughout his work. For an early statement, see Jacques Derrida, "Differance," in Derrida, *Speech and Phenomena, and Other Essays on Husserl's Theory of Signs*, trans. David Allison (Evanston: Northwestern University Press, 1973).

56. "Without impairing its veneration for Moses as a prophetic figure," Brown writes, "[the Qur'an] endorses the eschatological longing and mystic revelations associated with the figure of Elijah, without naming him." The figure of Elijah is, rather, metamorphosed in *Sūrah* 18 into "Khidr, the Green (the sacred color of Islam) . . . the eternal protector of the community [who] will appear at the Return as the head of the armies of the Mahdi, who will fill the earth with justice even as it is now filled with injustice." Khidr is, according to Brown, the angelic servant of God who initiates the prophetic figures of Islam, including Abraham, Moses, Jesus, and Muhammad, bypassing entirely the period of God's absence posited by Paul in which a historical narrative of past loss and future redemption replaces any further need for direct prophetic revelation (Brown, "Apocalypse of Islam," pp. 82–83). Cf. Paul Berman's description of "the bright green Islamist color" as a "flower of evil" and a "politics of slaughter" (*Terror and Liberalism*, p. 110). On the figure of Khidr/Elijah, see Henry Corbin, *Creative Imagination in the Ṣūfism of Ibn 'Arabī*, trans. Ralph Manheim (Princeton. Princeton University Press, 1981), pp. 53–67.

57. In arguing that there is in Islam "another reality, knowledge of which is a struggle" (*itjihâd*), Brown follows Henry Corbin's account of Docetism. "Docetism is an alternative to the Incarnationism inherent in Christianity from the start, an undercurrent which became the mainstream in Islam. . . . Docetism, as the Greek root of the word indicates, is devotion to appearances, to apparitions, to visionary experience, to vision. In Eternity all is vision . . . In other words, Islam is a theology which rejects incarnation and instead has theophany" (Brown, "The Prophetic Tradition," p. 55); Brown, *The Challenge of Islam*, lec. 3). See also Henry Corbin, "Divine Epiphany

and Spiritual Rebirth," in Corbin, *Cyclical Time and Ismaili Gnosis*, trans. Ralph Manheim (London: Kegan Paul, 1983).

58. Max Weber, *The Sociology of Religion*, trans. Hans Gerth and Talcott Parsons et al. (Boston: Beacon, 1993).

59. Girard, Oughourlian, and Lefort, *Things Hidden*; Girard, *I See Satan Fall Like Lightning*.

60. For a recent development of this view, see Gauchet, *Disenchantment of the World*.

61. "There is in the Qur'ān a nihilistic exposure of the senselessness of plots, and the meaninglessness of history. . . . What is really going on is not a story . . . with a beginning, middle, and end. God is not the actor in an eschatological drama of Exodus or redemption. God makes no promises, there is no promised land. . . . Islam abruptly retracts the historicity of God" (Brown, *The Challenge of Islam*, lec. 4, p. 55).

   This explanation of the Qur'anic text as *post*narrative explains what the Shiite theologian Seyyed Hossein Nasr calls the "incoherence" sometimes found there by scholars accustomed to the narrative project that dominates the Bible. Some Islamist *tafsirs* take a similar view. In commenting, for example, on *Sūrah* 18, Qutb says, "The *sūrah* does not give details of where this episode took place. . . . Nor does it define the period in Moses' lifetime when the events took place. Thus we do not know whether the events related took place when Moses was still in Egypt. . . . Was it after they had begun their forty years of wandering?" It does not, moreover, "give us any details of the identity" of the person with whom Moses conversed. "Was he a prophet, a messenger, a scholar, or a person favored by God for his strong faith" (Qutb, *In the Shade of the Qur'ān*, 11:287–88). For a more extended non-narrative interpretation of revelations to Moses, Adam, and others, see Qutb's commentary on *Sūrah* 20, vol. 11, pp. 370–462.

62. "How can he who died to sin still live in it?" (Rom.: 6:4).

63. Jonathan Lear, *Therapeutic Action: An Earnest Plea for Irony* (New York: Other, 2003), esp. chap. 3; Hans W. Loewald, "On Internalization (1973)," in *The Essential Loewald: Collected Papers and Monographs*, ed. Jonathan Lear (Hagerstown, Md.: University, 2000); Loewald, "On the Therapeutic Action of Psychoanalysis (1960)," ibid.; Loewald, "The Experience of Time (1972)," ibid.

64. Rieff, *Charisma*, pt. 1.

65. Adam does not commit an original sin; he is considered impeccable and revered as a Prophet (like Noah, Moses, Jesus, and Muhammad) to whom much (but not all) was revealed. The philosopher Tariq Ramadan notes that, in the Qur'an (2:37–38), "Adam and Eve have been forgiven" and their offspring are "born innocent." Tariq Ramadan, "Prometheus and Abraham," in Ramadan, *Islam, the West, and the Challenges of Modernity*, trans. Saïd Amghar (Leicester: Islamic Foundation, 2001), p. 214. Corbin notes that the Qur'anic tenet of "Adam's impeccability "turns the Biblical narrative upside down" and "puts us at the antipodes of the Pauline typology." He attributes its origin to the pre-Pauline, Ebionite sect of Judeo-Christianity. Ebionite Adamology is characterized by a doctrine (unique in Christian, Jewish, or Gnostic literature) that absolves Adam of all sin and also affirms his impeccability (Corbin, "Divine Epiphany and Spiritual Rebirth," pp. 67, 76–77).

66. According to Corbin, this idea "is far removed from the attribute of Compassion

known to exoteric theologies as pity or mercy toward servants, as indulgence or forgiveness toward sinners. This is no moral or moralizing conception, but a metaphysical conception . . . a passion lived and shared with the understood object" (Corbin, *Creative Imagination*, p. 116).

67. "Compassion acts and determines, it causes things to be and to become like itself, because it is a spiritual state" (ibid., p. 119). According to Corbin, Islamic philosophy aims to illuminate the revealed existence of the unseen creation that "emanates" from God. In this respect it is indistinguishable from theology. See Henry Corbin, *History of Islamic Philosophy*, trans. Liadain Sherrard, with the assistance of Philip Sherrard (London: Kegan Paul International, 1993).

68. Corbin, *Creative Imagination*, pp. 212–13. See also pp. 184–215. According to Corbin, "the divine name Al'-Lāh becomes purely and simply equivalent to al-Rahmān, the Compassionate" (p. 115). Creation is, in effect, God's prayer, a manifestation of Al'-Lāh's name, and in praying to him—which is essentially reciting his name—humans express sympathy for God's loss of all the divine names that must remain unknown. (pp. 112–20, 246–71). Danielle Celermajer has directed me to a similar idea in the Lurianic Kabbalah. See Gershom Scholem, *Kabbalah* (New York: Meridian, 1978), pp. 148ff.

69. Corbin, *Creative Imagination*, p. 113.

70. Massignon goes on to say that the "mental decentering" required for such compassion has more in common with the stigmata of St. Francis than with his alms for the poor or, indeed, with any transfer of worldly goods. Louis Massignon, "Transfer of Suffering through Compassion," in *Testimonies and Reflection: Essays of Louis Massignon*, ed. Herbert Mason (Notre Dame: University of Notre Dame Press, 1989), pp. 156–57.

71. Corbin, "Divine Epiphany and Spiritual Rebirth," p. 62. In *Creative Imagination*, Corbin says, "To become a Compassionate One is to become the likeness of the Compassionate God experiencing infinite sadness over undisclosed virtualities" (p. 118).

72. In his article, "The Prophetic Tradition," Brown notes that "Islam discards the notion of vicarious atonement: there is no world-historical drama of original sin and sacrificial redemption; no "Death of God," no Oedipal drama (old Nobodaddy), no sacrifice of the Son to appease the wrath of the Father" (p. 52). For a more extensive discussion of sacrifice and its annulment, see Brown, *The Challenge of Islam*, pp. 15–18.

73. Ibid. Brown's late work suggests a Gnostic grand alliance between the Sufi elements in Islam, Kabbalistic Judaism, and Christian mysticism against all institutional (immanent) forms of monotheistic religion.

74. Matt. 20:16. See also Matt. 19:20; and Mark 10:81.

Conclusion

1. In many languages nouns also have a gender—masculine, feminine, or neuter.

2. "The 'third person' is not a 'person'; it is really the verbal form whose function is to express the *non-person*." Emile Benveniste, "Relationships of Person in the Verb," in Benveniste, *Problems in General Linguistics*, trans. Mary Elizabeth Meek (Coral

Gables: University of Miami Press, 1971), pp. 197–98; see also Benveniste, "The Nature of Pronouns," in ibid.

3. For present purposes, I shall leave aside the vocative case (in which a noun is used to call upon or invoke) and the genitive case (in which the noun is related to another noun as a matter of belonging, origin, and so forth. (According to Benveniste, Indo-European had eight cases in all.)

4. So called because the nominative is also used as the verb's object when the sentence performs an act of naming.

5. In many languages verb conjugations also include person and number—whether the verb's subject is first-, second-, or third-person singular/plural. For my purposes here, I leave aside a verb's *voice*, which in English is either active or passive. In the active voice the verb's subject performs the action and in the passive voice receives it. The Golden Rule involves a reversal of voice (from active to passive) as well as a reversal of case.

6. "The forms of anteriority do not have a temporal relationship among themselves … but can only enter into opposition with those similar forms of which they are the syntactic correlatives" (Benveniste, "Tense in the French Verb," pp. 212–13).

   Such temporal substitution, he says, is the poetic underpinning of narrative prose. See Emile Benveniste, "Remarks on the Function of Language in Freudian Theory," in Benveniste, *Problems in General Linguistics*.

7. Since Kepler, astronomical time has been based on the distinctions between cycles and successions—essentially, the orbit and the count. The idea that orbits can be counted gives us two *spatial* models of time as infinite—the circle and the line. This conception of infinite time does not address the time awareness produced by narratives, myths, and so on. See Reinhart Koselleck, "Time and History" and "Concepts of Historical Time and Social Identity," in Koselleck, *The Practice of Conceptual History*; Hans Blumenberg, "On a Lineage of the Idea of Progress," *Social Research* 41 (1974).

8. Reinhart Koselleck, "The Temporalization of Utopia," in Koselleck, *The Practice of Conceptual History*.

9. Hayden V. White, "Auerbach's Literary History: Figural Causation and Modern Historicism," in White, *Figural Realism: Studies in the Mimesis Effect* (Baltimore: Johns Hopkins University Press, 1999), p. 96. White goes on to sum up historicism as "nothing other than the discovery that human life and society found whatever meaning they might possess in history, not in any metaphysical beyond or transcendental religious realm" (pp. 96–97). See also Atwood, *Payback*, chap. 3 ("Debt as Plot"). For analysis of the plot structure of Human Rights Discourse, see Joseph R. Slaughter, *Human Rights, Inc.: The World Novel, Narrative Form, and International Law* (New York: Fordham University Press, 2007), chap. 2.

10. White, "Figural Causation," pp. 88–90. See also White, *Metahistory*, introduction.

11. Erich Auerbach, "Figura," in Auerbach, *Scenes from the Drama of European Literature* (Minneapolis: University of Minnesota Press, 1984), pt. 3.

12. White, "Figural Causation," p. 96.

13. For analysis of the contrasting uses of grammatical time in narrative, mythic, and prophetic forms of expressions, see Henry Corbin et al., *Man and Time*, ed. Joseph

Campbell, trans. Ralph Manheim, Princeton/Bollingen Paperbacks (New York: Pantheon, 1957).

14. To accomplish this, however, temporal insufficiency must be grammatically *constructed* by narrative prose itself, which relates, for example, the completed, repeated, and continuing aspects of past action to the present of enunciation. See Burke, *The Grammar of Motives*, pt. 1; Erich Auerbach, "Vico and Aesthetic Historicism," in Auerbach, *Scenes from the Drama of European Literature*; Roman Jakobson, "Linguistics and Poetics," in Jakobson, *Selected Writings*, ed. Stephen Rudy, vol. 3 (The Hague: Mouton De Gruyter, 1962); Jakobson, "Poetry of Grammar and Grammar of Poetry," ibid.

15. In a messianic moment, "we are the chosen ones . . . whose present time was once the promised future of the past, and it is our responsibility to remember and redress the injustices suffered by those who made it possible for us to live." Niall Lucy, *A Derrida Dictionary* (Malden, Mass.: Blackwell, 2004), p. 74 (expounding Derrida on spectrality in relation to Benjamin's concept of "weak messianic power").

16. White, "Figural Causation," p. 88.

17. We first encountered a joint emphasis on paradigm and syntagma in our discussion of Lévinas, who found similar issues of nonpresence in temporality and otherness. "Time," he says, is "this *always* of noncoincidence," which also characterizes the gulf between us and even the most proximate others. He uses the term "diachrony" to express the common "non-presence" of other times and other persons, both of which we "await" but which we cannot "comprehend" all at once. Lévinas, *Time and the Other*, trans. Richard A. Cohen (Pittsburgh: Duquesne University Press, 1987), p. 32. See, generally, chapters 4 and 5 in this volume.

18. Cf. John Milton, *Paradise Lost and Paradise Regained*, ed. Christopher Ricks (New York: Signet, 1968); Gottfried Wilhelm von Leibniz, *Theodicy: Essays on the Goodness of God, the Freedom of Man, and the Origin of Evil*, trans. E. M. Huggard (New Haven: Yale University Press, 1952).

19. Parfit, *Reasons and Persons*. Page references cited parenthetically are to this text. Although Parfit wants to answer Nietzsche's call for values that assume the *death* of God, he finds his strongest precursors in the writings of Hume and Sidgwick (as atheological utilitarians), and Rawls, Nagel, and Nozick (as atheological Kantians).

20. A further complication with utilitarian justifications of suffering, according to Parfit, is that the interpersonal dimension of concern for "the other" affects our moral calculus about intertemporality. One would not, Parfit suggests, be *completely* relieved to learn for the first time that one's mother's painful medical procedure had already happened—even if one would be entirely pleased to know that one's own procedure is in the past. There is thus a way in which the separateness of other persons is different from that of other times. The absence of a strong time bias with respect to the suffering of others introduces what Parfit calls an "asymmetry" between our moral feelings for persons whom we love and our feelings toward ourselves (pp. 181–84). Here Parfit comes close to recognizing what Lévinas regards as an ethical responsibility to suffer *for* the other, perhaps *in the other's place*. But, unlike Lévinas, Parfit does not directly consider the *trans*temporal and *trans*personal aspects of ethical responsibility, confining himself to the question of whether pres-

ent suffering can be justified as a sacrifice for the benefit of "Future Generations" (pt. 4).

21. "Non-utilitarians take the question of 'Who?' to be quite unlike the question of 'When?' If they are asked for the simplest possible description of the morally relevant facts, their description may be tenseless, but it must be personal" (p. 340).

22. Neo-Kantians, such as Rawls, Nozick, and Nagel, would have me treat the other as I would treat my*self*—while treating myself as another *other*. On the concept of "impersonal reasons," see Thomas Nagel, *The Possibility of Altruism* (Oxford: Clarendon, 1970); Nagel, *The View from Nowhere* (New York: Oxford University Press, 1986).

23. "Not in all ways," Parfit continues, "for beyond these events the person has earlier or later selves. But it may be only one out of the series of selves which is the object of some of our emotions, and to which we apply some of our principles" (p. 328).

24. He replaces these concepts with an analogy between "persons" and "nations," which David Hume describes as collections of many possible persons who regard themselves differently over time. Parfit asserts that "we do not regard nations as the morally significant unit" and argues that we should take a similar view of persons, and "relieve suffering . . . whatever its distribution" (p. 341).

25. See Ramadan, "Prometheus and Abraham." Ramadan describes Isaac as a consenting participant in his own prospective sacrifice to whom God's beneficent purpose was previously revealed (p. 213, citing Qur'an, 37:102–9).

26. The Muslim concept of *Tawhid* means that God is *all* that can be worshiped. For a substantially similar Shi'ia interpretation, see Shari'ati, *On the Sociology of Islam*, pp. 832–37. The view that God *alone* should rule is also a central tenet of the Jewish Bible (*Tanakh*), and the foundation of all theocratic rejections of the idolatry of state forms. See Herbert N. Schneidau, *Sacred Discontent: The Bible and Western Tradition* (Berkeley: University of California Press, 1977). See also Brown, *The Challenge of Islam*, lec. 2; and Brown, "Shi'ite Islam: The Politics of Gnosticism," in Brown, *The Challenge of Islam*.

27. Ramadan, "Prometheus and Abraham," pp. 212–18.

28. On monotheism's implicit hatred of God, see chapter 4 in this volume. Ramadan illustrates his account of the "questioning," "tension," and "existential anxiety" underlying the human relationship to God in Western (Judeo-Christian) culture by long-standing Judeo-Christian ambivalence about the near-sacrifice of Isaac, the near-omnicide of the Flood, and the seemingly genocidal punishments God decrees for subsequent disobedience.

29. Brown, *The Challenge of Islam*, lec. 1.

30. Brown may well have objected to the Sunni Islamism of Qutb and Maududi, not as Berman does for being anti-Promethean but for being anti-Dionysian. He is critical of Islamic legalism in which the Prophet must be followed by a caliph, rather than an imam who has the power to release his initiates from religiously prescribed taboos. For Brown's stress on the antinomian (permissive) side of the imamate, see *The Challenge of Islam*, lec. 6. See also Norman O. Brown, "The Turn to Spinoza," in Brown *Apocalypse and/or Metamorphosis*; Brown, "Philosophy and Prophecy: Spinoza's Hermeneutics," in ibid.

31. According to Brown, "Trinitarian Christianity takes God's incarnation as a historical fact. As a literal historical fact. . . . If, as orthodox Trinitarian Christianity says, the Crucifixion is not only a historical fact, but the decisive event of world history, then God takes charge of history. History is God's act, and God redeems us from that original sin" (Brown, *The Challenge of Islam*, lec. 2). "Thereafter prophets are no longer needed to save the world: all that is left to us is our personal salvation" (lec. 3).

32. Badiou introduces his book by comparing Paul to Lenin (see *Saint Paul*, preface and chap. 1). Brown similarly focuses on what Jay Cantor calls "the Leninist or Islamist project" which is to destroy theocratic hierarchies. "Islam reveals some of its archetypal meaning, then, by the parallax view with Leninism" (Cantor, "Introduction," in Brown, *The Challenge of Islam*, p. xxv).

33. Cf. Brown, *The Challenge of Islam*, lec. 6; Alain Badiou, "Truth and Justice," in Badiou, *Metapolitics*, trans. Jason Barker (London: Verso, 2005); and Badiou, *Saint Paul*. Badiou himself would disagree about Islamism, which he equates to generic fascism (because it is anti-Marxist and antimodern). Here he sides implicitly with those on the left who see the struggle to defeat Islamo-fascism as akin to an earlier generation's fight against Franco. For criticisms of Badiou by his translator, see Toscano, "The Bourgeois and the Islamist," pp. 29–37.

34. For a description of generic fascism, see, e.g., Umberto Eco, "Ur-Fascism," *New York Review of Books*, June 22, 1995. The concept is further developed in Roger Griffin, "The Palingenetic Core of Fascist Nationalism," in *Che Cos'è Il Fascismo? Interpretazioni E Prospettive Di Ricerche*, ed. Alessandro Campi (Rome: Ideazione, 2003). Cf. Badiou, *The Century*.

35. Berman, *Terror and Liberalism*, pp. 60–120.

36. Berman thus takes the following to be a knock-down argument against the Islamic philosopher Tariq Ramadan: "In Islam, Ramadan tells us, there is no . . . temptation to rebel. In Islam, submission is all. Submission to God . . . is the road to social justice, to a contented soul, and to harmony with the world" (*Terror and Liberalism*, p. 17). Cf. Paul Berman, "Who's Afraid of Tariq Ramadan?" *New Republic* 236, no. 4814 (2007). For the connection between death and absolute mastery, see Mikkel Borch-Jacobsen, *Lacan: The Absolute Master* (Stanford: Stanford University Press, 1991).

37. Berman directly invokes the inner freedom necessary to resist false gods on which the prophets also called (*Terror and Liberalism*, p. 43).

38. Gauchet, *Disenchantment of the World*, esp. chap. 5.

39. The Islamic conception of "granular" time, and justice in the instant, stands as a philosophically coherent rebuke to this view that is no less grounded in Greek and Jewish ideas than is Human Rights Discourse. See Corbin, "Divine Epiphany and Spiritual Rebirth."

40. Eusebius, *Eusebius—the Church History: A New Translation with Commentary*, trans. Paul L. Maier (Grand Rapids: Kregel, 1999); Augustine, *The City of God Against the Pagans*; Dante Alighieri, *Monarchy* (Cambridge: Cambridge University Press, 1996). For discussion of the Christian emperor as *Katechon* (Restrainer of the Anti-Christ), see Schmitt, *Nomos of the Earth*, pp. 59–62; *Political Theology II*, chap. 2 (esp. p. 92). In these writings God does not yet rule on earth, and the religious role

of secular power is to postpone apocalypse, preserve life, and thus allow more sinners the opportunity to find their personal salvation. As a successor to the secular power of Rome, the Holy Roman Emperor would thus be charged with providing *security* to Christendom so that the Pope had more time to save souls before the final struggle comes.

41. Cf. Eugen Weber, *Apocalypses: Prophesies, Cults, and Millennial Beliefs through the Ages* (Cambridge: Harvard University Press, 1999).

42. For historical accounts of early Islamic theocracy, see Crone, *God's Rule*; Marshall G. S. Hodgson, "The Role of Islam in World History," in *Rethinking World History: Essays on Europe, Islam, and World History*, ed. Edmund Burke (Cambridge: Cambridge University Press, 1993); Brague, *The Law of God*, chaps. 3, 5–6 10–11, 15; Marshall G. S. Hodgson, *The Venture of Islam: Conscience and History in a World Civilization*, 3 vols. (Chicago: University of Chicago Press, 1974), esp. vol. 1.

43. Cohen, *Religion of Reason*, pp. 189–92. The seminal text on this point is Ezekiel 18–19 ("The righteousness of the righteous shall be his own, and the wickedness of the wicked shall be his own.") This passage marks a shift in Jewish (and later Judeo-Christian) thought from collective to individual responsibility—a decisive first step toward ethics. Ezekiel does not explain, however, why those born free of sin should inherit the fruits of past iniquity (such as property, advantage, and even national territory) without being tainted by the evil of earlier generations. But what are the external and internal costs of allowing those who benefit from historical injustice to assert that birth (or rebirth) has cleansed them of collective guilt? Is there something further that they must do or forswear? These are questions of moral urgency posed by the prophetic call to justice that present-day Human Rights Discourse largely suppresses.

44. Lynn Hunt suggests that, in its eighteenth-century form, the appeal to "human rights" was not a claim about the moral responsibility of violators but rather about the moral intelligibility of bearers. Her authorities are figures such as Rousseau and Condorcet, who stressed empathetic identification with the interior lives of others. Their argument for distinctively *human* rights is that the difference between the self and others is *least* in the domain of inner feelings, where all humans are essentially the same (*Inventing Human Rights*, chap. 1).

45. Luther, *Lectures on Romans*, pp. 174–75.

46. Why call such intelligibility *moral*? Surely we must not if we believe that morality is limited to the domain of what is right and must exclude those wishes and beliefs that are unconscious because morality forbids us from acting on them. Freud himself described the moral standpoint in Kantian terms as a prohibition that blocks the path from wish to deed. This allowed him to deflect critics of the infant field of psychoanalysis by arguing that its domain (the unconscious) was utterly different from that of morality, the realm of deeds. Yet Freud also treated wishes and deeds as equivalent *within* the unconscious. I believe that the explanations provided by psychoanalysis persuade us (when they do) because unconscious desires track connections between emotion and thought that are visible in the genealogy of our moral concepts. See Stuart Hampshire, *Thought and Action* (New York: Viking, 1967); and Hampshire, *Spinoza and Spinozism*.

REFERENCES

Abraham, Nicolas, and Maria Torok. "The Illness of Mourning and the Fantasy of the Exquisite Corpse." In *The Shell and the Kernel: Renewals of Psychoanalysis,* pp. 107–24. Trans. Nicholas T. Rand. Chicago: University of Chicago Press, 1994.

———. "Mourning or Melancholia: Introjection *Versus* Incorporation." In *The Shell and the Kernel: Renewals of Psychoanalysis,* pp. 125–38. Trans. Nicholas T. Rand. Chicago: University of Chicago Press, 1994.

Abram, Jan. *The Language of Winnicott: A Dictionary and Guide to Understand His Work.* Ed. Harry Karnac. Northvale, N.J.: Aronson, 1997.

Acemoglu, Daron, and James A. Robinson. *Economic Origins of Dictatorship and Democracy.* Cambridge: Cambridge University Press, 2006.

Ackerman, Bruce A. *Before the Next Attack: Preserving Civil Liberties in an Age of Terrorism.* New Haven: Yale University Press, 2006.

———. *The Future of Liberal Revolution.* New Haven: Yale University Press, 1992.

———. *We the People.* Vol. 2. Cambridge: Belknap Press of Harvard University Press, 1991.

Ackerman, Bruce A., and Anne Alstott. *The Stakeholder Society.* New Haven: Yale University Press, 1999.

Adam, Heribert, F. van Zyl Slabbert, and Kogila Moodley. *Comrades in Business: Post-Liberation Politics in South Africa.* Cape Town: Tafelberg, 1997.

Adarand v. Peña, 515 U.S. 200 (1995).

Adorno, Theodor W. *Negative Dialectics.* Trans. E. B. Ashton. New York: Seabury, 1973.

Agamben, Giorgio. "Beyond Human Rights." In *Means Without End: Notes on Politics,* pp. 15–28. Trans. Vincenzo Binetti and Cesare Casarino. Minneapolis: University of Minnesota Press, 2000.

———. *Homo Sacer: Sovereign Power and Bare Life.* Trans. Daniel Heller-Roazen. Stanford: Stanford University Press, 1998.

———. *Remnants of Auschwitz: The Witness and the Archive.* Trans. Daniel Heller-Roazen. New York: Zone, 2000.

———. *State of Exception*. Chicago: University of Chicago Press, 2005.

———. *The Time That Remains: A Commentary on the Letter to the Romans*. Trans. Patricia Dailey. Stanford: Stanford University Press, 2005.

Akenson, Donald H. *Surpassing Wonder: The Invention of the Bible and the Talmuds*. Chicago: University of Chicago Press, 2001.

Alchian, Armen A. "Cost." In *Choice and Cost Under Uncertainty*, pp. 180–201. Ed. Daniel K. Benjamin. Indianapolis: Liberty Fund, 2006.

———. *Property Rights and Economic Behavior*. Ed. Daniel K. Benjamin. Vol. 2, *The Collected Works of Armen A. Alchian*. Indianapolis: Liberty Fund, 2006.

Alchian, Armen A., and William R. Allen. *Exchange and Production: Theory in Use*. Belmont, Calif.: Wadsworth, 1969.

Alchian, Armen A., and Harold Demsetz. "The Property Rights Paradigm." *Journal of Economic History* 33, no. 1 (1973): 16–27.

Alford, C. Fred. *Melanie Klein and Critical Social Theory: An Account of Politics, Art, and Reason Based on Her Psychoanalytic Theory*. New Haven: Yale University Press, 1989.

Alighieri, Dante. *The Divine Comedy*. Trans. Mark Musa. Harmondsworth: Penguin, 1984.

———. *Monarchy*. Cambridge: Cambridge University Press, 1996.

Aloni, Udi. *Local Angel: Theological-Political Fragments*. London: ICA, 2004.

Aly, Götz. *Hitler's Beneficiaries: Plunder, Racial War, and the Nazi Welfare State*. Trans. Jefferson Chase. New York: Metropolitan, 2007.

Amar, Akhil Reed. "Abraham Lincoln and the American Union." *University of Illinois Law Review*, no. 5 (2001): 1109–33.

———. *America's Constitution: A Biography*. New York: Random House, 2005.

———. "The Bill of Rights and the Fourteenth Amendment." *Yale Law Journal* 101, no. 6 (1992): 1193–1284.

———. *The Bill of Rights: Creation and Reconstruction*. New Haven: Yale University Press, 1998.

———. "The Case of the Missing Amendments: R.A.V. v. City of St. Paul." *Harvard Law Review* 106, no. 1 (1992): 124–61.

———. "Remember the Thirteenth." *Constitutional Law Commentary* (1993).

Amar, Akhil Reed, and Daniel Widawsky. "Child Abuse as Slavery: A Thirteenth Amendment Response to Deshaney." *Harvard Law Review* (1992): 105.

American Law Institute. *Restatement of the Law of Restitution: Quasi Contracts and Constructive Trusts, as Adopted and Promulgated by the American Law Institute at Washington, D.C., May 8, 1936*. 3 vols. St. Paul: American Law Institute, 1937.

Améry, Jean. "Resentment." In *At the Mind's Limits: Contemplations by a Survivor on Auschwitz and Its Realities*, pp. 62–81. Trans. Sidney Rosenfeld and Stella P. Rosenfeld. Bloomington: Indiana University Press, 1980.

Anbinder, Tyler. *Nativism and Slavery: The Northern Know Nothings and the Politics of the 1850's*. New York: Oxford University Press, 1992.

Anderson, Benedict R. O'G. *Imagined Communities: Reflections on the Origin and Spread of Nationalism*. London: Verso, 1983.

Anidjar, Gil. *The Jew, the Arab: A History of the Enemy*. Stanford: Stanford University Press, 2003.

———. "Lines of Blood: *Limpieza de Sangre* as Political Theology." In *Blood in History and Blood Histories*. Ed. Mariacarla Gadebusch Bondio. Florence: Galluzzo, 2005.

———. "Terror Right (Carl Schmitt)." *CR-the New Centennial Review* 4, no. 3 (2004): 35–69.

Annan, Noel. *Changing Enemies: The Defeat and Regeneration of Germany.* New York: Norton, 1996.

Antin, Mary. *The Promised Land.* Ed. Werner Sollors. New York: Penguin, 1997.

Arendt, Hannah. *Eichmann in Jerusalem: A Report on the Banality of Evil.* Rev. ed. New York: Penguin, 1994.

———. *Hannah Arendt/Karl Jaspers Correspondence, 1926–1969.* New York: Harcourt Brace Jovanovich, 1992.

———. *The Human Condition.* Chicago: University of Chicago Press, 1958.

———. "Irreversibility and the Power to Forgive." In *The Human Condition,* §33. Chicago: University of Chicago Press, 1998.

———. *The Jewish Writings.* Ed. Jerome Kohn and Ron H. Feldman. New York: Schocken, 2007.

———. *On Revolution.* New York: Viking, 1963.

———. *The Origins of Totalitarianism.* New York: Harcourt Brace Jovanovich, 1973.

———. "Some Questions of Moral Philosophy." In *Responsibility and Judgment,* pp. 49–146. Ed. Jerome Kohn. New York: Schocken, 2003.

———. "Thinking and Moral Considerations." In *Responsibility and Judgment,* pp. 159–89. Ed. Jerome Kohn. New York: Schocken, 2003.

———. "The Tradition of Political Thought." In *The Promise of Politics,* pp. 40–62. Ed. Jerome Kohn. New York: Schocken, 2005.

Arrow, Kenneth J. *Social Choice and Individual Values.* 2d ed. New York: Wiley, 1963.

Asad, Talal. *Formations of the Secular: Christianity, Islam, Modernity.* Stanford: Stanford University Press, 2003.

———. "Redeeming the 'Human' Through Human Rights." In *Formations of the Secular: Christianity, Islam, Modernity,* pp. 127–58. Stanford: Stanford University Press, 2003.

———. "Reflections on Cruelty and Torture." In *Formations of the Secular: Christianity, Islam, Modernity,* pp. 100–24. Stanford: Stanford University Press, 2003.

———. "Thinking about Agency and Pain." In *Formations of the Secular: Christianity, Islam, Modernity,* pp. 67–99. Stanford: Stanford University Press, 2003.

Ash, Timothy Garton. "True Confessions." *New York Review of Books* 44, no. 12 (1997): 33–38.

———. "The Truth About Dictatorship." Review of *Transitional Justice,* 3 vols., ed. Neil J. Kritz, and other works. *New York Review of Books* 45, no. 3 (1998): 35–40.

Asmal, Kader, Louise Asmal, and Ronald Suresh Roberts. *Reconciliation Through Truth: A Reckoning of Apartheid's Criminal Governance.* 2d ed. Cape Town: David Philip, 1997.

Assmann, Jan. "Invisible Religion and Cultural Memory." In *Religion and Cultural Memory: Ten Studies,* pp. 31–45. Trans. Rodney Livingstone. Stanford: Stanford University Press, 2006.

———. "Monotheism, Memory, and Trauma: Reflections on Freud's Book on Moses." In *Religion and Cultural Memory: Ten Studies,* pp. 46–62. Trans. Rodney Livingstone. Stanford: Stanford University Press, 2006.

———. "No God but God: Exclusive Monotheism and the Language of Violence." In *Of God and Gods: Egypt, Israel, and the Rise of Monotheism,* pp. 106–26. Madison: University of Wisconsin Press, 2008.

——. *Of God and Gods: Egypt, Israel, and the Rise of Monotheism.* Madison: University of Wisconsin Press, 2008.

——. "Remembering in Order to Belong: Writing, Memory, and Identity." In *Religion and Cultural Memory: Ten Studies*, pp. 81–100. Trans. Rodney Livingstone. Stanford: Stanford University Press, 2006.

——. "What Is Cultural Memory?" In *Religion and Cultural Memory: Ten Studies*, pp. 31–45. Trans. Rodney Livingstone. Stanford: Stanford University Press, 2006.

Athanasius. *The Life of Antony.* Trans. Tim Vivian, Apostolos N. Athanassakis, and Rowan A. Greer. Kalamazoo: Cistercian, 2003.

Atwood, Margaret. *Payback: Debt and the Shadow Side of Wealth.* Berkeley: Anansi, 2008.

Auerbach, Erich. "Figura." In *Scenes from the Drama of European Literature,* pp. 11–78. Minneapolis: University of Minnesota Press, 1984.

——. "Vico and Aesthetic Historicism." In *Scenes from the Drama of European Literature,* pp. 183–98. Minneapolis: University of Minnesota Press, 1984.

Augustine, Saint. *The City of God against the Pagans.* Trans. R. W Dyson. Cambridge: Cambridge University Press, 1998.

Ayres, Ian. *Optional Law: The Structure of Legal Entitlements.* Chicago: University of Chicago Press, 2005.

Badiou, Alain. "The Adventure of French Philosophy." *New Left Review* 35 (2005): 67–77.

——. *Being and Event.* Trans. Oliver Feltham. London: Continuum, 2005.

——. *The Century.* Trans. Alberto Toscano. Cambridge: Polity, 2007.

——. "The Cultural Revolution: The Last Revolution?" *Positions-East Asia Cultures Critique* 13, no. 3 (2005): 481–514.

——. "Democratic Materialism and the Materialist Dialectic." *Radical Philosophy*, no. 130 (2005): 20–24.

——. "Eight Theses on the Universal." In *Theoretical Writings*, pp. 143–52. Ed. Ray Brassier and Alberto Toscano. Trans. Ray Brassier and Alberto Toscano. London: Continuum, 2004.

——. *Ethics: An Essay on the Understanding of Evil.* Trans. Peter Hallward. London: Verso, 2001.

——. "Further Selections from 'Theorie Du Sujet' on the Cultural Revolution." *Positions-East Asia Cultures Critique* 13, no. 3 (2005): 649–58.

——. *Logics of Worlds: Being and Event, 2.* London: Continuum, 2009.

——. "Philosophy and Mathematics." In *Conditions*, pp. 93–112. Trans. Steven Corcoran. London: Continuum, 2008.

——. "Philosophy and the 'War against Terrorism.'" In *Infinite Thought: Truth and the Return to Philosophy*, pp. 141–64. Trans. Justin Clemens and Oliver Feltham. London: Continuum, 2003.

——. *Pocket Pantheon: Figures of Postwar Philosophy.* Trans. David Macey. London: Verso, 2009.

——. "Politics as a Truth Procedure." In *Metapolitics*, pp. 141–52. Trans. Jason Barker. London: Verso, 2005.

——. *Saint Paul: The Foundation of Universalism.* Trans. Ray Brassier. Stanford: Stanford University Press, 2003.

——. "Selections from 'Theorie Du Sujet' on the Cultural Revolution." *Positions-East Asia Cultures Critique* 13, no. 3 (2005): 635–48.

———. "A Speculative Disquisition on the Concept of Democracy." In *Metapolitics*, pp. 78–95. Trans. Jason Barker. London: Verso, 2005.

———. "Truth and Justice." In *Metapolitics*, pp. 96–106. Trans. Jason Barker. London: Verso, 2005.

———. "Truth: Forcing and the Unnameable." In *Conditions*, pp. 129–44. Trans. Steven Corcoran. London: Continuum, 2008.

Badiou, Alain, and Bruno Bosteels. "Can Change Be Thought? A Dialogue with Alain Badiou." In *Alain Badiou: Philosophy and Its Conditions*, pp. 237–61. Ed. Gabriel Riera. Albany: State University of New York Press, 2005.

Baker, Nicholson. *Human Smoke: The Beginnings of World War II, the End of Civilization*. New York: Simon and Schuster, 2008.

Balakrishnan, Gopal. *The Enemy: An Intellectual Portrait of Carl Schmitt*. London: Verso, 2000.

Balibar, Étienne. "Is There a Neo-Racism?" In Étienne Balibar and Immanuel Wallerstein, *Race, Nation, Class: Ambiguous Identities*, pp. 17–28. Trans. Chris Turner. London: Verso, 1991.

———. "My *Self* and My *Own*: One and the Same." In *Accelerating Possession: Global Futures of Property and Personhood*, pp. 21–44. Ed. Bill Maurer and Gabriele Schwab. New York: Columbia University Press, 2006.

———. "The Nation Form: History and Ideology." In Étienne Balibar and Immanuel Wallerstein, *Race, Nation, Class: Ambiguous Identities*, pp. 86–106. Trans. Chris Turner. London: Verso, 1991.

———. "Racism and Nationalism." In Étienne Balibar and Immanuel Wallerstein, *Race, Nation, Class: Ambiguous Identities*, pp. 37–67. Trans. Chris Turner. London: Verso, 1991.

———. "Racism and Universalism." In *Masses, Classes, Ideas: Studies on Politics and Philosophy Before and After Marx*, pp. 191–204. Trans. James Swenson. New York: Routledge, 1994.

———. "'Rights of Man' and 'Rights of the Citizen': The Modern Dialectic of Equality and Freedom." In *Masses, Classes, Ideas: Studies on Politics and Philosophy Before and After Marx*, pp. 39–59. Trans. James Swenson. New York: Routledge, 1994.

Banner, Stuart. *How the Indians Lost Their Land: Law and Power on the Frontier*. Cambridge: Belknap Press of Harvard University Press, 2005.

Barkan, Elazar. *The Guilt of Nations: Restitution and Negotiating Historical Injustices*. New York: Norton, 2000.

Barry, Brian, and Robert E. Goodin. *Free Movement: Ethical Issues in the Transnational Migration of People and Money*. University Park: Pennsylvania State University Press, 1992.

Barry, Brian M. *Justice as Impartiality*. Oxford: Oxford University Press, 1995.

———. "The Public Interest." *Proceedings of the Aristotelian Society* Supplementary Volume 38 (1964): 1–18.

Bartlett, Robert. Review of *The Myth of Nations: The Medieval Origins of Europe* by Patrick J. Geary. *Journal of Modern History* 75, no. 4 (2003): 919–20.

———. *The Making of Europe: Conquest, Colonization, and Cultural Change, 950–1350*. Princeton: Princeton University Press, 1993.

———. "Medieval and Modern Concepts of Race and Ethnicity." *Journal of Medieval and Early Modern Studies* 2, no. 1 (2001): 39–56.

Bartlett, Thomas. "'What Ish My Nation?'" In *Irish Studies: A General Introduction*, pp. 44–59. Ed. Thomas Bartlett et al. Dublin: Gill and Macmillan, 1988.

Bartov, Omer. *Mirrors of Destruction: War, Genocide, and Modern Identity*. Oxford: Oxford University Press, 2000.

———. *Murder in Our Midst: The Holocaust, Industrial Killing, and Representation*. New York: Oxford University Press, 1996.

Bass, Ellen, and Laura Davis. *The Courage to Heal: A Guide for Women Survivors of Child Sexual Abuse*. New York: Perennial Library, 1988.

Bass, Gary Jonathan. *Freedom's Battle: The Origins of Humanitarian Intervention*. New York: Knopf, 2008.

———. *Stay the Hand of Vengeance: The Politics of War Crimes Tribunals*. Princeton: Princeton University Press, 2000.

Bataille, Georges. *Theory of Religion*. Trans. Robert Hurley. New York: Zone, 1989.

Battersby, John. "Academic Slams Mbeki for Neglecting the Poor." *Sunday Independent* December 12, 2002.

———. "The ANC Is Not a Socialist Movement." *Mercury*, December 12, 2002.

Bauer, Bruno. "The Jewish Problem." In *The Young Hegelians, an Anthology*, p. xiii. Ed. Lawrence S. Stepelevich. Cambridge: Cambridge University Press, 1983.

Bauer, Yehuda. "Comparisons with Other Genocides." In *Rethinking the Holocaust*, pp. 39–67. New Haven: Yale University Press, 2001.

———. "From the Holocaust to the State of Israel." In *Rethinking the Holocaust*, pp. 242–60. New Haven: Yale University Press, 2001.

———. *Rethinking the Holocaust*. New Haven: Yale University Press, 2001.

Bauman, Zygmunt. *Modernity and the Holocaust*. Ithaca: Cornell University Press, 2000.

Bazyler, Michael J. *Holocaust Justice: The Battle for Restitution in America's Courts*. New York: New York University Press, 2003.

Bazyler, Michael J., and Roger P. Alford. *Holocaust Restitution: Perspectives on the Litigation and Its Legacy*. New York: New York University Press, 2006.

Bell, Derrick A. *And We Are Not Saved: The Elusive Quest for Racial Justice*. New York: Basic Books, 1987.

Bell, Terry, and Dumisa Buhle Ntsebeza. *Unfinished Business: South Africa, Apartheid, and Truth*. London: Verso, 2003.

Belz, Herman. *Reconstructing the Union; Theory and Policy during the Civil War*. Ithaca: Cornell University Press, 1969.

Benigni, Roberto. *Life Is Beautiful*. 1997.

Benjamin, Walter. "On the Concept of History." In *Selected Writings (1929–1940)*, pp. 389–400. Ed. Howard Eiland and Michael William Jennings. Trans. Edmund Jephcott et al. Cambridge: Belknap Press of Harvard University Press, 2003.

———. "Paralipomena to 'on the Concept of History.'" In *Selected Writings (1929–1940)*. Ed. Howard Eiland and Michael William Jennings. Trans. Edmund Jephcott et al. Cambridge: Belknap Press of Harvard University Press, 2003.

———. *Selected Writings, Vol. 2 (1927–34)*. Ed. Michael William Jennings. 4 vols. Cambridge: Belknap Press of Harvard University Press, 1999.

Bensaïd, Daniel. "Alain Badiou and the Miracle of the Event." In *Think Again: Alain Badiou and the Future of Philosophy*, pp. 94–105. Ed. Peter Hallward. London: Continuum, 2004.

Bentham, Jeremy. "Anarchical Fallacies: Being an Examination of the Declarations of Rights Issued During the French Revolution." In *The Works of Jeremy Bentham*, pp. 489–534. Ed. William Tait and John Bowring. Edinburgh: Simpkin, Marshall and, 1843. Reprint, Elibron Classics Replica Edition, 2005.

Benveniste, Emile. *Indo-European Language and Society.* Trans. Elizabeth Palmer. Coral Gables: University of Miami Press, 1973.

——. "The Linguistic Functions of 'To Be' and 'To Have.'" In *Problems in General Linguistics*, pp. 163–79. Trans. Mary Elizabeth Meek. Coral Gables: University of Miami Press, 1971.

——. "The Nature of Pronouns." In *Problems in General Linguistics*, pp. 217–22. Trans. Mary Elizabeth Meek. Coral Gables: University of Miami Press, 1971.

——. "Relationships of Person in the Verb." In *Problems in General Linguistics*, pp. 194–204. Trans. Mary Elizabeth Meek. Coral Gables: University of Miami Press, 1971.

——. "Remarks on the Function of Language in Freudian Theory." In *Problems in General Linguistics*, pp. 65–75. Trans. Mary Elizabeth Meek. Coral Gables: University of Miami Press, 1971.

——. "Tense in the French Verb." In *Problems in General Linguistics*, pp. 205–15. Trans. Mary Elizabeth Meek. Coral Gables: University of Miami Press, 1971.

Bercovitch, Sacvan. *The American Jeremiad.* Madison: University of Wisconsin Press, 1978.

Beresford, Dave. "TRC Slams ANC, PAC and Winnie." *Electronic Mail and Guardian,* October 27, 1998.

Beringer, Richard E., et al. *Why the South Lost the Civil War.* Athens: University of Georgia Press, 1986.

Berkowitz, Michael. *Zionist Culture and West European Jewry Before the First World War.* Cambridge: Cambridge University Press, 1993.

Berlant, Lauren. "Poor Eliza." In *The Female Complaint: The Unfinished Business of Sentimentality in American Culture*, pp. 13–68. Durham: Duke University Press, 2008.

——. "The Subject of True Feeling: Pain, Privacy, and Politics." In *Cultural Pluralism, Identity Politics, and the Law*, pp. 49–84. Ed. Austin Sarat and Thomas R. Kearns. Ann Arbor: University of Michigan Press, 1999.

Berlin, Isaiah. "Benjamin Disraeli, Karl Marx, and the Search for Identity." In *Against the Current: Essays in the History of Ideas*, pp. 252–86. Ed. Henry Hardy. New York: Viking, 1980.

——. "The Life and Opinions of Moses Hess." In *Against the Current: Essays in the History of Ideas*, pp. 213–25. Ed. Henry Hardy. New York: Viking, 1980.

Berman, Paul. "Books: Who's Afraid of Tariq Ramadan?" *New Republic* 236, no. 4814 (2007): 37–63.

——. "The Other and the Almost the Same." *New Yorker,* February 12, 1994, pp. 61–71.

——. "The Passion of Joschka Fischer." In *Power and the Idealists; or, the Passion of Joschka Fischer and Its Aftermath*, pp. 1–97. Brooklyn: Soft Skull, 2005.

——. "The Philosopher of Islamic Terror." *New York Times Magazine,* March 23, 2003.

——. *Power and the Idealists; or, the Passion of Joschka Fischer and Its Aftermath.* Brooklyn: Soft Skull, 2005.

——. *Terror and Liberalism.* New York: Norton, 2003.

Binder, Guyora. "Did the Slaves Author the Thirteenth Amendment? An Essay in Redemptive History." *Yale Journal of Law and Humanities* 5 (1993): 471–505.

———. "The Slavery of Emancipation." *Cardozo Law Review* 17 (1996): 2063–2102.

Bion, Wilfred R. "Attention and Interpretation: A Scientific Approach to Insight in Psycho-Analysis and Groups." New York: Basic Books, 1970.

———. *Experiences in Groups, and Other Papers*. London: Tavistock/Routledge, 1989.

———. "Second Thoughts: Selected Papers on Psycho-Analysis." London: Heinemann Medical, 1967.

Birks, Peter. "Unjust Enrichment and Wrongful Enrichment." *Texas Law Review* 79 (2001).

Birnbaum, Pierre, and Ira Katznelson. *Paths of Emancipation: Jews, States, and Citizenship*. Princeton: Princeton University Press, 1995.

Blackburn, Robin. "Finance and the Fourth Dimension." *New Left Review*, no. 39 (2006): 39–70.

Bloomfield, Morton W. *The Seven Deadly Sins; an Introduction to the History of a Religious Concept, with Special Reference to Medieval English Literature*. East Lansing: Michigan State College Press, 1952.

Bloxham, Donald. *Genocide on Trial: War Crimes Trials and the Formation of Holocaust History and Memory*. Oxford: Oxford University Press, 2001.

Blumenberg, Hans. *The Legitimacy of the Modern Age*. Trans. Robert M. Wallace. Cambridge: MIT Press, 1985.

———. "On a Lineage of the Idea of Progress." *Social Research* 41 (1974): 5–27.

———. *Shipwreck with Spectator: Paradigm of a Metaphor for Existence*. Trans. Steven Rendall. Cambridge: MIT Press, 1997.

Bond, Patrick. "Reply to Johnson." *New Left Review*, no. 58 (2009): 77–90.

Boraine, Alex. *A Country Unmasked: Inside South Africa's Truth and Reconciliation Commission*. Cape Town: Oxford University Press, 2000.

———. "Truth and Reconciliation Commission in South Africa: The Price of Peace." In *Retribution and Reparation in the Transition to Democracy*, pp. 299–316. Ed. Jon Elster. Cambridge: Cambridge University Press, 2006.

Borch-Jacobsen, Mikkel. *Lacan: The Absolute Master*. Stanford: Stanford University Press, 1991.

Borgwardt, Elizabeth. *A New Deal for the World: America's Vision for Human Rights*. Cambridge: Belknap Press of Harvard University Press, 2005.

Bourdieu, Pierre, and Loïc Wacquant. "On the Cunning of Imperial Reason." *Theory, Culture and Society* 16, no. 1 (1999): 41–58.

Bowersock, Glenn W. *Martyrdom and Rome*. Cambridge: Cambridge University Press, 1995.

Bowlby, John. "Pathological Mourning and Childhood Mourning." *JAPA* (1963): 500–541.

Boyarin, Daniel. *Dying for God: Martyrdom and the Making of Christianity and Judaism*. Stanford: Stanford University Press, 1999.

———. *A Radical Jew: Paul and the Politics of Identity*. Berkeley: University of California Press, 1997.

Boyarin, Jonathan. "Reading Exodus into History." *New Literary History* 23, no. 3 (1992): 523–54.

———. "Space, Time, and the Politics of Memory." In *Remapping Memory: The Politics of Timespace*, pp. 1–38. Ed. Jonathan Boyarin. Minneapolis: University of Minnesota Press, 1994.

Bracher, Mark. *Lacan, Discourse, and Social Change: A Psychoanalytic Cultural Criticism.* Ithaca: Cornell University Press, 1993.

Brague, Rémi. *The Law of God: The Philosophical History of an Idea.* Chicago: University of Chicago Press, 2007.

———. "The Political Theology of Paul: Schmitt, Benjamin, Nietzsche and Freud." *Critique* 56, no. 634 (2000): 214–20.

Branch, Taylor. *At Canaan's Edge: America in the King Years, 1965–68.* New York: Simon and Schuster, 2006.

———. *Parting the Waters: America in the King Years, 1954–63.* New York: Simon and Schuster, 1988.

———. *Pillar of Fire: America in the King Years, 1963–65.* New York: Simon and Schuster, 1998.

Brealey, Richard A., and Stewart C. Myers. *Principles of Corporate Finance.* 7th ed. Boston: McGraw-Hill/Irwin, 2003.

Bredekamp, Horst. "From Walter Benjamin to Carl Schmitt, Via Thomas Hobbes." Trans. Melissa Thorson Hause and Jackson Bond. *Critical Inquiry* 25, no. 2 (1999): 247–66.

Brennan, Teresa. *The Transmission of Affect.* Ithaca: Cornell University Press, 2004.

Breytenbach, Breyten. *The True Confessions of an Albino Terrorist.* San Diego: Harcourt Brace, 1994.

Brilmayer, Lea A. "Carolene, Conflicts, and the Fate of the 'Inside Outsider'." *University of Pennsylvania Law Review* 134 (1986): 1291–334.

———. "Consent, Contract, and Territory." *Minnesota Law Review* 39 (1990): 1–35.

———. "Shaping and Sharing in Democratic Theory: Towards a Political Philosophy of Interstate Equality." *Florida State Law Review*, no. 15 (1987): 389–416.

Brooks, Peter. *The Melodramatic Imagination: Balzac, Henry James, Melodrama, and the Mode of Excess.* New Haven: Yale University Press, 1976.

———. *Troubling Confessions: Speaking Guilt in Law and Literature.* Chicago: University of Chicago Press, 2000.

Brown, Norman O. "Apocalypse: The Place of Mystery in the Life of the Mind." In *Apocalypse and/or Metamorphosis*, pp. 1–7. Berkeley: University of California Press, 1991.

———. *The Challenge of Islam: The Prophetic Tradition (Lectures, 1981).* Ed. Jerome Neu. Santa Cruz: New Pacific, 2008.

———. "Dionysus in 1990." In *Apocalypse and/or Metamorphosis*, pp. 179–200. Berkeley: University of California Press, 1991.

———. *Love's Body.* New York: Random House, 1966.

———. "Philosophy and Prophecy: Spinoza's Hermeneutics." In *Apocalypse and/or Metamorphosis*, pp. 95–116. Berkeley. University of California Press, 1991.

———. "The Prophetic Tradition." In *Apocalypse and/or Metamorphosis*, pp. 46–68. Berkeley: University of California Press, 1991.

———. "Shi'ite Islam: The Politics of Gnosticism." In *The Challenge of Islam: The Prophetic Tradition (Lectures: 1981)*, pp. 89–106. Ed. Jerome Neu. Santa Cruz: New Pacific, 2008.

———. "The Turn to Spinoza." In *Apocalypse and/or Metamorphosis*, pp. 117–41. Berkeley: University of California Press, 1991.

Brown v. Board of Education, 349 U.S. 294 (1955). Brown II.

Brown, Wendy. *Regulating Aversion: Tolerance in the Age of Identity and Empire*. Princeton: Princeton University Press, 2006.

———. "Wounded Attachments." In *States of Injury: Power and Freedom in Late Modernity*, pp. 52–76. Princeton: Princeton University Press, 1995.

Browne, Robert S. "The Economic Case for Reparations to Black America." *American Economic Review* 62, no. 1/2 (1972): 39–46.

Brzezinski, Zbigniew, and Samuel P. Huntington. *Political Power: USA/USSR*. New York: Viking, 1964.

Bull, Malcolm. *Seeing Things Hidden: Apocalypse, Vision, and Totality*. London: Verso, 1999.

Burg, Avraham. *The Holocaust Is Over, We Must Rise from Its Ashes*. New York: Palgrave Macmillan, 2008.

Burke, Kenneth. *A Grammar of Motives, and a Rhetoric of Motives*. Cleveland: World, 1962.

Burns, Stewart. *To the Mountaintop: Martin Luther King, Jr.'s Sacred Mission to Save America, 1955–1968*. San Francisco: Harper, 2004.

Butler, Judith. "Moral Sadism and Doubting One's Own Love: Klein's Reflections on Melancholia." In *Reading Melanie Klein*, pp. 179–89. Ed. Lyndsey Stonebridge and John Phillips. London: Routledge, 1998.

———. *Precarious Life: The Powers of Mourning and Violence*. London: Verso, 2003.

Calabresi, Guido, and A. Douglas Melamed. "Property Rules, Liability Rules, and Inalienability: One View of the Cathedral." *Harvard Law Review* 85, no. 6 (1972): 1089–1128.

Calder, Angus. *Revolutionary Empire: The Rise of the English-Speaking Empires from the Fifteenth Century to the 1780s*. New York: Dutton, 1981.

Canny, Nicholas P. "Identity Formation in Ireland: The Emergence of the Anglo-Irish." In *Colonial Identity in the Atlantic World, 1500–1800*, pp. 159–212. Ed. Nicholas P. Canny and Anthony Pagden. Princeton: Princeton University Press, 1987.

———. *Making Ireland British, 1580–1650*. Oxford: Oxford University Press, 2001.

———. "Migration and Opportunity: Britain, Ireland." In *Kingdom and Colony: Ireland in the Atlantic World, 1560–1800*, pp. 61–102. Ed. Nicholas P. Canny and Anthony Pagden. Princeton: Princeton University Press, 1988.

———. "The Passage to Maturity: Colonial Ireland and Colonial America, 1650–1790." In *Kingdom and Colony: Ireland in the Atlantic World, 1560–1800*, pp. 103–33. Ed. Nicholas P. Canny and Anthony Pagden. Princeton: Princeton University Press, 1988.

———. "The Permissive Frontier: The Problem of Social Control in English Settlements in Ireland and Virginia, 1550–1650." In *The Westward Enterprise: English Activities in Ireland, the Atlantic, and America, 1480–1650*, pp. 17–44. Ed. Kenneth R. Andrews, Nicholas P. Canny, P. E. H. Hair et al. Detroit: Wayne State University Press, 1979.

———. "The Theory and Practice of Acculturation: Ireland in a Colonial Context." In *Kingdom and Colony: Ireland in the Atlantic World, 1560–1800*, pp. 31–68. Ed. Nicholas P. Canny and Anthony Pagden. Princeton: Princeton University Press, 1988.

Cantor, Jay. "Introduction." In *The Challenge of Islam: The Prophetic Tradition: Lectures, 1981*, pp. ix–xxxi. Ed. Jerome Neu. Santa Cruz: New Pacific, 2008.

Card, Claudia. *The Atrocity Paradigm: A Theory of Evil*. Oxford: Oxford University Press, 2002.

Carroll, James. *Constantine's Sword: The Church and the Jews, a History.* Boston: Houghton Mifflin, 2001.

Carter, Jimmy. *Palestine: Peace, Not Apartheid.* New York: Simon and Schuster, 2006.

Cassian, John. *John Cassian, the Conferences.* Trans. Boniface Ramsey, O.P. New York: Paulist, 1997.

———. *John Cassian, the Institutes.* Trans. Boniface Ramsey, O.P. New York: Newman, 2000.

Caygill, Howard. *Levinas and the Political, Thinking the Political.* London: Routledge, 2002.

Césaire, Aimé. *Discourse on Colonialism.* Trans. Joan Pinkham. Ed. Robin D. G. Kelley. New York: Monthly Review Press, 2000.

Chatterjee, Deen K., ed. *The Ethics of Assistance: Morality and the Distant Needy.* Cambridge: Cambridge University Press, 2004.

Chatterjee, Deen K., and Don E. Scheid, eds. *Ethics and Foreign Intervention.* Cambridge: Cambridge University Press, 2003.

Cheng, Anne Anlin. *The Melancholy of Race: Psychoanalysis, Assimilation, and Hidden Grief.* New York: Oxford University Press, 2001.

Chipman, N. P. *The Tragedy of Andersonville; Trial of Captain Henry Wirz, the Prison Keeper.* Sacramento: Author, 1911.

Chirac v. Chirac, 2 Wheat. 259 (1817).

Chomsky, Noam. *Year 501: The Conquest Continues.* Boston: South End, 1993.

Chow, Rey. "Sacrifice, Mimesis, and the Theorizing of Victimhood (a Speculative Essay)." *Representations* 94, no. 1 (2006): 131–49.

Churchill, Ward. *A Little Matter of Genocide: Holocaust and Denial in the Americas, 1492 to the Present.* San Francisco: City Lights, 1997.

Claude, Inis L. *National Minorities: An International Problem.* Cambridge: Harvard University Press, 1955.

Coase, R. H. "The Problem of Social Cost." *Journal of Law and Economics* 3 (1960): 1–44.

Cochrane, Charles Norris. *Christianity and Classical Culture.* New York: Oxford University Press, 1957.

Coetzee, J. M. *Disgrace.* New York: Penguin, 2000.

———. *Elizabeth Costello.* New York: Viking, 2003.

Cohen, G. A. *If You're an Egalitarian, How Come You're So Rich?* Cambridge: Harvard University Press, 2000.

Cohen, Hermann. *Deutschtum und Judentum.* Giessen: Töpelmann, 1916.

———. "The German and the Jewish Ethos II." In *Reason and Hope; Selections from the Jewish Writings of Hermann Cohen*, pp. 185–88. Trans. Eva Jospe. New York: Norton, 1971.

———. "Religion and Zionism." In *Reason and Hope; Selections from the Jewish Writings of Hermann Cohen*, pp. 170–74. Trans. Eva Jospe. New York: Norton, 1971.

———. *Religion of Reason: Out of the Sources of Judaism.* Trans. Simon Kaplan. Atlanta: Scholars, 1995.

———. "Thou Shalt Not Go About as a Slanderer." In *Reason and Hope; Selections from the Jewish Writings of Hermann Cohen*, pp. 192–93. Trans. Eva Jospe. New York: Norton, 1971.

———. "The Transcendent God: Archetype of Morality." In *Reason and Hope; Selections from the Jewish Writings of Hermann Cohen*, pp. 57–61. Trans. Eva Jospe. New York: Norton, 1971.

Cohen, Jeremy. *Living Letters of the Law: Ideas of the Jew in Medieval Christianity*. Berkeley: University of California Press, 1999.

Cohen, Josh. *Interrupting Auschwitz: Art, Religion, Philosophy*. New York: Continuum, 2003.

Cohen, Stanley. *States of Denial: Knowing About Atrocities and Suffering*. Malden, Mass.: Blackwell, 2001.

Cole, David. "What to Do about the Torturers?" Review of *Torture Team: Rumsfeld's Memo and the Betrayal of American Values* by Philippe Sands; *The Trial of Donald Rumsfeld: A Prosecution by Book* by Michael Ratner et al.; *Administration of Torture: A Documentary Record from Washington to Abu Ghraib and Beyond* by Jameel Jaffer and Amrit Singh. *New York Review of Books*, January 15, 2009.

Coleman, James S. "The Concept of Equality of Educational Opportunity." *Harvard Educational Review* (1968).

———. *Equality of Educational Opportunity*. Washington, D.C.: U.S. Department of Health, Education, and Welfare, Office of Education, 1966.

———. "Equality of Educational Opportunity—Reply." *Journal of Human Resources* 3, no. 2 (1968): 237–46.

Coleridge, Samuel Taylor. *The Rime of the Ancient Mariner*. Ed. Gustave Dore. Edison, N.J.: Chartwell, 2008.

Colonomos, Ariel, and Andrea Armstrong. "German Reparations to the Jews After World War II: A Turning Point in the History of Reparations." In *The Handbook of Reparations*, ed. Pablo De Greiff. Oxford: Oxford University Press, 2006.

Commons, John Rogers. *Legal Foundations of Capitalism*. Clifton, N.J.: Kelley, 1974.

Conot, Robert E. *Justice at Nuremberg*. New York: Harper and Row, 1983.

Copjec, Joan. "Evil in the Time of the Finite World." In *Radical Evil*, pp. vii–xxviii. Ed. Joan Copjec. London: Verso, 1996.

———, ed. *Radical Evil*. London: Verso, 1996.

Corbin, Henry. *Creative Imagination in the Ṣūfism of Ibn 'Arabī*. Trans. Ralph Manheim. Princeton: Princeton University Press, 1981.

———. "Divine Epiphany and Spiritual Rebirth." In *Cyclical Time and Ismaili Gnosis*, pp. 59–150. Trans. Ralph Manheim. London: Kegan Paul International, 1983.

———. *History of Islamic Philosophy*. Trans. Liadain Sherrard, with Philip Sherrard. London: Kegan Paul International, 1993.

———, et al. *Man and Time*. Trans. Ralph Manheim. Ed. Joseph Campbell. New York: Pantheon, 1957.

Costigan, George P., Jr. "The Classification of Trusts as Express, Resulting, and Constructive." *Harvard Law Review* 27, no. 5 (1914): 437–63.

Coughlan, Patricia. *Spenser and Ireland: An Interdisciplinary Perspective*. Cork: Cork University Press, 1989.

Craig, Gordon A. "An Inability to Mourn." Review of *Wages of Guilt* by Ian Buruma. *New York Review of Books*, July 14, 1994.

Critchley, Simon. *Infinitely Demanding: Ethics of Commitment, Politics of Resistance.* London: Verso, 2007.

Crone, Patricia. *God's Rule: Government and Islam.* New York: Columbia University Press, 2004.

Cronin, Jeremy. "Á Luta Dis-Continua: The TRC Final Report and the Nation Building Project (Paper Delivered at the Conference, "TRC: Commissioning the Past," University of the Witwatersrand, June 11–14, 1999.)." http://www.trcresearch.org.za/papers99/cronin.pdf (accessed January 31, 2010).

Cryer, Robert, Håkan Friman, Darryl Robinson, and Elizabeth Wilmshurst. *An Introduction to International Criminal Law and Procedure.* Cambridge: Cambridge University Press, 2007.

Curtis, L. Perry. *Anglo-Saxons and Celts: A Study of Anti-Irish Prejudice in Victorian England.* New York: New York University Press, 1968.

D'Amato, Anthony. "Peace vs. Accountability in Bosnia." *American Journal of International Law* 88 (1994): 500–7.

Dagan, Hanoch. *The Law and Ethics of Restitution.* Cambridge: Cambridge University Press, 2004.

———. "Restitution and Slavery: On Incomplete Commodification, Intergenerational Justice, and Legal Transitions." *Boston University Law Review* 84 (2004).

Dagan, Hanoch, and James J. White. "Governments, Citizens, and Injurious Injuries, Part I." *New York University Law Review* 76 (2001).

Daley, Suzannne. "South African Panel's Report Arrives in Swirl of Bitterness." *New York Times,* October 30, 1998.

Dallaire, Roméo, and Brent Beardsley. *Shake Hands with the Devil: The Failure of Humanity in Rwanda.* New York: Carroll and Graf, 2004.

Dallen, James. *The Reconciling Community: The Rite of Penance.* New York: Pueblo, 1986.

Dalrymple, Theodore. "The Specters Haunting Dresden." *City Journal* (winter 2005).

Dane, Perry. "The Maps of Sovereignty: A Meditation." *Cardozo Law Review* 12 (1991): 959.

Danley, John. "Liberalism, Aboriginal Rights and Cultural Minorities." *Philosophy and Public Affairs* 20, no. 2 (1991): 168–85.

Danner, Mark. "Abu Ghraib: The Hidden Story." *New York Review of Books,* October 7, 2004.

———. "Torture and Truth." *New York Review of Books,* June 10, 2004.

———. "The Logic of Torture." *New York Review of Books,* June 24, 2004.

———. "We Are All Torturers Now." *New York Times,* January 6 2005.

———. "U.S. Torture: Voices from the Black Sites." Review of ICRC Report on the Treatment of Fourteen "High Value Detainees" in CIA Custody. *New York Review of Books,* April 9, 2009.

Dawn, Karen. "Moving the Media." In *In Defense of Animals: The Second Wave,* pp. 196–205. Ed. Peter Singer. Malden, Mass.: Blackwell, 2006.

Dawson, John P. "'Negotiorum Gestio': The Altruistic Intermeddler." *Harvard Law Review* 74, no. 5 (1961): 817–65.

———. "Restitution Without Enrichment." *Boston University Law Review* 61 (1981): 563ff.

———. "The Self-Serving Intermeddler." *Harvard Law Review* 87, no. 7 (1974): 1409–58.

Dawson, John Philip. *Unjust Enrichment: A Comparative Analysis.* Boston: Little, Brown, 1951.

de Kock, Eugene. *A Long Night's Damage: Working for the Apartheid State.* Saxonwold: Contra, 1998.

Dean, Carolyn J. *The Fragility of Empathy After the Holocaust.* Ithaca: Cornell University Press, 2004.

———. "Indifference and the Language of Victimization." In *The Fragility of Empathy After the Holocaust,* pp. 76–105. Ithaca: Cornell University Press, 2004.

Degler, Carl N. "One among Many: The Civil War in Comparative Perspective." In *Lincoln the War President,* pp. 89–119. Ed. Gabor S. Boritt. New York: Oxford University Press, 1992.

Deloria, Philip Joseph. *Playing Indian.* New Haven: Yale University Press, 1998.

Demsetz, Harold. "Toward a Theory of Property Rights." *American Economic Review* 57, no. 2 (1967): 347–59.

———. "Wealth Distribution and the Ownership of Rights." *Journal of Legal Studies* 1, no. 2 (1972): 223–32.

———. "When Does the Rule of Liability Matter?" *Journal of Legal Studies* 1, no. 1 (1972): 13–28.

Derrida, Jacques. *Adieu to Emmanuel Levinas.* Trans. Pascale-Anne Brault and Michael Naas. Stanford: Stanford University Press, 1999.

———. *Archive Fever: A Freudian Impression.* Trans. Eric Prenowitz. Chicago: University of Chicago Press, 1996.

———. "Differance." In *Speech and Phenomena, and Other Essays on Husserl's Theory of Signs,* pp. 129–60. Trans. David Allison. Evanston: Northwestern University Press, 1973.

———. "Interpretations at War: Kant, the Jew, the German." In *Acts of Religion,* pp. 135–90. Ed. Gil Anidjar. New York: Routledge, 2002.

———. "On Absolute Hostility: The Cause of Philosophy and the Spectre of the Political." In *The Politics of Friendship,* pp. 112–37. Trans. George Collins. London: Verso, 2005.

———. *On Cosmopolitanism and Forgiveness.* Ed. Simon Critchley and Richard Kearney. London: Routledge, 2001.

———. *The Politics of Friendship.* Trans. George Collins. London: Verso, 2005.

———. *Rogues: Two Essays on Reason.* Trans. Pascale-Anne Brault and Michaell Nass. Stanford: Stanford University Press, 2005.

———. *Sovereignties in Question: The Poetics of Paul Celan.* Ed. and trans. Thomas Dutoit and Outi Pasanen. New York: Fordham University Press, 2005.

———. *Specters of Marx: The State of the Debt, the Work of Mourning, and the New International.* Trans. Peggy Kamuf. New York: Routledge, 1994.

———. "Violence and Metaphysics: An Essay on the Thought of Emannuel Levinas." In *Writing and Difference,* pp. 79–153. Trans. Alan Bass. Chicago: University of Chicago Press, 1978.

Deutscher, Isaac. *The Prophet Armed: Trotsky, 1879–1921.* New York: Oxford University Press, 1954.

Dewar, Diana. *Saint of Auschwitz: The Story of Maximilian Kolbe.* San Francisco: Harper and Row, 1982.

Diamond, Jared M. *Collapse: How Societies Choose to Fail or Succeed*. New York: Viking, 2005.

Dickinson, Emily. *The Complete Poems of Emily Dickinson*. Ed. Thomas H. Johnson. Boston: Little, Brown, 1960.

Dijk, Paul van. "Final Time and the End of Time: The Philosophy of History Under Nuclear Threat." In *Anthropology in the Age of Technology: The Philosophical Contribution of Günther Anders*, pp. 52–60. Amsterdam: Rodopi, 2000.

Diner, Hasia R. *A New Promised Land: A History of Jews in America*. New York: Oxford University Press, 2003.

Dormandy, Thomas. *The Worst of Evils: The Fight Against Pain*. New Haven: Yale University Press, 2006.

Dorris, Jonathan Truman. *Pardon and Amnesty Under Lincoln and Johnson: The Restoration of the Confederates to Their Rights and Privileges, 1861–1898*. Chapel Hill: University of North Carolina Press, 1953.

Douglas, Ann. *The Feminization of American Culture*. New York: Knopf, 1977.

Douglas, Lawrence. *The Memory of Judgment: Making Law and History in the Trials of the Holocaust*. New Haven: Yale University Press, 2001.

Douzinas, Costas. *The End of Human Rights: Critical Legal Thought at the Turn of the Century*. Oxford: Hart, 2000.

——. *Human Rights and Empire: The Political Philosophy of Cosmopolitanism*. New York: Routledge-Cavendish, 2007.

——. "Theses on Law, History, and Time (the Cultures of Human Rights)." *Melbourne Journal of International Law* 7, no. 1 (2006): 13(15).

Driscoll, Jeremy. *Steps to Spiritual Perfection: Studies on Spiritual Progress in Evagrius Ponticus*. New York: Newman, 2005.

du Toit, André "The Moral Foundations of the South African TRC: Truth as Acknowledgement and Justice as Recognition." In *Truth Versus Justice: The Morality of Truth Commissions*, pp. 122–40. Ed. Robert I. Rotberg and Dennis F. Thompson. Princeton: Princeton University Press, 2000.

Dujack, Stephen. "Animals Suffer a Perpetual 'Holocaust.'" *Los Angeles Times*, April 21, 2003.

Dworkin, Ronald. *Sovereign Virtue: The Theory and Practice of Equality*. Cambridge: Harvard University Press, 2000.

Eco, Umberto. "Ur-Fascism." *New York Review of Books*, June 22, 1995.

Eggen, Dan. "Bush White House Cast Assails Obama." *Washington Post*, February 7, 2009.

Ehrenfreund, Norbert. *The Nuremberg Legacy: How the Nazi War Crimes Trials Changed the Course of History*. New York: Palgrave Macmillan, 2007.

Elster, Jon. *Closing the Books: Transitional Justice in Historical Perspective*. Cambridge: Cambridge University Press, 2004.

——. "Majority Rule and Individual Rights." In *On Human Rights: The Oxford Amnesty Lectures, 1993*, pp. 175–216. Ed. Stephen Shute and Susan. L. Hurley. New York: Basic Books, 1993.

——, ed. *Retribution and Reparation in the Transition to Democracy*. Cambridge: Cambridge University Press, 2006.

Ely, John Hart. *Democracy and Distrust: A Theory of Judicial Review*. Cambridge: Harvard University Press, 1980.

Eng, David L., and David Kazanjian, eds. *Loss: The Politics of Mourning*. Berkeley: University of California Press, 2003.

Epstein, Lawrence J. *The Haunted Smile: The Story of Jewish Comedians in America*. New York: Public Affairs, 2001.

Erdman, David. *Blake, Prophet Against Empire: A Poet's Interpretation of the History of His Own Times*. 2d ed. Princeton: Princeton University Press, 1969.

Erikson, Erik H. *Gandhi's Truth: On the Origins of Militant Nonviolence*. New York: Norton, 1969.

Eusebius. *Eusebius—the Church History: A New Translation with Commentary*. Trans. Paul L. Maier. Grand Rapids: Kregel, 1999.

Evagrius. *Evagrius of Pontus: The Greek Ascetic Corpus*. Trans. Robert E. Sinkewicz. New York: Oxford University Press, 2003.

Evans, Gareth. "Crimes against Humanity and the Responsibility to Protect." International Crisis Group, http://www.crisisgroup.org/home/index.cfm?id=6140&l=1 (January 31, 2010).

———. *The Responsibility to Protect: Ending Mass Atrocity Crimes Once and for All*. Washington, D.C.: Brookings Institution, 2009.

———. "The Responsibility to Protect and the Use of Military Force." International Crisis Group, http://www.crisisgroup.org/home/index.cfm?id=5209andl=1 (accessed January 31, 2010).

Everson v. Bd of Educ., 330 U.S. 1 (1947).

Fairman, Charles, and the Oliver Wendell Holmes Devise. *Reconstruction and Reunion, 1864–88. History of the Supreme Court of the United States*. Vols. 6–7. New York: Macmillan, 1971.

Fanon, Frantz. *Black Skin, White Masks*. Trans. Charles Lam Markmann. London: Paladin, 1970.

———. *The Wretched of the Earth*. Trans. Constance Farrington. Harmondsworth: Penguin, 1967.

Faulkner, William. "Requiem for a Nun." In *Novels, 1942–1954*, pp. 471–664. New York: Library of America, 1994.

Feher, Michel. *Powerless by Design: The Age of the International Community*. Durham: Duke University Press, 2000.

———. "Terms of Reconciliation." In *Human Rights in Political Transitions: Gettysburg to Bosnia*, pp. 325–38. Ed. Carla Hesse and Robert Post. New York: Zone, 1999.

Fehrenbacher, Don Edward. *The Slaveholding Republic: An Account of the United States Government's Relations to Slavery*. Ed. Ward McAfee. New York: Oxford University Press, 2001.

Ferenczi, Sandor. *Final Contributions to the Problems and Methods of Psycho-Analysis*. Ed. Michael Balint. Trans. Eric Mosbacher et al. New York: Brunner/Mazel, 1980.

Finkelstein, Israel, and Neil Asher Silberman. *The Bible Unearthed: Archaeology's New Vision of Ancient Israel and the Origin of Its Sacred Texts*. New York: Free Press, 2001.

Finkelstein, Norman G. *Beyond Chutzpah: On the Misuse of Anti-Semitism and the Abuse of History*. Berkeley: University of California Press, 2005.

———. *The Holocaust Industry: Reflection on the Exploitation of Jewish Suffering*. London: Verso, 2000.

———. "Israel: The 'Jew Among Nations.'" In *Beyond Chutzpah: On the Misuse of Anti-Semitism and the Abuse of History*, pp. 32–65. Berkeley: University of California Press, 2005.

Fiss, Owen. "Human Rights as a Social Ideal." In *Human Rights in Political Transitions: Gettysburg to Bosnia*, pp. 263–76. Ed. Carla Hesse and Robert Post. New York: Zone, 1999.

Fitzpatrick, Joan. *Irish Demons: English Writings on Ireland, the Irish, and Gender by Spenser and His Contemporaries*. Lanham, Md.: University Press of America, 2000.

Foner, Eric. *Reconstruction: America's Unfinished Revolution, 1863–1877*. New York: Harper and Row, 1988.

Foucault, Michel. *"Society Must Be Defended": Lectures at the Collége de France, 1975–76*. Ed. Mauro Bertani and Alessandro Fontana. Trans. David Macey. New York: Picador, 2003.

Fredrickson, George M. *Black Liberation: A Comparative History of Black Ideologies in the United States and South Africa*. New York: Oxford University Press, 1995.

———. "Reform and Revolution in American and South African Freedom Struggles." In *The Comparative Imagination: On the History of Racism, Nationalism, and Social Movements*, pp. 135–48. Berkeley: University of California Press, 1997.

Freud, Sigmund. "Analysis Terminable and Interminable." In *The Standard Edition of the Complete Psychological Works of Sigmund Freud*, 23:209–53. Ed. James Strachey and Anna Freud. London: Hogarth, 1957.

———. *"Civilization and Its Discontents."* In *The Standard Edition of the Complete Psychological Works of Sigmund Freud*, 21:59–148. Ed. James Strachey and Anna Freud. London: Hogarth, 1957.

———. "The Economic Problem of Masochism." In *The Standard Edition of the Complete Psychological Works of Sigmund Freud*, 19:157–72. Ed. James Strachey and Anna Freud. London: Hogarth, 1957.

———. *"Group Psychology and the Analysis of the Ego."* In *The Standard Edition of the Complete Psychological Works of Sigmund Freud*, 21:57–146. Ed. James Strachey and Anna Freud. London: Hogarth, 1957.

———. "Inhibitions, Symptoms, and Anxiety." In *The Standard Edition of the Complete Psychological Works of Sigmund Freud*, 21:77–175. Ed. James Strachey and Anna Freud. London: Hogarth, 1957.

———. *"Moses and Monotheism."* In *The Standard Edition of the Complete Psychological Works of Sigmund Freud*, 23:1–138. Ed. James Strachey and Anna Freud. London: Hogarth, 1957.

———. "Mourning and Melancholia." In *The Standard Edition of the Complete Psychological Works of Sigmund Freud*, 14:237–58. Ed. James Strachey and Anna Freud. London: Hogarth, 1957.

———. "Paper on Metapsychology." In *The Standard Edition of the Complete Psychological Works of Sigmund Freud*, 14:105–216. Ed. James Strachey and Anna Freud. London: Hogarth, 1957.

———. "Some Character Types Met with in Psychoanalytic Work." In *The Standard*

Edition of the Complete Psychological Works of Sigmund Freud, 14:309–36. Ed. James Strachey and Anna Freud. London: Hogarth, 1957.

———. "Totem and Taboo." In *The Standard Edition of the Complete Psychological Works of Sigmund Freud,* 19:161ff. Ed. James Strachey and Anna Freud. London: Hogarth, 1957.

Fried, Barbara. *The Progressive Assault on Laissez Faire: Robert Hale and the First Law and Economics Movement.* Cambridge: Harvard University Press, 1998.

Friedländer, Saul, ed. *Probing the Limits of Representation: Nazism and the "Final Solution"* Cambridge: Harvard University Press, 1992.

Friedrich, Carl J. *Totalitarianism: Proceedings of a Conference Held at the American Academy of Arts and Sciences, March 1953.* New York: Grosset and Dunlap, 1964.

Friedrich, Carl J., and Zbigniew Brzezinski. *Totalitarian Dictatorship and Autocracy.* Cambridge: Harvard University Press, 1956.

Frye, Northrop. *Anatomy of Criticism; Four Essays.* Princeton: Princeton University Press, 1957.

Fuller, Lon L, and Perdue, William R., Jr. "The Reliance Interest in Contract Damages, Parts I and II." *Yale Law Journal* (1936–1937): 52ff., 373ff.

Fuller, Lon L. "Positivism and Fidelity to Law: A Reply to Professor Hart." *Harvard Law Review* 71, no. 4 (1958): 630–72.

Funkenstein, Amos. "Franz Rosenzweig and the End of German-Jewish Philosophy." In *Perceptions of Jewish History,* pp. 257–305. Berkeley: University of California Press, 1993.

———. "Theological Responses to the Holocaust." In *Perceptions of Jewish History,* pp. 306–37. Berkeley: University of California Press, 1993.

Futch, Ovid L. *History of Andersonville Prison.* Gainesville: University Press of Florida, 1968.

Gabler, Neal. *An Empire of Their Own: How the Jews Invented Hollywood.* New York: Crown, 1988.

Gaddis, John Lewis. *The Cold War: A New History.* New York: Penguin, 2005.

Gager, John G. *The Origins of Anti-Semitism: Attitudes Toward Judaism in Pagan and Christian Antiquity.* New York: Oxford University Press, 1983.

Gandhi. *Hind Swaraj.* Ahmedabad: Navajivan, 1946.

Gandhi, Mohandas K. *An Autobiography: The Story of My Experiments with Truth.* Trans. Mahadev Desai. London: Jonathan Cape, 1966.

Gauchet, Marcel. *The Disenchantment of the World: A Political History of Religion.* Trans. Oscar Burge. Princeton: Princeton University Press, 1997.

Geary, Patrick J. *The Myth of Nations: The Medieval Origins of Europe.* Princeton: Princeton University Press, 2002.

Gellately, Robert, and Ben Kiernan, eds. *The Specter of Genocide: Mass Murder in Historical Perspective.* New York: Cambridge University Press, 2003.

Gergen, Mark. "What Renders Enrichment Unjust?" *Texas Law Review* 79 (1999).

Gerwel, Jakes. "National Reconciliation: Holy Grail or Secular Pact?" In *Looking Back, Reaching Forward: Reflections on the Truth and Reconciliation Commission of South Africa,* pp. 277–86. Ed. Charles Villa-Vicencio and Wilhelm Verwoerd. Cape Town: University of Cape Town Press, 2000.

Gibbard, Allan. *Reconciling Our Aims: In Search of Bases for Ethics.* Ed. Barry Stroud. Oxford: Oxford University Press, 2008.

———. *Wise Choices, Apt Feelings: A Theory of Normative Judgment*. Cambridge: Harvard University Press, 1990.

Giddins, Gary. *Visions of Jazz: The First Century*. New York: Oxford University Press, 1998.

Gilman, Sander L. *Jews in Today's German Culture*. Bloomington: Indiana University Press, 1995.

Gilmore, Grant, and Charles Black. *The Law of Admiralty*. Brooklyn: Foundation, 1957.

Girard, René. "The Bloody Skin of the Victim." In *The New Visibility of Religion Studies in Religion and Cultural Hermeneutics*, pp. 59–67. Ed. Michael Hoelzl and Graham Ward. London: Continuum, 2008.

———. *I See Satan Fall Like Lightning*. Trans. James G. Williams. Maryknoll, N.Y.: Orbis, 2001.

———. *Job: The Victim of His People*. Stanford: Stanford University Press, 1987.

———. "Mimesis and Violence." In *The Girard Reader*, pp. 1–19. Ed. James G. Williams. New York: Crossroad, 1996.

———. "The Myth of Oedipus, the Truth of Joseph." In *Oedipus Unbound: Selected Writings on Rivalry and Desire*, pp. 107–14. Ed. Mark Rogin Anspach. Stanford: Stanford University Press, 2004.

———. *The Scapegoat*. Trans. Yvonne Freccero. Baltimore: Johns Hopkins University Press, 1986.

Girard, René, Jean-Michel Oughourlian, and Guy Lefort. *Things Hidden Since the Foundation of the World*. Trans. Michael Metteer (book 1) and Stephen Bann (books 2 and 3). Stanford: Stanford University Press, 1987.

Glover, Jonathan. *Humanity: A Moral History of the Twentieth Century*. New Haven: Yale University Press, 2000.

Goldhagen, Daniel Jonah. *Hitler's Willing Executioners: Ordinary Germans and the Holocaust*. New York: Knopf, 1996.

Goldsmith, Jack L. *The Terror Presidency: Law and Judgment Inside the Bush Administration*. New York: Norton, 2007.

Gordimer, Nadine. *July's People*. New York: Viking, 1981.

Gourevitch, Philip. "The Return: With a Million Exiles Coming Home, Killers and Genocide Survivors Are Being Forced to Live Together (Letter from Rwanda)." *New Yorker*, January 20, 1997, pp. 44–51.

———. *We Wish to Inform You That Tomorrow We Will Be Killed with Our Families: Stories from Rwanda*. New York: Farrar, Straus, and Giroux, 1998.

Greenblatt, Stephen. *Hamlet in Purgatory*. Princeton: Princeton University Press, 2001.

Greenstone, J. David. *The Lincoln Persuasion: Remaking American Liberalism*. Princeton: Princeton University Press, 1993.

Gregory of Nyssa. *The Lord's Prayer. The Beatitudes*. Trans. Hilda C. Graef. Mahwah, N.J.: Paulist, 1954.

Griffin, Roger. "The Palingenetic Core of Fascist Nationalism." In *Che Cos'è Il Fascismo? Interpretazioni E Prospettive Di Ricerche*, pp. 97–122. Ed. Alessandro Campi. Rome: Ideazione, 2003.

Griffith, D. W. *Birth of a Nation*. 1915.

Griswold, Charles L. *Forgiveness: A Philosophical Exploration*. Cambridge: Cambridge University Press, 2007.

Gruber, Ruth Ellen. *Virtually Jewish: Reinventing Jewish Culture in Europe*. Berkeley: University of California Press, 2002.

Grutter v. Bollinger, 539 U.S. 306 (2003).

Guatemala, Never Again! Maryknoll, N.Y.: Orbis, 1999.

Guinier, Lani. *The Tyranny of the Majority: Fundamental Fairness in Representative Democracy*. New York: Free Press, 1994.

Gunther, Gerald. *Learned Hand: The Man and the Judge*. New York: Knopf, 1994.

Gutmann, Amy. *Why Deliberative Democracy?* Princeton: Princeton University Press, 2004.

Gutmann, Amy, and Dennis F. Thompson. *Democracy and Disagreement*. Cambridge: Belknap Press of Harvard University Press, 1996.

Habermas, Jürgen. "Citizenship and National Identity: Some Reflections on the Future of Europe." *Praxis International* 12, no. 1 (1992): 1–19.

———. *The Inclusion of the Other: Studies in Political Theory*. Trans. Ciaran Cronin and Pablo De Greiff. Cambridge: MIT Press, 1998.

———. "Struggles for Recognition in Constitutional States." *European Journal of Philosophy* 1, no. 2 (1993): 128–55.

Hacking, Ian. *Rewriting the Soul: Multiple Personality and the Sciences of Memory*. Princeton: Princeton University Press, 1995.

Hadas, Moses, and Morton Smith. *Heroes and Gods: Spiritual Biographies in Antiquity*. New York: Harper and Row, 1965.

Haidu, Peter. "The Dialectics of Unspeakability: Language, Silence, and the Narratives of Desubjectification." In *Probing the Limits of Representation: Nazism and the "Final Solution,"* pp. 277–99. Ed. Saul Friedländer. Cambridge: Harvard University Press, 1992.

Hale, Robert Lee. *Freedom Through Law: Public Control of Private Governing Power*. New York: Columbia University Press, 1952.

Hall, Anthony J. *The American Empire and the Fourth World*. Montreal: McGill-Queen's University Press, 2003.

Hallward, Peter. "Order and Event: On Badiou's *Logics of Worlds*." *New Left Review*, no. 53 (2008): 97–122.

Hamdan v. Rumsfeld, 2749 S. Ct. 2006 (2006).

Hampshire, Stuart. *Spinoza and Spinozism*. New York: Oxford University Press, 2005.

———. *Thought and Action*. New York: Viking, 1967.

Hannaford, Ivan. *Race: The History of an Idea in the West*. Baltimore.: Johns Hopkins University Press, 1996.

Harrison, John. "Reconstructing the Privileges and Immunities Clause." *Yale Law Journal* 101 (1992): 1385–1473, §§1 and 2.

Hart, H. L. A. *The Concept of Law*. Oxford: Clarendon, 1961.

———. "Positivism and the Separation of Law and Morals." *Harvard Law Review* 71, no. 4 (1958): 593–629.

Hartman, David. "Halakhic Sobriety and Inclusiveness." In *Israelis and the Jewish Tradition: An Ancient People Debating Its Future*, pp. 123–65. New Haven: Yale University Press, 2000.

Hartman, Geoffrey. "Holocaust and Hope." In *Catastrophe and Meaning: The Holocaust and the Twentieth Century*, pp. 232–49. Ed. Moishe Postone and Eric L. Santner. Chicago: University of Chicago Press, 2003.

Hartz, Louis. *The Founding of New Societies: Studies in the History of the United States, Latin America, South Africa, Canada, and Australia*. New York: Harcourt, 1964.

——. *The Liberal Tradition in America: An Interpretation of American Political Thought Since the Revolution*. New York: Harcourt, 1955.

Hattam, Victoria. *In the Shadow of Race: Jews, Latinos, and Immigrant Politics in the United States*. Chicago: University of Chicago Press, 2007.

Hausherr, Irénée. *Penthos: The Doctrine of Compunction in the Christian East*. Kalamazoo: Cistercian, 1982.

Hayner, Priscilla. "Fifteen Truth Commissions, Impunity, and the Inter-American Human Rights System." *Boston University International Law Journal* 12 (1994): 321–70.

——. "Same Species, Different Animal: How South Africa Compares to Truth Commissions Worldwide." In *Looking Back, Reaching Forward: Reflections on the Truth and Reconciliation Commission of South Africa*, pp. 32–41. Ed. Charles Villa-Vicencio and Wilhelm Verwoerd. Cape Town: University of Cape Town Press, 2000.

——. *Unspeakable Truths: Facing the Challenge of Truth Commissions*. New York: Routledge, 2002.

Hechter, Michael. *Internal Colonialism: The Celtic Fringe in British National Development*. New Brunswick, N.J.: Transaction, 1999.

Held, David. *Democracy and the Global Order: From the Modern State to Cosmopolitan Governance*. Stanford: Stanford University Press, 1995.

Held, Paul. "Bondsmen into Bondholders." University of California, Santa Cruz, 2005.

Hempel, Carl Gustav. "Deductive-Nomological Versus Statistical Explanation." In *The Philosophy of Carl G. Hempel: Studies in Science, Explanation, and Rationality*, pp. 87–145. Ed. James H. Fetzer. Oxford: Oxford University Press, 2001.

Herbstrith, Waltraud. *Edith Stein, a Biography*. Trans. Fr. Bernard Bonowitz. San Francisco: Ignatius, 1992.

Herf, Jeffrey. *Divided Memory: The Nazi Past in the Two Germanys*. Cambridge: Harvard University Press, 1997.

——. *The Jewish Enemy: Nazi Propaganda During World War II and the Holocaust*. Cambridge: Belknap Press of Harvard University Press, 2006.

Herrnstein, Richard J., and Charles A. Murray. *The Bell Curve: Intelligence and Class Structure in American Life*. New York: Simon and Schuster, 1996.

Hertzberg, Arthur. *The Jews in America: Four Centuries of an Uneasy Encounter: A History*. New York: Simon and Schuster, 1989.

Hertzberg, Arthur, and Aron Hirt Manheimer. *Jews: The Essence and Character of a People*. San Francisco: Harper, 1998.

Herz, John. *From Dictatorship to Democracy: Coping with the Legacies of Authoritarianism and Totalitarianism*. Westport, Conn.: Greenwood, 1982.

Hess, Moses. *The Holy History of Mankind and Other Writings*. Ed. and trans. Shlomo Avineri. Cambridge: Cambridge University Press, 2004.

——. *The Revival of Israel: Rome and Jerusalem, the Last Nationalist Question*. Ed. Melvin I. Urofsky. Trans. Meyer Waxman. Lincoln: University of Nebraska Press, 1995.

Hesse, Carla, and Robert Post, eds. *Human Rights in Political Transitions: Gettysburg to Bosnia*. New York: Zone, 1999.

Hesseltine, William Best. *Lincoln's Plan of Reconstruction*. Chicago: Quadrangle, 1967.

Hill, Jason D. "Forgetting Where We Come From: The Moral Imperative of Every Cosmopolitan." In *Becoming a Cosmopolitan: What It Means to Be a Human Being in the New Millennium*, pp. 95–120. Lanham, Md.: Rowman and Littlefield, 2000.

Hinshelwood, R. D. *A Dictionary of Kleinian Thought*. 2d ed. Northvale, N.J.: Aronson, 1991.

Hinton, William. *Fanshen: A Documentary of Revolution in a Chinese Village*. New York: Monthly Review Press, 1967.

Hirsch, Fred. *Social Limits to Growth*. Cambridge: Harvard University Press, 1976.

Hirsch, Fred, and John H. Goldthorpe, eds. *The Political Economy of Inflation*. Cambridge: Harvard University Press, 1978.

Hitler, Adolf. *Mein Kampf*. Trans. Ralph Manheim. London: Hutchinson, 1969.

Hochschild, Adam. *King Leopold's Ghost: A Story of Greed, Terror, and Heroism in Colonial Africa*. Boston: Houghton Mifflin, 1998.

Hodgson, Marshall G. S. "The Role of Islam in World History." In *Rethinking World History: Essays on Europe, Islam, and World History*, pp. 97–125. Ed. Edmund Burke III. Cambridge: Cambridge University Press, 1993.

——. *The Secret Order of Assassins: The Struggle of the Early Nizârî Ismâ`îlîs Against the Islamic World*. Philadelphia: University of Pennsylvania Press, 2004.

——. *The Venture of Islam: Conscience and History in a World Civilization*. 3 vols. Chicago: University of Chicago Press, 1974.

Hohfeld, Wesley Newcomb, and Walter Wheeler Cook. *Fundamental Legal Conceptions, as Applied in Judicial Reasoning*. New Haven: Yale University Press, 1964.

Höhne, Heinz. *The Order of the Death's Head: The Story of Hitler's SS*. Trans. Richard Barry. New York: Penguin, 2001.

Honneth, Axel. *The Struggle for Recognition: The Moral Grammar of Social Conflicts*. Trans. Joel Anderson. Cambridge: Polity, 1995.

Horton, James Oliver, and Lois E. Horton, eds. *Slavery and Public History: The Tough Stuff of American Memory*. New York: New Press, 2006.

Horton, Scott. "Justice After Bush: Prosecuting an Outlaw Administration." *Harper's*, December 2008, pp. 49–60.

——. "When Lawyers Are War Criminals." http://balkin.blogspot.com/2006/10/when-lawyers-are-war-criminals.html (accessed January 31, 2010).

Huhndorf, Shari M. *Going Native: Indians in the American Cultural Imagination*. Ithaca: Cornell University Press, 2001.

Hunt, Lynn Avery. *Inventing Human Rights: A History*. New York: Norton, 2007.

Huntington, Samuel P. *The Clash of Civilizations and the Remaking of World Order*. New York: Simon and Schuster, 1996.

——. "The Clash of Civilizations?" *Foreign Affairs* 72, no. 3 (1993): 22–49.

——. *The Third Wave: Democratization in the Late Twentieth Century*. Norman: University of Oklahoma Press, 1991.

Hurd, John Codman. *The Law of Freedom and Bondage in the United States*. 2 vols. Boston: Little, Brown, 1858, 1862.

Hutchins, Francis G. *Spontaneous Revolution: The Quit India Movement*. Delhi: Manohar, 1971.

Ignatieff, Michael, ed. *American Exceptionalism and Human Rights*. Princeton: Princeton University Press, 2005.

———. *Empire Lite: Nation Building in Bosnia, Kosovo, and Afghanistan*. London: Vintage, 2003.

———. *Human Rights as Politics and Idolatry*. Ed. Amy Gutmann. Princeton: Princeton University Press, 2001.

———. "Human Rights: The Midlife Crisis." *New York Review of Books*, May 20, 1999, pp. 58–62.

———. *The Lesser Evil: Political Ethics in an Age of Terror*. Princeton: Princeton University Press, 2004.

Ignatiev, Noel. *How the Irish Became White*. New York: Routledge, 1995.

Iklé, Fred Charles. *Every War Must End*. New York: Columbia University Press, 1971.

"Indictment in the Major War Criminals Trials (Count I)." Yale Law School, http://avalon. law.yale.edu/imt/count1.asp (accessed January 31, 2010).

Institute for Justice and Reconciliation. "Statement: Actions Required to Ensure the TRC Success." Paper presented at the the TRC: Ten Years On, Iziko South African History Museum, April 20–21, 2006.

International Commission on Intervention and State Sovereignty. *The Responsibility to Protect*. Ottawa: International Development Research Center, 2001.

Isaacson, Maureen, and Jean Le May. "Human-Rights Group Slams ANC," *Sunday Independent (SA)*, November 1, 1998.

Israel, Jonathan. *Enlightenment Contested: Philosophy, Modernity, and the Emancipation of Man, 1670–1752*. Oxford: Oxford University Press, 2006.

———. *Radical Enlightenment: Philosophy and the Making of Modernity, 1650–1750*. Oxford: Oxford University Press, 2001.

Jackson, Robert. "Opening Statement (Nuremberg Trials)." http://www.yale.edu/lawweb/ avalon/imt/proc/11-21-45.htm (accessed January 31, 2010).

Jackson, Stanley W. "Acedia the Sin and Its Relationship to Sorrow and Melancholia." In *Culture and Depression: Studies in the Anthropology and Cross-Cultural Psychiatry of Affect and Disorder*, pp. 43–62. Ed. Arthur Kleinman and Byron Good. Berkeley: University of California Press, 1985.

———. *Melancholia and Depression: From Hippocratic Times to Modern Times*. New Haven: Yale University Press, 1986.

Jacobson, Arthur J., and Bernhard Schlink, eds. *Weimar: A Jurisprudence of Crisis*. Berkeley: University of California Press, 2000.

Jakobson, Roman. "Linguistics and Poetics." In *Selected Writings*, 3:18–51. Ed. Stephen Rudy. The Hague: Mouton De Gruyter, 1962.

———. "Poetry of Grammar and Grammar of Poetry." In *Selected Writings*, 3:87–97. Ed. Stephen Rudy. The Hague: Mouton De Gruyter, 1962.

James, C. L. R. *The Black Jacobins: Toussaint L'Ouverture and the San Domingo Revolution*. 2d ed. New York: Vintage, 1989.

Jankélévitch, Vladimir. *Forgiveness*. Trans. Andrew Kelley. Chicago: University of Chicago Press, 2005.

———. "Should We Pardon Them?" Trans. Ann Hobart. *Critical Inquiry* 22, no. 3 (1996): 552–72.

Jaspers, Karl. *The Question of German Guilt.* Trans. E. B. Ashton and Philip Lamantia. New York: Capricorn, 1961.

Jencks, Christopher. *Inequality: A Reassessment of the Effect of Family and Schooling in America.* New York: Basic Books, 1972.

Johnson, Barbara. *Persons and Things.* Cambridge: Harvard University Press, 2008.

———. "Using People: Kant with Winnicott." In *The Turn to Ethics*, pp. 47–63. Ed. Marjorie B. Garber, Beatrice Hanssen, and Rebecca L. Walkowitz. New York: Routledge, 2000.

Johnson, Chalmers A. *Blowback: The Costs and Consequences of American Empire.* New York: Metropolitan, 2000.

Johnson, R. W. "False Start in South Africa." *New Left Review*, no. 58 (2009): 61–76.

———. *South Africa's Brave New World: The Beloved Country Since the End of Apartheid.* London: Allen Lane, 2009.

Jordan, June. "Poem for South African Women." In *Passion: New Poems, 1977–1980.* Boston: Beacon, 1980.

Judt, Tony. *Past Imperfect: French Intellectuals, 1944–1956.* Berkeley: University of California Press, 1992.

Kagan, Robert. *Dangerous Nation: America's Place in the World from Its Earliest Days to the Dawn of the Twentieth Century.* New York: Knopf, 2006.

Kahane, Meir. *Never Again! A Program for Survival.* Los Angeles: Nash, 1971.

———. *They Must Go.* New York: Grosset and Dunlap, 1981.

Karatani, Kåojin. *Transcritique on Kant and Marx.* Trans. Sabu Kohso. Cambridge: MIT Press, 2003.

Kateb, George. "A Life of Fear." In *Patriotism and Other Mistakes: Individualism and Contemporary Culture*, pp. 60–92. New Haven: Yale University Press, 2006.

———. "On Political Evil." In *The Inner Ocean*, pp. 199–221. Ithaca: Cornell University Press, 1992.

Katz, Jacob. *Out of the Ghetto; the Social Background of Jewish Emancipation, 1770–1870.* Cambridge: Harvard University Press, 1973.

Kecskemeti, Paul. *Strategic Surrender: The Politics of Victory and Defeat.* Stanford: Stanford University Press, 1959.

Kellogg, Robert H. *Life and Death in Rebel Prisons: Giving a Complete History of the Inhuman and Barbarous Treatment of Our Brave Soldiers by Rebel Authorities, Principally at Andersonville, Ga., and Florence, S. C.* Hartford, Conn.: Stebbins, 1866.

Kelsen, Hans. *Introduction to the Problems of Legal Theory: A Translation of the First Edition of the Reine Rechtslehre or Pure Theory of Law.* Trans. Bonnie Litschewski. Oxford: Clarendon Press of Oxford University Press, 1992.

———. *Pure Theory of Law.* Trans. Max Knight. Berkeley: University of California Press, 1967.

Kendall, Willmoore. *John Locke and the Doctrine of Majority-Rule.* Urbana: University of Illinois Press, 1940.

Kennedy, David. *The Dark Sides of Virtue: Reassessing International Humanitarianism.* Princeton: Princeton University Press, 2004.

————. "The "Rule of Law," Political Choices, and Development Common Sense." In *The New Law and Economic Development: A Critical Appraisal*, pp. 95–173. Ed. David Trubek and Alvaro Santos. New York: Cambridge University Press, 2006.

Kennedy, Duncan. *The Rise and Fall of Classical Legal Thought*. AFAR, 1975, 1998. http:// duncankennedy.net/legal_history/essays.html#RandandF (accessed April 2, 2010).

————. "The Stakes of Law, or Hale and Foucault!" In *Sexy Dressing, Etc.*, pp. 83–125. Cambridge: Harvard University Press, 1993.

————. "The Structure of Blackstone's *Commentaries*." *Buffalo Law Review* 28 (1978).

————. "Three Globalizations of Law and Legal Thought: 1850–2000." In *The New Law and Economic Development: A Critical Appraisal*, pp. 19–73. Ed. David Trubek and Alvaro Santos. New York: Cambridge University Press, 2006.

Kennedy, Ellen. *Constitutional Failure: Carl Schmitt in Weimar*. Durham: Duke University Press, 2004.

Kerényi, Carl. *Dionysos: Archetypal Image of the Indestructible Life*. Trans. Ralph Manheim. Princeton: Princeton University Press, 1976.

Kettner, James H. *The Development of American Citizenship*. Chapel Hill: University of North Carolina Press, 1978.

Keynes, John Maynard. *The Economic Consequences of the Peace*. New York: Harper and Row, 1971.

Kiernan, V. G. *America, the New Imperialism: From White Settlement to World Hegemony*. London: Verso, 2005.

Kimchuk, Dennis. "Unjust Enrichment and Reparations for Slavery." *Boston University Law Review* 84 (2004)): 1257ff.

Kimmerling, Baruch. *The Invention and Decline of Israeliness: State, Society, and the Military*. Berkeley: University of California Press, 2001.

————. *Politicide: Ariel Sharon's Wars Against the Palestinians*. London: Verso, 2003.

King, Charles. "Trouble in the Balkans." Review of *Explaining Yugoslavia* by John B. Allcock. *Times Literary Supplement*, July 20 2001, pp. 3–4.

King, Martin Luther. *Strength to Love*. New York: Walker, 1996.

Kirchheimer, Otto. "Decree Powers and Constitutional Law in France under the Third Republic." In *Politics, Law, and Social Change: Selected Essays*, pp. 110–59. Ed. Frederic S. Burin and Kurt L. Shell. New York: Columbia University Press, 1969.

————. *Political Justice: The Use of Legal Procedure for Political Ends*. Princeton: Princeton University Press, 1961.

————. "Weimar—and What Then? An Analysis of the Constitution." In *Politics, Law, and Social Change: Selected Essays*, pp. 33–74. Ed. Frederic S. Burin and Kurt L. Shell. New York. Columbia University Press, 1969.

Klein, Melanie. "A Contribution to the Psycho-Genesis of Manic-Depressive States." In *Love, Guilt, and Reparation and Other Works, 1921–1945*, pp. 262–89. New York: Delacorte/S. Lawrence, 1975.

————. "Love, Guilt, and Reparation." In *Love, Guilt, and Reparation and Other Works, 1921–1945*, pp. 306–43. New York: Delacorte/S. Lawrence, 1975.

————. "Mourning and Its Relation to Manic-Depressive States." In *Love, Guilt, and Reparation and Other Works, 1921–1945*, pp. 344–69. New York: Delacorte/S. Lawrence, 1975.

———. "Notes on Some Schizoid Mechanisms." In *Envy and Gratitude, and Other Works, 1946–1963*, pp. 1–24. New York: Free Press, 1984.

———. "Some Reflections on the *Oresteia*." In *Envy and Gratitude, and Other Works, 1946–1963*, pp. 275–99. New York: Free Press, 1984.

Kleinman, Arthur. *The Illness Narratives: Suffering, Healing, and the Human Condition.* New York: Basic Books, 1988.

Knohl, Israel. *The Messiah Before Jesus: The Suffering Servant of the Dead Sea Scrolls.* Trans. David Maisel. Berkeley: University of California Press, 2000.

Kochavi, Arieh J. *Prelude to Nuremberg: Allied War Crimes Policy and the Question of Punishment.* Chapel Hill: University of North Carolina Press, 1998.

Koh, Harold Hongju, and Ronald Slye, eds. *Deliberative Democracy and Human Rights.* New Haven: Yale University Press, 1999.

Koselleck, Reinhart. "Concepts of Historical Time and Social Identity." In *The Practice of Conceptual History: Timing History, Spacing Concepts*, pp. 115–30. Trans. Todd Samuel Presner et al. Stanford: Stanford University Press, 2002.

———. "The Modern Concept of Revolution." In *Futures Past: On the Semantics of Historical Time*, pp. 43–57. Trans. Keith Tribe. New York: Columbia University Press, 2004.

———. "The Temporalization of Utopia." In *The Practice of Conceptual History: Timing History, Spacing Concepts*, pp. 84–99. Trans. Todd Samuel Presner et al. Stanford: Stanford University Press, 2002.

———. "Time and History." In *The Practice of Conceptual History: Timing History, Spacing Concepts*, pp. 100–14. Trans. Todd Samuel Presner et al. Stanford: Stanford University Press, 2002.

Kramer, Jane. "The Politics of Memory (Germany Struggles with Its Past and a Proposed Holocaust Memorial) (Letter from Germany)." *New Yorker*, August 14, 1995, pp. 48–64.

———. *The Politics of Memory: Looking for Germany in the New Germany.* New York: Random House, 1996.

Kritz, Neil J., ed. *Transitional Justice: How Emerging Democracies Reckon with Former Regimes.* 3 vols. Washington, D.C.: United States Institute of Peace Press, 1995.

Krog, Antjie. *Country of My Skull.* Johannesburg: Random House, 1998.

Kuhn, Thomas S. *The Structure of Scientific Revolutions.* Chicago: University of Chicago Press, 1962.

Kuznets, Simon. "Economic Growth and Income Inequality." *American Economic Review* 45, no. 1 (1955): 1–28.

La Capra, Dominick. *History and Memory After Auschwitz.* Ithaca: Cornell University Press, 1998.

———. "Reflections on Trauma, Absence, and Loss." In *Whose Freud? The Place of Psychoanalysis in Contemporary Culture*, pp. 178–204. Ed. Peter Brooks and Alex Woloch. New Haven: Yale University Press, 2000.

———. *Representing the Holocaust: History, Theory, Trauma.* Ithaca: Cornell University Press, 1994.

Laber, Jeri. "Witch Hunt in Prague." *New York Review of Books* 39, no. 8 (1992): 5–8.

Lacan, Jacques. *The Ethics of Psychoanalysis, 1959–1960.* Ed. Jacques-Alain Miller, Trans. Dennis Porter. New York: Norton, 1988.

———. "The Mirror Stage as Formative of the *I* Function." In *Ecrits: A Selection*, pp. 3–9. Trans. Bruce Fink, Heloise Fink, and Russell Grigg. New York: Norton, 2004.

———. *My Teaching*. Trans. David Macey. London: Verso, 2009.

Lakatos, Imre. "Falsification and the Methodology of Scientific Research Programs." In *Criticism and the Growth of Knowledge*, pp. 91–196. Ed. Imre Lakatos and Alan Musgrave. Cambridge: Cambridge University Press, 1970.

Lang, Berel. *The Future of the Holocaust: Between History and Memory*. Ithaca: Cornell University Press, 1999.

Laor, Yitzhak. "Children of the State." Review of *Israel's Holocaust* by Idith Zertal. *London Review of Books*, January 26 2006.

Laplanche, Jean, and Serge Leclaire. *The Ego and the Id: A Volume of Laplanche's Problematiques*. Trans. Luke Thurston and Lindsey Watson. New York: Other Press, 1999.

Laplanche, Jean, and J. B. Pontalis. *The Language of Psycho-Analysis*. Trans. Donald Nicholson-Smith. New York: Norton, 1974.

Laqueur, Walter. *The Changing Face of Antisemitism: From Ancient Times to the Present Day*. New York: Oxford University Press, 2006.

Laufer, Steven, et al. "ANC in Court Bid to Block Truth Report." *Business Day (SA)*, October 29, 1998.

Laycock, Douglas. "The Scope and Significance of Restitution." *Texas Law Review* 67 (1989).

Le Goff, Jacques. *The Birth of Purgatory*. Trans. Arthur Goldhammer. Chicago: University of Chicago Press, 1984.

Lear, Jonathan. *Radical Hope: Ethics in the Face of Cultural Devastation*. Cambridge: Harvard University Press, 2006.

———. *Therapeutic Action: An Earnest Plea for Irony*. New York: Other Press, 2003.

Lemann, Nicholas. *Redemption: The Last Battle of the Civil War*. New York: Farrar, Straus and Giroux, 2006.

Lemkin, Raphaël. *Axis Rule in Occupied Europe: Laws of Occupation, Analysis of Government, Proposals for Redress*. Washington, D.C.: Carnegie Endowment for International Peace, Division of International Law, 1944.

León-Portilla, Miguel, ed. *The Broken Spears: The Aztec Account of the Conquest of Mexico*. Trans. Lysander Kemp. Boston: Beacon, 1992.

Lepore, Jill. *The Name of War: King Philip's War and the Origins of American Identity*. New York: Knopf, 1998.

Levi, Primo. *The Drowned and the Saved*. Trans. Raymond Rosenthal. New York: Vintage International, 1989.

———. *If This Is a Man: The Truce*. Trans. Stuart Woolf. Harmondsworth: Penguin, 1979.

———. "A Self-Interview: Afterword to *If This Is a Man*." In *The Voice of Memory: Interviews 1961–1987*, pp. 184–207. Ed. Marco Belpoliti and Robert Gordon. Trans. Robert Gordon. New York: New Press, 2001.

Lévinas, Emmanuel. "Diachrony and Representation." In *Entre Nous: On Thinking-of-the-Other*, pp. 159–78. Trans. Michael B. Smith and Barbara Harshav. New York: Columbia University Press, 1998.

———. "Ethics and Politics." In *The Levinas Reader*. Ed. Seán Hand. Trans. Jonathan Romney. Oxford: Blackwell, 1989.

———. "From the One to the Other: Transcendence and Time." In *Entre Nous: On Thinking-of-the-Other*, pp. 91–102. Trans. Michael B. Smith and Barbara Harshav. New York: Columbia University Press, 1998.

———. "Ideology and Idealism." In *The Levinas Reader*, pp. 235–48. Ed. Seán Hand. Trans. Seán Hand. Oxford: Blackwell, 1989.

———. "The Nations and the Presence of Israel." In *In the Time of the Nations*, pp. 92–108. Trans. Michael B.Smith. Bloomington: Indiana University Press, 1994.

———. "Peace and Proximity." In *Emmanuel Levinas: Basic Philosophical Writings*, pp. 161–69. Ed. Adrian Theodor Peperzak, Simon Critchley, and Robert Bernasconi. Trans. Simon Critchley, Tina Chanter, and Nicholas Walker. Bloomington: Indiana University Press, 1996.

———. "Politics After." In *Beyond the Verse: Talmudic Readings and Lectures*, pp. 188–88. Trans. Gary D. Mole. Bloomington: Indiana University Press, 1994.

———. *Time and the Other and Additional Essays*. Trans. Richard A. Cohen. Pittsburgh: Duquesne University Press, 1987.

———. *Totality and Infinity: An Essay on Exteriority*. Trans. Alphonso Lingis. The Hague: Kluwer, 1979.

———. *Totality and Infinity: An Essay on Exteriority*. Trans. Alphonso Lingis. Pittsburgh: Duquesne University Press, 1969.

———. "Useless Suffering." In *Entre Nous: On Thinking-of-the-Other*, pp. 91–102. Trans. Michael B. Smith and Barbara Harshav. New York: Columbia University Press, 1998.

Lévinas, Emmanuel, and France Guwy. "What No One Else Can Do in My Place: A Conversation with Emmanuel Levinas." In *Religion: Beyond a Concept*, pp. 297–310. Ed. Hent de Vries. New York: Fordham University Press, 2008.

Levine, Bruce. *Confederate Emancipation: Southern Plans to Free and Arm Slaves during the Civil War*. New York: Oxford University Press, 2007.

Levinson, Sanford. "They Whisper: Reflections on Flags, Monuments, and State Holidays, and the Construction of Social Meaning in a Multicultural Society." *Chicago-Kent Law Review* (1995): 1079–1119.

———, ed. *Torture: A Collection*. Oxford: Oxford University Press, 2004.

———. *Written in Stone: Public Monuments in Changing Societies*. Durham: Duke University Press, 1998.

Lévy, Bernard Henri. *War, Evil, and the End of History*. Hoboken: Melville House, 2004.

Lewis, David K. *On the Plurality of Worlds*. Oxford: Blackwell, 1986.

Licklider, Roy E. "The Consequences of Negotiated Settlements in Civil Wars, 1945–1993." *American Political Science Review* 89, no. 3 (1995): 681–90.

———. "Ending Civil Wars: The Implementation of Peace Agreements." *Journal of Democracy* 14, no. 3 (2003): 174–77.

Lijphart, Arend. *Democracy in Plural Societies: A Comparative Exploration*. New Haven: Yale University Press, 1977.

Lincoln, Abraham. "Address Delivered at the Dedication of the Cemetery at Gettysburg, November 19, 1863." In *Abraham Lincoln, His Speeches and Writings*, p. 734. Ed. Roy P. Basler. New York: Da Capo, 1990.

———. "Second Inaugural Address, March 4, 1865." In *Abraham Lincoln, His Speeches and Writings*, pp. 792–93. Ed. Roy P. Basler. New York: Da Capo, 1990.

Lindqvist, Sven. *Exterminate All the Brutes*. Trans. Joan Tate. New York: New Press, 1996.

———. *A History of Bombing*. New York: New Press, 2001.

Lloyd, David. *Ireland After History*. Notre Dame: University of Notre Dame Press, 1999.

Loewald, Hans W. "The Experience of Time (1972)." In *The Essential Loewald: Collected Papers and Monographs*, pp. 138–47. Ed. Jonathan Lear. Hagerstown, Md.: University, 2000.

———. "On Internalization (1973)." In *The Essential Loewald: Collected Papers and Monographs*, ed. Jonathan Lear, pp. 69–86. Hagerstown, Md.: University, 2000.

———. "On the Therapeutic Action of Psychonanalysis (1960)." In *The Essential Loewald: Collected Papers and Monographs*, ed. Jonathan Lear, pp. 221–56. Hagerstown, Md.: University, 2000.

Loving v. Virginia, 388 US 1 (1967).

Lucy, Niall. *A Derrida Dictionary*. Malden, Mass.: Blackwell, 2004.

Luther, Martin. *Lectures on Romans: Glosses and Scholia*, vol. 25: *Luther's Works*. Ed. Hilton C. Oswald. St. Louis: Concordia, 1972.

Lyons, David. "The New Indian Claims and Original Rights to Land." *Social Theory and Practice* 4 (1977): 249ff.

Lyotard, Jean-François. *The Differend: Phrases in Dispute*. Trans. Georges Van Den Abbeele. Minneapolis: University of Minnesota Press, 1988.

———. " 'the Jews.' " In *Heidegger and "the Jews,"* pp. 1–48. Trans. Andreas Michel and Mark S. Roberts. Minneapolis: University of Minnesota Press, 1990.

Lyotard, Jean-François, and Eberhard Gruber. *The Hyphen: Between Judaism and Christianity*. Trans. Pascale-Anne Brault and Michael Naas. Atlantic Highlands, N.J.: Humanity, 1999.

MacDonald, Michael. *Children of Wrath: Political Violence in Northern Ireland*. Cambridge: Polity, 1986.

———. *Why Race Matters in South Africa*. Cambridge: Harvard University Press, 2006.

MacDonnell, Francis. "Reconstruction in the Wake of Vietnam: The Pardoning of Robert E. Lee and Jefferson Davis." *Civil War History* 40, no. 2 (1994): 119–33.

Mack Smith, Denis. *Cavour*. New York: Knopf, 1985.

MacKenzie, Donald A. *An Engine, Not a Camera: How Financial Models Shape Markets*. Inside Technology series. Cambridge: MIT Press, 2006.

Macklem, Patrick. *Normative Dimensions of Aboriginal Self-Government*. Ottawa: Royal Commission on Aboriginal Peoples, 1994.

Maier, Charles S. "A Holocaust Like the Others? Problems of Comparative History." In *The Unmasterable Past: History, Holocaust, and German National Identity*, pp. 66–99. Cambridge: Harvard University Press, 1988.

———. *The Unmasterable Past: History, Holocaust, and German National Identity*. Cambridge: Harvard University Press, 1988.

———. "Unsafe Haven: Why Minorities-Treaties Fail." *New Republic* 207, no. 16 (1992): 20.

Malamud Goti, Jaime E. *Game Without End: State Terror and the Politics of Justice*. Norman: University of Oklahoma Press, 1996.

Malan, Rian. *My Traitor's Heart: A South African Exile Returns to Face His Country, His Tribe, and His Conscience*. New York: Atlantic Monthly Press, 1990.

Malan, Wynand. "Statement by Mr. Wynand Malan, Deputy Chair of the Human Rights

Violations Committee of the Truth and Reconciliation Commission, 16 May 1997." http://www.justice.gov.za/trc/media/pr/1997/p970516a.htm (accessed January 30, 2010).

Mamdani, Mahmood. "Amnesty or Impunity: A Preliminary Critique of the Report of the Truth and Reconciliation Commission of South Africa." In *Identities, Affiliations, and Allegiances*, pp. 325–61. Ed. Seyla Benhabib, Ian Shapiro, and Danilo Petranovich. New York: Cambridge University Press, 2007.

——. *Citizen and Subject: Contemporary Africa and the Legacy of Late Colonialism*. Princeton: Princeton University Press, 1996.

——. *From Citizen to Refugee: Uganda Asians Come to Britain*. London: Frances Pinter, 1973.

——. *Good Muslim, Bad Muslim: America, the Cold War, and the Roots of Terror*. New York: Pantheon, 2004.

——. "The New Humanitarian Order: Is the ICC's 'Responsibility to Protect' Really Just an Assertion of Neocolonial Domination?" *Nation*, September 29 2008, pp. 17–22.

——. "Now Who Will Bell the Fat Black Cat." Review of *Comrades in Business* by Heribert Adam, Frederik van Zyl Slabbert, and Kogila Moodley, *Electronic Mail and Guardian*, October 17,1997.

——. "The Politics and Political Uses of Human Rights Discourse." Columbia University, November 8–9, 2001.

——. "The Politics of Naming: Genocide, Civil War, Insurgency." *London Review of Books*, March 8, 2007.

——. "Race and Ethnicity as Political Identities in the African Context." In *Keywords|Identity: For a Different Kind of Globalization*, pp. 1–24. Ed. Nadia Tazi. New York: Other Press, 2004.

——. "Reconciliation Without Justice." *Southern African Review of Books* 46 (1996): 3–5.

——. *Saviors and Survivors: Darfur, Politics, and the War on Terror*. New York: Pantheon, 2009.

——. "When Does a Settler Become a Native? Reflections on the Colonial Roots of Citizenship in Equatorial and South Africa." In *Inaugural Lecture, University of Cape Town*, new series no. 208, May 13, 1998.

——. "When Does Reconciliation Turn into a Denial of Justice?" Pretoria: Human Sciences Research Council, February 18, 1998.

——. *When Victims Become Killers: Colonialism, Nativism, and the Genocide in Rwanda*. Princeton: Princeton University Press, 2001.

Mandel, Ernest. *Late Capitalism*. Trans. Joris De Bres. Rev. ed. London: NLB, 1975.

Mandela, Nelson. "Speech in National Assembly, 15 April, 1997." http://www.doj.gov.za/trc/media/1997/9704/s970415e.htm (accessed January 30, 2010).

Mandelbrot, Benoit B., and Richard L. Hudson. *The (Mis)Behavior of Markets: A Fractal View of Risk, Ruin, and Reward*. New York: Basic Books, 2004.

Mann, Charles C. *1491: New Revelations of the Americas Before Columbus*. New York: Vintage, 2006.

Mann, Michael. *The Dark Side of Democracy: Explaining Ethnic Cleansing*. New York: Cambridge University Press, 2005.

Mansfield, Mary C. *The Humiliation of Sinners: Public Penance in Thirteenth-Century France*. Ithaca: Cornell University Press, 1995.

Manvell, Roger, and Heinrich Fraenkel. *The Hundred Days to Hitler*. London: Dent, 1974.

Margalit, Avishai. *The Ethics of Memory*. Cambridge: Harvard University Press, 2002.

Markovic, Milan. "Lawyers Aren't Special: Why It's Legitimate to Investigate the Bush Lawyers Who May Have Approved War Crimes." *Slate*, http://www.slate.com/id/2206518/ (accessed January 31, 2010).

Martin, Randy. *An Empire of Indifference: American War and the Financial Logic of Risk Management*. Durham: Duke University Press, 2007.

Marx, Karl. "On the Jewish Question." In *Karl Marx, Frederick Engels: Collected Works*. Vols. 3, 5. Trans. Richard Dixon et al. New York: International, 1975–2001.

Massignon, Louis. "Transfer of Suffering Through Compassion." In *Testimonies and Reflection: Essays of Louis Massignon*, pp. 155–64. Ed. Herbert Mason. Notre Dame: University of Notre Dame Press, 1989.

Mastnak, Tomaž. *Crusading Peace: Christendom, the Muslim World, and Western Political Order*. Berkeley: University of California Press, 2002.

Matthiessen, F. O. *American Renaissance: Art and Expression in the Age of Emerson and Whitman*. London: Oxford University Press, 1968.

Mayer, Arno J. *The Furies: Violence and Terror in the French and Russian Revolutions*. Princeton: Princeton University Press, 2000.

——. *Plowshares Into Swords: From Zionism to Israel*. London: Verso, 2008.

——. *Why Did the Heavens Not Darken? The "Final Solution" in History*. New York: Pantheon, 1988.

Mayer, Jane. *Dark Side: The Inside Story of How the War on Terror Turned Into a War on American Ideals*. New York: Doubleday, 2008.

Mazower, Mark. "The G-Word." *London Review of Books* 23, no. 3 (2001): 1–5.

McGrath, Alister E. *Iustitia Dei: A History of the Christian Doctrine of Justification*. Cambridge: Cambridge University Press, 1986.

McPherson, James M. *Abraham Lincoln and the Second American Revolution*. New York: Oxford University Press, 1990.

——. *Battle Cry of Freedom: The Civil War Era*. New York: Oxford University Press, 1988.

Mearsheimer, John J., and Stephen M. Walt. *The Israel Lobby and U.S. Foreign Policy*. New York: Farrar, Straus and Giroux, 2007.

Mehta, Uday Singh. *The Anxiety of Freedom: Imagination and Individuality in Locke's Political Thought*. Ithaca: Cornell University Press, 1992.

Meier, Heinrich. *Carl Schmitt & Leo Strauss: The Hidden Dialogue; Including Strauss's Notes on Schmitt's Concept of the Political and Three Letters from Strauss to Schmitt*. Trans. J. Harvey Lomax. Chicago: University of Chicago Press, 1995.

Meinecke, Friedrich. *Machiavellism: The Doctrine of Raison d'État and Its Place in Modern History*. New Brunswick, N.J.: Transaction, 1998.

Meister, Robert. "Anticipatory Regret: Can Free Speech Be Protected When It Matters?" Review of *Perilous Times* by Geoffrey R. Stone. *boundary 2* 32, no. 3 (2005): 169–97.

——. "Beyond Satisfaction: Desire, Consumption, and the Future of Socialism." *Topoi* 15 (1996): 189–210.

———. "Discrimination Law Through the Looking Glass." Review of *Competing Equalities* by Marc Galanter. *Wisconsin Law Review* (1985): 937–87.

———. "The Logic and Legacy of *Dred Scott*: Marshall, Taney, and the Sublimation of Republican Thought." *Studies in American Political Development* 3 (1989): 199–260.

———. "N. O. Brown." In *In Memoriam: Norman O. Brown*, pp. 65–71. Ed. Jerome Neu. Santa Cruz: New Pacific, 2005.

———. "'Never Again': The Ethics of the Neighbor and the Logic of Genocide." *Postmodern Culture* 15, no. 2 (2005).

———. *Political Identity: Thinking Through Marx*. Cambridge: Blackwell, 1991.

———. "Sojourners and Survivors: Two Logics of Non-Discrimination." *University of Chicago Law School Roundtable* 3, no. 1 (1996): 121–84.

———. "Two Concepts of Victimhood in Transitional Regimes." In *TRC: Commissioning the Past*. Johannesburg: University of the Witwatersrand, 1999.

———. "Vigilante Action against Pornography: The Symbolic Destruction of Symbols." *Social Text*, no. 12 (fall 1985): 3–18.

———. "Ways of Winning: The Costs of Moral Victory in Transitional Regimes." In *Modernity and the Problem of Evil*, pp. 81–111. Ed. Alan D. Schrift. Bloomington: Indiana University Press, 2005.

Meltzer, Donald. *The Kleinian Development*. Pitlochry: Clunie Press for the Roland Harris Trust Library, 1985.

Melville, Herman. *White-Jacket; or, the World in a Man-of-War*. Ed. Harrison Hayford, Hershel Parker, and G. Thomas Tanselle. Evanston: Northwestern University Press, 2000.

Mendelsohn, Daniel. *The Lost: A Search for Six of Six Million*. New York: HarperCollins, 2006.

Menzies, Gavin. *1421: The Year China Discovered America*. New York: Perennial, 2004.

Meredith, Martin, and Tina Rosenberg. *Coming to Terms: South Africa's Search for Truth*. New York: Public Affairs, 1999.

Merleau-Ponty, Maurice. *Humanism and Terror: An Essay on the Communist Problem*. Boston: Beacon, 1969.

Milbank, John. *Being Reconciled: Ontology and Pardon*. London: Routledge, 2003.

———. "The Soul of Reciprocity Part One: Reciprocity Refused." *Modern Theology* 17, no. 3 (2001): 335–91.

———. "The Soul of Reciprocity Part Two: Reciprocity Granted." *Modern Theology* 17, no. 4 (2001): 485–507.

Mill, John Stuart. *Considerations on Representative Government*. London: Routledge, 1905.

Miller, David. *National Responsibility and Global Justice*. Oxford: Oxford University Press, 2007.

Miller, Perry. *Errand Into the Wilderness*. Cambridge: Belknap Press of Harvard University Press, 1956.

Milsom, S. F. C. *Historical Foundations of the Common Law*. London: Butterworths, 1969.

———. *The Legal Framework of English Feudalism*. Cambridge: Cambridge University Press, 1976.

Milton, John. *Paradise Lost and Paradise Regained*. Ed. Christopher Ricks. New York: Signet Classics, 1968.

Minow, Martha. *Between Vengeance and Forgiveness: Facing History After Genocide and Mass Violence.* Boston: Beacon, 1998.

———. *Breaking the Cycles of Hatred: Memory, Law, and Repair.* Ed. Nancy L. Rosenblum. Princeton: Princeton University Press, 2002.

Mitscherlich, Alexander, and Margarete Mitscherlich. *The Inability to Mourn: Principles of Collective Behavior.* Trans. Beverley R. Placzek. New York: Grove, 1975.

Moeller, Susan D. *Compassion Fatigue: How the Media Sell Disease, Famine, War, and Death.* New York: Routledge, 1999.

Molebeledi, Pule. "SA Still Needs Economic Liberation." *Business Day*, 2003.

Moltmann, Jürgen. *The Crucified God: The Cross of Christ as the Foundation and Criticism of Christian Theology.* Minneapolis: Fortress, 1993.

Moore, John, Jr. "Problems with Forgiveness: Granting Amnesty Under the Arias Plan in Nicaragua and El Salvador." *Stanford Law Review* 43, no. 3 (1991): 733–77.

Morgan, Edmund S. "The Big American Crime." Review of *Many Thousands Gone* by Ira Berlin; *Slave Counterpoint* by Philip D. Morgan, and other works. *New York Review of Books*, December 3 1998.

Morris, Benny. *The Birth of the Palestinian Refugee Problem Revisited.* 2d ed. Cambridge: Cambridge University Press, 2004.

———. *Righteous Victims: A History of the Zionist-Arab Conflict, 1881–2001.* New York: Vintage, 2001.

Morris, Herbert. "Shared Guilt." In *On Guilt and Innocence: Essays in Legal Philosophy and Moral Psychology,* pp. 111–38. Berkeley: University of California Press, 1976.

Morton, J. "The Cunning of Recognition: Indigenous Alterities and the Making of Australian Multiculturalism; Taking Responsibility for the Past: Reparation and Historical Justice." *Thesis Eleven* 85, no. 1 (2006): 122ff.

Mosteller, Frederick, and Daniel P. Moynihan, eds. *On Equality of Educational Opportunity.* New York: Random House, 1972.

Müller, Ingo. *Hitler's Justice: The Courts of the Third Reich.* Trans. Deborah Lucas Schneider. Cambridge: Harvard University Press, 1991.

Mueller, John E. *Overblown: How Politicians and the Terrorism Industry Inflate National Security Threats, and Why We Believe Them.* New York: Free Press, 2006.

Mufti, Aamir. *Enlightenment in the Colony: The Jewish Question and the Crisis of Postcolonial Culture.* Princeton: Princeton University Press, 2007.

Mulgan, Richard. "Should Indigenous Peoples Have Special Rights?" *Orbis* 33 (1989): 375–88.

Murphy, Jeffrie G. *Getting Even: Forgiveness and Its Limits.* Oxford: Oxford University Press, 2003.

Murphy, Jeffrie G., and Jean Hampton. *Forgiveness and Mercy.* Cambridge: Cambridge University Press, 1988.

Murray, Ian. "Tame Day for New Boys in School of Democracy." *Times*, October 5, 1990.

Mydans, Seth. "Myanmar Faces Pressure to Allow Major Aid Effort." *New York Times*, May 8, 2008.

Myers, Bob. *Is This Really What We Fought For? White Rule Ends, Black Poverty Goes On.* London: Index, 1997.

Nadler, Jennifer. *Oxford Journal of Legal Studies* 28, no. 2 (2008): 245–75; doi:10.1093/ojls/gqn011 (accessed March 23, 2010).

Nagel, Thomas. *The Possibility of Altruism.* Oxford: Clarendon Press of Oxford University Press, 1970.

———. *The View from Nowhere.* New York: Oxford University Press, 1986.

Naimark, Norman M. *Fires of Hatred: Ethnic Cleansing in Twentieth-Century Europe.* Cambridge: Harvard University Press, 2001.

Neely, Mark E. *The Last Best Hope of Earth: Abraham Lincoln and the Promise of America.* Cambridge: Harvard University Press, 1993.

Negri, Antonio. *Insurgencies: Constituent Power and the Modern State.* Trans. Maurizia Boscagli. Minneapolis: University of Minnesota Press, 1999.

Neier, Aryeh. *War Crimes: Brutality, Genocide, Terror, and the Struggle for Justice.* New York: Times/Random House, 1998.

Neiman, Susan. *Evil in Modern Thought: An Alternative History of Philosophy.* Princeton: Princeton University Press, 2002.

Ngai, Sianne. "Irritation." In *Ugly Feelings,* pp. 174–208. Cambridge: Harvard University Press, 2005.

Nichols, Roy Franklin. "United States vs. Jefferson Davis, 1865–1869." *American Historical Review* (January 1926).

Niebuhr, Reinhold. *Moral Man and Immoral Society: A Study in Ethics and Politics.* Library of Theological Ethics series. Louisville, Ky.: Westminster John Knox, 2001.

Nietzsche, Friedrich Wilhelm. *The Anti-Christ, Ecce Homo, Twilight of the Idols, and Other Writings.* Trans. Judith Norman. Ed. Aaron Ridley. New York: Cambridge University Press, 2005.

———. *Beyond Good and Evil: Prelude to a Philosophy of the Future.* Trans. Walter A. Kaufmann. New York: Vintage, 1989.

Nino, Carlos Santiago. *Radical Evil on Trial.* New Haven: Yale University Press, 1996.

Nora, Pierre, et al. *Rethinking France.* Trans. Mary Trouille. Chicago: University of Chicago Press, 2001.

Norris, Kathleen. *Acedia and Me: A Marriage, Monks, and a Writer's Life.* New York: Riverhead, 2008.

Novick, Peter. *The Holocaust in American Life.* Boston: Houghton Mifflin, 1999.

Nozick, Robert. *Anarchy, State, and Utopia.* New York: Basic Books, 1974.

Nunca Más (Never Again): A Report by Argentina's National Commission on Disappeared People. London: Faber, 1986.

Olin, Mallory. "The Political Theology of the Civil Rights Movement: Martin Luther King, Jr. and St. Paul." Undergraduate paper. 2006.

Omar, Dullah. "Justice in Transition." http://www.doj.gov.za/trc/legal/justice.htm (accessed January 31, 2010).

Ophir, Adi. "The Identity of the Victims and the Victims of Identity: A Critique of Zionist Ideology for a Post-Zionist Age." In *Mapping Jewish Identities,* pp. 174–200. Ed. Laurence J. Silberstein. New York: New York University Press, 2000.

———. *The Order of Evils: Toward an Ontology of Morals.* Cambridge: Zone, 2005.

———. "A Response to Benny Morris: Genocide Hides Behind Expulsion." *Counterpunch* (2004). http://www.counterpunch.org/ophiro1162004.html (accessed January 31, 2010).

Oren, Michael B. *Power, Faith, and Fantasy: America in the Middle East, 1776 to the Present.* New York: Norton, 2007.

Orentlicher, Diane F. "Settling Accounts: The Duty to Prosecute Human Rights Violations of a Prior Regime." *Yale Law Journal* 100, no. 8 (1991): 2537–2615.

Osiel, Mark. *Mass Atrocity, Collective Memory, and the Law.* New Brunswick, N.J.: Transaction, 1997.

Otto, Walter Friedrich. *Dionysus, Myth, and Cult.* Trans. Robert B. Palmer. Bloomington: Indiana University Press, 1965.

Oz, Amos. "The Tender Among You and the Very Delicate." In *In the Land of Israel,* pp. 85–100. Trans. Maurie Goldberg-Bartura. San Diego: Harcourt Brace Jovanovich, 1983.

Pakenham, Thomas. *The Scramble for Africa, 1876–1912.* New York: Random House, 1991.

Palmer, Robert Roswell. *The Age of the Democratic Revolution.* 2 vols. Princeton: Princeton University Press, 1959.

Paludan, Phillip Shaw. *A Covenant with Death: The Constitution, Law, and Equality in the Civil War Era.* Urbana: University of Illinois Press, 1975.

Parfit, Derek. *Reasons and Persons.* Oxford: Clarendon Press of Oxford University Press, 1984.

Patterson, Charles. *Eternal Treblinka: Our Treatment of Animals and the Holocaust.* New York: Lantern, 2002.

Patterson, Orlando. *Freedom.* New York: Basic Books, 1991.

Paz, Octavio. "Critique of the Pyramid." In *The Labyrinth of Solitude: Life and Thought in Mexico,* pp. 284–326. Trans. Lysander Kemp. New York: Viking Penguin, 1985.

Pflanze, Otto. *Bismarck and the Development of Germany: The Period of Unification, 1815–1871.* Vol. 2. Princeton: Princeton University Press, 1963.

Phalane, Charles. "Victims Have Waited Too Long, Says Tutu." *Independent On Line,* March 21, 2003.

Phillips, Adam. "Superiorities." In *Equals,* pp. 3–31. New York: Basic Books, 2002.

———. *Winnicott.* Cambridge: Harvard University Press, 1988.

Pines, Malcolm. "Bion and Group Psychotherapy." In *International Library of Group Psychotherapy and Group Process.* London: Routledge, 1985.

Pogge, Thomas. *World Poverty and Human Rights: Cosmopolitan Responsibilities and Reforms.* Cambridge: Polity, 2002.

Pomorski, Stanislaw. "Conspiracy and Criminal Organization in the Nuremberg Trial and International Law " In *The Nuremberg Trial and International Law,* pp. 213–48. Ed. George Ginsburgs and V. N. Kudriavtsev. Dordrecht: Nijhof, 1990.

Posner, Eric A., and Adrian Vermeule. "Reparations for Slavery and Other Historical Injustices." *Columbia Law Review* 103, no. 3 (2003): 689–748.

———. *Terror in the Balance: Security, Liberty, and the Courts.* New York: Oxford University Press, 2007.

———. "Transitional Justice as Ordinary Justice." *Harvard Law Review* 117 (2003).

Posner, Richard A. *Not a Suicide Pact: The Constitution in a Time of National Emergency.* New York: Oxford University Press, 2006.

Postone, Moishe. "The Holocaust and the Trajectory of the Twentieth Century." In *Catastrophe and Meaning: The Holocaust and the Twentieth Century*, pp. 81–114. Ed. Moishe Postone and Eric L. Santner. Chicago: University of Chicago Press, 2003.

Power, Samantha. "Bystanders to Genocide." *Atlantic Monthly* 288, no. 2 (2001): 84–108.

————. "Never Again: The World's Most Unfulfilled Promise." PBS *Frontline.* http://www.pbs.org/wgbh/pages/frontline/shows/karadzic/genocide/neveragain.html (accessed January 30, 2010).

————. *"A Problem from Hell": America and the Age of Genocide.* New York: Basic Books, 2002.

Powers, Thomas. "The Nestor of the Rockies." *New York Review of Books* 48, no. 17, November 1, 2001.

Premachand. *Nirmala.* Trans. Alok Rai. Delhi: Oxford University Press, 1999.

The Promotion of National Unity and Reconciliation Act. No. 34 of 1995, Amended in 1997 and 1998.

Prucha, Francis Paul. *The Great Father: The United States Government and the American Indians.* 2 vols. Lincoln: University of Nebraska Press, 1984.

Przeworski, Adam. *Capitalism and Social Democracy.* Cambridge: Cambridge University Press, 1985.

Truth and Reconciliation Commission. *Public Discussion: Transforming Society Through Reconciliation: Myth or Reality*, March 12, 1998.

Putnam, Hilary. "Lévinas and Judaism." In *The Cambridge Companion to Levinas*, ed. Simon Critchley and Robert Bernasconi, pp. 33–62. Cambridge: Cambridge University Press, 2002.

Quinn, David Beers. *The Elizabethans and the Irish.* Ithaca: Cornell University Press for the Folger Shakespeare Library, 1966.

Qutb, Sayyid. *In the Shade of the Qur'ān.* Trans. Adil Salahi. Vol. 11. Markfield: Islamic Foundation, 2005.

————. *Milestones.* Rev. ed. Salimiah, Kuwait: International Islamic Federation of Student Organizations, 1978.

Rabinbach, Anson. "'The Abyss That Opened Up Before Us': Thinking About Auschwitz and Modernity." In *Catastrophe and Meaning: The Holocaust and the Twentieth Century*, pp. 51–66. Ed. Moishe Postone and Eric L. Santner. Chicago: University of Chicago Press, 2003.

Rae, Douglas W., and Douglas Yates. *Equalities.* Cambridge: Harvard University Press, 1981.

Rai, Alok. *Hindi Nationalism.* Hyderabad: Orient Longman, 2001.

Ramadan, Tariq. "Prometheus and Abraham." In *Islam, the West and the Challenges of Modernity*, pp. 203–12. Trans. Saïd Amghar. Leicester: Islamic Foundation, 2001.

Ranciere, Jacques. "Who Is the Subject of the Rights of Man?" *South Atlantic Quarterly* 103, no. 2–3 (2004): 297–310.

Randall, John G. *Constitutional Problems Under Lincoln.* Rev. ed. Urbana: University of Illinois Press, 1951.

————. *Lincoln, the President.* New York: Dodd, Mead, 1945.

Ravitzky, Aviezer. *Messianism, Zionism, and Jewish Religious Radicalism.* Trans. Michael Swirsky and Jonathan Chipman. Chicago: University of Chicago Press, 1996.

Rawls, John. *Justice as Fairness: A Restatement.* Ed. Erin Kelly. Cambridge: Harvard University Press, 2001.

———. *The Law of Peoples; with, the Idea of Public Reason Revisited.* Cambridge: Harvard University Press, 1999.

———. *A Theory of Justice.* Cambridge: Belknap Press of Harvard University Press, 1971.

Reed, Gary Frank. "Freedom as the End of Civilization: Studies in the Troubled Relationship Between the Ideas of Liberty and Civility." Ph.D. diss., University of California, Santa Cruz, 1977.

Rehnquist, William H. *All the Laws But One: Civil Liberties in Wartime.* New York: Knopf, 1998.

Remnick, David. "The Apostate: A Zionist Politician Loses Faith in the Future. (Letter from Jerusalem)." *New Yorker,* July 30, 2007.

Resnik, Judith. "Dependent Sovereigns: Indian Tribes, States, and the Federal Courts." *University of Chicago Law Review* 56 (1989): 671–759.

"The Responsibility to Protect Coalition." http://r2pcoalition.org/ (accessed January 30, 2010).

"Responsibility to Protect: Engaging Civil Society." http://www.responsibilitytoprotect.org/ (accessed January 30, 2010).

Rév, István. *Retroactive Justice: Prehistory of Post-Communism.* Stanford: Stanford University Press, 2005.

Ricoeur, Paul. *Memory, History, Forgetting.* Chicago: University of Chicago Press, 2004.

———. *The Symbolism of Evil.* Trans. Emerson Buchanan. New York: Harper and Row, 1967.

Rieff, David. "An Age of Genocide." In *At the Point of a Gun: Democratic Dreams and Armed Intervention,* pp. 59–94. New York: Simon and Schuster, 2005.

———. *Slaughterhouse: Bosnia and the Failure of the West.* New York: Simon and Schuster, 1995.

Rieff, Philip. *Charisma: The Gift of Grace, and How It Has Been Taken Away from Us.* New York: Pantheon, 2007.

Robbins, Bruce. "Temporizing: Time and Politics in the Humanities and Human Rights." *boundary 2* 32, no. 1 (2005).

Robertson, Ritchie. *The German-Jewish Dialogue: An Anthology of Literary Texts, 1749–1993.* Oxford: Oxford University Press, 1999.

Robinson, Randall. *The Debt: What America Owes to Blacks.* New York: Dutton, 2000.

Roediger, David R. *Working Toward Whiteness: How America's Immigrants Became White: The Strange Journey from Ellis Island to the Suburbs.* New York: Basic Books, 2005.

Rogat, Yosal. *The Eichmann Trial and the Rule of Law.* Santa Barbara: Center for the Study of Democratic Institutions, 1961.

Rogin, Michael Paul. *Blackface, White Noise: Jewish Immigrants in the Hollywood Melting Pot.* Berkeley: University of California Press, 1996.

Rogozinski, Jacob. "It Makes Us Wrong: Kant and Radical Evil." In *Radical Evil,* pp. 30–45. London: Verso, 1996.

Roht-Arriaza, Naomi. *The Pinochet Effect: Transnational Justice in the Age of Human Rights*. Philadelphia: University of Pennsylvania Press, 2005.

Roht-Arriaza, Naomi, ed. *Impunity and Human Rights in International Law and Practice*. New York: Oxford University Press, 1995.

Roht-Arriaza, Naomi, and Javier Mariezcurrena, eds. *Transitional Justice in the Twenty-First Century: Beyond Truth Versus Justice*. Cambridge: Cambridge University Press, 2006.

Rorty, Richard. "Human Rights, Rationality, and Sentimentality." In *On Human Rights: The Oxford Amnesty Lectures, 1993*, pp. 111–34. Ed. Stephen Shute and Susan. L. Hurley. New York: Basic Books, 1993.

———. "Justice as a Larger Loyalty." In *Cosmopolitics: Thinking and Feeling Beyond the Nation*, pp. 45–58. Ed. Pheng Cheah and Bruce Robbins. Minneapolis: University of Minnesota Press, 1998.

Rose, Jacqueline. "Apathy and Accountability: The Challenge of South Africa's Truth and Reconciliation Commision to the Intellectual in the Modern World." In *On Not Being Able to Sleep: Psychoanalysis and the Modern World*, pp. 227–31. Princeton: Princeton University Press, 2003.

———. *The Question of Zion*. Princeton: Princeton University Press, 2005.

———. *States of Fantasy*. New York: Oxford University Press, 1996.

Rosen, Gary, ed. *The Right War? The Conservative Debate on Iraq*. New York: Cambridge University Press, 2005.

Rosen, Jeffrey. "The Conscience of a Conservative." *New York Times Magazine*, September 9, 2007.

Rosenberg, Tina. "Afterword: Confronting the Painful Past." In *Coming to Terms: South Africa's Search for Truth*, pp. 325–270. New York: Public Affairs, 1999.

———. *The Haunted Land: Facing Europe's Ghosts After Communism*. New York: Random House, 1995.

Rosenzweig, Franz. *The Star of Redemption*. Trans. Barbara E. Galli. Madison: University of Wisconsin Press, 2005.

Rossiter, Clinton. *Constitutional Dictatorship: Crisis Government in the Modern Democracies*. New York: Harcourt, 1963.

Rotberg, Robert I., and Thomas George Weiss, eds. *From Massacres to Genocide: The Media, Public Policy, and Humanitarian Crises*. Washington, D.C.: Brookings Institution, 1996.

Rotherham, Craig. *Proprietary Remedies in Context: A Study in the Judicial Redistribution of Property Rights*. Oxford: Hart, 2002.

———. "Restitution and Property Rites: Reason and Ritual in the Law of Proprietary Remedies." *Theoretical Inquiries in Law* 1, no. 1 (2000): 205–31.

Rousseau, Philip. *Ascetics, Authority, and the Church in the Age of Jerome and Cassian*. Oxford: Oxford University Press, 1978.

Ruane, Joseph, and Jennifer Todd. *The Dynamics of Conflict in Northern Ireland: Power, Conflict, and Emancipation*. Cambridge: Cambridge University Press, 1996.

Ruether, Rosemary Radford. *Faith and Fratricide: The Theological Roots of Anti-Semitism*. New York: Seabury, 1974.

Rummel, R. J. *Death by Government*. New Brunswick, N.J.: Transaction, 1994.

Ryback, Timothy W. "Forgiveness: Annals of Religion." *New Yorker*, February 6, 2006, pp. 66ff.

Sa'adah, Anne. *Germany's Second Chance: Trust, Justice, and Democratization*. Cambridge: Harvard University Press, 1998.

Said, Edward. "Michael Walzer's 'Exodus and Revolution': A Canaanite Reading." *Arab Studies* 8, no. 3 (1986): 289–303.

Said, Edward W. *Culture and Imperialism*. New York: Vintage, 1994.

Salvadori, Massimo. *Cavour and the Unification of Italy*. Princeton: Van Nostrand, 1961.

Sand, Shlomo. *The Invention of the Jewish People*. London: Verso, 2009.

Sands, Philippe. *Torture Team*. New York: Palgrave Macmillan, 2008.

Santner, Eric L. *Stranded Objects: Mourning, Memory, and Film in Postwar Germany*. Ithaca: Cornell University Press, 1990.

Sartori, Giovanni. *Democratic Theory*. Westport, Conn.: Greenwood, 1973.

Sartre, Jean-Paul. *Being and Nothingness: An Essay on Phenomenological Ontology*. Trans. Hazel E. Barnes. New York: Philosophical Library, 1956.

——. "Genocide." *Ramparts* (February 1968): 36–42.

——. "Merleau-Ponty *Vivant*." In *The Debate Between Sartre and Merleau-Ponty*, ed. Jon Stewart, pp. 565–625. Evanston: Northwestern University Press, 1998.

Sassen, Saskia. *Territory, Authority, Rights: From Medieval to Global Assemblages*. Princeton: Princeton University Press, 2006.

Savage, Kirk. *Standing Soldiers, Kneeling Slaves: Race, War, and Monument in Nineteenth-Century America*. Princeton: Princeton University Press, 1997.

Scarry, Elaine. *The Body in Pain: The Making and Unmaking of the World*. New York: Oxford University Press, 1985.

——. "The Difficulty of Imagining Other Persons." In *Human Rights in Political Transitions: Gettysburg to Bosnia*, pp. 277–309. Ed. Carla Hesse and Robert Post. New York: Zone, 1999.

Scheppele, Kim Lane. "Emergency Powers and the Constitution: Comment: Small Emergencies (Symposium)." *Georgia Law Review* 50 (2006): 835.

——. "Terrorism and the Constitution: Civil Liberties in a New America: Law in a Time of Emergency: States of Exception and the Temptations of 9/11." *University of Pennsylvania Journal of Constitutional Law* 6 (2004).

Schermers, Henry G., et al. *Free Movement of Persons in Europe: Legal Problems and Experiences*. Dordrecht: Martinous Nijhoff, 1993.

Schmemann, Serge. "United German Parliament Assembles." *New York Times*, October 5, 1990.

Schmitt, Carl. *The Concept of the Political*. Trans. George Schwab. Chicago: University of Chicago Press, 1996.

——. *Constitutional Theory*. Trans. Jeffrey Seitzer. Durham: Duke University Press, 2008.

——. *Die Diktatur, Von Den Anfängen Des Modernen Souveränitätsgedankens Bis Zum Proletarischen Klassenkampf*. Munich: Duncker and Humblot, 1921.

——. *Four Articles, 1931–1938*. Trans. Simona Draghici. Washington, D.C.: Plutarch, 1999.

———. *Legality and Legitimacy.* Trans. Jeffrey Seitzer. Durham: Duke University Press, 2004.

———. *The Leviathan in the State Theory of Thomas Hobbes: Meaning and Failure of a Political Symbol.* Trans. George Schwab and Erna Hilfstein. Westport, Conn.: Greenwood, 1996.

———. *The Nomos of the Earth in the International Law of the Jus Publicum Europaeum.* Trans. G. L. Ulmen. New York: Telos, 2003.

———. *On the Three Types of Juristic Thought.* Trans. Joseph W. Bendersky. Westport, Conn.: Praeger, 2004.

———. *Political Theology II: The Myth of the Closure of Any Political Theology.* Trans. Michael Hoelzl and Graham Ward. Cambridge: Polity, 2008.

———. *Political Theology: Four Chapters on the Concept of Sovereignty.* Trans. George Schwab. Cambridge: MIT Press, 1985.

———. "Total Enemy, Total War, and Total State." In *Four Articles, 1931–1938,* pp. 28–36. Trans. Simona Draghici. Washington, D.C.: Plutarch, 1999.

Schmitt, Jean-Claude. *Ghosts in the Middle Ages: The Living and the Dead in Medieval Society.* Trans. Teresa Lavender Fagan. Chicago: University of Chicago Press, 1998.

Schneidau, Herbert N. *Sacred Discontent: The Bible and Western Tradition.* Berkeley: University of California Press, 1977.

Scholem, Gershom. *Kabbalah.* New York: Meridian, 1978.

———. *The Messianic Idea in Judaism and Other Essays on Jewish Spirituality.* Trans. Michael A. Meyer and Hillel Halkin. New York: Schocken, 1971.

———. "Sabbatianism and Mystical Heresy." In *Major Trends in Jewish Mysticism,* pp. 287–324. Trans. George Lichtheim. New York: Schocken, 1995.

Schwager, Raymund. *Must There Be Scapegoats? Violence and Redemption in the Bible.* San Francisco: Harper and Row, 1987.

Schwartz, Regina M. *The Curse of Cain: The Violent Legacy of Monotheism.* Chicago: University of Chicago Press, 1997.

Scott, Austin Wakeman. "Constructive Trusts." *Law Quarterly Review* 71 (1955).

———. "The Right to Follow Money Wrongfully Mingled with Other Money." *Harvard Law Review* 27, no. 2 (1913): 125–38.

Scott, David. *Conscripts of Modernity: The Tragedy of Colonial Enlightenment.* Durham: Duke University Press, 2004.

Scott, Eben Greenough. *Reconstruction During the Civil War in the United States of America.* Boston: Houghton, Mifflin, 1895.

Scott, Walter. *Ivanhoe: A Romance.* New York: Modern Library, 2001.

Seavey, Warren A., and Austin W. Scott. *Notes on Certain Important Sections of Restatement of Restitution by the Reporters.* St. Paul: American Law Institute, 1937.

———. "Restitution." *Law Quarterly Review* 54 (1938): 29–45.

Sebald, W. G. "Against the Irreversible: On Jean Améry." In *On the Natural History of Destruction,* pp. 143–67. Trans. Anthea Bell. New York: Random House, 2003.

———. "Air War and Literature." In *On the Natural History of Destruction,* pp. 1–104. Trans. Anthea Bell. New York: Random House, 2003.

———. *On the Natural History of Destruction.* Trans. Anthea Bell. New York: Random House, 2003.

Sebok, Anthony J. "Two Concepts of Injustice in Restitution for Slavery." *Boston University Law Review* 84 (2004).

Sedley, Stephen. "Settlers v. Natives." *London Review of Books*, March 8, 2001.

Seed, Patricia. *American Pentimento: The Invention of Indians and the Pursuit of Riches*. Minneapolis: University of Minnesota Press, 2001.

———. *Ceremonies of Possession in Europe's Conquest of the New World, 1492–1640*. Cambridge: Cambridge University Press, 1995.

Seery, John Evan. *Political Theory for Mortals: Shades of Justice, Images of Death*. Ithaca: Cornell University Press, 1996.

Segal, Hanna. *Introduction to the Work of Melanie Klein*. London: Hogarth, 1973.

Segev, Tom. *1967: Israel, the War, and the Year That Transformed the Middle East*. New York: Metropolitan, 2007.

———. *The Seventh Million: The Israelis and the Holocaust*. Trans. Haim Watzman. New York: Hill and Wang, 1993.

Segev, Tom, Roane Carey, and Jonathan Shainin, eds. *The Other Israel: Voices of Refusal and Dissent*. New York: New Press, 2002.

Sen, Amartya. *Collective Choice and Social Welfare*. San Francisco: Holden-Day, 1970.

Seth, Vanita. *Indians of Europe: Producing Racial Difference 1500–1900*. Durham: Duke University Press, 2010.

Seward, Deborah. "Lawmakers of Unified Germany Hold First Session." *Associated Press* (1990).

Shapiro, Ian. *The State of Democratic Theory*. Princeton: Princeton University Press, 2003.

Shatz, Adam. *Prophets Outcast: A Century of Dissident Jewish Writing About Zionism and Israel*. New York: Nation, 2004.

Shavit, Ari. "Survival of the Fittest? An Interview with Benny Morris." http://www.counterpunch.org/shavit01162004.html (January 21, 2010).

Sherwin, Emily. "Reparations and Unjust Enrichment." *Boston University Law Review* 84 (2004).

Shiller, Robert J. "Measuring Asset Values for Cash Settlement in Derivative Markets: Hedonic Repeated Measures Indices and Perpetual Futures." *Journal of Finance* (1993): 911–31

———. *Macro Markets: Creating Institutions for Managing Society's Largest Economic Risks*. New York: Oxford University Press, 1993.

———. *The New Financial Order: Risk in the Twenty-first Century*. Princeton: Princeton University Press, 2003.

Shirer, William. *The Rise and Fall of the Third Reich*. New York: Simon and Schuster, 1990.

Shklar, Judith N. "A Life of Learning." In *Liberalism Without Illusions: Essays on Liberal Theory and the Political Vision of Judith N. Shklar*, pp. 263–79. Ed. Bernard Yack. Chicago: University of Chicago Press, 1996.

———. *American Citizenship: The Quest for Inclusion*. Cambridge: Harvard University Press, 1991.

———. *The Faces of Injustice*. New Haven: Yale University Press, 1990.

———. *Legalism: An Essay on Law, Morals, and Politics*. Cambridge: Harvard University Press, 1964.

———. "The Liberalism of Fear." In *Liberalism and the Moral Life*, pp. 21–38. Ed. Nancy L. Rosenblum. Cambridge: Harvard University Press, 1989.

———. "Putting Cruelty First." In *Ordinary Vices*, pp. 7–44. Cambridge: Belknap Press of Harvard University Press, 1984.

Sider, Robert D. "Credo Quia Absurdum?" *Classical World* 73, no. 7 (1980): 417–19.

Singer, Isaac Bashevis. "The Letter Writer." In *The Séance and Other Stories*, pp. 239–75. Trans. Aliza Shevrin and Elizabeth Shub. New York: Farrar, 1968.

Singer, Joseph William. "The Legal Rights Debate in Analytical Jurisprudence from Bentham to Hohfeld." *Wisconsin Law Review* (1982): 975ff.

———. "The Reliance Interest in Property." *Stanford Law Review* 40, no. 3 (1988): 611–751.

———. "Starting Property." *Saint Louis University Law Journal* 46 (Summer 2002): 565–80.

———. "Well Settled? The Increasing Weight of History in American Indian Land Claims." *Georgia Law Review* (1994): 481ff.

The Slaughter-House Cases, 83 U.S. 36 (1873).

Slaughter, Joseph R. *Human Rights, Inc.: The World Novel, Narrative Form, and International Law*. New York: Fordham University Press, 2007.

Slezkine, Yuri. *The Jewish Century*. Princeton: Princeton University Press, 2004.

Slotkin, Richard. *The Fatal Environment: The Myth of the Frontier in the Age of Industrialization, 1800–1890*. New York: Atheneum, 1985.

———. *Regeneration Through Violence: The Mythology of the American Frontier, 1600–1860*. Norman: University of Oklahoma Press, 2000.

Slotkin, Richard, and James K. Folsom, eds. *So Dreadfull a Judgment: Puritan Responses to King Philip's War, 1676–1677*. Middletown, Conn.: Wesleyan University Press, 1978.

Smith, Bradley F. *Reaching Judgment at Nuremberg*. New York: Basic Books, 1977.

———. *The Road to Nuremberg*. New York: Basic Books, 1981.

Smith, Rogers M. *Stories of Peoplehood: The Politics and Morals of Political Membership*. Cambridge: Cambridge University Press, 2003.

Sollors, Werner. *Beyond Ethnicity: Consent and Descent in American Culture*. New York: Oxford University Press, 1986.

———. *The Invention of Ethnicity*. New York: Oxford University Press, 1989.

———, ed. *Theories of Ethnicity: A Classical Reader*. New York: New York University Press, 1996.

Solnit, Rebecca. *A Book of Migrations: Some Passages in Ireland*. London: Verso, 1997.

Sontag, Susan. *Regarding the Pain of Others*. New York: Farrar, Straus and Giroux, 2003.

Spitz, Elaine. *Majority Rule*. Chatham, N.J.: Chatham House, 1984.

Stampp, Kenneth M. "The Southern Road to Appomattox." In *The Imperiled Union: Essays on the Background of the Civil War*, pp. 246–69. New York: Oxford University Press, 1980.

Stannard, David E. *American Holocaust: Columbus and the Conquest of the New World*. New York: Oxford University Press, 1992.

Stedman, Stephen John. "The End of the American Civil War." In *Stopping the Killing: How Civil Wars End*, pp. 177ff. Ed. Roy E. Licklider. New York: New York University Press, 1993.

Steele, Shelby. *White Guilt: How Blacks and Whites Together Destroyed the Promise of the Civil Rights Era*. New York: HarperCollins, 2006.

Steiner, George. "Zion." In *My Unwritten Books*, pp. 86–116. London: Weidenfeld and Nicholson, 2008.

Stendahl, Krister. *Paul Among Jews and Gentiles, and Other Essays*. Philadelphia: Fortress, 1976.

———. "Paul and Israel." In *Final Account: Paul's Letter to the Romans*, pp. 1–8. Minneapolis: Fortress, 1995.

Stern, Frank. "German-Jewish Relations in the Postwar Period: The Ambiguities of Antisemitic and Philosemitic Discourse." In *Jews, Germans, Memory: Reconstructions of Jewish Life in Germany*, pp. 77–98. Ed. Y. Michal Bodemann. Ann Arbor: University of Michigan Press, 1996.

———. *The Whitewashing of the Yellow Badge: Antisemitism and Philosemitism in Postwar Germany*. Trans. William Templer. Oxford: Oxford University Press, 1992.

Sternhell, Ze'ev. *The Founding Myths of Israel: Nationalism, Socialism, and the Making of the Jewish State*. Trans. David Maisel. Princeton: Princeton University Press, 1998.

Stewart, Columba. *Cassian the Monk*. New York: Oxford University Press, 1998.

Stone, Elaine Murray, and Patrick Kelley. *Maximilian Kolbe: Saint of Auschwitz*. New York: Paulist, 1997.

Stone, Geoffrey R. *Perilous Times: Free Speech in Wartime from the Sedition Act of 1798 to the War on Terrorism*. New York: Norton, 2004.

Story, Joseph. *Commentaries on the Conflict of Laws, Foreign and Domestic, in Regard to Contracts, Rights, and Remedies, and Especially in Regard to Marriages, Divorces, Wills, Successions, and Judgments*. Clark, N.J.: Lawbook Exchange, 2007.

Strauss, Leo. "Reason and Revelation." In *Leo Strauss and the Theologico-Political Problem*, pp. 141–80. Ed. Heinrich Meier. New York: Cambridge University Press, 2006.

———. "Why We Remain Jews." In *Jewish Philosophy and the Crisis of Modernity: Essays and Lectures in Modern Jewish Thought*, pp. 311–57. Ed. Kenneth Hart Green. Albany: State University of New York Press, 1997.

Taubes, Jacob. *The Political Theology of Paul*. Ed. Aleida Assmann and Jan Assmann. Trans. Dana Hollander. Stanford: Stanford University Press, 2004.

———. "The Price of Messianism." *Journal of Jewish Studies* 33, no. 1–2 (1982): 595–600.

Tavuchis, Nicholas. *Mea Culpa: A Sociology of Apology and Reconciliation*. Stanford: Stanford University Press, 1991.

Tawney, R. H. *Equality*. 4th ed. New York: Barnes and Noble, 1965.

Taylor, Telford. *The Anatomy of the Nuremberg Trials: A Personal Memoir*. New York: Knopf, 1992.

———. *Nuremberg and Vietnam: An American Tragedy*. Chicago: Quadrangle, 1970.

Teitel, Ruti. "Bringing the Messiah Through Law." In *Human Rights in Political Transitions: Gettysburg to Bosnia*, pp. 177–94. Ed. Carla Hesse and Robert Post. New York: Zone, 1999.

———. "From Dictatorship to Democracy: The Role of Transitional Justice." In *Deliberative Democracy and Human Rights*, pp. 272–90. Ed. Harold Hongju Koh and Ronald Slye. New Haven: Yale University Press, 1999.

———. *Transitional Justice*. Oxford: Oxford University Press, 2000.

———. "Transitional Justice Genealogy." *Harvard Human Rights Journal* 19 (2003): 69–94.

Terreblanche, Christelle. "Apartheid Victims and State Clash." *Independent On Line*, January 22, 2006.

Terreblanche, Sampie. "Dealing with Systematic Economic Injustice." In *Looking Back, Reaching Forward: Reflections on the Truth and Reconciliation Commission of South Africa*, pp. 265–76. Ed. Charles Villa-Vicencio and Wilhelm Verwoerd. Cape Town: University of Cape Town Press, 2000.

———. *A History of Inequality in South Africa, 1652–2002*. Pietermaritzburg, South Africa: University of Natal Press, 2002.

———. "The Production of the Past." Paper presented at the Institute of African Studies, Columbia University, April 1, 2000.

———. "Testimony Before the TRC During the Special Hearing on the Rule of the Business Sector." Carlton Hotel, Johannesberg, November 11, 1997.

Tertullian. "On Penance." In *Treatises on Penance: On Penitence and on Purity*, pp. 3–37. Trans. William P. Le Saint. Westminster, Md.: Newman, 1959.

Thomas á Kempis. *The Imitation of Christ in Four Books*. Trans. Joseph N. Tylenda. New York: Vintage, 1998.

Thompson, E. P. *The Making of the English Working Class*. Harmondsworth: Penguin, 1968.

Thompson, Janna. *Taking Responsibility for the Past: Reparation and Historical Injustice*. Cambridge: Polity, 2002.

Tocqueville, Alexis de. *The Ancien Regime and the French Revolution*. Trans. Stuart Gilbert. New York: Collins, 1969.

Todorov, Tzvetan. *The Conquest of America: The Question of the Other*. Trans. Richard Howard. New York: Harper and Row, 1984.

———. *On Human Diversity: Nationalism, Racism, and Exoticism in French Thought*. Trans. Catherine Porter. Cambridge: Harvard University Press, 1995.

———. "What Went Wrong in the Twentieth Century." In *Hope and Memory: Lessons from the Twentieth Century*, pp. 1–47. Trans. David Bellos. Princeton: Princeton University Press, 2003.

Torpey, John C. *Making Whole What Has Been Smashed: On Reparation Politics*. Cambridge: Harvard University Press, 2006.

Toscano, Alberto. "The Bourgeois and the Islamist; or, the Other Subjects of Politics." *Cosmos and History: The Journal of Natural and Social Philosophy* 2, no. 1–2 (2006): 15–38.

Trafzer, Clifford E. *The Kit Carson Campaign: The Last Great Navajo War*. Norman: University of Oklahoma Press, 1982.

Trefousse, Hans Louis. *The Radical Republicans; Lincoln's Vanguard for Racial Justice*. New York: Knopf, 1969.

Truth and Reconciliation in South Africa: 10 Years On. Cape Town: Institute for Justice and Reconciliation, 2006.

Truth and Reconciliation Commission Report. Cape Town: Juta, 1998.

Tusa, Ann, and John Tusa. *The Nuremberg Trial*. New York: Atheneum, 1984.

Tutu, Desmond. *No Future Without Forgiveness*. New York: Doubleday, 1999.

———. *The Rainbow People of God: The Making of a Peaceful Revolution*. New York: Doubleday, 1994.

Tuveson, Ernest Lee. *Redeemer Nation: The Idea of America's Millennial Role*. Chicago: University of Chicago Press, 1968.

Ulam, Adam. *The New Face of Soviet Totalitarianism*. Cambridge: Harvard University Press, 1963.

Uris, Leon. *Exodus*. Garden City, N.Y.: Doubleday, 1958.

Villa-Vicencio, Charles. "The Complex Legacy of the TRC: Unfinished Business Needs to Be Addressed." *Cape Times*, April 5, 2006.

———. "Getting on with Life: A Move toward Reconciliation." In *Looking Back, Reaching Forward: Reflections on the Truth and Reconciliation Commission of South Africa*, ed. Charles Villa-Vicencio and Wilhelm Verwoerd, pp. 199–209. Cape Town: University of Cape Town Press, 2000.

———. "Restorative Justice: Dealing with the Past Differently." In *Looking Back, Reaching Forward: Reflections on the Truth and Reconciliation Commission of South Africa*, pp. 68–76. Ed. Charles Villa-Vicencio and Wilhelm Verwoerd. Cape Town: University of Cape Town Press, 2000.

Villa-Vicencio, Charles, and Wilhelm Vervoerd. "Constructing a Report: Writing up the 'Truth.'" In *Truth Versus Justice: The Morality of Truth Commissions*, pp. 122–40. Ed. Robert I. Rotberg and Dennis F. Thompson. Princeton: Princeton University Press, 2000.

Vital, David. *A People Apart: The Jews in Europe, 1789–1939*. Oxford: Oxford University Press, 1999.

Vlastos, Gregory. *Socrates, Ironist and Moral Philosopher*. Ithaca: Cornell University Press, 1991.

Volkan, Vamik D., Terry C. Rodgers, and George Kriegman. *Attitudes of Entitlement: Theoretical and Clinical Issues*. Charlottesville: University Press of Virginia, 1988.

von Leibniz, Gottfried Wilhelm. *Theodicy: Essays on the Goodness of God, the Freedom of Man, and the Origin of Evil*. Trans. E. M. Huggard. New Haven: Yale University Press, 1952.

Waldron, Jeremy, ed. *"Nonsense Upon Stilts": Bentham, Burke, and Marx on the Rights of Man*. London: Methuen, 1987.

———. "Redressing Historic Injustice." *University of Toronto Law Journal* 52, no. 1 (2002): 135–60.

———. "Superseding Historic Injustice." *Ethics* 103, no. 1 (1992): 4–28.

Wallace, Anthony F. C. *Jefferson and the Indians: The Tragic Fate of the First Americans*. Cambridge: Belknap Press of Harvard University Press, 1999.

Walzer, Michael. "The Duty to Rescue." In *Arguing About War*, pp. 67–81. New Haven: Yale University Press, 2004.

———. *Exodus and Revolution*. New York: Basic Books, 1985.

———. "Nation and Universe." In *The Tanner Lectures on Human Values, XI*, pp. 57–56. Ed. Grethe B. Peterson. Salt Lake City: University of Utah Press, 1990.

———. *Regicide and Revolution; Speeches at the Trial of Louis XVI*. Cambridge: Cambridge University Press, 1974.

————. *Spheres of Justice: A Defense of Pluralism and Equality*. New York: Basic Books, 1983.

————. *Thick and Thin: Moral Argument at Home and Abroad*. Notre Dame: University of Notre Dame Press, 1994.

Warschawski, Michel. *On the Border*. Trans. Levi Laub. Cambridge: South End, 2005.

————. *Toward an Open Tomb: The Crisis of Israeli Society*. Trans. Peter Drucker. New York: Monthly Review Press, 2004.

Webb, James H. *Born Fighting: How the Scots-Irish Shaped America*. New York: Broadway, 2004.

Webb, Sidney, and Beatrice Potter Webb. *A Constitution for the Socialist Commonwealth of Great Britain*. London: London School of Economics and Political Science, 1975.

Webb, Stephen Saunders, ed. *1676, the End of American Independence*. Syracuse: Syacuse University Press, 1995.

Weber, Eugen. *Apocalypses: Prophesies, Cults, and Millennial Beliefs Through the Ages*. Cambridge: Harvard University Press, 1999.

Weber, Mark C. "Taking Subrogation Seriously: The Blue Cross–Blue Shield Tobacco Litigation Reconsidered." *Brooklyn Law Review* 67 (2002).

Weber, Max. *The Protestant Ethic and the Spirit of Capitalism*. Trans. Talcott Parsons. New York: Scribner, 1958.

————. *The Sociology of Religion*. Trans. Hans Gerth and Talcott Parsons et al. Boston: Beacon, 1993.

Wechsler, Herbert. "Toward Neutral Principles of Constitutional Law." *Harvard Law Review* 73 (1959).

Weigel, George. "Their Lustration—and Ours." *Commentary* 94, no. 4 (1992).

Weintrobe, Sally. "Links between Grievance, Complaint, and Different Forms of Entitlement." *International Journal of Psychoanalysis* 85 (2004): 83–96.

Weitz, Eric D. *A Century of Genocide: Utopias of Race and Nation*. Princeton: Princeton University Press, 2003.

Wenzel, Siegfried. *The Sin of Sloth; Acedia in Medieval Thought and Literature*. Chapel Hill: University of North Carolina Press, 1967.

Westley, Robert. "The Accursed Share: Genealogy, Temporality, and the Problem of Value in Black Reparations Discourse." *Representations* 92 (2004): 81–116.

————. "Many Billions Gone: Is It Time to Reconsider the Case for Black Reparations?" *Boston College Law Review* 40 (1998).

White, Hayden V. "Auerbach's Literary History: Figural Causation and Modern Historicism." In *Figural Realism: Studies in the Mimesis Effect*, pp. 87–100. Baltimore: Johns Hopkins University Press, 1999.

————. *Metahistory: The Historical Imagination in Nineteenth-Century Europe*. Baltimore: Johns Hopkins University Press, 1973.

Wiesel, Elie. *Against Silence: The Voice and Vision of Elie Wiesel*. Ed. Irving Abrahamson. 3 vols. New York: Holocaust Library, 1985.

————. *Night*. Trans. Stella Rodway. New York: Bantam, 1989.

Wieseltier, Leon. "The Demons of the Jews." *New Republic*, November 11, 1985.

Williams, Bernard A. O. "Deciding to Believe." In *Problems of the Self: Philosophical Papers 1956–1972*, pp. 135–51. Cambridge: Cambridge University Press, 1973.

———. "Left-Wing Wittgenstein, Right-Wing Marx." *Common Knowledge I* 1, no. 1 (1992): 41–52.

———. "The Liberalism of Fear." In *In the Beginning Was the Deed: Realism and Moralism in Political Argument*, pp. 52–61. Ed. Geoffrey Hawthorn. Princeton: Princeton University Press, 2005.

———. "Moral Luck." In *Moral Luck: Philosophical Papers, 1973–1980*, pp. 20–39. Cambridge: Cambridge University Press, 1981.

———. *Shame and Necessity*. Berkeley: University of California Press, 1993.

———. *Truth and Truthfulness: An Essay in Genealogy*. Princeton: Princeton University Press, 2002.

———. "Truth, Politics, and Self-Deception." In *In the Beginning Was the Deed: Realism and Moralism in Political Argument*, pp. 154–64. Ed. Geoffrey Hawthorn. Princeton: Princeton University Press, 2005.

Williams, Tom. "Diagnosis and Treatment of Survivor Guilt: The Bad Penny Syndrome." In *Human Adaptation to Extreme Stress: From the Holocaust to Vietnam*, pp. 319–36. Ed. John P. Wilson, Zev Harel, and Boaz Kahana. New York: Plenum, 1988.

Wills, Garry. *Lincoln at Gettysburg: The Words That Remade America*. New York: Simon and Schuster, 1992.

———. *Under God: Religion and American Politics*. New York: Simon and Schuster, 1990.

Wilson, John P., and Beverley Raphael. *International Handbook of Traumatic Stress Syndromes*, New York: Plenum, 1993.

Wilson, Woodrow. "The Fourteen Points." In *The Political Thought of Woodrow Wilson*, ed. Edmund David Cronon, pp. 445–46. Indianapolis: Bobbs-Merrill, 1965.

———. *A History of the American People*. New York: Harper, 1918.

Winnicott, D. W. "Aggression in Relation to Emotional Development." In *Through Pediatrics to Psycho-Analysis*, pp. 129–44. New York: Brunner/Mazel, 1992.

———. "Hate in Counter-Transference." In *Through Pediatrics to Psycho-Analysis*, pp. 194–203. New York: Brunner/Mazel, 1992.

———. "The Manic Defense." In *Through Pediatrics to Psycho-Analysis*, pp. 129–44. New York: Brunner/Mazel, 1992.

———. "The Use of an Object and Relating Through Identifications." In *Playing and Reality*, pp. 86–94. London: Tavistock, 1980.

———. "The Use of an Object in the Context of *Moses and Monotheism*." In *Psycho-Analytic Explorations*, pp. 240–46. Ed. Clare Winnicott, Ray Shepherd, and Madeleine Davis. Cambridge: Harvard University Press, 1989.

Winter, Cécile. "The Master-Signifier of the New Aryans: What Made the Word 'Jew' Into an Arm Brandished Against the Multitude of 'Unpronounceable Names.'" In Alain Badiou, *Polemics*, pp. 217–29. Trans. Steve Corcoran. London: Verso, 2006.

Wolin, Sheldon. "Political Theory from Vocation to Invocation." In *Vocations of Political Theory*, pp. 3–22. Ed. Jason A. Frank and John Tambornino. Minneapolis: University of Minnesota Press, 2000.

Wyman, David S. *The Abandonment of the Jews: America and the Holocaust, 1941–1945*. New York: Pantheon, 1984.

Yerushalmi, Yosef Hayim. *Zakhor: Jewish History and Jewish Memory*. Seattle: University of Washington Press, 1996.

Yoshino, Kenji. *Covering: The Hidden Assault on Our Civil Rights*. New York: Random House, 2006.

Young, James Edward. *The Texture of Memory: Holocaust Memorials and Meaning*. New Haven: Yale University Press, 1993.

Zagorin, Perez. *How the Idea of Religious Toleration Came to the West*. Princeton: Princeton University Press, 2003.

Zakaria, Fareed. *The Future of Freedom: Illiberal Democracy at Home and Abroad*. New York, Norton, 2003.

Zalaquett, José. "Balancing Ethical Imperatives and Political Constraints: The Dilemma of New Democracies Confronting Past Human Rights Abuses." *Hastings Law Journal* 43 (1992): 1425ff.

——. "Confronting Human Rights Violations Committed by Former Governments: Principles Applicable and Political Constraints." In *State Crimes: Punishment or Pardon*, pp. 23ff. Ed. Alice Henkin. Queenstown: Aspen Institute, 1989.

Zangwill, Israel. *From the Ghetto to the Melting Pot: Israel Zangwill's Jewish Plays: Three Playscripts*. Ed. Edna Nahshon. Detroit: Wayne State University Press, 2006.

Zertal, Idith. *From Catastrophe to Power: Holocaust Survivors and the Emergence of Israel*. Trans. Chaim Watzman and Gila Svirsky. Berkeley: University of California Press, 1998.

——. *Israel's Holocaust and the Politics of Nationhood*. Trans. Chaya Galai. Cambridge: Cambridge University Press, 2005.

Zertal, Idith, and Akiva Eldar. *Lords of the Land: The War for Israel's Settlements in the Occupied Territories, 1967–2007*. New York: Nation, 2007.

Zerubavel, Yael. *Recovered Roots: Collective Memory and the Making of Israeli National Tradition*. Chicago: University of Chicago Press, 1995.

Žižek, Slavoj. "Afterword: Lenin's Choice." In *Revolution at the Gates: Žižek on Lenin (the 1917 Writings)*, pp. 167–336. London: Verso, 2002.

——. "Neighbors and Other Monsters: A Plea for Ethical Violence." In *The Neighbor: Three Inquiries in Political Theology*, pp. 134–90. Ed. Slavoj Žižek, Eric L. Santner, and Kenneth Reinhard. Chicago: University of Chicago Press, 2005.

——. *The Parallax View*. Cambridge: MIT Press, 2006.

——. "A Plea for Ethical Violence." *Umbr(a)* (2004): 75–89.

——. *The Sublime Object of Ideology*. London: Verso, 1989.

——. *The Ticklish Subject: The Absent Centre of Political Ontology*. London: Verso, 1999.

Zupančič, Alenka. *Ethics of the Real: Kant, Lacan*. London: Verso, 2000.

——. "When Surplus Enjoyment Meets Surplus Value." In *Jacques Lacan and the Other Side of Psychoanalysis: Reflections on Seminar XVII*, pp. 155–78. Ed. Justin Clemens and Russell Grigg. Durham: Duke University Press, 2006.

INDEX